Alexandria
Adieu

To Adrian
Happy Birthday 2022
Love Aadel Darwish

Alexandria Adieu

A PERSONAL HISTORY
1939 - 60

Adel Darwish

NOMAD PUBLISHING

*To all of Alexandria's
children in the diaspora*

ALEXANDRIA ADIEU
A Personal History: 1939 - 1960

Published by Nomad Publishing in 2022
Email: info@nomad-publishing.com
www.nomad-publishing.com

ISBN 978-1-914325-00-7

© Adel Darwish 2022

All rights are reserved. No part of this publication
may be reproduced, stored in a retrieval system or transmitted in any form or by any means,
electronic, mechanical, photographic or otherwise, without prior permission of the copyright
holder

CIP Data: A catalogue for this book is
available from the British Library

Contents

Prologue: Alexandria…Where?	7
Usage and Glossary	11

Part I – The City that Dinocrates Built
1. The Trianon – and a Trio of Writers	17
2. Gare-Ramleh: Alexandria's Heart and History	23
3. The Hotel Cecil	35
4. The Hyphenated Alexandrians	45
5. *Doctors and Dayas*	56
6. The Annual Flower Parade	70
7. Tram Number 4, Old Alexandria	75
8. Rue France, Stamps and Homework	87
9. 1,000 Guinnieh, and a Home in Moharrem-Bey	93
10. A Tale of Two Cities	102

Part II – Alexandria's Identity and her Vandalism: Language, Identity and Cosmopolitanism
11. Language	120
12. Invasions and New Expressions	126
13. Alexander: the Democratisation of Knowledge	130

Part III – Sidi-Bishr
14. The 'Devil's Hole'	136
15. *Plages* and Policemen	140
16. My Love Tutor	150

Part IV – The Inclusive City
17. A Mischievous Generation	157
18. Schoolchildren Grow Up Fast	165
19. The War Generation	176

Part V – The Foundations of Modernity
20. Hats, *Hantours* and Harlots	187
21. The Railways: Politics and Play	190
22. Cairo Interlude	197

Part VI – The Twentieth Century
23. Film Houses: a Way of Life	209
24. Youssef Chahine: Alexandria's Struggle with Internal Egypt	215
25. Naguib Mahfouz, Censorship and 'Alexandrian Man'	222
26. Change and 'Uglification'	227
27. Heikal's Paradox: a Schizophrenic Attitude to Culture	230

Part VII – Love, Faith, and Culture
28. Alexandria and God — 236
29. Miss World — 244
30. Love Songs: Alexandria's Hymns — 250
31. Songs Move Closer to Allah's Politics — 257
32. Leila Murad: Alexandria's Songstress — 262
33. Cosmopolitan Festivities — 271

Part VIII – Exodus
34. Alexandria's Jews – a Second Exodus — 277
35. The Rest of the 'Mosaic' — 290

Part IX – 26 July 1956: The Day Alexandria Changed Forever
36. Sleepy Streets — 295
37. Treaty Journals — 301
38. Evacuation Day — 310
39. *Fuul*, Ration Books and Smugglers — 315
40. Memories of the North Coast Road — 320
41. The Kites Battle — 325
42. Nasser Betrays Eden — 328
43. Eden's Miscalculation — 336

Part X – Countdown to Conflict
44. A Country Divided — 342
45. Tawfik–Ourabi: the Constitution — 350
46. The British Bombardment – and Occupation — 357
47. The Alexandria–Misr Rift — 364
48. The 'Voice' of the Coup — 367
49. The Spy, the Officer, his Dancer and her Lover — 371
50. Plotters, Assassins and Fascists — 378
51. The Officers' Conspiracy — 382
52. The Move Against Alexandria — 387
53. Alexandria's Identity: Durrell — 393
54. Nasser's Defiance: the Suez War — 399

Part XI – The Fall of Alexandria
55. The Ethnic Cleansing of Alexandria — 403
56. The Second Arab Conquest — 407
57. Paving the Way for Sadat's Islamisation — 410
58. A Tale of Two Daughters — 413

Epilogue: the Gods Abandoned Alexandria — 416
Notes — 421
Index — 444

Foreword

What a magnificent portrait of a city! Adel Darwish has given us an achingly nostalgic memoir of his native Alexandria – a bustling port that since Greek and Roman times has been a beacon of learning, culture and religious inspiration, the cosmopolitan capital of the eastern Mediterranean. Once a flourishing international centre, the city has seen better days. The Jews, Greeks, Europeans and hotchpotch of nationalities proudly identifying as Alexandrians have been expelled or drifted away; the patisseries and cake shops, the salons and ballrooms where sophisticated society and intellectuals gossiped by day and danced by night have closed; the tramways that ran along the coast, linking monuments, public gardens and elegant villas, are dilapidated; and the public buildings, former emblems of civic pride, are now drab, neglected and decaying.

Adel grew up in the prosperous middle class of Alexandria in its heyday – the late 40s and the 1950s – and cannot but regret the uglification of his city, the expulsion of so many people who gave it life and soul and the cultural and economic vandalism that followed Colonel Nasser's seizure of power. He blames the Arab nationalists of the 1960s for spurning Alexandria's colourful past as an international melting pot. And he fears that today's climate of puritanical Islamism and extremism has made it harder not only to drink, dance, flirt and enjoy life, but to continue quaint, age-old traditions that so vividly shaped his boyhood.

But his book is more than regret. It is also a celebration of a city made famous by the writers E.M. Forster and Lawrence Durrell and the Greek poet Constantine Cavafy. He remembers in detail all the buildings, street signs and shops, with an encylopaedic explanation of each name, family and quirky incident stamped on the city's memory. He recalls the dedicated physicians and the quacks, the nicknames for the trams and the railway that ran on coffee beans, the snacks in the evening breeze of sea urchins and cold Stella beer, the flower parades and society beauties as well as the girls he dated in his lusty youth.

He brings also sharp political judgments, formed from many return visits as a British journalist and commentator, on Egypt's challenges and politicians, the venal as well as the venerated. In short, he gives us a rich travelogue and unrivalled biography of himself and his beloved Alexandria, a city the world deserves to know better.

Sir Michael Binyon[*]
January 2022

---

[*] Sir Michael Roger Binyon OBE is a well-known international British foreign correspondent who served in Berlin, Washington, Moscow as well as several Africa and Middle East capitals. He was for a long time leader writer of *The Times* and is widely respected for his insights on world affairs. He was rewarded and OBE by HM the Queen for his service to international journalism; and was given to British Press Awards in 1979 & 1980.

Prologue: Alexandria...Where?

The drive from Burg el-Arab, where I landed at night, to the civilised Royal Alexandria took an hour and a half rather than the ten minutes or so from Nuzha Airport, where I had arrived on a previous visit a decade earlier. The journey took me through what more closely resembled Afghan villages than the Alexandria I knew. Perhaps it was symbolic of how quickly Alexandria was moving further from herself. Nuzha, which had served the city for over seven decades during her cosmopolitan epoch, was shut for renovation in 2011, when the military who were in charge of the country set the election rules and criteria that empowered the Islamists, enabling them to easily take over. Burg el-Arab, originally an RAF airbase where Churchill had lunch with its commanders before the Battle of Alamein in 1942, is far away from the city both geographically and culturally. The airport's name was alien, associated with Bedouin culture rather than Alexandria's European ethos. Nuzha – European in design, layout and service – did for twentieth-century Alexandria what Muhammad Ali's harbour expansion had done for the nineteenth-century city, strengthening her links with Europe and underpinning modernity. The conceptual contrast between the two airports symbolised the regression of Alexandria. Alexandria, which had held out to the last breath before falling into the hands of strangers who never understood her culture, deceived me on my long interval visits into believing that my Hellenistic city would, by some miracle, survive the ugliness crusade of the barbarians who might have been on Cavafy's mind when he asked, 'Why this sudden bewilderment, this confusion? Why are the streets and squares emptying so rapidly,...?" when the city was 'waiting for the barbarians'.[1]

'Alexandria is slipping through our fingers', my father repeatedly warned when noticing the city's post-war decay, from broken chandeliers in building hallways to the ugliness creeping into fashion, manners and architecture – and then the accelerated demographic bleeding out, when Alexandria was shedding her children in the late 1950s and throughout the 1960s.

But my journey also raised another question. There was more than one Alexandria – several, in fact. As a teenager, I had become aware of parts of the city I have never imagined existed; another world of poverty, inhabited by poor countryside migrants. Could those quarters have expanded and taken over the city with the population having grown fivefold in 50 years.

It was one of my motivations in writing this book: to explain that there was European Alexandria, there was trade and commerce, and there were the quarters that were exclusively inhabited by people who treated their fellow Alexandrians (who happened to be ethnically different) with suspicion and cynicism. But there was another Alexandria, my own, the smelter that infused all races, saints and sinners into one culture: the Alexandrian culture. This, too, was a motive to write this book – besides other more important reasons, of course.

My autumn 2012 visit had been to participate in a Swedish Consulate-sponsored seminar on democracy: Egypt had been ruled for 18 months by the extremist Muslim Brotherhood, with their 60-year history of violence and terrorism. What prevailed from participants in the 2012 forum, and what I noticed in the Western media and several academic circles, was an Orwellian rewriting of Alexandria's history – and that of Egypt in general – to deceive the world into believing that Alexandria was always what they presented today: Arabised, ugly and controlled by an Islamic culture with no trace of her recent Europeanism. With a body of literature and superficial studies by revisionist neo-orientalists, Islamist sympathisers in the Western media and academic circles, and (economically motivated) Pan-Arabists proliferating in Egypt, there is an attempt, almost a campaign, to erase a 180-year chapter of Alexandria's story from the history books, an advanced crusade to erase Alexandria from memory.

The Western mainstream media (out of ignorance peppered with the customary racism) have deluded themselves into believing the lie they were party to concocting, thanks to a drop in professional standards and a laziness in checking facts, a false picture of Alexandria that they continue to misrepresent to their readers, listeners and viewers. But these misleading presentations bear little resemblance to the reality I have witnessed. Nobody in Alexandria (and the rest of Egypt) thought of their city or their country as Arab, in the way that Western media erroneously characterise them. Alexandrians and Egyptians did not even call people from the Arabian Peninsula 'Arabs' but referred to them rather as *Higazies*; the Arabs, as seen by Egyptians, were only desert-dwelling Bedouins who occasionally came to towns and the Nile Delta to carry some tasks or get temporary employment during the harvest season.

This was my most decisive motive for writing this eye-witness account of the Alexandria I lived in: to preserve her memory from the revisionists' rewriting of history and Western media ignorance. I also wanted to make the book a reference for history students by placing personal encounters and events in their historical context.

Several years elapsed between my last visit to Alexandria and the book appearing in print, but they were not all spent at the keyboard, in library reading rooms or taking notes from archives. I was also working as a self-employed full-time journalist and political commentator to earn a living – and over the past eight years, I have also faced several challenges.

Since 2016, I have suffered two serious cardiac problems, five extended hospitalisations, and three surgeries then a battle with cancer. However, what impeded my work most significantly was the medication's devastating side effects. The treatment affects my eyesight – especially one particular medicine, which blocks my vision for 20 hours out of each 48. Thanks to modern technology, I have been able to dictate to an iPhone and Microsoft Word program over 90% of the copy. This, in turn, presented more challenges. Using a Kindle app to enlarge the text made it impossible in most cases to find the exact page numbers for citations. Dictated text also required a great deal of editing while the medication aggravating arthritis joint pains. Friends came to the rescue: my dear long-time friend Pat Lancaster, the editor-in-chief of the *Middle East* magazine group, despite her own health issues, assisted with two long sections of over 25,000 words. Daniel Nayrouz, postgraduate at the London School of Economics, assisted with research and dealt with 40,000 dictated words.

Another blow came in 2017 when a fire in my old family home in London destroyed cabinets full of my files, university essays, a 40-year accumulation of notebooks from the time when I was a foreign correspondent, and my notes of visits to Alexandria and Egypt since the 1960s. Most upsetting was the destruction of my parents' papers and correspondence, picture albums and family objects. Other friends, old and new, also rode to the rescue. A great deal of information about the architecture and history of royal Alexandria – references and publications – was provided by Egypt's top medieval manuscripts expert Dr Khalid Azab, former executive head of the Bibliotheca

Alexandrina's special projects and information centre, to whom I am extremely grateful. I would also like to extend my thanks to the Bibliotheca's staff, past and present particularly Dr Islam Asem for his parcel of documents, Shaymaa Elsherif and her colleague Susan Abed, for the valuable assistance they provided to my researcher Naadirah Vali, postgraduate at SOAS, who retrieved newspapers and publication-archive material going back over 200 years and used in this book. I am also grateful for assistance provided at short notice by specialists in the Bibliotheca like the Subject Matter Expert Manar Badr and Mark George Kyriakos of the library's centre for Hellenistic studies.

I would also like to thank the great Alexandrian Harry Tzalas, president of Athens' *Hellenic Institute of Ancient & Mediaeval Alexandrian Studies, whose correspondence jogged my memory and who provided maps and other valuable information from his team's excavation in Alexandria.*

My gratitude to old friends, family and relatives who also jogged my memory and filled in gaps regarding this prosperous, colourful period in Alexandria's history. Special thanks to dear friends: thinker and author Dr Tarek Heggy, for many long telephone calls and meetings discussing Egypt's twentieth-century events and interpreting them; the Muscovite- Egyptian scholar and thinker Adel Elramly, for his enlightening correspondence about left-wing Egyptian intelligentsia and cultural changes in Egypt; and special thanks to Dr Sherif Helmy, who, in addition to his valuable medical care and assistance with my health challenges, also helped in filling gaps and provided useful information about social life in Egypt in the period after I left. Most important, I would like to thank Max Scott, director of Nomad Publishing for his patience and assisting me when getting stuck on using Microsoft Word, and special thanks to Ian McDonald for his editing, suggestions and positive ideas in reorganising some sections of the book.

Finally, this book is dedicated to all of Alexandria's children in the diaspora.

Usage and Glossary

Usage
I use 'she' and 'her' to refer to Alexandria – and 'Alexandrianism' as an identity; a soft nationalism.

I also use the (unfamiliar) term 'Alexandrinology', which is used by a few academics and historians. It is separate from Egyptology.

I only use Christian names (forenames) without surnames. I have also changed names on the subjects', or their families', request. There are ugly forces and Islamist extremists who retrospectively punish people or their descendants for actions that they do not accept today but were the norm in in the past.

I have also respected the wishes of some Alexandrians who have changed faith and who insisted on concealing their identity by changing both locations and names.

The spelling of words and expressions in the book adopt the Alexandrian and Egyptian spelling as used and sounded at the time, not the Arabic spelling (*higab* not *hijab*, Hessein not Hussein etc.). This doesn't apply to non-Egyptians.

However, there are a few exceptions to help academic researchers; I kept both spelling for example when people whose work is published in multi-languages: Dr Taha Hessein is also Taha Hussein/Hussayn.

Also some spelling appears French or Italian because it copies the Alexandria municipality signs which were in French (sometime Italian) and in Arabic texts like Rue Princesse Fawzia, or Princesse (not Princess) Faiza School

Some readers might find expressions 'outdated' according to current fashion. Since I am not a Winston Smith rewriting the past to fit the present, I prefer to be like a producer religiously sticking to fashion and visual symbols in a period drama, in the same way that you wouldn't expect to see William Ewart Gladstone using a mobile phone in a film about his premiership.

The same goes for behaviours, ethos and attitudes that might read as odd, outdated or insensitive for millennial readers but were normal, acceptable and even welcomed during the period.

I am using the lingua-franca, the lexicon of Alexandria and Egypt during the period covered in the book. As explained in a long chapter, the language is part of the identity. I have deliberately used Alexandrian terms of the period from the Second World War to 1960, to reflect the culture and way of thinking prevailing in *my* Alexandria.

Some of the names and phrases which were Alexandrianised Italian, French or Greek, might appear grammatically incorrect but they were the shortened versions used at the time – e.g. *Légaré Due Ramleh* is called *mehatet Ramleh* or *gare elrmaleh*, *salon de coiffure* is simply *le coiffure*, while the British are always referred to as *Les Anglais*.

On biographical dates of historical figures and Egyptian dynasties, I abide by the dates mentioned in *Britannica*. Of hundreds of people mentioned, a small minority have conflicting (and some not found) dates of birth and death; in these instances, I have left the dates out.

The order of prime ministers and presidents of Egypt is by person and by their first time of taking office. So, when the 25th prime minister (1942) is re-elected in 1949 and forms another government in 1952, he is still the 25th prime minister at all those dates.

On notes and citations: source and page(s) cited for specific quotes, or mention. For general background or extended information, a section, chapter, a full article, essay, or a book is referred to. Some exceptions in citations from online/kindle editions when and where there are no page numbers we cite ' location number' when possible.

Glossary
a'am Although the Arabic dictionary refer to use for 'uncle' in Egypt it is how working-class people, like the caretakers or milkmen, were addressed.
*abieh*a chap, as addressed by younger ones.
abla 'mademoiselle', as addressed by people younger than her; also a female school teacher, while female teachers address their headmistress as *Abla el-Nazerah*
…*agi*a dded to end of a profession name, like '…man' in 'postman' is *postagi*
Arab/sin Egyptian means Bedouins unless indicated otherwise in the text. The word 'Arab/ic' hadn't been added to the country's name during the period covered in the book.

Usage and Glossary

Arabic refers to the written language only; the correct term is 'Arabised-Egyptian' (not Egyptian Arabic) and in most cases 'demotic Egyptian', 'demotic Alexandrian' (I also use 'Alexandriaspeak').

Azhar, al- the official Egyptian Muslim 'Church' (see below*).

balad al-balad 'downtown'/town centre.

balday (indigenous).

ibn-balad(m.) *bint-balad* (f.) an indigenous Alexandrian who isn't of European or *chami* (*chewam* – meaning Levantine: Syrian, Lebanese Palestinian) ancestry; but outside Alexandria, *ibn-balad* meant a Nilotic Egyptian.

balayeure/-balyeur / elbalayeury street sweeper, derived from French.

Belediye the Municipality.

carro long, narrow wagon.

chellah exclusive group of close friends (either single- or mixed-sex).

Currency£€ Egyptian pound: at time of writing, roughly equal to £1.15 (sterling); £€ = 100 PT (*piastres*), five *ryals* (5 x 20PT), 10 *prezas* (10 x 10PT) or 20 shillings (20 x 5PT); 1 PT = 10 (*millièmes*); there was also *nos-franc* = 2 *piastres*, since the French franc (worth 4 *piastres*) was accepted in shops.

daya (plural: *dayat*) trained local midwife; I used *dayas* for plural.

DükkanıDükkan, Dükkana shop, store.

ebenosa walking stick (from the Ottoman *Abanoza* for ebony, used in Victorian times to make walking sticks).

effendis Europeanised Alexandrians/Egyptians.

eczane pharmacy.

fellah (plural: *fellaheen*) peasant, illiterate country-dweller.

fisiekh salted, fermented and sun-dried grey mullet.

forno bakeries.

galabiyaa loose-fitting tunic (also *qaftan*) – long garment worn by *fellaheen*, some women used as an indoor gown when alone.

gizyah poll tax on non-Muslims first imposed under Arab occupation in 7th century (abolished in 1798) (Arabs write *Jizyah*).

hanem Ottoman title ('dame'/'lady') in demotic to address/refer to middle-/upper-class married women.

Internal Egyptthe rest of Egypt, outside Alexandria.

kharabh waste land (also a bomb site).

khawaga alien/foreigner, but often used by Muslims to alienate non-Muslims.

mannequin demotic Egyptian (and Arabic text in Egyptian media) use this term for a fashion model.

masarwah non-Alexandrians from Egypt, so-called by Alexandrians (from the word *Masr/Misr*; see below).

Misr/Masr Egypt or, alternatively, Cairo.

monologist Egyptian demotic definition is broader than 'stand-up comedian' – it is a solo performer, delivering a song, a soliloquy, demotic poetry or even giving a talk.

Mukhabarat Nasser-era intelligence service.

mukhber plain-clothes policeman, *mukhbers* were generally corrupt and most of the time had arrangements with criminal gangs.

mutreba a higher level of female singer/songstress – a celebrity/'diva';(m: *mutreb*).

Nahda 'renaissance'; the 19th early 20th century modernity project of *laïcité*.

néo-natifs migrants who settled in the 'resurrected', nineteenth-century Alexandria – included Europeans, Ottomans and Nilotic Egyptians.

Nilotic Egyptians: I use this term instead of 'natives'.

sa'idie Upper Egyptian *fellah*; hard-working, strong but naive – and a central character in Alexandrian folklore's equivalent of the 'Irish joke' in the UK.

sa'ie(s) office Messenger, train foot-man, postal service assistant etc.

sufragie a household footman.

ulama the Islamic priestly class/ Azhar clergy.

usta master of a profession – like a tailor, barber or mechanic; also a chauffeur or 'cabbie'.

ustaza male teacher.

War/the War unless indicated otherwise, 'the War/post-war' refers to the Second World War and 'the Great War' means the First World War

Zappal private domestic rubbish (*zepallah)* collector, derived from the Italian *carro-dell-spazzatura* – refuse cart.

---

* Defining al-Azhar, the 970s AD-founded Islamic university, as a mosque or a seat of learning is shallow and fails to reflect its full institutional influence on society, education and culture or its role in legislation. In the context of modern Egyptian realities, it is the 'Islamic Church' like the Church of England but has a greater influence and enforceable role than the latter. A mosque is a building in every context, and there is no other definition for it but a structure: in Egyptian, it is *Game'h* – from *gama'h* (group) and *gome'h*, meaning 'congregating'. Egyptians never use the term employed by Arabs, *masged/masjed* (from *sajad*: to kneel or prostrate oneself), which represents only a location in the Egyptian language. In Egypt *Masged* is simply a consecrated building equivalent to a chapel, and cannot be used in the institutional sense of 'Church', like in 'Church of England'. In this book, al-Azhar is treated as an institution for Muslims like the Church of England for Anglicans. It is constitutionally part of the Egyptian state structure, funded by the taxpayer through the state (to the tune of £€ 15.708 billion in 2019 and expected to rise to £€ 17.5 billion in 2021 budget). The Egyptian Constitution specifies Islam as the official faith of the state, and al-Azhar also has a constitutional jurisprudence function; a death sentence only becomes valid with endorsement from the head of al-Azhar. Many of al-Azhar's *fatwas* are religious rulings, but acquired a de facto legal status (e.g. the serving of alcohol inside hotels and licensed premises, and to non-Muslims only; the criminalisation of suspected homosexuality – even extending to non-practising homosexuals; and the banning of organ transplants without al-Azhar's permission).

PART I

THE CITY THAT DINOCRATES BUILT

CHAPTER 1
The Trianon – and a Trio of Writers

'*Stella a'ranah, s'il vous plaît*', I asked for a chilled bottle of Alexandria's 'national' drink, the famous Birra Stella. In his white jacket, black trousers and starched shirt with a small ready-knotted bow tie, the young garçon looked at me hesitantly.

'I am originally *Iskandrani*', I said in demotic Alexandrian; 'long before your parents got together', I added, 'Now get a glass from the Frigidaire. I pointed at the revolving glass doors of the Trianon.

The Trianon sits on the site where the two 'Cleopatra's Needles' once stood. They marked the entrance to the temple that Egypt's last queen (69–30 BC) began constructing, in 30 BC, in honour of her lover Mark Antony (83–30 BC). The square used to be named after the needles: Place des Obélisques.[1] One obelisk stands today on the Thames Embankment between Waterloo and Westminster bridges. It was a gift from Muhammad Ali Pasha (1761–1829), the founder of modern Egypt, to Britain. Its voyage, loss at sea and recovery became part of the Alexandrians' folklore, as they believed it was Cleopatra's magic that saved the day.[2] The other was given to the United States by Viceroy Tawfik Pasha (1852–1892) as promised by his father, Khedive Ismail (1830–1895). In 1869, Ismail noticed the absence of the US flag among the assembled world ships at the inauguration of the Suez Canal, according to New York journalist Henry Hulbert (1827–1895). In conversation with the khedive, the obelisk was mentioned as a gift opening a new chapter of friendship between the two nations.[3] In 1880, it was moved to New York, where it still stands in Central Park.

I placed my Panama hat on a varnished 1930s superfine-twill cane chair and my bundle of newspapers on the round marble-top table on the deserted pavement on the northern side of the landmark café. I was the only customer spreading my accessories on the table and chairs as the clock hands were about to chop the hour ten into halves. God knows how many times those chairs had been re-caned in the Trianon's cycles of reincarnation since its first redecoration in the Art Deco style a century ago. They remained in their original First World War design, made of bamboo, narrow-braided straw and bulrush straps.

The establishment was first known as Athinèos when established in 1905 by two Greek Alexandrians, Andrea Drikos and George Pericles. It started as a pâtisserie and chocolatier with a café section, where customers could enjoy a cake with their tea or coffee, as well as bar section with high ceilings and large windows, the café has three fronts overlooking La Gare de Ramleh, Boulevard Sa'd Zaghloul and Place Sa'd Zaghloul. The cakes and chocolates remained very much Alexandrian delights, in the same way as the city's pâtisseries and salons de thé had been over the decades. The Athinèos expanded over the years – with its beautifully designed interior, wood panelling and Art Deco painting on the panels – was refurbished 20 years later and renamed 'Trianon'. The Trianon, like all similar Alexandrian cafés until the late 1990s had a bar, and some had barman or a barmaid, serving wine, beer and spirits. The drinking culture changed beyond recognition with Islamists starting to control public life from around the turn of the twenty-first century, which explained the young waiter's hesitation when I ordered Birra Stella to drink on the shady pavement as had been the custom in Alexandria for generations. It was my overwhelming desire because I had not had this pleasure since a flying visit in 1998. A previous trip in November 2000 had coincided with one of Alexandria's well-known *nawat* (storms), during which the rain goes on forever, limiting my choice of venues to indoors only. On the occasion, I had taken my pre-lunch Stella 90 metres away at the current Athinèos, looking out of its northern windows at one the best views in the Mediterranean: the entire Eastern Harbour, the open sea and the ruins of time gone by.

The City of Cavafy, Forster and Durrell
The Trianon is part of the 1890 block of Hôtel Métropole (formerly Hotel Lorio Palace), designed by Italo-Alexandrian architect Corrado Pergolesi. A century earlier, the block housed the Department of Irrigation offices, in which a particular civil servant sat: Alexandria's poet, Constantine Peter Cavafy (1863–1933, Konstantinos Petrou Kavafis). The poetry of the ethnically Greek, Egyptian national, culturally Hellenistic and spiritually Alexandrian Cavafy became the throbbing heart of the city's intellectual and cultural society during her *belle époque*.

CHAPTER 1 The Trianon – and a Trio of Writers

'A Greek gentleman in a straw hat, standing absolutely motionless at a slight angle to the universe', mused the English historian, essayist and novelist Edward Morgan Forster (1879–1970) upon his once encountering Cavafy going into the Trianon (Athinèos). Forster's 1922 book *Alexandria: A History and Guide* is perhaps the most insightful account of the modern 'golden age' of Alexandria (1810–1970) as he interweaves the city's 3,000 years of history into her twentieth-century tapestry.[4]

Forster was a controller, censoring correspondence and publications for the British military, during the Great War. He also assisted in translating into English the information guide to the Greco-Roman Museum in Alexandria (originally opened in 1892) after it was relocated from its cramped location on the Rue Rosetta into more extensive premises comprising 27 halls designed by Italian-born Alexandrian architect Ernesto Verrucci Bey (1874–1945).

The 1922 museum guide had been written in French by the museum curator, Egyptologist and Alexandrinologist Annibale Evaristo Breccia Bey (1876–1967) – the same Professor Breccia Bey who, famously, was forced in 1930 to publicly deny rumours that Howard Carter (1874–1939), of Tutankhamun fame, was to excavate for the Tomb of Alexander.[5]

While sitting at The Trianon thinking of putting into prose what had been bubbling in my head for many years. It was time to develop a mental photographic film that had been taken of my Alexandria but had remained in its darkroom canister for over 50 years. Forster's fame in Britain rests mainly on novels like *Howards End* (1910) and *A Passage to India* (1924); in Alexandria, he was better known for his writing and serialised stories in the *Egyptian Gazette* and the *Egyptian Mail* – the papers that also published Cavafy's poetry, inspired by his memories of sexual adventures and Hellenic glories.

The introduction to the edition of Forster's guide that I reread was penned, in a tone conciliatory to the then Nasser regime, by non-other than Lawrence Durrell himself (1912–1990).

Cavafy, Forster and Durrell were the best-known trio, out of a selection of several writers, whose quills reintroduced the modern reincarnated city-state to the twentieth-century-world's readers: Alexandria the magical; romantic; exotic; hedonistic; and, as many lately like to claim, mythical cosmopolis. Jane Lagoudis Pinchin suggests that Alexandria – as a bridge between east and west, Europe and the Orient – was Forster's own 'passage to India' and his literary wealth.[6] She describes the profound influence exerted by the city's spirit and by her poet, Cavafy, on both Forster (especially his 1924 masterpiece) and Durrell, in his *Alexandria Quartet* (1957–1960).

Between the 1880s and the late 1960s, men of letters like Cavafy,Forster, Durrell and scholar John Robert Liddell (1908–1992)[*] – and, later, Michael Haag (1943-2020, author of *The Durrells of Corfu*) – present us with a unique portrayal of pre-1970 modern Alexandria. The tableaux they drew form perhaps the best antidote to attempts by revisionists to erase the existence of a real part of Alexandria's *belle époque* memory and replace it, in an Orwellian sense, with a picture suggesting that the ugly present has been the reality of the past. The manifestations in women's dress (reminiscent of their Afghan counterparts in Kandahar), or in religious festivals or hideous new architecture, that you see in Alexandria today bear no resemblance to the reality of 40 years ago: of a cosmopolis that was culturally and, in many aspects also socially and economically, an extension of Europe. The city opened Egypt up to 160 years of modernity (1810–1970), development and economic prosperity. This dynamic city of the modern Western mind, with a culturally and ethnically pluralistic hybrid at heart and a Hellenistic soul, kept both Ottoman-Islamic and static Coptic-Christian traditions at bay.

Perhaps the photographic collections of Haag[7] are a visual equivalent of what had been expressed in the collective works of these writers. Nobody can imagine or fully understand the city, as reflected in those images, except its inhabitants themselves with their life experience before 1970. Alexandrians' senses were inseparable from their city's soul; their thoughts were part of her mind. Their knowledge came from the vibes in her body, and their culture came from her genes. 'From/in Alexandria', we diasporic Alexandrians, without thinking but instinctively, answer the question, 'Where do you come from?' or 'Where were you born?' *Not* 'Egypt'.

Few, if any, metropolises can claim a status of cosmopolis like Alexandria can. She experienced two golden ages, making her one of history's wonders. Her first golden age – following her laying out in 332 BC by Alexander the Great's architect, Dinocrates – was as the intellectual capital of the Classical ancient world and the seat of culture, medicine, philosophy and science under the Ptolemies (323–30 BC) – ruling over Egypt, Cyprus, Jordan all around the Mediterranean from geographical Palestine to the Adriatic coast, and Libya to the west – followed by the Roman period (30 BC–619 AD).

---

[*] Liddell was the type of scholar who sits quietly to write essays; he was a lecturer with the British Institute – now the British Council – in Athens, but, like Durrell, moved to Alexandria (where he became a university lecturer) when the Germans invaded Greece in 1941. He moved back to Athens in 1953 after the coup in Egypt. Liddell wrote several novels; his 1952 *Unreal City* is set in Cairo and based on Cavafy's work and life.

CHAPTER 1 The Trianon – and a Trio of Writers

The second golden age, that of royal Alexandria, was as the largest port in the eastern Mediterranean in the nineteenth and early twentieth centuries, under Muhammad Ali's dynasty (1805–1953).

Only if you had grown up in the reincarnated Alexandria (1810–1970) and knew her sites, ancient and modern, could you understand her multiple cultures. If you had roamed her Dinocratian streets and moved inside her circles, dived within her layers and vaulted her fences – which were not physical barriers but cultural, intellectual, ethnic and philological boundaries – you would have discovered that you, like me and like Alexandria herself, were a hybrid and a mongrel of numerous cultural and ethnic genes. Alexandrians might belong to one ethnic group or another; in reality, they were like the city herself in the mindset of daily life and trade. Like Durrell's character Justine, Alexandrians were neither entirely European nor fully Levantine – nor Egyptian nor African nor like any other assemblage or single, racially hegemonic Mediterranean group. Each one of us was, in a way, an individual mini-biological clone of the city, a minuscule model of Alexandria – and we Alexandrians collectively, in our similarities and diversities, were also a group-Alexandria: a 'we-Alexandria'.

In a geographical, ethnographical, historical and cultural sense, Alexandria was an island, surrounded by water except for a tiny narrow link to Africa's land mass, and with an invisible (cultural) umbilical cord connecting her to Europe. Her bubbling inner soul always wanted her to break away and drift with the Mediterranean currents, gliding to where she had been conceived by Greek gods and philosophers, to finally snuggle into Europa's bosom.

The closest personification to *my* Alexandria was Durrell's character Justine.[8] 'Justine is the spirit of Alexandria', wrote Cyril Connolly (1903–1974)* on the first-edition cover. Symbolising Alexandria herself, Justine was alluring and seductive, and always seemed like she was mourning her future death – predisposed to dreary, cryptic pronouncements; confused and ever searching for what, inevitably, had been repeatedly lost. Justine was neither Nilotic-Egyptian nor European nor Levantine but Alexandrian. She mirrored the city with her complex intricacies: a mixture of elegance and decadence, a lavish wealth next to extreme poverty, to which Justine moves at the end. Alexandria's ancient Hellenistic periods revived after peeling away layers of time laid down by Romans, Christians, Arabs, Mamluks and Ottomans. Their legacies of sometimes religiously induced strict and backward ways

---

* Cyril Vernon Connolly was a respected English critic who founded and edited the influential literary magazine *Horizon* (1940–50) to replace T.S. Eliot's *The Criterion*, which folded in 1939.

were entwined with modern European mores, making the city unique. They all co-existed, with certain traditions ghettoised in some quarters and many opposing ones in others, yet blended into one hybrid. During the time I lived there, I have been in several Alexandrias within astonishingly close geographical proximity to one another.

The married Justine with her past life which, we know through her former husband, and her affair with the novel's narrator (Darley) and continuing the pattern with her current spouse, Nessim, is also like Alexandria in a pervasively continuous triangular love affair. Alexandria's three lovers are the gentle, attractive, modern Europe; the abusively controlling, fundamentalist, oriental, predominantly Muslim Internal Egypt; and the ancient past with its memories of greatness, wealth and knowledge.

In *Justine*, Durrell introduced Cavafy, the poet of Alexandria, to the outside world of the 1950s. Alexandrians in the diaspora carry Cavafy's poetry within themselves. Many hold onto the intellectual feeling in his 1894 poem 'The City'. Ask any exiled Alexandrian what is in their innermost thoughts when they long for Alexandria, and they will express what sounds like Cavafy's 'The City' because she no longer exists where we left her. Still, she lives, with all her harmonies and contradictions, inside us.

The City[9]
You said: 'I'll go to another country, go to another shore,
find another city better than this one.
Whatever I try to do is fated to turn out wrong
and my heart lies buried like something dead.
How long can I let my mind moulder in this place?
Wherever I turn, wherever I look,
I see the black ruins of my life, here,
where I've spent so many years, wasted them, destroyed them totally.'
You won't find a new country, won't find another shore.
This city will always pursue you.
You'll walk the same streets, grow old
in the same neighbourhoods, turn grey, in these same houses.
You'll always end up in this city. Don't hope for things elsewhere:
there's no ship for you, there's no road.
Now that you've wasted your life here, in this small corner,
you've destroyed it everywhere in the world.

CHAPTER 2

Gare-Ramleh: Alexandria's Heart and History

I flipped through my newspapers on the southern pavement of Place Sa'd Zaghloul, formerly Place des Obélisques, the Italian consulate on its eastern side designed in 1880 by Enrico Bovio.* He also created the Greek School in Attarin, the city's Italian School and several other landmarks. The square remains one of the rare nineteenth-century open spaces unsavaged by modern architects, whose vandalism of Alexandria has been tenfold what post-war architects inflicted on northern English towns. Structured on the Italian Renaissance model of a piazza with four equal sides, the square was renamed after Zaghloul Pasha (1857–1927), Egypt's seventeenth prime minister following a landslide election victory for his Wafd party in 1924.†

Zaghloul Pasha's *wafd* (delegation) led the 1919 revolution against the British occupation. The national drive for independence included Jews and ethnically European-Egyptians, and gained sympathy from European and British residents like Forster. Although this

---

* Bovio and Pietro Avoscani (1816–1891) were part of a group of ethnic Italian-Alexandrian architects. They built some impressive landmarks, like the Ras el Tin Palace, the international market in Mina el-Basal in 1871; and Teatro Zizinia in 1863 (all by Avoscani). In Cairo, they designed the palaces of Abbasiyya and Hilmiyya in 1849 for Abbas Helmi I (1812–1854), the Gazira (1860) and Chubra (1861), and the Royal Opera House in 1869.

† The 1924 vote was the first after the 1922 removal of British protection. It was the seventh parliamentary election in Egypt to elect a full parliament: *maglis-el-newab* (house of representatives); the previous elections had been held in 1883, 1889, 1895, 1901, 1907 and 1913. The first modern council was established under Muhammad Ali in 1805: it comprised judges, clergymen and significant landowners, and half of its members were elected heads of villages.

23

quasi-democracy was short-lived (1922–54), it was the most advanced – and longest-lasting – liberal multi-party parliamentarian democratic experiment in the entire region.

Paradoxically, Egypt's first post-independence constitution damaged this fragile egalitarian equality and sowed the seeds of discrimination, creating a tier of second-class citizens. It named Islam as the primary source of legislation and Arabic as the official language of the state.[*] Cosmopolitan Alexandria, like other urban trade and industrialised centres, had been established by multi-ethnic and multi-faith Egyptian-born second- and third-generation migrants, while a quarter of her population at that time were Christian-Copts, whose civilisation predated Muslim rule by seven centuries. Street names were in French and Arabic, and remained so when I left in 1960; so were documents like passports. This was the legacy of Muhammad Ali, who founded the modern state by relying on French expertise.

Returning from exile in 1923, Zaghloul Pasha landed in Alexandria to a hero's welcome. Most of the city's performers, including *balady* dancers (emulated by Turks as belly dancers), formed his entourage of scores of horse-pulled *hantours* (cabriolets) with their instruments and singing *Salma, ya, Salamah* (safe return); it has become one of Egypt's most popular songs, often in multilingual performance. The song's opening lines were initially recited in the 1890s by prostitutes who passed their medical examination following their arrest for working without a health-clearance licence. The more extended current-version lyrics were penned by the dramatist, poet and actor Badi'e Khairy (1893–1966) for a 1919 musical by Alexandrian composer Sheikh Sayyed Darweesh[†] (1892–1923). Darweesh, better known by his common name Sheikh Sayyed, was for Nilotic-Egyptians what Cavafy was for Greco-Alexandrians. He composed 25 songs and 5 operettas on 13 different scales in 18 years, before dying of a cocaine overdose aged 31.

After the Great War, Alexandria enjoyed the fastest-growing economy in the Mediterranean region. She became a mecca for European business investors and individuals seeking a new life, and artists, intellectuals and writers experiencing an atmosphere of tolerance and freedom and a more open-minded society than hitherto. The city remained a

---

[*] None of the four constitutions drafted between 1866 and 1902 or their precursor, the Egyptian equivalent of a bill of rights granted by the Ottoman sultan in Istanbul in 1848, gave preference to one faith or one language.

[†] He acquired the title 'sheikh' after graduation from the Alexandria Institute of Theology in 1905; like many young sheikhs, he studied music. Playing the lute, Darweesh sang at cafés, bars and private parties before going on a tour in Syria and subsequently joining several theatrical companies.

CHAPTER 2 Gare-Ramleh: Alexandria's Heart and History

'summer capital', the gateway to Egypt and its economic engine until the military takeover in 1952.

La Gare de Ramleh, built in 1887 by Italian-Slovene architect Antonio Lasciac (1856-1946), became the centre of activities. It is an asymmetrical rectangle, its western side occupied by the Trianon while its longer northern and southern sides embrace the tram tracks and narrow at its eastern tip where the Ibrahim Pasha Mosque stands since 1949; it was built by Mario Rossi (1897-1961). Like many places in Alexandria, it endured its share of Luftwaffe bombing between 1940 and 1942.

The space's northern side is made up of six blocks, with buildings in a style similar to that of London's St Pancras Station. The ground, mezzanine and first floors of these blocks were home to nightclubs, several bars, cafés and casinos like the Belle Vue, established in 1929, which until 1904 had been the booking hall of the 1883 Italian-style Gare de Ramleh. Some bars, restaurants and pâtisseries had an entrance on the tram-tracks side and another on the corniche like Athinèos which was more extensive and with larger windows overlooking the Eastern Harbour. It had an orchestra and a dance floor, with jazz and other popular bands most nights. In the afternoons and on Sundays it played classical music; Mozart and Schubert pieces could often be heard drifting out of this iconic salon de thé.

The farther, eastern two blocks were home to insurance, shipping and airline agencies like Alitalia and TWA, but the biggest office belonged to BOAC (British Overseas Airways Corporation, later merged with BAE – British European Airlines – to form British Airways). There were also offices and private doctors' surgeries, a convenient location for the latter since many of them were teaching staff at the medical school on the opposite southern side, next to the old British Consulate.

There was a cricket field behind the consulate used by several schools' boys. Tests were played against visitors, mostly from the Commonwealth and British teams. The Scottish School, which overlooked the cricket field, was sequestrated by Colonel Gamal Abdel Nasser (1918–1970) and renamed Ramleh Secondary School.

The greater Mehatet el-Ramleh area was Alexandria's downtown. A semicircular area a little under a kilometre across covered Rue Safia Zaghloul, Rue Fuad, Rue Sultan Hessein, Rue Ancient Boruse and scores of smaller roads as laid on Dinocrates' original grid. It was like Leicester Square, Piccadilly, Haymarket, Soho and the Strand were for London. The district boasted two dozen cinemas and scores of Greco-Alexandrian eating, drinking and leisure places – from the traditional affordable tavernas serving the famous retsina, ouzo and Birra Stella to more upmarket restaurants and cafés, where you could order Metaxa Reserve cognac, and more Alexandrian-Italian bars, bistros and takeaway outlets. My favourite takeaway was from the vetrina counter of A'la keifak ('As-you-like-it'), a bar-*bistrot* next to the Strand cinema. Massech, a wine merchant on the opposite corner, had every type of imported and locally produced wine and spirit you could think of. Whether luxury Armenian and French cognac, single malt or blended whisky, rum or various central European fruit brandies – Massech had them all. It spared shoppers the time of going around Italian, Greek, French, Armenian and Syro-Lebanese grocers, who mostly stored drinks imported from their ancestral lands while excluding other imported wines.

Turning left into Boulevard Sa'd Zaghloul, you come to Banque Belge on the corner of Rue Chakour Pasha, named after Alexandrian-born Joseph Chakour, the first elected *directeur general* of the *belediye* (municipality). The French-educated pasha, born to migrant Lebanese Maronite parents, was popular among Alexandrians for modernising projects during his term in office (1892–1903). He introduced services and made many improvements like the enlargement of the Eastern Harbour, the installation of filters in city abattoirs, the expansion of the tramway network and several municipal parks, and the initial planning of the corniche.

Some iconic landmarks on Rue Chakour Pasha were part of Alexandria's modern identity, like Cinéma Majestic and Cinéma Park, and an entrance to the large hall indoor food market of *Sou'e el-Misallah* ('the Obelisk Market') and the billiard hall. Next to the market was the best-known *fuul medames* and falafel restaurant in the city, opposite the Israeli Girls School. Fuul Benyamine was founded by Benyamine, an Alexandrian Jew of Yemeni ancestry. The head waiter, Mohammed Ahmed, would serve the dish in a variety of forms: mashed *fuul* with tahini, with olive oil, or with tomatoes – sometimes with boiled or fried eggs, and with pastirma. The falafel, too, was sometimes stuffed with an egg. Besides these delights, it also served Sephardic and Mizrahi dishes – and *shakshuka* was one of Benyamine's specialities. It was made of cooked tomatoes with green peppers and olives; onions were optional, but eggs floating in the thick red soup were essential. When pressure increased on the Jews, Benyamine, to avoid sequestration, gave the majority shareholding to his Muslim head waiter, Monsieur Ahmed, and then the rest of the business when he left in 1957.

It is now a tourist attraction known as 'fuul Mohammed Ahmed', and the founder's name has been erased from official tourist guidebooks, but many Alexandrians still call it 'Benyamine'. Benyamine's was frequented by many European royals and celebrities in Alexandria during the War. Queen Sofia of Spain – who grew up in Alexandria where her late

CHAPTER 2   Gare-Ramleh: Alexandria's Heart and History

father, King Paul of Greece (1901–1964), was exiled during the Nazi occupation of his native country – made a high-profile visit to the *fuul* restaurant in 1989. The Spanish queen remembered the new owner, who, in turn, remembered her favourites when she used to visit the restaurant with her brother, Constantine (later, Constantine II).

There were dozens of small stalls and tiny shops specialised in repairing watches and radios, and in filling and repairing cigarette lighters, in addition to tobacconists' and newspaper kiosks and the stalls of lottery-ticket and cigarette vendors.

The 1952 coup regime changed the street name and sequestrated the Jewish school. The two cinemas were demolished in the 1990s and replaced by ugly blocks.

Place Sa'd Zaghloul, where I sat reading the papers, was an extension of Mehatet el-Ramleh. This opens onto the sea corniche, itself rebuilt in 1906 as a road with pavements either side and a metre-high stone fence along the Eastern Harbour curve. Once the new quay of Ptolemaic Alexandria's main anchorage and the site of the Ptolemies' palaces, this area had been overlooked and neglected by successive governments until 1906. Mehatet el-Ramleh became a hub for both revellers and commuters from the city's western, southern and eastern quarters, thanks to the replacement of the steam train that linked the city centre to the eastern suburbs of Ramleh (which means 'the sand', because it was just sand all the way to the Bay of Abukeir) with electric-powered trams in 1904. We used to sit on the upper deck of tram el-Ramleh to and from Sidi-Bishr *Arrêt*. As the line arches south towards al-Siouf and Victoria Terminus you could see, from the upper deck, a sea of sand and dunes stretching to the horizon and dotted with windmills powering water pumps for cottages, bungalows, huts and chalets behind the one- and two-storey villas with their back gardens hugging the tramline.

Tramway el-Ramleh: a Ride into History
The tram, running from Victoria Terminus east to Gare de Ramleh, was a living organ in Alexandria's body. It almost had invisible glands emitting unique cultural pheromones, attracting some types of passengers to colonise certain areas while releasing repellents keeping away other types. Until the mid-1960s, few – if any – migrants from the Egyptian countryside residing in the city's southwestern quarters would be seen on Tramway el-Ramleh. It was like a monster scaring them, a psychological electric fence they feared touching. For others, the Ramleh tram was an institution, a ride into the history of Alexandria, her growth and development over 150 years – not only in the spheres of culture, arts, engineering, architecture and archaeology but also in commerce, business and military affairs.

While the military regime's renamed stops are meaningless, the original tram *arrêts* names marked chapters of Alexandria's 3,000-year history. Soter was named after Ptolemy I, who oversaw Alexander's dream of building the great city and started on the lighthouse and the magnificent Bibliotheca Alexandrina. Appropriately, Soter was the stop for both the Greek Community Club and University College of Arts and Classics. Known as the 'stilettos-campus' because its female students, who competed in fashion and in showing leg, outnumbered male students by three to one, it also had one of the university's best-known cafeterias. The indoor buffet, with its three-sided ceiling-high glass windows, had a well-stocked bar serving varieties of wines, spirits, cocktails and the famous Alex ice-cold Stella. Soter was also the *arrêt* for one of the city's true icons: Casino de Chatby, a 1920s end-of-pier restaurant and café by day and entertainment restaurant at night. French musicians and singers like Louis Charles Augustin Trenet (1913–2001) and Maurice Chevalier (1888–1972) performed there. It exchanged performers of variety shows, magicians and dancers with a nightclub on the cornice road called Monte Carlo. I used to watch Suad perform there. She was a lovely dancer, who was the most genuine and honest among many girls I dated over the years.

West of Soter was Lazarietta (originally Lazaretto, meaning 'isolation from contagious infection'), where the first health quarantine was built by Muhammad Ali. Arrivals to Alexandria were to quarantine before travelling inward. Some 400 metres east of Soter lay *Arrêt* Dinocrates, named after the architect whose 332 BC plan for Alexandria became a blueprint for modern town planning. Without chalk, he improvised the use of barley grain to mark roads and the angles of crossroads, competing all the while with seagulls swooping down to eat them. At the time, some said it was a bad omen; others said, a sign from the gods that the great city would nourish and sustain the whole planet. Three kilometres east, the tram travels 300 years 'forward' into Bain Cleopatre (Cleopatra's *hammamamt*, although in reality she never bathed there). In all, two tram stops, a *plage*, an urban quarter and several Alexandrian landmarks are named after history's most glamorous queen, whose mind exceeded her beauty, charm and (alleged) seductiveness. Cleopatra, the wise and much-loved ruler who introduced festivals, parades, leisure and enriched knowledge. Cleopatra the warrior, plotting her next manoeuvre. The survivor. The strategic gambler who spoke Greek, the language of the ruling class and the Old World's superior knowledge masters; demotic Egyptian, the language of her people – Christians, Jews, pagan-Hellenes and Amunites of many races – and Latin, the tongue of the emerging lesser-cultured superpower.

CHAPTER 2   Gare-Ramleh: Alexandria's Heart and History

Between Bain Cleopatre and Dinocrates stops, the tram passes Chatby, named after a Muslim saint from Andalucía and the location of three landmarks. At the University Littorie Campus on Rue Plato, the other best-known university cafeteria stood by the Art Deco swimming pool. Named after its founder, the modernist Regie Scuole Littorie the project was entirely funded by the Mussolini government. It was opened in 1933 by King Victor Emmanuel III and turned into a military hospital for the allies during The War, but seven years later was bought by Alexandria University. Chatby is also the *arrêt* for Al-Ittihad, the Alexandria United sports club (established 1914). The AUFC has become inseparable from the twentieth-century Alexandrian identity since Alexandrians hold AUFC in their hearts like Liverpudlians cherish Liverpool FC.

Opposite the club on Rue Plato's western side, there is a large plot extending south to Rue Abukeir and west to *Arrêt* Soter. It was home to several connected cemeteries with tombstones of different ethnicities telling the story of Alexandria: a Greek Orthodox cemetery and museum, Armenian Orthodox graves, Greek Catholics, Armenian Catholics, Eastern Orthodox graves around the Coptic church of Mar Gerges (Saint George) and a military war memorial near the Anglican cemetery. There are some great works of art here, in stone, alabaster and marble. Latin Catholics, Syriac Catholics and Jews all lay in a harmony and peace that didn't always exist during their lives. They are proof of Alexandria's centuries-old cosmopolitanism. The names on some of the tombstones are those of men who built modern Alexandria. One is the Franco-Greco-Alexandrian Sir John Antoniadis (1818–1895), creator of Nuzha Palace and gardens, who was knighted by Queen Victoria for his services to culture and archaeology. Others are the businessmen, bankers, investors, industrialists and philanthropists who developed the city's economy and prosperity – Bianachi, Glymonopoulo, Anastasi – and, of course, Alexandria's poet, Cavafy.

On the northern side of the tram tracks, opposite the cemeteries, stands Collège Saint-Marc, one of Alexandria's top elitist boys' schools. It was established in 1928 by the sixteenth-century Catholic order, the De La Salle Brothers, and among the school's graduates are some internationally recognised names: Dodi al-Fayed (1955–1997), the late Princess Diana's death-partner; and former Egyptian foreign minister and Arab League secretary-general Dr Esmat Abd-el-Meguid (1923–2013).

The next stop, *Arrêt* Camp de Cesar, served the university stadium and college of civil engineering on the highest hill before approaching Old Alexandria, where Octavian pitched his camp in the summer of 30 BC after defeating Mark Antony and the Egyptian fleet a year earlier at the Battle of Actium (2 September, 31 BC). This is also an *arrêt* for the iconic Lycée Français d'Alexandrie school for girls, established in 1909 by the Mission laïque française. Its parents' association used to hire a special double-decker tram for the two daily school runs. The school remained the city's top girls' educational establishment until it was 'nationalised' by the Nasser regime, and standards took a nose-dive. Like Saint-Marc's, it has a good theatre, cinema auditorium and sports teams.

A kilometre northeast of Bain Cleopatre, the tram screeches its way back into the twentieth century. The track arches, hugging the coast as it passes the tram-maintenance works before stopping at Mustaf Pasha Army Barracks. This military installation was founded in the mid-nineteenth century by one of Muhammad Ali's officers who went to America to serve there and later returned. The barracks were named after Khedive Ismail's younger brother, the French-educated Mustafa Bahgat Fazil Pasha (1830–1875). When the Porte in Istanbul changed the line of succession, depriving him of the throne, he left Egypt in protest and became the patron of Yeni Osmanlilar (the 'Young Turks' opposition). He returned to Egypt when his nephew Tawfik ascended the throne, becoming a finance minister then justice minister in 1871. The barracks witnessed historic military actions twice. In 1882, Khedive Tawfik stayed there during the bombardment of Alexandria, marking the highpoint of the Ourabi-led army revolt culminating in the British occupation.[*] During the Second World War, the barracks searchlights crisscrossed the city's skies along with others from five hills around Alexandria, searching for Luftwaffe bombers. My mother, whose stepmother was injured by shrapnel from a German bomb and died later of septicaemia, had many stories about the 'sounds of war' during the blackout nights, when Allied anti-aircraft guns thundered during the air raids. Children were still finding their fragmented cases in 1960 near the camp.

The Ramleh tram tracks continue for another nine kilometres eastwards, running between 500 and 70 metres back from the coastline – the widest gap at the east end of the barracks and the start of a fashionable quarter full of large villas, including the British ambassador's summer residence. *Arrêt* Rushdy Pasha is named after Hessein Rushdy[†] (1863–1928), Egypt's eleventh prime minister (1914–19) and the location of his massive summer house. Rushdy Pasha, under pressure

---

[*] Ahmed Ourabi Pasha (1839–1911), from a peasant background, joined the army aged 14 and was promoted quickly. When a colonel, he led an army mutiny beginning in 1881 against Khedive Tawfik, who wanted to be independent from the Ottoman caliphate. The Ourabists opposed modernity and symbolise the military alliance with traditional Islamists.

[†] In some reference books it is written Hussien, and/or Roshdy.

CHAPTER 2   Gare-Ramleh: Alexandria's Heart and History

from the British, declared war on the Central Powers in the Great War. He had to resign to recognise al-Wafd – the delegation led by Zaghloul Pasha – as representatives of the Egyptian people on the world stage, demanding official legal independence and ending British protection. Rushdy's French-born wife, Eugenie le Burn-Rushdy, was one of the pioneering Egyptian feminists, joining Egyptian women like Huda Shaarawi (1879–1947), the daughter of a speaker of parliament. The movement's early impact was mostly intellectual; like her fellow women's-movement leaders, le Burn-Rushdy had her influential salon hosting writers, artists, poets and journalists of both sexes.

The tracks reach their closest point to the Mediterranean at *Arrêt* Laurent. Édouard Laurent was a nineteenth-century industrialist and philanthropist who built a school, local housing and a mosque, and donated to local public services. Rue Laurent led to *Plage* Laurent, marking the start of the famous golden sandy *plages* of Sidi-Bishr, where Cleopatra's bath really was located – four kilometres northeast of *Arrêt* Sidi-Bishr in a sand-rock island. The last queen of Egypt used to bathe in a small lake inside the rocks of an island 650 metres off *plage* Miami's sands. I once swam to the rocky isle and dived into the lagoon where she bathed under a full moon.[1]

Other tram stops were named after people who contributed to Alexandria's history, wealth and built realm. Zizinia was named after the dynastic founder, Count Stephen Zizinia (1794–1868). Zizinia epitomised the complex and nebulous identity of cosmopolitan Alexandrians. He was born in Chois, arrived as a slave from Greece with Ibrahim Pasha after the 1822 Massacre of Chios. Ibrahim promoted Tsisinia (Zizinia); he later acquired French citizenship while conducting business in Marseilles.[2] He became Belgian consul but was also elected president of the Greek community in Alexandria, and invested in and contributed to Alexandria as an Egyptian national building his city. Comte Menandre de Zizinia (1832–1907) constructed the Ramleh district bearing his name, building a theatre in 1862–63. Teatro Zizinia on Rue Rosette (later Rue Fuad) was designed by Italian architect Pietro Avoscani (1816–1891), who emigrated to Alexandria in 1837. Only in Alexandria could a slave become army officer, a consul general (later ambassador) and a minister. Alexander the Great, whose spirit resides in the city's genes, had set an example to follow. The founder of Alexandria, the greatest general in history who ruled most of the known world from Macedonia to India by the time he was only 32, married Roxana, the daughter of a captured barbarian tribesman from Bactria of no political significance, making her his equal.

Zizinia Senior also erected a church in 1863 dedicated to St Stephen, giving its name to the famous iconic Hotel San Stephano, which in turn gave its name in turn to another tram stop. The hotel, where the Egyptian cabinet used to meet in the summer, was demolished in 2000 and replaced by an obnoxious shopping mall.

The stop before San Stephano, *Arrêt* Mazloum Pasha, was named after Ahmed Mazloum (1878–1928), who was chief justice of *les tribunaux mixtes* and twice speaker of the Egyptian parliament, a minister of justice (1893–4) and finance minister (1894–1908). His large residence, built in 1898 by Lasciac, opposite the tram stop, was donated by his family to house the Alexandria College of Fine Arts. Proceeding southwest on another branch of the tramway el-Ramleh an *arrêt* carries the name of Nestor Gianaclis. He was the founder of a cigarette factory for exports, with a world trademark. Gianaclis, who came to Alexandria in 1864, revived the almost dying viticulture that had started in 3000 BC, expanded vine growing after spending 18 years searching for the perfect soil.[3] The Greek settler started new vineyards in 1882 using ancient Egyptian vines, and founded modern wine distilleries using thousand-year-old recipes.

The tram terminates at Victoria, where Victoria College is located. Named after the famous British queen in 1900, it became known as the 'Eton of the Mediterranean'. Many celebrated names were to be found among Victoria graduates: King Hussein of Jordan (1935–1999); Omar Sharif (1932–2015); Youssef Chahine (1926–2008); Tsar Simone-II (Simone Saxe-Coburg-Gotha) of Bulgaria (b.1937); the author of the 1938 book *The Arab Awakening*, George Antonius (1891–1942); the Palestinian- American scholar Edward Said (1935–2003); British mathematician Michael Atiyah (1929–2019); Saudi billionaire arms dealer Adnan Khashoggi (1935–2017); and the Egyptian-Israeli-Swiss inventor of the open-architecture model, Gilbert de Botton (1935–2000).

There is a great contrast between the southern and northern branches of the tram-track areas. The sand dunes, palm trees and bulrushes on the edge of swamps around the newish quarters dominate the landscape near Victoria. To the west – towards central Alexandria, where the tram-track branches at Sporting's – you are in early twentieth-century Europe. *Arrêt* Sporting's services both the *plage* and a residential area to the north and, to the south, the racecourse and sports club (founded 1890) including tennis, squash and cricket facilities.

A kilometre south is *Arrêt* Ibrahimiyah, a stop between Sporting's and Camp de Cesar, which was named after Muhammad Ali's great-grandson, Ibrahim Rifaat Pasha (1855–1932), who developed the area, drained its marshes and modernised the quarter, which was established by Greek migrants in the 1820s. General Ibrahim Rifaat

CHAPTER 2   Gare-Ramleh: Alexandria's Heart and History

led the Egyptian *mahmal* twice (in 1901 and 1903), the annual aid allocation, including supplies and covers for the Ka'ba in Mecca's grand mosque.

The 700-year-old tradition of sending assistance to *Higaz* (Arabia) was started by Shagart el-Dur[†] in 1250. It continued annually until interrupted by Ottoman rule in 1617. The custom was re-established by Muhammad Ali in 1818 after his sons, Ibrahim Pasha and Toson Pasha, quelled the Wahhabi rebellion between 1813 and 1818. The *mahmal* tradition continued until it was stopped in 1929. There was a dispute on who leads the Muslim world after the end of Ottoman Caliphate, with Egypt refusing to recognise Abdul Aziz Ibn-Saud's (1875-1953) taking over *Higaz*. In 1926, the Wahhabi Ikhwan, who considered the customary music-band accompanying *mahmal* an ungodly innovation, attacked the procession in Mana on the outskirts of Mecca. The Egyptian soldiers opened fire, killing 23 and injuring many. Three years later, Ibn Saud closed down the Egyptian Consulate in Jedda, and King Fuad I (1868–1936) cut the annual aid. The *mahmal* returned under his successor, Farouk, when Maher Pasha's government recognised Saudi Arabia in 1936. But it was stopped by King Faisal (1906–1975) of Saudi Arabia in 1966, in a dispute with Colonel Nasser.[4]

Ibrahim Rifaat was a traveller, and his book *Mira'at el-Harmaine* (The Holy Shrines' Mirror) was the earliest detailed geographical description of Arabia, its western coast, the Nagd mound, Mecca and medina, as well as customs and the culture of the people there. He also added detailed maps and photographs in later editions.[5]

Other tram stops' names – like Bacos (Bacchus), the Roman god; or Sidi-Gaber, referring to a saint's shrine – were associated with folkloric myth without much historical evidence. Glymenopoulo stop was named after the wealthy Greek-Alexandrian family who built a hospital and founded charities, and was also associated with an iconic *plage*. Carlton, Fleming, Buckley, Saba Pasha and Schultz were named after engineers who constructed the tram network or contributed to the areas carrying their names, and most were committee members of the late nineteenth-century semi-independent *belediye*, the richest in the region.

---

[*] A *mahmal* is a pyramid-shaped carriage with gifts sitting on top of a camel, referring specifically to a train of camels that Egypt sent to Arabia with an annual aid allocation including clothes, supplies and payments for the officials there. After raids by Arab tribesmen, the *mahmal* mission became part of the military's responsibility.

[†] Shagart al-Dur ('Aṣmat ad-Dīn 'Umm-Khalīl d.1257) became ruler of Egypt following the death of her husband, Sultan Saleh Ayyub (1205-1249), the last Egyptian sultan of the Ayyubid dynasty, and later of Izz al-Din Aybak (d1227; r.1250-57), the first sultan of the Bahri Mamluk dynasty (1250-1382).

Alexandria Adieu

Only in cosmopolitan, kaleidoscopic Alexandria could you have a tramline with stops carrying such historical, geographical and economic names: a Roman Caesar, the ancient world's top architect, a Ptolemaic king, the last Egyptian queen, a British queen, warriors and travellers of different races and faiths, Egyptian pashas and prime ministers, English gentlemen, a Belgian consul, Muslim and Catholic saints of both Egyptian and European background, and a Roman god of wine.

CHAPTER 3
The Hotel Cecil

The warm autumn morning had started pleasantly when I left Hotel Cecil, but now I took refuge in my memories. I became H.G. Wells's unnamed time traveller, but with my machine remaining in Place Sa'd Zaghloul, whose architecture I knew, while the Alexandria of 2012 was like a science-fiction fantasy. A colony controlled by a race of invaders with a queer ethos and an alien culture. When, rather than where, was I? The regal palms, Zahgloul Pasha statue and the Italian Consulate were still there, caressed by the familiar sea breeze from the Eastern Harbour.

This site had, for several years, been the busiest in the ancient world. It was the quay where building materials had unloaded during the construction of the 138-metre high Lighthouse of Alexandria, completed in 12 years starting around 280 BC. The Pharos was one of the Seven Wonders of the Ancient World, radiating rays of light and of Alexandria's superior episteme to the whole world for 1,600 years. It also projected a mixture of real events and myths, together making up Alexandria's story: Cleopatra's defenders of the city re-angling the giant mirrors atop the lighthouse to focus the strong sunrays, burning the Roman ships; or the light dying when the keeper vanished (he has originally been the only surviving mariner from a shipwreck whose sailors were blinded by the Pharos' light).

The last dip I had taken in the Eastern Harbour had been in 1959; Alexandria was convulsing then in pain and confusion, while losing her children. Everyone we knew had left Alexandria – deported, chased out, fled – or were planning to go. My cousins and I used to take a sailboat, at sunrise, to the Eastern Harbour wave barrier and spend the whole day with our fishing rods landing a handsome Mediterranean

35

catch. We unhooked still-living fish and placed them in baskets made of bamboo and netting, dangled in the water to keep them alive until we left around six each evening. We used to throw the fish that didn't survive to the circling seagulls.

Pharos Island and Legends
The Eastern Harbour is the bay to the east of the Heptastadion. This causeway, spanning 1,399.95 metres – equivalent in length to seven Greek stadia, hence the name – was created by Dinocrates in 332 BC to link Pharos Island with the mainland and the fishing village of Rhakotis a kilometre to the south.

Homer described Pharos as an 'island in the surging sea…lying off Egypt. It has a harbour with good anchorage; hence they put out to sea after drawing water'.[1] Homer's island is now the peninsula of Ras-el Tin, Bahary, Anfoushy and part of the city's Turkish quarter. There were no traces of any early human settlement in its soil. But in the sea around its shores, the stonework of a pre-historic harbour has been found.

Homer tells us how Menelaus was marooned on Pharos when he returned home from Troy; he only got away when he entrapped Proteus, the divine king of the island, and exacted a favourable wind from him. A related legend was found in an ancient Egyptian papyrus. In it, the king followed a reference as Prouti, interpreted by many as 'Pharoah'. But there was no mention of a pharaoh (meaning great house or palace, to imply a 'king'), engraved on temples or tombs. But the two biliteral hieroglyphs referred to the 'office of the great house' during the Eighteenth Dynasty's Thatmos III (1479–25 BC).[2]

Throughout a 700-year period starting with Dinocrates laying her foundation, Alexandria was the Hellenic world's 'mind'. The city would lose her political influence after coming under Roman sovereignty in 32 BC, but retained her dominance in culture, science, medicine and philosophy for another four centuries.

The Heptastadion divided the natural bay into two harbours, and by extending the islands east and west Dinocrates created wave barriers for both ports. In 332 BC, Rhakotis and five other villages stretched along the strip between the Mediterranean Sea and the marshes of Lake Mareotis. The lake had a greater depth than it currently does and was directly connected to the Nile, making a waterway to the sea. The lake harbour was an integral part of the plan when Alexander ordered his architect to build the city between the marsh and the sea, according to Diodorus Siculus (90–30 BC).[3]

The eastern side of Place Sa'd Zaghloul is occupied by the aforementioned Italian Consulate; the western side was rebuilt between

CHAPTER 3   The Hotel Cecil

the mid-nineteenth century and the Great War, replacing terraced houses dating back to the seventeenth century. On its northwestern corner sits the Cecil Hotel, where I stayed overnight. I had a welcome drink at Montgomery's Bar – so named for its association with the Allied Eighth Army commander-in-chief, Field Marshal Bernard Law Montgomery (1887–1976). 'Monty', as he was known to his soldiers and the press, stayed in the hotel for a few days with his officers while drawing up plans for the defence of Alexandria against the advancing mechanical divisions of Field Marshal Erwin Rommel(1891-1944). They planned the final confrontation in El-Alamein, 106 kilometres west of Alexandria. Monty defeated 'the Desert Fox' Rommel in November 1942 – a turning point in the War, reversing the German advance's tide in what Sir Winston Churchill (1874–1965) called 'the end of the beginning'. The defeat at El-Alamein prevented the Nazis from taking the strategic Burg el-Arab airport, where I had landed 12 hours earlier. Instead, it became Alexandria's operational airport in 2011 while Nuzha, the main airport, was undergoing renovation and still closed to international flights. Had Rommel occupied Alexandria, he would have also taken the Suez Canal, giving him access to the oil of Arabia.

The Iconic Hotel
Alexandria witnessed the grand opening of the Cecil Hotel just as the world was entering the Great Depression. The iconic hotel, first called Le Palais Regina and built in the Moorish style by Alexandrian-Jewish architect Giacomo Alessandro Loria (1879–1937), was completed in 1929. Loria was commissioned by Albert Metzger, a Jew from Alsace, who acquired British citizenship. Renamed The Cecil a year later by Metzger, the hotel was the last building to be constructed on the square opposite an open space: a Great War campsite for Allied soldiers and a launch base for the ill-fated Gallipoli campaign. The Cecil was immediately recognised as the best hotel in Alexandria, and for Lawrence Durrell it was always preferable to Cairo's Shepheard's Hotel because of its proximity to the sea. Colonel Nasser seized the hotel in 1956; the Metzgers were expelled from Alexandria, where their children had been born, with the permissible one suitcase each.

Albert began a new life with his family in Tanzania. He bought the New Africa Hotel in the capital, Dar-es-Salaam, running it successfully. It was nationalised in 1964, perhaps confirming the old superstition from Jewish folklore that a Jew was doomed to lose his fortune twice. He died in 1971. His daughter-in-law, Patricia Metzger (who had held her engagement party at Hotel Cecil a few months before the family's 1956 expulsion), fought a nightmare decade-long battle through the Egyptian courts. In 1996, the court ruled in her favour but the ruling was never implemented. John Metzger and his mother Patricia signed a deal with the Egyptian-state-controlled Egoth hotel chain to buy back their very own property for an undisclosed sum. The Mubarak Government (1981–2011) opposed the transaction, fearing setting a legal precedent for the tens of thousands of expelled Alexandrians who had also had their property sequestrated. In a bizarre arrangement, the Metzgers sold the iconic hotel back to the Egoth group, which had been dragging its feet in paying the agreed $10 million price tag, as John Metzger (now a Canadian citizen) told non-government-controlled Egyptian newspapers.

The Changes

It was my first stay at the landmark Cecil since December 1992, when I spent Christmas Day and had Turkey and crackers with two of my children, then aged ten and eight. The mood was sombre until someone remembered that *our* Christmas was on 25 December and played some tracks of Christmas hits from the 1970s, and there were little signs of festivities. Egyptian Christmas is on 7 January following the Eastern Church, I explained to my children, but I should have noticed even then, in 1992, that Alexandria was 'slipping through our fingers'. There were fewer of the seasonal decorations than I was used to seeing as a child on every street since the last week of November. The 1990s witnessed the acceleration of Islamisation, with increasing social intolerance of other cultures and faiths. The Mubarak regime gambled dangerously in the 1990s, attempting to appear more Muslim than the armed Islamist terrorist groups it was battling. Regime apologists in the Western media claimed Mubarak was competing with the well-funded and well-organised Muslim Brotherhood. However, although the current near-total Islamisation of Egyptian society has always been the objective of the terrorist groups, in reality the regime itself had Arabo-Islamist components within its political foundation.

Although such thoughts were disturbing, the view of the Eastern Harbour was calming – and the memory of a taste of Stella was a return to my Alexandria: the Alexandria of the corniche, the manicured lawns and flower beds on the square, and the *Roystonea regia* palms with their creamy trunks rising up to 20 metres. In the 1950s, thousands of these regal palm trees, many over 100 years old, stood tall, guarding Alexandria's clean avenues, boulevards, squares, circuses and open spaces. There was hardly any quarter without giant mature trees and green spaces in their open areas.

The avenues and boulevards stretched east–west on Dinocrates' grid, on the narrow strip between the Mediterranean and the three lakes and the swamps to the south. The strip today stretches 40

CHAPTER 3   The Hotel Cecil

kilometres, marking a city over eight times the size of the one founded by Alexander. But the man who carried out his vision was his general, Ptolomy I (Soter; 367–283 BC),* whose plan for Alexandria was so much admired later by Strabo (63 BC–21 AD):

> *'The city has magnificent public precincts and royal palaces which cover a fourth or even a third of the entire area. For just as each of the kings would, from a love of splendour, add some ornament to the public monuments, so he would provide himself at his own expense with a residence in addition to those already standing.'*~4

At the southern end of Hotel Cecil terrace, Café Pullman fanned out its tables and chairs on the sunny pavement. Horse-drawn *hantours* lined up on one side of the slip-road separating the green from the terrace, and taxis waited on the other side. The café served passengers who waited for the hourly Pullman service to Cairo via the desert route. The silver-coloured Pullman, with air-conditioning and comfortable leather seats, was a luxurious way to travel when replacing the loaded coaches of the 1930s.

In the morning, I passed the café, crossing the square by the Chambre du Commerce to al-Ma'arif bookshop, which had stood on the southern side of the square for 100 years.

Books, Coffee and Omar Effendi

It was my favourite as a schoolboy because its books were cheaper than anywhere else, thanks to state subsidies. I was always a bookworm as a teenager; perhaps this is what turned me into a writer – leading to individual thinking and the isolation of burying my head in books, bottling up my emotions only to pour them out onto pages. I have always been self-employed, except for a total of 11 years dotted throughout a 53-year career.

I picked up the newspapers from al-Maarif, and a few books that London stores claimed were out of print. A £€50 tip ensured the shop assistant would drop them at my hotel. I exited from the store's southern entrance into Boulevard Sa'd Zaghloul, right next door to the Brazilian Coffee Stores.

Founded in 1928 by the Greco-Alexandrian Sedaris family, the Brazilian Coffee Stores became a popular meeting place in Alexandria. Not only could one order at the bar the best freshly roasted *café turc* in town but also, my favourite as a schoolboy, a delicious iced-chocolate drink, the taste of which still resides in my mouth's memory. As the world economy was heading for depression in 1929, there was a surplus

---

* Also known as Ptolemy Lagos, Ptolemy Lagides and Ptolemaïos Sōtḗr, while modern Alexandrians and Alexandrinologists call him *Sōtḗr*.

of Brazilian coffee production – such that it was said that the railway locomotives used to run on coffee beans instead of coal.

After scanning the front pages over two cappuccinos, wondering about their mini-size cups, and a bottle of Evian, I put my Panama hat on and turned left towards Omar Effendi (Orosdi Back) department stores. I was looking specifically for 100% cotton socks, impossible to find in England. With their headquarters in the French capital, Omar Effendi, founded in 1856 by a former Hungarian army officer, had once been a match for any elegant department store in Paris or Rome. However, they had fallen on bad times and the premises looked poor and shabby; little wonder I was the only customer on a Saturday morning. While the bookshop and Brazilian Coffee Stores were still characteristically Alexandrian shops, Omar Effendi looked like a different planet. First were the chubby, scruffy *higabb*ed* shop assistants. This headcovering was never seen in Alexandria in the 1950s or 1960s, when female headgear arose from practicality, not faith or coercion. Domestic staff and factory girls used a tightened *écharpe* around the head to keep dust off their hair, or for hygiene when handling food. The *écharpe* was practical for ladies of all ages and ethnic backgrounds to visit *le coiffure*, or on wet or windy days. It was an essential accessory in spring – the worst season in Alexandria, when the *khamaseen* wind blows in carrying fine desert sands. Older ladies used a single-colour *écharpe* while widows sported a black one during mourning.

In Omar Effendi, my mother had exchanged words with a serving mademoiselle in the Alexandrian tongue, Franco-Italian-Ottoman and some Egyptian words, while I had tried on new wristwatches with automatic windup triggered by hand movement. My young teen nose was tracking the shop assistant's stimulating perfume, like a beacon guiding my eyes to follow her dance-walk negotiating the glass display boxes.

The shop assistants of the post-war years took pride in their appearance. They were the power behind the efforts of department stores such as those on Boulevard Saad Zaghloul, Rue Tawfik, Rue Cherif and Place St Katherine to match their equivalents in Europe. The mademoiselles showed you the goods with beautifully manicured hands and smiling faces in simple but most attractive maquillage, a magnet for gentlemen shoppers. Chicorille, la Maison des Cadeaux, Hannux, Oreco, La Maison Francaise, Franco, Etam, Salone de Vere, Old England, Sednaoui, Omar Effendi and the like only employed educated mademoiselles on the shop floor. Like all Alexandrian girls, they were multilingual, cheerful, polite and friendly to customers.

---

* The Muslim headscarf, known by Arabs as the *hijab*, is called *higab* in Egypt.

CHAPTER 3   The Hotel Cecil

A gentleman who stops to buy a feminine gift on his way home would seek the mademoiselle's advice. Besides the *parfum*, he ends up buying *bas-de-soie*, and *soutien-gorge* using the attractive sales girl's assets as a reference point for his girlfriend's or wife's size.

Maman, annoyingly, ended the session, dragging me out of Omar Effendi. She must have noticed a young adolescent's sexual arousal caused by the kind of spark that Alexandrian stores instilled in most boys' subconscious – their awareness of the epitome of femininity through the senses: a mix of *parfum* and details like *maquillage* and perfect *manucure*, and the sound of high heels.

I smiled, remembering how annoyed I was by *Maman* cutting short the enjoyable session of trying-wristwatches choice with touches of sexy feminine fingers. Did my mother spoil the encounter when she noticed how red-cheeked I became at the pats of this most feminine mademoiselle?

Was I clutching at memories of 1950s-scented images like holding onto a lifebuoy while Ommar Effendi's ship was sinking in the waters of 2012's ugliness?

With the urge to escape the slaps of the present, I grabbed a few of the half-dozen-sock bundles and handed a £€100 tip to the shop assistant to deliver them to my hotel in her break. Why did I give her double the bookstore assailant's tip? Was I, subconsciously, sorry for her? Whether she had been brainwashed or forced by Islamists to turn herself into a Taliban peasant made little difference; the poor girl was a victim.

The alienating feeling that I caught with every visit to the city of my birth began to bite, but the ugliness-induced nausea sunk deeper this time; Alexandria has become much less Alexandrian.

I tried to adjust to the rhythm of a tram belling its way towards Rue Vieille Bourse. The modern trams looked hideous, like boils continually oozing pus on a landscape that nineteenth-century architects had laboured to make an aesthetic model to follow.

No Ice-cold in Alex?
'Birra Stella', I repeated to the frozen waiter, 'Birra Stella, *a'ranah*'. Didn't this dumb-garçon know what *a'ranah* (sweaty) was? The ice-cold green bottle with the moisture condensation on it?

There had been a public outcry when dark-brown glass replaced the iconic green bottle after the nationalisation of the brewery, once managed by Chakour Pasha, when he had left the municipality. Negative feedback from vendors to the renamed Birra al-Ahram company alarmed its long-term staff, who, in the old days, collected data about customers' satisfaction and cared about product quality and public image. Soviet-style public-sector apathy had not become the prevailing attitude yet. The iconic old green bottle was restored, and the brown glass was allocated to another variety called Birra al-ahram (piramidale), something between a stout and the Irish Guinness.

The more sophisticated cafés kept tall glasses, about two-thirds of a pint, in the freezer – and, of course, charged more for them. Cafés – regardless of the area's affluence, or even with a mosque around the corner – served Birra Stella. Grocers, corner shops, refreshments vendors with their traditional wooden iceboxes on street corners – all must store Alexandria's national drink, the two sizes of Stella: the 'sweaty' 1-litre bottle or the chilled, smaller 300cl one on a marble-top table. Stella before lunch, or before sunset, was often accompanied by some sea harvest. A passing vendor would offer delights of the Mediterranean: what he had spent the morning sea-diving to harvest from the rocky bottom using snorkels and an old army knife, and relying on his breath. When he gets older, he uses local boys to dive for a fee of a shilling a shift. The vendors pass by cafés carrying two bamboo baskets with seaweed algae in the bottom and around the edges, with wet hessian and crunched ice covering the sea harvest over another layer of crushed ice and salt. They offered *ritsa* (sea urchins), clams, oysters, mussels and *glagola* – shellfish varieties peculiar to Alexandrian rocks. Sea urchins were the favourite, with their spikes still moving. Customers choose between half to two dozens. The vendor squats, use scissors or a frogman's knife to cut the top, squeezes fresh lime and presents to customers. The waiter would bring small teaspoons for the punters to scoop the sea urchin, washed down with Stella.

I could taste the memory waltzing in my mouth. I shook my head, thinking of the economics of this very Alexandrian feature. The variation in the price depended on the season; on location, as the further east you went – into areas frequented by holidaymakers – the more you paid; and, of course, on your haggling skills. It was a common pastime for students native to Alexandria to dive, harvesting their own urchins, to impress their girlfriends waiting on the rocks with a basket to collect the catch; then consume them with friends and share with students from outside Alexandria who, in return, would pay the 6 *piastres* for the Stella. Most shellfish is now banned by the health authorities. Some idiot in charge of drainage and sewage linked raw-sewage outlets to the rainwater-drainage network. Since Roman times, the latter had been draining into the sea; the former, installed in the nineteenth century, used to go to a pumping station to treat and reuse for irrigation. A quarter-century after the disaster was discovered, they still hadn't determined precisely when the mix-up took place or found solutions.

CHAPTER 3 The Hotel Cecil

I lifted my head from the *Egyptian Gazette*, the paper in whose columns, and in those of the *Egyptian Mail*, Cavafy and Forster had first published works a century ago – and which had been daringly liberal and ahead of its time. That kind of poetry and prose had landed writers like Oscar Wilde (1854–1900) in jail in Britain. I wasn't concentrating on the poorly subbed news items; the ancient city's scenes had weaved themselves into my bewilderment about the waiter's inability to understand the significance of an ice-cold in Alex.

An ice-cold Stella waiting in Alex was enough reward for Allied soldiers to make a last stand, blocking Rommel's advance in the scorching Libyan desert. This overwhelming desire for a cold beer in the heat of battle was vividly described in John Lee Thompson's 1958 wartime movie *Ice Cold in Alex*, based on the 1957 novel of the same name by the late British novelist Christopher Landon (1911–1961).

'*Iskandriah nawarret* [flooded with light] Buongiorno. Ya Monsieur Darweeche'. A shriek snatched me from the late-morning swim in my memories. The café manager, with his arms wide open, was welcoming me in typical demotic Egyptian, French and Italian in one sentence.

I don't know this smartly dressed manager. He must have recognised me from television commentary thanks to satellite service everywhere. He offered the first drink on the house. I said I was delighted to be here and couldn't wait for my first Alexandrian Birra Stella in 15 years.

'Wouldn't Monsieur Darweeche be more comfortable inside?' said the manager as he continued to clear a nervous frog in his throat, 'quieter and bigger table?'

What was wrong with sitting outside? I was the only customer on the pavement. How often do I get this opportunity to sip Stella in open-air on a marble-top table overlooking the Eastern Harbour?

'The mosque', he whispered, pointing behind his back with his right thumb.

The nearest *gami'eh*, where he pointed past the tram terminus, was Gami'eh Ibrahim Pasha (Ibrahim Mosque), named after the son of Muhammad Ali, Ibrahim Pasha (1789–1848). The Greek-born Ibrahim famously commanded the Egyptian Army in 1813 to subjugate the Wahhabis of Nejd, the central mound of Arabia. His father had the foresight to recognise the danger of fundamentalist Islam founded by their ideologue and leader, Muhammed Ibn- Abd- al-Wahhab (1703–1792).

Was the Trianon not in direct sight of the mosque at the next tram stop?

'…Ah but those *Agitateurs islamiques* fools could pass by', explained the manager.

Seriously? Islamist agitators, who weren't even visible, have forced a lily-livered Trianon manger to change his Alexandrian way of life?

Alexandria was becoming ruralised, like Inner Egypt.

In 1998, I was commissioned, by a London-based Arabic newspaper, to write a feature about my experience as a foreign correspondent in the MENA region.*

In one paragraph, I quoted a pun by veteran foreign correspondent Julian Nundy during the 1982 Beirut siege. He said at the time that the taste in his memory of a famous 'ice-cold beer on Alexandria's corniche' made him prepared to risk the Israeli shells raining on Beirut harbour to sail immediately to Alex for another.

The 'beer' was voluntarily censored by an Egyptian sub changing it into 'chilled orange juice', leaving the readers clueless as to why the film title had been quoted in the first place.

The likes of that beer-allergic subeditor, invading Alexandria in the company of officials with deep fundamentalist Islamic beliefs, has turned the European city into a bastion of Islamists controlling the Mosque of Ibrahim, the very pasha who had pushed them back into their desert burrows 200 years earlier.

---

* MENA (the Middle East and North Africa region) is, geographically, an area between the Atlantic Ocean north of sub-Saharan Africa going all the way to the Khyber Pass.

CHAPTER 4
The Hyphenated Alexandrians

The Italo-Alexandrians
Sipping my Birra Stella at the Trianon, after the manager had moved me inside the iconic café to avoid offending any Islamists, I gazed at another Alexandrian feature: the beautiful facades of the city's nineteenth-century Venetian- and Moorish-style architecture. These were built by pioneering Italo-Alexandrian architects like the aforementioned Alessandro Loria. Indeed, much of Loria's work was still visible in central Alexandria around Place Mehatet-el-Ramleh: iconic buildings like the National Bank of Egypt, with its mosaic medallions and ascending arabesques on Rue Tawfik.

Loria was born in 1880 in Mansoura, around 300 kilometres southeast of Alexandria, home to a thriving Jewish community. Another prominent Mansoura native was my late friend Victor Nachmias (1933–2004). He would have featured in the next chapter, as a medic, had his pharmacology studies in Cairo's Qasr-el-Ainy not been prematurely interrupted: in 1957, he was deported with his family by Colonel Nasser's regime despite their centuries-long presence in Egypt. Like many Egyptian Jews, the Nachmiases were issued a single-trip passport with no right of return. They became refugees and eventually settled in Israel, where Victor later became head of the Arabic section on Israel television's Channel One.

The 16-year-old Loria started as a draftsman at the Alexandria Municipality's technical office before attending the Politecnico di Torino. After returning to Alexandria two years later, he was awarded the municipality's first prize for his Italian community hospital. Loria also built Alexandria's Jewish-community school and hospital at 40 Rue Moharrem-Bey; the Italian orphanage Constantine and Elena Drosso, and many buildings around Place Mehatel el-Ramleh.

45

La-Maternità, the Italian community hospital, later became the city's General Military Hospital during the Second World War but was still run and administered by Italian doctors and nurses. It continued to house a maternity unit, specifically for the wives of Allied army officers. Alexandrians still call the erstwhile Italian hospital –*Lamaternitàeh* – and refer to a hospital as *espidalà*.

The Italo-Alexandrians, renowned for their extroversion and affability, were different from the city's other races, like the overwhelmingly numerous Greeks, the self-isolating British or the aloof Germans. The Italians comprised Alexandria's one of the oldest immigrant communities; there had been mentions of them by Venetian merchants back in the sixteenth century.[1] They were concentrated around Attarin Mosque, built on the ruins of the Church of Saint Athanasius (296–373), protector of the old town.* By the nineteenth century, they had dispersed across most quarters of the city in order to find work, assimilating well with other communities in the process. The Italo-Alexandrians worked in every sphere: fashion, barbering, restaurants and catering, manufacturing and construction, civil engineering, and academia. They also worked successfully alongside others – particularly, more impoverished Egyptian immigrants like the countryside *fellaheen*. Besides architecture, the arts (especially music) and establishing a budding film industry, their contribution to Alexandria was a vast and enduring one.

Thousands of Italian words became integrated into the spoken demotic Alexandrian. The city's inhabitants never use Arabic in place of many (Italian-)Alexandrian like *Teatro* or *lampa* (lamp). Train, cinema and hotel classes alike are *primo*, *secondo* and *terzo*, while motor-car parts are frequently referred to by their Franco-Italian names. The Italo-Alexandrians were, in fact, the most ingenious motor mechanics and dominated motor-service depots and repair workshops throughout the city.

However, it is the Italo-Alexandrian architects whose achievements still visibly stand out today, resisting the winds of hideous change. One such building, by Loria – the aforementioned Lamaternità, where I was born on a cold, rainy December night after Rommel had been driven back from the gates of the city – was where my mother first met Peggy, an English lieutenant's wife, who would become her friend. The two young mothers pushed their Silver Cross prams, carrying their two boys

---

* Athanasius the Apostolic, also known as the Confessor, served as the twentieth Bishop of Alexandria (346–373). He spent over 17 years in a total of five exiles ordered by four different Roman emperors, and had to flee Alexandria on six other occasions to escape assassins.

CHAPTER 4 The Hyphenated Alexandrians

born one hour and one room apart, along the Challalat municipality gardens' neat paths. They would pass the waterfalls and ponds, then, on warm days, head north along Rue Champollion – named after the French scholar, Jean-François Champollion (1790–1832), who deciphered the Rosetta Stone hieroglyphs – towards the seafront.

Two years later, my mother witnessed the beginning of a significant demographic change in Alexandria when the British officers' regiment, and her La-Maternità friend, were relocated to the Far East. (Their emotional goodbye was a prelude to many, sadder, more shocking and even tragic farewells ten years later as Alexandria became the scene of the largest exodus from the land of Misr since Moses led his people across Sinai.) However, I never managed to solve the puzzle of why, when her waters broke, my mother telephoned La-Maternità requesting an ambulance instead of the Jewish Hospital just down the road from where she was buying Christmas decorations at Boutique Eureka on the corner of Rue Greene and Rue Moharrem-Bey. (Boutique Eureka specialised in toys, ladies' accessories, cosmetics and bric-à-brac – all in short supply during the War.) Perhaps it was the Italian doctors' reputation; the name La-Maternità even overrode the institution's new official title when it had become a military hospital. My mother – who moved between different jobs in education, social services and charities – also volunteered as an army-hospital nurse during the War. However, her dementia progressed in the last 15 years of her life, leading to a total memory loss. One day in 2003, a final loss of consciousness culminated in her death, and I never managed to get the full story from her.

I was not able to find out from my father, either. His death at a relatively young age in 1979 did not provide much opportunity for investigation since the family had been scattered across five continents. In the 20 years between the 1960 exodus and my father's death, I only saw him on three occasions. A stroke he suffered in the bathtub almost drowned him before he was taken to hospital, where he remained in a coma while I was overseas reporting from troubled regions.[*] Furthermore, the deterioration in my father's health coincided with a news-crowded, eventful period – particularly in the Middle East. The Egyptians and the Israelis signed their historic peace treaty, ending 30 years of intermittent war. Tensions were high in the Gulf, with Arab leaders alarmed by Iran's 1979 revolution culminating in Ruhollah Khomeini's (1902–1989) Islamist-extremist faction taking over and threatening the region. And Western intelligence agencies

---

[*] I was a foreign correspondent covering the Middle East and North Africa, and most of the time I was a freelancer; freelancing 'hacks' cannot afford the luxury of turning down an assignment.

were plotting in Cairo, Arab capitals, and Islamabad to undermine a new government in Afghanistan following a Marxist-flavoured coup in Kabul that later led to Soviet intervention. The unintended consequence of the CIA unwisely plotting with some Arab countries' intelligence agencies was the birth of a jihadist 'Frankenstein's monster', still rampaging decades later as it evolved into al-Qaeda and its splinter ISIL (the Islamic State in Iraq and the Levant). A telegram informing me of my father's critical condition and his placement on life-support equipment didn't reach me in time to say goodbye to Papa on his deathbed and to ask for his final forgiveness. I still endure the lashes of guilt every Father's Day.

The flight of most families from Alexandria under pressure from the Nasser regime was brutally swift, hasty and chaotic. Tens of thousands were scattered all over the globe. None of my mother's close friends was still around to ask when I wanted to know why she had risked transportation to the La-Maternità instead of the Jewish Hospital down the road in Moharrem-Bey. I also never found out what became of the English boy with whom I shared sandpits, toys, swings, and the first shock to little toes on wet sand when overwhelmed by the cold Mediterranean water.

The Judaeo-Alexandrians

A coincidence took me, in 1949, to a different hospital built by Loria. I had dislocated my left elbow and shoulder and broken the bone in my upper arm in two places. Papa was so appalled by the sight of the dirty floor at the entrance to the Alexandria University School of Medicine (al-Espetalia Almeery's Accident and Emergency unit) that he took me, in the middle of the night, to the Israeli hospital on Rue Abu-Kier.

This renowned hospital had been founded by the Austro-Hungarian Bekhor de Menasce (1807-1887), the head of a famous Alexandrian Jewish family, who built most of the northeastern part of the Moharrem Bey quarter. The de Menasces established many charities and created thousands of jobs, donating their property to become schools for the disadvantaged. People still call the tree-lined avenue Share'h Menasce Pasha, even 60 years after the Nasser regime removed the white calligraphed name 'Rue de Menasce Pasha' from the blue metal sign.

The Rue Abu-Kier Jewish Community Hospital – its name, *el-mustashfa el-Israélie* was engraved in large, black Arabic script on its plaster facade – was regarded as the best in the Middle East and among the world's best. In addition to first-class private care facilities, it also provided treatment to the needy for free, regardless of religion

CHAPTER 4   The Hyphenated Alexandrians

or ethnicity. Baron de Menasce* also built a museum and library at the eastern end of Rue de Menasce. He had a huge villa that people referred to as Saray Menasce (Menasce Palace), which he eventually donated to the Ministry of Education to house Al-Faroukyiah (King Farouk) Secondary School.

By the early hours of the following morning, back in 1949, my arm had been put back together and my joints reset by the Jewish orthopaedic consultant Dr Orvand, who had been called out of bed to attend to me. He had a private clinic on Rue Fuad. Its reception window overlooked the landmark salon de thé Pastroudis, where Durrell took Eve (Yevette) Cohen (1918-200) on their first date in 1943. Piano and soft music played in the afternoon in Pastrouids where a music band sometimes entertained diners in its upmarket restaurant. Another window overlooked the soon-to-be-opened Cinéma Amir, leased to 20th Century Fox. After its opening in 1950, it screened cartoons on Saturday mornings and always gave out presents to visiting children. The cinema kept a record of families and children attending, and I recall the manager arranging a surprise birthday cake, complete with balloons and music celebration for my sister's birthday.

Dr Orvand's clinic was located one floor above the private radiography clinic of another Jewish practitioner, this time of Italian descent, the radiologist Dr Polanyi, who X-rayed my arm and shoulder before and after it was plastered. Dr Orvand examined my arm and finger movements weekly, while Dr Polanyi X-rayed my arm twice at his private practice when it was in a cast for over two months.

The Israeli hospital was part of a charitable organisation, and accepted voluntary donations when offered. However, the staff – mostly, but not exclusively Jewish – never asked for donations to avoid embarrassing less-affluent patients. Both Dr Orvand and Dr Polanyi treated patients at the Israeli hospital on a voluntary basis, and Dr Orvand oversaw physiotherapy after my cast was removed, but both refused to charge my father any fees. My grandfather later donated to the hospital fund.

This incident came at a time of growing anti-Jewish sentiment and propaganda encouraged by the British, who were angered by Jewish groups' attacks in Palestine. British Intelligence was disturbed by some Egypt-based Zionist organisations supplying arms and funds to 'Jewish gangs' – a term coined by *les Anglais* and parroted by Egyptian media. It became a theme, among many, in Lawrence Durrell's *Alexandria Quartet*, underlying the complexities involved when the British

---

* Jacob De Menasce was given the title from the Austro-Hungarian Empire in 1873, a year after being granted its protection in Alexandria by Emperor Franz Joseph I (1830–1916).

diplomat Percy Pursewarden is let down by his Egyptian friends. As his relationship with prostitute-turned-lover Melissa develops, she advises him that his (non-Jewish) Egyptian friends were among those secretly donating to militant Jewish groups in Palestine. At this time, most Alexandrian Jews – especially the elite snobs – dismissed the notion of supporting militancy to establish an independent Jewish homeland as a 'silly idea'. This rejection by notable Alexandrian Jews was also explored by my late friend and renowned Alexandrian filmmaker, Youssef Chahine, in *Alexandria… Why?* – the first part of his Alexandria Trilogy. In Alexandria, Jews enjoyed the most extended, safest and most prosperous period in their modern history, from the early nineteenth century right up until the 1956 Anglo–French Suez blunder.

A few months before I broke my arm, Egypt's King Farouk had led and financed a military coalition of the newly formed Arab League nations in a war to block the Jewish state's independence. Despite the open anti-Jewish propaganda, the Israeli hospital continued to treat poor Alexandrians, mostly Muslims from the poor neighbourhood of Hadra, named after Emperor Traianus Hadrian (76–138 AD), who had stayed in the area when visiting in 128 AD. Here, migrants from the countryside lived in an area detached from European Alexandria socially, economically – and geographically by the railway line running from the central station, Gare du Masr, eastwards to Sidi Gaber before the tri-junction to Cairo, the Western Desert and Rosetta.

The hospital's policy of equality did not give preferential treatment to Jewish patients over non-Jewish ones. My own preferential treatment was a gift of my plaster cast, especially at school and within family circles. It aroused the curiosity of other children, who delighted in scribbling notes or drawings with pencils and coloured chalk on it while I threatened to hit them with my 'iron arm'.

I guess 1949 was a watershed year in both my family's fortunes and in Alexandria's history, marking the beginning of the end of the great city and a way of life that would disappear for good. Army officers – mostly from rural, *fellaheen* families – were politicised and began to conspire against King Farouk. Upon ascending the throne in 1936, Farouk opened the country's military school, police academy and the navy and air force to sons of the *fellaheen*. Like the judiciary, the military school had been very much a closed club for the sons of aristocrats, landowners and the upper classes. This was a longstanding tradition going back to the nineteenth century, on the understanding that a sense of duty to the nation rather than financial gain should be a motive for occupying public office. Prestige and a higher status in society were the real rewards, and many careers – particularly in medicine, the judiciary, the army and the police – became family

CHAPTER 4   The Hyphenated Alexandrians

traditions, with sons following fathers and grandfathers. Many would donate what they considered a meagre salary to charities associated with the lower ranks of their profession.

In addition to officers conspiring, a previously hidden or suppressed anti-Semitism began to manifest itself through hostile propaganda aimed at Jews from small political groups as well as from Islamists. While Islamists held a deep, historical hatred for the Jews, other political tendencies – especially nationalists – were stirring up anti-Semitism and anti-Western sentiment. It is the case today, and was the case then. Arab nationalism was not an adopted idea in Egypt at the time, nor was it a subject covered by the Egyptian media; Egyptian nationalism was the only focus. For Alexandrians and most Egyptians, the word 'Arab' then meant Bedouin. Only the Islamists held on to a caliphate concept akin to that of the Ottoman Empire.

Alexandrian Jews did not think of themselves other than Egyptian citizens, and in 1949 continued their enormous contribution to the city's economic, commercial and cultural landscape – as well as to medicine, as I witnessed during my broken-arm episode. One dentist, regarded as the best in the field in the ethnically heterogeneous neighbourhood of Moharrem Bey, was Dr Max Salama (1914–2008), who was, from 2000 until his death, leader of the now-decimated Alexandrian Jewish community.

Born into an old Alexandrian family, Dr Salama was both the 'King of Alexandria's Jews' (especially in later years) and her favourite dentist. The famous doctor was so popular that his patients included King Farouk's relatives and another Alexandrian socialite, Ellithy Nasser[*], President Nasser's brother. Dr Salama refused to leave at the peak of anti-Jewish propaganda and harassment when Jews came under pressure to do so. His patients always loved him; his reputation and service to the community at large protected him from the fate that befell most of Alexandria's Jews. The military regime did not touch Dr Salama during their decade-long ethnic-cleansing campaign, which started with the Suez War and ended with the Six-Day War and its conclusion – the Yom Kippur War.

Dr Salama extracted some of my milk teeth. At that time, children tended to be given many sweets and sugary drinks, accelerating their milk teeth's decay. They used anaesthetic spray on the trickier gums in those days, and Dr Salama also carried out filling and gum-treatment work. Like most of his generation, he saw medicine not just as a vocation and a career to advance one's fortune but also as a mission and a service to the community. His fees remained low compared with those of other

---

[*] Al-Leithi/elLithy in some sources

practitioners, and he often did not charge the needy – especially the parents of schoolchildren. This charitable outlook remained with him after retirement and into the last few years of his life, which he devoted to serving what was left of the city's Jewish community. From tens of thousands in the early 1950s, only a few hundred Jews were left in Alexandria when Dr Salama became the head of her Jewish community in 2000.

Although many Alexandrians of all faiths attended his funeral, no Kaddish was recited for him since very few Jews were left in the city. A Kaddish at funerals must be delivered by a minimum of 10 males over 13; women don't take part. Salama's memory lives on amongst Alexandria's last-remaining Jews – especially in the Eliahu Hanvi Synagogue, which he helped save and rebuild, on Rue Naby Daniel – and among those of all other faiths, including Muslims, whose parents had passed down details of his generosity.

The Greco-Alexandrians

Next door to the Eliahu Hanvi Synagogue was the clinic of my grandfather's cardiologist. Dr *Caracatsanis* was among a few elderly Greco-Alexandrians who remained in the city until his retirement in the late 1960s.

The ethnic Greeks were the most numerous among the many Alexandria communities and seemed more prevalent and significant through their activities. In his *Histories,* Herodotus (484/490 - 430/420 BC), who visited Egypt during the twenty-seventh dynasty rule (the Persian occupation), wrote that the Greeks were one of the first migrant communities who lived there, and even under 700 years of Roman administration, Greek culture remained dominant in Alexandria.

With the Mahmoudiyah canal's construction and expansion in the harbour in the early 19th century, migration increased to Alexandria. The Greeks, a small orthodox community in the 18th century, were not on good terms with the Catholic Church, so the monastery of St Sabbas (Savvas) the Sanctified served then as a school for their children. They came in larger numbers than any other ethnic group from the then Ottoman provinces around the Mediterranean.

Unlike the Syro-Lebanese who spoke French, most of the Greeks spoke Turkish, like Muhammad Ali and his officials who did not learn Arabic until years later. The Greeks took any jobs offered, manual labour, commerce, service work, catering and cabbing. The Greeks founded nine primary and two secondary schools and their own chamber of commerce, charitable hospitals, clinics, medical and social institutions, sports clubs and schools for over a hundred years restoring Alexandria, culturally to what she was for 900 years until the Arab invasion in the

CHAPTER 4   The Hyphenated Alexandrians

seventh century. And they became the backbone of the cotton exports and the trade in le Bourse, the Alexandria stock exchange.

Most institutions like hospitals, orphanages, schools and community centres were founded by non-Nilotic migrant communities, especially the Greeks who outnumbered the others.

The first modern orphanage in Alexandria was established near St Katharine's Cathedral in 1847 by the French Sisters of Mercy Association, which founded a second one in Chatby in 1880. The British subsequently established two, in 1897 and 1901. The Belteseus Orphanage for the Disabled was established on Rue Missalla (Rue Safiya Zaghloul) by the German community in 1899. Greek migrants, however, built many more like La Philoptochos Orphanage for Disabled Children in 1894 and the 1905 Ashley Orphanage in Moharrem-Bey, which was relocated in 1907 when incorporated into the Bianchi Orphanage in Chatby, which also had had two schools and two ateliers attached to it. It was funded by the Bianchi Foundation, the charitable establishment of the banking-and-investor Bianchi family who came from Chio and whose names appeared in a famous Alexandrian rhyme:

> Chio, famous for its raki,
> Is even more so for its great men,
> Who sent as Benaki,*
> Chio famous for its raki~²

Another Greek orphanage for the disabled was established in Antoniadis Park in 1925, followed by the L'Asile de Sananbi Orphanage for Women in Attarin in 1926 and the Manna Orphanage, founded by the Greek Women's Association.

Alexandria's population increased almost fivefold from 12,528 in 1821 to 60,000 in 1840 and quadrupled to 170,000 by 1863³. All the increased population was immigrants. The vast of majority of the 170,000 there immigrants; there were 15,000 Greeks and a similar number of Italians and 10,000 French. There were also thousands of Maltese, Russians and Balkans of no fewer than 20,000, and at least an equal number, if not more, of other subjects of the Ottoman Empire, who weren't all ethnically European; but labelled as such. The last-named came mostly from greater Syria, North Africa, around the Black Sea and other Ottoman provinces in total, at least another 90,000

---

* The famously rich bankers, cotton merchants and investors also had their name written as pronounced Benakis (silent 's'); Emmanuel Binachi was known as the 'king of the bourse'.

53

were classified as Europeans. Indigenous Alexandrians numbered about 10,000 – descendants of 4,000 to 5,000 counted by the French in 1798 – but the rest were immigrants, including Nilotic Egyptians. The latter arrived later mostly during the reign of Said Pasha (1854–63).

There were 62,400 Greeks in Egypt in the official census of 1907, most of them in Alexandria. However, the Greek Alexandrian Committee suggests a figure of 120,000 in Alexandria alone[4] – and that the census excluded the ethnically Greek, who were classified as Ottomans or under other nationalities. By the Second World War, their number exceeded 300,000 and over two-thirds were in Alexandria, according to Paris Macris, a member of the Committee of Greek Alexandrians, with lesser communities beginning to flourish in Port Said, Cairo and other trade towns in the Delta.[5]

Many Greeks also arrived in Alexandria as slaves during, and after, Ibrahim Pasha's 1826 campaign in the Peloponnese. The most notable was Zizinia, who quickly became the most prominent and wealthiest Alexandrian.[6] Other Alexandrian Greeks came from Smyrna (today's Izmir) seeking fortune or investment in the vast and growing city on the Mediterranean – especially during their war of independence (1821–32) and more after it ended. Although ethnically Macedonian, Muhammad Ali Pasha was born in Greece and maintained strong connections, encouraging many of his compatriots to come over. The Pasha's friend since their days in Kavalla, (Baron) Michel Tossizza (1787-1850) became the first Greek consul general to the city and later the head of her Greek community.[7] The community organisation was founded in 1843 and became a model to follow by other migrant organisations.[8] The brothers Michel and Theodore Tossizza helped construct the first Greek school (1810) and hospital (1825) in Alexandria and many institutions that developed into modern ones and are still standing in the city today.[9] Tossizza commissioned Pietro Avoscani to design his grand house on Place des Consuls (Muhammad Ali Square).

Cotton, which had been introduced by Muhammad Ali and become Egypt's 'white gold', generated fortunes for many similarly to the way in which oil made many Texan millionaires in the twentieth century. Cotton exports made Greek millionaires families like the Kotsikas, the Rodochanakis and the Choremis who went into partnership with Emmanuel Bianchi (Benaki) establishing a giant cotton export empire. In 1857 the Choremis joined the Zervudakis and another wealthy Greek, Panteli Salvagos to found the General Bank of Alexandria. The Kotsikas* built a large hospital on Rue Abukeir in 1885, still known

---

* also written Cozzika

CHAPTER 4 The Hyphenated Alexandrians

by its original name even after being seized by the military regime and renamed 'Nasser's Hospital' after his death in 1970. Emmanuel Benakis (1843–1929) came to Alexandria from Liverpool in 1863, and within a few years became the 'king of the bourse' through his firm, Choremis, Benaki and Company. The Alexandria-based company was known as the most significant cotton exporter in the whole of Egypt[10]. In 1872 Bianchi became the governor of the General Bank of Alexandria.

The Greek-merchant Sunadinos family founded the Anglo-Egyptian Bank in 1827 (taken over by Barclays in 1924) and became partners in the General Bank of Alexandria. Another Greek, Nestor Gianaclis, established distilleries, vineyards and the famous cigarette factory.[11]

Older Alexandrians would recognise these names in the titles of hospitals, schools, banks, social and sports-services clubs, and centres named after their founders and benefactors. One of the earliest of many sports clubs founded in Alexandria was the 1910 Greek Club, located on the corner of Rue Soter and Rue d'Alexandre le Grand at the Soter Ramleh tram *arrêt*. I played as a centre-halfback with my school team, winning a football game against the Greek Club 2–1 in 1958.

The decade following the defeat of Ourabi and his Islamic-tainted military-Ottoman-nationalist rebellion[12] by the British in 1882 witnessed an influx of Greeks, who became the city's most successful community – amongst them were many of the wealthiest Alexandrians. In 1950, the number of Greek Alexandrians registered as shop owners stood at 2,300.[13] The community were among the most loyal Alexandrians, and Egyptians in general. Many Greek- and Italian-Alexandrians held angry protests outside the British and French embassies and consulates following the 1956 Anglo–French ultimatum given to Egypt. Many, especially communists, volunteered to fight against the British in Port Said. Greek Orthodox priests in churches like St Savvas prayed for Egypt's victory and condemned the Anglo–French attacks. In summer 1956, when Britain and France pressurised European pilots and guides to leave the Suez Canal zone in response to Nasser's nationalisation, the Greek captains refused to follow them and kept the canal open for navigation. In autumn 1956, Greeks in the southern coastal towns of Sinai fought alongside local Egyptians against Israelis trying to land from the Gulf of Akaba.[14]

Even after hostilities by the Nasser regime towards non-Muslim settlers and the wave of nationalisations, the numbers of Greeks (who did not have Egyptian nationality) remained relatively high compared with other ethnic-European Alexandrians. In 1963, there were 24,600 of them in Alexandria and 13,600 in Cairo, as registered with the Greek Consulate. The numbers dropped to 8,000 and 6,500 respectively after The Six-Day War.

CHAPTER 5
Doctors and Dayas

When my grandfather's health worsened, he followed Dr Caracatsanis the cardiologist's advice onto a low-cholesterol diet and exercise, taking me with him on his long seafront walks, but lacked the will on smoking, drinking and caffeine. Dr Caracatsanis stopped sending my grandfather invoices for treatment when he became aware of our family's financial misfortunes. My grandfather received a state pension, which, although sufficient for a comfortable retirement back in 1948, became worthless a few years later when the military-coup regime's shock economic policies caused him to lose a considerable fortune in stocks. It also froze a scheme introduced in the 1940s, when the War pushed prices up, that index-linked state and public-sector pensions (i.e. increasing them by the annual rate of inflation). Matters were made worse by the regime's catastrophic economic policies as inflation began to rise, making pensioners poorer. As a retired headmaster, my grandfather also lost his additional income from the illiteracy-eradication scheme of which he was in charge: the military regime, suspicious of a literate working class, abolished the project.

'*Ma'alhish mon chéri, ba'edeen…ba'edeen, habibty*' (never mind, my darling – later…later), the Greco-Alexandrian cardiologist would reply in typical demotic when my mother would ask about my grandfather's treatment invoices.

This charitable outlook prevailed amongst Alexandria's doctors, regardless of their background or training. My mother's French-trained dentist, Dr Hassan Fathy, worked one day and three evenings a week at his central Alexandria surgery on the western end of Place Mehatet Masr, charging regular fees. He had another practice in the predominantly working-class neighbourhood of Raghib Pasha, and

CHAPTER 5   Doctors and Dayas

also attended emergencies on weekends. The good doctor treated needy patients for free, and arranged with a local *eczane* not to charge them but to add the bill to his account. His upmarket dental surgery was in a central-Alexandria building that housed several lawyers and doctors, including one who left a lasting impression on the post-war generation.

Docteur Labib was an Alexandrian Copt, married to an Italian nurse whom he had met during his training. He opened his surgery one Sunday evening to re-attach the top part of my sister's middle finger, which had been almost severed. She had sneaked into the kitchen to stuff the meat grinder with some plasticine. Luckily, *Maman*, alerted by the screams, had the presence of mind to reverse the grinder handle gently. It was past nine in the evening when *Docteur* Labib started working on my sister's hand. He refused even to discuss fees, although he must have paid overtime to Mademoiselle Alice, the Alexandrian-born nurse with a French heritage who was his clinic's part-time manageress.

I remember *Maman* telling my sister to be quiet because the surgical stitches could not possibly hurt, since she had just had a local anaesthetic injected into her finger. Obviously, she was screaming hoping for more chocolate and bonbons, which Mademoiselle Alice gave her in return for her compliance. Doctors and nurses handing out bonbons – mostly citrus flavour – were commonplace in the practice of sweetening children to let the doctor examine the back of their throat or give vaccines, and no wonder: injections and immunisation were quite barbaric in the post-war years! The needle was often longer than the child's finger, and the syringe could easily have been a prop in one of today's horror movies. Some immunisations consisted of three scratches made to the upper arm with a serrated blade dipped into the vaccine bottle, and scratches sometimes became infected when children rubbed these itchy scrapes.

I guess the tradition of giving sweets to bribe children into compliance was also part of Alexandrian folklore, associated with treatments that did not involve doctors. Such remedies were scary and often unpleasant – I am willing to wager that some of them would be labelled child abuse today. They included the use of ventouses to treat chest infections – they were suction cups: short, transparent glass tumblers engraved with some mystic script – which were believed to draw out mucus from the bronchial tubes. Some families had them at home; others would call upon some quack self-styled 'practitioners' like Um Shlomo el-Daya. This Jewish midwife and unofficial district nurse was nicknamed after her eldest son, Shlomo, a Jewish primary-school teacher. Nobody called her by her real name, Esther – only the sobriquet *Um Shlomo*, meaning 'mother of Shlomo'. Later, especially after the Suez War, she instructed all to call her Um-Salamah. Salamah, as opposed to Shlomo, is both a

Jewish and a Muslim name – and her son became the 'Salamah *Ibber*' that we shall meet in the following section.

There was also a kind Nubian school *farrasha*, a nurse-aide who helped with general duties like hygiene and the serving of school dinners, Dadah Na'imah, who also possessed a set of ventouses. Her husband, *A'am* el-Dhawwah, would apply the treatment to men who were uncomfortable with a woman touching their naked backs.

The unqualified osteopath El-Dhawwah had learned skills and knowledge handed down from fathers and grandfathers for generations. He knew how to reset dislocated joints and support fractured bones using simple splints from local natural materials such as dried branches from palms and other bushes growing in the mounds of Nubia. By chance, luck or genuine skill, he always made the correct diagnosis and named the suitable treatment. El-Dhawwah once told a worried father to give his limping toddler some penicillin shots since her hip joint didn't need resetting. It later transpired that the girl had an abscess in her thigh muscles; the antibiotic injections treated it.

For chest infections, Um Shlomo would light a cotton tissue soaked in surgical spirit inside the upside-down ventouse cup for a few seconds before pressing it firmly against a child's back. The air inside the cup shrinks as it cools, forming a vacuum. Children hated it: the cup was too hot, and the vacuum would pull the skin up inside it; the blanket or quilt placed over the cups was heavy for a child. Removing the ventouses, with a popping sound, pinched the skin, leaving red circles that often invited ridicule and bullying at school for days afterwards.

I remember undergoing this treatment on at least three occasions when I had contracted chest infections. But my poor, late sister was frequently subjected to it as she was plagued by such infections and respiratory problems. 'The girl's breathing organs aren't right; we must never stop praying for her', Um Shlomo used to whisper to *Maman* as though the old Jewish community nurse could read the future. My sister died of lung cancer in Germany following two surgeries in 2009, although the cancer had been treated successfully when first appeared in her colon three years earlier. She had spent eight months in bed in 1952–3 with a rare infection and lungs full of fluid. The treatment recommended then was experimental and expensive. Although the Franco-Alexandrian doctor never charged for his frequent visits or the treatment he provided, the imported injections were costly. To pay for the medicine, my father had to sell his car and shares at a fraction of the price he had paid for them, as the market had nose-dived following the military regime's disastrous meddling in the economy.

After the disagreeable ventouse application, the next phase was quite a relief as Um Shlomo rubbed the chest with warmed camphorated oil.

CHAPTER 5   Doctors and Dayas

I guess inhaling the vapour helped unblock the often-congested nose and cleared the sinuses, but when coming into contact with moisture it forms a protective layer that lines the respiratory tract and helps sleep.

Unpleasant as it was, the ventouse treatment and its skin-pinching, was bearable compared to the horrible antiphlogistine. Containing glycerine, boric acid, salicylic acid, methyl salicylate, peppermint oil, eucalyptus oil and kaolin, this thick, grey, sticky stuff had an irritating, strong odour once its tins were opened. It was then placed in a bowl of ludicrously hot water. Um Shlomo would spread a thick coating of the gooey stuff on a cloth, put the slimy pad on the chest and another one on the back. This gooey damn thing dried overnight into vile, grey droplets turning bedsheets into a bed of nails like the one featured in the *Al-Hawy* show.* The feeling on my skin was similar to that caused by a sunburn I had one summer when the skin on my shoulders and back turned into blisters that peeled off painfully after bursting when my clothes rubbed against them. And my poor, late sister suffered these horrendous treatments countless times.

Other therapies were equally tormenting. For a cold, especially a head-cold or sinusitis, quackery concoctions made from camphor oil, eucalyptus oil, menthol and capsicum were dripped into a bowl of steaming boiling water. *Maman* would hold my face just inches from the scarily scalding water, covering my head and shoulders with a big towel while paying no attention to my protests. I was instructed to inhale the steam deeply through the nose. Although this torture would last only a few minutes, it felt like a lifetime. The hot water would be topped up and the process repeated until I managed to blow all the horrible green mucus out of my nose.

For earaches, paraffin oil was heated in a teaspoon over a cigarette-lighter flame or a candle before a cotton-wool ball was soaked in it and inserted into the ear. The oil was usually uncomfortably hot, and because you would be made to lie on your side with the sore ear facing upwards, the seeping oil made crackling sounds as the cotton wool was pushed into the ear. The sound was creepy and terrifying, reminding me of the sound in my head when Dr Salama had extracted my first molar.

Fever and abdominal aches were my most dreaded afflictions because the treatment for both was often humiliating as well as painfully torturing. Headache alone was not too bad because *eau de cologne* or surgical spirit was sprayed onto cotton handkerchiefs and placed on

---

* This Alexandrian street performer did magic tricks accompanied by a pianola; one of his amusing feats involved the pianola dancing girl walking across his bare chest as he stretched out on the bed of nails.

the forehead. The same method was also used on the belly if there was no temperature. But if there were a fever, especially accompanied by constipation, then the dreaded Um Shlomo's enema would follow. She filled a container with a mixture of boiled *Artemisia herba-alba*, chamomile and more of her 'secret' ingredients from various little jars that she carried in her bag. The child was held face down while administering the enema, then made to stay still for what felt like an eternity. You were not allowed to go to the toilet but were forced to use a chamber pot to enable efficient examination of the bowels' evacuated contents – God knows for what, exactly: I never found out.

These medieval treatments, which had no medical basis to them, often did make the children feel better. I am not sure if this was true, but they always told us so. I confess that, on several occasions, I have imposed the steaming-water treatment – with added drops of Olbas Oil and menthol – on my children, as well as warm olive oil to clear earwax. But I never subjected them to ventouses or the horror of antiphlogistine and enemas.

Sweets were also good bribe when taking a child's temperature – especially when inserting a thermometer into the child's anus, as was the favoured practice of French and French-trained nurses and doctors like *Monsieur Eldocteur*, whose full name I never discovered. All other doctors were just called *eldocteur*, except for this older, kindly, popular Franco-Alexandrian who must have covered the whole of the city as a one-district practitioner making home visits. Parents called *Monsieur Eldocteur*, who was in his sixties, before any other medic. He spoke demotic Alexandrian fluently; more importantly, he was loved by the children who might otherwise have been reluctant to be seen by other practitioners. In the post-war years, clinical encounters put children off. A visit to the dentist meant teeth extractions or fillings, while school nurses meant dusting hair with nasty anti-lice powders or swallowing ghastly tasting laxatives and other unpleasant mixtures to get rid of intestinal parasites and worms.

My mother joked that *Monsieur eldocteur* must have had a discount contract with the Nadler bonbon factory, as he gave their sweets to young patients just before their penicillin injections. He also let them use his stethoscope while their mothers boiled syringes and needles to ensure sterility. I guess it was also another trick by the wily old *docteur* to chat with the child alone. All the mothers I came across would always answer the doctor's questions instead of letting the children answer for themselves. Besides handing out sweets when he visited, *Monsieur Eldocteur* often instructed mums to give the child some Coca-Cola for unexplained stomach aches. Predictably, children looked forward to his visits. Sadly, the ageing *Monsieur eldocteur* (classed as French) was among the first wave of Alexandrians to be expelled from Egypt in the immediate aftermath of the Suez Crisis.

'Mr Needles'

Monsieur Eldocteur's duties and patients were immediately taken over by *Docteur* Labib, who was less keen on handing out sugar to children. Labib was also wiser to children's trickery than his much-older predecessor, often suspecting that a child was faking illness to get out of doing their homework or to get some bonbons. Instead, he prescribed less palatable cough or iron mixtures, all made in the local pharmacy on the spot. Sometimes *Docteur* Labib would read loudly, pretending to prescribe penicillin injections – 'call Salamah *Ibber*' – making the child jump to their feet immediately, saying they were ready for school.

The self-styled *Infirmière extraordinaire*, Salamah acquired the title *Ibber* (Egyptian for needles) – first coined by Mademoiselle Alice – not only because he was the best-known male nurse giving injections but also because he could arrive swiftly at short notice, with an injection kit thoroughly sterilised and ready to use.

Shlomo had changed his Jewish name to the neutral 'Salamah' after marrying a Muslim sports teacher, Abla Zaynab. People gossiped that he didn't convert to Islam, but nobody bothered to ask him; my mother maintained that – according to his mother, Esther – he never did. Shlomo's father-in-law was in partnership with Italian car mechanics and motorcycle importers, so he got him a Vespa: a bribe to take his harsh, masculine, loud and quarrelsome daughter off his hands. *Oncle* Zohni, Zaynab's father, fitted his son-in-law's Vespa with two toughened leather boxes housing smaller compartments in which he carried his medical kit and books. When the al-Ma'arif (Department of Knowledge, Education, Arts and Culture) relaxed rules prohibiting teachers from getting a second job, Salamah underwent first-aid training followed by another nursing course. He went around on his bicycle, then Vespa, giving injections and acquiring the nickname *Ibbar* ('Needles'), and doing odd hospital shifts.

Mademoiselle Alice, by contrast, kept the bonbon tradition going. She too had to leave two years later, even though she had been born in Alexandria in the 1920s. Her only family, comprising a brother and father, came under a lot of pressure and harassment after the Suez War.

The different Egypt that emerged a couple of decades later saw a normalising of dishonesty amongst many medical practitioners, who displayed religious inscriptions and other faith-based ethical slogans all over their surgery waiting rooms. Regrettably, this continues to be the norm. In 1997, I was duped by a top Cairo orthodontist who quoted me a quarter of a Hampstead dentist's price. He was recommended to me by another celebrated Alexandrian, the late movie star Omar Sharif. Omar didn't tell me at the time that his treatment had only been for a root filling and a set of capping crowns for cosmetic repairs to his famous front teeth.

The crook ruined my teeth and took out a perfectly healthy canine. I am still suffering 22 years later, and ended up having implants. In total, I must have paid over £25,000 thanks to a dishonesty that has become all too commonplace. Looking back, it would have been cheaper, wiser and less painful if I had paid the Cairo dentist the $10,000 to do nothing at all!

Social media are awash with stories of patients suffering – sometimes even dying – at the hands of dishonest con-doctors who took the Hippocratic oath in Alexandria – where the foundations of medical science were laid over 2,200 years ago.

The Alexandria School of Medicine

How and when did Alexandria's medical practitioners forget they were the heirs and guardians of the world first and most outstanding school of medicine of the Hellenic period – the school where disciples of Hippocrates (460–375 BC), the father of medicine, established the art of anatomy and identified human organs and their functions?

Herophilus (335–280 BC) performed dissections on human cadavers in public lectures at Alexandria – the practice the Vatican later banned as 'ungodly'. In addition to naming and describing the duodenum and the prostate, he provided detailed studies of organs including the eye, liver, pancreas, genital organs of both sexes and salivary glands.

Erasistratus (304–250 BC) succeeded Herophilus as head of Alexandria's School of Anatomic Medicine, where a large body of modern medical practice was born in Hellenic physicians' hands. He is credited with establishing the Methodic School of teaching medicine. Historians credit Erasistratus, together with Herophilus, as the potential founder of neuroscience due to his acknowledgement of nerves and their roles in motor control through the brain and skeletal muscles. He was one of the first scientists to conduct recorded dissections and, potentially, vivisections.

Modern medical studies were founded on work at Alexandria by Claudius Galen (129–216 AD), the Roman Empire's best-known physician and the father of the experimental medical investigation method. He moved from his native Pergamum to Smyrna, then to Alexandria to study and practice anatomy in the great school of medicine there. His treatises include *On Anatomical Procedures*, in which he meticulously demonstrated dissecting techniques; he was the first to master several anatomical investigations of the 'lower

CHAPTER 5   Doctors and Dayas

animals' like Barbary apes (African monkeys) and pigs. His work *Hygiene* became a useful handbook on staying healthy; his *Antidotes* included a substantial number of recipes implemented in disciplines including medical botany, toxicology and pharmaceutics. Galen in fact left behind a vast body of 500 treatises on subjects as varied as logic, ethics, grammar and medicine. In addition to the above, some of his medical texts include *On Medical Experience, On the Parts of Medicine, On Cohesive Causes, On Regimen in Acute Diseases in Accordance with the Theories of Hippocrates* and *On the Variety of Similar Parts of the Body*. Although he differed significantly with Hippocrates on his theories of the four humours that make up the human body (black bile, yellow bile, blood and phlegm), Galen, like most of his contemporaries, staunchly upheld the sacred oath of the father of medicine.[1]

In a tragic irony, the past 30 years have witnessed graduates of the Alexandria School of Medicine who – as students and trainee doctors attending operating theatres, anatomy labs, lecture halls and even hospital wards named after the likes of Galen and Erasistratus – have turned their backs on their medical school's great legacy. Their practices and attitudes reflect a rise in the manifestation of religious devotion, with doctors' clinics and medical centres allocating spaces for prayer and staff taking time off to pray rather than focusing on treating their patients. Hala Zayed, Egypt's *higab*-covered health minister since 2018, was reported to have ordered that all practitioners start their shifts at state hospitals with Islamic prayers. Today, doctors who try to separate faith-dominated politics from medical practice have become a whispering minority.

The story of an Egyptian woman who had to give up the contraceptive pill due to its side effects was case in point. She consulted a gynaecologist on whether practising some unconventional sex as a means of contraception during her marital lovemaking sessions carried medical risks of which she ought to be aware.

'Are you a Muslim?' the consultant asked the gobsmacked woman, before adding, 'then you should have realised that this practice was *haram* [religiously prohibited]…also, contraception was *makrooh* [religiously unpalatable] as ruled by the Prophet Muhammad'. (Muhammed invited his followers to marry and take pride in producing children.) Recovering from her surprise, the stunned patient told the doctor that she could have got a religious opinion on contraceptives from a clergyman without paying an overblown consultation *visita* (doctor's fees). The consultation ended in acrimony, with the doctor quoting eighth-century Islamic jurists and insulting the patient when she demanded her money back.

A 'Grand Canyon' separates the practices, medical ethics and bedside manners of the current generation from the subtle ways of older-generation physicians like *Monsieur Eldocteur*, Salama or *Docteur* Labib. As a young boy, I eagerly awaited the last-named's prescriptions for my sister so that I could volunteer to take them to the pharmacy and watch them mixing the ingredients. Fascinated by science at an early age, I had a chemistry set, given to me as a birthday present. I used to like watching pharmacists composing prescriptions from raw ingredients. Medicine was prepared in liquid form or, mixed with carriers like sugar and talcum powder, turned into pills or powder in sachets. The chemist wrote the name of the remedy, the patient's name and the dose on labels. I was over the moon when I was allowed to stick labels on little stained-glass jars that later became collector's items.

Some pharmacists let me watch them, like the younger of the two Mizrahi brothers who worked in the family founded Eczanet Mizrahi. I also loved to accompany my school friend Benjy Ciryakousy to his father's pharmacy to watch the preparation of prescriptions when made from scratch. But the best known in the business of constructing and mixing medicine on the spot was Eczanet Joannides on Rue Istanbul. When the family who ran the pharmacy left Alexandria around 1980, they sold it to a pharmacist already in their employment. He kept the original shop front, glass jars and display cabinets, leaving them just as they had been in 1900. Joannides, like most pharmacies, had retained the tradition of administering injections at reduced fees to patients who purchased their medicines from them – or free-of-charge to those, including diabetics and elderly patients, on longer courses of injections.

Injections in the old days were a bit of an ordeal for many. Post-war penicillin doses came in uniform packaging – a two-part combination box consisting of a two-inch narrow-necked jar containing the white powder with a sealed rubber stopper covered by tinfoil, and a brown-glass narrow-necked ampoule containing sterilised distilled water. After sterilisation in a container of boiled water over a methylene burner, the syringe sucked the distilled water from the ampoule before the top of the mini-jar was wiped with a surgical-spirit-soaked cotton pad. The needle pierced the jar's lid, injecting the water to dissolve the powder before it was sucked into the syringe to inject the child, who had by now grown anxious just watching the process. Preparing the injection was laborious compared with the modern, ready-made doses in disposable syringes available in abundance today. First, it was necessary to boil the dismantled syringe cylinder, piston shaft, needles, needles' cleaning wires and the two-inch serrated blade used to scratch the ampoule neck to break the tip. Middle-class families had their own stainless-steel box containing the injection kit and the boiling container for sterilisation. My mother, who helped as a nurse in various hospitals assigned to military efforts during the War, would start the process of sterilising the container on a spirit stove before the *docteur's* anticipated arrival. There were several *eczanes* within a moments' walk of our central Alexandria home and that of my grandfather near Boursa. At Sidi Bishr on the coast, finding a pharmacy was sometimes challenging. The nearest one was only open in the summer months, while the next nearest two closed in the evening and after midday on Saturday at weekends.

'Call the Midwife' (and thank Clot Bey)

Training *dayas* as midwives started in 1832 at the Medical School for Women in Cairo by Clot Bey, the founder of Western medical practice in modern Egypt. Antoine Barthelemy Clot (1793–1868), a Marseilles physician and surgeon, was invited in 1825 by Muhammad Ali Pasha to expand the medical school founded in 1799 by Napoleon Bonaparte in Cairo. Clot Bey, who had a street named after him in central Cairo, first recruited a dozen educated locals (all Christian – Copts, Armenians and Syrians) as interpreters, but he trained them from 1827 at the school of medicine and they became the first modern Egyptian doctors.

To combat the spread of venereal diseases in the Egyptian Army, Clot Bey decided to stem it at the source by treating women, which required training female medics. To circumvent Islamic-clerical objections to Muslim women being trained by men, let alone by non-Muslims, Clot Bey, with Muhammad Ali's approval, bought ten Nubian women from the slave market[*]. They were housed in an annex at the medical-school complex (guarded by two eunuchs), taught the fundamentals of medicine and trained on various treatments focusing on women's needs. The experiment exceeded Clot Bey's expectations; he started admitting Muslim women as patients to the hospital but secretly training them in medical procedures. Within a decade, Clot Bey-educated *dayas* proved to be quite efficient and have a more expansive medical knowledge than the Greek *dayas* – who passed their expertise on from mother to daughter – who oversaw birth and pregnancy issues[2]. Trained *dayas*, like Um Shlomo, were given a certificate as 'legal midwife'.

Besides delivering babies and administering primary postnatal care, the *dayas* helped with quackery prescriptions from *attarin* (herbalists) – waxing, treating visible spots and other feminine issues. They also changed dressings, lanced boils and treated cuts in emergencies, using iodine- and sulphur-based ointments to guard against infection. There

---

[*] Al-Azhar's clergy saw captured black African slaves as unequal, and they didn't require a female slave to cover her head with a *higab*.

were reports in the media about some *dayat* being arrested and charged with grievous bodily harm by performing *taharah*, the common name for female genital mutilation (FGM). Ironically, *taharah* means both purification and circumcision in Arabised-Egyptian.

While male circumcision, an ancient Egyptian custom carried forward by Jews as the *bris*, was practised by all faiths, some girls in the countryside were subjected to the barbaric clitorectomy. It often caused severe injury to the child's *labia minora*, leading to bleeding and infections. There was gossip about *fellaheen* migrants in the more impoverished outlying districts that served Alexandria's markets performing it. But I don't recall FGM incidents being reported in the press in Alexandria in the 1950s.

I understood from older retired Egyptian doctors that FGM was banned in the 1940s by the Ministry of Health and the medical practitioners' self-regulating union, the Egyptian Medical Syndicate (EMS).* This licensing body also acted as a disciplinary authority until the late 1970s, when it became increasingly politicised. However, the EMS had not given physicians clear instructions on FGM despite the harm caused by this barbaric practice and the need to back calls to ban it. Its executive committee – made up of a majority of Islamists and a minority of Nasserites, all hand-picked and approved in advance by the country's *Mukhabarat* – put their patients' welfare, clinical excellence and doctors' conduct below political issues (including national foreign policy) on their list of priorities as voted in their AGMs. Even in the UK, some Muslim families reported having paid some doctors inflated fees to perform the private clitorectomies, frowned upon by Alexandrians in the 1950s as another backward habit of the *fellaheen*.† Lesser-educated rural migrant families were secretive about girls' *taharah*, indicating they were aware of something objectionable about it. Indeed, all Alexandrian girls with whom I had teenage, or later, sexual encounters were anatomically intact.

When, in the 1980s, Islamists started calling upon Muslim families to 'purify' their pre-pubescent daughters through clitorectomy, most doctors were still refusing to perform a procedure that was backed up by no medical reason. A religious *fatwa* by the head of al-Azhar encouraged *taharah* as preferable and healthier for girls; it was a reply to an enquiring Muslim father after several Muslim doctors refused to

---

*According to the half-English half-Egyptian physician, communist writer and novelist Dr Sherif Hatata (1923–2017) and his former wife, the feminist writer Dr Nawal el-Saadawi (b.1931).

† Lloyd-Roberts, Sue, 'Hidden world of female genital mutilation in the UK', BBC Newsnight, 23 July 2012.

CHAPTER 5   Doctors and Dayas

perform clitorectomy on his daughters as emotionally and physically harmful.[3] On 6 February 2020, the International Day of Zero Tolerance for Female Genital Mutilation, al-Azhar issued a short online *fatwa* declaring FGM undesirable because of its harmful effect under Islam, while doctors also ruled it dangerous. And like al-Azhar's contrary reply 40 years earlier, this *fatwa* was followed by quotations from the Quran and Muhammad's lessons, legitimising the answer. Islamist activists took to social media and Muslim evangelists used Islamic broadcasting channels to launch a vicious attack on al-Azhar and its head, Sheikh Ahmed el-Tayeb, in response to his ruling protecting girls from FGM. 'They think it is normal to castrate infants to turn them into eunuchs, but they are averse to making corpses suffer?' Clot Bey had quipped back in 1828 when al-Azhar *ulama* objected to teaching dissection. Clot Bey circumvented their objection on that occasion by procuring cadavers belonging to black African soldiers, regarded by the Islamic clergy as inferior to Muslims.

Nursing-training courses were offered as more Egyptian medics were needed in clinics and health *mostousafs*. The latter were charity-run clinics, mostly free although always welcoming of voluntary donations. They dispensed medicine, carried out minor surgery and gave children vaccinations. Many were initially set up by European institutions for their own ethnic communities, but the clinics accepted anybody who needed treatment regardless of race or faith. Those established in predominantly migrant *fellaheen* areas were set up in buildings donated by Jewish charities. The Coptic Church also founded large Coptic Hospitals – one in Moharrem-Bey and another in Cairo; both treated patients irrespective of their faith or ethnicity. A third clinic was set up by the Coptic Church in the Kenyan capital, Nairobi. Other charitable facilities were opened by Italian Catholic schools, but offered care without enquiring about faith.

New Medical Ethics
The spread of Egyptian-founded *mostousafs*, which were small-scale hospitals admitting patients, was accelerated by the Egyptian Royal family's female members – particularly, King Farouk's sisters. Clinica Princesse Fawzia was one; others were named after princesses Faiza, Faika and Fathia as well as ones set up by the king's mother, Queen Nazli, along with her daughter-in-law, Queen Farida. The Nariman hospital for orthopaedic injuries was set up, in 1951, by Farouk's second wife when he married her following his divorce from Farida. These hospitals are still known today by their original names despite the republican regime's best efforts to erase royal achievements from the public memory.

The princesses had followed a tradition set by their late father, King Fuad I. As a young prince, Fuad established the Cairo Ambulance Service in 1902. Styled on its French equivalent, the service was staffed by uniformed volunteers. Farouk's great-uncle Prince Omar Toson (1872–1944), known as the Prince of Alexandria and the Prince of the Poor, was a European-educated moderniser who established free schools and orphanages, clinics and rehabilitation centres from 1900 onwards. He was one of the rare descendants of Muhammad Ali to have their name reinstated in Alexandria by military-republic officials – in the form of Rue Omar Toson – but only after erasing the title 'pasha'.

Most of these medical and charitable institutions were predominantly staffed by Alexandrians of European background. Doctors, pharmacists and nurses were highly respected members of society in those days, and doctors' orders were always followed. However, services and standards deteriorated rapidly after decades of demographic changes (in reality, ethnic cleansing) of Alexandria by the military regime, which did not spare medical staff when they happened to be Jewish or ethnically Anglo-French.

When reporting on the Yom Kippur War and diplomatic moves that followed, during 1974, I spent over eighteen months in and out of Egypt covering the negotiations. Part of my brief was to track the movement of British and American politicians and diplomats hosted by President Anwar Sadat (1918–1981) in the former royal palaces of Alexandria – or sometimes Cairo – that had been built by Muhammad Ali and his sons and grandsons. I preferred staying in Alexandria whenever I could, commuting to Cairo or staying there overnight as and when needed. During that period, I dated Mervit, a young Alexandrian dentist. One day she invited me to attend her morning clinic at Queen Nazli's Hospital in Anfushi, the Turkish quarter at the far northern end of Alexandria, before going to a pre-arranged lunch at the Marine (Greek) Club at the northwest tip of the Eastern Harbour. The 1920s hospital, overlooking the Eastern Harbour, had had the late queen's name removed and had become the Anfoushi site of Alexandria University's Medical School. But Alexandrians, to this day, still call it Ospedalia-el-Malikah Nazli.

I was shocked by the drop in standards compared with the 1950s and by the disorder. Most surprising was the cavalier – almost contemptuous – attitude towards patients whose taxes funded the hospital and paid the staff's salaries. My dentist girlfriend's patients who could not afford private treatment were shoved into the room by a rough-looking *tumargy* (male nurse). A half dozen or so sat inside her examination room on a row of rusty metal chairs with fixed, brown vinyl seats. I sat behind Mervit's desk in the corner as she instructed me.

CHAPTER 5   Doctors and Dayas

After examining a woman in her forties, Mervit told her she would need immediate surgery on her lower gums to treat a severe infection before it spread further, increasing the risk of septicaemia. Her female assistant gave the woman an antibiotic injection, as instructed – in English – and the dentist gave the moaning and tearful patient a local anaesthetic with short stabs to her gums and under her tongue. I felt a bit squeamish, and my facial expression showed it. Mervit asked me, in English, to move to an inside room which was cleaner and also had a professional dentist's chair and treatment equipment. The young dentist telephoned a colleague named Samir and, in English, asked him to join her, using some Latin medical terms during the conversation. Neither the dentist nor her assistant said a word to the other patients still waiting in the examination room. They left them sitting there as they moved the shaking, tearful woman into the surgery where I sat. I do not recall anyone asking the patient to sign a consent form. When Samir arrived, the two of them started to operate on the poor woman's gum, slicing it into a rectangular shape and pulling it down like a flap. I must have blacked out at the bloody sight, as the next thing I remember was Mervit and her colleague, Samir, leaning over me. Samir was pushing a sharp odour pad under my nose while Mervit held my hand to her lips. Both of them had turned their backs on their bleeding patient in the middle of an unpalatable surgical procedure.

CHAPTER 6
The Annual Flower Parade

The annual parade, with floats and wagons decorated with flowers and pretty girls dancing on them, was an old Alexandrian tradition revived by Greek settlers in the nineteenth century. My post-war happy childhood days included visits, with my late sister, to *Tante* Ralia and *Oncle* Niroop, whose home overlooked the Eastern Harbour where the parade passed. Ralia was a pet name – short for Coralia, the mermaid. She was always angry but had a sharp sense of humour on the rare occasions when she was not fuming or chastising someone. My quick-witted late sister also had a wicked sense of humour, with her one-line puns – most unusual for a German-educated physics academic. The highlight of visits to *Tante* Ralia's was watching the parade from her balcony. My three cousins, Ralia's boys, were the closest to me among 12 immediate and 8 second cousins. *Tante* Ralia's youngest was a year my junior, until she had a fourth son in 1957. They lived in a massive apartment in a 1920s six-storey block. Two reception and dining rooms with two balconies overlooked the Eastern Harbour Corniche and four bedrooms overlooked a small road where some businesses were located. One was an Indian tea- repacking warehouse.

Tea and Toys
The repackaging sector benefitted from both the Suez Canal project and Alexandria's free-marketing trade mentality, and favourable taxation laws became one of the major engines of the city's economy. Imports from the Far East in bulk industrial quantities would be repackaged into smaller, more attractive quantities either to be sold nationally or exported to European destinations. The sector also relied on the related export industries involving cotton, onions, refined rice and

CHAPTER 6   The Annual Flower Parade

refined sugar, which had been growing rapidly since the early 1900s. On the eve of 1960 nationalisations, annual rice exports were 550,000 metric tonnes. There were 45 cotton-exporting companies in Alexandria alone, 25 owned by Jews and half the rest by Greco-Alexandrians.[1]

Related to this sector was The Profitable Economic Repackaging Industries. The idea was the brain-child of the *wafd* industrialist Talaat Harb Pasha (1867–1941), whose Egyptian shareholders at his Banque Misr (established with assistance from Egyptian-Jewish investors) financed entrepreneurs and new industries.

What was initially industrial waste was thus turned into material for secondary industries, providing jobs and growth, with profitable repackaging. Oil was extracted from cottonseeds, while crushed seeds were processed into animal feed; soap production, packed for local and export markets was set up as part of the oil-extraction industry.

The tea-warehouse workers behind *Tante* Ralia's home repacked the loose tea leaves that came in chests into varied-sized packs, jars and tins for export and local markets. We exchanged the Hollywood movie-star photos that came in some cigarette packets left by the grown-ups with the warehouse workers for the foil lining from tea chests. Both foil and photos were popular currency among post-war Alexandria children. We exchanged the foil with other boys for marbles, postage stamps and mechanical parts used with the foil to make toys for the make-belief reacting of scenes from the American movies.

Children made their own toys in the post-war years. They utilised their imagination and initiative in a skilful reuse of spare parts discarded by mechanics, electricians and visiting repairmen – and packaging like tins, jars, pots and drink-bottle tops – to make toys. Clockwork toys were too expensive and only given on birthdays or Christmas, or on rare occasions like a hospitalisation for surgery (as when I broke my arm). And purchased toys were mostly educational, like Meccano kits or a chemistry set. I was given a chess set on my tenth birthday. It had been milled from blocks of bronze by a family friend, *Oncle* Selim, an engineer at the tram workshop.

We often found the odd fag in the box, which, along with the movie-star pictures, were valued currency to exchange with the tea-exporting workers. Mae West, Doris Day, Marlene Dietrich, Lana Turner, Jean Harlow, Marilyn Monroe, Jayne Mansfield, Greta Garbo, Jene Seberg, Veronica Lake, Barbara Lang and Greta Gynt were bigger hits with male workers than Gene Tierney, Ingrid Bergman, Vivien Leigh, Ava Gardner, Lauren Bacall, Judy Garland, Susan Hayward or Hedy Lamarr. Grace Kelly's photos topped the inflated-value list after she became a cover girl, and her love story via long-distance correspondence with Prince Rainier of Monaco (1923–2005) filled gossip columns. They met while Kelly was filming the Hitchcock movie *To Catch A Thief* on the French Riviera. Boys, with their testosterone flowing before growing into gentlemen, preferred blondes.

Female workers on the packaging line were mad about Clark Gable, Cary Grant, James Stewart and Humphrey Bogart – especially if you had his photo in a 'here's looking at you, kid' pose. John Wayne's photos were not that popular with the tea-warehouse workers of either sex. But he was well-liked by some school-playground boys, and among western movie fans in third-class film-houses.

Parade Day, and Children's Alexandria
Apart from *plage* events, the parade day at *Tante* Ralia's witnessed the congregation of most of my cousins. The 29 July public holiday marked King Farouk's 1937 official coronation. The 1952 coup regime appropriated the event and moved it to 26 July in 1957, marking Nasser's nationalisation of the Suez Canal a year earlier.

We would spend the afternoon on *Tante* Ralia's balcony, watching the parade with its carnival floats passing in an ocean of flowers. The day ended with fireworks in the evening, launched from the military observation post on the Silsilah promontory at the Eastern Harbour's far end.

Such revelries were in Alexandria's DNA, going back to the Ptolemaic era (332–30 BC). They peaked during Cleopatra's reign, especially in the heydays of her love affair with Mark Antony. The first dynastic festival of the Ptolemies, around 280 BC, would cost millions of dollars today; the parade was a phantasmagoria of music, incense, blizzards of doves, camels laden with cinnamon, elephants in golden slippers and bulls with gilded horns. Among the floats was a 4.5-metre Dionysus pouring a libation from a golden goblet.[2] Cleopatra's merriments were reincarnated when parades were revived by the Greeks in the nineteenth century, and continued growing with Alexandria's commercial and industrial expansion in the twentieth. They cost much less than Ptolemaic extravaganzas but kept the third-century BC's original spirit; what started in the stadium moved into the streets. The colourful flower-decorated floats carrying music bands and dancers, and embellished by the prettiest girls in Alexandria, proceeded along the Eastern Harbour Corniche, becoming a family day out for over 100 years.

The view of the old Eastern Harbour was stunning as *Tante* Ralia's balconies, located in the middle of its curve, gave us a full view of the entire corniche – east to west, where carriages headed for the Ras el-Tin Palace. People would be lining up or taking seats on the corniche stone wall. All balconies and windows were full, and some makeshift cafés

CHAPTER 6   The Annual Flower Parade

sprang up on the corniche pavement. Traffic police would tolerate it for the day: vendors selling sweets, popcorn, candyfloss and drinks – including the two sizes of Birra Stella. Onlookers in flats overlooking the parade route would use the public holiday as a party day: champagne for the well-off and sparkling wines for the majority toasted and exchanged with next doors' balcony and all in good humour, like any other European parade used by businesses, traders, banks and companies (national and international), and sports clubs to advertise by competing in decorations and designs. By the early 1950s, the parade's innovations were becoming more daring with a hedonistic touch.

Department stores hired attractive models to parade their latest collections. The models must have been gymnastic athletes parading on high heels on narrow four-metre-long makeshift catwalks on moving floats, while pretty girls gave out coupons for discounts and cards with the winning numbers of valuable items. Tobacco companies like Matossian and Gianaclis sometimes hired models, each dressed as a cigarette, to dance on the firm's float while handing out packets. Confectioners and chocolate firms like Ika and Nadler copied the idea, using their own female employees: they dressed as chocolate bars, nougat and bonbons. They were skilled in targeting less well-off families and underprivileged children, ensuring they got the lion's share of the gifts.

Drinks franchises and indigenous Alexandrian firms – like Coca-Cola, Pepsi-Cola, Sinalco, Spathis and Stella – appropriated the Ptolemaic Dionysus trick – giant bottles with drinks pouring into large tubs or glasses, and bubbles lit by coloured lighting, while good-looking girls handed out free drinks in wax-coated paper cups or danced on the edge of the giant goblet.

I often wanted to stay the rest of the public holiday for a sleep-over with my cousins. The boys conspired to fake a fight with my sister and another, half-Italian, girl whose mother called her Metta. But children used neither Metta nor Fiammetta, calling her 'Fiat' instead after the Italian car make. It was coined by a cousin, who said her face with a flattened nose and round spectacles resembled the Fiat automobile front. My cousins swore they witnessed the girls starting the fight. The grown-ups believed the three boys and dismissed the two girls' account – except for my father, who sternly said that perjury was a crime in law with a look meaning 'I know what you have been up to'. The dispute ended with a compromise, with me staying overnight with the cousins and Fiat going with my sister back to the home we happened to be staying in. If it was a weekend, I'd stay a second night or my younger cousin would return home with me. And we would travel alone, without mothers telling us off throughout the journey.

Alexandria Adieu

Those post-war years were safe for children: social boundaries were well defined, and children respected figures of authority and trusted them – whether policemen, doctors, the district nurse or teachers. Spot your teacher on the street and you immediately stood still, since running away or hiding would put you under suspicion. We also feared older, local shopkeepers reporting us to our parents or teachers. There were no mobile telephones or other instant ways to check on us. Yet the family had no worries if two boys travelled across Alexandria independently, knowing that a *commissario* (tram conductor) or a grown-up would always be at hand if needed.

My cousin and I would walk to the French Gardens if going to my grandfather's place, which lay behind them. If we were going to Moharrem-Bey we caught Tramway *Quatre*. The fare was 0.4 of a *piastre* for second class and 0.6 *piastres* for first class. It was half the fare for a child under 16. We never paid; the *commissario* never asked us. *Commissario-el-Tramway* would recognise by speech and clothing *wilad-elnas* (middle-class children of *effendis* or European Alexandrians). But he shooed off dirty-looking, underprivileged children, thinking they would cause trouble or were working with pickpockets.

Going to Sidi-Bishr on the coast took longer, and the journey was more scenic and enjoyable. We would walk along Rue Tatweeg, with its magnificent Italian architecture, and pass the Jardins Francais, as my mother called Place du Ismail. She followed my grandfather, who always used the pre-Great War names instead of the contemporary ones. The military-coup regime renamed it Place Ourabi. By tram or on foot we would reach La Gare de Ramleh for the iconic Tramway el-Ramleh with its double-decker second-class wagon, which was famed for its 'balconies' at the front and rear of the top deck (first class had only one deck). And on the balcony, we sat all the way until we reached *Arrêt* Sidi-Bishr, getting off to look at the old fort of al-Sarraiyah's military base with its big guns pointing towards the sea. Then, at the foot of the rock, we would plot our next plan to get my sister and Fiat into trouble.

CHAPTER 7
Tram Number 4, Old Alexandria

If the Tramway el-Ramleh ride was a route into the city's illustrious history, the older El-Balad tramway routes tracked Dinocrates' main roads, where history continued its march into the present. Tram Number 4 was my own childhood 'gateway' into the heart of 'Old Alexandria' and her tales.

'Selling the Tram'
Carrying gifts to *Tante* Ralia, my mother wanted to go by cab; however, if we were staying at Moharrem-Bey I insisted on going by Tram Number 4. It had a symbol of the red heart from the *cautchina* (playing cards); Tram Number 3 was a black club, 5 was a red diamond and 2 was a black spade. They added other symbols and shapes – so Number 1, the longest route from the shipyards at Muxx on the western outskirts to Nuzha Park near the airport, had a yellow star and Tram 6 was a red circle, and so on for all the routes. In the 1860s, Alexandria's tramlines were extended by the municipality to serve the city's southern and western areas where migrants from the countryside lived, to connect to factories south of Mahmoudyiah Canal, to access the Muxx shipyards and Western Harbour docks, and to services and trade areas in the city centre. The symbols were thought to be easier to recognise by the mostly illiterate *fellaheen* migrants. The trams, run by a Belgian company, went everywhere – generating the Alexandrian saying '*dokhet-el-Belgiky*' ('as dizzy as a spinning Belgian') – getting dizzy trying to figure out the *belgiky* (another name for the tram) and its circular routes, in one version of Alexandria's folklore. But there was another, more amusing version:

Alexandria Adieu

An Alexandrian conman approached a *sa'idie* arriving in the city for the first time and offered to guide him to reach his cousin in Karmouz. They climbed aboard the *belgiky*, which the *sa'idie* was seeing for the first time. The conman handed the *commissario* a *priza* note (10 *piastres*) for two tickets of 1 *millième*; one tenth of a *piastre* and whispered in his ear, apologising that he had nothing smaller. The conductor, who didn't have the full 98 *millièmes* change, would come back after every stop, handing the conman loose change he collected from other passengers. Finally, the Alexandrian satisfied the guest's curiosity, whispering that he owned the *Belgiky*, and the *commissario* was his employee. The conman had the paperwork – written in French – ready, signed and witnessed by another passenger, and the illiterate visitor used his brass seal and kept a copy after parting with £€15 (30 times the monthly rent of a whole villa in Alexandria) and having 'bought' the tram. As expected, the figure went up with inflation when the story was retold over the years. In one version, the *sa'idie* spent his holiday in Alexandria going around in circles on the *belgiky*, trying to find the conman until he was dizzy.

I wanted to go by tram as an excuse to get gateaux and a drink from the Italian pâtisserie next to the tram stop, while the shop assistant wrapped gifts for *Tante* Ralia. But Tram 4's route was also a journey through the history of the original Hellenic Alexandria, ending at Anfouhsi, the Pharos island, where the story began with Alexander standing there 2,200 years earlier. Maybe a subconscious' premonition that all will be lost, and I had to capture Alexandria on a mental film – a film that, one day, would be shown to the memoryless generations?

As it left the wide Rue Mohrrem-Bey with its giant trees, some older than the Italian- and French-designed nineteenth-century buildings themselves, Tram 4 circled the large Place Mehatet-Masr with its manicured gardens designed by Lasciac assisted by the Greek civil engineer Leonidas after the Great War, then passed the western edge of Kom-el-Dikka Hill. This promontory had military installations like communications towers, searchlights and anti-aircraft guns that had seen action during the War. When the nineteenth-century mound was removed in 1970, a Polish archaeological team searching for Alexander's mausoleum found an unusual U-shaped Roman amphitheatre. It was later used for live performances by the Alexandria Theatre Company like their 1973 production of Albert Camus' *Caligula*. The actors used the mounds around the stage to gallop on horseback. In 2004, Alexandria university archaeologists reclassified the site as study rooms and reading rooms, and the amphitheatre had been a multi-use lecture theatre, music hall and a debating arena.

CHAPTER 7   Tram Number 4, Old Alexandria

North of Kom-el-Dikka Hill lies in a district bearing the same name, where Cavafy lived and where his home has become a museum.

Books, Fashion, Saints and Miracles
The tram then slides north down Rue Naby Daniel, rebuilt in the 19th century by Alfonso Maniscalco, running south to north as central to Dinocrates' original urban grid. The name by which the street is known to Alexandrians, 'Rue Allah's prophet Daniel', refers to mosque built by Muhammad Ali in 1823. It replaced a small shrine sketched in a drawing plan of Alexandria by the Russian monk Vassili Grigorovich Barskij in 1727.[1]

But Daniel was a Jew who fled persecution in Syria to Alexandria in another version of the tale by ninth-century astronomers, the Uzbek Ibn Kathir (Alfraganus) and the Afghani Albumasar. Many Alexandrians believe the mosque was built above Alexander's original mausoleum. Early Arab travellers called it the shrine of 'Dhu'l-Qarnayn' (the Sire with the two horns), the title given to Alexander in the Quran.*

Rue Fuad Junction was the next *arrêt*. Formerly Rue de la Porte de la-Rosette, it runs west to east as laid out by Dinocrates and was named the Canopic Way back in 332 BC. It connects the Gate of the Sun in the east (today, Bab-Sharqi) and the Gate of the Moon in the west (today, Western Harbour).

Rue Fuad was like London's Bond Street at one end and South Audley Street at the other. Off Rue Fuad to the northern side, there were several arcades similar to those off Piccadilly and Jermyn Street in London. Several iconic salons de thé, pâtisseries and chocolatiers for which Alexandria was famed were located on Rue Fuad or on these passages and arcades branching off from it. There was another patisserie – Athinèos – with a tearoom, restaurant and bar with dancing floor and raised-stage rostra where jazz bands played on some evenings. This space used to be turned into a ballroom on occasion and its events rivalled the tea dances held on the roof garden of Claridge's Hotel, west on Rue Fuad.

Further east was Pastroudis, a salon de thé and restaurant; and 50 metres away, *confiseur* Flückiger on Phatios Street, off Rue Fuad, famed for serving several flavours of *crème glacée* and delicious, minuscule

---

* Quran 18: 83–94: 'I am Dhu'l-Qarnayn, who is mentioned in the earlier Scriptures.' The Greek text was written 1,000 years after Alexander consulted the Siwa Oracle (hence, the earlier scripture) and became convinced he was son of the god Amun. The priest gave Alexander the crown/helmet of the god Amun, with what looked like two horns.

gateaux. Past the Claridge's was another iconic tea room, Baudrot, at the corner of Rue Fuad and Rue Chérif Pasha, whose eclairs and other French specialities were served with *chocolat chaud* topped with crème fraiche. It was in Baudrot where Cavafy had met Forster for the first time during the Great War and where Durrell met Even Cohen first during the Second World War. Down the road, on Rue Cherif, Pâtisserie Unica was famed for serving brioches and *pains de Venise*, which were also delivered on order to traders' stores, offices and hotels.

Opposite Pâtisserie Athinèos was the grand nineteenth-century home of the British Institute, later the British Council, with its library and hall-cum-theatre-cum-cinema. When Nasser severed relations with Britain and France, deporting their nationals and Jewish dual nationals, the institute remained opened but deserted. A skeleton anglophile Egyptian staff kept the union flag conceptually flying thanks to journalist, academic and author Dr Mursi Saad-el-Dine CBE (1921–2013), who managed the institute after the British staff left in 1956. Its activity was mostly concentrated in Cairo, but the institute's service continued in Alexandria. The library resumed lending books to students and anglophile readers while also assisting amateur groups putting on Shakespeare plays and providing free English classes taken by volunteering British subjects, mostly spouses of Nilotic-Egyptian nationals.

Colonel Nasser tolerated the institute's activities because Dr Saad-el-Dine provided him with a weekly summary report of English press coverage and analysis. Later Saade-el-Dine became President Sadat's spokesman before serving as a cultural attaché in London. He was awarded CBE (Commander of the Order of the British Empire) by HM the Queen for his outstanding work in the field; he kept the British Council service for those who needed it when Anglo–Egyptian diplomatic relations were severed (1956–9). From 1959, Sir Colin Crowe (1913–1989) was only a charge d'affairs, not a full ambassador, until diplomatic relations were fully elevated to ambassadorial level with Sir Harold Beeley (1909–2001) and the British Council staff started returning to Alexandria and Cairo from 1961 onwards.

For over six years, visitor numbers to Alexandria's British Institute library dropped to fewer than a tenth of their 1956 tally. The few visitors always came in groups, never an individual on their own. Those who held a library-membership card kept it secret during the years of hostility to Britain and the fear of denouncement as *a'meel les Anglaise*, a pro-British traitor, if one was caught with such an 'incriminating' document. The institute's visitors were almost exclusively students from Alexandria University Department of English Literature and Anglo-Saxon Studies. Far fewer in number were the secondary-school pupils of teachers who dared to suggest the British Library as a source

CHAPTER 7   Tram Number 4, Old Alexandria

of knowledge, risking denunciation or worse – with informers framing them as collaborators of *les Anglais*. Nasser's propaganda encouraged people to become informers as 'a patriotic duty', but most were driven by ambition for personal gain within the regime's ideological organisations or an axe to grind against a neighbour or employer. In the days after the Suez War, we would turn off the radio if tuned to the BBC World Service or the French Mediterranean service Radio Monte Carlo when the doorbell rang, fearing a delivery boy would report us as spies or collaborators.

However, the search for knowledge, driven by intellectual curiosity, was in Alexandria's genes and in the grains of her saffron soil, on which scholars and philosophers had left their footsteps – among them Hypatia, her father Theon, Euclid and Callimachus.*

Despite isolationist barriers put in place by the anti-Western regime to discourage contacts with *allstimar* (European colonialists) and to switch allegiance to Arab countries and the Soviet bloc, anglophile Alexandrians kept going to the institute's library and the francophones to *l'Institut français*. Students of modest means, who either had a church-school education or had been tutored by enlightened staff, kept borrowing English and French books and periodicals from Rue Naby Daniel and Rue Mehatet Masr (location of the Institut français). The surrounding area – with its numerous bookstores, map shops and small independent printers – provided for Alexandria what Charing Cross Road, Fetter Lane and Fleet Street gave London in the eighteenth and nineteenth centuries. French culture was still dominant among educators and the intelligentsia until 1970; the term *librarie* was used by Alexandrians for a bookshop. Even after Arabisation and the influence of Muslim Internal Egypt, they still use the French concept in the Egyptianised-Arabic *maktaba*. This also meant a public or private library, a bookcase or fixed bookshelves.

The wrought-iron railing and fencing of gardens along the eastern pavement and above the stone guard wall of Naby Daniel's mosque served as backdrops of *de bibliotheca Mundi*, displaying thousands of local and imported books and periodicals in French, English, Italian, Greek, Armenian, Russian and other languages as well as Arabic. There were smaller clusters of bookshops near the university campuses; modern Alexandria University colleges were scattered across many quarters: Moharrem-Bey, Chatby, Camp de César, Bachus, Anfoushy, Rue Abukeir and Rue Champollion.

---

* Hypatia, philosopher, astronomer, and mathematician (350/70–415 AD); Theon the mathematician (335–405 AD); Euclid, the father of geometry (325–265 BC); and Callimachus of the Bibliotheca Alexandrina (305–240 BC).

Alexandria Adieu

Readers' Clubs

Nobody knows how or when an ingenious scheme evolved between students, bookshop keepers and periodical sellers, enabling the most impoverished pupils and teenagers to access up-to-date knowledge. Whether course reading books or simply classics, literature or world-authors' works that had been beyond their means came within reach. The students established a readers' club – paying, collectively, a monthly subscription of between 10 and 20 *piastres* to a bookshop to borrow books to read over a few days, then return them and take a fresh bunch. The shops and kiosk keepers' strict condition was that the books and publications be kept clean: no writing on the margins or folding of pages was allowed. Subscribers also borrowed periodicals like *Reader's Digest*, *National Geographic*, *Life Magazine*, the *Spectator* and *Paris Match*, to read and return within a couple of days. It was common among the poorer clubs in migrant areas to have pupils share the monthly subscription (about 2–3 *piastres* each) and to read in groups in one of the teenagers' homes.

The best Arabic language version of education and horizon-broadening was the weekly magazine *Sindbad*, sold at 2 *piastres* (£€ 0.02). Newspaper kiosks would lend the magazine to boys and girls on the same scheme. *Sindbad* was like a mixture of a children's *Reader's Digest*, concise encyclopaedia and historical reference book. It expanded in 1950, employing researchers and contributors, when the Ministry of Education under Dr Taha Hussein (Hessein in dometic Alexandrian) (1889–1973) took hundreds of thousands of copies, on an annual subscription, making the magazine accessible to more children in classrooms – especially in remote rural areas. It ceased publication when the military regime Minister of Education, Major Kemal-el-Dine Hessein, cancelled this subscription, leading to its bankruptcy.

Miracles of Saints and Queens

Tram Number 4 then stops at Rue de l'eglise Copts, leading to the 42 AD Cathedral of Saint Mark the Evangelist (5–68 AD), the second Gospel author. It was still a small chapel when, in 311 AD, Pope Peter I, the seventeenth pope of Alexandria, knelt for his final prayers before his martyrdom by the side of St Mark's grave. He became Pope of the Last Martyrs during the Diocletianic Persecution of Christians, as recounted by Severus of Ashmunain.[2] Peter's beheading (as ordered by the emperor) was delayed by the soldiers fearing a riot as Christians gathered at the jail. Protecting his flock from Rome's fury, Peter plotted with soldiers to smuggle him out of prison to St Mark's Chapel to be executed quietly. Fearing the wrath of God, so the story goes, the six soldiers 'drew straws' using coins to see who would perform the bloody

CHAPTER 7 Tram Number 4, Old Alexandria

task. Saint Mark himself had his body stolen from the site in 828, but his head remained in Alexandria. Venetian merchants Buono da Malamocco and Rustico da Torcello worshipped at the chapel when trading in the city; the relic custodians, monk Staurazio and priest Theodore, told them the chapel was next on the Arab occupiers' list.[3] The Arabs, who were plundering Christian churches to build mosques, were about to profane the church. The two merchants, along with Italian sailors, overcame Staurazio and Theodore. They replaced the evangelist's body with the nearby body of Saint Claudia and loaded it aboard a ship, concealed in wicker baskets and protected by cabbage leaves and pork to deter Arab guards from searching the boat in the harbour.

St. Mark's body was received in Venice by Doge Giustiniano Particìaco (Participazio), who ordered the building of the Basilica di San Marco around his sepulchre, where a mosaic depicting the recovery of the body is on the wall.[4] When the ship on which it travelled almost sank after hitting rocks near Sicily but reached Venice by some miracle, the saint's 'headless' voyage became part of Alexandria's folklore. It was also credited to the saint's celestial powers, just like an older legend granting extraordinary powers to Alexandria's last queen, the beloved Cleopatra, who is credited with saving her obelisk twice from sinking in stormy seas on the voyage taking it to its final destination in England.[5]

British engineers came up with the idea of a 29-metre-long by 5-metre-wide floating cylinder – built by engineers the Dixon brothers and named 'Cleopatra' – to contain the excavated 21-metre, 224-tonne obelisk, which was given as gift to Britain in 1820[6] by Muhammed Ali. This cylinder was towed by a steamer (the *Olga*) manned by Captain Henry Carter and crew in September 1877. A Force-8 gale in the Bay of Biscay led to the temporary loss of 'Cleopatra'. Six sailors from the *Olga* who volunteered to rescue the Cleopatra crew and their skipper, Captain Booth, perished when their boat capsized. Finally, after several attempts, Booth and his sailors were lifted on to the *Olga*. On 14 October, Captain Carter had to cut the towing ropes following a mutiny by his sailors because of 'bad spirits' that they believed were on the floating cylinder and had caused the storm. The voyage's own 'albatross', so the folk tale goes, was the armour and bones of a Roman soldier found buried with the obelisk, which a sailor had stolen and put in the cylinder along with the needle. After it was widely believed that the 'Cleopatra' had sunk, she was – miraculously – found once the storm ended by the *Fitzmaurice*, bound for Valencia, and was towed into Ferrol, Spain.[7] Negotiations regarding the salvage rights and cost took another three months, but finally the Alexandrian queen's supernatural powers rescued her famous needle, and the 'Cleopatra' was towed – by another steamer, the Carter-captained *Anglia* – into

81

London's East India Docks in January 1878.[8] In September that year, it was moved to its current location by the Thames.[9]

St. Mark's Church, enlarged by Achillas, the eighteenth pope of Alexandria (r.312–313), was ruined in 641 by the invading Arabs. It was rebuilt in 680 by Pope John III of Samanoud (fl.680) with permission from the Umayyad Governor of Egypt, Abd-al-Aziz ibn-Marwan, son of Caliph Marwan ibn al-Hakam (623–685), but was destroyed again in 1219. Naturalist and traveller Pierre Belon (1517–1564) mention the church's founding in 1547.[10] Just like the synagogue on Rue Naby Daniel, the church was destroyed by French bombs during the Napoleonic invasion in July 1798. It was repaired and reopened in 1819 by the 109th pope of Alexandria, Peter VII,* under Muhammad Ali Pasha.

Sultans, Kings and Independence

The tram turns east on Rue Sultan Hessein, where the finest French-style furniture is displayed in showrooms with workshops behind the southern side of the street. Hessein Kamel Pasha (1853–1917) – the second son of Khedive Ismail Pasha, the great moderniser – became sultan of Egypt in December 1914. He succeeded his uncle, Khedive Abbas Helmi II Pasha (1874–1944), who was forced by the occupying British to abdicate since Egypt, although practically independent, was officially part of the Ottoman Empire. Egypt became a sultanate under British protection, joining the Allies against the Ottomans and Central Powers. When Hessein Kamel died in 1917, his son, Prince Kamal el-Din Hessein† (1874–1932), declined the succession and his uncle, Ahmed Fuad, became Sultan – later King – Fuad I in 1922.

Abbas Helmi II became popular among those resisting the influence of *les Anglais* – influence exerted by their consul generals in Alexandria, the reformist Lord Cromer (Evelyn Baring, 1841–1917) and his successors Sir Eldon Gorst (1861–1911) and Herbert Kitchener (1850–1916).

From Rue Sultan Hessein, Tram Number 4 turns north into Rue Safiya Zaghloul. This used to be Rue al-missallah (*Obélisque*), and Alexandrians still call the area al-Missallah. The road was renamed in 1947 after *um-el-masrien* ('mother of nationalists'), the wife of Sa'd Zaghloul Pasha. The daughter of an Egyptian politician who served in several governments, Safiya Fahmy (1876–1946) was an activist in the 1919 revolution and a leader in the feminist movement. She

---

* Known as Peter El-Gawly, his papacy started in 1809 and lasted until his death in 1852. Coptic Orthodox Church Network – https://www.copticchurch.net/ – retrieved 16 August 2020.

CHAPTER 7   Tram Number 4, Old Alexandria

married Saad Pasha in 1896. I used to tease *Maman* and my siblings with tram-journey quizzes about street names.

The Modern Alexandria
Continuing north, the tram stops at Mehatet el-Ramleh before turning westwards by the Trianon and past the Café Pullman. It heads west between magnificent Italian architecture on the north side and the Marconi building on the south – then past Cinéma Rex and Cinéma Concordia, stopping the corner of the Jardins Français. So-named when reopened around 1890 by the French Consulate, which financed their repairs after the British bombardment eight years earlier, the French Gardens connected Place Muhammad Ali to the seafront of the Eastern Harbour when initially constructed in the 1870s.

The next stop is by Café vue-Splendide, on the corner of Rue Tatwig, and the French Gardens opposite the Court House on the northwest corner with the French Consulate on the other, northeast side. The wide space between the two building is home to the marble stairs lead to the memorial with Ismail Pasha statue in the centre making a splendid view from both the seafront and the café.

The square around the French Gardens was known as Place Ismail after the modernising Khedive Ismail 'the Magnificent'. During his reign (January 1863–June 1879) he built and modernised more than any other head of state in Egypt's modern history. He also created a prime minister's office in 1878,[*] when Egypt was still loosely associated with the Ottoman Empire.

The first prime minister of Egypt was Nubar Pasha (1825–1899). Born Nubar Nubarian in Smyrna to an Armenian merchant, Mgrdich, he was French- and English-educated, served as transport and foreign minister, was sent as an envoy to London and Vienna, and forged links with India. He was instrumental in constructing the Cairo–Suez railway line. His statue, known as 'the rusted Nubar Pasha', was moved to several places – from outside the Zizinia Theatre to near St Katherine's Cathedral, to a park near the medical school.

Ismail also modernised the national assembly (parliament). It evolved from a 1829 consultative assembly, formerly the higher council of 1824, formed of 99 directly elected and 57 selected members.[†] By 1866, the

---
[*] The post of prime minister, as a president of the council of ministers, was created by Khedive Ismail Pasha in 1878 and Nubar (its first holder) resigned when Ismail abdicated in favour of his son, Tawfik, in 1879. He served again under Tawifik 1884–8, and under Abbas Helmi II 1894–5.
[†] Headed by Speaker Mohammed Lazhogly Bey, it comprised 24 clergy and Islamic university scholars; two members nominated by the chief of Cairo merchants; two accountants; and two members representing each of the ten administrative provinces of

assembly was the first parliament in the region with representative and legislative functions. Its standing orders and procedure were highly influenced by its contemporaries in Europe, particularly the French Assemblée nationale. Ismail's architectural boom added more features to European Alexandria alongside a massive expansion in cultural and artistic activities.

As the tram carries on along Rue Tatwig, passengers have a choice of two stops at which to alight – either at Cinéma Couronnement, renamed in 1937 on Farouk's coronation, or at *Arrêt* Café Farouk, one Alexandria's oldest such establishments, which was initially named after its founder Panayiotis until its name was changed by his daughter, Maria Panayiotis, in 1938. When King Farouk's motorcade was passing on its way to Ras el-Tin Palace, she intercepted the cavalcade, calling, 'your majesty king of Egypt and Sudan'. The king stopped the driver to ask her what she wanted.

The 18-year-old Farouk accepted her invitation and sat at the café, having *chai* and smoking *shisha* with the people gathering around their popular king, who passed silver coins to children. Maria duly changed the cafe's name to *Kahavat* Farouk and the story is still told, with the usual folkloric editions. Until I left Alexandria, photographs of the king – smoking *shisha* and otherwise – still adorned the walls along with much royal regalia. Maria Panayiotis left Alexandria in 1963, selling the café to the local merchant Sayyed Hammam. He kept the photos, which gave credence to the café's name, but *had* to hang the portrait of each president of Egypt next to that of the late king.

The Canals

Travelling in the other direction on Rue Moharrem-Bey were Trams Number 6 and 1, and Number 4 made a journey into areas that had sprung up during the reigns of Muhammad Ali and his four successors over seven decades.*

Tram Number 4 circles back on Rue Rassafah, a scenic location with giant trees and also the *arrêt* for passengers to change to Tram Number 1 going east to Nuzha. Nuzha was mostly a green, leafy district and was inhabited in ancient times by notables like the Bibliotheca Alexandrina's great scholar Callimachus. The Nuzha bridge on Mahmoudiyah Canal severed a sizeable industrial complex and the Nuzha International

---

Egypt (known as directorates) as well as thinkers, intellectuals and community leaders.
* Muhammad Ali's son Ibrahim Pasha (1789–1848), who only ruled for three months; Ibrahim's nephew, Abbas Helmi I (1812–1854); Ali Pasha's fourth son, Muhammad Said Pasha (1822–1863); and Ibrahim's son, Ismail Pasha (1830–1895) who ruled until 1879.

CHAPTER 7   Tram Number 4, Old Alexandria

Airport. Part of Lake Mareotis, on the edge of Nuzha, served as an airfield for floating planes and seaplanes, with regularly scheduled flights. I accompanied my father twice and was taken into the cockpits of the aircraft; I also visited with my school for an educational trip.

Another primary-school visit, to the zoo on the north bank of Mahmoudiyah Nuzha Park, proved unforgettable for all the wrong reasons when I was seven years old. Our teachers had asked us to sit for a lunch break and distribute sandwiches after the first tour around the big-cats and bear cages and the chimpanzee enclosures. I gathered with a bunch of children under a giant palm with miniature fruit, when some large bird, disturbed by the noise, sprang out of the branches, letting a sharp stone drop on my head. Next, my face was covered in blood and one of the teachers rushed with me to the zoo admin's office to call for an ambulance. The duty manager got out the first-aid kit but couldn't stop the deep cut from bleeding. Fearing an ambulance delay, the zoo vet took me to his surgery and stitched the cut, stopping the bleeding. And for a long time, I didn't live down the teasing for being treated by a vet – especially by the children who witnessed my mishap.

Most of Tram Number 4's passengers would alight at Moharrem-Bey terminus, especially in the late afternoons and evenings, to enjoy a walk unique to the area – to stroll along Canal *la-Farkha* (chicken canal, named after the chicken-farm quarter on its east bank) or Canal Mahmoudiyah by giant eucalyptus and *Salix babylonica* (weeping willow), with their branches dangling in the water. Lovers walked hand in hand, shielded from prying eyes by the shadows of trees. Couples would also hire boats for a trip, mostly upstream towards Nuzha. They rowed past the industrial area and the inhabited districts for a picnic in the fields. The *marakbie* (boatman) would charge the couple a *piastre* for half an hour or *nus-a-franc* (2 *piasters*) for an hour, stretching to 80 minutes. But most couples paid full shilling (5 *piastres*) for a whole afternoon, giving them the privacy of empty fields and orchards far away. Tariffs would double or triple at weekends, in summer and during festivals, but would even drop lower on cloudy days in winter. Since nobody in those days had the three guineas for the deposit demanded by *al-usta-al-marakbie* (the boatman) to ensure the safe return of his dinghy, a wristwatch, an expensive fountain pen or the girl's gold chain would have to suffice.

Couples, especially school boys and girls, who didn't have the money to hire a boat opted for another route. They went north to dimly gaslit *strada dell' amore* along the west bank of Canal *la-Farkha*, shielded by the shade of the old trees.

Regardless of these diversions, without the construction of the Mahmoudiyah Canal by Muhammad Ali and Ibrahim Pasha there would have been no nineteenth-century rebirth of Alexandria.

The 72-kilometre-long canal starts at the Mahmoudiyah port junction with the Rosetta Branch of the Nile, tracing its silted Canopic branch, the seventh branch that reached the Nile Delta.[11] When completed in 1820, Mahmoudiyah connected the Nile to the Western Harbour – thus concentrating most of the exports and imports shared with Damietta and Rosetta in Alexandria's larger port. It linked Alexandria to Cairo's markets and the Delta, and to Upper Egypt's crop and cotton fields.

Many races settled in Alexandria, but most were Greeks trading in cotton exports and imports, and working within the harbour. By the end of Muhammad Ali's reign in 1848, the ethnically European's wealth was out of all proportion to their numbers (described as ' foreign nationals in that year's census) they numbered 11,666 or 11.2% of a population of 104,189; but, immigration from outside Egypt was growing faster than from the countryside was making Alexandria a European city more akin to Barcelona, Genoa or Marseilles than to Cairo. The ' foreign nationals' more than quadrupled to 46,118 or 21.5% of Alexandria's 231,396 population in 1882 census.[12]

CHAPTER 8
Rue France, Stamps and Homework

An Exotic Thoroughfare
Place Muhammad Ali designed by Francesco Mancini, with its open symmetrical gardens and lanes, epitomised Alexandria's cosmopolitanism and European taste, commercial success and modern history. Its rows of currency-exchange kiosks, and multiple stores and businesses, fronted magnificent Italian architecture like that of the *Saraya-hakanyiah* (mixed courts-palace of justice), built by Maniscalco who also built Boulevard Cherif Pasha next to the Mancini built bourse (stock exchange) at its eastern end, and Rue France at the *place's* western end. Part of Dinocrates' original plan, Rue France, connecting the square to the old island of Pharos, boasted hundreds of bars, cafés, stalls and bakeries, making the street's mixed aroma part of my Alexandrian memory. Parmesan cheese, spice-wrapped pastrami, pickles and many exotic smells became familiar in one section; in another, the scents of perfumes from *zankat el-sitat* ('the girls' market') and burning incense tickled your nose as it plucked unforgettable aromas from different ethnic bakeries: vanilla, cinnamon, and other species. There were countless races and ethnicities of traders and residents along that famous road.

My last visit was in early 1959, when the street was still Alexandrian, with Papa to see Monsieur Artinian, the wholesale groceries supplier. He was a second-generation Armenian-Alexandrian whose grandparents had fled Damascus for Alexandria in the wake of the 1850 massacre of Aleppo when Muslims, including Arab Bedouins, Kurds and Turkmen under Ottoman rule attacked and killed Christians, mostly Armenians.[1]

Monsieur Artinian invited Papa to his office upstairs, and they discussed the deteriorating situation in Alexandria and Egypt as a whole – especially economically. This included the negative effects on social cohesion and the threats to Jews and the naturalised or born Alexandrian of non-Nilotic ethnicity; they were the city's commerce and trade 'engines.' Nasser's security forces had rounded up the communists and the left-wing intellectuals, of all races, including many Greek and Italian Alexandrians, on New Year's Eve and in the following weeks. Political threats and disastrous economic management had pushed thousands to flee. Merchants like Artinian had started paying extortionist bribes to officials in the Egyptian General Export and Import Agency to facilitate import licences. Those costs and a drop in the Egyptian currency's value put imported goods beyond the reach of poorer Alexandrians, making Artinian's profit margin too slim to remain in business.

I stayed in the shop, exchanging pictures of Hollywood goddesses with Artinian's son, Edmond, and sneaking puffs from cigarettes supplied by Joe, whose father owned a tobacconist's shop off Rue France. Joe's father was a second-generation Alexandrian born to Jews who had migrated from Smyrna in the nineteenth century, and he had joined the two other gentlemen in Monsieur Artinian's office upstairs. We boys took swigs from Stella bottles while giving passing girls marks on the beauty scale – to giggles, or protests at low marks.

The currency with which Edmond paid us, and willing girls, was his father's merchandise: delicious pastrami, which his family specialised in making; salamis; shaves from giant Parmesan cheese tablets; olives; and valued Armenian cognac. Edmond's supply and Joe's cigarettes added to my collections of the useful pocket and handbag items with which my father would be flooded every Christmas from businesses: gifts like manicure boxes or Swiss Army-knife-style tools, retractable pencils, keyrings and playing cards. Exchanging these 'currencies' with flirting Alexandrines for teenage sexual petting round the back of the warehouse was a popular pastime.

We kept bits of this delicatessen fare to share with several cats when we spotted girls crossing from Souk el-Khiet, knowing their excuse to stop and chat was playing with the felines. Cats had been recruited over the years by shopkeepers as a natural defence against rodents, following traditions handed down by Egyptians for millennia when a large part of ancient Egypt's economy was based on cereal production; they worshipped the feline deity, Bastet. But in the reborn Alexandria of the nineteenth-century, Bastet's descendants were still serving the economy in the Western Harbour warehouses and around Rue France with dozens of wholesale groceries and stalls selling live quails, rabbits, chickens and ducks. Joe's cigarettes were also a good bait for girls, we found.

CHAPTER 8   Rue France, Stamps and Homework

King of the Stamp Collectors
Like my father, Joe's dad was one of the city's top philatelists. Alexandria had many shops displaying stamp-collection albums and rare stamps, mostly owned by Greek and French-Alexandrian philatelists. Papa was popular within collectors' circles but wasn't allowed to stand for the philatelic association committee because of La Poste Egyptienne rules. His senior postal-service position gave him rare access to stamps with faults like misspelling or wrong dates, or printers using the wrong dye. Such rarities often slipped past the quality-control check stage and found their way into circulation. Nineteenth-century rules permitted Papa to purchase stamps for private collection as long as he didn't trade them to make a profit. He exchanged rare stamps with other philatelists in Alexandria or by correspondence with collectors worldwide. With a Bolshevik attitude towards the Egyptian monarchy, the new regime ordered La Poste printers to withdraw all stamps issued from 1822 until 1952 and print straps over the faces of King Farouk and his father, King Fuad I. The non-defaced stamps became collectors' items alongside those commemorating great occasions, like the birth of Prince Ahmad Fuad (King Fuad II of Egypt) in January 1952 or the 1938 £€1 stamp marking Farouk's and Farida's wedding (it had become a collector's item after its withdrawal from circulation following their 1948 divorce). Papa's huge stamp collection (most of it, like his properties and antiques, were tragically left behind in Alexandria), and his philatelic knowledge made him a king among Alexandria's philatelists.

I loved visiting my father's office at La Poste Egyptienne, going through an arch of the great Italianate building by Mancini. I was fascinated by the Sudanese guards with the three deep-scratches on their black, shiny, clean cheeks as they stood holding their rifles with bayonet attached. The archway led to an open basalt-stone courtyard and stone-and-marble steps like those of the Foreign Office building on King Charles Street in Whitehall, then up the steps to Papa's office. The afternoons I enjoyed best were trips to Rue France or to visit *Oncle* Constantine, who shared his stamp passion, or to *Oncle* Farid's stores or Justo's workshop which shaped glass tubes for neon signs. Justo once helped me to make one with my name. We would stop first for afternoon tea at Athinèos, the Trianon, or Café le Bourse.

Rue France was associated with '*Les trois jokers – chellah*' – Joe, Edmond, me – and the flirting girls. I can only remember two names: Aurora, the tailor's daughter, and the Sephardic Jewess Viva, who lived up to her name with her energetic, lively, naughty games. In the last three years of Alexandria's cosmopolitan life as we knew it, I spent more late afternoons at my father's office than anywhere else. The working day was styled on the French system of a morning shift, afternoon break and a shorter late-afternoon session. I needed to type Arabic composition for school homework at my father's bureau of postal information, the 'brain' of the postal service's communications. They had a row of typewriters, each for one of the city's commercial languages: English, French, Italian and Greek. The Arabic-letter typewriter was one of only three in the whole of my Alexandrian world then. The second was with Monsieur Sabani, a chain-smoking Levantine Sephardic Jew who taught Arabic as a supply teacher.

Arabic, A Second Language
Contrary to common misconception, Arabic has always been a second (rather than first) language for Egyptians – and in the 1950s it was like a foreign language to most Alexandrians, including Muslims who were supposed to know the Quran. It is not the Egyptians' mother tongue since nobody speaks or thinks in Arabic; it is written only in books. However, pupils from all schools, including those of the *Ma'arif* (Ministry of Education) benefitted from Sabani's private lessons at his home in the Attarin district south of St Katherine's Cathedral. A sudden presidential decree that classical Arabic language, grammar, and Arabic studies was to become known as *igbary* (compulsory) in schools after the 1957–8 academic year had come into effect. Failing the Arabic exam meant retaking all other subjects, losing an academic year.

The third Arabic typewriter I encountered was at the office of Ustazh Ra'ouf, a shabby dressed solicitor-assistant trying to pass his law degree in evening classes while assisting a second cousin on my mother's side. The cousin was a French-educated barrister who had an office by Splendide, the café where lawyers and clerks gathered to select cases for sitting judges. I used to accompany my grandfather to Café Splendide, where he consulted with lawyers. He would often leave me at Cinéma la Concorde, screening cowboy movies or Hollywood-mutilated Greek mythologies or Biblical stories. Daytime admission was discounted, at 1–2 *piastres*, but paying a full shilling or sometimes *perizah* (10 *piastres*) to Demetrious, the usher, my grandfather would ensure he kept me safe, since cinemas popular with young teens were targeted by, mostly Italian, paedophiles. The larger tip was given when the attendant needed to accompany me back to Café Splendide, where my grandfather made three years of Sisyphean visits consulting lawyers in futile attempts to save what was left of his shrunken wealth.

Presidential decrees rendered some laws organising commercial property rental and trade inapplicable while the military regime also purged independent-minded judges; the cousin-barrister himself lost his business, like thousands whose lives were ruined by Nasser's policies, and took to the bottle. He remained in Alexandria, living on the assets

CHAPTER 8   Rue France, Stamps and Homework

of his rich, indigenous Alexandrian wife from a family dating back to the seventeenth century. Although my mother and other female relatives seldom said a good word about her, children and teenagers loved *Tante* Sonia.

What she lacked in looks, she compensated for with elegance and feminine charm in her sense of *la mode*. Sonia *hanem* was generous as we received useful and fancy gifts from her, not just on seasonal occasions like Christmas and birthdays but also on visiting her stylish home or when she visited *Maman*. *Tante* Sonia was quite attentive if we youngsters happened to accompany mothers to one of her impressive receptions, and we would be spirited away in a separate flat in the same five-story building owned by her family opposite Café Farouk. The host was the only adult who popped in a few times to check that we were well looked after, given refreshments and had plenty of games to keep us occupied.

Her family's influence, combined with bribery and shielding behind a Muslim name, saved the barrister from a fate that turned thousands of prosperous Alexandrians into exiles scattered around the globe. But such privileges and cunning couldn't save the barrister with a brilliant mind who would once discuss modern art trends, poetry, classical music and Greek tragedies with the confidence with which he used to win most cases in court. Depression and liver failure dogged his final years, and he died after a short illness following the demise of *Tante* Sonia herself in 1977.

'Viva the green-leaves meaty casserole'

My compulsory Arabic course work for that term in 1959 was a humourless homework composition titled 'The United Arab Republic, a new influential regional power with a historical mission'. Monsieur Sabani wore a sardonic smile as he chalked the script on the blackboard while we played a one-second-long round of a favourite pastime: using wooden rulers to flick little balls of bolting papers soaked in the inkwells at the boys in the front rows. Some students, including myself, were instructed to type our homework since our handwritten Arabic was illegible to the eyes of Monsieur Sabani, who had to hold papers or books close to his nose even with his thick spectacles on. Unfortunately, my Arabic calligraphy still, in the words of Monsieur Sabani, 'resembled the footprints of a drunken seagull'.

With my father's help and subtle hints from the teacher, I learned a young teenage lesson that came in handy later in life when writing freelance pieces bearing no relation to reality, commissioned by idiotic ignoramuses of editors. It was an exercise in the imaginative writing of pretence – using subtle, symbolic metaphors as coded signals that the main message in the piece was total nonsense. These were essential survival tools to show subordination to the imposed orthodoxy of the day or to bypass an ignorant censor – somewhat similar to post-Millennial exaggerated political correctness, leading to a mental straitjacket of self-censorship. Like my composition for Monsieur Sabani in 1959, one learned how to deploy literary tools to create a parallel reality shoring up a fantasy political entity that nobody in the Arabic classes, including the teachers, believed existed.

This charade was also evident in the morning assembly at schools. We were forced to salute the new entity in unison: '*Tahya al-Gomhouria al-Arbiah al-Muthadeda*' ('Viva the United Arab Republic') but the students instead chanted '*Tahya al-Mulkkhia al-Matboukha be-lahmah*' ('Viva the green-leaves meaty casserole'), while the teachers remained indifferent or stifled giggles in handkerchiefed fake coughs. We soon discovered that '*Tahya al-Mulkkhia*' became the morning assembly's sarcastic hymn in all Alexandria schools – for boys and girls alike – without any prior conspiratorial plotting.

These types of jokes – playing on verbal puns, quipping jibes at the regime – were part of the typical Alexandrian humour. The tram conductor Ra'ouf used to make his own rhymes with the whistle, which indicated 'Tram ready to depart' and alert the driver. Alongside taxi drivers, tramway conductors in Alexandria were an informative barometer for gauging the public mood and the people's reaction to ridiculous changes imposed by the regime.

CHAPTER 9
1,000 Guinnieh and a Home in Moharrem-Bey

'May I win *alf* (£€1,000) *guinnieh* and a home in Moharrem-Bey', was an Alexandrian folk saying. A villa in Moharrem-Bey, in the early twentieth century, was a sign of success and of dreams fulfilled. The fashionable quarter with leafy streets had more open space than the crowded city centre, but has badly deteriorated since the late 1960s. Its most sought-after parts were the northern and eastern roads of Moharrem-Bey, known as the 'Latin Quarter' due to its colourful ethnic and multicultural mix.

The bey himself, Moharrem (1795–1826), was the admiral of the Egyptian Navy established by Muhammad Ali in 1810. Ali built a strong navy as a powerful tool to serve his regional policy; sometimes he used it to assist the Ottoman Porte in quelling rebellions. But it was employed mostly for advancing Egypt's own interest independently, just as Cleopatra did 1,800 years earlier. This strategy raised the suspicions of European powers, who did not want to see an independent state emerging in Egypt. It ended with the Battle of Navarino in 1827, with British, French and Russian naval forces jointly inflicting heavy losses on the Egyptian Navy led by Admiral Hassan el-Iskandrani Pasha (1790–1854).[1] The pasha's name was given to another main road off Rue Moharrem-Bey, and the battle led to the 1827 Treaty of London granting Greece's independence.[2]

European migrants started expanding the city east to Ramleh and attracting Moharrem-Bey residents in the early twentieth century. The land in Ramleh was much cheaper than in Moharrem-Bey, and the area also started to gain attention when the 1860 Ramleh tram was electrified in 1902.

Alexandria Adieu

Like most central-Alexandria roads, Rue Moharrem-Bey was washed overnight with seawater from specially designed tank-lorries. While the avenues and boulevards with tramlines had electric lights, other streets off them, like Rue Iskandrani and Rue de Menasce, were lit by gaslights atop ornamental, decorated cast-iron posts with glass lanterns. Their light cast giant tree shadows resembling mythical monsters, scaring us children when they moved on breezy evenings. But we used to beg the gasman to let us hold the end of his long lighting rod during his rounds to light the gas lanterns at sunset.

Moharrem-Bey buildings were typically Italian-designed villas with gardens, large classic *okalle*, a French- or Italian-style blocks with a central courtyard like ours. Others had side and rear entrances from back streets instead of the central yard. This classic nineteenth-century architecture was prevalent in Rue Menace Pasha, Rue Greene, Rue Rassafah, on the Mahmoudiyah Canal banks and around Canal *la-Farkha*. The latter took the same path as the ancient canal built by Dinocrates, linking the Canopic branch of the Nile with the Eastern Harbour where the Ptolemaic royal places were located. Farkha Canal supplied fresh water to Alexandria's water-purification station, known as *wabour-el-maiyah* (the waterworks). Nowadays, water reaches the station via a wide concrete tunnel built under the Farkha, which turned into a road in the 1960s – the work of the philistine, unelected governorate that replaced the enlightened nineteenth-century, elected municipality council. The giant trees along Rue Tirea'atl-farkha that gave it the romantic name *Strada dell' amore* were savagely cut down in the 1970s when the banks were incorporated into a new four-lane road link to *Autostrade* Alexandria–Cairo. Alexandrians born after 1960 have no memory of how Moharrem-Bey used to look.

Celebrities – Villa Ambron

The area was home to many prominent personalities, investors and bankers. Barone de Menasce lived on the road later named after him. Ismail Hafez Pasha – the court chief of Hessein Kamel, Sultan of Egypt from 1914 to 1917 – was a resident of Moharrem-Bey. Hafez Pasha's daughter, Bahigah Hafez, was born in his Moharrem-Bey villa on 4 August 1908. Educated in Alexandria's *École franciscaine* and *mier du dieux*, she went to France for training at the Conservatoire de Paris. She was the first female composer of a film soundtrack in 1930 and a prominent actress in the Alexandria-based film industry. She owed her success to her music coach, another Moharrem-Bey-based composer: the maestro of Conservatoire d'Alexandrie, Giovanni Burgazzi. Many industrialists who built Alexandria, like Ioannis Lagoudakis (1851-1919) who founded a paper mill in Moharrem-Bey, resided in

CHAPTER 9   1,000 Guinnieh and a Home in Moharrem-Bey

the quarter. Lagoudakis had a villa with a large garden overlooking the 'chicken canal' (Farkha Canal's local nickname).

The leafy chicken-canal neighbourhood was full of European-styled residences like Villa Ambron on Rue al-Ma'amoun, where Lawrence Durrell lived after fleeing the Nazis in Greece. He moved into an apartment in the upper part in 1943 with his girlfriend, later his wife, Eve Cohen. She was an Alexandrian-born Jewess and the muse-inspiration for the character Justine, after whom he titled the first book of his *Alexandria Quartet*.

The landlord, architect and civil engineer Aldo Ambron lived in the flat below with his wife Amelia and their daughter Gilda, who was later killed in an air crash. The historian Michael Haag notes that Gilda Ambron was the only Alexandrian whose real name would appear in Durrell's *Alexandria Quartet* – twice in the second part, *Balthazar*, as its list of the fictional names ends with the only real one, Gilda Ambron:

This was Alexandria, the unconsciously poetical mother city exemplified in the names and faces which made up her history. Listen.
Tony Umbada, Baldassaro Trivizani, Claude Amaril, Paul Capodistria, Dmitri Randidi, Onouphrios Papas, Count Banubula, Jacques de Guery, Athena Trasha, Djamboulat Bey, Delphine de Francueil, General Cervoni, Ahmed Hassan Pacha, Pozzo di Borgo, Pierre Balbz, Gaston Phipps, Haddad Fahmy Amin, Mehmet Adm, Wilmot Pierrefeu, Toto de Brunel, Colonel Neguib, Dante Borromeo, Benedict Dangeau, Pia dei Tolomei, Gilda Ambron.... The poetry and history of commerce, the rhyme-schemes of the Levant which had swallowed Venice and Genoa.

(Names which the passer-by may one day read upon the tombs in the cemetery.)[3]

Signore Ambron, patron of the arts, was also president of the Club Italiano and the founder of many Alexandrian institutions that helped the city flourish, like the Banco Italo Egiziano; he also held the title of Grand Uffiziari of the Italian Royal Court. King Vittorio Emmanuele III stayed as his guest at Villa Ambron when he was in exile in Alexandria after his abdication in 1946. (Ironically, when King Farouk was deposed by the military six years later, he sailed in the opposite direction – choosing Italy for his exile, where he was allegedly poisoned by the military regime and later died. The Italian king passed away in Alexandria in 1947.) Signore Ambron helped the family engineering company of his wife Almagia, also known as Amilia, which built the splendid front of the corniche in Alexandria's Eastern Harbour – its design held by historians and Alexandrinologists alike to reflect the Ptolemies' spirit in its magnificence.

Alexandria Adieu

Durrell's writing den was a room on top of the Tower, an octagonal addition projecting eastwards at the villa's corner. He penned *Prospero's Cell* and started working on the *Quartet*, but he didn't complete it until he returned to Greece after the War. His leaving Alexandria relatively soon gave faultfinders reasons to suggest he let his imagination get the better of him in writing about the city, which, allegedly, didn't exist in reality.

Durrell's critics comprised mainly left-wing Anglo-Saxon historical revisionists; and, most dangerously, modern (non-Alexandrian) Egyptian academics and researchers of an Arab-nationalist and Islamic persuasion. The majority of them missed the irony that they themselves were writing about Durrell and his contemporaries retrospectively. Given the ages of nearly all these authors and critics, hardly any of them can have known the Alexandria about which they were writing in refuting Durrell's description: some, especially the revisionists, were only born after the *Quartet* was published, and most were not even born until 30 or 40 years after the Villa Ambron events took place.

The exceptions among Durrell's critics were Alexandrians born before the War, like scholar Harry Tzalas (b.1936):

'You cannon come to know a city during war – she does not show you her face at such times – and Alexandria of the war years, was changed for a while was adrift.'[4]

This exception aside, the motives of most *Alexandria Quartet* critics seem to be ideological and political, particularly in accusing Durrell of excluding Egyptians from the scene. This is total nonsense: Nessim and his family, central to the narrative in all four books, are Nilotic-Egyptians with ancestry predating Islam and Christianity; so are characters like Semira and Claire.

Isn't a non-Muslim born in Egypt an Egyptian national?

In addition to Nessim's family, there were other Egyptians: Balthazar, Justine, Melissa, Claire, Samira and Layla to name but a few; but they happened to be non-Muslim. Several personae were mixed race, hybrid, like Alexandria herself. However, claiming that those who had built Alexandria since 1810 were not Egyptians would rationalise the illegal seizure of their property, investments, banks and businesses.

Durrell's critics thus included those intent on an Orwellian rewriting of Alexandria's history in order to erase a chapter of her life. These revisionists chose to ignore demographic facts created by economic and historical realities. Alexandria's population grew twenty-fold in 100 years; thus, in fact, almost all Alexandrians but an indigenous few were immigrants.

When the French landed in 1798, there were fewer than 5,000 inhabitants, mostly migrants – half of whom were also migrants from the Egyptian countryside – whom we might call indigenous Alexandrians;

CHAPTER 9 1,000 Guinnieh and a Home in Moharrem-Bey

all the rest, who made post-war Alexandria a one-million-strong metropolis, were second- or third-generation immigrants and settlers. They were all Alexandrian but of different ethnicities, from Europe and the Levant mostly. Other migrants were Armenian, Russian or members of many other ethnic groups from the provinces of the former Ottoman Empire, or investors from British Empire nations and Muslim and Coptic Egyptians from the countryside. The latter group were the last to arrive, as workers or students, decades after the Europeans – especially the Greeks and the Italians – had already built Alexandria's residential and commercial districts. Internal Egypt's immigrants were attracted by the prosperity created by non-Nilotic migrants and the massive public projects of Muhammad Ali and his son, Ibrahim Pasha – like the shipyards, the arsenal, the railways, the Mahmoudiyah Canal, the enlargement of the harbour, and the palaces and state buildings.

The Jews of Alexandria were Sephardim (those expelled from Spain in the fifteenth century and settled in Ottoman provinces); Mizrahim (the geographical definition of Jews originally from the MENA region, often including Sephardic Jews); and, although not widely known, many Ashkenazim (Yiddish-speaking Jews from eastern Europe) who had fled earlier Russian pogroms but who also began to arrive as refugees in large numbers in the 1930s and early 1940s.[5] Meanwhile, the Karaite Jews had been indigenous to Alexandria and Internal Egypt for hundreds of years.*

Villa Ambron had been home to dignitaries like the leading Alexandrian-born Egyptian painters Saad el-Khadim (1913–1987) and Effat Nagui (1905–1984), both of whom have a museum dedicated to their works. For a short while, another resident was Max Debbane, considered to be the authority on Alexandrinology. His *Bulletin of the Société Archèologique d'Alexandrie* was a great reference on the subject; he had thousands of files on Alexandria, which he had written himself. After his death, the American University in Cairo bought 3,300 of his books, but the valuable files disappeared.[6]

Eve (Cohen) Durrell told Michael Haag that she would sit and watch Durrell writing in the Tower and he wasn't disturbed. 'I kept silent, I hardly ever spoke, because I was still coming out of my past…I wasn't sure what my part was doing, but I was happy to observe.'[7]

Villa Ambron, part of Alexandria's soul and body, has tragically and deliberately been allowed to fall apart in order to facilitate its barbaric demolition to erect another monument to ugliness.

---

* Karaite, Hebrew *Miqra* meaning the Hebrew bible and the root of the verb *qara* meaning to proclaim through reading – and the same in Arabic, as Mohammed first word in his Quran was: Iqra – read.

By the middle of the twentieth century, Moharrem-Bey – especially the grid of roads north of Rue Moharrem Bey – was home to a mix of middle-class Copts; Muslims; and European Egyptians like Hungarians, Albanians, Italians, French, Russians, Greeks, Syrians, Cypriots, Georgians and Armenians. I am sure there were more ethnicities, but I list the ones I encountered. There were also mixed-marriage families: Europeanised Egyptian *effendis* and *hanems*, middle-class professionals and academics. The further north or west you went along Rue Moharrem-Bey the more European the quarter was, demographically. Like us, some families had more than one home: a Moharrem-Bey apartment or villa, and another villa or chalet in one of the Ramleh districts near a *plage*. We referred to each abode by geography, not by the exact address. The El-Balad (central Alexandria) home meant my grandfather's flat in his building on Rue-Falaki, or when my mother said, 'We'll spend the half-term in Sidi-Bishr', she meant Villa Alexandrine in Sidi-Bishr. This was built in the 1930s on land my grandfather bought for 20 *piastres* (9d or 45p in new British money) per square metre. When the family purchased an extra 50 square metres to build an extension in 1950, War inflation pushed the price up fourfold per square metre.

A Cosmopolitan Block

Our Moharrem-Bey home was in a four-storey French-style block with a central courtyard. It was on a junction summarising Alexandria, bounded by roads named after a Jew, a Macedonian Ottoman, an Egyptian Muslim and an Italian – leading to Abbasiyah Hill-park, home to the university's college of sciences.

The block had been built in the late nineteenth century by Italian architects with French taste. All the surrounding dwellings projected beautiful facades with balconies, and had shops below them. In our building, at street level there was a café run by a Maltese, an Armenian grocer, a Muslim butcher, an Upper Egyptian ice vendor, a Cypriot bread outlet and a Greek fruit shop displaying most exotic products from all over the world when in season: avocados, mangos, pineapples, American and Levantine apples, all varieties of citrus, custard apples, coconuts. The residents were Albanian Macedonians, Italians, indigenous Alexandrians, Levantines, migrants from Upper Egypt and the Delta, Jews, Coptic Christians, Catholics, Muslims, non-denominations and mixed-ethnic marriages; the *bawab* (*portier* – caretaker) was Nubian. Opposite the block was a pharmacy and a two-storey building housing an Italian pâtisserie.

Our Moharrem-Bey abode was a seven-room apartment laid out around a spacious central hall reached through a smaller one

CHAPTER 9   1,000 Guinnieh and a Home in Moharrem-Bey

accommodating an *entrée suite* and tall mirror stand for coats and walking sticks. We stayed the winter months (mid-November to late April) while the rest of the summer months, Christmas, Easter half-term and all other holidays were spent at our Sidi-Bishr home, Villa Alexandrine. The third home, El-Balad, was my grandfather's smaller, four-bedroom duplex on top of a four-storey building near *la Borsa*. He let out the rest of the buildings to businesses and offices. The fixed rent, which averaged £€1–4 a month per unit, was a handsome income in the early 1900s but, by the middle of the century, was hardly covering the overhead cost of keeping the building or paying the *bawab's* wages.

The apartment had high ceilings with cornices and plaster roses. It had four French windows opening onto two balconies. One balcony, with three doors to three rooms, ran along two street facades – making it nearly 20 metres long and a metre and a half wide. The other, about eighteen square metres, had French windows into two rooms. Internal room balconies overlooked the courtyard. There were services stairs from all kitchens into a back street with fence and climbing vine. The kitchen, bathroom and separate toilet, and two smaller rooms used for serving staff, were all inside one enclosure divided from the great central hall. The hall was used as a living and casual room if we didn't have guests on weekdays. Three of the seven rooms opened to one another through dividing Georgian-style glazed doors. The middle room had a giant glass panel of four doors opening to the hall and the other room with the corner balcony – and, in turn, it too opened to a fifth room. Children loved to run through and play hide-and-seek.

There were seven spacious flats in the block, of the type you see in central Paris. On the very top lived an Italo-Alexandrian family: *Tante* Carlota and *Oncle* Luca, their daughter Francesca and her older brother Filippo. Theirs was the only flat on the top floor; thus, they had the entire roof, which they turned into a lovely garden with endless potted flowers, climbers, roses, jasmine and garlands dangling halfway down the courtyard.

On the ground and lower-ground floors on the east side lived *Oncle* George and *Tante* Tina (Kristina), an Alexandrian couple in a mixed marriage – from the Egyptian Coptic and Armenian churches – with their three boys and one daughter. Opposite, on the western side, lived a Jewish family: *Tante* Fortune and *Oncle* Bishara and their son Sammy. When they left due to the harassment of Jews, their flat was occupied by people who seemed different: a non-Alexandrian shipyard shift foreman. He had only migrated to Alexandria from Kafr-el-Zayat, 104 kilometres southeast in the Delta, after the War and still spoke the *fellaheen* tongue.

There was something queer about the contrast between these two families; perhaps it was the teenager's instinct that we were losing our sophisticated, cosmopolitan Alexandria to the new invaders from inward-looking oriental Egypt?

The new occupier sounded foreign to the ears of children and teenagers – unlike the Jewish family, who spoke like everyone else and sounded normally Alexandrian. The exception was the shipyard foreman's much-younger wife, Patty, from his second marriage: she was Alexandrian, born in Bahary. She was also a stunner of pale complexion with freckles, standing over 179 centimetres tall with a model's figure and symmetrically perfect face with dark-green eyes. If Patty (Pattiah – 'Patience') had been blonde instead of having long, brown hair that reached her hips, she would have been the spitting image of Nicole Kidman except for her eye colour. A son from his first marriage moved in with the couple.

Patty, about whom us teenage boys fantasised, was submissive to her husband. She was ready for him at the end of the day with a deep bowl of warm salt water that he would put his tired feet into, and she would massage them with her sexy hands' long, slim fingers. I overheard Bellitta, the housekeeper, reporting to my mother – saying the milkman's daughter, Souso, had seen them. My mother told her that Souso was a naughty, unreliable gossip and it was nobody's business.

'Couples expresses their affection in different ways', she said, adding that what might seem weird to us could be someone else's usual way of life. 'If she is happy, then leave her alone' was my mother's final verdict on the subject. It took me years, and experience, to understand what she meant, in the same way that it took me a while to understand how class and other prejudices sneak their way into children's subconscious.

Awakening to Class Discrimination

Although it wasn't vocalised, all subtle signals indicated that the new occupiers were different: a working-class Muslim family. Children were learning the boundaries of class hierarchy subtly through prefaces and titles that the grown-ups guided them to use. The middle class and neighbours like us were *oncle* and *tante*. From the same social class, a young man was *abieh*, a mademoiselle was *abla*; female teachers, in turn, addressed their headmistress as *Abla-el-Nazherah*, with the same fearful respect that young Catholic nuns accorded their mother superior. A lady was referred to as *hanem* in the third person ('Madame' when addressed directly); mademoiselle (if not married), and the same for a serving waitress or a female shop assistant; *ustaz* was a male teacher. All *ustaz* were gentlemen role models in their manners and sartorial fashion; so were middle-class professionals, *effendis*. They always wore

CHAPTER 9   1,000 Guinnieh and a Home in Moharrem-Bey

a three-piece suit and tarboosh in winter, and a summer suit with Panama or some sort of light straw hat in the summer. *Ustaz* also denoted a learned lawyer.

Our new neighbour had moved from a working-class district near Mina-el-Basal (the 'onion docks' – although they were for exporting cotton, not onions!) to the middle-class side of Moharrem-Bey (there were less-attractive neighbourhoods to the south of Rue Moharrem-Bey). Children registered he was 'different' when my mother and everyone else referred to him as '*Usta* A'ati', short for his name, Abd-el-A'ati (child of god, the provider). The other known *ustas* in the area were Manolli (Emmanuel) the barber and Paolo the tailor who worked from a ground-floor flat below his residence on Rue Iskandrani. A third was *Usta* Franco, the cleverest motor mechanic in Alexandria, who seldom ordered new automobile parts as he always managed to repair original ones. His brother-in-law, *Usta* Giovanni, was a body-repair genius who could panel-beat a car wing crushed like an old sandwich wrapping back into its original shape. We youngsters sussed out that A'ati was different; he was not an *effendi*, thus he won't qualify to be *Oncle* A'ati. I remembered Alexandria days when my local London corner shop was sold to a Turkish family. The owner's sons started calling me *oncle* while everyone else was mate, mister or darling. Their father addressed me, without exception, as 'sir'.

Interestingly, *Usta* A'ati's wife was plainly referred to as Patty and addressed as such by everyone. She was a proper Alexandrian like the rest of us, but not entirely – thus, not qualified to be a *hanem* or *Abla* Patty for the children. Just Patty; even the prettiest Alexandrian female on the block could not break through the class-title barrier. 'Don't you know how to address a hanem *ya fellah*?' my mother lectured a post-office clerk for daring to call her *hagah* (someone who had performed the Mecca pilgrimage) instead of Madam or *Hanem*.

A'ati's son was the only boy on the block named Mohammed. Poor Mohammed was often put to an impossible test in a cruel show asking if one has to be put to *dabh* (like when cooks kill birds before cooking), whom to choose: Patty or Bunny? Bunny was his biological mother, who, so the story went, abandoned the boy to his paternal grandmother who subsequently passed him to his father. There was something unusual about the story, something the grown-ups pretended to ignore (and some, unkindly, laughed at) but the children didn't miss and thus didn't laugh about. Even the younger children – who didn't know terms like cruel, sadism or psychological abuse – realised it wasn't right.

CHAPTER 10
A Tale of Two Cities

Dickensian Alexandria

Economic and fiscal gaps between extreme riches and extreme poverty were a feature of cosmopolitan, kaleidoscopic Alexandria. A short journey from affluent, middle-class, Europeanised Alexandria opened my eyes to another Alexandria that I didn't know. After subjecting *A'am* Mahmoud, the milkman to one of her Gestapo-style inquisitions about his product's freshness, my mother instructed Bellitta to go with his daughter and inspect the cows he milked daily. I accompanied Bellitta to check two cows, Riya and Sakinah, named after two villainesses who ran a brothel frequented by officials and allied army officers; they became part of Alexandria folklore after murdering many women whom they lured into a secrete den, concealed next to a police station.

After walking half a kilometre southward off Rue Moharrem-Bey we approached the Mahmoudiyah Canal café opposite the palace of Iskandrani Pasha whose family donated to become a school.

The café was located by stone steps leading to the canal bank where I had earlier rescued a kitten from drowning and carried it home, ruining my school jacket. I named it Puskas, after the Hungarian footballer Ferenc Puskás (1927–2006). Bellitta and I took the flat-deck ferry, powered by human muscle. Two men completed the operation, pushing a long punt to the canal's bottom then walking bent forward to the other end of the boat with the punt wedged against their shoulders. In the morning and evening rush hour, each bank saw lines of rural and Upper Egyptian migrants who had moved to Alexandria searching for a better life.

Workers crossed to the south bank to start their shift in the factories, railway works and industrial complexes that had sprung up between

CHAPTER 10   A Tale of Two Cities

1860 and the Great War. On the southern bank would stand a shorter queue of people carrying vegetables, fruit, eggs, live birds and rabbits, as well as dairy and other produce to sell. Street pedlars with pushcarts, tricycles and donkey-pulled *carros*. They delivered produce to street markets like Rue Pawalino a kilometre to the east, or further north to the indoor Souk-el-Missallah near Ramleh station. The ones who travelled on into European Alexandria, or Ramleh, got higher prices, but none escaped the haggling of housewives or maids – many of the latter would have come from the same impoverished areas as the vendors themselves.

Many vendors came from Gheit-el-Enab, where the 1937 Mar-Gerigus (St George) church is located to serve the majority Christian migrants from Upper Egypt, giving the quarter the name Gezirat-el-Appat (the Copts' island). The island produced some folk-tale villains, and *fittewat* (gangsters) controlled many neighbourhoods and ran protection rackets. They featured in literary works and dramas, like the 1961 novel-turned-movie *The Thief and the Hound* by Naguib Mahfouz (1911–2006). Gheit-el-Enab also gave birth to many writers and thinkers, like novelist Edwar al-Kharrat (1926–2015) who wrote in Classical Arabic, Demotic Egyptian and French.* It was the location for Ibrahim Abdel Meguid's moving and well-researched historical novel *No-One Sleeps in Alexandria* about the War years and the air raids on Alexandria.

Mahmoud, the milkman, wasn't enough a master of craft to be an *usta*, nor was he a *me'alem* (merchant) because it was a title reserved to business owners employing several subordinates; he was a non-status *a'am*, as we called doorkeepers and street sweepers. Like a fate stamped by Greek Gods, his label was '*A'am* Mahmoud the milkman' – even to people decades his senior, like my grandfather. Mahmoud, in turn, would enquire about the welfare of *el Bey, el kebier* (the senior master), while *el-bey elsogheir* (the lesser bey) was my father, who was also older than the milkman but called him *A'am* Mahmoud. The milkman put his stainless-steel containers in a *carretta* (box wagon) pulled by his donkey Allenby, named after Field Marshal Edmund Allenby (1861–1936), commander of the Allied Forces in the Great War. He upgraded it to a tricycle after Allenby retired to comply with health calls following typhoid and cholera outbreaks. While the milkman lost Allenby, others continued to use draught animals to serve or transport fresh food. *Carros* (long, narrow wagons), carried gridded wooden cages

---

* His novels, like *Girls of Alexandria* and *Rama and the Dragon* – as well as his semi-autobiography, *City of Saffron* chronicling the life of poorer Coptic Alexandrians during the War years – are an excellent account of Alexandrian life between 1930 and 1950.

full of live poultry and eggs past Mahmoudiyah Canal on their way to market, while scores of sub-contractors used horses and mules to pull carts taking ice blocks from Raheem's store next to our Moharrem-Bey home. Raheem once argued with Papa that ice wasn't classified as fresh food; thus, it wasn't his problem if irresponsible vendors used it with food and drink.

'I can't sell it with end-user instructions, can I?' he said full of astonishment, rolling up his eyes at the smartly dressed educated *effendi's* lack of common sense!

Although Mahmoud found the tricycle to be a more cost-effective vehicle, he missed Allenby. I only remember the donkey vaguely, but I was told I loved being put on its back. Mahmoud also used it as a chat-up pretext, flirting with housemaids and female street pedlars with bawdy puns about Allenby's organ. Milkmen in Alexandria were central characters in the type of coarse folklore equivalent to British milkmen jokes. And the widower *A'am* Mahmoud lived up to such a reputation, according to Bellitta's gossip.

Bellitta was the one I trusted as a child; she injected the human understanding of the poorer Alexandria into my social consciousness thanks to her own experience, kindness, patience and the time she allocated to me. 'Bellitta' was a diminutive of Bella, the name by which an Italian deserter from the Great War had called her late mother, who became his close friend when he hid near their village 90 kilometres east of Alexandria. When her mother died, the father, suspecting Bellitta was not his biological child, threw her out and she was taken to an orphanage run by Italian nuns. They found her a home with my grandfather, as a *cameriera*, a serving companion, for his wife, Dora, who had become depressed following the death of her only child and a lengthy illness that rendered her infertile. As a toddler, I sometimes called her Dada, but later just Bellitta like everyone else. She addressed my grandfather as *ya Bey*, or *el-padrone* in the third person; she referred to my mother as *el-signora* and my father as *el-bey elsogheir* (just as Mahmoud did).

In addition to home, food and clothing, my grandfather provided the orphaned Bellitta with books after realising that her orphanage lessons put her far ahead of the elementary education provided at state schools. Two years into her service, my grandfather banned Bellitta's drug-addict brother from coming to the house to collect her meagre wages. He placed them in a post-office savings account instead, where it was added to the dowry for her unfortunate marriage in 1954. She continued to drop by frequently to help wash and clean, and take me out to railway depots to spot steam locomotives that I loved. She had two girls by two successive husbands, who both ill-treated her. After a short illness, she died, leaving the young girls to fend for themselves at

CHAPTER 10 A Tale of Two Cities

a time when most ethnic Europeans had left Alexandria. European-Alexandrians were the first-choice employers for those less-fortunate migrants who only served in the daytime. The worse-off ones – children of countryside migrant families living south of Mahmoudiyah Canal – became lesser-educated live-in maids.

Needy parents would send a child as young as eight to work as a live-in housemaid or boy servant. Their cruelly painful calculation was to pass the child's clothing, food and medical costs on to the employing family. In exchange, the stepfather, the widowed mother or her boyfriend would collect the wages, which were as low as 50 *piastres* to a pound per month. Ethnically European employers paid better than their Nilotic counterparts. The needy domestic child would often register with *mekhaddem*: these unregulated domestic-service agents were kings in a Dickensian world of exploited children. They usually kept the larger part of the child's meagre wages as commission. The children's families preferred ethnically European and Jewish employers to Nilotic and Muslim Egyptians. Most *mekhaddems* wouldn't deal with the latter, who paid less and treated their domestic serving children poorly.

This cruel practice of child servants was, reportedly, still going on well into the 1990s. Housemaids in their teens were sexually exploited by male members of the household. When a wife caught her husband with the housemaid, she threw the poor girl out – while a mother would punish the maid found in a son's bed but often kept her in service. My sister overheard mothers preferring this arrangement to the son catching some disease in a brothel. Often, a pregnant maid would be thrown out. She'd be lucky if she got a few pounds instead of threats with a theft report to the police if she didn't go quietly.

Domestic-service children kept by Nilotic-Egyptian families were often beaten up by cruel children of their own age or older. Child servants were forced to carry shopping half their body weight, deprived of sleep and overworked with no specified fixed hours. It was slavery in all but name. I am still ashamed to have witnessed those abuses and exploitation on an industrial scale. Although my family treated servants relatively better than many I knew, I still wake up at night with guilt and shame at the treatment of some child-servants I witnessed over 60 years ago.

The younger of Bellitta's two daughters married a sailor, and the older one took a longer, complicated route. She became pregnant at the age of sixteen and managed to contact my mother via family members who hadn't signed a non-return pledge with the Nasser regime, thus travelling back to Egypt with relative ease. My mother hurried to the girl's rescue and arranged a safe house, where she gave birth in secret;

with her old school friend *Tante* Oni, *Maman* plotted and bribed to get the necessary paperwork, and the one-day-old bastard was adopted before the poor teenage mother could hold it in her arms. Those conspiring, old-fashioned Alexandrian ladies kept the money the childless couple gave the girl and invested it in a bond saving account. She graduated a few years later and became a schoolteacher. They also found her a good husband – another teacher. I saw the girl again in 2003, at a memorial service for my mother held by her surviving Alexandrian friends – mostly wartime nursing volunteers. Bellitta's daughter was accompanied by her husband and their two children. She said she was grateful to my late mother for 'many favours in her life, especially education', but there were mixed feelings in her tears. Only she and I understood what they meant.

The Other Alexandria
On the other side of the Mahmoudyiah Canal, I thus discovered another Alexandria different from the European city and the middle-class way of life. Bellitta was on a mission to inspect *A'am* Mahmoud's health- and-hygiene credentials, as instructed by *Maman*, who had become a hygiene freak after a post-War cholera outbreak. Vegetables and fruits had to be soaked in deep containers of diluted, purple potassium permanganate while shoes had to be left outside the door and their soles washed with disinfectant, with a total ban on takeaway food among other dictatorially imposed measures.

We walked seemingly forever, passing through several 'worlds' that I was discovering. The first was an ugly, industrial wasteland with scrapyards and dirty, barefoot children sorting through piles of discarded metal. Then we passed the western railway line that served the docks, the Muxx shipyards and the Libyan Desert. It was lined with casuarina trees on each side, which gradually became denser. No smartly dressed *effendis* or elegant ladies were present, but railway-maintenance workers in dark-blue overalls covered in dirt, and the odd barefoot child or woman carrying weights of vegetables or baskets of fruits heading north to Mahmoudiyah Canal. We also passed smaller fields with men and women bent down tending lettuce shoots. Bellitta followed instructions given by Mahmoud's daughter, Souso, a flirtatious, naughty teenager who had inherited her father's classic milkman genes. The little minx was ahead of her years, advanced on the womanly side of things and well-endowed with a nice figure. She was no different from any Alexandrian mademoiselle on weekends. On Saturdays, she dressed in a tight garment in heels and matching handbag, wearing perfume and full maquillage, flirting with boys while queuing for the cinema or a dance hall.

CHAPTER 10   A Tale of Two Cities

Souso was in a flowery dress, flat brown shoes and a straw hat, waiting for us by a pig-farm entrance. I wanted to inquire whether we could buy a piglet to keep in the Sidi-Bishr garden, but Bellitta firmly put me off. We were led through a narrow path of tall banana plants, giving off a nose-destroying smell of fertiliser. When the trees became as dense as a forest, the fertiliser stench gave way to a more pleasant fragrance. We entered a dense grove of acacia, eucalyptus, fig and Ficus bonsai trees surrounding an orchard of citrus-fruit trees and vines on raised poles and wires, before passing a plot of vegetables and strawberries.

We reached an opening with a tiny muddy pond, where some ducks splattered next to a single-storey cottage that doubled as *A'am* Mahmoud's home and dairy workshop. Riya and Sakinah, the two milk cows, were munching under a shed roof while some chickens were picking grains from the ground. The open yard also held a chicken coop and enclosure where many grey rabbits grazed and ran. Once inside, Souso invited us to sit on a sofa with tatty but beautifully embroidered cushions. She placed an engraved old oak table with ivory patterns, covered in an overused but clean lace tablecloth, before us. She brought a faded silver tray with a china teapot, matching milk jug, teacups and saucers, sugar jar, silver spoons and a tea strainer, then placed another tray with a tub of fresh cream and two china bowls of biscuits and *kahak*, the traditional cookies that dated back to ancient Egyptian times. All seemed part of a tasteful set of china and silverware: Souso, who also placed three pretty embroidered serving napkins, came from a struggling third generation of Upper Egyptian migrants but had acquired something of Alexandria's European ethos. This must have been her mother's set and beautiful laces, which had helped the widower and his daughter add touches of good taste and beauty to their simple home.

The manner in which Souso greeted and invited us in and presented the tea reflected Alexandria's European etiquette with no trace of the peasant life that her grandparents had lived. Regardless of their wealth, Alexandrians added touches of beauty and taste to their homes; those who lived in flats with no gardens had window boxes and flowerpots on their balconies.

A blue-and-gold china vase held freshly cut blooms that I recognised from flower beds we had just passed with Souso: chrysanthemum, ceanothus, lilac and lavender. Then there was a framed picture of King Farouk and Queen Farida on one wall, and a framed photo of a much younger *A'am* Mahmoud and his late wife on their wedding day. He wore a suit and bow tie, and she was in a white bridal dress wearing beautiful maquillage, looking extremely pale next to his darker complexion. '*Maman – allah yerhamha*' (My mother – God bless her soul), said Souso, smiling as we looked at the photo. There was also a framed print of Van Gogh's *Sunflowers*. The painting was loved by her mother, said Souso, giggling cheekily (albeit incorrectly) that the Dutch artist, whom she called *vansan gookh*, had had his ear injured by a jealous girlfriend who caught him painting another naked mistress!

'*Itfadalo, s'il vous plaît*', said Muslim Souso, who had only attended the first three years of elementary education at Mar Girgis Coptic School in Gheit-el-Enab, in Franco-Egyptian-Alexandrian, inviting us to have tea. Bellitta poured two cups without adding any milk. I understood that this was because we weren't sure it had been boiled.

Souso – and thousands of other poor Alexandrian mademoiselles living in makeshift accommodations on the outskirts of Alexandria, of the kind that we had passed on our way from Mahmoudiyah Canal – maintained standards and ambitions. Although less well-off than middle-class Alexandrians, they managed to enjoy culture, arts and entertainments like they did. The milkman, who had a comfortable home by his class standards, had an attractive daughter. She went to the cinema and downtown dance halls at weekends and had good taste, as her clothes reflected on special occasions. The only connection to her *fellaheen* grandparents was her milking the yellow-brownish cow, Riya, which I now watched in fascination. Bellitta stood behind me, placing a protective arm on my shoulder while Souso, who had changed into a shorter brown working dress, pulled out a low wooden stool. Her legs opened as she sat down. I felt a twinge of sensation: Souso had no knickers on. She smiled and winked at me. 'Look out!', I shouted, alerting her as Riya suddenly kicked, but the milkmaid didn't flinch, only swiftly rearranging her body away from the kick with a smile and a wink of someone confident in how to deal with the hazards of the job. More surprises awaited me when I wanted to visit the toilet. Bellitta asked for *l'Kabineht*, the term used by less-sophisticated Alexandrians from the Italian *gabinetto*. 'We also call it *toilette* here', said Souso, with perfect French pronunciation but indignantly; 'This way, sir', she led me. Bellitta drowned her embarrassment in tea, pouring another cup.

The *Kabineht* was a 15-centimetre raised square-shaped platform with a hole in the middle and stone around it with two pads for the feet of the unfortunate *désespéré*, a high cistern and a chain. It was a clean but scary construction. I encountered its like in Turkey and the French countryside in the 1980s, and these inconvenient Ottoman loos were also to be found in most Egyptian railway stations in the countryside and in third-class train carriages. They were hazardous, as only a fit yoga enthusiast could execute a 'number two'. Even standing without slipping on the wet stones needed a tightrope balance.

CHAPTER 10   A Tale of Two Cities

Souso's *toilette* contrasted with the clean 1920s Art Deco public conveniences, whether run by the railway board or by *belediye* in *plages* and central Alexandria. By the late 1970s, they had been forgotten by municipality health inspectors. Visitors to the staffed ones at Egyptian airports, public buildings or railway stations were subjected to customary *baksheesh* to use the always-locked and relatively cleaner cubicles with proper bowls and seats. The attendant's trained eye spots the Bey or the elegant *hanem* a mile away, presenting them with fresh-out-of-the-box toilet paper and a towel at the handwash basin later. The encounter with *A'am* Mahmoud's loo made me realise why my mother ensured she left the house with an empty bladder and declined drinks offered when visiting poorer homes on her charitable rounds.

I later noticed that most Egyptians outside European Alexandria didn't pay much attention to this vital service, and this indifference soon overwhelmed larger parts of the city after 1960s Arabisation. Alexandria's biographers, like Ricardo Wahby Tapia and Dr Abd el-Fattah Abdellah wrote about the contrast between the clean sanitary conveniences of European Alexandria and the inadequacy of toilet and wash facilities to which Muslims from countryside background were accustomed as long as the facilities fitted within Islamic jurisprudence. The two authors recorded seeing countryside migrants in dirty clothes, many with grimy bare feet and filthy hands all day, but only when it was required by Islam would they wash for prayer. Abdellah says his observation also supported his 'conviction of the inimitable nature of the Islamic religion as it mandates washing before each prayer. Muslim jurists classified the act according to the type of external body grime that required washing, including body secretion, excrement, urination and passing gas.' He was appalled and couldn't comprehend how those southern migrants weren't embarrassed by defecating or urinating in the ruins of collapsed buildings behind the air-raid shelters in full view of any curious onlooker.[1] Exiled Alexandrian Whaby Tapia recalled seeing, in 1964, one of those *fellaheen* migrants urinating on empty land then drying his 'long penis with a small sandstone, totally oblivious to anyone that might have seen him'.[2]

As a boy, I often felt nauseated when retrieving a racketball from behind a row of beach huts and found evidence of human defecation. The beach had gates, and entry was by a fee; they must have climbed the fence during the night. Why go through this trouble when free public toilets were available? Was it a social protest by a twisted-minded interpretation of Islamist-indoctrinated hatred towards Alexandria's European sections?

Observation of post-Millennial London rekindled these thoughts. I have often seen teenagers from council estates deliberately lead their dogs to defecate on Hampstead house gates by the Heath. Was the case in post-war Alexandria, also part of a protest by anti-urban *fellaheen* pushing through the separating cultural barriers into European Alexandria? By the 1990s, they finally overran the whole city, which has now been entirely ruralised apart from its old city-centre architecture. That part, too, has had its beautiful Italian and central European facades pockmarked by an array of signs.

- *The milkmaid's offer*
Showing me the way to the *toilette*, Souso squeezed my hand and brushed her moistened lips against my ear, murmuring, 'I saw your eyes feeling between my legs', she bit on my ear; 'did you like my smooth waxed c***?'. She suddenly grabbed my chin and gave me a kiss on the mouth; I blushed.

'I know how to milk a bull too; shall I show you?' I declined the offer, pushing her hand away from my groin. Perhaps I was concerned because Bellitta was on the other side of the wall, but later I realised it was something else. Souso repeated her wish to milk a bull after I had finished, but I declined once more – just like I did two weeks later when I encountered her on the stairs in our house, and even when the coast was clear in our kitchen when we were alone.

She was puzzled why I turned down the service of an attractive girl. I realised I was put off by her hands despite her good looks and sexy figure. Looking back on this unforgettable encounter, I realised how minute details can make a pretty girl desirable or turn a man off. Souso's hands were clean, but her fingernails were short and shaped in a masculine fashion, just like those of *A'am* Abdouh, the school caretaker. I have always been put off by women with non-feminine or ugly hands or feet. I cannot even look at women's hands with the Millennial French manicure, with nails filed like the tip of a plumber's screwdriver. I wonder whether women realise how off-putting this fashion has been – especially for gentlemen who grew up during the pinnacle of femininity, represented by glamorous icons like Brigitte Bardot, Grace Kelly, and Alexandria stores mademoiselles?

It remains one of the inexplicable mysteries of the universe: why women follow the fashion of the day, which were mostly introduced by gay men, even when the so-called *moda* undermined their femininity and often made a girl less attractive?

- **The dividing canal: the dividing lines**
The Mahmoudiyah Canal was another barrier – like Kom-el-Dikka Hill, the railway line and the Ramleh tram – dividing Alexandria into two cities and several communities. In contrast to poverty, scrapyards, industrial sites and inadequate housing south of the canal, a walk

CHAPTER 10   A Tale of Two Cities

eastwards along the northern bank of Moharrem-Bey towards Nuzha was as pleasant as a stroll along any European canal with tall trees.

The 'other' Alexandria on the south bank had an extension that started on the northern bank, to the west towards Karmouz and Ragheb into working-class areas. I went a few times with my teenage auntie, Milla, sitting at the downmarket café by the ferry steps while vendors carrying bamboo-and-rush baskets brought fresh fish caught early in the morning from Lake Mareotis. The youngest of the five siblings was called Milla Giada because of her unusual piercing green eyes. She was only 14 when her mother died, and she moved with us since my father was the eldest male family member. I also went on the ferry with my grandfather to inspect illiteracy-combatting classes in the afternoon and evenings for workers in the south-bank factories. Like many services in Alexandria, the essential and much-used punting ferries filled gaps not covered by public bodies.

Public Services

- La Poste
Letter and telegram services were provided by La Poste and delivered by the postman (he was *el-postiono* to Bellitta and Francesca but *A'am* Shenouda – *el-postagy* to everyone else). *A'am* Shenoudah would shout the names from the courtyard all the way up in a voice that would have shattered the skylight four floors above had its glass not been toughened during the War. But when it came to delivering our letters, he would climb the back stairs and ring the kitchen doorbell. He had been told off the first time he shouted our names some years earlier, according to Bellitta. More plausibly, he made the ascent for the refreshment in our kitchen, jam sandwiches and cakes, like several service- and tradesmen did.

- Streetlights and cleaning
As well as paving and resurfacing streets and laying down sewage and water pipes, the *belediye* laid gas pipes for streetlights in 1865, installed by the Compagnie de Gaz et d'Électricité Lebon. The French gas engineer and industrialist Charles Lebon had set up gasworks and gas streetlights in his home town of Dieppe, other gasworks in Spain and Italy, and streetlights in the capital of French Algeria in 1841. After signing a 75-year concession in 1873 to construct a network of street lights powered by town gas from processing imported coal,[3] Lebon built the first gas plant in Karmouz by Mahmoudiyah Canal. Although town gas was still used for many streetlights in the 1950s, the municipality and Lebon started using electricity generated from the Karmouz

plant back in 1892. The first customer to have an electric meter (number 61448) with 2-ampere power installed on 11 May 1895 was the *avvocato* Manouzdi on Rue Cherif. Many wealthy merchants, royal villas and palaces had their own electric lights supplied by private generators and powered by Lebon town gas. The second, with a 16-amp meter, was the Ottoman Bank on Place Muhammad Ali – after which, hotels and homes started contracting Lebon's service.

I recall a 'Lebon man' visiting our premises for the monthly gas and electricity meter readings. In Moharrem-Bey, Remon (Raymond) was suddenly replaced in 1957 by Alexandrian *ibn-balad* Ishak, who kept the same uniform but swapped the beret for a *casquette* when ambulance crews, tram conductors and policemen sported it instead of the tarboosh on the orders of Nasser regime. Lukas, the older Belgian man who used to read the meters located in the basement of the block in my grandfather's downtown place, continued to visit but disappeared in 1959, and nobody replaced him until I left Alexandria. Like the rest of the eastern part of Ramleh, there was no gas service in Sidi-Bishr.

Services like street cleaning and rubbish collection from fixed points on street corners were quite efficient until I left. I noticed accelerated deterioration over the years with my infrequent visits between 1962 and 1998. By my last visit in 2012, the service, performed twice daily for 80 years, had become non-existent in many parts of the great city.

The municipality had employed street sweepers in central Alexandria since the 1830s, but their deployment in other areas was not enhanced until the 1870s. *A'am* Gad *el-balayeur* was the street sweeper in Moharrem-Bey. Like his Sidi Bishr colleague, *A'am* Hassan, he had a *belediye*-issued uniform and a cap. Unlike Hassan, who had a larger plot made up of over two dozen streets, Gad had a smaller area but was always busy. There was the tram, two bus routes, many shops, cafés, restaurants and greengrocers – all generating a considerable amount of refuse. He also collected handsome sums in *baksheesh*. In the summer months, *A'am* Hassan in Sidi-Bishr had an assistant as the plot's residents would increase sixfold. Each sweeper had a hand-pushed cart with two barrels for what they swept, and holders for disinfectant – a thick, black liquid with an awful smell they poured into the open rain drains to kill the cockroaches. In reality, nothing worked with those devilish brown insects (*Periplaneta americana*), which could also fly short distances.

The *belediye* rubbish truck made two collections in central Alexandria. The morning round picked what street sweepers had in their barrels and the large steel boxes on corners. After midnight, the truck (which Alexandrians called *cumune*) picked packaging and boxes left by restaurants. The rubbish collection by *cumune el-zepallah* in Sidi

CHAPTER 10   A Tale of Two Cities

Bishr and other beach areas only took place once a day during the summer months, and every second day in winter. Central Alexandria streets used to be washed overnight with cleaning foam and seawater sprinkled from special trucks. The last time I saw those trucks in action was during my year as an external student at Alexandria University in the mid-1960s. Then this service too disappeared for good, leaving Alexandria's streets matching the viciousness of the unsightly high-rise blocks that replaced the city's villas and gardens.

- **Recycling and fashion**
Despite a good street-cleaning service provided by the *belediye*, its refuse collection didn't extend to private homes' waste. However, decades before the term recycling was invented, the most organised domestic rubbish collection and reuse of items were independently organised in Alexandria without intervention from officialdom.

In Moharrem-Bey, the *zappal*, *A'am* Ghattas, and his two boys would come in a mule-pulled *carro-l-zepallah*, a wagon box with high sides (a corruption of the Italian *carro-dell-spazzatura* – refuse cart). They collected the daily rubbish tins or large buckets left outside kitchen doors on *sellem-khadameen* (or sellem-de-service – servants' stairs) landings. The boys would empty the bins into a large, soft basket made of dried bulrushes, straps and a leather belt going around their shoulder and waist, and empty it into their wagon. In Ramleh villas, there were usually back or side alleyway entrances to the kitchen, unlike in central Alexandria's block buildings. The service subscription was anything between *nos-guinea* (50 *piastres*) and 15 shillings (75 *piastres*) for flats in densely populated areas, but would jump to a full guinea for a villa. Bellitta joked that we paid three times for rubbish collection in Sidi-Bishr what we did for the similar service in Moharrem-Bey, where we generated twice as much rubbish since we burned some refuse and threw food scraps in the giant compost barrel at the far end of the villa's back garden.

The *zappals* received additional tips during festivals and holidays. Given Alexandria's ethnic mix and multiple faiths, they would get up to a dozen tips a year – doubling their income. The monthly fee and *baksheesh* tips were usually collected by Rerrie, who insisted on sounding the French 'R', shortening Myriam. She was *A'am* Ghattas's teenage daughter, who, in addition to helping her father, took over domestic duties when she was only 12 after her mother died. By the time I left, she was 19 and studying for university entry.

Collecting the monthly fee, Rerrie came to the front door – not sellem-de-service – greeting the family with a card relating to the particular faith or event. She had a spark in her eyes whenever she encountered my grandfather, who gave her books and inquired about her school progress while encouraging her to study for university. She was about two years behind her peers due to her family's challenging conditions. Rerrie used to dress in a dark-blue frock in winter or in a bright flowery dress in the summer, or Sham-Ennessim, the oldest Egyptian spring festival coinciding with Easter Monday. She wore a two-inch gold crucifix on a chain on her chest, standing tall on three-inch heels with a matching leather handbag. Her dark hair in two long braids was a far cry from the hair stuffed under a cap and the masculine blue salopettes she sported when she happened to help her father during the sons' absence. But Ghattas never let her carry anything, only allowing her to sit on the wagon's driver seat holding the reigns of Barhoom, the mule. Just like any other working-class Alexandrian mademoiselle, she would work as hard as any tough man long before #MeToo and feminism were heard of. Then she would change into the latest *mode-Parisienne*, with attractive but straightforward maquillage and a head-turning, feminine hairstyle. The poorer working-class girls also followed *moda*; the Egyptian textile and fashion industry provided cheaper versions from affordable quality cotton, wool or linen.

Local Alexandrian women of all faiths were historically used to working next to men long before the European phase of the twentieth century. It was reported when reconstructions and repairs started following the British bombardment of central Alexandria in summer 1882 that 'male workers were joined by women in long bluish gowns, [who] could be seen climbing up ladders with their loads'.[4]

Since the late 1920s, many Alexandrian girls had already been able to acquire affordable versions of Paris's newest mode by making their own frocks – a skill learned from their mothers and taught at girls schools – or by hiring affordable seamstresses in popular quarters. An ageing Jewish seamstress, Ronita (Ronit), in the working-class Karmouz quarter could make a spitting image of any *fustan* (frock*)*, *jupe* or ensemble after eyeing its photograph in a fashion magazine.

Zappal service in Sidi-Bishr was provided by descendants of Coptic migrants from Upper Egypt who were based in Ras el-Soudah, four kilometres south of Sidi-Bishr Railway Station. The mule-pulled tipper-*carro* could empty its load by tilting backwards once unhooked from the pulling animal. The *zappals* made collections daily except on weekends. It was a socio-economic service that went beyond just disposing of domestic waste; it became an environmentally self-sustaining industry long before the concept of 'recycling' became a Millennial belief. It sprang up spontaneously as an industry organised by Alexandrians themselves, and grew to provide thousands of jobs in a long chain of services and supporting trades.

CHAPTER 10   A Tale of Two Cities

The rubbish was taken into *ma'alb* (a turnover), a fenced empty space between the railway line and Rue Abukeir (now a hospital-complex car park). Scores of children sifted through tipped piles, separating and rearranging items in wooden or tin boxes and hessian bags supplied by contractors working for several factories. Broken glass went to the Yassin glass and crystal works south of Mahmoudiyah Canal; cans and bottle tops went to metal workshops and smelters in the industrial areas further to the southeast; wrapping, cardboard and rags went to the Lagoudakis paper mill. Food scraps fed pig farms or, with organic material, were placed in old oil drums and sold as fertiliser to banana plantations and farms on Alexandria's outskirts and along the railway line to Cairo.

No newspapers or magazines were put in the rubbish. Periodicals were culturally and visually rich, full of pictures and exciting reports, features and analysis of national and international events. They had stories about Hollywood stars whose movies were screened across Alexandria's many film houses, so they were handed down from better-off to lower-class households, barbershops and popular restaurants where you could have a hearty breakfast for under *nos-franc*. Newspapers and magazines were collected by boys in the neighbourhood. Glossy magazines and coloured periodicals in good condition were sold to news kiosks outside second-hand bookshops near the central railway station or Rue Naby Daniel to be re-resold. Newspapers were neatly folded into four and compacted into foot-high bundles tied with string that the boys' mothers collected from parcels. They sold them by the weight to local shops to pack loose merchandise such as flour, grains, roasted nuts, falafel, bread and crêpes. Vendors, cut a newspaper page into A4 size sheets and would skilfully wrap each folio round their forearm in cone-shaped *kurtas*, to pack their products for customers.

Recycling was perfected during the war years. Like other ladies of her war generation, *Maman*, until her terminal illness in 1998, didn't dispose of things that modern households happily throw away. Brown paper and Christmas wrappings were neatly folded and kept in a drawer, elastic bands were put in washed oat tins, strings would all be placed in a ball in a jar. Jars were always cleaned to store the jams and marmalades made in winter. Fruits in the season were turned into thick jelly-jam, and many vegetables pickled and stored in jars for use throughout the year – dates, guavas and pears in autumn; oranges in winter months. Narring – a bitter, sour, small orange that only appeared in January – was my mother's favourite. It was turned into thick marmalade by cutting the fruit's rinds and boiling them for hours. Vegetables and roots – peppers, tomatoes, cucumbers, onions, beetroots, lemons, limes and aubergines – were pickled; some needed to be soaked, others boiled first then stored in jars. Tins and other boxes were used to store ingredients or handed to children to turn into toys – especially in primary school classes, when supervised by teachers.

Administering Alexandria

- European Alexandria: the financial capital
Public services, like street lighting and drainage, were organised by La Municipalité, so-called in Muhammad Ali's French guide organisation in 1810. Street names and documentation were all in French then, a legacy of Bonaparte's 1798 expedition – as were the first public-services organisations, some basic civil laws and courts modelled on the modern European style after centuries of neglect under Ottoman rule. Called the *Belediye* (municipality) when Muhammad Ali added Turkish to French in the official documentation, it went through different organisation stages. It was fully established as a modern institution in 1869 when run by 13 elected members, who became 28 within two decades. It started as a Mixed Provisional Municipal and Commercial Committee (MPMCC), set up with the Cairo government's help to resurface roads and serve the harbour.[5] By 1820, Alexandria was the de facto diplomatic, financial and economic capital of Egypt. The country was then – officially, and in name only – part of the Ottoman Empire; hence, there were ambassadors in Constantinople and consuls representing their nationals in regional cities like Smyrna and Alexandria.

Alexandria became the economic and cultural engine of a modern Egypt. Muhammad Ali was building and pushing for her independence from the Ottomans. Ali and his successors set the tradition of making Alexandria their summer capital.[6] The summer months were extended to almost half of the year by Muhammad Ali himself, who started spending more time in the *Palais* Ras el-Tin, the oldest of Egypt's royal palaces, first built between 1811 and 1817, redesigned in 1834 and overlooking the Western Harbour on the ancient island of Pharos north of Bahary. Bahary was known as the Turkish quarter because it resembled Istanbul in its architecture, erected during Ottoman rule. Ras el-Tin Palace was named after the land where it stands today, *ras el-tin* meaning the Cape of Figs; it saw fig trees growing in Ptolemaic-era orchards on the western edge of a narrow promontory sticking out into the sea as the most northwesterly tip of Old Pharos island. The Cape of Figs is almost totally surrounded by water and, like Alexandria herself, is not quite part of Egypt or of Africa but a slice of land accumulated from Nile and sea deposits of Mediterranean life forms over millions of years – persisting it belonged to no continent out of the Old World

CHAPTER 10 A Tale of Two Cities

three but to the sea.* It was a fitting location for the founder of modern Egypt with his massive ambitions and Mediterranean roots to build the very first palace in what to become his unofficial capital.

The Palace of Ras el-Tin was built in the Italian Renaissance style – with wood and plaster, projecting eaves and protruding rectangular window frames and panels – by craftsmen, architects and master builders summoned from Ali's native Macedonia. Its 17,000-square-metre original design resembled a Roman fort, and was also influenced by Moorish style and Ottoman taste in boasting a harem section; the Pasha, Muhammad Ali, had a divan to receive the consuls of foreign powers.[7] But European interior designs began to take over the palace within a few years. Architect Pietro Avoscani made many changes, both inside and outside. Avoscani was later to design Alexandria's central railway station, among many other landmarks. Gas lights, made by a local Alexandrian firm, were installed in Ras el-Tin by Scottish engineer Thomas Galloway. He was a lieutenant in the British Army before working for Muhammad Ali in 1824, supervising over 40 British engineers in the Great Foundry of Bulaq.[8] In 1827, marble bathrooms and staircases were installed – and European bedrooms replaced oriental floor beds.[9]

The pasha received gifts like mosaic table and chandeliers from the British East India Company and world leaders like the pope and King Louis-Philippe I (1773–1850) of France.† By 1848, all the furnishing, decor and interiors were totally European. A semaphore point was erected in the palace square as part of an organised optical telegraph system that took Muhammad Ali's orders to Cairo in 45 minutes.[10]

The historian Dr Alfred Joshua Butler (1850–1936), a Fellow of Oxford's Brasenose College, was hired to tutor young royals enjoyed Ras el-Tin's beautiful gardens, 'shaded by palm and acacia glowing with flowers of rare scent and splendour, freshened with cool streams and fountains', he recorded in his *Court Life in Egypt*.[11] The pasha made the palace the centre of Alexandria's political and social life, inviting cultured European visitors at short notice.[12]

- The independent Belediye

European and other powers of the time were represented by their consuls based in Alexandria. Alexandrian exporters and importers urged the government to establish a *commission municipale* with the

---

* See Map R; also Chapter 14 – 'The "Devil's Hole"' for Europa and the Bull, and the connection with *L'ancienne Méditerranée*.
† King of France from 1830 until the monarchy was abolished in the 1848 revolt.

power of taxation to organise police, health, road maintenance and commerce. Khedive Tawfik supported the proposed *belediye* commission (comprising 13 members, 8 representing European settlers). Objecting to their nationals paying a suggested 8% tax, the consuls opposed the plan, which would have also given Cairo more power with the government appointing the council's president. Paradoxically, some of those consuls were Alexandrians – for example, Max de Zogheb, representing Portugal, and Menandre de Zizinia of Belgium. Several businessmen behind the proposals were also subjects of powers represented by the consuls objecting to giving the metropolitan civil body more powers.

This predicament weakened the consuls' position, enabling a compromise for a mixed municipal and commercial committee to liaise with the Egyptian Government. But it did not have the power of taxation, which only came into effect in 1890 with pressure from the British consul general, the reformist and progressive Evelyn Baring, first Earl of Cromer. The *belediye* committee comprised three-quarters elected members in equal numbers by registered municipality taxpayers, importers and exporters, and property owners; a quarter were appointed by the Egyptian Government. To harmonise ethnic representation in Alexandria's racial mix, a maximum of three from the same nationality would be among the elected members.[13] But in those days, 'British' or 'French' could also have meant someone from those nations' colonies, and 'Ottoman' included Egyptians, Greeks and Syrians. The appointed members were usually Egyptian – but, equally, that didn't mean they were necessarily ethnically Nilotic-Egyptians.

The Egyptian Army's founder who was cast as Egyptian was a French born general with Napoleon's army, who converted to Islam and changed his name from Joseph Anthelme Sève to Suleiman (1788–1860). Rue Suleiman Pasha in central Cairo is named after him. Muhammad Ali commissioned him to help build the Egyptian Army on a European model; he was placed in charge of a new military academy at Aswan to train a 'new model army' of Sudanese slaves. He married the Greek Muslim Myriam Hanem, with whom he had three children: Aasma, Mahadi and Nazli, a maternal great-grandmother to King Farouk.

Not only was Alexandria Municipality the first in Egypt, but it also remained for a long time the only autonomous metropolis council in the region. When Chakour Pasha was elected as its first *directeur general*, Nubar Pasha sent him his warm wishes on his appointment in 1892: 'You will occupy a post that is not completely equivalent to a Vice Secretary of State, but that is definitely superior to the presidency of the Council [PM]'.[14]

CHAPTER 10   A Tale of Two Cities

The council's structure reflected Alexandria's cosmopolitanism. The elected members included four British, eight Nilotic-Egyptians and six Greek-Alexandrians. Some of these names made history: streets, residential areas, parks and tram stops were named after them. A district was named after Ambrose Georgios Ralli (also written Ambroise – b.1874)[*]; another was named after Baron Jacques de Menasce; and Antoniadis Gardens, a miniature version of Versailles laid out around a palace, named after the founder Sir Jon Antoniadis[15] who is buried there. He donated his gardens and estate in the Nuzha district to the municipality.

The municipality documents were always in French, explaining why the Alexandrian street names were in French. Their communiqués were also published in the official papers in Arabic and French.

---

[*]Ambroise/Ambrose George Ralli (Jr), member of the the municipality committee, was born in 1874 (no death date can be found); his father was Georgios Ambrouzis Ralli (1845–1922) – Ralli, Tony, Family Tree: Gw.geneanet.org/tralli

Part II

ALEXANDRIA'S IDENTITY, AND HER VANDALISM:
LANGUAGE, IDENTITY AND COSMOPOLITANISM

CHAPTER 11
Language

Cosmopolitanism was more than a feature of Alexandria; it comprised the city's identity as an epitome of modernity. Its post-Ottoman inhabitants constructed their identity from various components, accumulated over decades by the Alexandrians themselves: architecture, fashion, arts and etiquette – and, of course, how they intercommunicated and expressed themselves. Here, I deliberately use the term 'demotic' instead of 'colloquial'. Demotic Alexandrian – the language used on her streets, spoken and often written – has been more than a medium of communication; it was an essential component of the city's identity. A language is also a primary tool for programming (and reprogramming) the human mind. Therefore, it is vital to correct the misconception regarding the Egyptian Alexandrian language. Arabic, a written-only text for many Egyptians, has always been a second language for them and is never used as the daily, spoken demotic tongue. Thus, it is not the language in which Egyptians think or dream, nor how their toddlers pick up the vernacular as they grow.*

Changes in the patois used over the past half-century in the everyday language of a country like Egypt have been inseparable from alterations in the collective national mindset. It joins confusion about the national identity, which was until the late 1960s uniformly Egyptian. Changes in a language come gradually, sometimes too slowly to be noticed from within, but they are easy to spot for someone visiting the place between long intervals.

---

* Ethnic minorities who don't speak general demotic Egyptian also often use the Arabic script as their written language for documentation and correspondence: for example, Nubians would speak Nilo-Saharan sub-languages (like Nile Nubian or western Nubian), while Greco-Egyptians would speak and think in mixed Egyptian and Greek.

CHAPTER 11   Language

George Orwell's (1903–1950) 'Newspeak', in his novel *Nineteen Eighty-Four*, was a classic example of changing national identity through linguistic reprogramming. The particularities of Newspeak make it impossible to translate most older remnants of the language: 'In fact, there is no word for "science", with "Ingsoc" [the name of the fictional ruling party of the totalitarian state of Oceania] covering any meaning that such a concept could possibly have.'[1]

As in *Nineteen Eighty-Four*, the Nasser regime's 'Newspeak' was a powerful tool for modifying the nation's identity. The military coup diminished Alexandria's political status as a summer capital and was followed by its socio-cultural and commercial annexation by Inner Egypt, as represented by ruralised Cairo. And those who had the economic upper hand managed to vandalise cosmopolitan Alexandria within three decades. By the twenty-first century, Alexandria's unique individual characteristics had all but changed. She had been crushed under a stampede of *fellaheen* taking over the most beautiful parts of fragrant Alexandria, which once were replicas of European towns. 'The City was invaded by neo-Hyksos'*, Old Alexandrian Dr Abdelfattah Abdallah, who biographised life in Alexandria between the 1930s and the 1990s, lamented, 'Unsophisticated and backward fellaheen who made fortunes in oil-rich Gulf countries and invested them in ugly tower blocks that defaced the most beautiful parts of Alexandria.'[2]

Unlike nineteenth- and twentieth-century European migrants and cultured Egyptians returning from schooling or long trips in Europe saturated with its culture, the 1990s *nouveau riche* spent years accumulating wealth by working in rich Arab countries with little to offer in culture, knowledge or social etiquette. Like many Old Alexandrians, Abdallah calls them 'neo-Hyksos' and new Tartars, likening their takeover of Alexandria to the thirteenth-century Mongols' sacking of Mesopotamia and the Levantine cities.

Two changes in language accompanied the 1956–1990 demographic turmoil: the first was Nasser's deliberate reprogramming of the collective mind along Newspeak-style lines. His syntactical change was ideological, replacing the simply defined Egyptian identity with a confusing, unclear pan-Arab one. The second wave – the more dangerous of the two – was the Islamisation of his successor, Sadat, which evolved from the first in an ideologised culture underpinning a belief system. And the language began playing its role in transforming the Egyptian identity by adding a pan-Islamic layer.

---

* The rise of the Hyksos kings in Egypt was made possible by an influx of immigrants from Palestine and area south of the Jordan valley into Egypt beginning about the eighteenth-century BC.

The first wave excluded non-Nilotic ethnic Egyptians and relabelled them *Aganeb* (foreigners/aliens) by stretching the meaning of the term in an unmistakably hostile way. At the same time, Nasser, who controlled all media outlets, banned the adjective 'Egyptian' and replaced it with 'Arab' – a label embracing outlanders while excluding hundreds of thousands of fellow Egyptians. Sadat's changes thus marginalised and antagonised millions of non-Muslim Egyptians.

The slogan 'One common language' meaning written Arabic only) has formed the primary 'evidence' in Arab nationalists' propaganda to propel their ideological fantasy of a hegemonic, single 'Arab nation' corresponding to the former Ottoman provinces. However, their illusion is not supported by convincing geographical, cultural, historical or demographic facts. For example, post-Millennial genetic studies have found that Egyptians have only 17% Arab genes (below 2% in areas inhabited by Nilotic- Coptic Christians), while the Lebanese have 56% Arab genes.[3, 4]

Pan-Arabists[*] have been desperate to undermine national languages predating any documented Arabic, sometimes by millennia, while referring erroneously to those countries' national and demotic tongues as regional *Lahgat* (accents or dialects) of Arabic. Speaking one language doesn't make an Australian, a Scotsman and an American automatically Englishmen – although there is, in fact, far less difference between their English vernaculars than in the enormous gap separating an Iraqi and a Tunisian, who would barely understand one another. Nonetheless, fanatical Arab nationalists (and mostly uniformed mainstream media) would claim that they are one race speaking one language.

Alexandria's tongue

Demotic Alexandrian is the spoken language for the period covered by this book before the Arabisation process: this vernacular has changed considerably in half a century (1970–2020). An influx of newly Arabised Muslim migrants from the countryside, many of whom had spent decades in the Gulf countries and Libya, have swelled Alexandria's population fivefold to near six million.[5] They brought with them rural *fellaheen* expressions that mixed with the mostly Mediterranean *lingua franca* Alexandrian. Lesser-educated newcomers also copied their sponsors' or employers' patois, subconsciously associating the vast wealth of oil-rich Arabs with the orthodox Islamic thinking reflected in their vernacular.

---

[*] Pan-Arabism as a political ideology emerged in the 1940s within the Ba'ath (Arabic: 'renaissance') party founded by Syrian sociologist Michel Aflaq (1910–1989) and politician Salah al-Bitar (1912–1980).

CHAPTER 11   Language

The 2020 demography of Alexandria bears no resemblance to the ethnically diverse composition of its pre-1980 population. The populace then consisted of two groups: the indigenous Alexandrians of the rapidly growing modern city from the early 1800s, who were descendants of the native Alexandrians (numbering under 5,000 in 1798), and *néo-natifs*. The latter embraced two subgroups: European and Europeanised Ottoman migrants, who built modern Alexandria's (and Egypt's) economy before her independence in 1922; and a smaller grouping of migrants from Internal Egypt, whose numbers accelerated with the growing industries around and after the Great War. Many of the latter integrated into Alexandria's society and her way of life, except for some *fellaheen* living in their cultural ghettos on the southern outskirts (these were the first to flee Alexandria during the Luftwaffe air raids on the City from 1941 to 1942;[6] most didn't return until 1946). The demographic composition began to change a decade later, after Suez. Between 100,000 and 200,000 expelled, fled or departed under political and economic pressure were second- to sixth-generation *neo-natif* Alexandrians. They were replaced with 780,000–830,000 migrants, mostly from rural Egypt (and Dr Abdallah's neo-Hyksos and neo-Tatars).

During my subsequent visits to Alexandria, especially for extended periods between 1963 and 1981, I did not notice a significant change in Alexandriaspeak on a scale comparable with the accelerated linguistic transformation during the two decades that followed.

While demotic Alexandrian in the 1940s and 1950s was different from the language spoken in Internal Egypt, Millennial popular Alexandrian is increasingly becoming a subset of the modern (contemporary) Egyptian vernacular. Ideological Arab nationalists, wrongly, call modern demotic Egyptian *Al-lahgah al-Masryah* (Arabic in Egyptian accent) – and are parroted by many Western academics (with laughably superficial knowledge of the Arabic language – and its subsets and subdivisions – and a shallow understanding of Egypt), whose ignorance is second only to that of journalists. Their categorisation is unrelated to the real usage of the language. The difference between demotic Egyptian and Arabic is not like the difference between Kent and Birmingham accents in British English, or even that between Toronto, Sydney and Glaswegian patterns of intonation. The closest taxonomy – if we insist on using the term 'Arabic' – would be 'Arabic-Egyptian'.

When a word or a phrase conveys identical meaning in every place but only sounds different, then it is an accent; when the term and the structure of the sentence vary but still convey a similar meaning, it is a dialect. If a substation quantum of the vernacular in daily use doesn't fit within this definition, then we *are* talking about two *different* languages and not merely accents of one tongue.

Alexandria Adieu

In Alexandria (and Egypt generally), only the official written script of books and state documents is Arabised-Egyptian (Egyptian in Arabic script); the spoken, demotic language is just Egyptian as it evolved over the millennia. And there is a massive body of input from French, Ottoman-Turkish, Greek, Italian and some English and Persian contributing to modern Egyptian; its non-Arabic inputs are greater in volume than the Arabic ones. Foreign invaders – namely, the Arab conquerors – introduced their tongue to an existing indigenous Coptic language predating Arabic by millennia.

Except for geographical Arabia, Arabic has never been the indigenous language of the large area now lazily (and often meaninglessly) referred to as 'The Arab World'. Some new Arabic phrases were introduced to Egypt through foreign military occupation but was absorbed into and added to a rich, existing language. It had minor impact on the existing Demotic language since the main body of the idiom remained Egyptian while the text of the occupying power, namely Arabic writing, started replacing the demotic letters. It was a process similar to the way the Middle (Ptolemaic) Demotic (440-30 BC) had replaced early Demotic (650-400 BC) which in turn started appearing next to, and often replacing, the hieroglyphic text during the Twenty Fifth Dynasty rule (790-656 BC), as illustrated on the 196 BC engraved Rosetta Stone.

Today, a phrase written in Arabic letters in Sudan or Morocco has a different meaning to that in Arabia, where it originated. *Doulab* in Arabic is a wheel but a wardrobe in Egyptian. *A'gallah* is a wheel in Egyptian but haste in Arabic. *Me'arras*, a groom in North Africa, is a pimp in Egyptian. If you ordered *harissa* in Egypt you would receive a honey-soaked cake topped with *crème fraîche*; in Arabia and North Africa, you would get a hot chilli paste instead. The difference between *harissa* in Alexandria and *harissa* in Arab countries cannot be accounted for by 'accent'; it denotes a different vernacular with distinguished meanings – originating from, and accumulated through, the usage of an indigenous language over centuries.

An identical script (like Welsh and English for example) is not evidence of one cross-border language either. All of western Europe uses the same Latin script, but even fanatical European federalists never claim this as evidence of a single 'Eurospeak' to forge an ideological identity in the way that Arab nationalists do with Arabic letters.

Historical upheavals following invasions and colonisation when the invaders become the ruling elite do not necessarily lead to a replacement of the existing language with that of the invaders. In many cases, the invaders' and the natives' tongues merge or the ruling elite imposes its own as the 'official language', and the pre-existing tongue runs in parallel as the demotic one. However, the hybridisation of languages

CHAPTER 11 Language

into one Alexandriaspeak was the city's resistance to assimilation into a larger Arabo-Islamic (later Ottoman) body by having her own pidgin language – an echo of Felipe Guaman Poma de Ayala's (1535–1616) *First New Chronicle and Good Government*[7] seen as an example of autoethnography.[8] Professor Mary Louise Pratt (New York University) coins the phrase authethnographic text: 'a text in which people undertake to describe themselves in ways that engage with representations others have made of them'.[9]

CHAPTER 12
Invasions and New Expressions

Egypt was invaded, in part or whole, by Nubians (728 BC), Assyrians (676 BC) and Persians (525 BC), with each of these invaders' lexica seeping into the Egyptian language. Alexander, *Alexandros ho Megas*, standing on Pharos Island in 332 BC was a historical event. His Ptolemaic Dynasty (332/305–30 BC)[*] established Alexandria as the capital of an independent and powerful nation-state, with Greek running for centuries in parallel with the two varieties of Egyptian language: the dying official hieroglyphics and the thriving demotic Egyptian.

The Romans – following the battle of Actium in 31 BC – annexed Egypt without an actual invasion, introducing Latin. The Arabs occupied Egypt in 642 AD, beginning the Arabo-Islamic period, which evolved into the Mamluk era (1250–1517 AD). The fastest philological change during that period was the move to suppress expression in the Coptic language following Egyptian revolts and uprisings between 724 and 832 AD, culminating in the Bashmurite Revolution (824–31) and the massacres of the Egyptians in the northern Delta by the colonial Arab Abbasid caliphate armies in 831–32 AD.[†] The Baghdad-based

---

[*]The Macedonian dynasty begins with the building Alexandria, 331–330 BC, but history books mark the start of their rule as 305 BC (the year Ptolemy I became king/pharaoh, because Alexander was the king until his death in 323 BC): the start of the larger Egypto-Ptolemaic kingdom with Alexandria as its capital. The official religion was Greco-Egyptian syncretism established by Alexander, but there was also the common Egyptian polytheism (based on Isis rituals), as well as Judaism and worship of Greek deities and others throughout the kingdom.

[†]Bashmur was a region of marshland with sandbanks and a dense cover of reeds. In Egypt, nowhere else was more propitious for armed rebellion against Arab occupation, which started in 712 AD, reaching a peak in 749 and lasted until 767. It subsided

CHAPTER 12 Invasions and New Expressions

Caliph Al-Ma'moun (786–833 AD) banned Egyptians from speaking their own demotic Coptic language. Families reported to be speaking it at home had their houses destroyed.[1]

The other wave of repression behind the mass conversion to Islam in tenth and eleventh centuries, was an aggressive collection of *gizyah**, a poll tax on non-Muslims, with more Arabic finding its way into the new converts' demotic Coptic language. The Ottomans, who invaded and annexed Egypt in 1517 AD, kept the *gizyah* practice, appropriated the Egyptian economy's central activities and moved skilled workers to Constantinople, causing economic and social decline back home.

Not only did the Napoleonic expedition (1798–1801) end this licensed fiscal raid, it also introduced a large body of French vernacular into the Egyptian language. The French campaign was the most enlightened military-backed intervention in Egypt since Alexander's conquest. Napoleon planted the seeds of modernity in the country, bringing with him the French ideals of *liberté, égalité, fraternité*. He also rolled back the oppressive dominance of Islamic jurists and the backwardness associated with the Ottoman Caliphate's tendency to treat non-Muslims in the conquered lands as second-class citizens. The *corps d'intellectuels*, which grew out of this historic clash of civilisations, associated French phrases and ideas with the dawn of modernity and emancipation from the Islamic caliphate's restrictions on freedom of thought and speech.

In turn, Egypt's nineteenth-century *corps d'intellectuels* passed this collective subconscious on to the succeeding generations, as Muhammad Ali sent the brightest of Egypt's students to be educated at the Sorbonne in Paris within 20 years of Napoleon's departure. Government bursaries for Egyptian students in French universities, became known as *be'tha*, became a tradition for generations – both *be'tha* and French learned men remaining behind after Bonaparte's departure, founding modern Egyptian education and culture. Later in the nineteenth century, *be'tha* graduates were sent to Italy for art, music, opera and architecture – and much later to Britain and America for engineering and science. Napoleon's short-lived regional project had a broader long-lasting Enlightenment effect. It consequentially paved the way for 160 years of European-based Egyptian modernity under the rule of another outsider, the Macedonian-born Muhammad Ali, and his dynasty (1805-1953), with an effect comparable only with that of the first Macedonian, Alexander, 2,130 years earlier.

---

rather than being totally suppressed, and again flared up in 831–832 and was brutally put down by three Arab armies.
* *Jiyzah* in Arabic.

Alexandria Adieu

Egypt's Arab invaders didn't conquer a demographic vacuum. They didn't establish a new nation-state – as was the case with the New World's colonisation, with French or Spanish becoming the new states' languages. Instead, the Arabs invaded a sophisticated nation-state of an ancient civilisation, more advanced than that of its subjugator. The existing native Egyptian language, both written and spoken, had been in use for millennia, documenting and administering a complex, centralised bureaucracy running organised systems of taxation, education and trade as well as an army.

Between 300 BC and 400 AD, the ancient hieroglyphics were still in use and began to be absorbed into the local demotic and mixed with Greek when Alexandria became the world capital of thought, sciences, philosophy and progress until the fifth century AD. The three languages were engraved on the Rosetta Stone, carved around 196 BC. Perhaps the demotic text on the Rosetta Stone illustrates Egyptian rejection of the invader's dominance, a mass defence mechanism that lasted for centuries. Demotic began to evolve in its written form alongside the elite's hieroglyphics during the Twenty-Fifth Dynasty (744-656 BC),* probably because the Nubian rulers appropriated the hieroglyphic language as they told their story in stone for centuries. Demotic Egyptian developed into middle (Ptolemaic) demotic (400–30 BC) and late Roman Demotic (30 BC).

Languages do not suddenly die; demotic Egyptian didn't disappear with the seventh-century Arab occupation. General Amr Ibn-al-As (573–663) led a few thousand Arab warriors, most of whom were illiterate. They were joined on the way by many mercenaries – including Roman deserters, Assyrians and Persians – who spoke other tongues. The idea that Ibn-al-As's warriors could have imposed their language on a civilisation like Egypt's is a fantasy. In contrast, the French expedition of 1798 had a lasting effect that even 70 years of British controlling presence in Egypt couldn't wash out. Today, the French school of journalism is dominant in Egypt, while clothes, cuisine and most home items are also known by their French or Franco-Demotic names.

The Bibliotheca Alexandrina (founded in 300 BC with translations of hundreds of books from hieroglyphics) became a hub of scholarly studies as the most advanced university globally for 700 years, the birthplace of the body of knowledge and thought from which seeds of the Renaissance grew some 1,000 years later.[2]

---

*There are several dates for this: some begin with the Kushite invasion of 744 BC by Piye, but other Egyptologists mark the start with his successor, Shebitku, who ruled 714–705 BC and was destabilised in 656 BC with the Assyrian invasion and the establishment of the 'puppet' Twenty-sixth Dynasty, starting with Psamtik I's unification of Egypt.

CHAPTER 12   Invasions and New Expressions

Scholars, philosophers, theologians and mathematicians spoke, held conversations, read and wrote in many languages in order to translate this world knowledge into Greek. Books were brought from other shores when Alexandria's population was around 330,000 during Cleopatra's reign (51–30 BC). There was a sizeable population of international commercial traders who spoke various tongues, with their ethnic vocabularies becoming absorbed into Alexandria's demotic-speak in addition to these translations.

Cleopatra (69–30 BC) was popular with Alexandrians not just by virtue of her extravagant festivals and self-indulgent parties. She mastered the Egyptian people's Ptolemaic demotic and the Kemet hieroglyphics, and spoke Greek and Latin. She could communicate effectively in Persian and Assyrian,[3] and most probably also Hebrew since she corresponded with, and visited, King Herod of Jerusalem when she leased part of Judaea to him.[4] At the time, there was a vibrant, established Jewish community in Alexandria dating back to 300 BC. By the end of the last queen's reign, Alexandria's Jews occupied two of the five quarters of Alexandria. This led to Hebrew words seeping into the City's demotic, similar to the way in which Sephardic Jews introduced many ladino expressions 1,800 years later – especially when haggling in Alexandria's markets.

CHAPTER 13
Alexander: the Democratisation of Knowledge

Of the figures who invaded Egypt, only two were outward-looking; they aimed to project Alexandria – and with her, the rest of Egypt – into the outside world, thus introducing additional foreign languages into the Egyptian patois. They were both Macedonians, 2,100 years apart: Alexander and his Ptolemaic dynasty, and Muhammad Ali and his dynasty.

The Ptolemies established an independent Egyptian state as a leading power in the ancient world and, for decades, its wealthiest. Muhammad Ali's dynasty found its *lapis philosophorum* in Alexander's spirit left in the great city's saffron soil; they evoked the spirit to resurrect Alexandria in the nineteenth century.

Great cities like Alexandria typically have a distinct body of architecture, a work ethic and a market with its trading ethos and customs, forming the citizens' identity and the place's character; history adds to these citizens' interactions, forging a city's soul. Alexandria was unique: her position as the Hellenic world capital of knowledge made her the only city that has experienced this identity of character, soul and also a mind twice in its history.

Alexandria was conceived in a dream, a revelation given by the gods to Alexander. She was built and designed from scratch to hold the philosophised knowledge and mind of the universe when ancient Egypt's achievements met Greek philosophy. Alexander's godly dream wasn't just a smart theo-political plan but a philosophically driven divine mission.

Alexander was more than a great military strategist; he was also a politician with the stuff of philosophers engraved on his mind by his tutor. He was most likely influenced by the ideas and politics of

CHAPTER 13 Alexander: the Democratisation of Knowledge

Pericles of Athens (495–429 BC). Alexander's spiritual encounter with the geography and history of the place resulted in the dream-vision that grew out of a subconscious mind refined by the great philosophy that was the foundation of the modern Western open mind. It was a philosophy whose reincarnation, 2,000 years later, heralded Egypt's Age of Enlightenment. Alexander was tutored by Aristotle (384–322 BC), who in turn was taught by Plato (428/427–348/347 BC), and Plato by Socrates (470–399 BC). Those philosophers were celebrities in Greece as they debated with their opponents in marketplaces. With this philosophy-based democratisation of knowledge, Alexander set out to conquer most of the then civilised world, armed with education and philosophy before horsemen and spears. In the lands he ruled, Alexander was keen on establishing binary cultures in which Greek philosophy and thinking married with the local, indigenous ethos and wisdom.

The Egypt of the fourth century BC was inward-looking, shut off, strictly centralised and hierarchal – her priceless treasures of learning in medicine, architecture, astronomy and mathematics controlled by the elite priests in her temples. The population remained ignorant of those treasures; only their manual labour and skills were needed for building monuments, farming and combat in the army. Controlled by religion and their obsession with the afterlife, the Egyptian masses had no concept of democracy, open debate or public philosophy. Their conscious and collective minds were confined in a triangular structure of power with the god-king on top resting on the other two sides: religion, with its priestly class; and the army. Alexander's concept of binary culture democratised knowledge, making wisdom, philosophy and science accessible to the people of Alexandria – which became the seat of world learning and the cultural, political, spiritual and commercial capital of Egypt.

Until the fourth century AD, books were gathered from every corner of the known, civilised world – not just Greece, Rome, and Egypt. Ptolemy I began sending for books to be brought to Alexandria from as far afield as India, Armenia, Persia, Babylon, Georgia and Judaea. Ships docking in Alexandria had their books temporarily confiscated in order to be copied for the Bibliotheca before the original was returned to the vessel with a handsome reward; the practice went on for centuries.[1] The tradition was set by Alexander: with every conquest of an eastern kingdom, he strove to collect rare books and send them back to Aristotle.[2]

Alexander's mysterious trip in 332 BC to Siwa Oasis, 600 kilometres southwest of Alexandria, was political, philosophical and spiritual: he regarded the Egyptian gods as far more illustrious ancestors than those of Macedonia. He was taken by the high priest into the Holy of Holies, the inner sanctum of the temple, to consult the oldest oracle in the world – that of the Egyptian god Amun, as described by Arrian of Nicomedia in his *Anabasis*. Nobody really knew the exact details of the priest or the oracle's information.[3] Alexander emerged believing that he was the son not of Philip of Macedon but of Amun, who had impregnated his mother by supernatural powers. He even saw in a dream that his father, Amun, commanded him to build the great city of Alexandria and instructed him to push further eastward with his conquests.

A divine power was needed to confirm Alexander's status as an Egyptian king conceived by the god Amun for the Egyptians to accept him. But he might have genuinely believed that Amun was his father. Alexander and the Ptolemies joined Amun with the king of their gods to make Zeus-Amun, establishing Alexandria's modern (Hellenic) religion. His last wish was to be buried in Siwa to be near his father Amun, not with his worldly ancestors in the Greek town of Aigai.[4] Alexander's godly status was cemented by a myth stating that six days after his death there were no signs of decay on his body in Babylon despite the extreme heat, as reported by the first-century historian Quintus Curtius Rufus, who chronicled developments when the Egyptians came to visit and examine the body.[5]

The Egyptians believed Alexander to be their king, a son of their god Amun; thus, he should be buried as one. Aiming to secure the Egyptians' loyalty and legitimise his rule, Ptolemy I plotted and manoeuvred to have the sarcophagus with Alexander's body brought to Alexandria on a golden carriage within two years of his death. And finding Alexander's tomb in the city became the dream and quest of many archaeologists, scholars, Alexandrinologists and Alexander-obsessed Alexandrians over the years.

Muhammad Ali: Alexandria Resurrected

Like Ptolemy-Soter and Cleopatra, the Macedonian-born Muhammad Ali was outward-looking with a global (commercial) mindset. His international policies and strategies were inseparable from his internal plans to build a modern independent state. Like Cleopatra, Muhammad Ali had broader regional ambitions after re-establishing the modern nation-state with the rebirth of Alexandria, which became his de facto capital from 1820, given her commercial and political importance as a seat for the world powers' consuls. This kick-started process in commercial success, economic growth and greater independence from Egypt – which was, in turn, becoming more independent from the Porte in Constantinople.

CHAPTER 13   Alexander: the Democratisation of Knowledge

With these changes, migrants from Europe, Armenia, Circassia, Central Asia and from other Ottoman provinces flocked to the city. They came with refined culture and taste, and injected yet more linguistic diversity into the predominantly Turco-Franco demotic lexicon of nineteenth-century Alexandria. Even before the French landing in 1798, this Mediterranean *lingua franca*[6] formed the larger part of the polyglossia forming Alexandriaspeak. Under Muhammad Ali, the city revived her ancient status in trade, wealth and cultural: a linguistic 'contact zone'[7] of races and tongues. His first *be'tha* spiritual guide, Sheikh Rifa'ah el-Tahtawi (1801–1873), passing through Alexandria for the first time to sail to France in 1826, found it hard to understand Alexandrians. '[M]ost of the city's common dwellers speak bits of Italian or something similar',[8] noted the Azhar graduate, who later learned French and translated several works.

Hellenic Alexandria, where Greek philosophy had been the foundation of the ancient world's highest seat of learning – namely, the Biblioteca Alexandrina – was cynical towards theological teaching. The Church, despite its power, failed to impede the progress of thought, philosophy and science. And if Hellenic Alexandria had a problem with the Church, her trouble with Islam was more significant in the twentieth century. Al-Azhar's traditional scholars usually don't accept critical thinking or questioning the nature of the universe when philosophical thought contradicts their scriptures (as shown by court cases they initiated against Muslim philosophers in Egypt);[9] the inevitable clash was only delayed by pragmatic accommodation,[10] and was due to European Alexandria's wealth and trade subsidising the existence of the weaker oriental parts of Internal Egypt. Unlike its strong influence there, Islam's lexical and social impact on nineteenth- and twentieth-century European Alexandria was minimal.

Post-Great War growth and industrialisation attracted mass migration from the Egyptian countryside, and with it Islamic words began to seep into Alexandriaspeak – especially its overuse of Islamic adjectives and Allah references in spoken form. But French remained the language of commerce, finance and local politics, which it had been since 1868. Alexandria's multiple-language newspapers (French, Greek, Italian, Turkish, Armenian, Spanish and Arabic) often used multilingual journalists cross-working on different publications, contributing new, peculiarly Alexandrian, expressions to the city's patois.

Alexandria was overlooked by the Arabs, who preferred Inner Egypt and thought that the city was bad-spirited. Meanwhile, the Mamluks and Ottomans neglected basic maintenance operations such as dredging the various branches of the Nile regularly, as carried out by the ancient Egyptians and Ptolemies. As a result, this major trade route

Alexandria Adieu

from Egypt to the sea silted up. Alexandria, the Hellenic world's mind, was reduced by the end of eighteenth century to a population of 5,000 – who spoke the latest version of demotic. Only with the construction of the Mahmoudiyah Canal and the port under Muhammad Ali and Ibrahim Pasha did the modern city – with the spirit of Hellenistic Alexandria – rise like a phoenix, with French the official language of register and trade.

Hundreds of thousands of migrants from many lands brought phrases and expressions into the demotic Alexandrian that was used when I last lived there. The city's inhabitants mostly recognised one identity – Alexandrian – as expressed by Cavafy, celebrating the numerous languages spoken in Hellenic Alexandria in the first century AD in his 1907 poem *Alexandrian Kings*:

The Alexandrians were gathered
to see Cleopatra's children,
Caesarion, and his little brothers,
Alexander and Ptolemy, whom for the first
time they lead out to the Gymnasium,
there to proclaim kings,
in front of the grand assembly of the soldiers.[11]

Cavafy, accused of turning Alexandria into a mythical land, succeeded in linking this outpost of European civilisation and culture to the city's glorious Hellenistic past. Cavafy, who wrote poetry in Greek, was born in Alexandria in 1863 to a Greco-British father and moved with his family to Liverpool following his father's death. Due to the economic depression in Britain, they returned to Alexandria. He called Alexandria ('the City of exiles and immigrants') home; to her bosom, the poet was 'Returning from Greece', as he titled his 1914 poem, with many key words of owning and belonging. He writes of 'our own countries', from which Alexandrians' ancestors and parents migrated:

At least we're sailing our seas,
the waters of our own countries - Cyprus, Syria, Egypt -
waters we know and love.
Why so silent? Ask your heart:
didn't you too feel happier
the further we got from Greece?

Cavafy is here on the return voyage with a key word, 'return'; you only 'return' to your 'home', a place whose people were a mosaic of cosmopolitanism given the mixed blood in their veins, which Cavafy calls 'our':

We simply can't be ashamed
of the Syrian and Egyptian blood in our veins;
we should really honour it, delight in it.

CHAPTER 13 Alexander: the Democratisation of Knowledge

Cavafy, proud of Alexandria's mixed genetic culture in her neo-Hellenistic epoch, reminds us of what it was like during the Ptolemaic era. The Greeks reached Hellenic greatness not by remaining in Greece but by presiding over a cosmopolitan Alexandria – Cavafy's real home, and the right home for the pinnacle of their achievement in building a neo-Alexandria, as expressed in *Alexandrian Kings*' third stanza:

...*the Alexandrian Gymnasium was*
a triumphant achievement of art,
the opulence of the courtiers was extraordinary,
Caesarion was full of grace and beauty
(son of Cleopatra, blood of the Lagidae;

Again, Cavafy emphasises who his fellow Alexandrians really were and the languages they spoke when they

...*rushed to the ceremony,*
and got enthusiastic, and cheered: in Greek, and Egyptian,
and some in Hebrew.

PART III
SIDI-BISHR

CHAPTER 14
The 'Devil's Hole'

Sidi-Bishr *plages* and the activities associated with them were inseparable from my Alexandria and her identity. Alexandria was a daughter of the Mediterranean, and we Alexandrians always identified with the sea – as did our life in Sidi-Bishr.

The suburb was named after the thirteenth-century Sufi saint Bishr el-Gowhari, who came from Andalusia to join a mystic Sufi school growing in North Africa and was buried on the sandy hill with a mosque erected around his shrine in the nineteenth century. After the expansion of the Ramleh tram network in the 1860s, people started making a day trip to the *plages*. With the tramline's electrification in 1902, Sidi-Bishr *Plage* became so popular that it began extending eastwards to include more coves along the coastline.

Until the late 1970s, the Sidi-Bishr quarter would only come alive during the summer months – a legacy of the state's traditional government moving to Alexandria, the summer capital.

Arrêt Sidi-Bishr, the farthest east on the Ramleh tram, was, as urban characteristics went, different from the Classical European architecture of older central Alexandria. It was a modern quarter, neither included in the original plans of Dinocrates nor considered by nineteenth-century Italian architects when they busied themselves building modern Alexandria 12 kilometres to the west.

The district's streets were mainly known by numbers and many were still unpaved sand, while some were covered with crushed chalkstone rather than being totally paved and asphalted. My grandfather built Villa Alexandrine before the War and, although it was among the earliest on Rue Dix-Neuf, it had access to a paved, clean, smooth-asphalted surface. Rue Dix Neuf (Nineteen) had been laid out around

CHAPTER 14   The 'Devil's Hole'

the turn of the twentieth century, after a few villas had begun to emerge over the sand dunes and rocks. The northern section of the hilly street was the most elevated in Sidi-Bishr with a breathtaking view of the sea, where the ever-changing colour of the sky – from blue to green to grey to orange – bowed to kiss the waves miles beyond l'île Sidi-bishr, a deserted rock-islet about three kilometres off the coast. As my little child feet tapped the slopes leading from the highest point down to the *plage*, I used to look, beyond the immeasurable distance, at the white-lined waves of *le mer méditéranéen* toying with Lilliputian fishermen's boats. I tried to count them, or guess what they caught, and gazed beyond the horizon to Europa. Was her world an extension of ours, or the other way around?

Avrupa, or *Evrópi* for the most numerous ethnic group of Alexandrians, Europa – as others called Europe – was, so the myth goes, the ancestral human mother of Alexandria from a union with Zeus: the island beyond the Sea of Darkness commanded by Proteus, the sea's prophetic old man doing the work of Poseidon, god of all waters. Proteus, who dwelled in the island of Pharos, near the mouth of the Nile, was the figure that Greek myths called Alexandria. The connection with *l'ancienne Méditerranée* and her coming into being was symbolised by *Europa and the Bull*, a modern statue created by French-trained sculptor Fathy Mahmoud (1918–1982). A white sculpture with the beautiful, naked, pale Evrópi carried by Zeus, who shapeshifted into a bull and swam with her to Crete. On the island, he revealed himself as god of gods in order to ravish this human beauty, the daughter of the king of Tyre, and left her on Crete to give birth to Minos and his, later exiled, brothers. Evrópi herself settled on the land mass, giving it her name; she later came to Alexandria, with the Macedonians, Greeks and Romans whose descendants built the modern royal city. Unlike his blackness in the myth, the Bull, Zeus, was, in Mahmoud's sculpture, white like Europe. And behind the Bull and the Maid of the Mediterranean, Mahmoud added brilliant high, white sails. They symbolised both the voyage from Tyre to Crete to Europe to Alexandria and the light of Alexandria that rolled back the sea's darkness and illuminated the Hellenic world with knowledge and progress.

This landmark sculpture, also known as *The Maid of the Mediterranean*, was erected near Cape Silsilah at the far end of the Eastern Harbour where the Ptolemies had built their palaces. The sculpture was vandalised by Muslim Brotherhood extremists during their 2012–13 rule, which ended with a mass uprising culminating in their overthrow by the army. Ironically, the unenlightened Islamists understood the significance of the Europa and the Bull sculpture far better than did most Alexandrians who drove by the figure daily.

Alexandria Adieu

The former were trained to destroy whatever threatened their world of ignorance; the latter had had their collective memory erased by the education system of Nasser and his successors.

As a source of light and life, the sea has always been where Alexandria belonged, and where Alexandrians baptised themselves and washed away their troubles. Nothing of today's ugliness was there to block our sea view from the sand rock at the north end of Rue Nineteen. The short distance to the *plage* was dotted with a few chalets that only came alive in the summer season and were occasionally used in the empty Sidi-Bishr winter nights for hedonistic sex parties or stag nights where 'everything went'. The view as you entered the *plage* was a live tableau of Alexandria: frothy, silver waves flirting with the pedicured toes and waxed, sun-tanned legs of happy, playful mademoiselles, the volume of whose shrieks and giggles automatically adjusted to the distance at which some young men flocked. The chaps engaged in racketball contests and some lined up paddle-pads ready for a race – both groups performing the instinctive, centuries-old game of attracting the other sex's attention.

The daily summer activities and warm, sunny days revolved around the beach. The *plages* of Sidi-Bishr comprised a whole cosmos of culture, leisure, love, games, sports and fun where you heard a mix of accents in one Alexandrian sentence, chewing four or five languages into one. Nobody would bat an eyelid at the familiar sight of women sunbathing or swimming in different types, colours and shapes of *maillots*, one-pieces or bikinis (in reality, two-pieces and nothing like the Brazilian version).

Young ladies and chaps strolled along the pier, licking their gelato or drinking their pop from long straws, wearing summer hats, sunglasses and fashionable *maillots*. One jetty was by Casino Miami and a longer one was at 'Sidi-Bishr Number One'; this free-entry *plage*, curving over a kilometre, had a 50-meter-long pier lifted on pillars with a casino and bar serving food, wine, beer and spirits. Many of these casinos hosted performances with singers and *balady* dancers. Entertainers from Spain, Mexico, Italy, India and Africa also presented their dances in colourful costumes. 'Sidi-Bishr Number Two' *plage* curved for a kilometre from the edge of the casino to a rock where the Royal Automobile Club of Egypt stood. 'Royal' was dropped after the officers declared a republic in 1953.

The *plages* were given numbers but geographical or other characteristics also fed into popular names, different from the official numbering. Number One was free-entry, but the metropolis municipality charged a tax of 1 (then 2) *piastres* for the beach umbrellas. *Plages* Two, Three and Sarraiyah levied entry fees during the summer months. Locals

CHAPTER 14   The 'Devil's Hole'

argued and seldom paid, knowing that it was a policy to raise revenue from holidaymakers. Sidi-Bishr Number Three comprised a trio of beaches as it included *Plages* Miami and Beir Masoud, also known as the 'Devil's Hole'. The latter had the tiniest stretch of sand; most of its area consisted of rocks with a cliff-edge drop into the sea. With no sandy space for noisy ball games, Beir Masoud was favoured by those seeking a little peace – like sunbathers, chess enthusiasts and readers.

Relating its name to the devil perhaps had to do with the sudden change in the sea's mood – caused, according to folkloric belief, by the dead's spirits when disturbed. The 'devil's hole' itself was discovered in 2000 to be a man-made ventilation shaft of a large hypogeum tomb in a submerged ancient necropolis.[1] The sea swells and waves high slamming the rocky cliff generate a fountain of water, exploding out of the hole high up in the air and often jumping over beach *cabanas*, splashing the corniche road and passing automobiles. The phenomenon repeatedly catches unexpected non-Alexandrians off guard, ruining beautiful hairstyles, hats, dresses and summer suits.

But the Arabic-Egyptian name, Masoud, denotes the lucky man's well. One of several folk stories indicates that it was named after Masoud Effendi, a *belediye* surveyor mapping the beaches, who set up his work tent by the hole – although there is no record of an official by that name. The cavity was linked by an underwater tunnel to a smaller well 20 or so metres to the northwest, then extending another 20 metres into the sea to an underwater opening that was visible at low tide from the edge of the bay's end. Boys would hold their breath, dive into the cave and then come up again for air in the middle cavity under the rock before diving back into the Devil's Hole to collect silver coins. The money had been tossed into the well by out-of-town couples whispering secret wishes with their romantic offerings; a rare, sudden wave splashing in response was a good omen, so the folklore went. This is a more plausible explanation behind the name Masoud: the lucky boys would find the silver *nos-francs*, either the hexagonal ones bearing the profile of King Fuad I or the rounded shillings (5 *piastres*) with his or, better still, Sultan Hessein's profile.*

The well was also a location for a teenager still shuttling between childhood mischief and adolescent sexual desires in the maze of tunnels under the rock. The ancient tunnels were thought to be man-dug for quarrying, since the necropolis area was used for cutting stones in ancient times.

---

* For details on Egyptian currency and coins, see: Azab, Khalid, Dr, *Memory and Future of History: The Secret of Egyptian Currency in Two Centuries*, *Awraq* Egypt-History III series, Bibliotheca Alexandrina Publications, Alexandria, 2015, pp. 51–7.

CHAPTER 15
Plages and Policemen

Beach umbrellas, deck chairs, rackets and tennis balls, badminton, shuttlecocks and spike-swingball made up Sidi-Bishr's *plage* scene. Besides playing ball, we surfed on flat-bottomed canoe like a paddleboard*, hired from *A'am* Khamis al-Ghattas (the *belediye* beach-guard). Each board was over 2 metres long, 60 centimetres wide and 25 centimetres deep, made from hardwood frames and covered in 10-millimetre marine plywood. *A'am* Khamis charged *nos-a-franc* (2 *piastres*) an hour, rising to 4 *piastres* for *masarwah*, but we only paid 1 *piastre* for an hour or a shilling for a whole day.

We invented 'surf-polo', with each team of three hitting a beach ball with the paddle while using the floating, red metal buoys as lines to score. the beach-guard was not too keen on the game because it meant taking half of his fleet on a reduced hire fee – so he would whistle, saying it was too dangerous for swimmers and threatening to complain to *Tante* Ralia. We reached a deal with his son, Fawzi, that our *chellah* never hired the full six boards but only three for our team for the 90-minute duration of the match for a full *priza* (10 *piastres*), while the opposition would be *masarwah* paying him what he could get away with. It took us two summers to discover that the rascal charged the *masarwah* between *rub'h*- and *nos-guinea* (25–50 *piastres*) for each board depending on the visitors' haggling skills and how much refreshments they bought from him – and he pocketed his cut before handing the money to his father.

A'am Khamis used to perch on his watchtower, barefoot in a roll-neck navy-blue long-sleeved top and khaki shorts exposing his

---

* Called Periswar, but nobody knew why

CHAPTER 15   Plages and Policemen

thin, sun-blackened, veined, bowed legs while sporting a white cotton *casquette*. He was equipped with a pair of Great War binoculars and an Edwardian Metropolitan Police-standard whistle around his neck. (This model was also issued to Alexandria's policemen, who, until 1947, served alongside British police officers and had a British chief inspector.) Khamis blew his whistle when the *drapeau rouge* was raised, indicating that the current was too dangerous for swimming beyond the buoys. There were other irritating hazards when the red flag was flying. Gooey tar, washed by the waves, stuck to our feet. It was a recurrent, hard-to-avoid nightmare as mothers never let their teenagers past the doorstep until the tar was removed using unpleasant substances. Bellitta used to leave jars and tins containing repulsive liquids by the kitchen door to dissolve the tar: cigarette-lighter fuel, nail-varnish remover, paraffin oil and white spirit. We would soak old rags in one or more containers and rub the tar off our feet, then hose our feet after frothing them with *savon debbah* block, a dull-looking brown-greenish cube of soap press-marked with an image of a dancing *debbah* (bear) used for washing floor tiles and patio stones.

Khamis would also blow his whistle warning boys diving dangerously from the top of the *zouhlia'ah*, the recreation slide that stood about 15 metres into the water, or to warn those using it who looked to be over 18. On rare occasions, he had to tell off young men annoying mademoiselles – but these were usually *masarwah*. Sadly, by the year 2000, none of those beautiful, once well-maintained recreation structures built in the 1920s and 1930s remained – only rusty iron poles left to injure swimmers since nobody bothered removing them.

Unruly young men undeterred by Khamis's whistle were dealt with by Police Sergeant Hareedy. Like most officials and *belediye* employees, Hareedy sported a King Fuad-style moustache. He would use his own British-constable-style whistle to alert his squad patrolling the beach, stretching between Beir Masoud and Mandra, to come to his immediate assistance if the mischievous young men did not follow his instructions.

We knew all the policemen by name, calling each of them Shawish (sergeant) regardless of rank except their boss – *the* real sergeant – whom we addressed as *A'am al-Shawish* Hareedy. The constables also knew us, and were somewhat relaxed about rules. They only became strict when danger was in sight, or if some idiot was playing with a wooden racket ball too close to children. We rarely got into trouble with *Shawish* Hareedy, but when we did our guardians (most of the time *Tante* Ralia, or occasionally my grandfather) were called. They would join the policeman in telling us off and imposing a type of punishment appropriate to the transgression in front of the police. Punishment varied from grounding to a deduction from pocket money, which we were given every evening as a means of parental behaviour control. In extreme cases, we had our *accessoire-el-plage* confiscated. This would include our rackets, balls, kites, snorkelling and diving kits. That said, our misdemeanours were light and innocent compared with what today's children and teenagers get up to. The parents never doubted the intentions or the word of the beach watch guard; the police; or, on rare occasions, the *sawahel* (coastguard). The last-named were a separate branch of the armed forces working in liaison with *belediye*, patrolling on foot with Lee–Enfield 303 rifles and bayonets. The force patrolled along the corniche and beach between sunset and 07:00, guarding against smuggling and reporting from telephone boxes reserved for their use only.

The confiscation of our diving kits, which lasted a full week, only happened once – and it was the most severe trouble we ever encountered with the authorities. We had gathered our usual harvest of *ritsa* by diving behind Miami Island's rocks with reed-braided soft baskets floated on makeshift airbags that we towed to the beach. There was a ban on diving for shellfish of any type – a rare measure, usually to do with accidents caused by injuries from rocks, drowning by diving or health issues. I think it was the last-named on this occasion because, later in the 1950s, more *masarwah* (and many *fellaheen*) came in and the Municipality Health Administration registered a rise in dysentery and other gastric infections caused by shellfish.

My father, whose advice I still follow, never consumed shellfish in months without an 'r' in their name (May to August). But like any Alexandrian, he made an exception when it came to freshly harvested *ritsa* picked from one of two places: a rocky islet opposite Saraya and *Plage* Sidi-Bishr Number One or the northern, open seaside of *Île de Miami*, about 600 metres off *Plage* Miami. This beach also served the bay as a natural wave barrier, extending longer than a football field with a width of 30 metres. To the west was an archipelago of small rocks – all of which could be seen at low tide – forming a western geological barrier to that natural mini-harbour, turning it into a makeshift marina over the years and providing extra income for *A'am* Khamis and his sons. Here, we would dive to a depth of three to six metres for sea urchins, where strong currents washed the water.

There was a natural lake – a mini lagoon in the centre of the rocky island. The water was always fresh but calm, and gentle waves moved on its surface while the sea was frothing its angry waves over the rocks. The water had a beautiful turquoise-blue colour with a golden rim that turned bright orange at sunset; it never got stagnant or smelly, and had fish. A Greek underwater archaeological team discovered, around 2005,

CHAPTER 15   Plages and Policemen

that the lake was on top of a deeply carved fish tank and extension of the Beir Masoud necropolis. The lake had magical powers, so Alexandrian folklore went, and Cleopatra bathed there regularly – especially on the days she set off to meet Mark Antony. According to the popular myth, the water's magic peaked in the full moon when the sea was calm.

As late as 1968 (I was in Alexandria frequently when I covered the region following the Six-Day War), some women were after that mystic power. They went some time between midnight and dawn after a full moon – and, particularly, a blue moon when the sea was as obedient as it was to their greatest grandmother, Cleopatra – to swim naked in order to ensure conception and increase their libido. One girl, eager to reclaim her boyfriend from a rival's bosom, nearly got into serious trouble by swimming there alone at midnight. Her family had to pay a handsome bribe to the *sawahel* patrol to convince them she was not a smuggling gangster but merely a foolish young lady. My last visit there in 1968 came as a shock – with picnic leftovers and signs of people relieving themselves in the mysterious caves and wells, one of which would have been where Cleopatra's maids helped her dry and change.

Our sea-urchin incident occurred with a new policeman who did not know us insisting on confiscating our sea harvest. *Tante* Ralia was so angry that she emptied our baskets into the sand and started crushing the sea urchins under her shoe. The policeman wanted to charge her with littering the beach. It took the intervention of his boss, *A'am el-Shawish* Hareedy, to let her with a verbal caution and an apology. We were made to scoop up the urchins, earning a few spikes and pricks to our fingers, to the amusement of the laughing policeman. We also had our diving equipment confiscated for a whole week in the last of the warm summer days – and lost some pocket money, but the grounding was cut short as the mothers did not want teenagers around the house. I personally did not mind because I had a list of books to read. Besides, I continued to sneak out from the back garden into the arms of my older lover, the Cairo University student next door, thanks to the intervention of an overzealous policeman. She returned in holidays and weekends to her grandfather's home; he was her only family following her parents' death when she was a child.

Despite widespread corruption in their ranks, the police performed their duties with admirable common sense. Alexandria police were better than any other force in Egypt, given their experience of dealing with a European city. They were in service of the people as opposed to the current force, which became a political tool after the officers took over. Even the most bent official in those days would not tolerate a public hazard or undermine safety. Several policemen, especially younger ones from an urban background who had some education and

143

a strong sense of responsibility, were often strict – like the one who stood guard until we cleared up *Tante* Ralia's mess.

There was a well-known story of a policeman on the beat who stopped the Austin Hillman driven by Lieutenant-Colonel Gamal Abdel Nasser at 21:00, 22 July 1952 on Rue Qasr-El-Nile in Cairo on his way to meet his fellow conspirators to execute their General Naguib-led coup. The offside brake light of the colonel's automobile was not working. In a scene that would never be repeated after the military takeover, a lieutenant-colonel in his full military outfit pleaded with a policeman down-rank by eight times to let him off. Finally, the young idealistic policeman let the army officer drive on after the future president lied, saying that he was in a hurry to take his sick wife to the doctor. Nasser had to leave his driving licence to be collected from Qasr el-Nile police station with proof of having fixed the faulty light within 48 hours. Whenever the Egyptian and Arab media use this story, it never occurs to journalists or presenters to point out the police discipline and zeal in imposing law and traffic regulations that existed before the army's takeover. Instead, they often frame it in terms of a meddling little policeman who could have changed the course of history.

When I included the incident in a column commissioned by a London-based Arabic daily in 2019, an Egyptian sub cut out the phrase 'an army colonel was pleading with a policeman'; the sub editor was following the publishers' instruction to keep the image of the military regime in Egypt sacred and untouchable. By the time Nasser died in 1970, a teenager driving dangerously along the Alexandria corniche could throw the name of his father, an army colonel, at the cowed policeman to let him go. Taxi and lorry drivers would have to cough up a few pounds from their meagre earnings for the same favour, and a policeman would be lucky if his punishment for daring to stop a speeding army officer stopped at an insulting *affa* (slap on the back of the neck) or a demeaning *shalloot* (a kick up the backside).

Nonetheless, in addition to the odd bribe when stopped by traffic police for jumping red lights, there was also laxity in dealing with black-marketeers, petty theft, local drug dealing or pickpocketing, with a wink and a nod from the police. A family guest was pickpocketed on his way to visit us; my father telephoned his *mamour* (chief of the district police force) friend to report it. The wallet was recovered the same evening. The *mukhber* who delivered the wallet (and was given a good dinner in our kitchen) said he made the head of pickpockets' gang on the tramway an offer he couldn't refuse. When the grateful guest got his wallet back, everything was there, including the exact sum of money, except that the notes were different from the original ones. Not all stories involving the police were positive or amusing, however.

CHAPTER 15   Plages and Policemen

I once witnessed two well-built *mukhbers* beating up a man in his twenties. He didn't protect his face from the heavy blows but held his pockets with both hands. My uncle explained: the man was scared they would plant some drugs on him. After giving a false name, my uncle called an ambulance from a public telephone at the post office, saying that a man had been left bleeding on the pavement. A few minutes later, the arrival of an ambulance from the charitable Italian clinic saved the bloke; the *mukhbers* pretended to be giving first aid after rescuing him from an imaginary gang, and he did not contradict their version. Police corruption grew several-fold during the Sadat regime (1970–1981); planted evidence was frequently used by Amn-el-Dawlah (the state-security investigations service) to frame activists – especially communists.

There were older villas, the two largest on Rue Nineteen, separated from ours by our two gardens. A few houses dotted the hill going north, but the largest on the street – Ghandour Pasha's, built in 1910 with an impressive dome and a tower – lay further south across Rue Cinquante surrounded by a sea of sand and dunes.

We hardly carried any luggage travelling between our different homes as each was fully furnished and equipped for our use. To reach our villa as a family, we often used the automobile or a cab from Moharrem-Bey since there was no direct transport. By tram, we got off at *Arrêt* Sidi-Bishr, with the Sarraiyah rock and its jungle of trees and vegetation on the north side to the left. On the right, the road led to Victoria; to the east were one- and two-storey villas with their back gardens hugging the tramline. From the tram stop, the choice was a good 30 minutes' walk along Rue Princesse Fawzia or to catch Bus Number 25, along the same road, or Bus Number 27 that linked the tram *arrêt* to Sidi-Bishr Railway Station, which was on the Abukeir line from the central rail station, Mehatet Masr. There was no sign of life for a mile between the station and the start of Rue Dix-Huit except for a few huts, chalets and the odd villa – only discernible by the steel tower of its windmill extracting underground water.

But from the El-Balad residence, there was the scenic route of *Autobus el-Bahr* (the corniche bus) running from the French Gardens along the corniche to Montazah, the palace built in 1892 by Ernesto Verrucci Bey(1874-1945) for Khedive Abbas Helmi II. It was not designed in the Italian style like other royal buildings but modelled on Austro-Hungarian designs. Helmi II spent many years in central European cities like Vienna, Marienbad and Budapest, where Alexandrian newspapers were sold daily all year round, and which were favoured by Alexandrians and wealthy Egyptians.

Alexandria Adieu

In the 1950s Rue Nineteen was so empty that even during the summer holidays children used it for *patinage* and ball games, pausing briefly for the odd passing automobile. In the winter – especially during the Suez War in 1956, when we stayed until after Easter 1957 as my mother didn't want to spend blacked-out nights in central Alexandria recalling her stepmother's death caused by an air raid during the War,[1] – no motor vehicles passed apart from the post office's and the rubbish truck.

Rue Nineteen was home to a mixture of old families who lived there permanently and visiting ones from central Alexandria, alongside some Caireans who had a second summer home, either on a long lease or owned; the latter were from old, known, respected, middle-class families. Only in the 1950s did some non-Alexandrians, of what my mother called the *nouveau riche*, started appearing on our road with their unfamiliar mores and queer habits.

Apart from a five-storey 1930s building on the corner of Place Sidi-Bishr, there was no building higher than three storeys in the 450-metre asphalted section of the kilometre-long Rue Nineteen.

Rue Nineteen was, like many typical Alexandrian streets, a bridge founded on and structured from geography; history; culture; love; and memories of life, sadness, hedonistic fun or adventures. It was a bridge between our childhood and the open, scary, alien, unknown world of adulthood growing in the four corners of the globe where Alexandrians were to be scattered following the post-Suez mass exodus.

At the northern end of the street was a barber's and a grocery; on the other side was a parade of shops – including the tyre-repair station where would buy a second-hand rubber inner tube for a *piastre* to use as a raft for our angling and diving gear when swimming to rocky islands. There was also a fancy-goods and odd-items shop that did best in the summer, selling fishing rods, snorkels, buckets and spades, sunglasses, parasols, tennis balls and other beach accessories. Here too was the post office, run by Hassan Effendi, who lived with his two daughters above it. It offered a part-time service in winter and opened five and a half days a week in the summer. To the south of the mosque square, ten steps led to an elevated terrace with a block of six flats owned by *Oncle* Wahbah, an estate agent who also ran Kazino-el-Samar. Although it was in full view of the mosque, the café served Birra Stella to punters who left God's work to his servants. The western side of Rue Nineteen had had more villas: a two-storey house and an older café owned by Ma'alem E'gilah, who owned the buildings and three shops. His brother, like him a migrant from Suhag in Upper Egypt, ran a *forno*. *Maman* and her school friend *Tante* Oni called him el-Shanab (*la Moustache*); he sported an impressive moustache, triple the size of Hercule Poirot's

CHAPTER 15   Plages and Policemen

whiskers, projecting – with the aid of heavy wax – a couple of inches from his face. He sold bread and baked the residents' dishes, mostly fish in large copper or tin trays. Many, like my mother, didn't like the smell of fish lingering in their homes.

We used to have fish delivered from Rue Zananiri market in Ibharimiyah, named after the Alexandrian George Zananiri Pasha (1863–1956). The pasha, who came from a Syrian Melachite family (the Byzantine Church) was the secretary-general of the Sanitary Maritime and Quarantine Department. Alexandrians checked the freshness of a fish by its bright-red gills. But fishmongers rubbed the gills with a piece of fresh animal's liver to keep it red; a good sniff for any traces of beef, pork or lamb was required. There was also the brightness of its wet eyes; the longer a fish has been out of the water, the dryer its eyes would get. Although all Sunday lunches, when guests came, were home-made, we had a baked fish feast on special Sunday occasions – like when *Tante* Ralia or Papa's best friend, *Oncle* Farid, and family came to dine. These usually comprised two large baking trays of sea bass and sea bream, about 25–30 centimetres long, laid regimentally on trays. One would be seasoned with lime and a spot of white wine, with the belly stuffed with salt, pepper, garlic and fresh parsley from the garden, and brushed with olive oil; strictly no onions. I inherited the onion intolerance from my mother; it caused us terrible stomach upsets. The other tray would have rings of onions and tomatoes, and slices of lime. Our kitchen oven didn't take the size of *la Moustache's* trays, which could feed a whole regiment.

There were no shops south of Monsieur Moustache's *forno*, only villas. The first belonged to *Tante* Bahiyah, a war widow who had several boys and girls. On the opposite side, on the higher level reached by steps, was the house of *Oncle* Emin Sorour, a police inspector, and his wife, *Tante* Oni. She came from an aristocratic family, and her father and grandfathers had all been police chiefs.

I don't remember her father, but my mother said he was, in looks and manners, the spitting image of Youssef Bey, the character played by Eric Portman (1901-1969) in the 1950 movie *Cairo Road*. This was a thriller about the Egyptian anti-narcotics police; it had a mixed-race cast reflecting life in Egypt in 1930s and 40s, with mixed marriages being common. Coincidentally, *Tante* Oni was the spitting image of Camellia, another of the *Cairo Road* stars. It was, in fact, the last film in which the Alexandrian-Jewish actress Camellia (1919–1950) participated before her tragic death at the age of 31 in August 1950 on the TWA Flight 903 from Cairo to Rome. She was born Lillian Victor Cohen in Alexandria in 1929 to a French father and Alexandrian-Italian mother. She attended the English Girls School (EGS) and started her career when 17, in the movie *Le masque rouge* followed by another 18 films. But she presented herself as Christian, most likely on the advice of filmmaker Ahmed Salem (1910–1949) who discovered her talent. Salem was also the first presenter at the birth of Cairo Radio in 1934, and the director of Cairo's first filmmaking industrial complex. He introduced Camilla to King Farouk when – among other actresses, singers and musicians – she entertained the monarch's guests. The king's praise for her performance generated gossip, fuelling rumours about a secret affair between them, spread by anti-Farouk Marxists, Islamists and British intelligence agents alike.

Another established old Alexandrian family, who owned a compound comprising five three-storey villas opposite Villa Alexandrine, were the Hibatallahs. Monsieur Hibatallah was a merchant of ironmongery and tools running an impressive store on Rue Nubar behind the mixed-tribunal building. I knew three of his many boys – one was my age, one younger and the other one was older, although he was closer in temperament to myself. We never referred to his wife as *tante* followed by a Christian name, the reason for which I never found out, but rather in typical, modern, demotic Alexandrian as *Tante* Madame Hibatallah.

She was elegant, well dressed and sported a great hairstyle; the *coiffeur* visited almost daily. On windy days, she sported an *écharpe*.

Rue Nineteen provided a snapshot of Alexandria's demographic mosaic: Copts, Jews, Muslims, Greek and Levantine Orthodox, and Roman Catholics; they encompassed indigenous Alexandrians, migrants from Internal Egypt and three generations of other ethnic immigrants – Armenian, Greek, Italian, French and mixed-race and -faith families. Vicky, an English nurse residing at Monsieur Hibatallah's compound, was the only grown-up who insisted on children calling her by her Cristian name without madam or *abla*. I grew fond of Vicky after one autumn when she nursed and bandaged my leg after I fell on the Devil's Hole rocks and hid the cuts from my parents, leading to their infection worsening. There was an Italian music teacher, in whose villa my sister spent most her time taking music lessons. Sloping south across Rue Cinquante (Rue Fifty), our road steepened again – passing Villa Gahndour Pasha. It cut across Rue Fifty and continued past the last two villas on the western side; one belonged to a retired Turkish headmaster, *Oncle* Nour-el-Dine, and his wife, Darriyah Hanem; the other was the last villa on the road before the asphalt ended and the sandy hills began. This house was home to the Jewish sisters *Tante* Mahalia and *Tante* Ella, with their many cats. One childhood pastime was competing in remembering the cats' names, but I only recalled *Mishmish* (apricot); had I encountered Boris Johnson at the time, I'd have called the cat Boris because of the remarkable resemblance.

CHAPTER 15   Plages and Policemen

The other was the black-and-white Clark – named after Alexandrian women's heart-throb, Hollywood star Clark Gable, because of a black line like Gable's moustache across its white mouth and under the eyes of its otherwise white face. We used to bring fish we caught to the cats and got some cakes and sweets from the two sisters, on our way up the street where the asphalt and pavement opened to the sand dunes' emptiness for another kilometre to the Abukeir–Alexandria railway line.

From the sun-scorched Rue-Mehatet-Sidi-Bishr to the east and the railway line to the south there was nothing but endless sand except for what was left of an old British camp and a few dotted windmills. We used to find some old war gasmask parts and spent ammunition there. We often encountered two familiar Arab girls in colourful dresses checking on their goats, which kept the growth of garden hedges and their flowers below a metre and a half high by standing on their hind legs and reaching for any vegetation. By the mid-1970s, the Arabs had disappeared; most were related to tribes in Libya, where they settled, attracted by the oil wealth.

I had many happy childhood memories playing at adventures with my cousins and friends on the dunes, flying kites or riding down the hill on bicycles hired at a *piastre* per hour.

CHAPTER 16
My Love Tutor

We played hide-and-seek among fruit trees and the thick, overgrown hedges making garlands from jasmine and honeysuckle in our younger years. All the villas on Sidi-Bishr's streets had gardens with lovely fragrances that passers-by inhaled all the way to the railway station whenever the sea breeze blew from the beach up the road from our villa. The last big two-storey house on Rue Nineteen – belonging to a seldom-seen, elderly, retired sea-captain – had a large, neglected garden like a jungle, separated from ours by a failing wooden fence. We had to sell a good chunk of our plot due to financial setbacks in 1950, but the two back gardens remained connected.

One never forgets the fragrance from childhood days; it often massaged my senses' memory when I made love to a brunette years later. I was dazed by a combination of fragrances; the strongest were jasmine mixed with feminine perfume and puffs from rolled joints shared with the seductive, older Cairo University student. She was the partner in my very first full-penetrative sexual encounter – in her secret den between the shady, dark fruit trees, their leaves moistened by the sea breeze. I sneaked out in the dark to the older student for long lovemaking sessions and smoking joints throughout the summer. I often brought some brandy or any bottles from the house to create our unique cocktails of mixed leftovers; flowers; half-ripe fruits like guavas, rosehip and mulberry; and other naughty ingredients.

She was experienced beyond her years and loved sexual experimentation with drinks, smoke and fruits. Little was left to the imagination when she played a fundamental role in shaping her underage lover's sensual direction. She led, and I obediently followed

CHAPTER 16 My Love Tutor

instructions, similar to the way in which Forster describes Cleopatra enthralling Antony:

Voluptuous but watchful, she treated her new lover as she had treated her old. She never bored him, and since grossness means monotony, she sharpened his mind to those more delicate delights, where sense verges into spirit. Her infinite variety lay in that. She was the last of a secluded and subtle race, she was a flower that Alexandria had taken three hundred years to produce and that eternity cannot wither, and she unfolded herself to a simple but intelligent Roman soldier.[1]

But I was a fast learner with an intellectual imagination, who reinterpreted the improvised script and developed it into pages in a future book. Among the fragrance of Alexandria's fences, shrubs, trees and flowers, I learned erotic innovative lovemaking with an older, experienced girl. Years later, I translated my instincts into words; I understood that eroticism was the Alexandrians' intellectualisation of love, the only ancient faith they truly believed in. Those evening visits to the secret garden, and adventures at Beir Masoud's caves and Miami's rocky island, granted me experience way beyond my years. It was an experience that came in handy later with many girls and attracted bullying and abuse from older, rough boys, who took their frustration of failed encounters with girls out on me. In my Alexandria school and later in England, jealousy of the frustrated losers generated bullying – often peppered with racism and anti-Semitism.

The older student was courageous and a follower of Alexandria's oldest religion: love, of every kind. Once, I wanted to impress her by showing off high-diving from the top of the dangerous rocky cliff of the Devil's Hole. She was accompanied by a friend reading Classics at Alexandria University. They came in their tight, black trousers tied below the knees with red ribbons, and their open blouses knotted above the waist, exposing green-and-pink top two-piece bras.

My older lover didn't hesitate when I invited her to high-dive with me from the shallow middle well. We swam in the tunnel, appearing in the Devil's Hole to wave to out-of-towners who crowded over the metre-high stone wall. In her excitement, my exhibitionist lover gave me a French kiss, to giggles and whistles from *masarwah*, as if watching a movie. Then we dived to the bottom for coins. The applause and cheers got louder when she kissed me again, but his time showed the onlookers a silver coin balanced on her tongue. We dived into the tunnel and climbed out on the rocky surface from the middle well. She ushered her friend to join but the other girl declined, preferring to watch over her friend's hat, clothes and Kodak camera. The small crowd followed us as we walked to the edge of the rock. I was becoming aroused by my girlfriend's sexy steps and her breathless whimpers. Her painfully arched feet with dark pink-painted toenails shyly negotiated the prickly rocks pockmarked by angry waves' millennia-long labour to shape Alexandria's coastline.

I held her hand on the edge of the rock and said, 'Let us dive'; she said, 'You go first'. I bowed to each crowd gathered on either side of the narrow bay, and snatched a kiss from her. I stretched out my arms and jumped, flying upwards copying diving athletes, made an arch in the air as I lifted my body a few feet up and dived with hands and head down to the gentle waves below. My lover adjusted her pink bonnet to tuck stray wisps of hair inside, held her nose and dived feet first followed by a round of applause. I encouraged her to take a deep breath and dive with me into the tunnel. It is only about a metre high in a low tide, but it fills up in high tide to the middle well. We swam in the tunnel to the middle well, then dived again to the Devil's Hole.

We repeated this a few times, picking coins until the crowd got bored of us and gathered around the gelato vendor, who was soon followed by the pianola man. Taking advantage of the diversion, we snatched a 'quickie' as she led the moves of an encounter that was excitingly powerful for a teenage boy. Women are astonishingly innovative in hiding silver, gold or jewellery, even when naked. She did some naughty things with the silver coin she had balanced earlier on her tongue, after producing it and another one from under her bonnet. She said I should keep one of the coins that carried 'a mixture of the two of us'. I still have it, among several from Alexandria's old silver.

This diving show and the wayward tunnel hiding became one, among several, summer pastimes. The risk that we might have been caught or told off by the beach police added a motivating excitement.

Alexandria teens didn't take much notice of the *belediye* signs that prohibited diving into the well. At the most, boys got a telling-off from the *plage* policemen, who would sometimes confiscate the silver coins collected from the 'lucky man's well' by the unlucky boy who got caught.

A few days later, I discovered why my older lover's friend didn't join us in the caves when I went bearing gifts of Greek Metaxa and French Martell into our secret den between her grandfather's garden trees. I was expecting a customary, improvised, cocktail-fueled hashish-smoking liaison, but the girl who was too shy to dive was naked in the arms of my lover: her bisexual girlfriend. She had invited the other student for a holiday, planning joint sessions with her love-apprentice.

A few years later, during my external study time at Alexandria University, my older lover had graduated from Cairo and was reading for her PhD in Alexandria. She continued her promiscuous adventures discreetly, but started a steady relationship with a senior lecturer. They

CHAPTER 16 My Love Tutor

became engaged by the end of the year. She kept the engagement ring on her finger when we rekindled our passionate encounters. Sadly, none of the memory-laden trees, homes or gardens remain; obnoxious high-rise blocks replaced them in the 1990s.

By the late 1960s, her grandfather could be seen confined to a wheelchair enjoying the sun on their veranda. The cruel local Egyptian children would tease him in a cowardly fashion, ignored by their ill-bred parents. His family, all living abroad, got him a full-time nurse before selling the villa after his death in 1970. Recalling those liaisons, I was then still legally underage – yet I surprise myself by how pragmatic I was, with a mature, cold attitude as I didn't mind her other lovers. Even after her engagement, I guess that I too, like all students, was promiscuous. I saw her again when she came to London for a shopping holiday for her 1967 wedding, which she called off at the last minute. She became the darling and target of English boys on the London 1960s scene – especially along the King's Road and in Earls Court clubs. She impressed and dated all of her London admirers.

The last time we had our naughty adventures was in a lovely nineteenth-century *dahabiya* (a river houseboat) that she inherited. It was the summer of 1968, a year after the Six-Day War, when I spent several months working as a stringer for some Fleet Street titles, travelling between Cairo and Alexandria. As I had predicted three years earlier, she cancelled her wedding to the devout *fellah* Muslim lecturer who couldn't handle her. She was working then for the regional UN cultural mission. Her houseboat, on one of the Nile's leafier Cairo stretches north of Zamalek, was a two-storey floating structure: a mini-replica of her family's Alexandria villa. Her parties on the houseboat were attended by stars, artists and diplomats – half of whom were spies – and a few remaining Jews. And we had the time of or lives. As always, she never ceased to surprise me; when I mentioned I was seeing an Alexandrian nightclub dancer, she suggested I should invite her for a couple of days to the houseboat. She laughingly promised not to try to convert Suad, the dancer, to her bilateral liaisons and wouldn't even dream of joining in: 'We have been there before, and as a philosopher, I don't swim in the same river twice.' She was true to her word.

That was the end of it, as the next time I saw her it was lunch at the Groucho Club when she worked for a London PR agency using her multilingual skills. She had married an English chap working in the City; they had two children. She gave me the second silver coin, hidden within her many years ago the day she plucked it from the Devil's Hole – 'a mixture of the two of us' – before leaving London for Cairo, where her husband had relocated.

Alexandria Adieu

A Walk to Mandarah

I used to join my retired grandfather's morning walks along the beach when he joined some legendary Wafd party[*] politicians for morning coffee on *Plage* Mandarah, past *Plage* Miami. The entry would be by fee only, but my father and grandfather were too well-known among enforcement controllers from the *belediye* to demand money from us. My grandfather greeted policemen on the way to the casino to read his newspapers. One of the police chiefs used to be a pupil at his school. In the 1950s, we teenagers used to help the municipality *plage* controllers by running errands, especially on *Plage* Sidi-Bishr Number Three, Miami and Al-A'safrah Beach (the *plage* sandwiched between Miami and Mandarah).

The last-named was a short stretch, still unspoilt in the 1950s. On the other side of the corniche road were sandy plots were many chalets stood. They were economical alternative holiday accommodation – let out by the day, week, or month during the summer season at a fraction of the price paid for a Sidi-Bishr apartment or chalet. They were affordable to lower-income Alexandrians, whether indigenous or first- or second-generation migrants from rural and Upper Egypt. Most were not-too-well-off white-collar workers motivated by Alexandria's spirit of aspiration thanks to their general elementary-school education. A few of them attended secondary education, elevating many to *effendi* status. They lived in modest homes in southern quarters like Gheit-el-Enab and Karmouz, but they wanted the best for their children. They sent them to church schools or charitable missionary schools with more advanced and varying curricula than state schools (rather like the difference between grammar schools and comprehensive schools in the UK). They rented al-A'safrah and Mandarah chalets for a period from a long weekend to two weeks in order to give their children a taste of what those from the 'other Alexandria' enjoyed for most of the summer. In *The City of Saffron*, about his childhood in Gheit-el-Enab, Alexandria's celebrated novelist Edwar al-Kharrat recalls spending a summer holiday in a chalet rented by his uncle in Mandarah.

Mandarah was much quieter than other *plages*; hence, it was favoured by retired politicians and some movie stars avoiding unwanted attention from fans. Among them was actor, director, scriptwriter and film editor Stephan Rosti (1891–1964), whose career spanned 43 years from 1920. Rosti was a typical child of Alexandria. He was born to an Italian-Egyptian dancer who married the deputy Austrian consul

---

[*] The Wafd party (founded 1918) was the most popular in Egypt. It was in power seven times, winning the largest share of seats in every election since independence in 1922 until the 1952 coup overthrew the parliamentary system.

CHAPTER 16 My Love Tutor

in 1889 but refused to leave Egypt and join him in Austria when his mission ended. The estranged husband tried to get his son, Stephan, out of Egypt but his mother fled Cairo with her boy to Alexandria, where they hid. She enrolled Stephan at a local school under her maiden name, Rosti. After the Great War, Stephan went to Austria but couldn't trace his father and worked as a dancer in nightclubs in Germany and France, where he met Egyptian filmmaker Mohammed Karim (1886–1972)[2] in 1920, who persuaded him to return to Alexandria to work in the movie industry. His Mandarah escapade is part of the city's film-community folklore. Rosti, a womaniser with a Casanovan libido, believed in recharging his prostate battery with the power of Manadrah's sunrays before sunset. In the late afternoons, when the *plage* was quiet, he would slip his swimming trunks a few inches down and bend over his *cabana's* gallery with his backside facing the sun at a perfect angle, letting the sunbeams shine directly on the centre of his buttocks. He even admitted to a few well-chosen actresses that the Mandarah sunbeams on the right spot, rather than his Italian genes, were the secret of his high sexual power.

My grandfather and I would stop on the way, to have his *café turc* and buy me a soft drink like *Subia* (a rice drink with honey), pomegranate crush or sugarcane juice from a vendor next to Hôtel Bosporus. The owner, Metry, had installed a new electric sugarcane presser – the first of its kind in the area – which crushed the cane between revolving cylinders and extracted its juice to pass over refrigerated shiny plate exchangers. Metry's contraption gave you the fresh juice straight into your tall glass chilled at 7 degrees centigrade within seconds from extraction, with white foam on top and without adding crushed ice like other vendors did. My grandfather's justification, when my mother expressed displeasure at the purchase, was that it was clean since no ice was added to the liquid. Ice was a cause of infections like tummy bugs and hepatitis, she was convinced, but she was against having cold drinks made in cafés in general.

We would then continue on the way to Mandarah so he could have his political arguments. Sometimes, instead of Metry's place, we would go to Casino Sidi-Bishr, an Edwardian structure of wood and glass at the end of a pier. It had a top like a Victorian conservatory, a café, bar and restaurant on a square platform on cast-iron-and-wooden pillars. Alternatively, we would visit a similar venue – Casino Miami, on Miami Beach – a two-storey Art Deco villa with glass bricks, constructed on a shorter concrete pier. These were just slightly more elegant, upmarket and expensive cafés than *Oncle* Wahba's Kazino, where you can sit down and have a drink, coffee, ice-cream, snack or even lunch with a spot of wine.

Alexandria Adieu

The marble-topped tables had the Panama hats resting on silver-handled walking sticks of the handsomely dressed pensioners in bespoke but old-fashioned linen suits, and their shaky hands trying to steady the broadsheet newspapers in various languages. These gentlemen shooed off the odd insect with their horsetail fly-swats, while lifting a *café turc* to their lips. If it was a late morning just before lunch, and on hot days, you would see the 'sweaty' green Birra Stella bottles. I would then join my peers by the *plage* or in one of the *cabanas*, while my grandfather joined his – the elegant Great War-generation gentlemen, one of whom I could have hardly dreamed I would one day see staring back at me from the looking glass in a faraway land.

PART IV
THE INCLUSIVE CITY

CHAPTER 17
A Mischievous Generation

Teens' Games and Scandals
Our nearest neighbours in Moharrem-Bey were *Oncle* Wissa and *Tante* Magda (Magdalena). He was a devoted conservative Coptic Christian who worked as a clerk in an import-and-export company. *Tante* Magda excelled in making cakes, and her recipe for punch was a closely guarded secret. Other families of different faiths enlisted her knowledge and skills to make *kahak* or punch for their parties. The couple had five children with a wide age gap between the older three and the younger two. The senior daughter, Ziezi (Isis), was slim, with a Hedy Lamarr figure and looks except for her green eyes. She played the piano to a professional standard, and the whole block loved to listen to her playing – especially when accompanied by Filippo, the boy who lived on the top floor. She studied in Italian schools and had a great voice; she would have had a career with Alexandria Opera if it hadn't been for *Oncle* Wissa's strict puritanical rules, which, in turn, had disastrous consequences. Ziezi had joined a music band with Filippo (but kept it secret from her strict father), and got pregnant by a fellow musician – an Italian. She nearly bled to death trying a naive DIY abortion with some foolish girlfriends. The ladies, including my mother, managed to protect her reputation, keeping a lid on the affair, which broke her cheerful spirit. For a whole year, Ziezi only went out to church and Sunday school. A year later, the spark was back in her eyes; she regained her sense of humour, dropped the Sunday school and played cheerful tunes on the piano.

Her younger sister, Neta (Nenet, the Egyptian goddess of the Deep), was a few years my senior and had a great body. She went to French schools and, secretly, to dance classes. She later joined Madame Nichols' girls, the Anglo–French dance school *Les danseuses de Madame Nichol*.

Alexandria Adieu

During the eighteen months of Ziezi's positive transformation, Neta often invited us to watch her dancing to her sister's tunes accompanied by Filippo in the evenings and afternoon when *Oncle* Wissa was working late.

The export–import business was going through the crisis of the military regime's confusing change of trade rules. They were trying desperate measures to salvage what was possible, with poor *Oncle* Wissa working 14 hours a day. For a few years, most businesses classified as 'foreign' evaded the military regime's claws by shifting over 51% of their holdings into 'trusted' Muslim Egyptian employees' names. The political climate started to change again with the growth of political Islam, treating non-Muslims as *khawaga* – including Christian Copts, who predated the seventh-century Arab colonisation.

It is funny how we, in older age, remember snapshots, like video clips, of our childhood days glowing clearly in the memory from times well before we considered keeping a diary of exact dates. It must have been in winter, because of the shorter days, during the mid- 1950s; I was in my early teens, having already experienced the electric charge when touching a female body. I used to dance with my older neighbour, Neta, to Ziezi's piano beat. From memory, over 60-odd years ago, the slow dance developed into our adolescent 'dirty dancing'. Her rubbing against my groin increased with every piano party, holding me tighter.

It happened one evening when *Tante* Magda, escaped the teens' party to my mother's, and we danced in a dimmed light. Ziezi, Neta and their brothers created a makeshift stage, with the pianist in the low light of *abajourahs* (dimmed *abat-jour*) in the central hall while we danced in two intercommunicating rooms. In short skirts with no knickers, Neta, who was taller than me, went further as she pulled me behind the ceiling-to-floor French window curtains that Alexandrians had added to their lighter ones during the War blackouts. With French kisses, her hand led the way to the game of *fursha* ('painting brush') common among adolescents.

'Let us paint a tableau,' she whispered, in French, bending her neck down and biting my ear painfully, 'it is a new game'. God knows who coined the brushstrokes phrase, but it was an accurate description of how boys and girls had adolescent non-penetrative sex: rubbing genitalia like a draftsman's brushstrokes until the artist and his model finished their 'water painting'. Neta, who first offered a guiding hand, was surprised and impressed that a boy several years her junior managed to skilfully paint a tableau, to her satisfaction, in the dark.

My pulse was racing; I could hear my heart beating in my eardrums, worrying her brothers would kill me if they looked behind the curtains. But the older two, Sherrie (Sherif) and Mikha (Mikhail)

CHAPTER 17 My Love Tutor

were slow-dancing with two of the girls who were also neighbours. The other girls joined Neta's youngest brother Eda (Said), dancing in a circle around the piano singing with Ziezi. Needless to say, once we had painted our first picture behind the curtains, Neta always devised cunning ways to arrange more artistic sessions.

By the time of Chanukah that year, Ziezi's happy secret was revealed. She was in love with a Jewish boy, Danny, who restored her faith in men. And he knew all the sordid details of her brief encounter with the Italian rascal. We weren't sure whether her strict father, who was so angry, had slapped her, as the rumour went, or not – but she disappeared. She had run off with Danny, who, in turn, fell out with his family. His mother, reportedly, had a heart attack when learning that her son, who had already broken her heart by leaving dental college for the entertainment industry, was to marry a Christian. But my mother, typically, claimed that Carmy, Danny's mother, faked her heart attack and it was only a sever indigestion episode caused by her awful cooking!

Oncle Wissa never recovered from the shame, ageing ten years in one weekend. It was not the only scandal to befall that poor religious man, who was also staring economic ruin in the face. Further shame was authored by his eldest son, Sherrie, who was younger than Zippy Ziezi and older than Naughty Neta. As his mother used to say, Sherrie was not the brightest among the neighbourhood boys and was often conned by street vendors as he paid the asking price without the customary haggling.

He was teased at school at a time when bullying was the norm and seldom anyone complained to staff, as teachers only intervened if you were caught in the act. They called him *Cheri* with the French 'r' as pronounced by the French-trained Egyptian actress Zozou Madhi (1914–1982), who was typecast as the seductive scheming villainess brothel madame in black-and-white Egyptian movies.

His younger brother, Mikha (Mikhail), a name he adopted after failing to stop his and other mothers calling him 'Meeky' (Micky) within an earshot of other children as the school bus collected him – you can guess why. But Mikha (with a Scottish 'kh' sound) was ignored by other pupils who continued to tease him with Micky Mouse for the next two years. It only stopped when he took on two boys alone at the school toilets away from the main building. One had to get dental treatment, and the other bully had a black eye and swollen lips. They were too humiliated to even talk about it, and both swore it was their fault slipping and hitting sinks when playing rough on the wet-tiled floor. Since the incident, all the school switched to Mikha but our neighbours kept the old name – especially his mother, shouting 'Meeeekiee' from their balcony at the top of her voice.

Their younger brother, Said, who had no nickname at home, was called 'Eeda' at school, and obliviously adopted by the neighbourhood children, but I can't remember anything interesting about him. The teased Sherrie, whom we took as 'two slices short of a loaf', proved us wrong. He generated a scandal dwarfing that of careless Zippy Ziezi and her Jewish boyfriend – a scandal that could have led to severe trouble but for my parents' quick thinking and the police chief's sensitive response.

Another *personne étrangère* who came to Ziezi's piano parties was a shy Muslim girl called Safi, a school friend of Francesca, Filippo's sister (our neighbours on the top floor). Safiya (meaning 'the unadulterated one') lived on Rue Menasce Pasha but came with Francesca, especially when her brother Filippo was singing to Ziezi's playing. She was the eldest child of Mohsen Effendi, a clerk at Barclays Bank (renamed Banque de Port Said after nationalisation), and was a loner; we didn't know of any friends of hers except Francesca.

Safi was still underage when she ran off with Sherrie. Her father, *Oncle* Mohsen, and his wife, *Tante* Sohair, were beside themselves with worry over her whereabouts. The school also contacted the parents when she failed to attend for three successive days. Her father filed a missing-persons' report at the local *caracol* (sub-police station), south off Rue Iskandrani. Then, *Tante* Sohair overheard Souso, the milkman's daughter, gossiping with their housemaid about the possibility that Safi might be with Sherrie, saying she had seen them a few times making out at the back of Cinéma Moharrem-Bey.

There was an electrifying shouting when *Oncle* Mohsen and *Tante* Sohair visited *Tante* Magda and *Oncle* Wissa, and my parents were concerned that Mohsen Effendi might suffer a heart attack. My father took him to a quiet, secluded bar on Rue Iskandrani attached to a wine shop owned by middle-aged Cypriot Marika and her brother, Gergie. He promised to accompany Mohsen in the morning to the district *mamour* (police chief, equivalent to a major in the army). *Oncle* Wissa lit a candle and locked himself in his bedroom, praying, while the two mothers joined my mother for dinner. Like most of the ladies of that formidable generation, the ladies were a bit calmer than the gentlemen. They started scheming to find a tailor-made solution, confident in their ability to manipulate the two fathers into accepting their plans.

Mixed Marriages
The police chief's office, where *Oncle* Mohsen had filed the missing-minor report, departmentally oversaw smaller precincts known by their Ottoman name: *caracol*. Papa had become friends with the *mamour*

CHAPTER 17 My Love Tutor

through a mutual friend, *Oncle* Monier, who, in turn, tipped off his old police-academy colleague, outlining the problem to give him time to devise a plan to defuse the crisis.

The front-desk sergeant took Mohsen Effendi and my father to the *mamour's* impressive office, where President Nasser's framed picture had replaced that of General Naguib, which had substituted for King Farouk's for a whole year. The *mamour* ordered drinks and chatted and joked, to calm down the angry father. A *mukhber* was called. The *mukhbers* were a tough lot, each in a woollen cap and long, yellow coat and always holding a long, thin bamboo stick that they used freely; they were, corrupt and most of the time had arrangements with criminal gangs. The *mukhber* reported, verbally, that he had ended the gossip for good. He had compellingly persuaded *A'am* Mahmoud that if his daughter were to open her big mouth again, gossiping about Safi and Sherrie, his vendor's licence would be revoked. My father and Mohsen Effendi spent a long time chatting with the *mamour*, who complained about his own teenage children and let him fill in a form reporting his daughter's suspected kidnapping.

It later transpired that the form never left the wise police chief's locked desk drawer. He was wily and experienced, keeping the district safe and quiet by good community-based intelligence. He turned a blind eye to some petty corruption like his subordinates, accepting gifts for the odd breach of licenced opening hours or traffic violation as part of a broader strategy and *mukhbers* roughing people up. Letting his subordinates know that he knew what they were up to was, according to *Oncle* Monier, the leverage that the *mamour* used to move his subordinates and influential traders and businesses on his larger 'chessboard'. The police chief wanted to avoid an exaggerated version of a story of a Muslim girl running off with a Christian boy becoming the focus of broader gossip, and being exploited by Islamist troublemakers.

After the long meeting with my father and Mohsen Effendi, he ordered a junior officer to drive his guests home after agreeing to wait a few days until his detectives found out the runaway couple's whereabouts.

There were some sensitivities about cross-marriages between Muslims and non-Muslims, and clergymen would instruct against a Muslim woman marrying a non-Muslim man, insisting he must convert. But they didn't mind things the other way around.

Although there were examples of such situations spilling over into violence in Upper Egypt and parts of the countryside, they seldom caused incidents worth reporting in multi-faith, multi-ethnic Alexandria. The worst-case scenarios there were couples splitting up or the man converting to Islam reluctantly.

While Alexandria's ethnic mosaic had many positive aspects, there were also some negative features, especially when you started moving south of the line that divided European Alexandria from the rest of the demographic, predominantly Muslim, Egypt. An invisible line ran south of Rue Moharrem-Bey to the central railway station to Kom-el-Dikka: a line dividing Alexandria into two 'continents'. Migrants from Inner Egypt lived in the south, while the Alexandria north of the invisible line was buzzing with people living in a different world – led, controlled and managed by the European and Europeanised Alexandrians.

Less than a kilometre south of this imaginary fence, the mix of races and faiths showed the contradictions of intolerances bubbling under the calm surface of middle class multi-ethnic Alexandria, despite its easy-going atmosphere and general social acceptance of marriage of diverse religions. Muslim barmen and waiters who had no objection to serving alcohol or pork came from the modest parts of this area, while *fellaheen* migrants lived further south. However, their tolerance represented pragmatic accommodation rather than a modernised way of thinking. Ibrahim Abdel Meguid (b.1946) illustrated this situation in his novel *No One Sleeps in Alexandria*, through the central character, Sheikh Magdeldine – an al-Azhar-educated country landowner who migrates to Alexandria before the War to escape a vendetta in his village. Only once in his four years living among mostly Christian migrants from Upper Egypt in the Gheit-el-Enab quarter does he take his wife out to downtown Alexandria to walk by the corniche. Both are shocked by the ungodly ways of Alexandrians, their drinking and how the women of the other Alexandria dressed immodestly and expressed affection openly for men.[1]

Even some who became white-collar *effendis* through schooling could not shake off their profound *fellaheen* intolerance towards non-Muslims. I once overheard a gentleman visiting our neighbour, Oncle Yaqoub, whispering to his wife, 'Can't you wait? We should buy it from the Muslim grocery near the station instead.' My mother was once shocked by a similar comment from one of her acquaintances married to a top government official dropping in for tea after consulting a doctor nearby. The guest gave the prescription to a maid and instructed her to dispense it from 'the Muslim *eczane*', half a mile away, instead of the Christian-owned pharmacist opposite the house or the Jewish *eczane*, Mizrahi, on the next block.

If you went further south towards the Mahmoudiyah Canal Muslim children would sing '*eid-el-apat; zay el-zappat*' (Christian feast drowning in the mire) if it was raining on the Epiphany, as it often did.

This unspoken but existing tension motivated the *mamour* to plot with my father to keep the lid on the foolish runways' love story. After

CHAPTER 17   My Love Tutor

a few days, *Oncle* Mohsen was visibly calmer thanks to the influence of his bank work colleagues, who, as in many offices, were a snapshot of mosaic Alexandria. Mixed marriages across faiths and races were prevalent among them; thus, they wondered, what was the fuss all about?

Mohsen Effendi was also manipulated by his attractive, young-looking and always merry wife, *Tante* Sohair, who was talked into accepting the reality by my mother. In his second meeting with the *mamour*, Mohsen Effendi was exchanging jokes as the company included *Oncle* Monier, known among the police crowd as 'a police officer in service of the community (females)'. A shocking story involving him as a police lieutenant had become part of the police-ranks' folklore. His area *mamour*, on a surprise visit, found an attractive dancer who had been arrested for soliciting in a nightclub on his police desk shaving her long legs. His response was to quote the slogan of the day: 'The police in the service of the community, sir.' Seeing that the arresting officer had interrupted the dancer's feminine task, finishing the job was in the interest of hygiene and morale. 'Both', was the young lieutenant's reply when his superior asked whose morale this was – the suspect dancer's or the station constables'?

Mohsen Effendi was giggling loudly while the *mamour* spiced up his version of the embarrassed *Oncle* Monier's story as he sipped on his coffee and pulled on a cigar presented to him at the police station.

Safi's father was informed that the couple were living in Wabour-el-Maiyah, a quiet area of Bab-Sharki named after the nearby Alexandria waterworks. The police chief explained that the couple, who lived in a bedroom provided in a friends' house, would by now have consummated their civil marriage. The wise *mamour* patiently persuaded the 'bride's' father to drop the charges, saying that she would most likely have already conceived. If his son-in-law had to go on trial, he could spend two to three years behind bars.

'And then', like an ice-cold water bucket poured on the father's head, '...when the boy is in jail, and the court nullifies the marriage, who would take the damaged goods, and possibly holding a baby, off your hands?'

The father never pressed charges. A year later, the couple was seen at Safi's parents with their baby, Mohsen. I never had the chance to quiz Sherrie about the rumour that *Oncle* Mohsen slapped his face twice (or, in another version, gave him a *shalloot* up his backside) on his first visit to his in-laws?

I equally never found out whether Sherrie converted to Islam or not. There had been too many examples of this practice to count, as Alexandria was used to inter-faith and mixed-race marriages. Civil

163

Alexandria Adieu

marriages were certified in the registry section in mixed courts and later, after freezing the *tribunaux mixtes*, in the post office where they didn't bother asking about religion. The officials accepted a signed civil contract between the two parties and then added witnesses' signatures. Only a clergyman would bother, when the parents ask for baptism or similar. And in every story I encountered with someone converting for marriage, it was always the one marrying into a better-off family who would convert despite claims he or she was motivated by higher spiritual aspirations. But when there was no family pressure, mostly to do with inheritance, nobody bothered to go through the process of conversion as it would have involved bureaucrats and meddling clergymen – both detested and despised by Alexandrians. There was the story of a friend of an ethnically Italian friend of my mother, whose husband converted from Catholicism to Islam to marry a Muslim girl with whom he fell in love. Shielding behind exceptions permitting Muslim men to have a second wife, the husband refused to divorce his wealthy Catholic wife. She filed for divorce in the family court, but I never found out the outcome of the case after I left Alexandria.

A sister to Alexandrian novelist Edwar al-Kharrat remained happily married to a Muslim chap she met when both worked for the Alexandria Rice Refining and Export Company. Neither she nor her husband converted since there were no financial gains in either doing so.

A friend of my father, who was baptised Philipe, took the ambiguously multi-faith name Farid when he married the Muslim *Tante* Kuka (*kawkab*: star). They had homes in Alexandria and in central Cairo, and a large country house in the middle of a fruit orchard in the northeast of the Nile Delta, which *Tante* Kuka had inherited from her father. They also had a nineteenth-century chalet with a commanding view of Aboukir Bay, where Admiral Nelson (1758–1805) destroyed the French fleet in August 1798.

As they each, independently, had considerable wealth, besides his business in spare parts for precision machinery, neither bothered to change faith. We never found out which religion their children took; I assume none – like us. All of Alexandria accepted the groom's new name except his mother, *Tante* Georgette, who, until she died in 1968, insisted on calling him 'Phileepe' and correcting his sister, *Tante* Marie, every time she let the word 'Farid' pass her lips.

CHAPTER 18
Schoolchildren Grow Up Fast

The Harouns were another set of much-loved neighbours in Moharrem-Bey – *Oncle* Moheb Haroun, an inspector in the Department of Customs and Excise in the harbour, and his wife, *Tante* Kikki (Hikmat). She was an excellent cook and had various recipes for *lapin*, an attribute that fitted the couple's 'breeding like rabbits'. They needed a whole floor of two apartments to accommodate their six children, who became eight before I left Alexandria: three boys and five girls – three were stunners, one of them was my age and the others were two and three years my senior.

Boys would rush to their balconies when the wolf-whistles in the street announced the three girls' approach. Wolf-whistles were intended, at the time, as a sign of light-hearted appreciation as many girls responded in giggles or, occasionally, squelched the admirer with a witty quip.

The girl three years my senior (whose name, Hia'a, meant 'modesty') introduced me to French-kisses and the 'tongue tango' when I was barely 11. The following winter, her school friend, Shani, introduced me to *fursha* – enabling me to impress my older neighbour, Naughty Neta, behind the French-window curtains.[1] The schoolboys and girls played sexual fun-games in the back seats of cinema theatres or the deserted upper deck of the tramway Ramleh in winter. Those teens who looked older or had a bit of cash played the game in deserted winter seafront cafés and casinos; waiters would let them enjoy themselves for inflated prices. Those who preferred the warmth of a film theatre needed deeper pockets to bribe the usheresses. Our preferences were Cinéma Rio, Cinéma Royale and Cinéma Fuad; we didn't like those with wooden seats, like the Plaza and Alhambra. It was never a good practice to overlook the tipping ritual of leaving the full *riyal*-coin (20 *piastres*) after buying two drinks or gelato. The untipped usherette's torch would accidentally shine on the penny-pincher at an awkward moment while guiding a late arrival to sit right next to the young lovers, even when the cinema was almost empty.

Not having enough pocket money for cinema tickets or a deserted seafront café didn't impede school teens' quest for fun. They played the game in nature's lairs, between trees and shrubs in public parks – most famously, Challalat municipality park. This was conveniently located for a cluster of schools like the English Girls School (EGS), English Boys School (EBS) and the Italian School. The other famous secondary school, only 120 metres from Challalat, was Nabowiya Mousa Girls School.

Nabowiya Mousa (1886–1951) was an early twentieth-century feminist: the first Egyptian girl to study for a university degree, sitting the exams without attending classes in 1907 since females weren't permitted into seminars. Mousa wanted equal pay and got a degree to overcome the obstacle that female teachers lacked a university degree, thus being paid 40% less than their male colleagues. She had to face, and impress, a committee especially set for the only female student to sit the exam without attending university. Mousa was a writer, author and journalist, publishing under a pseudonym. When her real name was exposed, she almost lost her post because teachers were banned from taking another job. Only the praise of the popular nationalist first post-independence prime minister, Sa'd Zaghloul Pasha, for her work discouraged her headmistress from sacking her.

The Nabowiya Mousa's girls – along with those form other shools – would meet boys at Challalat Park to picnic or kiss and brush-paint in the bushes.

The Banat Haroun – *les filles d'Araroun* – were a classic representation of Alexandrian girls. With its wider, diverse gene pool, the city's girls were a world apart from any other females from Egypt. They were daring, of stunning beauty with a lighter complexion than other Egyptian females, and many would have blue, green, grey or light brown eyes, and European hairstyles.

A vivid picture of them was drawn by my late friend, Edwar al-Kharat in *Banat iskandriah*.[2] Al-Kharatt pens his poetic feelings, sketching a lover he encountered and adored as a secondary-school student at Abassiyah School, which later became Alexandria University College of Sciences and Technology in Moharrem-Bey. His romantic longing, love and admiration form a spiritual, prayer-like tribute given his early, religious upbringing in a family from a strict, conservative Coptic Upper Egyptian background. In Upper Egypt, church teaching

CHAPTER 18   Schoolchildren Grow Up Fast

remained in a time capsule dating back to the split between the Eastern and Western churches. Paradoxically, at the time of authoring *Banat iskandriah*, 1987–9, al-Kharrat was a secular atheist, but love was the only religion Alexandria recognised deep in her souls and let her Alexandrian children practice.

The Virgin Lady, bringer of light, *Sitt* [Saint] *Demiana* [Damiana], Santa Katarina all at once…What did I care what she did in life, who she was, what her relationships, what circumstances, whether she was a teacher at the primary school of the Anglican church where my sister Louisa studied?…Was she a salesgirl in a department store? Did she work at the mill with Mona's sister Gamalat? Was she married or not?… she was beyond that, she was not subject to the laws of this earth. The fire of her eyes in mine, just for an instant. …Still I see her face, faintly tinged with rose, finely sprinkled with scarcely distinguishable spots, her pursed lips a deep crimson. ….Her eyes which are a lake with wide-flung borders, golden-green-these are the eyes which shaft the boy and man at once with agony, which enduring passion while pillowing him in sung content. Silent Madonna of Ghobrial.* Her body is an altar, her legs two strong smooth draped columns with one secret and treasured capital. Baptism font and source of water of life from which I drink and never thirst. Her breasts dazzle as if blessed, suckling the world on the milk of human kindness, rounded beneath the hand-knitted pullover…[3]

Reading al-Kharrat's prose, first in Arabic when he gave me a copy, almost three decades after I left Alexandria, his words expressed emotions bubbling inside my head recalling my early adolescent encounters with the Harouns and other girls of Alexandria in the 1950s. The Banat Haroun were no exception: typical *filles alexandrines* – sexy, attractive, articulate and intelligent. I briefly dated one of them when I spent a year as an external observer at Alexandria University in 1963–4. Although we met in a flat that I had, we couldn't resist the allure of nostalgia for our early romantic teen years. We had fun and games at the back of cinemas, where, unlike in the 1950s, more Egyptians spoke with new, introduced Arabic words since filmgoers were, by then, mostly Inner Egypt migrants in auditoria dotted with a few European-Alexandrians who braved the new regime's 'weather'.

Although there were five Haroun girls, the three closest to my age had some stunning schoolmates from El-Amirah Faiza (Princesse Faiza), a prestigious secondary school for girls. El-Amirah Faiza School's corner on Rue Rasafah was like a honeypot attracting 'drones' from many other schools. Recognisable by their ties and uniform, the

---

* A Coptic-Chrstians-dominated area located south of Moharrem-Bey.

boys were on their toes, worried they might be spotted outside the girls' school gate by Abla Nafousah (also known as 'Miss Madhi'), Princesse Faiza's disciplinarian deputy headmistress. The sight of this old spinster standing at the huge, bow-fronted school bay window like a scary Egyptian goddess from a Hammer Horror movie – and she certainly had the face and hairstyle to match – would send the boys fleeing in panic. One-sixth former, Hosny, had a terrible accident, breaking his arm and injuring his head colliding with Tram Number 4, when he ran off frightened by Abla Nafousah shaking her forbidding index finger at his group of boys. When Miss Madhi identified boys by their tie, she would telephone their school and report them. A whole class – or, in some cases, an entire form – would get into trouble since nobody would snitch on their schoolmates. The school tie was a sacred tribal symbol, with all the macho-honour attributes that this entails. Mercifully, there were no digital cameras or mobile phones available to be weaponised by the authoritarian deputy headmistress in those days.

My school was far away from this central cluster, with no girls' schools located for miles around – so only at weekends, or when we stayed at Moharrem-Bey or El-Balad, did I have the chance to hook up with a Princess Faiza schoolgirl. For a new gramophone record or some cosmetics stolen from my mother's collection – or from some left on display after her Tuesday receptions – the Haroun sisters would introduce me to one of their more liberal-minded, naughty girlfriends: the type of girls who basked in their wayward reputation. On most occasions, the girls and I would exchange new adolescent games we had learned.

Different from their Egyptian counterparts, Alexandria girls were sophisticated and showed it from an early age. Their etiquette, like the rest of the Alexandrians, was Mediterranean European. The same went for their sense of *moda* and maquillage, their ability to dance to whichever music played. Even the poorest among them, who lived in humble conditions, would blend easily and mix quickly with upper-middle-class and European Alexandrians in her *chellah* without being exposed as of lesser breeding than the most privileged in the group. With strangers and new teachers, the girls were too polite; yet, some of their acquired nicknames, which fitted their decadent practices, painted a different reality. Names coined in a mixed-language glossary by our, or a rival, *chellah* depended on rhyming, on the similarity of first letters or on an adjective attached to the first name to amplify or reflect a lascivious speciality or a cavalier attitude to adolescents' sex games.

Such monikers included 'Handy Hadia', whose real name was Hedaia (meaning 'finding God'); she acquired the soubriquet reflecting her speciality when she was only 13. The quick-witted 'Sillyman', our

CHAPTER 18　Schoolchildren Grow Up Fast

own nickname for the half-Jewish half-Muslim Soliman, came up with the name Hadia, meaning pacifist, because it was the opposite of *haiga*, meaning 'permanently sexually aroused'. Since his father was Muslim and the mother was Jewish, both sides of the Abrahamic family claimed him as their own – but Sillyman cursed Yahweh and Allah with equal venom and frequency. The boy, who had obviously inherited his mother's sense-of-humour genes, was gifted in mixing names from different languages. He also 'held the copyrights' for some labels that are impossible to forget – such as 'FFF': Frustrtaingly Flirty Francesca, due to her continuous coquettish toying with boys without going very far; or his brand names for two cousins: 'Mouna-Mouth' and 'Shafikah Shafaief' (lips). Neta's label 'Naughty' was coined by her own sister, Ziezi, in response to Neta naming her 'Zippy Ziezi'. Ziezi, in a brainstorm with Sillyman, labelled Neta's friend 'Faiza Fassad' (the corrupting Faiza).

Faiza, the name meaning 'the winner', was the senior of the *chellah*; she came from a rich land-owning family east of the Delta. Her mother had died when she was seven, and her stepmother didn't like her. Her father sent her to school in Alexandria with a generous monthly allowance, to live with her maternal grandmother as her guardian. The French-educated Albanian-aristocrat grandmother was stuck in her post-Great War pleasure-seeking era. The easy-going Drita Hanem held bridge games and small concerts in her massive mansion and didn't bother disciplining her unruly granddaughter. The old lady didn't even knock on Faiza's room door when she had some of mixed-sex *chellah* with her. Faiza's room was more like an apartment, with a reception area seperate from her bedroom and a massive balcony as well as a vast en-suite bathroom that had a window onto the rear garden and a separate walk-in closet full of her clothes. She travelled to Europe with her grandmother during summer and Easter breaks, and became popular with pupils who all wanted to be her friends. Faiza always managed to get hold of any 'forbidden fruit', like hashish for our parties or drinks and cigarettes when shopkeepers refused to sell them to minors, and often guided girls and boys through their first sexual encounters. She always had money and an endless supply of maquillage from her careless grandmother's collections. Faiza would hold impromptu parties with a couple of hours' notice when one of the maids, whom she bribed, tipped her that the grandmother planned a long evening visit to one of her friends playing bridge.

All teens held parties, mostly improvised at short notice, when one of the spoilt better-off pupils invited us while their parents or guardians were away. With the coup regime's mismanagement of the economy, many businesses found Cairo more attractive than Alexandria. But this was a windfall for us teens, in the way of play and pleasure. Many families had started spending more time away from Alexandria. They had other homes on their country estates, mostly growing fruit or cotton for export, or in Cairo, to which the parents would go on long weekends, leaving the offspring in the care of exploited domestic staff who weren't much older than the children themselves. The domestic chaperone would join the fun when they fancied a boy, or turned a blind eye for a modest bribe – or, in most cases, both. As expected, the wildest of the parties was held by Faiza Fassad when her grandmother travelled to play bridge or stay with friends. Champagne would flow in the large mansion in Ramleh, and the venal domestic staff were just as wild as their young mistress.

By the time I was 16, I had reasonably good sexual experience – way ahead of most boys in my peer group. I also acquired a reputation for grown-up, intellectual conversation and a taste for sound films or music events, to which I invited girls. I learned from a young age that females love getting flowers and presents. I managed to give them gifts they appreciated – books, records, new French maquillage articles or stockings: such items became desirable after the Suez War when Nasser started banning imports. I often took flowers I picked from our or our neighbours' gardens in Sidi-Bishr to a girl on a first date. But what the Moharrem-Bey schoolgirls appreciated most was my discreet conduct; I never boasted about my conquests with the opposite sex. It was not a cunning device on my part but more of a cautious approach since my gateway to the gentler sex's skirts were the Haroun sisters, whose family knew mine. A wrong move could have resulted in grave consequences – especially bearing in mind Safi's and Sherrie's story, which was told with more editing, additions and alterations as time passed. (When I visited the area 35 years later, I ran into one of the Haroun sisters. Looking and sounding more like her mother, her recounting of the mixed-faith runaway couple's story was significantly different from the one I witnessed.) Besides, my school was geographically too far away for me to mix with Moharrem-Bey schools' boys and the ones I knew were relatives or brothers of many of the schoolgirls.

The Muslim ones and migrants from *fellaheen* families, including Christians from Upper Egypt, were hypocritically self-appointed zealous guardians of their sisters' and cousins' sexual purity. But the boys were themselves quite aggressive sexual predators. I witnessed how those brothers and cousins, who would engage in fist fights to protect the honour of the clan's females, behaved in a brattish way even by 1950s standards. At Faiza's wild parties, the same boys would engage in sexual encounters with classmates of their own sisters, as long as the sisters didn't attend the parties.

There were incidents of brothers attacking sisters' boyfriends physically. But my discreet ways earned me far more sexual encounters than most boys, thanks to my gifts of books and records; my sharp wit and sense of humour in telling amusing stories; and, most beneficially, I wasn't from a local school – and the 'grass is always greener on the other side'. But my semi-innocent adventures earned me the odd beatings, too; there is a scar still visible on my left eyebrow. One evening, Shani's older brother, who had a silver ring with a projecting scary skull, punched me as I dropped her off in a taxi, misinterpreting her adjusting of her school uniform and her peck on my cheek.

Puskas, Cruelty and Kindness
There were other stories about our neighbours – like Francesca and Filippo, who had a great singing voice, occasionally singing with different bands. On few memorable occasions, I accompanied Francesca to attend her brother's multi-ethnic singing band playing at Athinèos.[4] We also once nearly got caught when her mother unexpectedly came into the little roof garden of their apartment: we thought we were safe when *Tante* Carlota, accompanied by *Tante* Kikki, returned form a shopping trip. Quick-thinking Francesca pretended to be collecting the washing from the line on the roof. But in her haste, she took my trousers along with the bundle – leaving me shivering, mostly from worry and stress. It took me an hour of waiting for the opportunity to escape with some pink, female garment wrapped around my body.

Tante Carlota made beautifully decorated, delicious bread and cakes like *buccellato*, *ciambella* and her popular *pampaptio di ferrara*, which she must have been baking on an industrial scale since every neighbour seemed to have one or two. She frequently invited the neighbourhood teens to taste them with her children, especially the seasonal cakes. As soon as the chestnut vendors appeared on the streets pushing carts with charcoal grills, we knew we'd be treated to a delicious *castagnaccio*. On another unforgettable occasion, I was the only one left at the table pretending I was still hungry for more *torta caprese* and biscotti after the others had gone on the roof, singing with Filippo and his sister. Francesca's titillating hand had been busy under the table while her brother was blowing out his birthday-cake candles – and I had to remain still for ages, stuffing my face, before I could stand up, staggering with a bloated tummy, to join the others.

There were some less-memorable neighbours: one such couple was *Oncle* Yaqoub and *Tante* Sara. I can't recall exactly what *Oncle* Yaqoub did for a living, but I believe he was a civil servant. They were Muslims and more conservative than the rest of the neighbours, with no sense of fun. Their status was elevated when their eldest son Jimmy (Gamal) joined the military academy at the age of 16, soon after the military coup. They had two girls, Emma and Crème – the latter, with the French pronunciation, shortening her name, Karima (also Alexandrian for cream). Her brother, Meadow (I can't remember his real name), became an army officer. I don't recall many stories about them as they were a rather boring, humourless family. The only memorable anecdote was an encounter between *Oncle* Yaqoub and Bellitta, when he angrily accused her of deliberately letting Puskas, my cat, defecate on stairs near his flat. 'Don't you think I would've given Puskas some toilet paper to wipe his behind since I managed to train the cat when and where to do it?' Bellitta cheekily responded but she was told off by my mother just to mollify *Oncle* Yaqoub, the whole family – and then the rest of the neighbourhood – was amused by the encounter, which, as expected, was retold for many years to come in different edited versions.

Puskas wasn't the first cat I rescued. Both Bellita and my mother were getting irritated by my habit of carrying home any kitten I found wandering the streets. I mostly encountered the homeless felines south of Rue Moharrem-Bey, where more Egyptian immigrant families lived. We hardly saw a cat or a puppy abandoned in the Ramleh area, home to mostly European migrant families, except for the odd lost pet.

Egyptian children were cruel to animals. 'The Egyptian child's attitude toward dogs is unique. As soon as he spots a canine strolling peacefully, the child looks for a projectile to throw at the poor animal' was the accurate description penned by the late leading journalist Mustafa Amin (1914–1997). Amin's column often set the public agenda when it appeared in the weekly broadsheet *Akhbar-el-Youm*. He co-founded the paper, which became the country's highest-circulation weekly, in 1944 with his twin brother Ali Amin (1914–1976).

The only severe, memorable fist fight I had as a child was to protect a poor chameleon on the garden-wall climbers at Villa Alexandrine. The quarrel started with the eldest boy of next-door's *vulgaires du Caire*, who snatched the reptile over the garden wall. My sister had helped the poor lizard back to a branch for its own safety; it was slowly crawling up when the boy grabbed it. He was holding the chameleon by its tail and swinging it. As I tried to rescue the reptile, his brother and his cousin joined the fight: it was three against one, and with two boys older than me. I fought bravely, but I lost – so did the chameleon. When the poor creature's head was smashed to bits against the paving stones, I shouted at the older boy, *ya-Ibn-el-Kalb-*, ('son of a hound', a common Egyptian insult). Amazingly, his mother, a schoolteacher, complained to Bellitta about my swearing while ignoring his cruelty to animals. Bellitta told her that we had never seen any behaviour like that displayed by her boys, and she should pay more attention to their

CHAPTER 18 Schoolchildren Grow Up Fast

treatment of creatures and anti-social conduct. She then told her that my mother was too busy to see anyone, and we went inside.

We used to have street entertainers, like the pianola man and his dancing daughter, the *hawi* (illusionist), the *aragous* (Punch-and-Judy man), *ilvaso Pandora* (Pandora's box) and the *oradati* (the man with his chained baboon). This last-named poor animal danced to the rhythms of his master's tambourine and reed-pipe, and would occasionally get a lash from his bamboo stick when it hesitated.

The baboon man made stops every 100 metres or so – and especially outside Villa Alexandrine, since we tossed several coins into his upturned tambourine after each show and gave the baboon bananas, peanuts in shells and the odd bonbon. The abused animal loved cracking the peanut shells and cleverly unwrapping the sweets, while Bellitta kept the heartless *oradati* busy with a cup of tea and some cakes. Repeated incidents over the space of three weeks or so also revealed the cruel, nasty tricks played by *les vulgaires du Caire* on the poor baboon. We should have figured out, when they handed it wrapped bonbons, that it was contradictory to their nature to be generous to humans or animals. Within minutes of eating the sweets, the baboon became restless, attracting beatings from his master and protests from upset children. The sadistic Cairean boys had laced their bonbons with chilli powder and waited for the creature's reaction, enjoying its pain and the commotion their wicked prank generated. It was also noticeable that the Cairean *nouveau riche* were the only family on the street who did not have pets.

Pet animals and other creatures were a favourite pastime among children in our circle of European and indigenous Alexandrian middle-class families. Access to outdoor space determined the type of pet – whether rescued or litter cats and dogs, or rabbits and hamsters kept in enclosures. Moharrem-Bey was still full of villas and low-rise blocks surrounded by gardens, as were areas like Smouha, Sidi-Gaber and Rue Abukeir.

I had an Alsatian called Lucky, who died in a road accident when he chased a ball down Rue Nineteen to its junction with Rue Fifty and was hit by Bus Number 27. The driver and passengers hastily disembarked; some asked where the nearest vet was. Lucky, bleeding from the mouth and ears, died a few minutes later in my arms. We took him home and an older boy, Sabbi, made a coffin. Except for the *cairéens vulgaires*, all the neighbourhood children of both sexes and multiple faiths came to bid Lucky a final farewell. We decided to hold a proper funeral, but we couldn't agree on the sermon. The only accessible cemetery was the *turab*; its entrance was from Sidi-Bishr Mosque Square, where we had watched Muslim funerals. For convenience, the children voted to give the canine an Islamic burial. We copied Muslim funerals, carrying Lucky's coffin to the mosque and chanting words whose meaning we didn't quite comprehend. The mosque was closed, so we placed the coffin outside the building. Sabbi bowed, kneeled, touched the ground with his forehead; we copied him, then we proceeded to the *turab*. The *turabi* (gravedigger) blocked our way, cursing devilish children desecrating the graves with a dog. According to Muslim folklore, a Muslim licked or touched by a dog needs to be washed seven times before God accepts his prayer. Only the sight of our clothes stopped the rough *turabi* from hitting us, since social class was a deterrence in those days. But it was also an early wake-up call as I discussed the encounter with my older cousins later, noticing the *turabi's* attitude and we became aware of hidden feelings around religious rituals and folkloric beliefs.

We changed the funeral's direction, going up the hill to the empty sand dunes to the south beyond the Ghandour Pasha villa and the Jewish sisters' house. We had another discussion: a Jewish burial was ruled out as there were no ten Jewish males to read *kaddish*, and we opted for Christian burial instead. Lord Jesus never discriminated against any soul, and he accepts all god's creatures great and small into his kingdom. Since many of us went to English, French or Christian mission-run schools, we knew the Lord's Prayer. We sang 'Guide Me, Oh Thou Great Redeemer', to which only two or three of us knew the words, and got stuck on the second stanza 'whence the healing stream doth flow', quickly jumping into 'Feed me till I want no more'. We then repeated the Lord's Prayer and entrusted our brother, Lucky, to the Lord. Sabbi and an unusually tall, very skinny girl we called 'Olive Oyl'* had already dug a grave. We marked it with white stones and placed an improvised cross with Lucky's name and dates in Olive Oyl's neat handwriting (I can't even remember her real name after all these years).

I then had another dog, Ronnie, a Labrador. But I rescued several cats and even frogs that inhabited a little makeshift pond we created in the back garden; many of those frogs died as they left the pond in the mating season. It wasn't until a teacher, Mademoiselle Noura, explained to the class that fully-grown frogs would instinctively try to travel back to the ponds or waterways from which we had picked them as tadpoles weeks earlier. After that, we all gave up the practice of picking tadpoles in jars from the Ras-el-Souda marshes to bring home.

---

* The name of a tall, skinny female cartoon character created by E.C. Segar in 1919 for his comic strip *Thimble Theatre* – best-known as the girlfriend of Popeye, who became the strip's main character.

CHAPTER 18   Schoolchildren Grow Up Fast

Some children living in El-Balad flats without gardens, but which had balconies or roof terraces instead, opted for pigeons. Parents were not too keen on the birds, which were noisy and messy. They also got the occasional health inspectors' warning letter considering the birds to be a health hazard. The favourite post-war hobby for children dwelling in downtown Alexandria, however, was raising silkworms. This practice was encouraged by schoolteachers, which enabled children to follow the creatures' four life-cycle stages over six to eight weeks in a shoebox with holes for them to breath. The boxes were easy to carry between homes and school. Chalking on the blackboard, teachers explained the metamorphosis during the life cycle of those beautiful moths of that branch of hexapod. School children would trade-off the silk cocoons, which were in pink, white or greenish-yellow, or the white caterpillars grown from tiny larvae. Those larvae would also be exchanged for mulberry-bush leaves needed to feed the caterpillars and for the butterflies to lay eggs on for the next season.

Mademoiselle Noura once took the whole class to her uncle's orchard in Seiouf, a suburb southeast of Alexandria, for a lesson on bees and how honey was harvested. I failed to persuade my mother to have beehive boxes in our back garden.

CHAPTER 19
The War Generation

Formidable Ladies

Regardless of where we stayed, our home was always full of visitors. Some sought my father's advice or help, given his many contacts; others consulted my mother, who was mostly active in charitable organisations and within education circles. Like the city's other middle- and upper-middle-class *hanems*, *Maman* held her ladies' receptions on the second Tuesday of each month. This ritualised tradition was attended by beautifully dressed ladies and socialites of Alexandria. It was like a scene of the ladies' arrival at a modest, low-budget opera production of *Cinderella* – all beautifully dressed, maquillage applied by professional *coiffeurs*, *parfum* scenting the air and jewellery sparkling. It was exclusively a ladies' event; gentlemen weren't too keen on this arrangement but cordially accepted the tradition with cold respect. Papa learned to escape the fuss accompanying the preparations preceding the event; he made sure he would be travelling – or else stayed in Sidi-Bishr if the monthly event was in Moharrem-Bey, and vice versa.

Reception day was a big event for the hostess, who would hire extra domestic staff and spend lavishly on preparations. Many of the cakes and sandwiches for the afternoon tea were ready a day earlier and chilled champagne (which was, in later years, downgraded to economical sparkling wine) was served in coupes followed by various drinks – always coupes; never flutes, which were for the *plage*. Also the day before, coffee jars would be replenished with a new batch in the traditional way, the green coffee beans would be roasted and ground, and a few secret ingredients added. On the big day, preparation of the multiple dishes would start early in the morning. Several cakes would have been prepared days earlier, but some were baked only on the day – or even

CHAPTER 19   The War Generation

as guests arrived. Scones were the very last; my mother's motto was that they only went in the oven when you heard the front gate open.

A seamstress would make the hostess (and daughters) two dresses: one for the afternoon, when some were invited for lunch and afternoon tea, and an evening dress for cocktails. *Tante* Fortune would design new dresses or make alterations, turning older ones into that year's fashion – especially following our financial misfortunes. After her family left Alexandria for good, Fortune's duties were transferred to *Usta* Paolo, the tailor, who had a dumb son-in-law, Emilio, who had once been his apprentice. Among the team was also the Alexandrian Jewish hairdresser Diaa, who, like all *coiffeurs* I encountered, was gay – perhaps the only Jewish gay who didn't try to hide it in those days.

On the day itself, the close circle of friends would arrive early to have lunch. They would exchange gossip and plot against their husbands, to force them into paying for the latest fashion and passing fancies – Eve's tricks for charming her 'old man' into submission. *Moda* was always a favourite subject. Paris was the fashion world's throbbing heart, and the latest *moda* design from *La Ville Lumière* or Milan would appear in Alexandria virtually the next day.

I recall *Tante* Yvonne's London visit (as instructed by *Maman* to check on my accommodation and studies); she was horrified by the Englishwomen still in 1950s fashion.

'The war ended years ago', she shrieked, 'Why are *l'anglaisiat* still years behind Alexandria's moda?' She was trying on hats in Great Portland Street, which in the early 1960s was full of sweatshops making garments, hats, scarves and accessories exhibited in the street's small shops at a fraction of their prices down the road in Selfridges.

My mother referred to her reception as 'The Tuesday'. It wasn't just a party or a social visit but a mixture of a cultural, entertainment and political-discussion event – something like today's group therapy. There was always someone playing the piano, especially in the evening, since the instrument was part of the furniture in most of Alexandria's middle-class homes. Those without a piano played records on the electric gramophone, a piece of *mobilia* that was polished and cared for. When in Moharrem-Bey, *Tante* Carlota and Ziezi took turns playing and singing. The latest copies of fashion, gossip and intellectual magazines would be on the coffee tables of the *salle d'entrée* and on the salon's marble tabletops. The latter room had gold-leaf sofas, armchairs and chairs, all upholstered in *velours brodé*. I often wondered why all ladies' salons and *salles d'entrées* looked similar, the same as my mother's; 65 years later, I am none the wiser.

The latest copies of *Life, Paris Match, Al-Musawar* or *Moda* were always there – and often older copies of feminist publications, like the

Alexandria Adieu

weekly *L'Egyptienne*, which had stopped in 1940 after 15 years (although my mother later started keeping them under wraps), and the monthly *Bent-el-Nile* (the Nile's Maiden), launched by the activist lawyer and writer Doria Shafik (1908–1975). The earlier Egyptian feminist movement was a middle-class phenomenon led by French-educated intellectual ladies. Unlike modern feminists, they weren't ideological extremists nor encouraged divorce and splitting families but addressed real issues affecting the underprivileged woman. They tackled problems like inequality, sanitation in the countryside, women's health and free education for girls. These women's-movement activists were engaged in charitable work on the ground and actions to improve women's lot – especially the less fortunate ones – and address their needs.

The ladies' discussions varied; they might cover a published article, an issue, a short story or a film review, with someone using one of the publications on display to back up her view. Some of the more thinly attended afternoon sessions were group therapy or brainstorming to find solutions for those seeking help. They were often solutions to some feminine issues, openly discussed. My mother ensured that children, especially the boys, were temporarily exiled to the garden, a playroom or taken out of the house altogether to protect their virgin ears from penetration by sordid details. My sister; my cousins, who'd come with my aunties; and I used to devise ways of eavesdropping on the conversation, giving us thrills – the latest in body-hair removal or how to lose weight. The conversation often led to best tricks to keeping a husband interested instead of going out, or keeping him out if the woman concerned had gone off sex – or, worse, having an affair since all was permissible (with discretion) except the sole taboo: divorce. All advice and therapies aimed at avoiding divorce at all cost.

One of our favourite stories was that of 20-something Elham, who joined her mother at a Tuesday reception. Elham was, tearfully, seeking advice about whether to leave her husband, who was having an affair.

'Shut-up, silly little cow,' said my mother to the stunned girl, 'why do you let him go into another woman's arms?' Poor, shocked Elham wasn't used to the older lady using such terms in telling her off.

'What does the other girl have that you don't?' She advised the girl to focus on tarting herself up to win her man back, never to broach the subject with him and to take some champagne from our kitchen on her way home:

'Remove your body hair, play romantic music and exhaust the jackass in bed every night – and leave nothing for the other girl.'

Such instructions were one of the factors explaining some of the mystery surrounding Um Shlomo's visits. Um Shlomo, the Jewish *daya* who also doubled as a private beautician, had a weekly two-hour session

CHAPTER 19   The War Generation

with the household females. Sometimes a teenage girl in the family who was coming of age, mostly around 14, would join Um Shlomo's mysterious sessions. Later I understood it was the girl's initiation into grown-up femininity with its practice and endless preparation that, soon, would attract a suitable young man and also drive him mad after marriage. In our house, Um Shlomo's arcane rituals were held in the en-suite bathroom attached to my mother's bedroom, or a spacious upstairs room overlooking the back garden if we were in the villa. The men wouldn't be in the house, nor would the children – particularly boys; they would be on a day out, accompanied by Bellitta.

I was in my teenage years before I was let into some of the guarded secrets of womanhood – like the rituals of *halawah* (body-hair-removal technique). The *halawah* waxing method went back thousands of years to ancient Egyptian times: a mixture of sugary syrup, lemon and lime, and some secret ingredients passed down the generations. I was shown and told the details by Shams, a girlfriend from El-Amirah Faiza School. Shams described how women like Um Shlomo mixed the ingredients and heated them to the right temperature on a spirit stove, then moved and kneaded and squeezed and twisted them between the fingers before applying to the legs, thighs or pubic area of the female body. It was left for a few seconds then pulling off with the hair, roots and all. It left the skin smooth for days without the stubble left by shaving.

'Like my skin', said my girlfriend, mischievously guiding my hand from her toes slowly up her leg to her thighs.

'Make the *halawah* too hot, and it would be runny and sticky and impossible take off the skin, or too hard and cold, and it won't attach to the body hair' – Shams's sexy voice became the soundtrack to a silent movie I was watching.

It was a Thursday afternoon when she invited me to her room at the rear of their house in north Moharrem-Bey. We hid behind the shutters and watched across a narrow passage leading to a courtyard. The event was taking place in a home opposite hers on a lower level, giving us a full view of mostly naked women going through the *halawah* ritual, every step of which my girlfriend explained in detail like a 1950s beauty-contest television commentator. Some, especially younger ones, screamed in pain when the *halawah* pad was pulled from their pubic area, then giggled, hiding their faces in both hands. Their reaction and the scene itself made me think of poor Elham and what she must have gone through to win against a rival. I had to share Elham's story with my girlfriend, who chuckled, adding that pulling the *halawah* pad was a bit painful, 'but it is quite sensual, leaving one feeling sexy, with the urge to make love'. She tossed her blondish hair, the feature behind her name: Shams – 'sunshine'.

'So, it was a mixture of pain, pleasure and sensual arousal that Elham went through, then?' I asked.

'Your mother gave her the right prescription in the appropriate dose', said Shams, enquiring what was to become of Elham and her marriage.

I remembered that when Elham followed the instructions and headed to our kitchen for the champagne, my mother called after her, 'and never let him find out that you have found out about the affair'. The girl lived happily ever after.

'Of course,' said Shams, who was – like most Alexandrian girls – much wiser than her years.

My mother and her friends were a bunch of tough, wise, elegant ladies who had survived the War. Some had survived two world wars; others, concentration camps; some had even volunteered as nurses with the Allied troops, and served in the army or with the civil-defence forces. But they never lost touch with their feminine side, and made sure of their full maquillage, elegant dresses, perfect manicures and being there for their families. Being a wife and a mother while engaging in charitable work was a full-time job. Oozing femininity, they were strong – in command of their families and of any situation. They also knew how to deal with emergencies and unexpected crises.

They were no-nonsense ladies. And I often wonder what they would have made of today's 'snowflakes' or girls taking offence at a little affectionate name, innocently verbalised. I even recall occasions when girls were disappointed when not hearing a single wolf-whistle when riding a bicycle or playing ball on the beach. Marriage was sacred; a married couple from that generation would sacrifice anything and engage in all kinds of pretence just to keep the family together for the sake of the children.

'The BBC Woman's Hour destroyed more homes than the Luftwaffe managed to do', was one of *Maman's* immortal phrases.

The Great War Gentlemen
Some visitors who sought my grandfather's advice irritated my mother, who verbalised her dislike of countryside migrants, especially those who retained their *fellaheen* customs.

'Why couldn't they see him in his disused office in El-Balad' she often murmured. In fact, anyone from outside Alexandria – even from Cairo – was *fellah* in her book – a subconscious attitude, most likely inherited from her Ottoman migrant parents. My mother had been about four when her mother died during the Great War.

My grandfather retired in 1948; shortly thereafter, King Farouk gave his school an award – it came among the top ten best-performing

CHAPTER 19   The War Generation

schools in Egypt and Sudan – and for his service to the local community when he was its headmaster. He remarried in 1917 to the elegant, stone-hearted Dora (Dorotea) Hanem; she was half Maltese. Most migrants who were subjects of the defeated Ottoman Empire became naturalised Egyptians after independence in 1922. Many former Ottomans, including Jews, joined the Egyptian nationalist movement with Sa'd Zaghloul Pasha. My grandfather was among those activists of the 1919 revolution advocating reforms, and he became a passionate *wafdi*. Many of those Ottoman migrants now considered Egypt their home, and saw independence as an opportunity to progress and trade with new markets overseas. The Egyptianised migrants, in their passion for an Egypt independent from British influence, were 'more Catholic than the pope', as my mother used to cynically criticise my grandfather and his friends. Perhaps she had a Nostradamic vision, sensing how the Nilotic Egyptians would, within a few years, betray those who helped them win independence, build their country and to prosper economically.

Behind her strong front, my mother carried deep, painful scars and hurt from her childhood experiences. She was traumatised by her biological mother's death. The childless Dora – whose only boy died in 1920 and who suffered a complicated miscarriage, rendering her unable to conceive – took out her frustration and hurt on her stepdaughter. She ill-treated her and even physically abused her in a classic childless-stepmother scenario. Dementia erased 50 years from my mother's memory: in 1999, she treated me like a schoolboy, checking whether I did my homework, and instructed imaginary maids to assist her in getting ready for my father coming home 20 years after his death. But her memory of her stepmother's abuse was there in minute detail: she showed me imaginary bruises on her arms, and grimacing when I touched them. Dora had died during the War: she contracted septicaemia following a shrapnel injury when a bomb dropped on the house she sheltered in its doorway during a German air raid.

My grandfather often testified to European Jews' role in Egypt's nationalist independence movement as they shared other Egyptians' distrust of *les Anglais* and disliked their snobbish anti-Semitism and the superiority complex behind some of their more stupid actions. I was confused as a teenager by his British-educated friends sharing his anti-*Anglaises* sentiments; I only began to understand that generation's conflicting feelings towards Britain after I moved to England.

Deploying the subtle British racism that only non-born British individuals could spot, *les Anglais* often alienate you with small, elusive, subtle reminders that you might be British legally and culturally but you still weren't 'one of us' or you 'don't belong here' – an attitude that only gets worse when they assume you are of a Jewish heritage. Contrary to the common belief, the more left-wing and liberal the crowd you find yourself in, the more anti-Semitic, racist and xenophobic signals and alienating remarks they will throw at you.

In 1991, I sat in Broadcasting House's reception area waiting to go on the Radio 4 'World At One' programme when a journalist (who is now a top BBC TV star with his own slot) approached an African man in an open-necked shirt and inexpensive jacket, asking, 'Mr Darwish?' I have, for several years, appeared regularly on television current-affairs programmes, supposedly watched by journalists like him; yet the Cambridge-graduate BBC man was mentally blind to the idea that an ordinary-looking white gentleman in a Savile Row three-piece suit could replace the image his mind created for someone born in Egypt.

A month after the 2011 Egyptian uprising that overthrew President Hosni Mubarak (1928–2020), I was at the Groucho Club with two *Guardian* female journalists following my colleague Nick Cohen's book launch. We ran into a restless young man – the *paper's* news editor. He nagged me non-stop to know 'my feelings' about Egypt. I was puzzled, since my interest (not my 'feelings') was that of a journalist following a foreign news story. The young *Guardian* man kept insisting, in an impatient teenager's manner, that I must 'have feelings about [my] country, Egypt' (which, for me, has been a foreign country, like many I have reported on, since the 1960s.) The leftie's message was that I belonged not here but over there – further south – thus, I worked with my emotions rather than with my skills or experience, which, at the time, was longer than the years he had walked the Earth.

And the combination of racist-led stereotyping and lazy ignorance behind the BBC man's and the *Guardian* journalist's attitudes has been perpetuated over the years by a creative and media industry dominated by the liberal left. The 1991 ITV adaptation of Agatha Christie's 'The Theft of the Royal Ruby' in the third series of *Poirot* – directed by Andrew Grieve, and dramatised by Anthony Horowitz and Clive Exton – is a case in point. Prince Farouk was just under 16 when he succeeded his father, Fuad I, in 1936. The drama, set (in 1931) when Farouk would have been a boy of 11, inaccurately introduced the prince as 20 years old with the usual negative, racist stereotyping. Similarly to the *Guardian*-adolescent's and the BBC journalist's expectations, Grieve presented the heir to Egypt's throne as an emotional, excitable, old dark-skinned fool, portrayed by an Asian-British actor. Farouk was genetically white Caucasian from European stock. His mother was the great-great-granddaughter of the French Suleiman Pasha, General Joseph Anthelme Sève.[1] On his father's side, Farouk was the grandson

CHAPTER 19   The War Generation

of Khedive Ismail, who by marriage added Italian and Austrian blood to Farouk's grandfather's Macedonian and Greek genes. Prince Farouk, factually, had blue-grey eyes and was as pale in complexion as the 'European' detective Poirot. Farouk was sophisticated and calm thanks to his British tutor, Mrs Nayler, whose 'English influence' irritated his French-educated Alexandria born mother, Queen Nazli.[2] 'Farouk who spoke English well,' wrote British High Commissioner Sir Miles Lampson (1880-1964) in his diary on the eve of the young prince departure to England in October 1935, 'was in fact like an overgrown English boy.'[3]

The Retired Headmaster
It was paradoxical to see how cruelly my grandfather, an Egyptian patriot by choice, was treated by the Egyptian Muslims that he championed. He kept his political activities out of the staff room and the classroom, encouraging his pupils to debate freely and neutrally. Consequently, he had to seek the help of *les Anglais*, whom he actually wanted out of the country.

He was suspended without pay following a report from a corrupt Nilotic-Egyptian Education Ministry official from a rival party, who found out about his political affiliation. The ministry official tried to blackmail my grandfather, threatening to send a secret file about his activities during the 1919–22 movement to the inspector in charge of conduct. Teachers, judges and other civil servants were banned from political activities or taking a second job. The corrupt official carried out his threat when my grandfather showed him the door. When the ministry appeal board had procrastinated for nearly two years, my grandfather spoke to the British chief inspector about setting a hearing date. Despite their subtle racism and anti-Semitism, the wronged teacher admired *les Anglais*' 'sense of justice and fair play, and their championing of the underdog'. The tribunal unanimously reinstated my grandfather to his post. The reimbursement of two years' salary, with interest, enabled him to build Villa Alexandrine in Sidi-Bishr. It stood on a sandy plot that he purchased from the fabric merchant Monsieur Hammami, who had a magnificent three-storey shop on Rue Tawfik Pasha. My grandfather and my father had accounts with the fine-fabrics merchant, enabling Paolo the tailor to procure material for their winter and summer suits.

Enlisting the help of *les Anglais* while actively working to kick them out of Egypt was a blot on my grandfather's reputation, however. His enemies continued to exploit this, giving the military-coup regime another pretext to target him. My grandfather, the history teacher, alerted me early on to the components making up Alexandria's –and the country's – identity.

Alexandria Adieu

'Royal Egypt got its modern culture and civilised education from the French, while arts, music, and modern architecture came from the Italians', he often reiterated. The British strengthened political representation and a free press, and helped with massive engineering projects, 'although *les Angliases* did not finance them but, on the contrary, made huge profits from the ventures', was his verdict.

Strangely, what has been left over as a legacy of only three years of Bonaparte's expedition and 70 years of British presence is the classical French-style anti-Anglo-Saxon sentiment still prevalent in Egypt today.

The Tarboosh Prophecy

In 1953, my grandfather was angered by a front-page picture of the regime leader, General Naguib Bey, receiving a visiting foreign delegation while sporting a *casquette les Anglais* instead of the official Egyptian tarboosh. The old patriot interpreted Naguib's gesture as a betrayal of a long struggle against British occupation. He considered the ending of the tarboosh's status as the nation's official headdress to mark the beginning of a slippery slope of betrayal by the military regime and the abandoning of scared national symbols, a loss of Egyptian identity and a reneging on their promises to the people.

'Those misguided adolescent *fellaheen* will lose everything, mark my words; they will sell the nation's heritage, the pyramids and the Nile itself', he said, shaking his head and tossing the torn newspaper into the bin.

It was a sign that the officers' leader, Naguib, had become '*Les Anglais*' slave'. He kept repeating that he suspected the army officers were serving the British. It was rumoured then, in 1953, that the British had known about the 1952 military coup and had been in touch with the officers but were happy, without actually encouraging them, to get rid of the king. This account turned out to be true after documents were released years later and books were written on the subject.[4] In his negotiations with the then UK foreign secretary, Anthony Eden, in 1954, Colonel Nasser, who became president, relinquished Sudan to the British. Refusing to separate Sudan from Egypt had been a sticking point, causing Britain to fall out with the traditionally pro- *Anglais* Wafd party supported by King Farouk.

Until he died in 1976, my grandfather still sported his tarboosh in winter and a Borsalino straw hat in the summer with the rest of his attire – precisely as he had on the day he retired in 1948.

While a state-school headmaster, my grandfather had urged his staff to compete with top education institutions like Victoria College, St Marks and Lycée Français rather than other state schools.

CHAPTER 19   The War Generation

He encouraged foreign-language and history and music teachers, who were also giving drama lessons, to spend the school holidays in Europe and bring back the latest in books and music records. He bullied wealthy, local, often illiterate, merchants into funding a school play or hosting a concert. The hapless *me'alem* (merchant) would have little choice but to agree with the headmaster for the sake of his son who needed extra tuition time.

His school started a tradition copied by others, the alpha in exams of every class would go on educational trips to visit ancient monuments between Alexandria and Aswan, and from Sinai to Siwa, besides visiting the Opera and the Egyptian Museum in Cairo. When boys couldn't afford the trip's cost, the headmaster urged some wealthy merchants to donate, and he gave them classically framed paintings and pottery made by the pupils. The less-cultured traders would be embarrassed into outdoing each other, and coughed up enough funds for the trip. The boys had to hand over every *piastre* of their pocket money to teachers in charge, so nobody knew who was self-financed and who was funded by the school.

During his service, my grandfather never claimed overtime and took a Robespierrean anti-corruption stand all his life. He once threw out a wealthy landowner from the countryside who tried to bribe him, saying, 'Use your money to improve your son's fat head.' But he would, to the annoyance of my mother, have time and give hospitality to the poor *fellaheen* and dispense free advice, helping with filling in forms and running errands for them.

Many of my grandfather's predictions in 1953 about the damage the officers would inflict on Egypt came true. Among their early casualties was the illiteracy-eradication scheme, which had been running for many years. My grandfather ran the programme in the industrial areas of Nuzha, which generated extra income for him. In the 1940s, the Ministry of Education, in collaboration with businesses and industrialists, had launched a bold plan to combat illiteracy among less-fortunate migrant workers from the countryside. The industries had funded the larger part of the scheme by providing facilities such as classrooms and transport on top of various incentives – including rewarding participants with overtime pay on hourly classroom attendance, added to their weekly wages. The ministry provided textbooks, and educators (who were retired teachers) were paid extra on top of their pensions to take these classes in the evenings and at weekends. The military regime stopped the scheme. The move was widely interpreted as the officers preferring to deal with an illiterate working class than one that could read and write. The years 1952–4 witnessed civil unrest and protests – notably, a strike organised by union workers in a textile complex, which ended violently with the intervention of the security forces and the public hanging of workers' leaders only 11 days after the officers had taken power in the July 1952 coup.

PART V
THE FOUNDATIONS OF MODERNITY

CHAPTER 20
Hats, *Hantours* and Harlots

My first memorable train journey was with my grandfather in 1949. The retired headmaster was in his sartorial element – a three-piece summer suit, tarboosh and his essential *accessoires*: pocket watch attached to a silver *catena*, sliver-topped *ebenosa* (walking stick) and horsetail fly-swat with an ivory handle in the shape of a hoopoe-bird's head. The family was at Sidi-Bishr for the approaching Easter break while I stayed with my grandfather at his El-Balad home near the Bourse to finish some errands. We visited Dr Orvand for a check-up on my arm; I had had the plaster cast removed a few weeks earlier at The Israeli Hospital. My grandfather had a fitting appointment with *Usta* Paolo and also needed to pick up a summer pair from the shoemaker. We also visited Rue France to leave his tarboosh (one of his two winter-tarbooshes) for its annual service with *Usta* Zaki, the Jewish *tarabishi*, agent for P. & C. Habig.[*]

This Viennese firm had become Europe's largest tarboosh makers and exporters after the headgear became part of the Bosniaks Division of the Austro-Hungarian Army. Ibrahim Pasha made the tarboosh an obligatory part of the Egyptian Army uniform in 1820, importing 500,000 tarbooshes annually from Austria. The 1825 tarboosh workshops weren't enough for the growing demand. The tarboosh became a symbol of middle-class respectability, worn by civil servants and traders, and later part of Egypt's school uniform. *Usta* Zaki had a workshop off Rue France; his apprentices steam-cleaned the tarboosh felt, pressing it inside two-brass heated moulds, and replaced the tassel

---

[*] P. & C. Habig is a (now fifth-generation) hat manufacturer and former supplier to the Imperial and Royal Court in the Austrian capital.

and silk lining. My grandfather picked a readily serviced tarboosh in a box and a Borsalino straw hat.

We took a *hantour*, a horse-drawn four-wheel cabriolet also known as *A'rabia* (not to be confused with the post-1980 Arabised name for motorcar – an automobile for my generation). The *A'rabia* had a large, waxed leather *capote* (bonnet) folded back and forth by two steel levers on hinges. There were two oil lanterns on the sides of the *hantour* for night journeys. It could take four people comfortably and five at a pinch as it also had a folded seat behind the *a'rbagi's* (cabbie's/cabman's) raised seat. *Hantours* cost a few *piastres* more than a taxi ride, but fashionable gentlemen and ladies preferred them because, unlike taxis, they could get on and off without bending while keeping hats or tarbooshes on.

The *a'rbagi* used a *kurbag*, a nearly two-metre-long bamboo stick with a longer leather whip attached. He often needed to lash backwards at boys hitching a ride on the vehicle's back axle, whether in response to a 'Behind you' pantomime-style alert – '*kurbag wara*' – from a passer-by or as a genuine warning to a mischievous boy who had snatched something from a vendor. The *kurbag wara* action saw an *a'rbagi* taking his frustration out in response to naughty quips and vulgar puns from teenagers.

'Come back here!'
Hantour cabbies were traditionally a subject of bawdy jokes, a combination of reputation and folkloric memories. They were notorious for overcharging out-of-towners and couples going for a romantic ride on the deserted autumn corniche or along the leafy banks of Mahmoudiyah Canal with the carriage *capote* fully drawn, concealing the lovers. *Hantour* services generated sub-industries like wheelwrights' workshops and horse stables. The trade concentrated in two areas west of Ragheb Pasha and north of Karmouz called Gabaliyat-al-o'llel and Kom-bakir.

There was, in fact, no *gabaliya* (mound), and the *o'llel* (fired-clay water pot) shops had vanished in the eighteenth century. Neither was there a *Kom* (hill) or any character called Bakir in this flat area of narrow streets, part of the grid created by Dinocrates in the ancient village of Rhakotis 1,500 years earlier. That quarter had remained ill-reputed since it was reported as such by visitors to Alexandria in the seventh century. Brothels were legal until 1949, with regular medical check-ups on their working girls organised by the local health authority under the 1885 Medical and Public Health Act. Prostitution itself didn't become illegal until 1951, pushing the trade underground and coining a new term, *beit-serry* (a concealed house), for a brothel. It quickly replaced *beit-el-a'ya* ('handsome madam's house'); *a'ya* was

Chapter 20   Hats, Hantours and Harlots

the presentable madam in charge while *ma'toura* (a trailer) referred to the subordinate sex worker. The trade flourished throughout the Great War, with thousands of British and Empire soldiers gathering in Alexandria, waiting to be shipped to killing fields like Gallipoli. Half-naked women sat on doorsteps in the narrow streets of the area calling after the soldiers, if they didn't stop to examine the 'goods' displayed, to 'Come back here', pronouncing the call 'Kom-back-ir'. Australian and British soldiers began using the phrase in the high-pitch tone of the area's women as a destination to give the *hantour arbagis*, who started providing a shuttle service between *Kom-back-ir* and the camps, thus earning a pimping reputation in Alexandrian folklore.

It was a profession and a trade like any other in a metropolis's complex economy, creating jobs and providing a living for thousands: cabbies; local shop, café, bar and restaurant proprietors, landlords, seamstresses, cleaners, housemaids, doctors, nurses and pharmacists. They, in turn, generated more jobs for the chain of services and suppliers. The area and its vice had been mentioned repeatedly in Alexandria's literature. The adaptation of Durrell's *Quartet* into the 1969 movie *Justine* depicted the quarter's seedy, narrow, vice-ridden streets in 1938 Alexandria. Justine was played by the French actress Anouk Aimée while Melissa, the prostitute, was portrayed by the Danish actress Anna Karina (1940–2019). In one memoir, not only did the author give a colourful eyewitness account of life in 'Kom-back-ir' but he also detailed how his school friend led a double life. The friend, who studied Quranic reciting and basic Islamic creed under his mosque-imam father's influence, didn't follow in his footsteps but opted for a well-paid job at a crystal factory. But he fell in love with an attractive prostitute working in a Kom-bakir brothel and became her lover–pimp. When his father died, he came under massive pressure from the mosque foundation – run by his former tutors – to replace the old man as imam. The poor chap had to give up his foremanship at the crystal works but could not give up his *fille de joie*, sneaking out of her bed at dawn and rushing to the mosque to lead the morning prayers. It was a scenario reminiscent of that faced by the *gendarme*-cum-pimp Nestor Patou, played by Jack Lemmon in Billy Wilder's 1963 comedy *Irma la Douce*, who gets up at the crack of dawn for a day job to support his working girl but can't quite get her off the game. For years the lover–sheikh would spend the day teaching Quranic verses to children in the mosque's *kuttab* (madrasah) and leading the day's prayers before hurrying in the evening back to Kom-bakir to attend to his courtesan's needs.[1]

CHAPTER 21
The Railways: Politics and Play

The *hantour* dropped us at Mehatet-Masr, as Alexandria Central Railway Station was, and still is, known, with its impressive facade, colonnades and large glass windows. The station was rebuilt during the Great War by Lasciac assisted by the Greek civil engineer Leonidas Iconomopolous (Economopolous), when they designed a grandly scaled square for the terminus between 1915 and 1925. Lasciac's design replaced the original one built 60 years earlier by British Engineer Edwin C. Baines,[1] who was part of Stephenson Engineers team contracted to construct the Alexandria–Cairo railway line. The line itself became operational in 1854 but was officially opened in 1856, as the first in Africa and preceding the Ottomans' mainland network. Sidi Gaber,[2] 3 kilometres to the east, was the main terminal before Mehatet-Masr was completed and became operational in 1856.[3]

The railway project started in 1833, later than Muhammad Ali had planned. He brought the rails from England in the 1820s for a Suez–Cairo line to improve the mail service and transit between Europe and India.[4] The French, who were canvassing to build the Suez Canal, pressured him to abandon it. The connection to Suez, making the first modern transport link between the Mediterranean and the Indian Ocean, began in 1858 by Said Pasha (1822–1863), after whom the Mediterranean town by the northern entrance to the finished canal was named. The Alexandria–Suez continuous link was not completed until 1869; its route, going through agricultural areas with better access to fresh water,[5] was preferred to that of the 1858-built,[6] direct, shorter (144 kilometres) Cairo–Suez desert line.[7] The latter became operational again in 1930.

CHAPTER 21   The Railways: Politics and Play

Muhammad Ali had the foresight to be sceptical of the Suez Canal idea, fearing it would give the British a pretext to control Egypt. Construction on the Alexandria–Cairo line was started by his son, Viceroy Abbas Helmi I Pasha (1812–1854) in 1851, commissioning the British steam-engine pioneer Robert Stephenson (1803–1859).[8] It began operation in 1852, and started carrying goods and passengers the next year. In 1858, Said's 32-year-old heir, Ahmad Rifaat Pasha (1825–1858), drowned when the train taking him from Alexandria fell off the 24-metre river float designed by Stephenson and used to take the train across the Rosetta branch of the Nile to the Delta.[9] The tragedy accelerated the building of the 500-metre-long Kafr-El-zayyat swing bridge.[10]

Alexandria's terminus had space for carriages leading to two service roads, one along each side, with wrought-iron railings and arched gates – rather like the old King's Cross Station before philistine architects and London planners removed the gates on Euston Road in the 1960s.

Mehatet-Masr's main royal gate faced west to the great square, still called Place Mehatet-Masr by Alexandrians tired of the repeated square's renaming at the whim of Egypt's military presidents. Two other gates faced Kom-el-Dikka military hill and a further entrance at the northwest led to the *Terzo* (third-class) ticket hall for cars with wooden seats. Other gates faced Rue Moharrem-Bey and service slip road used by Post Office vehicles.

The northern slip road was an extension of Rue Grenfell, named after Field Marshal Francis Wallace Grenfell (1841–1925),* the second Sirdar of the Egyptian Army.† The first sirdar was Sir Evelyn Wood (1838–1919) and great names followed him, like that of Lord Kitchener. Sir Reginald Wingate (1861-1953) also had a street named after him in the Fleming district of Alexandria, and people still call it Rue Wingate, while stores and businesses also use the name of Wingate in same neighbourhood. The sentiment is not confined to Alexandria, either: Caireans still call Chubra General Infirmary by its original name, 'Hôpital Kitchener'. Kitchener requisitioned the hospital, soon after it had been opened in 1915 by the Austro-Hungarian Society, to treat British soldiers. It was renamed Lord Kitchener Memorial Hospital for Maternity and Children, with its reputable nursing and obstetrics school, by an Egyptian charity trust after buying the Kitchener estate

---

*Lord Grenfell GCB, GCMG, fought in the Anglo-Zulu War and with the Anglo-Egyptian Army in the Battle of Suakin against the Mahdists in 1888, and at the Battle of Toski the following year.
† The rank was equivalent to chief of the army although the constitutional head of the state was colonel of chief.

191

Alexandria Adieu

in 1925. The rank of sirdar, always occupied by a British general, was abolished after signing the 1936 Anglo–Egyptian Treaty. The last sirdar was Sir Charlton Spinks (1877-1959).

The rebuilt Art Deco station entrance from the Rue Grenfell slip road was first built with a glass canopy resembling the one between Marylebone station and the Landmark Hotel in London. The *primo* and *secondo* ticket hall was decorated in fine plasterwork, and its mosaic floor lead through to waiting rooms, the station master's offices and the *tashehillat* (the military facilitation bureau). The bureau, a legacy of the two world wars, was given prominence over any other facilities by the 1952 coup regime to remind the people who were the actual ruling elite.

The top, eastern stretch of the Grenfell slip road also led to the goods wagons and Post Office cars at the top of Platform II, where the express trains to Cairo and Aswan departed, pulled by powerful steam engines that became my childhood preoccupation. One train driver of Italian heritage had a crush on Bellitta, so he often let me sit in his steam-engine cabin. She would take cakes and sweets to bribe the driver and his *a'tashgi* (fireman/boilerman) to let me pretend to drive the engine. One weekend, I rode in Santo's engine facing Alexandria, which decoupled itself from the express when it departed for Cairo. The steam engine travelled backwards to Hadra workshop to be turned around to face north and refill with water and more coal. I was over the moon when Santo let me pull the cord to hoot as we approached level crossings, letting out three long whistles when we passed Helmy, the signal-box operator. I was helped by Fathy, the fireman, who lifted his heavy shovel to feed coal into the roaring fire. When we arrived at the railway works in Hadra, I ran straight to look at the machinery. Bellitta gave the engineers cakes and sweets, and we got a lift with another engine back to Mehatet-Masr. My neat Sunday clothes were covered in black soot, grease, coal dust and dirt; *Maman* was furious with Bellitta. But my grandfather told her it was an experience of which most boys could only dream.

Bellitta once persuaded a steamroller operator to let me ride with him, going up and down Rue Nineteen during its resurfacing. This time, my mother was angry not only because my clothes were beyond salvage but also because I had sticky tar in my hair and on my arms and legs.

Bellitta was great at organising those encounters. We also paid a few visits *to el-matafy*, the Kom-el-Dikka central fire station on Rue Tosson. The engines and ladders were Edwardian, painted red with brass fittings as shiny as the firemen's brass helmets. Besides the usual cakes and Bellitta flirting with the firemen, our family also used to donate to the service. They let me explore the fire-engine parts and help

CHAPTER 21   The Railways: Politics and Play

with turning the handle to swing the ladder. The real treat was to climb up the training tower and watching the firemen slide down the pole.

Another favourite was visiting the railway signal box above the 'chicken canal' bridge reached by a stone staircase. Bellitta also befriended *A'am* Helmy, the operator when, on a weekend shift, she would take cakes and a thermos flask with tea. He let me pull the points levers with him; then I would run to the smoke-covered windows as soon as I heard the train whistle, and wave at the train driver when he passed the kiosk. Helmy let me drop the brass tablet with the train number into a box with the words '*maslahat Sekka-hadid*" in Arabic and '*Intérêt des Chemins de fer*' in French.

An *intérêt* was, administratively, a sub-department of a ministry – like those for roads, bridges and canals; civil aviation, or ports and lighthouses. The railways were also a *maslahat* and, along with the post office and telegraph service, came under the Wizarat al-Mouasalat (Department of Communications and Transport).

When organising the civil service in a pyramidical bureaucracy as a managed system to collect taxes, Muhammad Ali employed French technocrats. They used names with French concepts, such as *maslahat* for 'the people's interest', for bodies that were run by permanent civil servants. The civil service expanded in 1848–54 during Abbas Helmi I's reign (1848–54) and that of Ali's fourth son, Said Pasha, and was completed under the moderniser Viceroy Ismail Pasha.

The post-coup military autocracy changed names to reflect its calamitous philosophy. *Maslahat* became *ha'ieah*, which had an imposing Kafkaesque subtext: 'He's of *a hai'eah*' implied an enforcer's appearance. The new regime was imposing its order on the people instead of serving them.

The Age of Glamour and Etiquette
'*Shayyal*', the *a'rbagi* called out in the direction of a queue of porters in shabby blue uniforms under a sign warning that luggage carrying was restricted to *maslahat*-authorised porters only. A porter placed our bags on his trolley, disappearing into the railway station. My grandfather handed his engraved silver cigarette case to the vendor at the newspaper-and-tobacco kiosk. The man returned it filled with cigarettes, and handed the retired headmaster his favourite papers: le *Bourse*, *L'Egyptien*, *al-Missa* – Alexandria's evening newspaper – and *al-Masri*. The last-named was the country's second-largest circulation paper and a platform for the Wafd party.

---

* There is no one word in English to convey the meaning of a service (in this case, the railways) in the service of the public.

Alexandria Adieu

The porter was waiting with our luggage by a *primo* (first-class) car, even though nobody had told him which class we were travelling. The uneducated poor often figured out passengers' social backgrounds, and impressively tailored their service to get the highest *baksheesh*!

The first-class compartments had sliding frosted-glass-panelled doors, engraved with the crown and the railways emblem, opening to the corridor, and roller blinds on the door and each side window (two windows to the outside). Three small *abajuras* (*abat-jour*) were positioned on either side by mirrors above the upholstered benches. My grandfather hung his hat on a hook under the brass-mesh shelf on which he placed the box with the other hat and his briefcase. He tried to switch on an *abajura* above his seat several times, tapping the small lamp unsuccessfully. A Nubian train *sa'ie* (footman and wagon guard), in a neat yellow-greenish railways suit and red tarboosh, entered carrying a tray with two glasses of chilled water and handed my grandfather a numbered brass tablets for our luggage. My grandfather complained about lamp; the *sa'ie* apologetically said that he would report it. He returned a few minutes later, ushering in a couple and placing a ladies' hatbox and a briefcase on the shelf. A glamorous lady with a model's figure in her early thirties entered; she had the looks of Rita Hayworth but was about a couple of inches taller than the Hollywood star. She wore a tight black-and-white skirt with a side slit above her knee, black-and-white high heels, and a white jacket with large black flower-shaped buttons. Sporting a white hat with a starched, wide, dotted-net brim and a shiny black-and-white handbag, she was followed by a gentleman in his fifties dressed in a light-blue three-piece suit with a silver watch-*catena*, holding an ebony-handled horsetail-hair fly-swat.

Instead of the fashionable *ebenosa*, the gentleman held, obviously, the lady's folded parasol. My grandfather stood up as soon as she stepped into the compartment and nudged me to do likewise. The gentleman behind her grimaced at the thought of sharing a compartment with others, let alone a young boy. But his frown changed into a smile upon seeing my grandfather, who greeted the arrival with 'Aha, Ramzi Effendi? I haven't seen you since the War blackouts; you haven't changed a bit.' Ramzi Effendi introduced the lady – she was not his wife because she was a mademoiselle – followed by her family name instead of the usual Alexandrian, *l'madame*, or *l'hanem*. My grandfather kissed her hand, as this was expected of gentlemen on first introduction in those civilised days of strictly observed etiquette. The lady was most likely Muslim from the way in which she replied to my grandfather's small talk checking on her wellbeing: '*Merci beaucoup, alhamdulillah, kwayessa kettir ya bey*' ('Thank you very much, sir; I am, praise to Allah,

CHAPTER 21   The Railways: Politics and Play

very well'). When my grandfather introduced me after the lady sat down by the window opposite me, I offered to swap seats since she was travelling in the opposite direction. She took out some chocolate from her handbag, praising the courteous attitude of a little boy. In reality, I had said the first thought that came into my head after she caught me staring at her long legs and sexy feet arched in open-toed high heels.

The deputy station master arrived in a green-grey suit with a white starched collar, black tie and a neat tarboosh, sporting a King Fuad-style moustache. He apologised for the defective light, promising it would be fixed at the next station. Sidi-Gaber was 15 minutes later on the timetable, and was where trains waited ten minutes for east-of-Alexandria passengers to board. The station served as the main terminal for 22 years before Mehatet Masr was built. It was also a hub connecting Rosetta with the Abukeir lines – and linking the Marsa Matruh line to the Libyan Desert, the transport 'backbone' that had served the Eighth Army, enabling it to make a stand at Alamein and prevent the Germans from overrunning Alexandria.

Ramzi Effendi and my grandfather unfolded their newspapers, exchanging views about the bourse, politics and the folly of launching a war against Israel in 1948. The lady asked her companion to get her reading material: French, Italian and Arabic magazines and a hardcover book. The book was closed on a thin ivory bookmark with a silver hook and a delicate red-silk tassel at the end of it. She told me it was over 60 years old and had been made in India.

A Sidi-Gaber electrician brought a spare lamp. He was followed by the station master himself, more impeccably dressed than his Mehatet-Masr colleague, repeating the *maslahat's* apologies. He had the same King Fuad-style moustache. This made me wonder whether it was a compulsory fashion for white-collar staff since the onboard ticket inspector also sported a similar one – and I later noticed that all officials sporting the tarboosh, along with police and army officers, shaped their moustaches in a similar style.

Looking back in dismay and sorrow on that period, the train journey with all its encounters printed Alexandria and her way of life on my childhood mind at a time when everyone was still talking about the War.

This was a cocktail of matchless ingredients: British railway infrastructure and engines; European train cars and furniture; French social culture, etiquette, newspapers, bureaucracy and education system. Alexandrian ladies preferred *Mode Parisienne* (while many added touches of the Hollywood look and hairstyle); architecture, arts, music, theatre and opera were mostly Italian – as was the gentlemen's fashion. However, gentlemen also retained a touch of Ottoman masculinity as symbolised by the King Fuad-style moustache. Paradoxically, they kept the tarboosh as a sign of Egyptian independence – after it had been banned by Mustafa Kemal Atatürk (1881–1938) in Turkey – while phasing out symbols of a sultanate and the concept of the caliphate. Egyptian officialdom was very attached to this national symbol; it was worn by British personnel seconded to the civil service in Egypt and Sudan, and in the Egyptian police and armed forces. Charles Gordon Pasha (1833–1885) always sported the tarboosh after joining Khedive Ismail's service in 1873 and serving as his governor-general of Sudan (1877–9 and 1884–5). Gordon was in his tarboosh when, unarmed, he faced an overwhelming number of Mahdist Ansar assassins in Khartoum.

CHAPTER 22
Cairo Interlude

When we got off the train at Cairo Central Railway Station, we stepped into another world – profoundly different from European Alexandria. Bab-el-Hadid (the Iron Gate) – as Caireans named the railway station because it had a sizeable, arched iron gate – was also the title of a 1958 movie by Alexandrian filmmaker Youssef Chahine. Entirely shot within the vicinity of the station, *Bab-el-Hadid* was the first Egyptian movie to be written exclusively for the screen, and its characters were created for this scenario by prolific *scénariste* Abd-el-Hay-Adib (1928–2007). All the movies made by the county's large film industry until then had been adaptations of Egyptian novels and folk tales, world classics, theatre plays, Greek tragedies or adaptation of Hollywood musicals and European films.

Like Chahine's depiction a decade later, Bab-el-Hadid was noisy, dusty and not as European as Mehatet-Masr in Alexandria with its manicured lawns and flower beds. There were more *fellaheen* in the Cairo station concourse alone than I had seen in my entire life. Countryside passengers in *galabiyas* were pouring out of *terzo* train cars carrying braided-rush and bamboo baskets; only the *effendis* and ladies had suitcases, wheeled ahead of them by porters. The outside yard was raucous, hot and dusty, with shabbily dressed men shouting over the traffic noise to attract passengers into their waiting taxis and *hantours*. We took a black-and-white Cairo taxi to Chubra to stay with my grandfather's friend; they had been together in schools in Upper Egypt and Sudan in the 1920s. He lived in a two-storey 1890s villa. His wife, Saniya Hanem, had arms totally concealed by her many gold bracelets and jewellery. Their house was dim and seemed unwelcome, but my mood changed when I discovered their two granddaughters; the younger girl, Lucy, was two years my senior.

Alexandria Adieu

The Egyptian Museum – Maspero Pasha

The older girl, Lola, who attended a French school, became my guide in my first visit to the *Antiquekhaneh*, the famous Egyptian Museum. The cramped old museum was first built in 1835 in central Cairo near the opera house. But it became too small for the many Egyptian antiquities found by European Egyptologists. Auguste Mariette Pasha (1821–1881), director-general of Egypt's *Maslahat al-Athar* (Intérêt des antiquités) began to list antiquities in 1850. They were later moved to the *Antiquekhaneh* in 1902 at the request of another great Egyptologist, Gaston Maspero (1846–1916). Maspero could read hieroglyphics and speak and write Arabic at 20, at the age of 34, he became assistant to Mariette and succeeded him as head of antiquities in 1881.

Maspero Bey removed the sand from around the Sphinx, discovered and restored over 4,000 ancient Egyptian scripts, and fought hard to end tomb robberies and the smuggling of artefacts encouraged by British dealers. This led to several stand-offs with *les Anglais*. He even resigned briefly in 1892, but returned to his post after Khedive Tawfik gave him the title pasha. His largest 'catch' came in 1881: arresting the heads of the Abd-el-Rasool clan, the largest gang of tomb robbers, which led to the recovery of scores of mummies of ancient Egypt's great kings including Rameses II (1304–1214 BC). The events were documented in the 1969 movie *The Night of Counting the Years* – a well-made, accurate documentary-drama by Alexandrian filmmaker, designer, photographer and screenwriter Shadi Abd-el-Salam (1930–1986).

Gaston Maspero was also behind the 1912 Excavation and Antiquities Act, criminalising excavations of archaeological sites without the prior permissions granted to academics under supervision. The Act banned archaeologists from keeping half of their findings, restricting them to samples of relics or replicas of items in the museum. It obliged archaeologists to keep their sites safe and tidy, and required visitors to the museum and archaeological sites to pay entry fees – with the income going exclusively to maintaining the antiquities budget. Maspero Pasha appointed Howard Carter as chief inspector of archaeological sites in southern Egypt in 1905. It was Maspero who, in 1907, introduced Carter to the Fifth Earl of Carnarvon (George Edward Molyneux, 1866–1923), who financed his excavations – enabling him to make the most famous archaeological discovery of all time: that of the intact tomb of Tutankhamen in 1922–3. Part of the Nile Corniche is named after Maspero, as is the Egyptian Broadcasting House.

The impressive museum entrance was guarded by large granite figures of the Sphinx. My grandfather pointed to a tomb containing Mariette Pasha's remains – a stone-casket in the foyer, where he had been buried at his own request. The massive entrance hall was like a

CHAPTER 22   Cairo Interlude

mythical world, with too many antiquities and statues to count – and they looked extraordinarily magnificent and imposing, with some even intimidating. On my last visit there in autumn 2000, I had the same feeling I had had as a boy half a century earlier: that I would not spend a night in this hall for all the world's gold. The mummies recovered by Maspero in 1881 were displayed on the first floor.

The main attraction was the famous Rameses II (1303 -1213 BC), the third king of the Nineteenths Dynasty (1292-1190 BC) who ruled for six decades (1279-1213 BC) and was known for his extensive building programme. The rest of the hall was occupied by the mummies of the Eighteenth Dynasty (1549-1292 BC)*, starting at the entrance with its sixth king Thumosis III (1485-1425 BC), who co-reigned – as a child from 1479 BC with his stepmother Hatshepsut (1507-1458 BC), who was also his aunt and regent, for 21 years then ruled on his own until 1425 BC. It was during his reign, the biblical stories claim, that the Exodus and the plagues took place.

The dynasty itself was founded by Ahmose I, who ruled between 1539 and 1524 BC. Ahmose, known as the 'first liberator', led his army – equipped with the latest weaponry including two-horse chariots, the sickle sword and the composite bow – to rid the Delta of its occupying oppressors, the Hyksos kings *(hekau-Kha-sut)*. The Hyksos invaded northern Egypt from the area that is today's southern Levant and Jordan Valley, as recorded by the Egyptian Hellenic historian and priest, Manetho, in the third century BC. Manetho also arranged the translation of over 800 of Egypt's ancient books, which were kept at the Temple of Heliopolis, from hieroglyphics into Greek for the Bibliotheca Alexandrina. The Hyksos were relabelled 'settlers' under Colonel Nasser following his ill-fated federation with Syria, part of the land from which these 'settlers' originated according to Manetho's writings. However, the term 'Hyksos' is today used by Egyptians to negatively refer to an uncultured crowd or a mass of football hooligans.

The northern end of the museum's first floor housed the treasures of the best-known Egyptian king, Tutankhamun (1342–1323 BC) – a magnet for all its visitors. The king's gold-lined internal burial chamber was inside a giant glass cage. During Carter's and Lord Carnarvon's opening of the chamber in 1923, the latter was bitten by a mosquito and the sting was infected by a razor, leading to blood poisoning. He died later in a Cairo hospital, spawning the folkloric belief in a 'curse of the pharaohs'. After admiring the relics of the boy-king, especially

---

* Some reference books will mark the start as 1539 BC because of Ahmos, who was fully Egyptian although he was proceeded by Kamose (either his brother or father) as the founder of the dynasty in 1549 BC.

the golden burial mask and his magnificent chariot, I wanted to go around and see more. I was also fascinated by the inter-connected galleries displaying thousands of treasures. But we spent ages by 'King Tut's' treasures because Lola sat forever drawing Tutankhamen items in a book of foolscap-sized rough papers using coloured chalk crayons for her school project. We had sandwiches for lunch and spent the entire day there.

My grandfather was waiting for us in front of the museum; we walked across the green (Tahrir Square) into the old Hotel Semiramis by the Nile. Hotel Rameses II was built in 1907 and, when it had a roof garden added in 1931, it was renamed after the Assyrian queen Sammu Ramat. Known as Semiramis, she ruled from 811 to 806 BC, and was famed for her obsession with hanging gardens. We had high tea, like a scene from an Agatha Christie novel set in an Art Deco surrounding. Sadly, the hotel was burned down along with many other magnificent buildings when rioters ransacked central Cairo in January 1952. They targeted cafés, bars, cinemas, theatres, hotels and beauty salons among 750 buildings designed and built by European architects during the reign of the visionary khedives, Ismail and his son Tawfik.

The Nile Bridges

The next day, we took a single-deck river cruiser with rows of seats from a Rodh-el-Farag pier, sailing up the Nile. First, we passed under the 495-metre *Kupiri*[1] Imbaba. Linking the Delta and Upper Egypt railway lines, this bridge was built in 1891 by French engineer David Trampley. It was upgraded in 1924 with an added two-lane elevated level for motor cars by Belgian railway specialists Baume & Marpent, who constructed 158 bridges in Egypt.[2] Some 15 minutes later, the boat passed the affluent Zamalek Island, connected to one of the city's poorest quarters by *Kupiri* Abu el-Ella. This steel bridge was constructed in 1908 by Alexandre Gustave Eiffel (1832–1923) to open and close, allowing tall ships to pass to the Delta. But the French engineer's giant machinery opened and closed the bridge just once before jamming the massive structure; it has badly affected navigation on this stretch of the Nile ever since.[3] According to Cairo folklore, Monsieur Eiffel's failure led to his depression and eventual suicide in 1923.

My grandfather raised his voice to be heard over the diesel engine, instructing us to pay attention to architecture as we passed the Egyptian Museum. The boat was approaching the 932-metre-long arched Ismailia (Khedive Ismail Bridge). But the 1931 structure – built by Sir Ralph Freeman (1880–1950), who also designed the famous Sydney Harbour Bridge (1932) – was renamed *Kupiri*

CHAPTER 22   Cairo Interlude

Qasr-el-Nile by General Naguib's regime in 1953. It had been built to replace *Kupiri* al-Gezira when the latter could no longer cope with traffic volume.

The 1869–1871 al-Gezira bridge was commissioned by Khedive Ismail, who built 180 large bridges and 250 smaller ones on the Nile and its branches and canals during his 15-year reign. In addition to the Suez Canal, Ismail's massive infrastructure projects included 112 freshwater canals, totalling 13,500 kilometres in length, reclaiming an additional 770,000 hectares from desert and saline terrain.

Ismail also expanded Egypt's railway network, from 443 to 1,908 kilometres, into Sudan after his army annexed Kurdufan in 1874. He modernised Suez and Alexandria harbours with advanced lifting equipment to export refined sugar from 64 processing plants that increased exports over threefold in eight years, and built an extra 15 lighthouses. He founded the first school for girls in the Ottoman Empire during his education-expansion plan, increasing schools' numbers from 185 in 1863 to 4,685 by the mid-1870s. *Kupiri* al-Gezira was built by Linant Pasha, the chief engineer of al-Ashghal Alo'moumia (the Ministry of Public Works). The French-born engineer – full name, Louis Maurice Adolphe Linant de Bellefonds (1799–1883) – also participated in the construction of the Suez Canal between 1859 and 1869.

Inaugurated by King Fuad I in 1933, the current Khedive Ismail Bridge is famed for its four replica obelisks, two at either end, each guarded by a large bronze lion statue. The four oversized lions, cast by French sculptor and animalier Henri Alfred Jacquemart (1824–1896), were initially planned to stand guard around Jacquemart's earlier creation – the statue of Muhammad Ali Pasha on his horse in Alexandria's Place des Consuls in 1872. According to Alexandrian folklore, the pasha's statue has, ever since, been a protector of the city he had resurrected over six decades earlier. When the British bombed Alexandria for two days in July 1882 – reducing the area to rubble and damaging the British, Greek and French consulates on the square – only the pasha on his horse remained standing high above the ruins. Muhammad Ali Pasha's protective magic also prevailed during the Second World War when the Luftwaffe subjected Alexandria to the worst air raid that an Allied city outside Britain was to sustain, as Rommel's panzers approached. None of the bombs fell on the square, and the one that dropped nearby failed to explode. The campaign by Colonel Nasser (who spent his childhood in Alexandria) to tear down the history and memories of *Alexandrie royale* stopped at the square that Muhammad Ali Pasha protects. The officers didn't dare remove his statue, as they had done with those commemorating the rest of his dynasty. Superstitiously, the street signs announcing its new name '*Midan-el-Tahrir*' were carefully placed away from where the pasha's gaze fell.

Leaving Muhammad Ali Pasha to guard his square, Jacquemart's lions were given another assignment in Cairo in 1931 – namely, to stand guard at each end of *Kupiri* Qasr-el-Nile. In so doing, they made it the most photographed modern monument in central Cairo. The republican regime, however, made it illegal to take photographs of any bridges anywhere in Egypt. This bizarre arrangement resulted in endless incidents of unsuspecting tourists being arrested for photographing of the lions until the comical ban was lifted in 2001.

The girls waved at the first Cairo hotel to be built on the Nile, where we had enjoyed high tea the day before. But grandfather redirected our attention, reminding us that we were sailing through Khediviate Cairo – built by Italian and French architects for Ismail Pasha's modernisation project, starting in the 1860s and continuing throughout the city's own *belle époque*.

Verdi's Aida

The pinnacle of Ismail's modernisation programme was the construction of Cairo's Royal Opera House in 1868 by Alexandrian architect Pietro Avoscani.

'My country is no longer in Africa; we are now part of Europe', said Ismail Pasha in November 1869, as he officially opened the building. This, together with the completion of the Suez Canal in the same year, tells the story of the Enlightenment chapter in modern Egypt's history. Ismail paid Giuseppe Verdi (1813–1901), 150,000 French francs to composed *Aida* for the inauguration of the opera house. Contrary to common belief, *Aida*'s premiere had to wait until 24 December 1871.[4] Instead, the Italian composer's 1851 *Rigoletto* was performed for the opening in November 1869.

It was the Siege of Paris, during the Franco–Prussian War, that blocked the shipping of *Aida*'s scenery and costumes to Egypt for the scheduled performance. Its 1871 Cairo premiere, for invited dignitaries only, was never recognised by Verdi, who was infuriated because the ordinary public could not attend. He considered its February 1872 performance at La Scala in Milan to be *Aida*'s official premiere. (Incidentally, Avoscani had copied the style of Milan's 1778-built La Scala for his Cairo Opera House designs, because he only had 18 months in which to get it ready.)[5]

Opera was new to Cairo at the time. There was no record of any Ottoman Egyptian Muslim composing or writing opera. And although some performances were held in rich merchants' houses in Alexandria, there is no history of public ones held in Cairo before 1869.

CHAPTER 22   Cairo Interlude

Paris Au Bord Du Nil – Modern Identity
Our boat now passed nineteenth-century palaces and large villas with gardens and trees on the riverbank.

'*Paris au bord du Nil*', said my grandfather, pointing to Ismail-built central Cairo, which looked much smaller than European Alexandria.

Ismail revisited Paris in 1867 (20 years after attending its military college) to inaugurate the Egyptian pavilions at the *Exposition Universelle*. Like the Bonaparte expedition 70 years earlier, this Franco–Egyptian encounter had a profound, lasting effect. The French were fascinated by the ancient-Egyptian-themed exhibition on a *dahabiya* moored on the Seine. The boat had been towed from Alexandria, and Mariette Bey had set up a mini-Egyptian temple with replica decoration, artefacts and antiquities loaned from the Cairo museum. A 2,000-year-old mummy was even unwrapped in the presence of the French royals. An oriental bazaar was also set up in another part of the pavilion. In their turn, technocrats, doctors and engineers among Ismail's entourage were impressed by French arts and culture. But the French perception of Egypt – and the respect they showed for Egyptian civilisation and culture, along with their treatment of their guests – changed many Egyptians' attitudes. Even the most conservative and reserved among them, who had treated Europeans with suspicion, returned embracing French culture after they 'saw the light' in Paris.[6]

Ismail wanted to do with Cairo what Napoleon III had with Paris. At the latter's command, Georges-Eugène ('Baron') Haussmann (1809–1891), prefect of the Seine, had replaced the French capital's winding medieval alleyways with long, straight gaslit boulevards and constructed attractive new buildings at main crossroads. The monumental *beaux-arts* Opéra Garnier (named after its architect, Charles Garnier [1825–1898]) caught Ismail's eye; he admired its facade during construction. Ismail chose Ezbekiya Gardens, where the new quarters of Khediviate Cairo meet the old central city, to erect a monument marking his vison. And nothing would encapsulate his vision of modernity and culture – or add the civilised complements of a new independent identity – more than an opera house: the first in Africa and the region.

Ismail had wanted an opera whose story was compatible with the identity he was forging for the nation: an original, Egyptian one. Mariette Bey was among the specialists consulted by Ismail: he had already written a story about an Egyptian princess, an army general and an Ethiopian female prisoner-of-war. The common belief was that Mariette guided his friend, French librettist and theatre director Camille du Locle (1832–1903), who, in 1869, suggested to Verdi an opera set in ancient Egypt. Mariette designed the costumes and accessories for *Aida's* original premiere while answering an avalanche of questions from due Locle.[7]

Art, ancient indigenous heritage (unearthed by the French), culture and architecture become inseparable from the newly emerging national identity, which was distinctively independent from the incoherent, pan-Islamic character enforced by the priestly class since the Ottoman invasion of Egypt in 1516.

Architecture and Identity

The nineteenth-century *resurrected* Alexandria was decades ahead of Cairo and Internal Egypt in the realms of culture and architecture, which were part of her Euro-Mediterranean identity. Alexandria's architecture was mostly hegemonic, overshadowing the odd *aléatoire* randomly emerging on the city fringes. Cairo's architectural themes were ambivalent, fluctuating between holding onto an oriental Islamic character and coyly accepting the European Franco–Italian designs introduced by Ismail – and thus reflecting a notion of transculturation.

'Alexandrianism' itself was different from Egyptian nationalism: it was not a conventional nationalism but was identity-inspired – a socio-economic-cultural identity underpinned by an entrepreneurial spirit of commerce and trade. Alexandrianism was a world away from the nationalistic aspirations simmering in Cairo, which manifested themselves through twin polarised representations. First was the Ottoman legacy of the Ourabists'[8] traditional Islamo-oriental resistance to British occupation, but because of this rooted Islamic influence,[9] it also, secondly, rejected all aspects of modernity as European colonialism (since they were associated with the 1798 French expedition). Other, less influential trends encompassed what I call enlightened nationalism – appreciating the progressive creative and intellectual transformation that began to take shape after the War before it was overwhelmed by the militaristic nationalism dominant in the second half of the twentieth century and by millennial Islamic nationalism. The difference between the two cities was reflected in the dominance of a European architectural identity throughout Alexandria, while in Cairo this remained at the level of a ghettoised 'Paris by the Nile', besieged on all sides by the massively growing oriental Cairo.

Cathedrals, railway stations, opera houses, bridges, viaducts and arcades represent history's brushstrokes on a city's canvas. A city's architecture can be a slow death or can continue to pump energy and growth into her living being; it constitutes an account of the accumulation of centuries and millennia of her life and her citizens' memories – no matter how painful, bloody or controversial the times have been, it remains part of the city's or the nation's story. Whether

CHAPTER 22   Cairo Interlude

ancient like the Pyramids and the Colosseum, medieval cathedrals like Canterbury and Notre-Dame de Paris, or testimonials to oppressive conquests like The Tower of London and *la Bastille*, all carry emotions and chronicle chapters of nations' histories.

Their 'bricks and mortar' collected fragments of the spirits of those who built them, dreamed and designed them as inspired by God's or man's ambition. The souls and heartbeats of architects from Dinocrates to Christopher Wren are stored in their creations. I once spoke with a Native American Egyptology student in Luxor's Karnak temple in 2000. She would meditate among the columns at sunrise.

'Close your eyes and let your other senses flow', she said, 'you may be able to read, feel and hear the thoughts, imagination and love of stonemasons, bricklayers and construction workers whispering'. The builders of monuments continued, for centuries, to speak to generations of visitors, the student-philosopher said. Hence, when such monuments face destruction, leaders who understand their nations' souls restore or rebuild them in a fashion retaining the identity they represented. When the Houses of Parliament were bombed during the War, Churchill insisted that the main Commons chamber be rebuilt exactly as it was, resisting enlarging and modernising it to accommodate all members.*

When Cairo Opera House was destroyed by fire in October 1971 (to cover up the theft from the Opera's props and costumes, or so several newspapers at the time claimed), musicians and composers expected their opera to be restored in its original La Scala style. UNESCO, and opera lovers worldwide would have contributed generously had the Egyptians built a replica of the old one or a modern, larger auditorium behind the facade of the original opera house to preserve their own history. However, the pan-Ottoman nationalism trend (which became a pan-Arab one) had already defeated the independent nationalism of Egyptian identity. Hardly any voices called for a campaign to restore the building to its original state – visually, architecturally and culturally safeguarding a chapter of the story of Egypt's modernity spanning 160 years. An ugly concrete multi-storey car park stands now in the place of Avoscani's creation. Instead of the Khediviate Opera House, a modern building designed not by Italian but by Japanese architects was erected in a location far removed, physically and conceptually, from the original symbolic choice of Ezbekiya Gardens. The new opera house was built on the other side of the Nile, on Gazira Island in the secluded national exhibition centre, where the public has only limited access to it – the very opposite of Verdi's principled stance on the people's accessing *Aida*'s first performance.

---

* Although there are 650 elected MPs, the seating capacity on the green benches is only 427.

205

Alexandria Adieu

In 1864, the nine-hectare Ezbekiya Pond had its size reduced by Ismail, who planted more trees to form the modern park. The French born planner and civil engineer Jean-Pierre Barillet-Deschamps Bey (1824-1873) who was commissioned by Ismail added a wrought-iron fence in 1872, with four gates facing the cardinal points. *Sour-l'Ezbekiya* ('fence') was like the northern edge of London's Green Park, on Piccadilly's south side, with book and paintings stalls and street craftsmen. Amateur artists would sit producing their work and selling them, or painting portraits of passers-by on their way to the opera or to one of the theatres on the other side of Place de l'Opéra. I went one afternoon with my grandfather to *Sour-l'Ezbekiya*, where he picked out some old books. I refused to sit for a street artist because the two girls' charcoal portraits made them look silly, but they were delighted with them.

Architectural changes and the destruction of landmarks as part of altering Egypt's identity has been going on since the officers took power; the 1952 central Cairo fires were started by Islamists and their officer-backers at Place de l'Opéra.[10, 11] The Nasser regime filled in the pond and destroyed most of Ezbekiya Park, leaving a small green with some trees little bigger than the Hogarth Roundabout on the A4 at Chiswick, and concreted over the rest, turning it into a bus terminus. But the traditions of old books and periodicals survived, although most of the books have become Islamic.

Alexandria's old guard also failed to protect her identity from deformation by losing her demographic richness, and could not save her language (or Egypt's in general) from mutilation. But could they have preserved her Italian-built architecture? The point was powerfully made by Alexandria chronicler and novelist Ibrahim Abdel Meguid in *Clouds Over Alexandria*, the finale of his Alexandria Trilogy. One of *Clouds'* main characters, the communist intellectual Iesa Salmawi, who has spent three years in Nasser's jails along with many who objected to the autocratic ruler changing the Egyptian identity, wanders Alexandria's old town streets on New Year's Eve 1975 admiring the city's nineteenth-century architecture.

'Anyone who didn't know the history of Alexandria's architecture didn't know the city', thinks Salmawi, setting a goal for himself – namely, rereading the history of the city and sharing it with university students, opening a magic cave for them. In the process, Salmawi cites examples as diverse as Greek mythology and Alexandria United football club losing its away games. The lesson was about losing when your feet aren't planted in your own soil, which was inseparable from identity. But then, will the soil remain saffron; will Alexandrians find themselves standing on another earth? Was the question swirling, in

CHAPTER 22   Cairo Interlude

1975, in Salmawi's injured and bleeding head after it was hit by a bottle thrown by an idiot an hour before the customary New-year's eve midnight rite (another signal of a generation losing identity by not knowing when exactly to toss the old out of the window)*: 'The desert and its sand had begun to creep into it [Alexandria's saffron soil] from the Arabian Peninsula. Yes. These Wahhabi ideas, which are gaining ground now, would later cover all of Egypt's soil and sink into it, and Egyptians would become estranged from their own history.'[12]

The Pyramids
Our boat was approaching the end of its Nile voyage by *Kupiri* Abbas, still known by its original title despite the Nasser regime renaming it *Kupiri* al-Giza. It was constructed in 1908 during Abbas Helmi II's reign to connect Giza on the west bank of the Nile to old, pre-Islamic Cairo. The bridge was made of three parts, with the middle section swivelling 90 degrees to let boats pass each other. It became notorious through the Cairo University students' 1946 clash with the police. The police foolishly ordered the bridge opened as the demonstration went over it, leading to several drownings and the resignation of Egypt's 27th prime minister, Fahmy el-Nakrashi Pasha (1888–1948).

We left the boat at a jetty by Abbas Bridge to take a taxi from the rank serving the Cairo Zoo, another legacy of Khedive Ismail Pasha. He established the zoo in 1870 on 21 hectares planted with exotic trees and plants imported from Africa and the New World; the original 180 birds and 78 animals were donated from Ismail's private menagerie. The zoo was expanded to 32 hectares by his son, Tawfik, and officially reopened in 1891. The taxi drove along Avenue de la Pyramide, home to several nightclubs featured in many movies, which leads to the Pyramids mound – known geographically as the Giza Plateau. Here, we seemed like ants next to the oldest and best known of the Seven Wonders of the World.

No photographs or films prepare you for the tremendous astonishment, almost shock, at the size of the Great Pyramid of King Cheops (Khufu)[†], second of the seven kings of the Fourth Dynasty (2575–2465 BC). With a height of 146.73 metres and a base measuring 230.35 metres on each of its four sides, the monument was visually in control of the entire mound. The Great Pyramid was built over 4,500

---

* A midnight New Year's Eve tradition in Alexandria – often involving crockery.
† Ruled for 63 years (2589-2566 BC) according to Manetho (Malek, Jaromir, The Old Kingdom, The Oxford History of Ancient Egypt, Oxford University Press, 2000, PP 88) but modern historians suggest between 46-26 years (Thomas Schneider: Lexikon der Pharaonen. Albatros, Düsseldorf 2002, PP 101-104)

years ago with its four corners facing the four cardinal directions with a precision of 0.067 degree of error. Twenty-first-century photographic technology has confirmed that the pyramid in fact has eight, not four, sides – and it is the only pyramid in the world with such features. This was first noticed by an RAF pilot who took a photo flying above the magnificent structure in 1940, when he spotted concavity on the pyramid that is invisible from the ground. Furthermore, it only becomes noticeable from the air above the Great Pyramid at four specific times – at either dawn or sunset exactly on the spring and autumn equinoxes – perhaps another mystery that one day might unlock the secrets of how the Egyptians managed to build such a grand monument with this stunning accuracy.

Like its two lesser neighbours, Khufu's Great Pyramid was originally covered in white polished limestone, reflecting the sun in a magnificent sight. The stones were plundered in the Middle Ages – mostly to build mosques and palaces during Arab, Mamluk and Ottoman rule. Only the middle Pyramid of Chephren (Khfre), the fourth of the dynasty's rulers, had some of the white stone left on its top. The third pyramid, further to the south and last to be built, is – at 61 metres high and 111.4 metres each side – the smallest; it was constructed by Mykerinus (Menkaure), the fifth king of the dynasty.

So far, this was the most fascinating day in that momentous year in my young life, which had started with the family's economic losses and my broken arm. But the peak moment was standing next to the Sphinx, one of the oldest and largest statues in the world at 73 metres long and 20 metres high. This enduring, 4,500-year-old[13] monumental sculpture, with a human face and a lion's body, was cut from the plateau's base rock. Touching the Sphinx and other monuments in those days was what we did, and nobody stopped you. So, it was an overly exhilarating day as we climbed the Great Pyramid and the giant claws of the Sphinx. But the scariest experience was getting on the back of a camel: when it raised itself, I thought I would fall on my face; then the camel straightened itself up, almost throwing me backwards. I think the presence of Lola and Lucy, who wisely opted for ponies, was what stopped me showing fear – although I struggled not to throw up with seasickness from the movement of that beastly 'ship of the desert'.

PART VI
THE TWENTIETH CENTURY

CHAPTER 23
Film Houses: A Way of Life

Film houses were central to Mehatet el-Ramleh, the beating heart of Alexandria. Some had a purely theatrical background – like the 1900 Teatro dell'Alhambra, which turned cinema in 1928 when the first speaking movie was screened. The 1931 Cinéma Roi – renamed 'Ferial' in 1938 after the birth, in Alexandria, of King Farouk's first daughter, Princess Ferial (1938–2009), 600 metres to the west of the 1921 Cinéma Rex – was hit during the Suez War by an RAF rocket that narrowly missed the Marconi communications centre next door. Closer to Cinéma Ferial, by the corner of Rue Safiya Zaghloul, sits Cinéma Strand. It started in 1906 as Aziz and Dorès Cinephone, but took the name of the Belle Vue nightclub nearby in 1908, and was renamed the Strand in 1950 before becoming a nightclub – in 1968. Now, like most Alexandria cinemas and clubs, it has been bought by an Islamist Arab sheikh, who closed it down. The Cinéma Rio on Rue Fuad (opened 1935) uniquely had a second, open-air, auditorium on its roof garden.

Cinemagoing was a way of life in Alexandria, especially before the launch of national television in 1957, and remained so for two decades afterwards. Admission was affordable for all, starting from as little as 9 *millièmes* (£€0.009)[1] in third-class wooden-seated cinemas in popular areas, where you got a pop drink as your change from the *sagh* (1 *piastre* [PT] coin). A top-balcony seat on a Saturday evening was a *shilling* (5PT), or a *rub'h-guinea* (£€0.25 or 25 PT) for a *loge* (box) in the city's 1930s Art Deco film houses. The average cinema seat throughout Alexandria was the hexagonal coin *nos-a-franc*.[2] The less well-off only headed for Mehatet el-Ramleh's film houses on special occasions; there were two dozen cinemas within a 750-metre semicircle in the area. I

209

have been inside no fewer than 50 cinemas in Alexandria, from luxury ones at Gare de Ramleh and summer open-air auditoria in Sidi-Bishr to those in fashionable, mixed areas like Ibrahimiyah and impoverished quarters Hadra and karmouz.

Independent cinemas, like the Cinéma San-Stephano (founded in 1907), catered for visitors to the city; others, like Cinéma Moharrem-Bey and Cinéma Star near Rue Naby Daniel, for local residents in Europeanised or mixed areas. Ibrahimiyah had four film houses: the 1953 Cinéma La Guitèe on Rule La Guitèe, Cinéma Riviera (opened in 1958) by Rue Abukeir, the 1940-built Cinéma Odeon by the Ibrahimiyah tram stop and Cinéma Sporting (founded 1949) on the opposite side 300 yards to the east. Lower-prices modest venues included the 1935 Cinéma Widad on Rue Anastasia, Cinéma al-Nile in Karmouz and Amir in Raghib Pasha for migrant dock workers – while Cinémas Muxx, Hadra, Muntazah, Karmouz and Anfoshui were all named after their local quarters.

Luxury Art Deco cinemas always had a bar and café, and they introduced air-conditioning in the 1940s. They had leather or upholstered seats in four seating categories. However, whether it was a downmarket establishment in popular areas like Hadra, Karmouz, Raghib, Gabbari, Wardian or Gheit-el-Enab or a top luxury film palace like Cinémas Rialto or Metro on Rue Obélisque (Safiya Zaghloul) they all had one feature in common: a bar or a cafeteria section selling all manner of drinks, including wine and beer – especially Stella. There were also numerous outdoor cinemas during the summer season and some theatres that would become cinemas in the summer, especially when air-conditioning became standard after the War (in those days, smoking was still permitted in cinemas). There were numerous cinema clubs like De Jésuites in Cleopatra or Armenian Club. Community centres, like the one ran by the Greeks in Chatby, and schools, municipality-subsidised public libraries and social centres also showed films daily or weekly.

The Egyptian film industry was quite significant in terms of volume of production. It often churned out the largest number of films outside Europe and Hollywood, except for India and the Soviet Union. The industry secured the dominance of demotic Egyptian as the tongue of modernity and culture throughout the Arabic-speaking spheres. Films were either original Egyptian stories or adaptations of Hollywood, French or British films. Egyptian scriptwriters and film producers adopted their plots, settings and characters, while casting directors searched thoroughly – often successfully – for actors and actresses who resembled the English, American or French stars in the original movies, copying their hairstyles, make-up and dresses.

CHAPTER 23   Film Houses: A Way of Life

Since the making of the first feature films in Alexandria in 1917, Egyptian movies had routinely been released with French subtitles added at the production studios. The best-known subtitling service was Ideal-Titra Film, a joint venture started the early 1930s using technology developed separately by the Swedish Ideal Film and (their later partners) the French Titra Film. The first in Egypt to pioneer the translation subtitle was the Alexandrian Leopoldo Fiorello in 1912, with slides in Arabic script next to silent movies in Il-cinema egiziano (El-Cinéma el-Masriyah) in Alexandria. By mid-1927 and early 1928, films had subtitles on the celluloid with the arrival of American technology developed for the 1927 movie *The Jazz Singer*. A few months later, this technique was trialled successfully at Teatro Alhambra in Alexandria.

Subtitles were annoying when they did not match speech or obscured some details of the picture. Even before the obligatory-translation rule (see below), distributors wanted subtitles to secure broader appeal among the lesser-educated filmgoers who often understood French better than English. Like migrants to Alexandria from the Egyptian countryside, many of the European or former Ottoman subjects of the nineteenth and early twentieth centuries understood spoken demotic Alexandrian but few of them could read or write Arabic – nor did they recognise Cairean expressions on a soundtrack. Unlike the former, the latter spoke and read French at home – and many studied English besides their own (mostly French, Italian or Greek) ethnic language. In the 1930s, movies released in Egypt added English subtitles to their French strap, thereby covering a good part of the screen. This irritated filmgoers, who were subsequently relieved by a new invention: Anis Ebeid (1909–1988), a French-trained Egyptian sound engineer, developed a multilingual machine to print the subtitles in hollow fonts.

Arabic subtitles on imported Hollywood French and Italian films were selective and voluntary. Illiteracy rates were high; thus, many Egyptians did not understand written classical Arabic; they spoke their own demotic Egyptian while, as we have noted, Alexandrians spoke a mix of sub-languages.[3] In 1939 Prime Minister Mohammed Mahmoud Pasha (1878–1941), a hardline nationalist, made Arabic (plus a second language) subtitles a condition for releasing imported films for public screening. French was added to Arabic on Italian and Hollywood movies on release, while Italian and Arabic went on French ones. Films showing in Alexandrian cinemas in the 1960s were still carrying the two-language subtitles. Youssef Chahine kept French and English subtitles on his movies with their dialogue in Alexandrian-influenced demotic Egyptian. Chahine was English-educated at Victoria College, studied film in America and Italy, and conversed in Alexandriaspeak (Franco-Italo-Alexandrian) at home and among friends.

211

The Birthplace of Egypt's Film Industry

Alexandria was the birthplace of Egyptian cinema. The city had the seeds of film awareness growing in her saffron soil, already rich with actors, artists, writers, singers and musicians. The first motion picture shot in Egypt, in 1897, was of the Place des Consuls in Alexandria by Italo-Alexandrian Eugene Promio, who was the Lumière brothers' cameraman.[4] In the same year, the first film house in Africa was launched: Alexandria's *Lumière Cinematographe* by the aforementioned film-pioneer brothers.[*] While promoting their equipment in Alexandria in 1896, they screened their first film in Toussoun Bourse, a Pall Mall-type members' club with various halls suitable for performances, concerts and social events.[5] Ten years later, Egypt's first music-accompanied projection, using a Gaumont gramophone, took place at Aziz Bandarli's and Umberto Dorès' cinema hall. Alexandrians Bandarli and Dorès, both film photographers, established Egypt's first film studio in Alexandria in 1907, and also shot the first Egyptian documentary – of Khedive Abbas Helmi II visiting the science institute – in the same year.[6]

Other films documented social events, like the 1912 opening of Cinéma Empire, attended by the elites of Alexandrian and Egyptian society, or sporting events at schools including the Frères School at Saint Catherine's Church and the Collège Saint-Marc in Chatby. They were a prelude to the first newsreel, *Le Journal Pathé*, screened at Cinéma Pathé (and the newsreel became known as 'Alexandria's Mirror'). The original Pathé newsreel had been launched in France in 1896 by Pathé Frères (Pathé Brothers Company).

Bandarli and Dorès, along with some Italian investors, were backed by Banco di Roma to found la Société cinématographique Italo-égyptienne (Sitcia), the very first film-production company in Egypt. They shot three films in their studio in the Nuzha area with Stelio Chiarini (-1943), who shot some iconic pictures later in the 1920s, as director of photography.[7] Sticia'a first films – *Nahw al-Hawiya* (*Towards the Abyss*, 1917); *Charaf al-Badawi* (*A Bedouin's Honour*, 1917); and *al-Zohour al-Katela* (*Deadly Flowers*, 1918) – failed to financially break even due to a lukewarm reception among the public.[8]

A Bedouin's Honour was the first feature film with a Nilotic-Egyptian actor, Mohammed Karim.[9] Nonetheless, Sticia suffered heavy losses and went into liquidation within three years – but Chiarini went on to make a massive contribution to the Alexandria-cum-Egyptian film industry as he became a mentor to the country's second generation

---

[*] Auguste Marie Loius Nicolas Lumière (1862–1954) and Louis Jean Lumière (1864–1948).

CHAPTER 23   Film Houses: A Way of Life

of filmmakers. He trained, as his apprentice, the Alexandria-born Alvise Orfanelli (1902–1961). When Sticia folded, Orfanelli took over the equipment and developing laboratories in return for his overdue wages to found Studio Alvis and, in turn, train the third generation of Alexandrian filmmakers like Togo Mizrahi (1901–1986), who became a giant of the Egyptian film industry.[10] He created the comic character of the clumsy Egyptian Jew Shalom, played by another Alexandrian, Leon Angel (1900–1945), and turned the Alexandrian-Jewish songstress Leila Murad (1918–1995) into the highest-paid movie star in Egyptian cinema. He came up with the shrewd idea of using her name, Leila, in the title of a series of movies.

Orfanelli became a mentor to my late friend Youssef Chahine when he hired him as an assistant and later became director of photography on all 16 of his apprentice's films until he died in 1961. Chahine, who made another 21 movies, often told me that he learned the art of the film camera from Orfanelli. Like his mentor, who died during the filming of *Ragul-fi-Hiyaty* (*A Man in My Life*) – letting his assistant, Robert Sa'ad, finishing the shooting – Chahine's terminal illness stopped him completing his last picture. *Hiya Fouda!* (*What a Mess!*, 2007) and was completed by his own assistant, apprentice Khalid Youssef.

The first specialised film periodical in Egypt was published in French in Alexandria in 1919, the same year in which the first Egyptian actor was to play a leading role in a full-length feature film – Alexandrian Fawzi el-Gazayerly (1886–1947) in *Madame Loretta* (he went on to star in another 16 moving pictures). The growing industry in Alexandria was attracting filmmakers from as far away as Latin America. Pedro La'ma (1907–1947) and his brother Abraham (1904–1953) arrived in the city from Chile with experience in acting, directing and producing. They changed their names to the faith-neutral Badr and Ibrahim when they established the Mina Club in 1926. A year later, they took over Studio Alviss's facilities, founding Condor Film. They produced the first full-length Egyptian movie – the racy, romantic *Qublah-fi-Alsahra'a* (*A Kiss in the Desert*). Fifteen years later they made *Cleopatra*, the first historical film in Egyptian cinema.

In 1927, the first union for the film industry was established in Alexandria. Two years later, the Alexandrine Aziza Amir (1901–1952) became the country's first female film director, with her *Fille du Nil* (*Daughter of the Nile*).[11] In 1930, Alexandrine music composer and actress Bahiga Hafez (1908–1983)[12] starred in the first ever film adapted from an original Egyptian novel in the Arabic language: *Zeinab*, by Egyptian novelist, writer, essayist and Sorbonne graduate

213

Dr Muhammed Hessein Heikal* (1888–1956). Amusingly, the director Mohammed Karim, insisted on disinfecting the cowshed and instructed assistants to wash the cow with luxury soap and water before shooting the farm-girl character Zeinab (played by Hafez) milking the animal.

In 1932, Mohamed Bayoumi (1894–1963) established Egypt's first cinema institute in Alexandria.[13] The first Greek-language films made in Alexandria in 1937 were by Orfanilli and by Mizrahi.[14] The outbreak of the War, with Alexandria coming under heavy air raids from the Luftwaffe, pushed the film industry out of the city and on to Cairo. Many films were shot at Studio Misr (established in the capital in 1935), leading to the majority of Egypt's performers, actors and film technicians moving out of Alexandria and settling in Cairo.

---

* He might appear as Hussein Heikal in Arabic publications and websites

CHAPTER 24
Youssef Chahine: Alexandria's Struggle with Internal Egypt

A row of Art Deco film houses once dominated the southern side of Place Mehatet-el-Ramleh: the Radio, Strand, Ritz and Cinéma Ferial. The last-named was the location of the opening scene in Youssef Chahine's 1978 picture *Alexandria... Why?* – the first of the filmmaker's celebrated trilogy of semi-autobiographical movies intertwined with the complex story of modern Alexandria.

First lieutenant Anwar Sadat is sitting with his comrade-in-arms, air force pilot Hassan Ezzat, in the front row of Cinéma Ferial. At the end of the 1941 newsreel about the War raging in Alamein, 128 kilometres to the west, Sadat angrily responds to a joke from a British army officer behind him. Deciding to do something about the likes of 'the English jackass', the two nationalists meet the Muslim Brotherhood leader Hassan Al-Banna (1906-1949), who invites them to join his group. Chahine's hint highlights the Islamists' influence on the politicised army officers who staged a coup in 1952. Many officers did in fact join the organisation.

The film was first released in New York before it was nominated for the Berlin, London and other film festivals. As Chahine told me in 1981, he wanted to show the movie to a broader international audience, and for film critics to review it, before the Egyptian censors mutilated it. The director had his run-ins with the authoritarian Nasser administration in a complex relationship, perhaps a masochistic one on the former's part. Chahine went into self-exile in Beirut when Nasser imprisoned left-wing activists and intellectuals from 1957 onwards, in a bout of persecution that lasted until 1964.

Nasser instructed his minister of culture to 'tell that crazy Alexandrian to return home to enrich the Egyptian cinema'. The eccentric

215

filmmaker had a love–hate affair with the Egyptian establishment and the country's film-industry community – and, most of all, with his fellow liberal-left intellectuals. They failed to understand Chahine's Alexandrian liberated, rebellious, decadent and Dionysian outlook on life. Most of his literati critics hailed geographically from Internal Egypt, with little socio-cultural connection to pre-1960s Alexandria; they had only read or heard misrepresentations of a city of ungodly European depravity.

Like Alexandria herself, Chahine's personality was a multi-layered construction of complexity and paradoxes; he was too open, too cosmopolitan and too liberal for Cairo's close-minded film community. Their deeply seated, subconscious *fellaheen* Islamic intolerance fogged their ability to see beyond the surface of hedonistic pleasure in Chahine's movies. They were disturbed by his recurrent subplot device of gay love. But the subplot was often Chahine's own vehicle to convey a sophisticated, intricate, historical message inseparable from Alexandria's story. The most Europeanised and open city in the region had a complicated relationship of multiple dimensions with modernity and its Ottoman legacy, with Islam and *laïcité*, Europe and Internal Egypt.

Alexandria's mores and Inner Egypt's values were mutually alien – each saw the other's culture as strange, bizarre and incompatible – but out of their clash something new was born, a theme that Chahine repeatedly explored in his subplots of gay love affairs. This theme was an appropriate vehicle because *shazth* (abnormal) is a negative Arabic term for a homosexual. But this word only began to be used disparagingly by Alexandrians more than half a century after Cavafy and Forster had been openly publishing poetry and prose about homosexual love in newspapers like the *Egyptian Gazette*, le *Phare d'Alexandrie* and the *Egyptian Mail*.

The love affair between an English soldier and his upper-class Egyptian-nationalist abductor annoyed the left-wing Egyptian critics reviewing *Alexandria... Why?* A similar affair, between an Egyptian youth and a colonel with the 1798 French expedition, in Chahine's later *Adieu Bonaparte* (1985) similarly irritated many Egyptian left-wing intellectuals and viewers, of both sexes, during its 1985 London screening. Chahine was challenging the regression of Egyptian liberalism and the reverse of modernity. He places the gay love affair between two races, classes and cultures in a socio-historic and political context – namely, the clash, in 1798, between Egypt and Europe. It was intercourse that gave birth to modernity, which progressed until reaching the end of the road in his *Alexandrie encore et Toujours* (*Alexandria Again and Forever*, 1989), the last of the Alexandria Trilogy.

CHAPTER 24   Youssef Chahine: Alexandria's Struggle with Internal Egypt

In *Alexandria... Why?* the Egyptian gay character was privileged upper-middle-class, educated and well-off while his British prisoner-cum-lover was a poor working-class boy. While a minority – on the wane in the 1970s, and almost non-existent in post-millennial Alexandria – of liberal-minded older Egyptians saw this gay-love subplot as progressive, most Egyptians saw it as unnatural – using the term *shouzthoz ginsy* (sexual abnormality). The lover, an *a'skari inglisy* (British soldier), was the enemy in the make-belief world of cinema and the collective mind of its Egyptian viewers.

Ten years later, the gay love affair in *Adieu Bonaparte* was the other way around: the French officer was cultured, intellectual and upper class while his Egyptian lover was a simple, deprived boy whose two brothers represent twin Egyptian trends. One wants to benefit from French culture and the other, influenced by the Islamic clergy, violently resists the French. This relationship symbolised real historical events when the 1798 French expedition advanced life in a dirty, disease-ridden, medieval backwater, coaxing it into a modern, cultured hygienic and clean existence.

In *Alexandria... Why?* – depicting a time when chic Alexandria was at her peak of elegance and glamour – the Egyptian-Alexandrian gay lover is a provider, more prosperous and more civilised than his lover, offering the English soldier what was beyond his reach back home: luxury lifestyle, etiquette, money, culture, and love. In *Adieu Bonaparte*, the Egyptian baker's son is the underdog, the deprived, the poorer partner while the French officer becomes his saviour and provider, guiding him towards progress. French army officers who remained behind after Napoleon were the founders of the modern Egyptian Army.[1]

By the mid-1980s, Egyptian graduates had been indoctrinated in the 1952 coup regime's schools to see *les Anglais* through one prism – as an occupation force whose meddling was unwelcome. Egyptian school curricula presented the British as having a warped view of historical events like the bombardment of Alexandria in 1882, through the exaggerated folklore of victimhood. As for the older generation, educated in pre-1958 schools during Egypt's period of modernity, the British were simply not culturally as 'chic as the French' – a phrase that my mother and her friends often repeated. The older Egyptian middle classes were culturally and socially Francophile – especially the Alexandrians, who were more interested in French etiquette and fashion (and Italian art and culture) than any British ethos. As a middle-class student in European Alexandria, Chahine noticed that it was customary to spend holidays in Venice, Vienna and other cultural cities beyond the reach of most of *les Anglais* because Alexandrians were culturally polished by French and Italian influence, and he emphasised this in his second film in the trilogy, *An Egyptian Story* (1982)

Alexandria Adieu

Non-Alexandrian critics' objection to Chahine's characters also had a socio-psychological cast, considering Egyptians' schizophrenic attitude to homosexuality in men – a sentiment that was not widely shared in tolerant, open-minded Alexandria. Most Egyptians (especially those from a *fellaheen* background) do not recognise a gay couple's relationship as being between two equals. One party, the 'submissive' one, is called *khawal* – a derogatory, demeaning insult making the wretched soul who acquired the label fair game for bullying. Paradoxically, there is no specific label for the other party: the 'macho-man', dominating the *khawal* during their brief encounter. This indicates that one party is accepted as 'normal' and the other as *shazth*. Men considering themselves 'normal' (heterosexuals) and with girlfriends often boast that they have 'f****d a *khawal*'.

It is hard to fathom this confused attitude within the Internal Egypt subculture; my circle of friends who attended European schools struggled to fully understand this paradox, although we laughed at *khawal* jokes. Quizzing one Egyptian university student from a rural background, who did not deny a rumour that he had seduced a first-year student *khawal*, he was upset by my suggestion that he too must be homosexual? Pointing to his buxom girlfriend was his masculine proof of not being a *khawal*. A bisexual, then? He refused to accept that definition either.

Between *Alexandria... Why?* – set in the 1940s, when Alexandria had reached her peak of European Judaeo-Christian cultural modernity – and *Adieu Bonaparte*, depicting the events of 1798 with the French landing in Alexandria, Chahine also emphasises the relationship between East and West, seen as *shoztouz* (abnormal, from *shazth*) by a backward ruling establishment comprising the *ulama* (Islamic priestly class) of al-Azhar, the judiciary and Ottoman representatives in Egypt's eighteen century. But this 'abnormal' relationship with the French ushered in a new dawn, with an advanced, liberal, progressive culture modernising 'Dark Age' Egyptian society. The French introduced hygiene, equality and education; they ended the extortionist *gizyah* tax, collected from non-Muslims since the seventh-century Arab occupation; and, for the first time, they published journals. The progressive and liberating cultural effect of the French expedition had lasting repercussions: it developed Egypt and changed the entire Levant, ushered the region into the age of modernity, and rediscovered ancient Egypt's treasures and knowledge with the unlocking of hieroglyphics. It thus demonstrated to the world the secrets of ancient Egypt's greatness for the first time since Alexander the Great democratised the knowledge and sciences that had been a closed monopoly of the priestly class.

CHAPTER 24   Youssef Chahine: Alexandria's Struggle with Internal Egypt

Chahine was a true child of Alexandria – born from her womb, carrying her Ptolemaic genes and suckling culture from her neo-Hellenistic breasts. Alexandria – with her cosmopolitanism, her racial hybridity, her deep-rooted progressive attitude to love (of any kind) – was always present and trackable, openly or subtly, in all of Chahine's films – whether set in Alexandria or on the Upper Nile 1,200 kilometres to the south.

Homosexual love in poetry and essays such as those of Cavafy was frequently published in Alexandrian newspapers in the late nineteenth and early twentieth century, when such writings would land authors in jail in London and most European capitals – perhaps excepting Paris. E.M. Forster was in love with Muhammed Al-Adl; to his passion he authored *Alexandria: A History and a Guide*, according to Michael Haag, basing his conclusion on Forster dedicating the book with the phrase ' to Hermes psychopompós' (in Greek Ερμής Ψυχοπόμπος).[2] Al-Adl was a conductor on the Ramleh tram; on it, Forster wrote, you meet people 'from all walks of life' – a code, at the time, for being sexually different. And the iconic Tramway el-Ramleh remained a vehicle for finding love, of any kind, when I lived there.

There was no English or German Cavafy: Forster stopped publishing novels as he felt unable in London, the largest city in the world, to write about homosexual love. Oscar Wilde was put in Reading Gaol for indecency in 1895 while Alexandria was celebrating love of all kinds. She was not only a city of political conflicts between khedives and consuls but also, socially, a city of culture and ahead of her time. Alexandria of the nineteenth and early twentieth century was far more progressive, tolerant and inclusive than the Alexandria of the twenty-first century. Even her rulers did not take rigid conservatives' complaints about the open articulation of gay love too seriously. When the Dutch Consul, Mr Ruyssenaers, complained to Said Pasha of the prevalence of homosexuality in Egypt, the pasha reportedly teased him by replying that the consul should try it himself before complaining.[3]

The Resistance to the Renaissance

Egyptian intellectuals of the early twentieth century called modernisation efforts *al-Nahda* (the renaissance). *Al-Nahda* remained under attack and, at best, was accommodative – a compromise to co-exist with the religiously entrenched theological influence of the Muslim 'Church', al-Azhar, and the Coptic Church of St Mark – reactionary, anti-modernity institutions dismissing secularism as ungodly. Today, forces like those of the Islamists and pan-Arab nationalists – including Nasserites – still perceive Europe with the same nineteenth-century mindset and suspicious intent. Words like *algharb* (the West) and *homma* (the others) continue to be used by these groups in a way that reflects a confusion of eighteenth- and nineteenth-century Enlightenment Europe with the colonial advances of the Western imperial powers of the same period.

The investment in education and move to modernity pioneered by Muhammad Ali and his sons and grandsons, the khedives, began to pay dividends in art, culture, education and social progress in what was known then as *Nahdat-Masr*, the renaissance of Egypt, around 1900. However, this wasn't entirely secular progress on the scale of the enlightened French *laïcité*. Liberal Islamic theology professor, Hamed Nasr Abu Zaid (1943–2010) insisted that the *Nahda* project was an attempt to blend Islamic heritage with Western European heritage and scientific discoveries.[4] This accommodative position led to a dualist understanding, (and often miscomprehension) of Western heritage. The compromise often suppressed philosophical and scientific tendencies, a practice more evident today in Egyptian translators omitting and censoring (by rephrasing) translations of European books into Arabic to fit their Islamic prejudices.

Those associated with a rationalist Islamic heritage (capable of complementing European Enlightenment values) remained on the periphery. Abu Zaid himself was accused of blasphemy and suspended from his university post in Cairo, and Islamists lawyers presented a petition to divorce him from his wife under the pretext that a Muslim woman could not stay married to a non-believer. The couple had to seek political asylum in the Netherlands.[5]

The accommodative position thus produced uncertainty, which undermined the project of enlightenment. Consequently, oriental Muslims imported technologies for two centuries but rejected attempts to understand the modernisation's philosophical and cultural background. This resulted in a failure, over the past two centuries, to develop a scientific environment – an attitude that gives credence to the claim (rejected by the European and British left as racist and Islamophobic) that this mindset limits many Islamic nations to a one-dimensional perspective on the Enlightenment and thus a misunderstanding of European modernity.

The claim that secularism has come under intense attack because most of the corrupt regimes that copied the Egyptian military-coup's autocracy fought their Islamic opponents under a secularist banner is disingenuous, misleading and factually untrue. In fact, those regimes ended modernity and secularism while competing with Islamists to claim the faith banner. Even during Nasser's power struggle with the Muslim Brotherhood, he was pouring subsidies into al-Azhar and other religious foundations in order to claim that Islamic and Arab regimes

CHAPTER 24   Youssef Chahine: Alexandria's Struggle with Internal Egypt

were copying him by injecting handsome doses of religiosity into all cultural and political spheres. In Egypt itself, this process was accelerated during Sadat's rule (1970–1981).[6] Religion has been incorporated into the modern state in Egypt and in Arabic nations, and in almost all countries with a Muslim majority, by the adoption of shari'a law within their legal systems. Subsidising the official 'Church', as Egypt's al-Azhar is with a $1.2 billion annual injection of taxpayers' money (2019/20 budget with an increase of another $102 m for 20/21), the clergy have been submitted to political authority rather than separated from it.

For example, in 1925, Judge Sheikh Ali Abd-el-Raziq (1888–1966), known as the father of secular Islam, published a book, *Al-Islam-wa-Osoul-Alhokm*[7] (Islam and the Foundations of Political Power), arguing for the abolition of the caliphate, which he described as a human innovation. Citing the Quran and other sources, he argued for the separation of state and religion and posed a simple question: 'Was the Prophet [Muhammad] a King?'[8] When a majority of his al-Azhar colleagues attacked him, a few came to his aid; however, a campaign against Raziq led to his expulsion from his judicial post.

Al-Azhar, a power centre and an institutionalised 'Church' in all but name, which Islamised this budding secularism, saw the likes of Raziq's attempts to secularise Islam as undermining their authority as a power centre. The Islamists were encouraged by the new 1923 constitution, which, for the first time since Egypt's democratic process had started 120 years earlier, specified one faith – Islam – as a source of legislation and the official religion of the state.

In 1947, Mohammed Ahmed Khalafallah (1916–1991) presented his doctoral thesis at Cairo University's Arabic Department on the art of literary narration in the Quran.[9] His approach led al-Azhar to pressurise the panel to reject the thesis' admission; he was transferred to a non-teaching job, while the professor supervising his studies was banned from teaching Islamic theological studies.[10]

Al-Azhar continued to attack modernising philosophers – like Dr Taha Hussein (1889–1973), who stood trial for blasphemy but whose case collapsed. When Dr Hussein joined Abd-el-Raziq in calling for Egypt to emulate Turkey in changing its Arabic alphabet to a Latin script, which would have simplified printing processes, al-Azhar accused them of attempting to undermine Islam; the calls to modernise Arabic-language printing eventually died out.

CHAPTER 25
Naguib Mahfouz, Censorship and 'Alexandria Man'

The buildings, designed by Italo-Alexandrian architects, project inspiring facades and have impressive entrances with marble staircases. They house offices and doctors' surgeries, and several *pensiones* often run by war widows. One, Pensione Miramar, was the location for the 1969 film *Miramar* – an adaptation of the 1967 novel of the same name by the 1988 Nobel laureate Naguib Mahfouz.

Egyptian censors delayed the film's release by a year over one word. *Toz* is salt powder, but it meant 'worthless' or 'Who cares?' in demotic Egyptian (salt was non-taxable in the country) – a little like saying 'Who gives a toss?' '*Toz*' is contemptuously uttered in the movie by the landowner-aristocrat character when Nasser's Socialist Federation* commissar introduces himself. Petrified by the thought that he might permit an insult to the Socialist Federation, the censorship chief kicked the problem upstairs to the minister of culture, who in turn played safe by sending the film celluloid reels to Nasser himself.

When the president eventually viewed it, months later in 1968, he did not mind *toz* being voiced by, in the regimespeak, 'a negatively painted character'. Nasser sought a second opinion from the rubber-stamp parliament's speaker, Anwar Sadat. Mahfouz turned down Sadat's invitation to join him for a private screening to discuss the movie. Sadat agreed with Nasser's assessment of *toz* but wanted to cut another 'disparaging to women reference'. Stories like this show Nasser's tight grip on all media of expression – spending two hours

---

* Nasser's Socialist Federation (founded 1961) was the single political party that ruled Egypt until Sadat rebranded it to serve his own regime (see Chapter 26 – 'Heikal's Paradox – a Schizophrenic Attitude to Culture').

CHAPTER 25   Naguib Mahfouz, Censorship and 'Alexandria Man'

watching a movie to decide whether to censor one word. They also indicate the centralisation of power, with officials and ministers terrified of making decisions without referring to Nasser – thus paralysing the government machinery. Sadat's input is also curious: while obediently approving his boss's ruling, he also added his mark. He could have been signalling his disassociation with his 1940s Islamist allies, but it was more likely to have been the influence of his second wife, Jihan,[1] on his way of thinking despite his rural background and tendency towards traditional Islamic teaching. After Sadat became president following Nasser's death in 1970, Jihan, as the First Lady,[2] played a crucial role in dusting off regulations prohibiting FGM – an issue that tend to be forgotten because few bothered to report incidents.

Miramar was Mahfouz's only novel set entirely in Alexandria and only one of two set outside the Old Fatimid quarter of Cairo, where all the events of his other 32 novels and most of his 350 short stories took place. Despite the narrow, almost-Dickensian localisation of most of his works, Alexandria has been an essential intellectual well from which Mahfouz filled his ink bottles. He spent every summer there in daily conversation with contemporary Egyptian thinkers and their visiting European friends.

I had a lucky encounter with the celebrated Nilotic scribe, not in one of Mehatet el-Ramleh's iconic bars or pâtisseries but much further east – in Sarraiyah, which marked the start of Sidi-Bishr district. Café and Casino Petruo, established in 1909 by Nikos Petrou as a restaurant, was from 1930 onwards managed by his son, Panayoti, and his wife, Caliope Manolagas. The premises, which hosted dance and music in another age, was located on the corner of the corniche and Rue Ikbal at the western foot of a large sandstone rock in Sidi-Bishr. Sarraiyah had been established as a military post in the nineteenth century,[*] and saw action in all the subsequent wars in which Alexandria was involved.

Three European-educated Egyptian intellectual giants followed Mahfouz in spending the morning in this quiet secluded café, hidden from holidaymakers and journalists during Alexandria's summer months. The first was French-educated philosopher, historian, novelist, dramatist and essayist, the Alexandrian half-Turkish Tawfiq El-Hakim (1898–1987), who had developed Egyptian drama with his 1933 *People of the Cave* and mocked society and the establishment in a series of philosophical dialogues with his imaginary jackass. His friend was travel writer and essayist Dr Hessein Fawzi (1900–1980), who 'deserted' his medical-surgeon post for the realm of letters and

---

[*] The name comes from the generic Ottoman Turkish term for palace, court-house, ministry building, hall, fortifications or castle.

Alexandria Adieu

published many travel essays under the pen name 'Sindbad'. His style was of the 'A letter from...' type with socio-political and historical analysis. Like El-Hakim, he was an Egyptian-identity patriot who resisted and ridiculed colonel Nasser's Arabisation of his country. I had been introduced to the trio by an anglophile I had met in the London Old Vic theatre a few years earlier: the Cambridge-educated academic who declared himself an enemy of academism, poet, literary and drama critic, and essayist Dr Louis (Lewis) Awad (1915–1990) – the third of our four illustrious figures.

The earlier trio did not, however, voice their criticism until 1968, following the humiliating defeat suffered by Nasser and his Arab allies in the 1967 Six-Day War. Awad was more noticeable and, time-wise, ahead of the others in criticising Nasser. He was briefly jailed in 1959 alongside patriots opposing Nasser's Arabisation of the country and erasing 'Egypt' as an official name.* Awad's 1965 book *An introduction to Arabic philology* was banned by court ruling: al-Azhar had petitioned the court, claiming the book was an affront to the sanctity of the language of the Quran, which Muslims believe to be the word of Allah.

Dr Awad presented evidence that Arabic, like any other language, evolved and developed, with many words acquired from various tongues. Not only did he dismiss as fanciful the idea that the Biblical Adam and Eve spoke Arabic, he also said that there was no mention by early historians and travellers of Arabs among the ancient civilisations predating Christianity. The moderniser-secularist Awad believed not in God or religion but in the concept of continuous Egyptianism as an identity.

Der Alexandria-Mann

As a disciple of Alexandrinology, I believe that Awad was the closest to fitting Nietzsche's description of *der Alexandria-Mann*. In Awad's life, I see the connection between Oscar Wilde's 'critical spirit of Alexandria' and the German philosopher's explanation. In his 1891 essay 'The Critic as An Artist', Wilde maintains that there is really not a single form that art now uses that does not come to us from Alexandria's critical spirit, where these forms were either stereotyped or invented or made perfect. I say Alexandria, not merely because it was there that the Greek spirit became most self-conscious, and indeed ultimately expired in scepticism and theology, but because it was to that city, and not to Athens, that Rome turned for her models.[3]

---

* Egyptians' objection was twofold: the confederation with Syria was unconstitutional as it was carried out by Nasser without debate or being voted on as a party manifesto; and Egypt as a name disappeared, the country becoming the 'Southern Province' of the United Arab Republic.

CHAPTER 25   Naguib Mahfouz, Censorship and 'Alexandria Man'

This connection was posed more sharply and more polemically by Friedrich Nietzsche (1844–1900) in his critique of 'Alexandrian culture' and 'Alexandrian man' in that great 1872 founding document of modern sensibility, *The Birth of Tragedy*.[4]

For Nietzsche, 'Alexandrian man' is 'theoretical man', who first achieved cultural supremacy in ancient Alexandria and dominates the modern world's culture. Alexandrian man is the inventor, the abstractor, the calculator, the scholar who believes he can guide life by 'science' and correct the world by reason and knowledge. He is an optimist, who turns his back on the profound Dionysian truths of life and on any metaphysics that would acknowledge them, and substitutes for metaphysics and metaphysical consolation an earthly consonance. He seeks to keep the individual forever safe by confining him within a limited sphere of soluble problems. The goal of the Alexandrian man is knowledge, science, scholarship – *Wissenschaft* in German. 'All our methods of education have this ideal primarily in view; any other form of existence has to struggle on laboriously beside it, as something tolerated, not intended.' Nietzsche's *Alexandria-Mann* subsumes ancient Alexandria but goes beyond her in a metaphor for a psycho-cultural condition submitting the old world's gods of creative arts to scholarly scientific knowledge.

Awad's work between 1959 and 1966 infuriated both non-religionists and Islamists. The former reported him to Nasser as undermining Arabisation (and, by association, Nasser's federation with Syria) and the latter accused him of atheism and belonging to communist organisations, whose members the autocratic Egyptian president incarcerated between 1957 and 1966.

Awad was not a communist but a liberal-minded modernist who belonged with early twentieth-century egalitarian reformists whose calls for social justice resembled the slogans of Marxist groups. By the 1950s, Awad's fellow liberals had already shifted their focus from poverty alleviation and equality, leaving the Marxists to own progressive and social causes. Unlike his fellow-Western-educated liberals, Awad kept the social-justice flag flying on, which gave Nasser's reactionary, anti-modernity and anti-free-thinking commissars an opportunity to label him a communist and lock him up.

These four thinkers – Awad, Fawzi, Hakim and Mahfouz – were now ordering, in demotic Egyptian, *hors d'oeuvres*, *pâtisseries* and *café au lait* by their French names in a Greek café. In 1968, French culture was still dominant in Alexandria before the English language slowly took over. Services like shoe polishing, cleaning and catering were done by impoverished, mostly uneducated, rural migrants, who learned many French words, as part of the lingua franca, in order to

225

communicate with the customers they served. It was a generational legacy: Egyptian postgraduates were sent to France and Italy on full government bursaries in the nineteenth and early twentieth centuries. Their influence was evident in culture, arts, media and literature; the educated British-Egyptians became politicians, engineers and industrialists.

In that summer of 1968, Mahfouz and his companions preferred Café Petrou's quiet veranda in the shade of tall trees and the vegetation of Sarraiyah's rocky fort, with its famous Navarone-type giant naval guns. I once witnessed a firing exercise in an early 1950s autumn while the corniche road was closed to traffic. We boys, copying war movies, hid behind a makeshift trench in an opening opposite the rock – waiting, with our fingers in our ears, for the massive guns to sound. Once fired, we ran across the road to the seafront, sharing two sets of binoculars between us, anticipating the huge column springing up with the shell exploding in the water several miles out to sea.

My last visit to Petrou was in January 1971 – a quick stopover when I lunched at the deserted café with Suad, the nightclub dancer, having snatched a day trip to Alexandria to see her during a short visit to Cairo.

The ancient Egyptian monolith of Cleopatra's Needle *(above)* stands on the Embankment in London today between Waterloo Bridge and the Golden Jubilee Bridge that crosses from Charring Cross.

A painting of the storm in the Bay of Biscay *(above and below)* depicts *The Olga* towing Cleopatra, following set off in more peaceful waters from Alexandria. A lithograph captures the arrival of the cylinder in the Thames some 5,000 km away.

The statue of Muhammad Ali Pasha *(above)* founder of Modern Egypt whose projects resurrected Alexandria. He is the protector of the city in Alexandrian folklore. A view of Alexandria's Menasciyah Square built by Francesco Mancini in the early 19th century *(below)* shows the extent of European architectural influence.

Baurdot on Rue Fuad *(above)*, the iconic patisserie where Durrell met Eve on their fi[rst] date and where Cavafy first met Forster. Villa Ambron in Moharrem Bey *(below)* whe[re] Lawrence Durrell lived with Eve Cohen and started writing the drafts of Alexand[ria] Quartet in the tower.

The iconic double deck Ramleh tram *(above)* that was in service from 1910 until late 1970s. The Bacus tram stop *(below)*, taken in 1918, the same year when Colonel Nasser was born, a stone throw from the tram stop.

Alexandria was the only city outside Britain to sustain relentless air-raids from the Luftwaffe and Italian air force until the end of 1942.

Alhambra Theatre *(above)* and cinema opened in 1900. Reflecting the cosmopolitan nature of Alexandria's society, the images here show the founding meeting of the Maltese Society *(left)* inside and a programme in Greek from 1921 *(below)*.

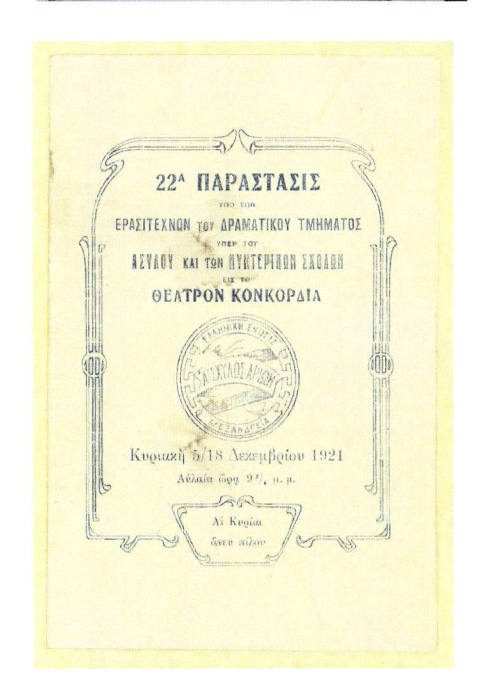

Gare de Masr, Alexandria's central Railway station, *(above)* rebuilt in 1915 to replace the one constructed in 1854 *(left)*, and the square in front of it completed in 1920 *(below)*.

Le Bourse in 1920 *(above)* was one of the busiest stock exchanges in the world made millionaires and history. The Muslim Brotherhood fired on Nasser on its balcony in 1954 and from the same balcony Nasser nationalised Suez Canal in 1956. Alexandria port *(below)* was once a major shipping hub.

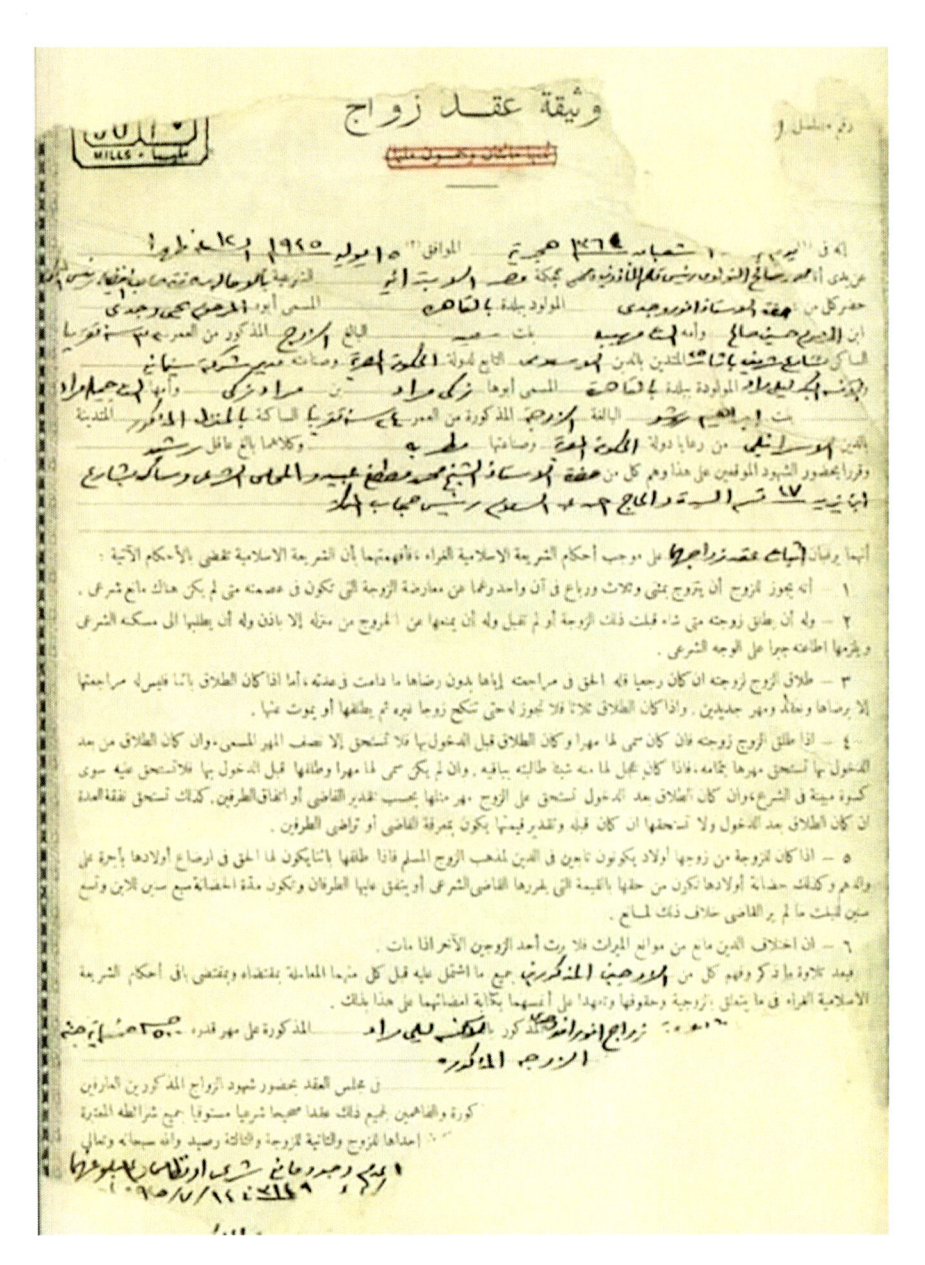

Alexandrian Jewish songstress and movie star Leila Murad 's marriage certificate to famous actor Anwar Wagdy *(above)* includes the entry in the religion section as "Israelite" for her and "Islam" was him. The whirlwind romance and wedding *(opposite)* seized popular imagination across the nation.

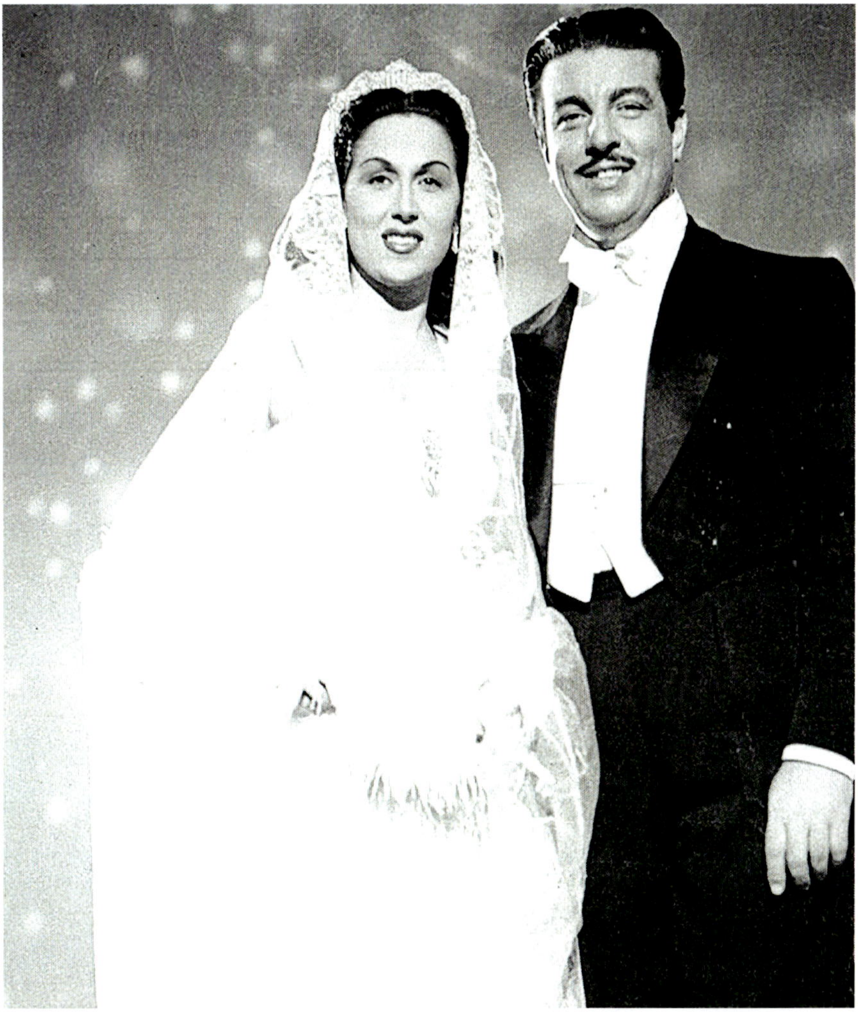

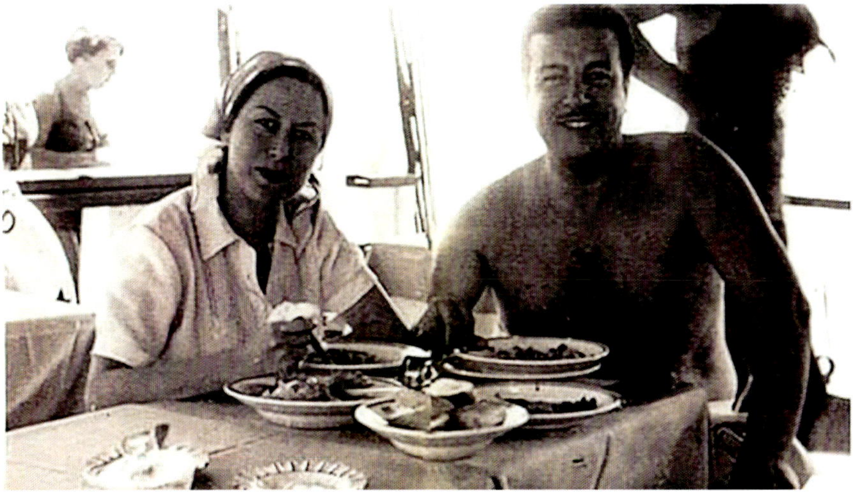

The Alexandria Israeli Hospital on Rue Abu Keir *(above)* and the leading medical Staff in 1933 *(below).*

רופאים, אחיות, רוקחים של בית־המרקחת, ועובדים של המעבדה, המשרד, חדר־הרנטגן, המטבח והמכבסה של בית־החולים היהודי באלכסנדריה — 1933. תאה באמצע השורה השניה

Eliyahu-Hanavi Synagogue on Rue Naby Daniel *(opposite)*, founded in 1354 by Sephardic Jews fleeing Spain. It was damaged by French bombs in 1798, and restored in 1850 *(above)* by funds from Viceroy Abbas Helmi I and money raised by local Jews and Sir Moses Montefiore. It still holds services today for the few remaining Alexandria Jews and many visiting Jews from around the world

> **I love bikinis, says Miss Egypt**
> By PAT TYLER
>
> FOURTEEN lovely girls, in London for the "Miss World" competition next Monday, were the best of friends yesterday—until the 15th contestant, Miss Egypt, arrived.
>
> The 14 girls, from all over the world, arrived at a Press lunch and reception wearing smart, simple dresses or suits. Miss Egypt wore a revealing, off-the-shoulder black cocktail dress.
>
> They all walked smilingly down a flight of stairs into the restaurant, shook hands with their hosts, and went to their tables.
>
> All, that is, except Miss Egypt. She blew kisses left and right and ignored her hosts.
>
> **SO BRIEF**
>
> After lunch the girls were asked to change into bathing suits for photographs. Miss Egypt—her name is Miss Marina Papelia, from Cairo—swept from the room . . . and the strapless top of her dress collapsed as she went.
>
> She is seen *in the dress in the picture on the right*.
>
> A few minutes later she was back in the briefest of brief bikinis. "Miss Egypt," pleaded the organiser, "bikinis are not liked in this country—or in this type of restaurant."
>
> **SHE SAID...**
>
> Miss Egypt looked at the other girls, all in one-piece bathing suits. Then, running her hands over her hips, she said loudly: "None of these girls have anything *here*—I have. Why shouldn't I wear a bikini?"
>
> The other girls ignored her, but the organiser tried again. "Miss Egypt, I am only trying to help you—this is not a bathing beauty contest. The judges will choose the girl who looks best in evening dress and a swim-suit. THEY WON'T LIKE BIKINIS."
>
> This time Miss Egypt went and changed.
>
> Meanwhile, the other girls were talking. Said Miss Israel —a quiet, graceful girl—" Do not ask me what I think of bikinis." Miss Ceylon—in a silvery-pink sari — said: "I only once before, for the Miss Ceylon contest. I am a little shy even in that."
>
> And Miss U.S.A.—in a smart white one-piece suit — commented: "That's something I just could not do—walk about in front of all these people in a bikini."
>
> But Miss Egypt had disappeared again, and returned wearing the bikini.
>
> "I like bikinis," she told the beauty contests wearing bikini. After this contest, I want to stay in Europe or America to do film work. I will not go back to Cairo—there is no scope for my talents there."

Alexandrian Marina Papelia who represented Egypt in Miss world 1953 *(left)* was disappointed she wasn't allowed to parade in bikini and caused scandals in London, leading the judges to award the crown to a French rival in the competition.

Palelia's fellow Alexandrian, Antigone Costanda, *(below)* won the 1954 Miss World Crown shouting it was a victory for Marina who had been cheated of the crown. Miss Universe 1935 was also Alexandrian: Charlotte Wassif.

Life Magazine cover, September 1942, carried picture of Alexandria born princess Fawzia taken by Cecil Beaton who described how, if Botticelli were reincarnated, she would be the subject of his Venus.

Europa and the Bull made by Fathy Mahmoud in the 1950s tells the story of Zeus who disguised himself as a bull to carry Europa, daughter of the King of Tyre, to Crete and have children with her whose descendants were to construct Alexandria.

CHAPTER 26
Change and 'Uglification'

Naguib Mahfouz's and Suad's favourite, quiet Café Petrou is no more. Sarraiyah rock – with its beautiful, fragrant climbers; mature Mediterranean pines; weeping willows; camphor; mulberry; and ancient climbing vine – and, of course, its guns – has also gone. The historic site was replaced by another monument to ugliness: a shopping mall with a few windowless, indoor cafés below a high-rise block and hotel, owned by the military who controlled Egypt since the 1952 coup. Disfiguring of the Maid of the Mediterranean, as Alexandria has been known, was accelerated from the 1990s onwards, when corrupt officials assisted property developers in unleashing their philistine architects on the city. The systematic destruction of magnificent Italian architecture, the villas with their fragrant hedges and trees meant that the visible foundations of Alexandria's modern identity were systematically erased to be replaced by suffocating concrete monsters.

The catastrophic mutilation of Dinocrates' beautiful 2,300-year-old street pattern resulted from cultural and political changes. The corruption that misinterprets building regulations (or circumvents them all together) outdated housing laws and demographic change forced by the military-backed republican regime conspired to deface Alexandria. The story of our old villa, where we had shared three generations of memories on a fragrant Sidi-Bishr street with delightful flowers and climber-covered fences, was a case in point. The two-storey 1930s building with its garden has become a modern 15-storey residential block. The once light, bright Rue Nineteen – continually refreshed by sea breezes carrying scents of jasmine, acacia, citrus and honeysuckle – now only sees the sun for a short time around midday. It

Alexandria Adieu

has been plunged into darkness by monstrous towers with heights ten times the width of the road.*

An Egyptian-national brother-in-law of mine went into partnership with an unscrupulous property developer in an attempt, so he claims, to save something. Our villa,[1] occupied at the time by my sister and himself, was part of what remained of the family portfolio, which had shrunk to below a fifth of its 1930s value and size, and the rental income – fixed by antiquated laws – wasn't covering overheads. A son of the *nouveau riche* Caireans who had bought the plot next to our villa cashed in his army retirement pension and started turning their modest one-storey lodge into a block of flats. He followed the prevailing practice of bribing officials for retrospective planning permission to add an extension swallowing up the front garden. The officials replace records in order to show that the building has always been a multi-storey block using a loophole permitting the addition of extra floors. The *nouveau riche* Cairean used cowboy-builders, digging next door and causing severe subsidence to our villa. My brother-in-law did not report the incident in time to halt the work, as instructed by his wife. My late sister was an academic in Germany (where she passed away in 2008), and spent little time in Alexandria. In practice, nobody reported building-regulations breaches since everyone flouted them. The people who invented bureaucracy thousands of years ago devised ways to prolong the rare planning complaints through endless litigation. Meanwhile, flats that replace villas have been already occupied, and the equally corrupt local councillors (or MPs) tell the media that demolishing unauthorised buildings will make residents homeless while there was a chronic housing shortage.†

A tragedy similar to that of Sidi-Bishr's Rue-Nineteen was inflicted on every suburb of Alexandria. Simultaneously, central El-Balad's great Italian and French eighteenth- and nineteenth-century building facades were degraded beyond recognition. To add eyesores to insult, their frontages have been covered with signs advertising everything from lawyers' practices to dentists' surgeries, *services de coiffeur*, escort agencies fronted by massage parlours, and basement garages turning into makeshift mosques. In the last-named case, balconies host the mosques' loudspeakers, adding incomprehensible deafening mixes with several muezzins competing in their calls to prayer.

---

*The initial municipality building regulations limit the height of building to no more than three times the width of the road, but local planners claim the national building regulations override 100 years old local planning laws.
†Alexandria's population grew from 1 million in 1950 to 1.5 million in 1960 – to 2.8 million in the following decade, and 5.281 million in 2020.

CHAPTER 26   Change and 'Uglification'

The outdated Housing Acts and regulations lead landlords to deliberately leave buildings to crumble, and then justify knocking them down. If a building is heritage-listed, the fines involved are too insignificant to dent a developers' profit margin; some escape the fine altogether by bribing officials.

Nasser's hostility towards Jewish and non-Nilotic Alexandrians led to a mass exodus of thousands who weren't the regime's initial target. Their vacated properties fell into the hands of newly created *al-Hirassah*,* the de facto landlords of thousands of empty buildings. The army officers and Nasser's commissars who managed the *al-Hirassah*, and their cronies, occupied the best of central Alexandria's classic buildings, which had been hastily vacated by the departed and the deported. The new residents paid the old rent, taking advantage of loopholes. Other houses were homes and businesses whose owners, leaving in a hurry in the aftermath of the Suez War, sold for as little as £€50 ($220 at the time) to ethnically Nilotic neighbours or employees. The new owners' aesthetic tastes and attitude to historic architecture were different from those of the old proprietors.

Nasser's socialist, anti-private-landlord laws enforced the concept of fixing rents at the date of signing the agreement; some of these went back to Ismail's reign. The country's Housing Acts allow tenancies to be passed to children and grandchildren without updating the rental agreement. Egyptian commentators' argument that reforming housing laws would be unpopular is disingenuous in a country where the unelected ruling autocracy has been making new laws, or repealing existing ones, on a whim for six decades.

---

* The military-run committees in charge of sequestrated assets.

CHAPTER 27
Heikal's Paradox –
A Schizophrenic Attitude to Culture

Egypt's celebrity *littérateurs* like Mahfouz actually owed a considerable part of their success to Colonel Nasser's authoritarian administration. The regime's propaganda chief, Mohamed Hassanien Heikal (1923–2016), provided them with financial security and facilities. Mahfouz penned 12 novels and short-story anthologies during 17 years of state subsidies. Heikal – as editor from 1957 to 1974 of *Al-Ahram*, the best-known Arabic-language daily for decades and the most influential in the region for 30 years – made top writers accessible to millions of Egyptians. He allocated generous space for them in the weekend literary-review section of the paper.

Traditionally, journals and newspapers rather than books had, since the nineteenth-century *Nahda*, made world literature – either in the original European languages or translated – accessible to Egyptians. Cavafy and Forster published first in Alexandria's newspapers years before writing books. The Egyptian press focused more on literature than on sections like sport or entertainment before maturing around the turn of the twentieth century, helped by two external factors. First, Christian Syrian journalists escaping conflict and Ottoman repression launched newspapers in Egypt, including *Al-Ahram*, which were less restricted by Islamic teaching than home-grown periodicals. Second, British control from 1882 onwards was a major modernising factor, introducing models of journalism that were copied locally. Whether in Arabic or several other languages, the Egyptian press became a public opinion maker in the political sense.[1]

By the 1930s, the country's Arabic-language publications had become a semi-academic arena for the advancement of an evolving literary Arabic language (written only, since no Egyptian speaks it)

CHAPTER 27   Heikal's Paradox – A Schizophrenic Attitude to Culture

with oriental characteristics, at the expense of the extensive demotic Egyptian lexicon. These publications' legacy helped Colonel Nasser to weaken the Egyptian identity by oriental Arabisation. Nasser's mission was continued by Heikal, who became the toast of Arab authoritarian regimes after his later rift with Sadat.

Throughout the 1960s, Heikal used his weekly column in *Al-Ahram* to promote the idea of moving Egypt away from the modern Euro-Mediterranean culture sphere into the embrace of Arab countries within a larger Islamic-world orbit. His crusade ran counter to the original role of *Al-Ahram* in the late nineteenth century. The paper had been founded in Alexandria by the Syrian migrant brothers Bisharah Takla (1852–1901) and Salim Takla (1849–1892), who supported the Alexandria-based Egyptian-identity-focused independence prevalent during the 1880s Ourabi-led officers' mutiny.[2] The newspaper was nationalised along with the rest of the media in 1960, becoming the official mouthpiece for Nasser's autocracy (1954–1970). Heikal kept Egypt's top intellectuals inside a Johnsonian tent.* Most were from the left, like playwright and short-story writer Youssif Idris (1927–1991);[3] playwright Lutfi el-Khouli (1929–1999), who edited the monthly *al-Taliaa* (Vanguard), a platform for Egyptian Marxists; and the late UN secretary-general, Dr Boutros Boutros-Ghali (1922–2016) editing *Assiyash-Aldawliah* (International Politics) (1965–1990). Those publications generated a carefully narrowed, indoctrinating awareness (viewing regional and international politics through national/socialist and pan-Arab lenses). The process confused the post-Suez generations about their independent Egyptian identity (forged and polished over 160 years of modernity) by adding imported Arabic and Islamic characteristics.

The Authoritarian Organs of Corruption

Egypt's republican era has been plagued by corruption and nepotism with a maze of apparatuses making ordinary people, especially the poor, too scared to approach the organs of officialdom. Injustice has been the norm, with the country's police and security forces acting brutally and relying on informers and informants from among the poor relations of targeted persons. While the regime was economically backward, it spent lavishly on art, cultural festivals and sports – as long as the relevant stars toed the line. Nasser's political apparatuses became a gravy

---

* US President Lyndon B. Johnson (1908–1973) is credited with the phrase: 'Better to have your enemies inside the tent pissing out, than outside the tent pissing in.'

231

train, thus institutionalising corruption. The one-party, Socialist Federation, SF (1961–78) evolved through several metamorphoses from the Liberation Rally, formed by the 1952 coup officers who had no popular base, to the *Hei'at el-Tahrir* (Liberation Board), rebranded *al-Ittihad-Al Qawmi* (Nationalist Federation, NF) in 1957. Searching for a base to back his socialist reforms (nationalisation and sequestrations), Nasser renamed NF *Alittihad al-Aishtraki* (SF) in 1961.

In 1957, Papa and his friends were concerned about the wave of 'Egyptianisation' (nationalisation) that was leading investors and businesses to flee the country. They reasoned that when no more assets remained to nationalise, the government would borrow – increasing public debt and raising taxes. They were proven right.

Further economic hardship was caused by a drop in the productivity of the workforce. Colonel Nasser's National Charter* made membership of a trade union a condition for obtaining a public-sector job, but joining the SF became a prerequisite to joining any trade union. Attending indoctrination courses was compulsory for new SF members. I observed a graduation seminar at Cairo University in spring 1968, invited by an SF member who asked me to remain quiet. The leaders on the stage were articulate in promoting socialism and justifying grabbing the industrialists' assets but were economically illiterate, exploiting young participants' naivety. A student questioned the justification of sequestrating a family-built business, and was asked in turn how the family had acquired that business in the first place without exploiting Egyptian *fellaheen*? Unsurprisingly, nobody answered, 'by raising capital through bank borrowing to start a business'. Astonishingly, their studies curricula did not include the basic economics of investment loans, which had been the known means of financing businesses in Egypt a mere decade earlier. Theirs was a generation of Soviet-style dependency on the state for employment and services, with little motivation for individual initiatives.

Nasser, the republic's authoritarian president, appointed himself both chairman and secretary-general of the party when it became the Arabic Socialist Federation (ASF) until he died in 1970. This move and the new name linked ideology with politics and the economy, pushing Nasser's pan-Arab ambitions – starting with the 1958 ill-fated

---

* Colonel Nasser replaced the 1956 'revolutionary' constitution (which made little legal sense) with the National Charter on 21 May 1962 at a mass rally labelled 'The National Congress of Labouring Forces' that emulated Soviet, Chinese and North Korean Communist party congresses, at which handpicked members applauded and unconditionally rubber-stamped the leadership's recommendations. It became the blueprint for Colonel Gaddafi's People's Committees and their congresses held every few years in his 'Libyan Arab Republic'.

CHAPTER 27   Heikal's Paradox – A Schizophrenic Attitude to Culture

federation with Syria: the United Arab Republic (UAR). The union ended with a military coup in Syria in 1961, yet Nasser kept its official name of UAR without 'Egypt'.

Nasser's Messenger
Nasser gave, Heikal a free hand and a considerable budget, enabling him to turn the aforementioned *Al-Ahram* group into a think tank. I visited the newspaper's massive building on Rue Ibrahim Pasha (renamed Rue République) during my trips to Cairo in the 1960s. Journalists used to drink in the *Al-Ahram* bar on the sixth floor, where they served *birra masriyah* (Egyptian beer) and Stella, rebranded *Birra al-Ahram* as well as whisky; gin; vodka; Egyptian, Greek, French and other European wines and cognac; and varieties of cocktails. The bar had a self-service cafeteria and a waiter-service restaurant.

The newspaper was respected nationally and internationally; news agencies and diplomatic missions awaited Heikal's Friday column. Entitled '*Bisarah*' ('Frankly speaking'), this comprised over 2,000 words of opinionated analysis using vivid metaphors. In reality, it reflected his master's mood of the week, which led observers and foreign diplomats searching between the lines to decipher Nasser's intentions. Sometimes Nasser's hidden message was a trial balloon.

Heikal was Nasser's confidante, and would have afternoon tea at the presidential palace each Thursday. The two were partners in brainstorming anti-European policies, which the former sold to the public. Together, they put an end to Muhammad Ali's 160-year epoch of modernity and reversed his outward-looking policies that opened up Egyptian society to European culture and free-market economics.

Following Muhammad Ali's example, Khedive Ismail and King Fuad I engaged in national projects that Europeanised Alexandria and modernised Egypt. In contrast to the khedives' vision, Heikal convinced Nasser to turn his back on European civilisation since 'the west will always treat him as a minor', as Heikal himself repeated to me, insisting that the Western nations would have never allowed Nasser to act independently. Wanting his leader to be a big fish in a small pond, Heikal persuaded Nasser to play a leading role within three geographical and ideological circles to which he alleged Egypt belonged – Africa, and the Arab and Islamic spheres – while leaning towards the Soviet bloc. He convinced Nasser that his widespread support within Arab countries would be similar to Hitler's popularity among German-speaking communities in central Europe. The result was regression and a reversal of the modernisation project. The African sphere, a geographical reality, was soon neglected by the regime because most Africans preferred to continue closer cooperation

233

with Europe – many remaining within the Commonwealth or *la Francophonie*.

The Arab sphere was more an ideological fantasy than a genuine geographical extension of Egypt, which, until Sudan broke away in 1956, had had a border with only one Arab-majority country (Libya) but bordered six African nations and Israel (mandate Palestine before 1948). After Sudan's separation, Egypt's geographical neighbours were one African country (Sudan), one Arab nation (Libya) and Israel. Confederation with Syria gave Nasser borders with Iraq, Jordan and Lebanon. Arabisation became inseparable from the Islamic domain, thus dangerously adding to the muddled new nationalism a powerful faith-based resistance to modernity – many Islamic teachings still present modernity as a hostile takeover by Judaeo-Christian Westerners.

In a bitter twist of irony, Heikal's own media empire fell victim to his successful mission – symbolising Egypt's disastrous journey from modernity to a backward, medieval culture. I was invited for lunch at *Al-Ahram* during a stopover in Cairo in 1998 by Egyptian author and veteran war reporter and military historian Abdou Mubasher (b 1937). We couldn't have the customary drink; the bar was gone. The once-stylish restaurant had turned into a shabby canteen with a dirty tiled floor like some third-world warehouse. My last visit to the building was in 2005, covering President Mubarak's reforms that allowed a contest between presidential candidates for the first time since the 1952 military coup – although, like every election since Nasser's 1956 vote, the outcome was known in advance. The lavish, luxurious 1950s wood-panelled *Ahram* editor's office was still there, as if in a time warp. But the occupier in 2005, Osama Sarrayiah (editor, 2005–11), said he hadn't stepped into that cafeteria for years due to poor hygiene; he ordered lunch for both of us from the nearby Hilton Hotel restaurant instead. As soon as Sadat became president in 1970, Heikal tailored his column to back this third military president. He justified the 1971 palace coup against his former allies, Nasser's men, in which Heikal's role had been instrumental. But he later turned against Sadat over peace with Israel.

Demonising the Jewish state and promoting a Zionist world conspiracy was a significant component in the Nasser–Heikal media message. Today, Heikal's disciples keep public opinion hostage to his legacy of rejecting normalisation with Israel despite signing a peace treaty in 1979.

I have often wondered whether Hekail tried to follow in the footsteps of two of his predecessors – the Levantine poet Khalil Mutran (1872–1949), who edited the paper from 1901 to 1902, or Daoud Barakat (1868–1933), its longest-serving editor (1902–33). While

CHAPTER 27 Heikal's Paradox – A Schizophrenic Attitude to Culture

toeing the official line, the two also gave space to Egyptian figures – especially the poets and writers who led *al-Nahda*, the enlightened movement and the drive to modernity that buit the foundations of the 1919 revolution. Or was Heikal just an opportunistic mouthpiece of two successive military-backed autocrats?

Heikal once said that keeping culturally Europeanised writers inside the tent and using them to counter the influence of Nasser's critics was his own idea. His claim remains uncontested, but according to Lutfi el-Khouli, Mahfouz and Fawzi were unhappy with the arrangement but saw this accommodation as the only way for them to be published. Mahfouz, after being awarded the 1988 Nobel Prize for Literature, made strong hints to this effect.

I couldn't glean conclusive answers from Heikal. My relationship with him turned cold after he accused me of turning into a 'Neo-Con' (neo-conservative) – a label the Anglo-American left gave the Bush Sr administration men who became advisers to his son, George W. Bush (b.1946). During the build-up to the 2003 Iraq invasion, I argued publicly that we must join with the Americans to keep British influence in the region. Heikal, like many Egyptians of his persuasion, viewed despots like Saddam Hussein (1937–2006) positively, as continuing Nasser's anti-Western pan-Arabism.

PART VII
LOVE, FAITH AND CULTURE

CHAPTER 28
Alexandria and God

Many, unjustifiably, accuse Lawrence Durrell of letting his imagination run away with him in his *Alexandria Quartet*, but in my view this is a strength, not a weakness. Durrell builds on Cavafy's and Forster's works; the intricacies and complexities of his characters' relationships manage to reflect Alexandria's spirit. Like the two *littérateurs*, he rediscovered what Cleopatra blessed about Alexandria: love before any religion.

In his analysis of Ptolemaic literature while writing notes for the exhibits of Alexandria's Greco-Roman museum,[1] Forster, the modern city's early twentieth-century biographer, presents us with love – the only faith that Alexandria held throughout the centuries:

The Alexandrians seldom sang of anything else but love: their epigrams, their elegies and idylls, their one great epic, all turn on the tender passion, and celebrate it in ways that previous ages had never known, and that future ages were to know too well. Darts and hearts, sighs and eyes, breasts and chests, all originated in Alexandria and from their intercourse between Palace and Mouseion*—stale devices to-day, but then they were fresh. *Who sculptured love and set him by the pool, thinking with water such a fire to cool?*† runs a couplet ascribed to one of

---

* The Mouseion was a building containing reading rooms and a lecture hall, founded by Ptolemy Soter as an institution that became a philosophical establishment but was financed and administered by the king's court and was considered the most significant intellectual achievement of the Ptolemian Dynasty.
† Forster is here quoting from Callimachus (305—240 BC), the Alexandrian scholar and poet who studied in the Bibliotheca Alexandrina and became assistant librarian but was never made a chief librarian. Forster, E.M., Alexandria: A History and a Guide, Whitehead Morris Limited, Alexandria, 1922. PP 19

CHAPTER 28   Alexandria and God

the early Librarians, and containing, in brief, the characteristics of the school—decorative method, mythological allusiveness, and the theme of love. Love as a cruel and wanton boy flits through the literature of Alexandria as through the thousands of terracotta statuettes that have been exhumed from her soil; one tires of him, but it is appropriate that he should have been born under a dynasty that culminated in Cleopatra.[2]

Since the times of debating in the Mouseion, and throughout her history, Alexandria handled and tamed one belief system after another that entered her walls. Whether 'the ancient religion of the Hebrews, the philosophy of Plato, the new faith out of Galilee',[3] she took each in turn, modifying it as she left her impression upon it. '[S]he extracted some answer to her question, the Alexandrian question of how can the human be linked to the divine?'[4]

Can God be loving and powerful too? Alexandria's strength and weakness were to answer the question by the conception of a link between man and God. Having always had to shift this link up and down was her weakness: if she got it too near to God, it was too far away from man, and vice versa. Her strength was that she clung to the idea of love, and much philosophical absurdity and theological aridity must be pardoned in those who maintain that the best thing on earth is likely to be the best thing in heaven.[5]

For the inhabitants of this city of saints, sinners and philosophers, the question must be raised by those who have a religious sense – but it was never asked by Islam, the faith that swept Alexandria physically and spiritually into the sea and today covers her features and allures with its *higabs* and *niqabs*.

'There is no God but God, and Muhammad is the messenger of God', says Islam, denying the need for a mediator. The man Muhammad has been chosen by the divine to tell us what God is like and what he thinks, wishes and commands – and there, at this point, all machinery ends, leaving us to face our creator. As a God of power, we encounter Him, who may temper his justice with mercy but does not stoop to the weakness of love, as experienced by humans.

With its all-powerful mighty, great, compassionate God, Islam could not be assimilated into Alexandria's soul because Muslim theologians never pondered the Alexandrian question. Words like 'love' or 'loving' were not among *al-Asma ul-Husna* – the 99 names recognised as being given to Allah in the Quran. The Muslims' 'gospel', which they believe to be Allah's own words, gave the creator names like 'Lasting', 'Victorious', 'Almighty', 'Vengeful' and even 'Merciful' – but not 'Love' or 'Loving'.[6] Unlike Christian theology and philosophy, which were studied and had their schools and splits for hundreds of years in

Alexandria, there were no similar schools or studies regarding Islam in a city that found the new faith alien to her mind and temper. It is noticeable that none of the scores of Muslim saints with shrines and mosques dedicated to them in the city was born in or originated from Alexandria – or Egypt, as a whole – but came from Andalusia, North Africa or the Levant. In contrast, Coptic and Catholic saints buried in the city were Alexandrians or Egyptians.

Forster stops at the question asked by Amr Ibin-al-As about closeness to God. Amr was the warrior and poet who led the army that conquered Egypt in 639–642 AD.* He would colonise Alexandria as the most highly valued and richest prize in the early Arabo-Islamic empire of 634–1258 AD.† As he lay on a sofa in his inland new small town of Fustat, 220 kilometres southeast of Alexandria, General Amr was asked how an intelligent man felt approaching death.

'I feel as if the heaven lay close upon the Earth and I between the two, breathing through the eye of a needle', he responded. Forster notes that this conversation 'could never have taken place between two Alexandrians' as *this* was alien to Alexandria's thinking.[7]

Alexandrians have always been sceptics by nature – especially regarding religion or a belief in a single, domineering God – which Durrell observed. 'People driven like this to the very boundaries of free will are forced to turn somewhere for help, to make absolute decisions. If she had not been an Alexandrian [i.e. sceptic], this would have taken the form of religious conversion', he writes in Clea's letter when describing her last brief meeting at Haifa with Justine.[8]

General Amr's 'heaven...close upon the Earth' answer was recalled some 1,200 years later, but in an earthly manner, by the nameless, impoverished Irish narrator of Durrell's *Justine* – later identified as Darley, in subsequent books in the *Quartet*. Darley was tempted to reply with Amr's 'breathing through the eye of a needle' quote when asked by the French consular official, Pombal, what was the matter with him. That evening he had walked about in Alexandria aimlessly 'as survivors must walk the streets of their native city after an earthquake, amazed to find how much that had been familiar was changed.' With the city crushing

---

* See Chapter 11 – 'Invasions and New Expressions'.
† The first Muslim Arab raids on the Levant started in 634 AD – with Damascus changing hands between the Arabs and the Romans no fewer than 635 times and a complete takeover of besieged Jerusalem, which surrendered in 641 AD. Caliph Omar (568–644 AD), true to his word, allowed the construction of churches and other faiths' places of worship – but of course, they all had to pay the *gizyah* poll tax to the ruling invaders. The Arabs were less successful in Asia Minor, but then took Egypt in 642; Mesopotamia and Persia in 633–51; the rest of North Africa, 647–742; Iberia in 711–88; Sindh in 711–14; and Transoxiana in 673–751.

CHAPTER 28   Alexandria and God

about his ears, Darley couldn't remember much – except running into Pursewarden and Pombal in a bar, and that the latter recited Cavafy's (whom he calls the old poet) famous 'The City', which struck him 'with a new force – as if the poetry had been newly minted', though he knew the verses very well.[9]

But the seventh-century Arab general inflicted a thousand years of dust and silence on the city after he turned his back on Alexandria, which did not entirely embrace the faith the conqueror had imposed on Internal Egypt. Unlike General Amr, Darley was not trapped between heaven and earth but between ideal love and how it was practised by Alexandria herself, as symbolised by Justine. What 'crushed [the city] about his ears' was the way in which he had parted earlier with Justine with one look – as if both wished 'to take up emplacements in each other's mind forever'.[10]

While Forster was Alexandria's curator and, like Cavafy, one of her biographers, Durrell was her storyteller: the one who intoned her epic song to the world; Durrell the soloist, who understood the city more than most who dwelled there. Perhaps, Durrell, the foreigner – portraying Alexandria with all her sects, gospels, cabals, contradictions and loves – had a more comprehensive view from the outside, while the city's insiders focused on details.

Perhaps he was fortune-reading into the city's near future; Justine *was* Durrell's Alexandria, as he saw her passing from her prime into her decay. The city was beginning, in the 1970s, to be crushed beneath the weight of a creed the Alexandrians could not reconcile with other traits they had tamed into their peculiar mix of races and tongues – the untameable faith that demolished Hellenistic Alexandria for the second time in 1,300 years.

All other religions to reach Alexandria's shores could be moulded by her to fit into her soul and mind; she had once possessed all the varieties of art, innovation and achievement of the time. For over 500 years, the city had represented the world's most refined accomplishments when the world was transforming from ancient into Hellenistic.

She [Alexandria] did cling to the idea of love. She was a sophisticated city, able to add new dimensions—new links—to the more primitive versions of the religions she met. The Alexandrian Jew, unsatisfied with an inaccessible God, created *Sophia* or Wisdom and then his *Logos* or Word, the messenger who bridges the gulf between Jehovah and man, just as the Ptolemies had created Serapis from Greek and Egyptian ingredients.[11]

Filles d'Alexandrie
Recalling my Alexandria years, love is among the most vivid memories that survived the upheavals of exodus and the mentally tormenting

experiences; it needs no notebooks, double-checking of references or newspaper archives to recall details, names, faces and places. Going back more than six decades, memories in that department are still alive in my head as if it were yesterday.

During my returns to Alexandria as a visiting reporter in 1967 and 1968 – covering the Six-Day War and its fallout, which would change the region's geopolitics – I rekindled earlier love affairs. I was 'in love' with two girls during my earlier semesters reading Arabic and Middle East History and carrying out a research project between 1963 and 1965 as an external observer at Alexandria University. The dalliances earned me the nickname 'Roika' (made up of *Roi Farouk* with a feminine 'a' added). There was a condescending, angry tone in the Egyptian students' voices when they called me by the nickname – especially the male students, who were not too amused by a *khawaga* dating girls beyond their reach.

One girl was the aloof, stylish and aristocratic Farida, named after Farouk's first wife, Queen Farida (1921–1988). The other lover was the attractive and extraverted Nariman, *ma-habiptite* (*habibty*, and *petite amie*), named after Queen Nariman (1933–2005) – the second wife of the late king and mother of Ahmad Fuad II (b.1952), the Switzerland-based exiled king of Egypt.

Adding 'Ahmad' to the prince's name was, so Alexandria folklore goes, a bad omen for the monarchy, which ended 18 months later. King Fuad I gave all his children names starting with 'F': Farouk, Fawzia, Faiza, Faika and Fathia – and printed the letter as his insignia. This was not only because he loved his mother, Ferial Qadin, but also because he was told by a mysterious fortune-teller that he should stick to names beginning with 'F' before she vanished like a mirage at the palace gates. Farouk followed his father – renaming his first wife, Safinaz, 'Farida' and calling his children Ferial, Fawzia and Fadia. But after divorcing Farida and remarrying, not only did the aforementioned Nariman keep her 'F-free' name but they also added 'Ahmed' to Fuad.

The Farida I dated had Greta Garbo's body and looks, but was a couple of inches taller than the movie star and was pale in complexion. She was an aristocrat of Macedonian heritage on her father's side and Austro-Hungarian ancestry on her mother's. Her family had lost considerable land and property to the military regime – but they still lived stylishly and, being Muslim Egyptians, faced no pressure to leave the country. Unlike Nariman, who enjoyed projecting her alluring feminine assets in the way she dressed and walked, Farida went to great lengths to conceal her beauty – which, predictably, only made her more appealing to the men she appeared to ignore. She always arrived at the campus in a vintage black 1950 Buick. The male students' eyes

CHAPTER 28   Alexandria and God

would zoom to the Buick's door as it was opened by her chauffeur, anticipating the sight of the first long, pale leg as she stepped out. After adjusting her hat and taking her bag of books from the chauffeur, she stood over 5 feet 10 inches tall, with the latest fashionable sexy heels adding to her already long legs.

This latter feature was voted – in absentia, and to the irritation of other female students – *agmal reglien* (the most attractive pair of legs) on campus, after an unofficially organised contest called during a drink-fuelled evening at the students' union bar. The next day, the then-sober student union officers reversed the decision. However, a closed group of students and willing girls held an unofficial competition on another campus: the Littorie, home to the School of Law and the School of Botanic Studies. These two buildings were separated by a *piscine* in the middle of a beautifully manicured lawn. The lively extravaganza was organised around the swimming pool, which was usually open (except for coldest winter weeks) and was surrounded by umbrellas, tables and chairs outside a café bar. Although the event was unauthorised, Nasser's repressive authorities did not intervene to ban it since it was not political. Still, a couple of *mukhbers* from state-security intelligence were spotted among attendants.

The impromptu, amateurish extravaganza was not advertised, and the *chellah* organising it had expected about ten friends or so – but surprisingly it attracted a good crowd, with several girls entering. Farida herself did not attend the event, yet she was nominated by (mostly male) students. Her entry was a life-size picture of a stunningly attractive pair of legs in a sexy pair of high-heeled shoes. Rivals claimed that the graphic artist, one of Farida's admirers, had cheated by using a photograph of Marlene Dietrich's legs. However, Fikri, the talented photographer and graphic designer from the Fine Arts college, always maintained that the poster *was* Farida's legs. His testimony was backed up by the (self-appointed) three judges whom Fikri had shown the negative of Farida's picture.

Although initially voted the 'Queen of Legs' – by a show of hands – other participants protested, demanding the non-attending contestant's disqualification. However, a counter, louder objection from revelling spectators who had been downing litres of Birra Stella all afternoon led to a compromise, pushing Farida into third place.

Despite the judge's decision, the students continued to refer to Farida's legs as *mulook el-reglien* ('the royal of all female legs'). The next day, she arrived on the campus in a pair of knee-length white boots and a black-and-white, below-the-knee *jupe*, not allowing any eyes a glimpse of her winning pins. Nor did she reveal them again for the remaining days before the late-spring half-term. However, they were

241

're-bared' in a short mini-*jupe* and a pair of FMS high heels after the break, when the contest was no longer a hot topic of discussion.

Doing the opposite of what others expected of her was just one strand of Farida's multi-layered, enigmatic personality. She was not a rebel but she would not join in what was generally popular, which, paradoxically, made her continually mysterious – fully known for being unknown. The classically conservative Farida deliberately limited the number of her friends to a carefully selected few: those that she might consider inviting to her birthday party, customarily held at Hotel San Stefano. Four was the maximum number of 'them' that she would tolerate at any one time – the term was her snobbish, misanthropic reference to everyone else.

Occasionally, I managed to drag her kicking and screaming to join my friends in one of Alexandria's top exclusive places like Beau Rivage or to listen to jazz at Pastroudis or the quieter Côte d'Or. She would insist on us first having an hour by ourselves, perhaps listening to the soft afternoon music at Santa Lucia. Her taste was typically Alexandrian Greek, and Athinèos was her favourite because we could have a private enclosure with a magnificent view of the Eastern Harbour. She also liked the Elite café, because the curtains were always drawn on this exclusively Greek-Alexandrian place whose head waiter, Stelios Koumoutsos, who knew little about archaeology, spent most of his time excavating in search of Alexander's tomb. His claim of having a secret code for maps to the lost *soma*, as Alexander's mausoleum was known, turned out to be a hoax after his documents were examined by Professor Harry Tzalas of the Hellenic Institute for Ancient & Mediaeval Alexandrian Studies.

After an hour of music and champagne, she would be in a better mood to tolerate my friends joining us for cocktails – but only when they were visitors from the UK or Europe; thus, meeting 'them' wouldn't become habitual. Unlike other girls, Farida never once accompanied me to Alexandria's oldest surviving bar, the iconic Cap d'Or, where time stood still around 1900. She considered it 'too sleazy' a place for the unique one to be seen in.

Ironically, in post-millennial – more Islamic – Alexandria, Cap d'Or remains *the* place to go and be seen, becoming a top visitors' attraction in recent years. The bar has never been updated or modernised since it was first opened as a watering hole for the nearby Bourse traders, some 120 years ago. It was not touched by the Muslim Brotherhood Islamists, who terrorised many of Alexandria's restaurants and cafés into ending alcohol sales – perhaps because it is a tourist attraction. Nonetheless, its new Muslim owner, nicknamed Sheikh Ali (because he closes his doors on the Muslim *shabbat* – Fridays), has been subjected to harassment, abuse and spitting, with rubbish frequently being dumped in front of

CHAPTER 28   Alexandria and God

his establishment. The one who loved going there with my in the 1960s was the free-spirit Nadiya; she also joined me on cabaret visits. Nadiya was an arts-and-culture socialite who earned a living in the enterprising Alexandrian way of making her omelette from different egg baskets. She gave talks in French, Italian and Alexandrian Egyptian in the city's art galleries, but was also a stand-up comedian at university events and occasionally freelanced for local publications.

Other girls frequently felt uncomfortable in Farida's presence at social gatherings – on the odd occasion when she accepted their invitations – because their boyfriends would usually pay more attention to the enigmatic, unapproachable Farida than to them. Few could dream of affording the fashions or accessories to match hers. Farida was always dressed in the latest *Mode Parisienne* and was never seen twice in the same outfit.

My other girlfriend at the time was a typically rebellious, strong-willed, head-turning and attractive *bint-balad* – *une fille d'origine alexandrine*. Despite her exhibitionist traits, no macho-man would even dare to wolf-whistle his admiration – except, perhaps, from inside a passing car or behind closed shutters. Alexandrian girls used to boast about how many wolf-whistles they collected walking down the road. Nariman was no exception as she tapped across the pavements in her sexy, open-toed high heels. She would turn heads regardless of whether her model-girl long legs were wrapped in tight black *pantalons* and a spotty white *chemisier* knotted at the waist or bared in a mini-*jupe* and elegantly-cut blouse – or an altogether more elegant ensemble, complete with a shiny patent-leather handbag when going out on a date.

Nariman was like a character who had danced on her high heels out of the pages of Edwar el-Kharrat's book *Filles d'Alexandrie*.[12] Attractive, feminine, witty, strong-willed and flirtatious, no boy could mess with Nariman. Yet, when she chose, she was warm and generous, with the ability to see through any would-be Don Juan imposter within seconds of striking up a conversation.

CHAPTER 29
Miss World

Alexandria girls...oh, Alexandria girls.
'Alexandria and its women. There are sketches here of Leonie, Gaby, Delphine...', wrote Durrell in *Justine*, 'But for the most part, these Alexandria girls are distinguished from women in other places by a terrifying honesty and world-weariness.'[1]

Alexandria girls were 'different', as Muslim men (and these were the open-minded ones!) from outside the great city would politely, but negatively, comment – meaning that the women of the historic city were too much for them: not women as they understood women to be, not like their own sisters or mothers.

But there were less-flattering names given to the *filles d'Alexandrie* by other strata of the male population. These were rural students, who descended upon the University of Alexandria like legions from another planet in 1964 after Colonel Nasser had, in a presidential decree the previous summer, abolished tuition fees without prior consultation with the Treasury or the university administration. After learning how to keep their jaws from dropping at the bevvy of beauties surrounding them, the first-year *fellaheen* students could be heard whispering to one another, 'Keep away from her, *di a'al-hal-sha'arha* [she's a loose woman]' when an Alexandrian girl smiled at them.

The sophisticated *mademoisellat Iskandriyah* were snobbish, regarding *masarwah* (non-Alexandrian) students from the rural provinces as inferior and less cultured than themselves. They allowed the odd one into the *chellah* just to make fun of him. Europeanised, even if not of European heritage, refined Alexandrian girls were undoubtedly on par with their European counterparts.

CHAPTER 29   Miss World

Miss Universe 1935, as winner of the-then 'International Pageant of Pulchritude' (also called the International Beauty Contest), was the 23-year-old Alexandrian Charlotte Wassef (1912–1988), who had been voted Miss Egypt 1934 and who went on to a career as a successful mannequin for 20 years. Miss Wassef won the international judges' unanimous vote in Brussels, where the extravaganza was held.

Two decades later in London, another Alexandrine, 20-year-old mannequin and designer Antigone Costanda won the 1954 Miss World pageant – beating Miss America, Karin Hultman, into second place while third place went to another Mediterranean mermaid – Elfi Mela of Greece. Seventeen nations from four continents and the Caribbean were represented at the event. Costanda, like Wassef, was also a former Miss Egypt, having taken the title in 1953.

In 1954, the Miss Egypt crown passed from Alexandria to Cairo and onto the head of 21-year-old Iolanda Christina Gigliotte, who was later the famous French singer Dalida, selling 170 million albums before her suicide in 1987.

She was born in 1933 to Italian immigrant parents – Pietro Gigliotti (1904–1945), who studied music, and the seamstress Filomena Giuseppina (1904–1971). They escaped the poverty of Serrastretta, in southern Italy's Calabria region, to Cairo where Gigliotti became a violinist with the Royal Opera Orchestra, setting up a family home in the city's northern Chubra district. Pietro was detained, with other Italians, in an internment camp run by Allied forces in Egypt between 1940 and 1944 – a traumatic experience that changed him into a heavy drinker, frequently becoming violent and abusive.

At the 1954 contest in London, Costanda screamed, 'It is a win for Marina [Myshi Marina] Papaelia' when crowned. She was referring to her 23-year-old fellow-countrywoman, who had taken second place in the previous year's pageant. The result had prompted reports that Papaelia's failure to take the crown had been the judges' punishment for her naughty behaviour. The Alexandrian, who was Miss Egypt 1952, represented her country in the 1953 Miss World contest, spoke five languages, and could fluently hurl insults in several others using words understood only by native speakers of those tongues.

Papaelia had initially shared a hotel room with Miss Denmark, Ingrid Anderson, who found her behaviour so objectionable that she ran screaming into the hall demanding a room or roommate change. Ultimately, the Alexandrine ended up with a room all to herself, since none of the other girls would share with her.

Like many participants at the Lyceum Ballroom in London, the Egyptian media in 1953 believed Papaelia was cheated out of the crown because of her foul mouth; according to popular opinion, the judges were making an ethical point. Instead of crowning the Egyptian girl, they awarded the title to Denise Perrier, a French convent-educated schoolgirl with a sedate personality, who had reportedly worn maquillage for the first time in her life for the contest. The decision to promote the demure French contestant over Marina and her colourful conduct became hot media gossip in the London tabloid press. Papaelia was disappointed that she could not sport a bikini in the parade, where the organisers allowed one-piece costume only. Whenever the event organiser, Eric Morley (1918–2000), took the participants on a carefully choreographed evening out to an exclusive West End club, the Egyptian girl would hold a spontaneous show with the press gathering around her. And to Morley's horror, she would be in outfits considered immodest by 1953's conservative standards.[2]

Fortunately, Marina quickly recovered from the shock of losing the Miss World crown, as became clear from her participation in subsequent media interviews and photo sessions. Pulling no punches, she told a news reporter who asked her opinion of the new, French, Miss World: 'I theenk she steenk!'

Her escapades are still talked about among pageant fans, and the event's organiser, Morley, confided in his 1967 book, *The Miss World Story*, 'Despite the headaches and frights Papaelia gave me at the time, I shall always remember her as one of the outstanding figures, in every way, among all those who have entered the contest at any time.'[3] Morley orchestrated the annual pageant every November from 1951 until his death, when his wife, Julia, took over. The London event began to be televised in 1959. The US launched the rival Miss Universe contest in 1951.

After redressing the wrong done to Marina Papaelia at the Lyceum in her 1954 winning speech, Costanda had a successful and varied career. She first went on to model in France, Egypt, Greece, Italy and throughout the Middle East before moving into interior design. At the age of 72, she was one of the judges at the 2006 Miss Egypt contest, a tradition that began in 1927 and was only interrupted for four years during the War.

Alexandrian Amour

Cleopatra's and Hypatia's spirits, and those of the beauty queens of Alexandria, whispered to my senses whenever I encountered their daughters, Farida, Nariman and a few less-colourful others.

They were the most noticeable and desired queens on the campus in the early 1960s when Alexandria of Cavafy, Forster and Durrell were still resisting Internal Egypt's deadly embrace.

Farida and Nariman, like Durrell's Justine – with her multiple-personality disorder – in a way symbolised Alexandria. They epitomised

CHAPTER 29 Miss World

the Alexandrian character's syncretism in her continuous attempt to fuse contradictory physiognomies into an alloy – a tasteful cocktail of harmony and liberalism – alongside her persistent and genuine belief in love as a virtue. The two *magnifiques femmes alexandrines* also exemplified Alexandria's age-old riddle as both, in their dissimilarity, practised the same religion - love.

Farida detested being with, let alone in, a crowd – preferring the quiet of exclusive settings. She swam with me a few times after sunset, and the darker it got the warmer and more affectionate she became. One night, under a full moon, we swam at midnight in the lagoon known as Cleopatra's Pond, located in the middle of the rocks of Miami Island, just as Egypt's last queen had done. We had the islet to ourselves because it was a chilly night when people thought the water was too cold for them to swim to the rocks (known as Gezirah Gabr-el-Khour). In reality, in the evening, Alexandrian seawater remains warmer than the sand, which cools down faster after sunset. However, getting out of the warm water into a goose-pimple-inducing breeze was another matter.

Still, the chilly evening kept swimmers away giving us a rare chance to swim naked in the moonlight. As if by some magic mastered by the last Ptolemaic queen, the water in Cleopatra's Pond was always refreshingly cold in the heat of summer days but warm and comforting on chilly spring and autumn evenings.

When Farida slipped out of the dark blue lagoon with silver streaks sliding down her naked, slim, fairy-white body and stood tall on the rock, tilting her head to inhale the rays of the full moon that impressed its face on the water, time stood still. I gazed in awe, mesmerised by a Greco-Roman alabaster version of the Birth of Venus. It was the moment Farida burned her love brand on my memory forever. Perhaps Cleopatra's magic – or the mystical, supernatural powers of Hellenistic maidens sleeping beneath the lake – had propelled Farida's allure to slide up the moon rays into a celestial beauty that night. Forty years after that full-moon midnight ritual, ancient tombs were discovered exactly beneath the rock where my Venus extended her arms to embrace the moon.

In contrast to Farida's overconfident indifference, Nariman would only venture into the sea in a two-piece *maillot* with me when we were with the *chellah*. Rarely would the two of us be seen alone on an open *plage* in the full view of onlookers, with her preferring concealed urban locations for what she called *séances intimes*. Perhaps this was to do with the influence of her father's Islamic teachings in childhood; maybe she was concerned about his reputation as a respected Muslim cleric or, worse, about gossip reaching him.

Alexandria Adieu

However, in our more intimate moments, she would bite my ear in a painful ecstasy. '*Allah, ya habibi. Allah, Allah,* don't stop, please – *ne vous arrêtez pas, s'il vous plaît*', stage-whispering her Alexandrian orgasm: a passionate, trilingual venting of joy, ecstasy and love. Our tender moments were sensual rituals brought to life in a modern epicurean temple of Cleopatra. Repressed or forgotten beliefs planted during early childhood never die but, as Freud observed, will somehow find a way to express themselves. For the daughter of an imam who led a congregation of hundreds in prayer, biting the ear of her lover and repeating the name of Allah showed how deeply buried formative beliefs rode on the back of her French liberal education. Our lovemaking left little to the imagination - only full vaginal penetration was a strict taboo for the extrovert Muslim clergyman's daughter.

Meanwhile, the introverted, ice-cold aristocrat Farida, who was not too keen on a prelude to lovemaking beyond a single French kiss, preferred going straight into full, conventional sex. On some rare occasions – especially on late winter afternoons when the sea was angry, the heavy Alexandria rain hammered the window and a bottle of champagne (of the correct, expensive label) had massaged the 'queen of legs" snotty throat – her face would surprise my unsuspecting groin in a typically unexpected move by the unique one. Within seconds, she was like a volcano. For Farida, actions expressed love more passionately than words: her entire lovemaking lexicon did not exceed six words: '*viens à moi*', she would whisper, opening her arms invitingly, and always signing off the long, hot session in cold English: 'Thank you, darling' – with a sisterly peck on my cheek, meaning get out of bed.

'Light me a cigarette, *s'il vous plaît*, there's a good chap', she would say, tapping her perfectly manicured fingernails on the bedside table where she had discarded her grandmother's long, black-and-silver cigarette holder with its ivory mouthpiece, next to her chic golden cigarette box. Sitting up cocooned in the bedsheets, she would puff out the smoke, blow me a kiss and order me out of the bedroom into the hall – or into the bar, if we were staying in a hotel – so she could get dressed in private. Never once did she dress and put on her maquillage in my presence. On one occasion, she called me into the bedroom to zip up her dress when she had misplaced the zip slider-pull hook, and I saw the contents of her, all-French-made, *boîtier de maquillage* spread across the dressing table. It was a super-classic display of femininity from a different age: the *époque glamour* of elegance and magical allure.

She spread several brushes, including two *pinceaux rouge*, alongside lipsticks, cheek blushers, pots of *poudre* and pads, golden *poudre compact* and *mascara-cils*. Then, for her eyeliners and eyebrows, there were two antique silver-and-ivory kohl *pots d'antimoine* with silver chain holders,

CHAPTER 29   Miss World

crayons à sourcils, nail vernis, crystal *parfum* containers and an Art Deco crystal perfume atomiser with a pump-ball and a braided cord.

Nariman, by contrast, was a fully Alexandrian *bint-bahary* – the affectionate folkloric term, loaded with connotations and watchful association, for indigenous Alexandrian girls from the city's Turkish quarter. She grew up in a part of Bahary called Anfoushy, a piece of the city surrounded by the Mediterranean on three sides; it was the old Pharos Island where Alexander landed in 332 BC following the instruction he received, in a divine vision, to build the great city. The sexually liberated, vociferous French-schooled Muslim clergyman's daughter was another story of what remained of twentieth-century neo-Hellenistic Alexandria.

Belief, culture, plus Alexandria's cosmopolitanism and decadence – all were assimilated in her *tête chic*. All sounded and seemed natural when, at the moment of true love expressed by senses, the faith's spiritual aspects, deeply implanted when forming her childhood identity, found a way to conform to Alexandria's true faith – love.

Love was the only religion into which Alexandria moulded the beliefs, that came with several gods, to her shores over the centuries – except for one. The latest one – which had arrived with General Amr's horsemen, complete with swords and spears – proved a bit of a challenge to handle and manipulate into blending with her faith, but at least, the name of its god was recoined in Alexandria's tongue. Alexandrians and many urban Egyptians of all religions, ethnic backgrounds and languages exclaim '*Alllaah*' to convey, sometimes, grief or disappointment but mostly admiration when encountering beauty, good taste or a pleasant surprise – and, some of them, in love, often when expressing pleasure.

CHAPTER 30
Love Songs: Alexandria's Hymns

The phrase '*Allah, ya habibi*' that my Alexandrian lover whispered rapturously in my ear was not her copyright. It was an expression frequently picked for romantic usage by Egyptian lovers, dating as far back as the 1930s and lifted from songs and films in a period when going to the cinema was the treat of the week.

Music, dance and singing were inseparable from Alexandria's spirit in hundreds of bars, pâtisseries and clubs. And because I was an external observer, not officially registered during the academic terms, I spent more time going to iconic cafés, bars and nightclubs than to student events. There were dozens of cabarets in Alexandria, especially on the seafront. Monte Carlo in Chatby and La Côte d'Azur on a rock surrounded on three sides by sea were favoured by Nadiya, my older guide and companion. Nadiya was an arts-and-culture socialite who earned a living in the enterprising Alexandrian way of making her omelette from different egg baskets. She gave talks in French, Italian and Alexandrian Egyptian in the city's art galleries, but was also a stand-up comedian at university events and occasionally freelanced for local publications. There were local singers with lovely voices and good performing dancers in the many nightclubs.

It was at La Côte d'Azur where, a few years later when I went to cover the aftermath of the Six-Day War, I met the dancer Suad and we had a short affair, but she kept in touch through longhand letters and postcards. I was with two high-spending Egyptian Air Force pilots hosting a pair of Russian airmen with a couple of escort girls when two performers came to our table: the songstress and the girl who had danced to her melody before the interval. The management encouraged this tradition because gentlemen would order champagne, at three times

CHAPTER 30   Love Songs: Alexandria's Hymns

the price of wine, for a performer joining the table; the performers were also trained to spot *wilad-elnas*. Not only I was the only one to stand up, thus embarrassing the other gentlemen into following suit when the two girls approached, but I also kissed each one's hand on the first introduction – a custom I picked from my grandfather, and hadn't discarded in the tasteless mannerless age of political correctness.

Noticing my behaviour, Suad enquired about the 'English gentlemen's' etiquette. I laughingly explained how I learned my manners long ago from my father and grandfather in Alexandria, not in England; and I didn't think much of it when she asked where I was staying. But she woke me up me at the crack of dawn with a phone call after she had finished her show, and asked me to take her for late lunch as she was going to sleep now. We went to Athinèos for lunch later that day, starting our affair. The other girl at La Côte d'Azur performed popular *tarab* (cheerful) songs like '*siret-el-Hob*' (love gossip), which included the verse containing *Allah, ya habibi* in its tune. Suad gave some inspiring performance with innovative, sexy steps that made her the toast of Alexandria's nightclubs.

The expression '*Allah, ya habibi a'ala hobbak*' (conceptually translated as 'Allah revealed himself in the way you love me') became fashionable in the 1960s: a launchpad for light-hearted puns with hints of sexual intimacy, exchanged between couples within their *chellah*. It had a subtle, socio-cultural origin as a line in a couplet (stanza) by poet Morsi Gamil-Aziz (1921–1980), written in demotic Egyptian-speak rather than the Arabic of scholarly books. His contemporary lyricists couldn't keep pace with his quill, waltzing on the page. Gamil-Aziz was nicknamed *gawahergy al-kalam* ('jeweller of words').

The '*Allah, ya habibi*' ('Wow, my love') verse was immortalised in Egyptians' public collective memory when first sung at private performances throughout 1963, before being officially launched in a live concert broadcast in 1964 by Umm Kulthum (1898–1975). This songstress gained fame across the Arabic-speaking nations, most of whom were weaned on a diet of Egyptian movies and performing arts since none of them had a film or entertainment industry to speak of.

Kulthum was among a handful of vocalists who had a *tarab* voice – a gift that elevates a singer to the higher echelons of a *mutreb*. *Tarab*'s connotations in demotic Egyptian went beyond the limits of its Arabic meaning, 'cheerfulness'. In Egypt, it denoted an atmosphere in time and place, a collective good feeling – both a state of mind and a state of the senses generated by vocal and music – and was sometimes visual too; in a live performance, it signified an energising and an engaging of several senses simultaneously. Miss Kulthum inherited her *tarab* voice from her father, Sheikh Ibrahim Beltagi, who was a village muezzin. He

251

Alexandria Adieu

needed merely the tone and a musical ear to recite the prayer call like a melody from a minaret.

Sheikh Beltagi coached his gifted daughter, who, aged ten, began singing in religious festivals in their home village. In 1921, he took her to Cairo, where she performed at private parties and concerts. Unlike European Alexandria – whose pashas, wealthy merchants and bankers held traditional classical music and opera-singing concerts in their large villas – many of Cairo's notables were from a rural background influenced by the Ottoman legacy. They preferred the long, drawn-out songs of that culture, with their accompanying music on Arabic, Turkish and Persian modal scales.

These parties often had *balady* dance performances, which – unlike belly dancing – require disciplined, harmonised, rhythmic moves with the music. Thus, in Cairo rather than Alexandria, the 25-year-old Miss Kulthum made a record – in 1924 – which would mark the start of a career spanning five decades and including 292 songs, an operetta and six moving pictures.

In 1935, she participated, alongside other singers and songstresses, in a live broadcast by the national broadcasting service al-Iza'a al-Masriyah (Radio Cairo). Launched the previous year, the service was run by Marconi's Wireless Telegraph Company on a 15-year contract with the Egyptian Government and broadcast throughout Egypt and Sudan. Several smaller private and commercial broadcast services, started up around ten years earlier, were also in operation at the time.

The diva Kulthum became Colonel Nasser's favourite performer. He weaponised her voice, turning her performances into a flagship of his regime's culture-propaganda armada and conquering the airwaves in Arabic nations throughout the MENA region. His strategy was to galvanise support among the less-sophisticated Arab masses – mostly east of Suez, where the peoples, except for some urban francophones, had little exposure to European culture. The popular songstress used the modern technology of the Egyptian Broadcast and Television Service, which was lavishly funded and modernised by the military regime, to advance her career beyond Egypt's borders. None of her rivals was given equal access to the service, or to the privileges with which she became accustomed, except perhaps for singer and music teacher Abd-el-Halim Hafez (1929–1977), who became the official male voice of the Nasser regime.

Politics and Performance

There were totalitarian parallels between the rituals and features of both Nasser's public speeches and Umm Kulthum's live concerts. Both were frequently broadcast live, were on a large scale and exceptionally long.

CHAPTER 30   Love Songs: Alexandria's Hymns

Colonel Nasser's orations were delivered to energetic crowds, packed into squares or giant marquees. They cheered and applauded on cue, sharing a common cross-border sentiment, screaming newly introduced, pan-Arab, jingoistic slogans against some external foe which, as in Orwell's *Nineteen Eighty-Four*, was frequently redefined at the whim of the ruler.

Kulthum's concerts were, like Nasser's speeches, designed to be overwhelming. The public was manipulated into regarding each event as some richly deserved and long-awaited reward. Whether Nasser's or Kulthum's, the event would be widely publicised in advance with a carefully managed campaign to generate a common sentiment

Egypt's state-controlled media created a demand and a mood of anticipation among the public for the songstress's concerts, which were transmitted live. Until Khulthum's last performance in November 1972, entertainment pages and diary editors filled acres of column inches gossiping about her music or paying for a stolen carbon copy of her handwritten lyrics. Several editors paid out handsomely to anyone who claimed to have attended one of her exclusive private performances preluding the public shows, and some journalists were repeatedly duped by con artists selling stories of phantom private shows. Sleazy tabloid reporters paid their police contacts or private detectives to spy on her dressmakers' workshop.

In the 1960s, millions beyond Egypt's borders tuned to Radio Cairo and television channels broadcasting Kulthum's concerts. Colonel Muammar Gaddafi (1942-2011) brought forward his 1969 coup d'état, which overthrew King Idris of Libya (1889–1983), in order not to clash with her monthly concert, raising suspicion about the role of Colonel Nasser's *Mukhabarat* (intelligence service) in the Libyan coup; he knew that majority of Libyans would be tuning to Cairo Radio for the concert.

The 'Jewellers of Words' – God is Love

The rhymester Gamil-Aziz started working at his father's greengrocer's before reading Law, Quranic Studies, and Pre-Islamic Poetry. He had a song broadcast by Radio Cairo when he was only 18. His style of simple phrases, often two words, from everyday usage to portray the intricacies of human emotions made his lyrics both popularly appreciable and challenging for composers, as Baligh Hamdy (1931–1993), one of the most celebrated composers of the era, once told me. We talked a great deal about Gamil-Aziz when we had afternoon tea in Paris in 1979 with his then-wife, singer Ourada Algazaeriayh (*Ouarda l'Algérienne*, 1939–2012) – a name, ironic for a French national, that was coined by the Nasser-controlled media. Ourada Fattookie was born in

Paris to Algerian–Lebanese parents. She shot to fame after moving to Cairo in 1960, playing various singing roles in Egyptian movies.

The celebrated vocalist told me that Gamil-Aziz's lyrics were the best among those of her 99 known songs, many composed by her husband, who continued to write tunes for her even after their divorce. Nasser himself ordered her deportation following a political run-in, of her own making, with his *Mukhabarat*. The feared General Intelligence Service had reported to Nasser that the songstress herself was behind the rumour of an alleged love affair with the defence minister, General Abd el-Hakim A'mer (1919–1967). Ourada returned home to Paris, where she married Hamdy in 1972. In the same year, she was invited to sing in a concert marking the tenth anniversary of Algeria's independence by President Houari Boumédiène (1932–1978), another Nasser-style autocrat, who blithely appropriated a French national's singing voice as belonging to a country she knew little about. Ourada wasn't allowed back into Egypt until Sadat reversed Nasser's deportation order in 1972. It was, in fact, Sadat who had introduced her to A'mer in 1960 during a champagne party in Syria, recorded by the *Mukhabarat* and reported to Nasser.

Gamil-Aziz's '*Allah, ya habibi*' verses were contained in his poem 'Siert-el-Hob', commissioned by Kulthum in 1962 for one of her monthly concerts, broadcast live two years later as a 55-minute-long link in a three-part show. It was one of Kulthum's most appealing odes to Alexandria because it elevated love, the city's only accepted religion, to heavenly levels. The final, five-minute-long stanza became known as the 'couplet Allah Allah'. Kulthum repeated 'Allah' over 40 times, mesmerising her audience in the auditorium and millions of her adoring fans over the airwaves – and associated the word, 'Allah', in the minds of Egyptians with physical love for the first time.

Until then, the word 'Allah' had only been verbalised for the exclamation of good feeling or the admiration of beauty, but never within the realm of the senses until it was accompanied by Baligh Hamdy's music. Always seeking any visual remnants of my Alexandria, I came across a black-and-white film recording – made a long time ago in a galaxy far, far away. In it, all the gentlemen in the Alhambra Theatre's auditorium (built 1900) in Alexandria are immaculately dressed. Not a single *higab* Islamic headdress is to be seen among the ladies who are in their *robes de soirée*, displaying their stylish jewellery with their hair in the latest *style de mode*. Some are holding their partners' hands, others swinging their heads to the rhythm of 'Allah… Allah', as if vibrating with sweet love moments, unexpectedly conjured up from their subconscious. Although the lyrics do not openly indicate an intimate scene between two lovers, Kulthum's *tarab* voice and her

CHAPTER 30   Love Songs: Alexandria's Hymns

playing with the repetition of the word 'Allah' take her audience's aural experience to new heights of sensuality.

Playing the recording in 2020 generated not *tarab*, however, but rather the blues. A combination of memories from a lost way of life and Kulthum's soul-penetrating voice vibrated the sad ambience into ecstasy. 'Vibrated into ecstasy?' Another phrase the recording had dusted-off from a dim corner of my memory. When? Who?

Eureka! The phrase was coined by Nadiya; how could I forget such an unforgettable *fille d'Alexandrie*?

Unrolling the evening newspaper, she read from the report on Kulthum's 1964 performance at the Theatre and Cinéma Alhambra. '…Vibrated into ecstasy reminding every woman in the audience who was once in love', she ran her finger down the column as she placed her kit on the unfolded newspaper on the coffee table. She spread some torn cigarettes, cigarette-rolling papers, small bits of foil, matches and tobacco wallet with its scented contents. Then, from a brown-paper bag, she emptied out an impressive mound of *mazag domestico* (homegrown cannabis). '…Ecstasy of the pleasure of love.' After taking a long drag, she puffed out a blue cloud of smoke into Nariman's face, which she had first grasped like a spinster auntie holding a restless child still, to pay it some unwanted admiration. She inserted the leviathan-sized joint between the girl's lips with her other hand.

'Ecstasy of *piacere d'amore* because the lyrics awakened in a woman her special love-making experience like worshipping rites with flowers and candles reaching a spiritual orgasm', said Nadiya in an over-dramatised tone, lifting a bubbling champagne coupe in one hand and gesticulating with the other, mimicking the motions and the voice of Hind Rustom (1931–2011), the 1950s and 60s Egyptian model and actress. Rustom specialised in playing sensual, seductive scenes and was nicknamed the 'Marilyn Monroe of Egypt'.

'The bit about love wasn't printed', she snapped, suddenly out of Rustom's character and becoming Zouzo Nabil (1920–1996) – an actress typecast in such roles as a disciplinarian prison warden, a foreign spy and a scheming nightclub owner, 'The f****** desk-sub cut it out', she downed the coupe in one go and snatched the joint (by now between my lips), replacing it with her champagne-laced lips in a long smooch before turning to Nariman and giving her a French kiss.

Her feature had been censored; Alexandria had already entered its downward spiral of weakness. It was the centuries-old weakness, the unsolved Alexandrian question of how to link the humans to the deity. Alexandria had shifted away from man, becoming dangerously close to God: Allah, the mighty, who may be 'just' and 'merciful' but who was altogether too powerful to be associated with the frailty of love.

Alexandria Adieu

When Gamil-Aziz joined forces with Hamdy and Kulthum again to sing about love and God, he borrowed from the New Testament. He deployed 'Allah' in the 1969 'Alf-lila wa-lilah' (One Thousand and One Nights), unrelated to the classic *Arabian Nights* tale. Telling a love story lasting a thousand and one nights, Kulthum sang Gamil-Aziz's verse, 'speak the name love; Allah is love', without indulging very far in sensual phrases.

'*Allah Mahabah*' (Allah is love) was customarily engraved in gold and framed by many Coptic Christian shopkeepers, as part of their centuries-long desperate clutching onto the faith without appearing to challenge the Muslims who had imposed their rule over the country since Egypt fell to the Arab army in the seventh century. Gamil-Aziz copied from 1 John 4:16: 'God is love; whoever abides in love abides in God, and God abides in him...'. The lyrics were penned when Egypt was dragging Alexandria closer to Allah, who was too powerful a God to succumb to the feebleness of love. A few years earlier, the transition had already been emphasised by a desk subeditor savaging Nadiya's feature.

Continuing to shed her gifted children by the thousands, like an old tree in autumn, Alexandria lost Nadiya too. The critic, cultural performer, socialite and monster-joint-rolling monologist moved to Montreal in 1969 to join a Franco-Jewish Alexandrian boyfriend, who jilted her at the altar. Perhaps it was the betrayal, delivered in a two-line folded note on the eve of her wedding, or maybe her heavy smoking, drinking and carefree lifestyle, but Nadiya died in 1975 of advanced lung cancer; it was too late to treat by the time it was detected. Listening to the famous couplet, I recalled that evening with the *chellah* of self-indulgent, Dionisian Alexandrian intellectuals – Nariman and Nadiya playing Hind Rustom, Zouzo Nabil and herself. I listened again and again to the 'Allah...Allah' recording, until the tears of the memory well ran dry. Whether seriously romanticising God or recalling his name in a mixture of pleasure, romance and joking – what Alexandrians could do with a word, a name of a god, that led other cultures towards slaughter and mass murder in his name instead!

CHAPTER 31
Songs Move Closer to Allah's Politics

Gamil-Aziz, who created lyrics for over 1,000 songs, never expressed regret – even when accused by Islamists, as early as 1957, of 'scribing lewd verses'. Instead, he remained proud of his work until he died in 1980.

In contrast, his contemporary, Ahmed Shafiq-Kamel (1929–2008), regretted writing for Miss Kulthum the suggestive love-scene verse: 'let me float in your eyes as your strokes comfort my being, o' lover do come to me' in the song 'inta-Omry' (You're my life), condemned by Islamists as 'immoral' in 1964.

The poet fell under the spell of Islamist preacher and television evangelist Sheikh Metwalli al-Sha'rawi (1911–1998), who for 20 years was the public face of hardline Islamic fundamentalism, and the godfather of many of its leaders in Egypt.[1] After his repentance, Shafiq-Kamel was rewarded by President Sadat's regime with a diplomatic post in Saudi Arabia on the recommendation of al-Sha'rawi. The poet protested angrily when a street in the Israeli kibbutz of Nev Illan, west of Jerusalem, was renamed 'Inta Omry', and issued public condemnations of the Jewish state for appropriating his song title. Shafiq-Kamel admired Nasser and was a devout believer in his pan-Arabism ideology. This weakness before a strong ideological charismatic leader explains Shafiq-Kamel's (and his contemporaries') journey on the Islamist path, which helped to reverse 160 years of modernity in Egypt.

In 1964, Alexandria's way of life was coming under attack by the likes of Sheikh al-Sha'rawi and his disciples. 'Women in licentious maillots on plage', Islamic preachers used to shriek from their pulpits during Friday prayers, 'shamelessly strolling flirtatiously near mosques'. This was an unprecedented attack at the time: many mosques overlooked beaches, and both bathers and worshipers had co-existed in close proximity for decades.

One mosque imam, Sheikh Ashour, shot to fame after complaining to Colonel Nasser during a political congress's live broadcast. The sheikh claimed that naked bathers were distracting his congregation near the *plage*, adding of one particular visitor that 'she comes into the mosque in short dresses to visit the Saint's shrine then kneels to pray and bend down prostrating displaying the goods in the rear *vetrina*.' Nasser and the meeting burst out laughing; the episode and the sheikh's antics subsequently became satirical material for cartoonists and stand-up comedians for a few weeks before he went quiet after the information minister instructed the media to ignore him. But the episode revived stories of the Islamic *maillot*-design contest held a few years earlier.[2] Condemning women in *maillohat* was no laughing matter because it was the first step on a slippery slope to a more sinister collapse of social values. The trend of Islamic evangelists' claiming to be protecting morals was part of their preaching subliminal messages of intolerance, misogyny and xenophobia that succeeded in infiltrating Muslims' collective minds. Among clerics who joined Ashour was another preacher, Sheikh Abdel Hameed Kishk (1933–1996) a founding member of al-Gma'a al-Islamia (Islamic Group, IG), an offshoot of the Muslim Brotherhood that recruited mujahideen for the CIA-funded Afghanistan operation. The IG, a sinister terrorist group, was behind vile acts like the 1997 Luxor Massacre, which left 64 people dead. Another founder, Sheikh Omar Abdel-Rahman (1938–2017), was jailed for life on terror charges arising from an early (1993) attack on New York's World Trade Center. Kishk was arrested in 1965 for Islamist terror-related plots, but there wasn't enough evidence to convict him in the trial and he was set free. All of IG founders and leaders were disciples of Sha'rawi.

The music for 'inta-Omry' was composed by Muhammed Abd-el-Wahab (1902–1991), then Kulthum's 30-year-long arch-rival. Wahab, a giant in the Egyptian worlds of music and film, had enjoyed a fanbase as broad as the entire MENA region since the late 1930s. Although he started modernising Egyptian oriental Arabo-Persian music in the 1960s by introducing Western modal scales, especially in Kulthum's songs, Wahab remained conservative in his own daily life, which was like a time capsule from the 1930s.

Out of superstition and for the sake of resisting modern innovations, Wahab never once travelled by air; he always voyaged by sea, which provided newspapers with a wealth of celebrity gossip. Reporters, both Egyptian and Arab, followed the eccentric, vegetarian, hypochondriac composer's peculiar lifestyle. He was famed for subjecting his carefully selected guests to strict hygiene training before attending private rehearsals at his Cairo home.

Getting the two – Wahab and Kulthum – together was Nasser's idea, since Wahab, like Umm Kulthum, Abd-el-Halim Hafez, and a few selected performers and composers like Shafiq-Kamel, was another weapon in the government's entertainment arsenal in a strategy designed to secure the regime's regional socio-cultural dominance. Wahab and Kulthum, like many other famous performers and stars, became projectors of Nasser's propaganda. Blending Stalin's use of arts and culture with Goebbels' art of mass indoctrination, Nasser's regime made full use of popular star performers. Financial incentives, like being given the leading role in a popular television series or film, as well as government subsidies for productions by those who toed the line became the carrot while waving a big stick against others. The constant threat of severe punishment, exile and marginalisation ensured that the majority were in the regime's camp.

The trio – Wahab, Shafiq-Kamel and Kulthum – cooperated further in transmitting the Nasserite message to a broader pan-Arab audience. While Gamil-Aziz's patriotic lyrics were love songs for his country and Egypt's rich history, Shafiq-Kamel's choruses were laced with endorsements of pan-Arabism – calling for armed struggle, especially against Israel.

Although the 1960s in Egypt were productive and financially rewarding for performing artists on the regime's gravy train, it was also a period of worry and concern for many non-Muslims and Alexandria's business fraternity and most of her residents. They felt the pinch and experienced a considerable change in their social lives; although they did not know it then, it was the start of an irreversible regression. The reversal of modernity and the loss of identity through a journey from pan-Arab nationalism to Islamic-nationalism in Egypt has been illustrated in Shafiq-Kamel's office. The pictures of the hardline Islamist preachers Sha'rawi and Kishk hang either side of Colonel Nasser's portrait behind his desk.

Food, Fun and Faith Festivities
With the power of inertia, Alexandria kept going, for a while. The Alexandrians continued their rites and practices, temporarily slowing the move away from man and nearer to God. The city resisted for another decade or so before falling into the Islamists' cultural grip. When the sun began to set on her second golden age, her Muslim residents were still calling their festivities by Alexandrian names – unlike the purely Islamic titles they would use 40 years later.

Alexandria Adieu

Eid al-Fitr, the ending of the fasting month of Ramadan, was never called as such by Alexandrians back then but instead was known as *Eid-el-Sughaier* (the lesser Eid). Meanwhile, *Eid al-Adha* (the feast of sacrifice, celebrating Abraham's sacrificing his son to God) was *Eid-el-Kebier* (the grand Eid). And *el-Eid*, without adjectives, meant Easter Sunday. Even Alexandrian Muslims used the term in respecting the six holy days of Easter week; Job's Wednesday (Holy Wednesday), *Jeudi Saint* (Maundy Thursday), Weeping (Good) Friday, (Holy) Saturday of Light, *el-Eid* and *ShamEneessim* (Easter Monday, but also the oldest Egyptian spring festival). Chanukah and Catholic Christmas were called as such, while the Orthodox Christmas on 7 January was called *eid-el-Abat* (the Coptic Eid). I did not begin to use these feasts' official Arabic names, like *Eid-el-Qiama* (Easter Sunday), or Arabo-Islamic names like *Eid al-Adha* until I started my university Middle East Studies course.

Prophet Muhammad's birthday (the Muslims' equivalent of Christmas), which is today known as *Mouled el-Naby* – was called *al-Mouled*, omitting the word '*Naby*'(prophet). The '*al*' article before *Mouled* was to distinguish it from other *mouleds* (birthdays) of various Muslim saints, such as Abu el-Abbas el-Morsi (1219–1287), an Andalusian-born scholar who established a Sufi sect in Alexandria in 1244. El-Morsi remains the patron saint of dockworkers, fishermen and Al Ittihad (Alexandria United), the city's largest football team and very much part of its identity. His shrine is located a mosque built in 1929 by Mario Rossi (1897-1961) and named after the saint on the east side of Pharos Island. There is a famous verse associated with the saint: 'hail the saint Abu el-Abbas, Alexandrians are *le crème class*'. Alexandrian fans (of any sport) chant the verse in games against outsiders.

Some of Alexandria's older 23 *plages* were named after Muslim saints (non-was originally Alexandrian) whose mosques hugged beaches like those of Sidi-Bishr, Sidi-Gaber or Chatby. Strangely, all the saints along the seafront had their birthday-*mouleds* held in the summer months when the evenings were warm and the districts' populations swelled six- to eightfold with the arrival of summer visitors – thus, coincidentally, maximising the trade that went with the celebrations.

Mouled Sidi Bishr, the largest and most spectacular, would last five days and nights in the middle of August; the saint was no more important than others, but geography and economics played their role. Sidi-Bishr Mosque had a large square, the Montazah Green on its other side by the sea and an empty plot opposite that accommodated a sizeable fairground larger than what mould-entertainment offered in many Egyptian towns.

CHAPTER 31 Songs Move Closer to Allah's Politics

The event was as busy as Brighton pier on a summer Bank Holiday. Game stalls gave out prizes like dolls, goldfish and little toys. The games themselves comprised tin-can-alley sets, hoopla, hook-a-duck, target practice with air rifles, darts with a spinning-wheel target, test-your-strength, mirror-labyrinths, swings and rides, merry-go-rounds, dodgems and trampolines. Street performers included a Pandora's box and a weightlifter taking bets on meeting new challenges. There was a tent with entry tickets where singers, *balady* dancers and magicians performed. Being a Muslim saint's birthday didn't stop vendors from selling non-halal food, or from serving alcohol like ice-cold Birra Stella. The stalls, takeaway-food vendors and performers represented a mosaic of cosmopolitan Alexandria. Italian gelato vendors and singers competed with the Spaniard pianola performers and tambourine dancers. Takeaway drink stalls represented European and oriental cultures; French cheeses, popcorn, multiple varieties of Italian salami and sausage and candyfloss sat alongside *fuul* and falafel, eggs and *basturma*, (a version of Pastrami) kebab and cakes – and sweets of all kinds. The stalls were run by Alexandrian Armenians, Greeks, Syro-Lebanese and Magharba (North African) settlers – the last-named with their famous couscous and green-leaf mint tea. While the middle classes enjoyed their Stella, the poor had the cheaper Bouza made from barley and old, stale bread.

Eids, before the Islamisation of Alexandria, were not observed but celebrated as festivals. Only the very devout male Muslims went to the mosque at sunrise, especially for *Eid el-Kebier*. Sunrise on this day, so the story claimed, was the moment when Isaac (Ismail in the Muslim version) was spared Abraham's blade by the Angel of Yahweh descending with the sacrificial ram. Most merry, decadent and indulgent Alexandrians, regardless of faith, hated getting up that early – except for making money.

The Mosque of Sidi-Bishr, up the road from Villa Alexandrine, only became busy with worshippers when *Eid el-Kebier* coincided with the summer holiday season. Holidaymakers from the interior provinces of Egypt, who outnumbered the locals by six to one, were keener on being nearer to Allah than Alexandrians were.

CHAPTER 32
Leila Murad: Alexandria's Songstress

On one occasion, Bellitta called me, and together we hurried up the sloping Rue nineteen to Sidi-Bishr Mosque square, where the media circus had gathered during the Eid rites to await a visit by celebrated movie star Leila Murad. Her story and that of her family encapsulated a sad chapter in the history of Alexandrian Jews, mostly indigenous Egyptian Karaites, Sephardim and Mizrahi who evolved, changed or even converted.

The movie star and *mutribah* (songstress) Leila Murad was born Lillian Mordechai in 1918, when the growing Alexandria film industry produced feature films. Her Alexandrian-Jewish Karaite father was Ibrahim Zaki Mordechai Effendi – a singer, composer, music teacher and hazzan (religious cantor); her mother, Gamilah Salomon, was of Polish descent. Miss Murad was educated at a French Catholic school on a charity *bourse* (scholarship). She was coached by her father, who had shortened his name to Zaki Murad. Many Alexandrians Egyptianised their non-Muslim-sounding names when their careers took them beyond the city's boundaries, where the Arabic-language media were less tolerant than Alexandria's journalists.

The nine-year-old Leila Murad made her first stage appearance at Cairo's best-known and most successful music hall, *Sala*[*] Badi'a Masabny (founded 1926). Miss Masabny (1894–1974), was born to a Syrian family who migrated in 1901 to Argentina, before returning to Damascus in 1912. She moved between Beirut, Damascus and Cairo[†]

---

[*] *Sala* is demotic Egyptian (from Italian) for a music hall.
[†] Bad'a Masabny told her story to Egyptian TV presenter Leila Rustom (b.1937) in the programme Nojoum-ala-alard on Beirut TV on 25 February 1969.

CHAPTER 32   Leila Murad: Alexandria's Songstress

where she settled late 1914 and learned acting, singing, and *balady* dance and established a performing company that dominated Egypt's musical shows for 30 years.

Besides her father, Miss Murad was also trained by another Egyptian-Jewish Karaite, the Cairo-born Daoud Hosni (1870–1937). Hosni composed music for over 500 songs, including two for Murad, and was the first musician in history to compose an opera in Arabic – *Samson and Dalila*.

At the age of 14, Leila Murad started singing at private events in Alexandria. In 1934, she managed to beat Umm Kulthum by performing at the launch of the national broadcasting service al-Iza'a al-Masriyah (Cairo Radio), before releasing her first record a year later. While Kulthum had initially been a village girl from a *fellaheen* background with a strong Islamic influence, Murad was an Alexandrian – exposed early to the city's European culture. She was also blessed with better looks than her contemporary rival. Kulthum's later melodies were lengthy and suited large-scale concerts and mass broadcasts; Murad's shorter songs were more appropriate for the new 'seventh art'* to which Egyptians were growing accustomed. Cinema became the country's most popular medium of entertainment, and a source of information for the illiterate masses before television was launched in 1958.

The cinematographic film was a medium through which the filmgoer, as an individual, becomes immersed in a dream connected with the film stars – as Woody Allen (b.1935) illustrated in his 1985 film *The Purple Rose of Cairo*, when the handsome movie star jumps out of the screen and spends the day with his adoring fan, the housewife-filmgoer. With a beautiful face and angelic voice, the 19-year-old Leila Murad shot to fame with her first film, *Yahia el-hob (Vive l'Amour)*, in which she starred with Egypt's celebrated singer and composer, Muhammed Abd-el-Wahab.[1] Murad had the leading role in another 27 talking pictures, becoming the highest-paid Egyptian movie star of all time (including up to the present day, taking inflation into account). Although she retired in 1955 and hid from the media until she died, she remained popular. A sea-rock off the coast of Marsa Matruh, 300 kilometres west of Alexandria, was named Leila Murad's Rock in 1950. It was the very one upon which she sat singing to the town's beach as 'the romance plage sought by les amoureux, while mermaids drift in its water' when filming her 1950 musical *Shat el-Gharam (Plage d'Amour)*.

---

* The Italian thinker Ricciotto Canudo (1877–1923) coined the phrase 'seventh art' for cinema. The five traditional arts were painting, music, architecture, poetry and sculpture – to which Canudo proposed adding dance as a sixth, meaning that cinema occupied the following slot.

Alexandria Adieu

Marsa Matruh Municipality erected a bronze statue of Murad in the town centre, where cafés, hotels and shops are named after her. The Alexandria question, how can the human be linked to the divine, was evident in Murad's case. This daughter of Alexandria was, in her early career, moving in her life, as often expressed in her songs and films, closer to humans with their love and their emotional feebleness. Later, she moved closer to God. One of the best known among her 1,200 recorded songs was '*Ya-raiheen lil-naby el-ghali*' ('Ye, on your way to the dear Prophet Muhammad'), hailing Muslim pilgrims on their way to Mecca. The song has been consistently aired in many Arabic countries during *Hag* (hajj) season for seven decades.

Marrying someone from a different faith was natural for Alexandrians; Murad was no exception when she fell in love with a Muslim actor. On her marriage certificate, dated 15 July 1945, the entry under faith was 'Israelite', while 'Islam' was the stated religion of Anwar Wagdy (1904–1955). The heartthrob of teenage girls, Wagdy was nicknamed the 'Clark Gable of Egypt' for his similarity with the Hollywood star's hairstyle and famous moustache. In reality, Wagdy 'got there first' in the racy 1927 romantic movie *Qubla fi al-Sahra'a* (A Kiss In The Desert). Starring in several films together, Murad and Wagdy became so popular that advertising agencies used them on posters for cigarettes, drinks, automobiles and family holidays. Ironically, in the year in which Miss Murad recorded the pilgrims' song (1952) for the film *Leila l'Aristrocrat*, released in 1953, Islamic fundamentalists spread a rumour accusing her of donating money to Israel. She went to great lengths to deny the accusations, and succeeded thanks to her popularity. Her publicists' press release included a copy of a letter from the army command addressed to the chairman of the Egyptian Film Industry Chamber (EFIC). Sent three months after the 1952 coup, the missive confirmed that the star had neither visited Israel nor donated money to the Jewish state.

Like most non-Muslims – whether indigenous Alexandrians, Nilotic-Copts or migrants from diverse backgrounds – the Murads took the army-coup leaders' assurances of equal treatment at face value. They viewed the ongoing changes as ushering in a new era of hope and progress. The majority of Alexandria Jews neither donated money to groups fighting the British in Palestine before 1948 nor expressed any wish to move from their country to Israel. Therefore, they did not see the changes as a threat and took a pragmatic view by adapting to the new reality and expressing loyalty to the new regime.

At first, the officers' regime chose Murad over Kulthum to vocalise their official propaganda song '*Al-itihad-w-al-nizham-w-al-a'mal*' (Unity, Order and Hard Work). The three words became the junta's

CHAPTER 32 Leila Murad: Alexandria's Songstress

slogan in the early years. The motto was displayed on signs shaped like fighter-aircraft wings sticking out from lamp posts and inscribed on *a'lam e-tahrir*, the military coup's *tricolore* (in red, white and black) which flew next to the Egyptian national flag and was to replace it five years later. The four-minute song mentioned Allah 12 times, five of which were as 'all-powerful'. The music, featuring a military march with drums and trumpets, was composed by Murad's younger brother, the actor and composer Maurice Murad (1922–1981). Like his sister, who married a Muslim movie star, Maurice, who changed his name to Mounir, married a Muslim actress, Soheir el-Bably (b-1937); she acted in over 60 movies, television dramas and theatre plays.

As well as confirming Murad's patriotism and loyalty, the army correspondence throws light on the anti-Semitism within trade unions and commercial bodies besides the post-war tendency to exclude Jews and boycott their businesses. As my own family experience confirms, most of Alexandria's Jews saw themselves as Egyptians; they found the idea of a Jewish state impractical and unappealing. Even those whom the horrors of the Holocaust persuaded of the need for a Jewish homeland were appalled by Jewish political groups' violence in Palestine. Film director Youssef Chahine examined the theme, confirming Alexandrian Jews' rejection of Jewish nationalist violence in his 1978 film *Alexandria...Why?*

Many political Jewish activists were seen to be unpalatable. My mother's friends found them '*inconvénient*' and the idea of an independent Jewish state '*pas chic*'. Political leaflet-pushing volunteers and donation collectors were seen then as a menace; their annoying doorstep calls could best be likened to Jehovah's Witnesses getting you out of bed on a Saturday morning.

Leila Murad was at the peak of her career and a beloved movie star when the military regime's letter became her *Certificat d'Innocence*. One wonders what the outcome would have been had it been during the Suez War itself – or, worse, the Six-Day War, when Egyptian-Jewish men were put in internment camps for three years. Her younger brother, Isak Zaki Murad, suffered such a fate, and her failure to visit him at any point during his detention caused a big rift in her family.

In the same year (1953) that Miss Murad got closer to the military regime, she secretly married Captain Wageih Abazah (1917– 1994), an Egyptian Air Force intelligence officer who joined the conspiring officers in 1952, after having had a child with him. The couple did not inform the captain's family. The ethnically Circassian Abazahs were one of Egypt's oldest aristocratic families, whose sons were mostly British- and French-educated.

265

Alexandria Adieu

The anti-Jewish feeling, which grew stronger in Cairo than in Alexandria, predated the Suez War and increased after the 1948 Arab–Israeli conflict. Monologist performers were openly making stereotypical anti-Semitic jokes on the national broadcasting service after the 1952 military coup, while Jews began to be negatively portrayed in films.

However, the severest blow against Alexandria, especially the city's Jewry, come not from within but from foreign governments – those of France, Britain and Israel. Following the departure and expulsion of thousands of wealthy Alexandrians, the city's destiny over the next two decades was to be looted like a treasure-house by thieves who do not know what they were after. In 1954, the Israelis recruited a handful of Egyptian Jews to firebomb public buildings like Alexandria's and Cairo's post offices.[2] The intention was to sow discord between the Egyptian Government and its Western allies and encourage more Egyptian Jews to emigrate to Israel.

As we have seen, most of Alexandria's Jews preferred to remain in Alexandria and Egypt in general, even after the 1952 coup. Only four months before Colonel Nasser nationalised the Suez Canal, Jewish donations enabled the opening of a new wing at the famous Israeli Hospital on Rue Abukeir. Charitable acts by Jewish philanthropic organisations providing for poor and orphaned Muslim children did not help reduce anti-Semitism; it was buried deep in the layers of Egyptian society – particularly in Internal Egypt outside Alexandria.

There were several elements behind this anti-Semitism. On the social level, there was the snobbery of the European-educated upper-middle-classes and aristocratic Egyptians. Additionally, there was a historical indoctrination rooted in Islamic teachings, particularly in the countryside. Meanwhile, the country's anti-British, urban, nationalist organisations had strong Nazi and fascist ingredients in their creed, while most political organisations held Britain responsible for 'handing Palestine to the Jews'.

By the start of the War, Leila Murad had become much favoured by Egyptian listeners and cinemagoers; and to attract them many of her film titles included 'Leila', the character she always portrayed. Her sixth film in 1946 was called simply *Leila*, and was directed by the Jewish Alexandrian-born filmmaker Togo Mizrahi, the son of Italian migrants. Mizrahi, the second generation of Alexandrian-born filmmakers trained in the city's growing film studios, was a pillar of the Egyptian film industry. Along with Muslim producer Ahmed Badrkhan (1909–1969), Mizrahi established the first film actors' and cinema workers' union in Egypt.

Mizrahi also created the character of Shalom (Shlomo), a clumsy Egyptian Jew in a series of comedy films including *Shalom el-Riady*

CHAPTER 32   Leila Murad: Alexandria's Songstress

(Shlomo the athlete) and *Shalom-fi-al-police* (Shlomo the policeman). Before the increase in anti-Jewish sentiment around Israel's independence (which was accelerated under the 1952 military regime), Mizrahi felt comfortable enough in the 1930s to declare his faith and heritage and to create a Jewish character that was a box-office hit. The Egyptian filmgoers, including Muslims and Coptic Christians, saw it as natural for an Egyptian Jew to serve in the police, the armed forces or the civil service.

Shalom was the *nom de scène* for Leon Angel, a clerk in the Alexandria Municipality. He performed comic sketches and films, especially after forming a Jewish-and-Muslim *duetto* with another comedian, Ahmed el-Hadad (1912–1982). The two became known as Shalom-wa-A'bdou. Since the so-called *Sah'ua* (Islamic awakening) and the theological struggle to reverse modernity, all copies of Shlomo films have disappeared apart from rare reels kept by the odd private collector.

The Egyptian Trinity

Egypt changed its 'official' religion only twice in over 6,000 years.* Egyptians' attitudes to religion are ancient and deeply rooted in their psyche, seeking security in their millennia-long belief in a centralised trinitarian nation-state: the trinity of 'The Father' (Pharaoh/King), 'The Son' (the human body of the Army), and (sanctified by) a 'Holy Spirit' (the Church).

The modern Holy Spirit, al-Azhar as a de facto official Muslim Church, is part of the state structure. Christians have the Coptic Church, whose bishops toe the state's line – set by al-Azhar with the military's collaboration. Both al-Azhar and the Coptic Church are robust institutions, with a firm grip on the lives of their followers. The latter wields that power thanks to the sheer strength of faith and belief, similar to the potency of the Catholic Church (the Vatican) in places like Ireland, Poland and Latin America. The former's power is consolidated by faith, the education system and the strong arm of the state. Ironically, indigenous Egyptian Jews (the Karaite, who only believe in the Five Books of Moses and reject the Talmud as an innovation) were luckier than their fellow Egyptian Christians and Muslims. They escaped the suffocating psychopathic embrace of al-Azhar and the Coptic Church as they enjoyed autonomy from official rabbinical authority thanks to state protection granted in the tenth century, continuing under Ottoman rule and beyond Egyptian independence in 1922.

---

* Christianity became dominant in the fourth and fifth centuries, while the majority converted to Islam between the eleventh and twelfth centuries under the economic pressure of the *gizyah*.

Alexandria Adieu

In the 1938 film *Hayat-wa-alam-alsayyed-al-massieh* (The Life and Pains of Christ the Lord) – the first drama film in Arabic-Egyptian about the life of Christ – Jesus was portrayed by Ahmed A'allam (1899–1962), a Muslim actor who starred in over 70 movies with multi-faith and multi-ethnic casts. The film's screenplay was co-written by an obscure Egyptian priest, Father Antwan Ebied. For the most part, it was scripted by the dean of Cairo University's School of Arts and Classics, later head of Alexandria University, the French-educated thinker, philosopher and novelist Dr Taha Hussein (Hessein).

As a Minister of the Ma'arif (the Department of Knowledge, Education, Arts and Culture) from 1950 to 1952, who returned to academia after the military coup, Dr Hussein, introduced free school education and expanded the illiteracy-eradication programme. He also funded the *alf-Kitab* ('thousand books') scheme of translating 1,000 books from many scholarly disciplines – including the sciences, literature, history, classics and economics – from European languages. Dr Hussein was an outstanding figure in Egyptian and Arabic literature. In the 1920s, he revolutionised the dull and frequently absurd literary criticism common in the Arabic language. He was an advocate of critical thinking, who urged the embracing of European culture. He had a run-in with Islamists and the clergy of al-Azhar. The religious establishment filed a petition to the state prosecution agency demanding he be put on trial for undermining the Islamic faith in his 1926 book *Fi-al-shi'r al-gahili* (On pre-Quranic Poetry). At the same time, they launched a media campaign accusing him of apostasy and heresy. With his application of modern European critical methods in the book, Dr Hussein contended that the vast body of poetry in Arabia presumed to be from the pre-Prophet Muhammad eras (570–632 AD) had been forged by Muslims at a much later date to give credence to Quranic myths. The Islamists lost when the case was thrown out because it related to linguistic and historical research rather than a theological study or a message intended to undermine the Islamic religion. This outcome would almost certainly have been the opposite in Egypt a century later.

Blind since childhood, Dr Hussein was, and still is, hailed by Egyptian nationalists for his 1938 book *Mustaqbal al-thaqafah fi Misr* (The Future of Culture in Egypt), which built on his earlier body of work advocating the assimilation of modern European culture into the Egyptian *intellectualis corporis* and argued that there were only two sets of civilisations: 'Western civilisation [which] originated from Ancient Egypt, Greek philosophy and Roman law; and the second from Indian philosophy'. He concluded, 'Egypt belongs by heritage to the first, to same broader Mediterranean civilisation that encompassed those of France, Greece and Italy; and not to Arabia.'[3]

CHAPTER 32 Leila Murad: Alexandria's Songstress

Togo Mizrahi directed all of Miss Murad's early films; it was he who came up with the idea of putting her name, Leila, into the film titles. Nine of them bore such titles – like *Leila at School*, *Leila the Country Girl*, *Leila in the Dark* and the aforementioned *Leila*. Unlike Murad, who had the documented backing of the military regime, Mizrahi, the Alexandria-born Egyptian national, faced growing false accusations of backing the Jewish state during the months leading up to war against Israel in 1948. The campaign against the Jewish state's independence was encouraged by sections of officialdom and the Muslim Brotherhood, whose influence on King Farouk was more potent and more effective than on his father, Fuad. Like many talented Egyptians, Mizrahi was forced by the growing anti-Jewish attitude to emigrate; he went to Italy in 1949, taking his remarkable skills with him. He subsequently made a few trips back to his home town of Alexandria, in the country of his birth, sparking speculation in the Egyptian media about the prospect of him making new films for Egyptian cinema. However, none materialised before his death in self-exile in 1986.

In her 1954 *Eid-el-Kebier*[4] charitable visit to Sidi-Bishr Mosque, to which Bellitta and I had hurried, Leila Murad was handing out money to the needy and sweets to their children as they gathered outside the Muslim saint's shrine – she was performing *waf'a bel-nadhr* (*nadhr* = fulfilling). *Nadhr*, in Egyptian folklore, is a pledge to give to the needy or perform a task of a religious nature, by someone believing God had answered their prayers. The Egyptians superstitiously believe that failing to fulfil a *nadhr* invites bad luck. Declining to sign autographs or to speak on microphones pushed into her car window outside the Sidi-Bishr Mosque, Murad was only blowing kisses followed by 'Bless you'. Perhaps her *nadhr* was to do with the Abazahs finally recognising her marriage to their son, or with the restoration of her patriotic credentials by the military regime – nobody ever found out. Miss Murad retired from acting and singing the following year, aged 37 and never once spoke to the media again until she died in 1995.

The Sidi-Bishr *nadhr* visit was reported as celebrity gossip and pictured in weekly magazines; there was nothing unusual about a Jewess appealing to a Muslim saint to put in a word in heaven. I recall Muslim women in Alexandria praying to *Sainte Thérèse de Lisieux* (1873–1897) for healing from some ailment. Women travelled to her basilica in Shubra, north of Cairo, to pray and leave icons in the shape of the afflicted organ made from gold or silver – framed and placed alongside hundreds of votive tablets all over the chapel. When healed, they would fulfil *nadhr* by donating to the chapel and praying there, regardless of their faith. For Alexandria's Muslim women seeking healing, St Thérèse was second only to the Holy Mother of God. The Virgin Mary was mentioned in their book as 'the most purified God's chosen female in the worlds' (Quran 3:42), not just on Earth but in the worlds of Earth and heaven – a status not bestowed even on Muhammad's mother, daughters or wives.

CHAPTER 33
Festivities Alexandria Style

Alexandria, until the late 1970s, was still mostly secular and culturally European. Devout Muslim families celebrating *Eid-el-Kebier* in the post-war city who wanted to stick to blood-sacrifice fundamentals instructed a butcher to perform them privately. *Eid-el-Kebier* marks the climax of the Mecca pilgrimage season. It wasn't unusual for enlightened Muslim scholars to debate the rites associated with the blood sacrifice on the pages of newspapers in a secular-critical fashion. They urged people to donate the cost to a charity and opt for a *dinde* or a *coqo-deek* (rooster) instead of a sheep; many Alexandrians did. I had an early childhood shock associated with the event. Said *el-kharoof* became the neighbourhood youngsters' pet when they discovered its distinctive 'Ba, ba, ba' one morning in the old sea-captain's garden.

'It is Said', said Helmy, the retired mariner's helper, chauffeur and minder, 'It is here for *Eid-el-Kebier*'. The children visited the sheep regularly, stroking it and feeding it *berseem* (green shoots). After *Eid*, Said's rope was still there – next to blooded rags. When the truth was revealed about the neighbourhood pet's departure, the children were in tears. I was very young but I remember being sick at the sight of the blooded rags, and I still dislike the taste and smell of lamb.

Most Alexandrians of all faiths were what we called 'Christmas Christians' or 'high-holiday Jews': they saw religious calendar days as a chance for some time off to enjoy social and cultural festivities rather than days of worship. The only exceptions I encountered were a few devout Jews, especially older ladies among the Mizrahi families. They insisted on traditional rituals like cleaning and cleansing the home before Passover, a task that makes a typical spring cleaning seem like an enjoyable picnic. The season was not looked forward to by most Jewish women. Women also had to get the kosher Passover Seder items ready – the tablecloths, the dishes (especially the small ones for dipping salt water), the flatware, water, wine glasses, napkins and the kiddush cup. Although Jewish schoolboys often made jokes about how Egyptian Jews still thanked God for the Exodus that had freed them from slavery and harsh conditions in Egypt, their de facto country where they enjoyed a high standard of living.

Marking the end of the Muslim fasting month of Ramadan, *Eid-el-Sughaier* celebrations were colourful, and focused on food, drinks and a party atmosphere for the middle classes. In poorer rural-migrant areas in south Alexandria, it was a chance for children to have a good time going out in colourful clothes and carrying paper wind-spinners and balloons. These impoverished families went out in groups of a dozen or more, riding on a horse-drawn *carro* for a *millième* or two, for picnics in Nuzha Park, where the zoo was located, or on Anfoushy *Plage*. The same, overall, went for the Coptic Christmas and el-Eid (Easter), marking the end of the 40-day Lent.

The celebrations were not exclusively for the particular faith festival's followers but for everybody, especially children. And like all festivities that were originally faith-rooted – like Christmas; Easter; the two eids (greater and lesser); Rosh Hashanah; or Egypt's oldest festival, Sham-Ennessim – everybody celebrated in a party-like atmosphere – particularly families with children.

Sham-Ennessim goes back thousands of years to the ancient Egyptian calendar: Shamu was then the season of harvest, after the season of emergence. Since Egypt's Christianisation, it has always coincided with the Monday after the Eastern Churches' Easter Sunday. Celebrated by Egyptians of all faiths and none, the ancient traditions carried on: colouring eggs; putting some eggs over ring-braided baked bread; and eating salt fish, like *fisiekh* (salted mullet) and salted sardines, as well as lettuce, scallions and *termis* (salted soaked lupini beans) – all of them the legacies of offerings that their ancestors had presented to their deities. And because it marked the start of spring, the open-air celebrations were held near vegetation, flowers, trees and water.

Families would go out all day until sunset to public parks and onto the Nile banks. They went to the Mahmoudiyah Canal or the green spaces near any *plage* in Alexandria – or hired boats for the occasion. *Maman*, with her hygiene-freak ways, didn't allow us to join public picnics. But because we were always in Sidi-Bishr for Easter, we used to have the traditional picnic in the back garden of the villa, sometimes joined by cousins or neighbours from my mother's circle of snobs for the Easter-egg hunt. It wasn't until my external year at Alexandria University that I joined a Sham-Ennessim picnic. It was held on a Nile

CHAPTER 33   Festivities Alexandria Style

felucca hired in Rosetta (64 kilometres east of Alexandria) with some students, since both Farida and Nariman were with their families. I got a horrible stomach and abdominal pains along with a fever, realising how right my mother was about *fisiekh* food poisoning.

Christmas festivities lasted up to two months in Alexandria, from Chanukah to *Eid-el-Ghatas* (the feast of the Epiphany), given that the Egyptian Christian calendar is two weeks behind the Catholic one. Egyptians referred to the whole season of eight weeks as '*al-kriesmas*'. Today, with the overwhelming Islamisation of life in Egypt, non-Christian Egyptians mean New Year's Eve when they say *al-kriesmas*. As children, we favoured the colourful atmosphere of Moharrem-Bey or our El-Balad home near Boursa as places to spend the season, while my mother preferred the quieter atmosphere of Sidi-Bishr. With a couple of exceptions when she wasn't well, *Maman* gave in and we would move to Moharrem-Bey or El-Balad at the start of Chanukah.

The Moharrem-Bey area's residents were mostly Coptic Christians, but included the usual mix of Muslims, Anglicans, Greek Orthodox, Catholics – mostly Italian – and Jews from different races and cultural backgrounds. This tapestry of diverse communities was again evident when owners or managers of stores, cafés, bars and restaurants added dishes of all origins to their menus, alongside the decorations and nativity set in their shop windows. The Christmas tree was the unifying symbol of the season for all, and was often placed next to the Chanukah menorah in early December. Fluffed cotton wool would be used for snow decorations. There would also be little candles or paraffin lanterns as well as glass baubles, which my mother hated as the children often broke them, letting tiny bits of shards go everywhere. Rue Moharrem-Bey, and the other shopping streets, were just a sea of lights in contrast to the dark, empty and deadly silent streets in Sidi-Bishr's winter months.

Middle-class women were full-time mothers and homemakers in those days, although they were also engaged in charitable work – and thus, children-focused. Each mother made sure all the neighbourhood children, irrespective of their parents' faiths, would receive gifts and the festival's symbolic sweets exactly like those given to her own children. Whether the festival was Christmas, Easter, Eid, New Year, Nowruz, Purim or Sham-Ennessim, presents, cakes, sweets, masks and toys, coloured eggs and chocolate eggs were handed to all youngsters. From the richest to the poorest, they all shared the custom. In some quarters, children were given new clothes, shoes and toys.

One tradition – associated with all, but taking on a ritual flavour with Muslims and Copts during other festivals – was the baking of *kahk*. Jews; Christians, of all churches; Muslims; and non-denominational neighbours all partook in *kahk* preparation, for this baking tradition went back to ancient Egypt. Muslims make *kahk*, marking *Eid-el-Sughaier*, regardless of whether they had observed a fasting Ramadan or not. *Kahk* are cookies that have remained in the same form and shape for over 5,000 years, just as they appeared on the walls of ancient Egyptian temples. The word meant 'dough' in hieroglyphic at a time when growing and harvesting corn and wheat, and trading in flour-based products and cereals, comprised the backbone of the Egyptian economy. It is known outside the country as *khak-misri* (Egyptian cookies). The Alexandrian version was the same shape but had its unique ingredients, reflecting the city's cosmopolitanism. It was made from a soft dough of flour, butter, milk, ground sesame, baking powder, instant yeast, sea salt and a particular spice mixture known as *rouh-el-kahak* ('the kahk's breath'), which the lady of the house would have kept in a jar to add to the mix.

Rouh-el-kahak was made of a wide a variety of ingredients: ground rose seeds or rosehip, ground laurel leaves, ground cloves, cardamom, tailed pepper (*piper cubeba*), Rosaceae, ground dried fennel, cinnamon and one or two more secret ingredients passed from mother to daughter. The dough was then kneaded into different shapes, like circles and ovals of around five centimetres' diameter. The knack was to roll the dough into long two-centimetre-thick cylinders and cut into strips, each shaped into a ring. Some *kahk* were stuffed with *malben* (Turkish delight), and some with *agamia* (sweetened date or other fruit paste); the latter was preferred in Internal Egypt.

Alexandrians also added other types of stuffing, like fig jam, salty caramel or dried mixed fruits. All kinds of *kahk* had to be *nakshed* (decorated) using short, brass, serrated-tipped tongs to emboss patterns and decoration while the dough was still soft. The grooved decoration also helped the baked *kahk* retain the dry icing sugar sprinkled on top of it. Ladies of each household developed their unique design as their family insignia. Other types of bakes and cookies included *petits fours* which were shaped by tools into flowers, balls and cubes, and were lightened by reducing the amount of butter in the dough. These *petits fours* had multiple flavours like vanilla, chocolate, almond, cinnamon and citrus.

Another type was called *bisküvit* (biscuit). It was slightly richer in dairy than the *petits fours*, and was distinguished by its sprinkled crystals of sugar on top. The *bisküvit*'s dough had flavours added like orange, lemon, ginger, aniseed and coconut. Then the dough was shaped by hand or by *fourmas* (tin moulds) into circles, rings, rhombuses, pentagons, hearts, triangles, semicircles, stars, crosses and soldiers

CHAPTER 33   Festivities Alexandria Style

to give to children. Muslim families still made cross-shaped biscuits because it was a legacy predating Islam, when cookies were baked for el-Eid (Easter Sunday).

Other cookies included *goraiybah*, shaped into circles and ovals. This was different from traditional *kahk* – hence the name *goraiybah*, meaning 'alien' – with a shortbread-like texture, but softer with a richer dough made using one-third butter and two-thirds flour, with hazelnuts or almonds on top. The *kahk* ritual sometimes went on for two days. When the extended family's women couldn't provide enough hands for the job, then the task force would be bolstered with girls from the neighbourhood of diverse faith and ethnicities – especially in mixed-race areas like Moharrem-Bey, Cleopatra, Azarita and Attarin. The *kahak* 'gang' would move through three or four households in the ten days running up to the festivities to make enough for all.

Nobody I can think of had large enough stoves in their home to bake the quantities of *kahk* and other varieties. The different kinds of dough were placed on *sagat* (baking trays) hired for a deposit from the local *forno*; the average was 20 trays per household! Children usually marked the trays with chalk, writing their name on each one, and the *furn* boys collect them. Those badly exploited boys used to make daily deliveries from the bakeries to *épiseriat* (*épiceries*), clubs and cafés early each morning: freshly baked *baladi* (flatbread); croissants; baguettes; and *fino*, the Alexandrian baguette, 8–9 inches long and narrowed at both ends. The shape and name of *fino* were unique to Alexandria, and not used elsewhere in Egypt or worldwide. There is no documented record of its origin, but folklore suggests it was introduced to Alexandria in the nineteenth century by a Greco-Italian baker called Fino. In his honour, the bakeries *La Panetteria di Fino* (Fino's Boulangerie) were founded in the Ibrahimiyah area. Hence, the Alexandrians named this unique type of baguette *fino*.

The *forno* boys were kept busy during the *kahk* season, collecting *sagat* from each household. Carrying them to the *forno* on foot or balanced on a bicycle required remarkable skill, but it also showed terrible child-labour exploitation. The boy would balance his body's weight in a tower of *sagat*, cycling to the *forno*. He would ensure that the trays went into the kiln in the correct, chalk-marked order as the baking time differed for each type of dough. He also undertook to return the same *sagat* to the same household to get a good tip.

Icing sugar would be sprinkled on the *kahk* while still warm, before storing them in lidded containers. Ladies would send a sample of each variety to neighbours. The gift was usually accompanied by chocolates and often with sweet wine.

Alexandria Adieu

Colourful Feasts
During their Eids (especially Easter, and sometimes Christmas or Epiphany), Copts, Greeks, Armenians, and other Christian denominations would offer wine with *kahk*. I witnessed Muslim families marking the end of Ramadan evening with champagne. On the morning of Eid, the middle classes, especially in Europeanised quarters of the city, celebrated with champagne, or the available sparkling wine, oysters and mussels, or salt fish when the festival fell during the summer months when many Alexandrians avoided shellfish. Some invited their non-Muslim neighbours because the neighbours would ask them to share their festival celebrations too.

Alexandria, who tamed faiths to fit into her way of life, also moulded new settlers, mainly from the Ottoman Empire provinces. The closest were Sephardic and Mizrahi Jews, Armenians and Greeks, and Italians and central Europeans – adopted her cultural convictions. Their cuisine was part of the city's ethos of assimilation, which bridged so many races and faiths.

In Alexandria, festival cuisine was marked by its cosmopolitanism, as more dishes were added over the years to the indigenous gastronomy to celebrate European Easter, Eastern Easter and the end of Ramadan. Indigenous Coptic and Muslim dishes included lime-salt fish; the *baccalà* (imported salted cod); salt-beef; and, my father's favourite, *aringhe*. This was smoke-dried Baltic herring, which needed particular skill to turn it quickly several times over a spirit stove's naked flame. Guests sometimes joined in, bringing in different offerings of their own depending on their cultural background. It could have been tins or jars of delicacies from their ancestral lands, wines, ouzo, arak, grappa, palinka, Armenian cognac or imported beer in addition to Birra Stella.

Nobody personified the city's of love and multifaith character like my father, the true Alexandrian. He never ceased to impress people, knowing which psalms to recite on any occasion. Whether it was a Muslim *ma'tam*, a Jewish Kaddish or Shiva, or a Christian memorial service, he spontaneously recited the prayer and knew how to bless a *bris*. And instead of imposing any faith on us, he encouraged us to grow up freethinkers. Like Papa, to whom I never had the chance to say goodbye before his death, I never managed to say a proper adieu to Alexandria. Neither I nor any other Alexandrians in our circle could put a date on when exactly the city we knew let out her last breath – the Alexandria who moulded numerous religions into one faith, the only one she truly practised: *agape, Amour, hob*, love.

PART VIII
EXODUS

CHAPTER 34
The Jews' Second Exodus

Our neighbours, a Mizrahi family – *Tante* Fortune (*Fortunieh*) and *Oncle* Bishara, a goldsmith, and their son Sammy – lived in the upper-ground-floor maisonette. Fortune, whose grandmother had emigrated from Syria in the nineteenth century, was a high-class seamstress, while Bishara's parents were of Mesopotamian ancestry. Like his parents and grandparents, Sammy was born in Alexandria before the War. *Tante* Fortune and my mother formed a special bond when the former became my sister's wetnurse. My mother had an infection following surgery to remove cysts from her breasts in 1946, and couldn't feed my newly born sister. Fortune also nursed my mother for months, with a good diet including, of course, chicken soup – also known as 'Jewish penicillin' – while continuing to breastfeed my sister.

On a whim, and without any parliamentarian or legal procedure, Nasser stripped thousands of their nationality or residency rights and ordered their deportation. Twenty-five thousand were deported immediately after the Suez War alone in a development that changed life in Alexandria for good. The tragic irony was that many rabbis in Alexandria actually criticised Israel in that fateful month – October 1956 – in their synagogue services. Most of the Alexandrian Jews saw themselves as Egyptians, and condemned the Anglo–French attack on their country to recapture the Suez Canal, which had been nationalised by Nasser three months earlier.

Within hours of the Anglo–French operation ending on 6 November 1956, thanks to the intervention of US President Dwight Eisenhower (1890–1969),[1] Colonel Nasser ordered the first wave of deportations. Those holding British or French passports were given as little as 48 hours to leave the country. Thousands of Jews who were imprisoned,

277

Alexandria Adieu

and many more who were harassed and came under pressure when they couldn't acquire travel documents from sympathetic consulates, found themselves stateless in the post-Suez drive. Many of them and their children knew no other country or way of life; they had been born and grown up in Alexandria. Hundreds were escorted to the city's harbour under the watchful eye of armed soldiers and put on ships sailing away. Other regional autocrats copied Nasser's treatment of Jews and ethnic minorities. King Idris of Libya rounded up his country's Jews, confiscated their assets and deported them to Italy during the Six-Day War.[2] Autocratic regimes in Algeria, Syria and Iraq behaved similarly.[3]

Like many Egyptian Jews who loved their country of birth, *Oncle* Bishara at first resisted threats, abusive phone calls and a raid by a gang of thugs as he was about to open his shop, following which it took the police until the end of the day to arrive on the scene. It later transpired that the attack had been organised by a secret apparatus within Nasser's Nationalist Federation. After this, Bishara finally gave in, signing a pre-prepared declaration that he was leaving of his own free will.[4]

The family had no other passport to travel on, so they became refugees on the move before eventually finding a new home in Israel. They wrote to my parents a few times. Parted Alexandrian Jews' letters were infrequent, taking months to arrive as they came by hand with travellers or were posted from a third country due to a state of war between Israel and Nasser. Neighbours used to gather at our home to read the letters; the women would burst into tears. Sophisticated Alexandrian Jews who became stateless and ended up in Israel found life there uncomfortable, not like European Alexandria.

Neighbourhood ladies, including Muslims and Christians, stayed up all night in 1958 helping *Tante* Fortune pack. Whether expelled or leaving 'of their own free will', Alexandria's Jews were not allowed to take cash with them although clothes were permitted. So for weeks, the neighbours had given her expensive material and helped make garments that she could sell abroad – they also sewed the odd gold chain into a dress lining for a rainy day. All the neighbours were concerned that these chains might be discovered at customs; some weeks later, they were delighted when my mother informed them that our good neighbour Fortune was safe. The post from abroad was frequently opened by Nasser's security agents; letters were either censored or used to put recipients under surveillance – they could also be deployed as evidence of the latter's collaboration with 'the enemy', placing pressure on them to flee the country in turn. The last letter arrived by carrier from Marseilles four months after it was dated. Fortune signed off, saying she was missing Alexandria's cocktail parties and my mother's monthly Tuesdays with their music, dance, champagne and gossip.

CHAPTER 34   The Jews' Second Exodus

I, too, left Alexandria, and my family lost touch with them. Almost 30 years later, I encountered Sammy, who was much older than me (he passed away in 2003), during a short stay in Israel. He recognised me from my television reporting. We drove to see the aged *Tante* Fortune. She hugged me for what felt like the entire three decades of separation, with her tears soaking my collar. She kept stroking my head and cheeks, and kissing me. It felt like we had gone back half a century. Apart from white hair and shaky hands, she was the *Tante* Fortune who had stayed up all night looking out of the window for my return with my father in the early hours from the Israeli Hospital, with my arm in a heavy, solid plaster cast. Not waiting for the *bawab*, who had a tiny apartment under the stairs, she ran down the 12 stairs into the courtyard, opening the automobile door and holding me in her arms, covering my head, face and the swelling hand sticking out of the plaster in motherly kisses. She had tucked my mother into bed three hours earlier after my father had sent her home in a cab around midnight, exhausted from the whole affair. Papa carried me to *Tante* Fortune's duplex apartment; she made us breakfast before we went home upstairs an hour later. Sammy, about 12 years old at the time, was the first to decorate my fresh plaster with his scribble. Our 1990s reunion was like a video clip from Alexandria found in a decommissioned time machine. Despite arthritis slamming their brakes on her joints, *Tante* Fortune kept bringing dishes, feeding me non-stop like she had four decades earlier. Her short-term memory was muddled, but she remembered details and names from her Alexandria.

My sisters, my mother, *Tante* Carlota, *A'am* Mahmoud and Souso. Speaking in the Alexandrian tongue, she remembered the nicknames like Monsieur *Ibber* ('Mr Needles'), Chéri (Sherrie), his brother Meeky, and tradesmen by profession: *Usta* Manolli, *el-mezain* (the barber); Raheem *beta'h eltalg* (the ice vendor); *Monsieur eldocteur*, and *el-hakim* Labib. Fortune's words flashed a snapshot of Alexandria; these memories of a 'slice' of her previous life were a raft keeping her afloat after *Oncle* Bishara's death, until she too passed away in 1997. Whenever I encounter old Alexandrians, regardless of the geographical diaspora, the experience is similar. Whether in the Old or the New World, ageing Alexandrians in the vicinity gather to meet someone they knew as children or whose parents they recalled. Some were fragile older ladies, others had been born in exile and only learned second-hand of the city and names whose faces they could only imagine. Then: an avalanche of questions – especially from the younger ones, eager to hear my version of stories told by their mothers and grandmothers about a city that lost her Jewish children long before they were born. The few surviving elders wanted to know: What was left of our Alexandria?

Alexandria Adieu

What had become of neighbours, of people, of shops, of cafés and the of the rest of the human topography of a city they carried in their hearts, whom they had left decades earlier. Memories were exchanged, although distorted, fuzzy and become more unclear with time. And on some occasions, there was singing and *balady* dancing from younger women (proving they had Egyptian genes in their rhythmically twisting bodies) to melodies by Umm Kulthum, Farid al-Atrash[*] and Leila Murad, played on scratched old records. And, of course, laughs at stories re-edited beyond recognition and at bawdy Alexandrian jokes – and also tears during those memorable soul-aching encounters. Like our Alexandria days, those encounters were phased out and no longer possible. With the passing away of personae like my parents, *Tante* Fortune, Sammy and *Oncle* Bishara, Alexandria continued to slip through our fingers, losing another living part of her body as it turned into a few pages in her 2,340-year-long story – with the danger of revisionists rewriting them. How many, if any, of those original Alexandrians who had left 70 or 80 years ago are still around?

Settlers and Stereotypes: a History of Anti-Semitism
Most of the Ottoman Jews who settled in Alexandria in the nineteenth century were Sephardic, descendants of those who left Spain in the fifteenth century. They made Spain prosper economically and culturally in the fourteenth and fifteenth century until the Catholic zealots Ferdinand and Isabella expelled them in 1492. Spain's loss became the Ottoman Empire's gain when Sultan Bayezid II (1447–1512) welcomed the Jews. Some settled in Constantinople, and many established a presence in Smyrna, Salonica and the Levant, making these places flourish economically and culturally. They introduced publishing by setting up printing workshops. Bayezid, who was a patron of art and culture, tried to marry Western and Eastern cultures. He granted the Spanish refugee Jews permission to set up a printing press in Turkey as long as publications were confined to Hebrew and European languages,[†] not printing in Arabic or Turkish.[5] Books in Turkish had to wait until 1729, during the final years of Ahmed III (1673–1736), whose reign (1703–30) was known as the Tulip Era, while the majority of historians date 1718 (Passarowitz Treaty)[‡] as the start of the Tulip reforms – and then only after Shaykh-al-Islam, Yenişehirli Abdullah Efendi, the chief mufti,

---
[*] Farid Atrash (1910–1974) was a Syrian-born Druze who migrated to Egypt to join the largest entertainment, film, music and performance industry in the eastern Mediterranean. His career spanned four decades.
[†] The Ottomans preferred limited handwritten texts.
[‡] The Treaty of Požarevac (a town now in eastern Serbia), signed on 21 July 1718 between the Ottomans, the Habsburg monarchy of Austria and the Republic of Venice.

CHAPTER 34 The Jews' Second Exodus

gave the sultan religious permission,* thus establishing the first Turkish printers in Constantinople.⁶

Until the late 1930s, many Jews in Egypt did what other minorities did: they applied for the nationality of countries that become independent from the Ottoman Empire or of the states that annexed the provinces where their ancestral families resided. Although the perceived advantage was benefitting from foreign protection, or tax incentives going back to the late-nineteenth century, there was another, more important, reason. Even before the Second World War, the Egyptian Government made it difficult for non-Muslims (or those labelled as 'of foreign extraction') to become naturalised.⁷

During this 'second exodus', the less well-off Jews were left stateless,† although they were supposed to be Egyptian by birth.

The drive to Egyptianise (and, later to Arabise) both public life and the economy harmed the country's non-Muslims and non-Nilotic ethnic minorities, but the Jews were to receive more blows against them than these other groups. Treating Egyptian Jews with suspicious also predated Nasser's autocracy.

There had been agitation against Jews in the late 1930s and the 1940s. Most of the attacks and ill-feeling directed at them in the latter decade were due to their real or alleged links to Jewish nationalist organisations in Mandate Palestine. Fascist and Nazi ideologies were also becoming attractive to Egyptians, especially in Cairo – although the drive was more anti-*les Anglais*, with the hope that Britain would be defeated in the War. But popularity for Rommel and the Nazis also carried with it anti-Jewish sentiment since the Jews were, naturally, in favour of the free-world Allies associated with *les Anglais*. Islamists and fascists like Young Egypt party members (known as the 'Green Shirts') called Jews 'the enemy'. Successive Egyptian governments also saw them as being behind communist activities. Unlike in Europe, Jews in Egypt in that period were still largely not discriminated against because of their religion or race but rather for political reasons.

But there were also incidents of traditional anti-Semitism predating the 1940s, including anti-Jewish propaganda by Catholics and Muslims. In 1932, leaflets containing anti-Jewish Catholic propaganda

---

* The first printings in Arabic and Ottoman Turkish (written then in Arabic letters) were set by the Hungarian Ottoman diplomat Ibrahim Muterferrika (1674–1745), but his workshop was closed in 1742 by the powerful lobby of scribe-publishers. Others, however, established Arabic letters (Ottoman Turkish) printers 40 years later.
† Only in 1961 did the UNHCR's Convention on the Reduction of Statelessness (for the implementation of the 1954 UNHCR Convention Relating to the Status of Stateless Persons) oblige countries to safeguard against statelessness; it entered into force in 1973, but Egypt remains a non-signatory.

Alexandria Adieu

was distributed to patients at Alexandria's Jewish Community Hospital. Seven years earlier, a Dominican monk at Saint Catherine's College called Brother Lèonce distributed leaflets at Passover accusing Jews of children's ritual murder. Hassan al-Banna, the founder of the Muslim Brotherhood and its assassination squad, declared in 1928 that non-Muslims were second-class citizens and should pay *gizyah*, which had been abolished by Napoleon in 1798. The Muslim Brotherhood thugs would go to Jews to ask for *gizyah* contributions, threatening to tell Sheikh al-Banna if they refused. Jews who ignored the threat sometimes found their stores and businesses set alight or plundered.

The Nasser regime's propaganda referred to Egyptians who were ethnically non-Nilotic and Jews by an older term: *mutamassirun* (Egyptian*ised*). This originally meant Egyptianised by choice; in later years, the phrase was negatively redefined as 'pretending to be Egyptian'. Emerging in the late nineteenth-century, *mutamassirun* referred to settled migrants and first-generation people born to them. By the early twentieth century, most of them considered themselves no different from Muslims or Copts in the rest of Egypt and Sudan – all of them, after all, were subjects of the Ottoman Empire. The difference perhaps, was socio-economic; the settlers were proportionally financially better off than the majority of indigenous citizens. The majority of *wilad-el-balad* (indigenous Nilotic Egyptians) preferred the safety of steady employment in the civil service or large firms to gambling with risks taken by the *néo-natifs*, (non-Nilotic migrants), who had borrowed to invest and established their own businesses. Like settling migrants everywhere, Egyptian Jews adopted the way of life and etiquette of their country's middle class – which in Egypt were uniquely Franco-Mediterranean. From the start of the twentieth century, the *mutamassirun* became an essential component of Egyptian society and pillars of the economy: they established banks and commercial ventures, and contributed to culture, education and medicine. Despite their diversity, they were seen by Egyptian nationalists (especially the Islamic-leaning ones) as a homogeneous group. The *mutamassirun* were referred to by the xenophobic term 'them': *aganeb* – often called *khawaga*. Although listed in dictionaries as 'alien – foreign', *Khawaga* had other folkloric associations meaning 'different' or 'not belonging here'. In the marketplace, Muslims referred to Levantine merchants, even a Muslim one, as *khawaga* – as they did Coptic Christians, who predated Islam by 700 years, and Jews, who predated both in Egypt.

After 1948, the character of a stereotypical *khawaga* took on a cynical twist. Unlike the earlier black-and-white movie depiction of the Egyptian *hara* (lane/alley), with its mosaic of ethnicities and faiths who all spoke one tongue and shared the same customs, the 1950s

CHAPTER 34   The Jews' Second Exodus

khawaga began to be portrayed differently. The new *khawaga* character had a foreign accent and got linguistic terms wrong; they didn't sound like other Egyptians (which was patently false in the case of the second and third generations), and in comic sketches was portrayed as cunning and deceitful – albeit always outwitted by Ibn-el-Balad (the son of Mother Egypt). And from 1953 onwards, the character became fair game for a new generation of monologists (solo-performers and stand-up comedians) who were increasingly racist, with an additional dose of vulgarity, and anti-Semitic even by 1950s standards. And the anti-Jewish stereotype –jokes about being a modern Shylock: an unscrupulous, penny-pinching and extortionist moneylender – were exchanged on the stage and during performances broadcast live on national radio. The phenomenon became widespread, and accelerated after 1956.

I was labelled *khawaga* myself, and endured negative stereotyping during my sabbatical year as an external observing student at Alexandria University. Students outside my close *chellah*, who would be discussing politics in the bar, would immediately change the subject when I approach. I was *khawaga* – working for the enemy, *les Anglais* – even though I spoke and understood demotic Alexandrian better than those cheeky Egyptian nationalists. I knew the city better than most of those *fellaheen*, who had only seen Alexandria for the first time when starting their courses.

The alienation of Alexandria's *mutamassirun* and Jews was a twentieth-century tragedy. Many who were in a loving relationship with partners who unexpectedly became 'other Egyptians' said a quick goodbye, or didn't manage to say it at all, when they fled with their families. There are heartbreaking stories by Alexandrians, particularly Jews, who chronicled the tragedy of the second exodus through their personal accounts or documentary novels. Alexandrian historical-novel author Ibrahim Abdel Meguid captured the mood in his moving account of brokenhearted experiences, with couples splitting as one partner deported or fled after the Suez War, in *Birds of Amber*, the second volume in his Alexandria Trilogy.[8]

In the novel, Katina, the ethnically Greek Alexandrian – third generation, born in the city, who knew no other country but Egypt – tearfully drinks her last night away while listening to Umm Kulthum before her final exodus. She holds Arabi, her Attarin shop-assistant Muslim soulmate and occasional lover, tight to her bosom as she is about to be uprooted from her life and memories. Her tears mix with Arabi's Metaxa cognac and with his tears, embracing each other for the last time. Throughout 1957, Arabi witnesses Alexandria haemorrhaging her most treasured (and richest) asset – namely, her children; her human wealth. The close friends from the meaningful years of his life are departing in droves: Asmahan – whose second-generation Italian parents named her after the songstress Amal Al-Atrash (1912–1944 and sister of Farid Al-Atrash), known as 'Asmahan'; Rachel Zahaf, the Alexandrian-born Jewess who loves Arabi but he turned down her repeated requests for marriage; and, finally, the woman he has truly loved for years and whose bosom becomes his last refuge, Katina – with whom he has shared pains, memories, pleasures and sorrows – is leaving too. Arabi is lost, cast adrift after those close to his way of life and thinking have departed Alexandria.

In addition to my own experience, reading Meguid's description of events was an additional reminder of Alexandria's pain. The character Arabi symbolised the less-fortunate Muslim Alexandrians. They are extrovert and outward-looking, holding onto Europeanised Alexandria and resisting being dragged inward towards Inner Egypt. But the Suez tragedy also transforms Arabi's character in order to symbolise Egypt itself after the departure of its 'estranged' citizens, who were given the alienating labels *khawagat* and *aganeb*. Arabi, now alone in an increasingly Egyptianised Alexandria without Katina's guidance, drifts aimlessly in bars and nightclubs and blows the money she left with him to help start a new life, as he did earlier with another 50 pounds gifted by Rachel, the Jewess who loved him. In 1957, hastily departing Jews and other *khawagat* (allowed £€20 for each adult over 21 – equivalent to $80 at the time) were selling entire business and property for as little as £€50. But Arabi, the jackass, as Katina kept calling him, lacks the common sense and the economic savvy to invest the capital in an enterprise and change his life for the better. Perhaps, in choosing the name Arabi, Meguid summarised how the Nasser regime (which Arabised Egypt) squandered the wealth sequestrated from Jews and other *khawagat* on pointless projects and political adventures in Arab countries, leaving Egypt gripped by an economic hangover after a high-spending night in the bar of ideology.

Another account was given by the Cairo-born American journalist Lucy Lagnado (1956–2019), a third-generation Jewess whose grandparents had migrated from Aleppo in the nineteenth century. She details her family's stateless status, becoming refugees living on charity handouts in France after leaving Alexandria in 1963. She was only seven years old, crying for Puspus, her cat left behind, when, aboard the ship taking them away for good at Alexandria harbour, she saw a lady taking her cat with her.[9] Since the entire family were Egyptian-born Jews, they had no other documented nationality and became penniless refugees until moving to America. The family was headed by her father, after whom the book – *The Man in The White Sharkskin Suit* – was

CHAPTER 34   The Jews' Second Exodus

named: the man known as 'The Captain', who once played cards with King Farouk but who later had to sell neckties out of a suitcase on the streets of New York to survive. He looked at the Alexandrian coast growing smaller, weeping with other Jews on the deck and crying out '*Raga'ouni masr*' ('Take me back to Cairo'). Many an Egyptian Jew's longing cry was later turned into a Franco-Arabic song, with English and Egyptian lyrics.

'Never to Return' – and Those Who Stayed
Egyptian-born Jews – like our neighbours *Oncle* Bishara, *Tante* Fortune and Sammy – were given a *laissez-passer*, a temporary travel passport valid only for one trip. For those against whom the regime could find no pretext for deportation, life was deliberately made difficult by harassments that included threats, abusive phone calls and pressure on or loss of their businesses.[10]

Many Jews were also forced to sign a declaration of no return, pledging to make no future claims on their property left behind in Egypt.[11] The 'never-to-return' policy was a condition that the regime demanded from Egyptian Jews who feared for their safety. This was scary and especially puzzling for these indigenous Jews because Nasser himself, until he was six years old, had grown up on Rue Khoronfoush, just around the corner from Haret-El-Yahud (the city's Jewish quarter) – as the late Egyptian-Jewish communist Youssef Darwish (1910–2006) pointed out.[12]

My father and his friends estimated the number of people whom Alexandria lost in a decade to be much higher than the official figure of 100,000. They suggested a total closer to 180,000 Alexandrians, who left the city during the period. Many obtained emergency passports from sympathetic consulates with whom they cited some connection. The regime registered these documents as nationalities, reclassifying Egyptian-born Alexandrians as *aganeb* and thus discounting them from the official figures. Counting their personal acquaintances who were legally Egyptian but listed as *aganeb* among all their contacts who left Alexandria, the ratio would have increased the official figure by 1.5 to 1.8 times. I never had a chance to explore their calculations, and modern equipment to make copies was not easily accessible 60 years ago – even if the topic interested a young university student. In addition, I only met Papa three times between leaving Alexandria and his death in 1979.

The official figure also excluded thousands of Egyptian-born Alexandrians whose status would have permitted them to remain in the country but who fled the regime's heavy hand. Others left under severe economic pressure when their assets or businesses were nationalised, or they lost their livelihoods when their employers or contractors were expelled.

The exodus continued after the Suez War until The Six-Day War, with the last indigenous Egyptian Jews leaving after the Yom Kippur War. When the Six-Day War broke out in June 1967, thousands of Egyptian Jewish men, mostly Karaite, were rounded up and placed in internment camps. They weren't released until after Colonel Nasser's death, more than three years later. But very few were arrested on the false charge of 'spying for Israel' compared with those during the Suez conflict. Between November 1956 and February 1957, hundreds of Alexandrian and Cairean Jewish men were arrested as *gawsis el-yahoud and les Anglais* (spies for the Israelis and British). Many were released after a few days, but many more were expelled from the country within a very short period.

Only the indigenous Egyptian-Jewish Karaites remained. Of the Karaite (meaning 'readers'), a majority lived in *harat-el-Yahoud* (the Jewish neighbourhoods of the cities – but not a ghetto, in the European sense). Karaite women wore *habaras* (long, plain, usually black headcovering)* and some sported *malayah-laf* (indigenous to Alexandria, but adopted in Cairo too: a wrapping sheet like the Iranian *chador* but not covering the face). The men dressed in *galabiyah* with a dark grey jacket on top, sometimes a short tarboosh on their head or a skullcap, and looked like Egyptian *fellaheen*.

The Karaites (*Qarraein* in Arabic) were the poorest among Alexandria's Jews. Their women did domestic service – working as cleaners, washerwomen and cooks – and school maintenance, assisting teaching staff; the men did menial jobs, either for better-off Jews or wealthy Alexandrian merchants and businesses. They had lived in Egypt for centuries, well before the Arab occupation in the seventh century. Their names were typically like those of their Muslim compatriots: Ratibah, Nazek, Nazily, Farida and Aminah for women; the men were Abdallah, Abdel Wahid, Abdel Nour, Mounir, Moussa, Nader, Yahia, Daoud, Whabah or Amin – like Ma'alem Amin who ran upholstery services, doing annual house calls to re-stuff mattresses and pillows with cotton. They avoided Coptic names that went back to ancient Egypt, like Ramses, Muheb, Aida or Isis.

Karaites' synagogues were like Islamic mosques: they did not have benches; worshippers knelt on carpets like Muslims, and when prayed they touched the ground with their foreheads.

Some of the indigenous Egyptian Jews go back to Ptolemaic Alexandria, when the city's Jewish quarter was almost as large as that of the Greeks.[13] It had its own sturdy walls and was governed by an

---

* A two-piece dress, usually black. The bottom part was almost like a skirt, the top a plain piece of material that covered the head and shoulders to the waist. It could also be used to veil the face

CHAPTER 34   The Jews' Second Exodus

ethnarch (Greek for 'leader of the people') under a Jewish council and laws. According to the historian Flavius Josephus (37–100 AD), Jews settled in Alexandria shortly after Alexander the Great's death.[14] At first, they dwelled in the eastern sector of the city, near the sea. During the Roman era, two of the city's five quarters (particularly the fourth, known as 'Delta') were inhabited by Jews. Their synagogues spread over almost every part of Alexandria.[15]

Egyptian Karaites only recognise the original five books of Moses and reject the Talmud (written compendium of laws) as an innovation. Additionally, they do not recognise *Mishnah* (the first written collection of oral law).[*]

Egypt was home to the largest number of Karaites in the entire diaspora. While pressure – economic, social and political – after the Suez War drove other Jews to leave, the Karaites were the last to leave and many among the remaining ones converted. I heard Amin, the upholsterer, telling my grandfather during his annual visit to our household in 1959 that his community preferred to stay in Egypt where they felt safer and independent from official rabbinical authority. This protection, by their rulers, from interference by the rabbinical authorities was a centuries-old tradition. Their religious autonomy had been granted to their ancestors by General Ibn-al-As when he occupied Alexandria in the seventh century. However, like all other non-Muslims, they continued to pay the *gizyah* tax to the ruling colonial Arabs and then to the Ottoman Caliphate until Bonaparte ended the practice in 1798. Their worst treatment was experienced under Colonel Nasser despite their loyalty to Egypt, their country. Their community included the last Jews to leave Egypt, and many of them settled in Israel.[16] In 1974, Amin followed his sister and nephews, who had left in 1971. He gave the upholstering business to his apprentice, Moussa, who married a local Muslim girl.

It is nearly impossible to put an exact figure on this second exodus due to multiple categorisations and the reality of faiths cutting across ethnic and national lines. Even nationalities listed on official Egyptian departure files weren't totally accurate, since they were taken from temporary travel documents obtained from sympathetic consulates during the post-Suez War flight. But it is generally accepted among my generation that Alexandria, in the mid-1950s, was home to an estimated 35,000–40,000 Jews, of various races and ethnic origins.

---

* More about Karaites: Anan Ben David (715–795) and his followers were called the Ananites (the Karaites are the later Ananites); a large number of Karaite works appeared in the tenth, eleventh and twelfth centuries; the best known and comprehensive work providing the code of practice and the origins of Karaism was that of Abu Youssef Jacob al-Qirgisani (890–960) – in Arabic: Kitab al-Anwar wal-Maraqib.

I recall in the 1950s alighting from Tram Number 4 at *Arrêt* Eliayhu Hanvi Synagogue on Rue Naby Daniel. Considered at the time to be the largest in the region, the synagogue had been founded in 1354 by Sephardic Jews fleeing persecution by the Inquisition in Spain and Portugal. The building sustained massive damage from French bombs in 1798 when Napoleon landed in Alexandria. Italian architects restored it in 1850 with finance from Viceroy Abbas Helmi I, local Jews and Sir Moses Montefiore (1784–1885).[17*]

The synagogue still holds services for the remaining few Jews, but nowadays under guard. When the head of the Alexandria Jewish community, Dr Max Salama, died in 2008, and the synagogue was full with mostly non-Jewish mourners, no Kaddish was read since no ten Jewish adult men could be found as required to recite the full prayer. Only 180 Jews were recorded as attending the synagogue regularly. Most Jews had left the country, converted to Islam or didn't dare to attend synagogue, keeping their heads down amongst the general population by adopting names unrevealing of their faith. Salama was succeeded as president of Alexandria's Jews by Ben Youssef Gaon, whose father once owned a tailoring workshop.

This iconic, historical place of worship was closed for the Rosh Hashanah of 5773 (2012) by the Muslim Brotherhood government (2012–13) under the pretext of 'security considerations'. Eliyahu Hanvi Synagogue was reopened in 2017 when the Egyptian Department of Antiquities footed the $7 million bill for its restoration. In a growing movement for keeping Egypt's Jewish heritage alive, the post-Islamist government allocated $37 million to the restoration of eight Jewish heritage sites. The synagogue was included in the World Monuments Fund's list in 2018 as 'at risk'. The Association Internationale Nebi Daniel continues to raise funds to help keep its activities alive and to assist visits, after the Egyptian Government turned down their offer to contribute to the repairs in 2017. The France-based association organised a visit in 2020 by 180 Jews of Alexandrian origin to the synagogue, reopening with the first *shabbat* service in eight years, after renovation.[18] Its grand reopening in February of that year was headed by Egypt's minister of antiquities, and many of the visiting Jews of Egyptian ancestry became quite emotional.[19]

The regime's claim that most Jews were not deliberately expelled might be technically correct, but it is factually disingenuous when put

---

* Born to a Sephardic Jewish-Italian family in Livorno, Sir Moses Haim Montefiore, 1st Baronet, was a British banker, financier and philanthropist. His grandfather had immigrated to London with the family in 1740s but maintained close ties with Livorno. He was elected for the ancient office of Sheriff of London for the year 1837.

CHAPTER 34   The Jews' Second Exodus

in its historical and social context. Not every Jew, especially those with no Anglo or French connection, was rounded up and ordered to leave. But the general atmosphere and hostility towards the Jews made them uncomfortable, if not scared. The Nazi concentration camps lay only a decade in the past, after all, and many recalled fleeing Alexandria to escape the Luftwaffe's bombs while Rommel knocked at the gates. The Nasser regime's propaganda generated a hostile pubic atmosphere, and many Jews felt unsafe – including those born in Alexandria.

CHAPTER 35
The Rest of the 'Mosaic'

The tragic exodus encompassed all communities – not just the Jews. Alexandrian-Egyptian-born non-Nilotic ethnic groups, Syro-Lebanese, Maltese, Cypriots and many former Ottoman subjects (Armenians, Balkan peoples, Greeks, North Africans and Russians) or European ethnic minorities also faced unfavourable odds. Economic pressure, the sequestration of assets and nationalisation – in addition to intimidation and hostile anti-Jewish and anti-European 'colonialism' propaganda, associating those communities with the 'enemies of Egypt' – forced them to depart. They tearfully left a country that they knew as home, leaving their parents, grandparents, spouses and loved ones in graves in Alexandria's saffron soil. Many took sand from the *plages* they loved; others, randomly, took the saffron soil itself in jars and tins. Their grip grew tighter on their little grains of Alexandria as her coast got smaller and smaller. Standing on the decks of ships, their view of the city was blurred by tears as the distance increased, with the vessels painfully ploughing the waves of the Mediterranean towards the unknown – uprooting their existence from the only home they knew: Alexandria.

Arabisation – Sout al-Arab
The largest exodus in Alexandria's modern history, whether by mass deportation and deliberate pressure from the regime's agencies and apparatus or as a by-product of the ongoing economic and social upheaval, went hand in hand with the most disturbing and irreversible damage – namely, cultural change: Nasser's deliberate Arabisation of the city, and Egypt as a whole, with a view to changing the nation's identity. This was steadily advanced by replacing or destroying the institutions

CHAPTER 35   The Rest of the 'Mosaic'

of modernity founded by Muhammad Ali's dynasty. The presence of multi-ethnic communities, mostly of European stock, was seen by Nasser as impeding his reversal of modernity. It was a deliberate policy to Arabo-Islamise Egypt's Europeanised parts, especially Alexandria and her European culture, and demographic hegemony made the job easier. Just as the Ourabists believed in the 1880s that European thoughts and ideas were linked to ungodly ideologies, so were Europeans and their culture associated in Nasser's mind with imported, alien concepts like liberalism and calls for restoring parliamentarian democracy, free speech and the individual's free choice. This explains his encouraging a pliant media to refer to their fellow Egyptians as *aganeb* because of their ancestral background.

After deporting the Jews, the British and the French, other ethnic groups who felt threatened began to leave. The second group to flee were the Italian-Alexandrians, followed by the descendants of former Ottoman subjects like the Armenians, the Syrians and communities from around the Black Sea; the Greco-Alexandrians were the last to go. The majority had been born in Alexandria, but they came under immense pressure – not just economic but also political. The Egypt-born Greeks and most Italians, who loved Egypt and supported Nasser, were confused and dismayed at their treatment by his regime. Scores of left-wing Italian-Egyptians and hundreds of Greco-Egyptians who had joined the armed resistance against the British in Port Said were the first to be arrested and jailed when the Nasser regime turned against the Egyptian communists a year later. It was a big shock to those communities – especially the Greeks. Although the arrest of communists was not broadcast on Egyptian national media or reported in the heavily censored newspapers, Alexandrians (not just Europeans but Egyptians too) were getting their news from the external European Broadcast, and from the eastern bloc radio stations.

Ethnic minorities realised they could not trust the military government. The officers broke the promises they made in July 1952, like holding elections and assuring foreign embassies, businesses and the non-Nilotic ethnic communities that they would be treated as equal citizens.[1] Even the non-communists in migrant communities and those who weren't interested in politics saw the move as a bad sign and accelerated their flight. While using a 'Newspeak' process of reprogramming minds in schools and in the media in order to alter the collective national way of thinking – as well as changing the names of streets, squares and buildings – demographic changes became another tool deployed to shift the nation's identity. And, subsequently, Alexandria's identity also started to change at astonishing speed.

Additional other factors contributed to these demographically generated cultural changes. Mass expulsion became one of Nasser's standard foreign-policy devices – no longer on the scale that followed the Suez War, when descendants of migrants from the Ottoman provinces who had connections with Western powers (especially Britain and France) were deported, but randomly expelling immigrants or workforces from countries with whom Colonel Nasser had fallen out. These changes of direction in foreign policy were unpredictable – as in Orwell's *Nineteen Eighty*-Four, in which the regime's propaganda redefines the national crusade of the day to fit such sudden switchbacks. Aside from the much-demonised Western powers, regional autocratic rulers retaliated in kind by deporting Egyptian citizens. This led many long-term residents to vacate premises, which were occupied by newcomers with an ethos alien to Alexandria's culture. This tit-for-tat policy, with its damaging socio-cultural consequences, continued after Nasser's demise in 1970.

Such foreign-policy inconsistencies caused harmful economic tremors, affecting the flow of money sent home by Egyptian expatriates – which didn't help the country's already-shaky economy. These abrupt changes often followed one of Nasser's public rants, broadcast on the 1953-founded *Sout al-Arab* ('Voice of the Arabs' – VoA) radio service. Years before Nasser fully controlled Egypt's traditionally independent newspapers, *Sout al-Arab* was his megaphone in the region.[2]

Broadcasting to the MENA region and Europe, VoA was the first significant and effective use of this influential mass-indoctrination tool since the demise of the Third Reich minister of propaganda, Joseph Goebbels. The VoA was the brainchild of Nasser's trusted propagandist, Abd el-Kader Hatem (1918–2015), whom Egyptian journalists nicknamed 'Dr A'tem' ('the endarkened'). Hatem, an army officer and member of the Naguib coup, became head of *intérêt et informations* in 1952. He was appointed by Nasser to head the Middle East News Agency in 1955, when the regime purchased 51% of the agency's shares a few months after it had been established by then-independent Egyptian newspapers. Nasser nationalised the agency along with the rest of the country's press in 1960. Hatem was behind the threats issued against Egyptians working for the BBC after the Suez War, following its Arabic-language broadcasts about the regime's heavy-handed treatment of the opposition. Most Egyptians first learned about the rounding up of opposition members and communists, including Jews, Greeks and Italians, from the BBC's external service in English and Arabic, and from Radio Monte Carlo broadcasting in French and Arabic. Hatem targeted Egyptians working for the two services and threatened their families at home. He refused to withdraw the threat when the BBC appealed to him.[3]

CHAPTER 35   The Rest of the 'Mosaic'

In addition to leading the VoA and the Middle East News Agency, Hatem became minister of state for broadcasting in the Ministry of Culture and National Guidance, then Minister of Information. Like most who shaped Nasser propaganda machine, Hatem was assisted by former Nazis[4] who had taken refuge in Egypt and were given Muslim names.[5]

The VoA was one of the most effective weapons in Nasser's political arsenal, receiving disproportionally high funding compared with other publicly funded sectors.[6] Not only did the radio service spread Nasser's influence among Arabic speaking nations, it also introduced listeners in Arab countries to vocabularies and political terminology still prevalent today. Arabic Wikipedia and its pro-Islamist equivalent, al-Maerifah, have pages relating to historical events from 1798 onwards that are full of jargon coined on the VoA's airwaves. Adjectives like 'nationalist hero' are added to Dr Hatem's name, praising his role in 'backing the national liberation struggle everywhere'. In reality, those 'liberation struggles' were just military coups with little or no popular support base. On the same pages, personae like Khedive Tawfik or regional leaders like Nouri al-Said Pasha of Iraq have terms like 'treason' and '*Les Anglais* collaborators' associated with them.

Part of the 1952 officers' xenophobic policy was to reverse commercial, primavera (the managing of contract clauses), trade and business-ownership laws. These laws, rules and practices formed the basis of Alexandria's commerce – upon which, in turn, Egypt's modern, prosperous economy had been built and flourished in the nineteenth and twentieth centuries. The very few who escaped expulsion or left under pressure only managed to salvage some of the business they or their families had established by going into partnership with Egyptian nationals, giving the latter majority shareholdings.

The Italian Garage – and the Italian Pâtisserie
Medhat unexpectedly found himself a majority shareholder in a car-hire and garage motor-repair business. He had failed to finish his secondary *Thaqafa* (the equivalent of the British O-level or GCSE examinations) and owed his career to his old headmaster. My grandfather was an old-fashioned educator who saw teaching as a lifelong mission, not just a career. He would not give up on students who lacked academic passion, but tried to find them apprenticeships to get into some trade based on their performance in *ashghal* (vocational-skill) classes.

These classes were designed to train pupils in practical skills. When Medhat failed to pass his exams, my grandfather fixed him up as a petty clerk and apprentice mechanic with his friend Salvatore, who had a garage and automobile-hire business. The garage owner's nephew,

293

Franco, was also a pupil of my grandfather's before becoming known as *Usta* Franco, one of Alexandria best automobile mechanics. The business owner employed Medhat as a bookkeeper, especially when Arabic script was required for dealing with customers' invoices and correspondence, and as an apprentice mechanic. A bizarre change of fortune made the failed student the majority shareholder of the firm since he was the only full-blooded Nilotic-Egyptian Muslim in the small family business with a relatively good education, reading and writing in Arabic, besides his mechanic-repair skills. The law changed in order to force those classified as *aganeb* to transfer majority shareholding to 'Egyptians'. Medhat started ordering his former bosses around, sitting on a leather armchair behind the business founder's desk.

Something resembling the old order would be temporarily restored during my grandfather's visits, however. Psychological conditioning and school discipline remain with us for the rest of our lives, and Franco and Medhat responded to the retired headmaster's visits as if he were entering their classroom with a cane in his hand. The old headmaster would sit in the boss's seat while his two former pupils stood to attention in front of the desk. They would turn the silver boxes of cigarettes and bonbons to face their old teacher, and ask which drinks to order. Refreshments varied according to season: cold Birra Stella followed by *café turc* in the summer; *café turc* with a double cognac on cooler days.

On occasions when I accompanied my grandfather, I would walk with an apprentice to the nearby pâtisserie to fetch the drinks. There were so many delights to dazzle a young boy's eyes: varieties of gâteaux, the maize-flour *biscotti-al-Cocco* and drinks like *cioccolata calda* or salep (*Orchidea calda*). The latter drink was made from orchid tubers with hot milk and maize starch, topped with whipped cream and crushed almond nuts and sprinkled with cinnamon and added flavours like vanilla or rosewater. Salep was typically sweetened with sugar, but Fabio, the pâtisserie waiter, added honey to mine instead. On hot days I would order gelato and *cioccolato ghiacciato* or Sobia Fredda – made from boiled, ground rice; coconut milk; honey; and vanilla – with ice cream. Following one episode, when I made myself sick with too many sugary cakes, my grandfather only permitted a takeaway drinks delivery to the automobile-rental office in order to keep an eye on me.

Overall, however, with no retired headmasters to check the excess of ungrateful Egyptian subordinates, the story of the businesses they came to control had many unhappy endings. Most deteriorated and fell into ruin when their founders left the country or their elderly owners died – as was eventually the case with the garage – or they were sold off for their premises to be knocked down and replaced by ugly tower blocks, leaving tens of thousands of Alexandrians unemployed.

PART IX
26 July 1956:
The Day Alexandria Changed Forever

What are we waiting for, assembled in the forum?
The barbarians are due here today.
Why isn't anything going on in the senate?
Why are the senators sitting there without legislating?
Because the barbarians are coming today.
What's the point of senators making laws now?
Once the barbarians are here, they'll do the legislating.
C. P. Cavafy, 'Waiting for the barbarians'

CHAPTER 36
Sleepy Streets

On the morning of 26 July 1956, my sister and I walked from Villa Alexandrine, heading south on Rue-Nineteen before turning into Rue Fifty eastwards. We passed the secluded Turkish War Cemetery for Ottoman soldiers killed in the Great War, then Miracolo, the *teinturerie* (dry-cleaner). We crossed the nameless dirt roads serving the *turab* (Egyptian cemetery), whose crumbling tombs of Egyptian Copts and Muslims in stark contrast to the marble and granite tombs in the neatly manicured Turkish war cemetery behind its Art Deco iron gate.

We saw the 'con-twins' by their seasonal watermelon marquee, an outlet for small vendors trading on hand-pushed carts. They carried on with their small-time trade even after a boost in status by which they became *wegha* (notable socialites) as the Liberation Rally's local commissars. They had been named the con-twins for duping clients as unlicensed estate agents – letting holiday chalets, rooms and flats to *masarwah* summer visitors. During the dead months of winter, they let out chalets at weekends for stag and other decadent parties while tipping off call girls about the locations. With the new-found fortune afforded by changes in the political winds, they gave up their odd manual jobs while delegating less-reputable pursuits to their *subian* (hired assistants). My mother kept them at bay – refusing to recognise their new political advancement as a passport to *société chic*. Her snobbery proved costly in the new order emerging in Egypt: our family were not looked upon favourably by the regime.

The con-twins were an example of the kind of opportunists who, within a decade, became the *nouveau élite* – the middle strata of a new class serving the 'pharaohs-in-khaki', as people nicknamed the junta officers, but an elite without the refined taste, education or etiquette of the old class. They climbed through Nationalist Federation (NF) ranks when it replaced the Liberation Board, then became group leaders in Colonel Nasser's Socialist Federation (SF).[1]

When Anwar Sadat took over following Nasser's death in 1970, he phased out the one-party monopoly on political life by dividing the SF into three parties. The twins left their top positions in the SF and joined Hezb-Misr (the Egypt party), founded by Sadat, but deserted it in 1978 to follow the president into his new Hezb-El-Watany el-Democrati (National Democratic Party – NDP). The NDP remained in power as the country's largest party until President Hosni Mubarak's removal in the 2011 uprising. The NDP was dissolved by Egypt's constitutional court later that year.

Cinéma Libération

On that day, Thursday 26 July 1956, the twins were loading an open-backed lorry with banners and chairs. We thought it was for a new film release opening at their makeshift Cinéma al-Tahrir (Cinéma Liberation), which the brothers had improvised on a *kharabah* (wasteland) on Rue Fifty immediately after the military coup. They had acquired two 16 mm projectors from the regime's Maslahet el-Isti'lamat (General Bureau of Information) to help spin the officers' message.

The cinema screened the *Isti'lamat* newsreels, heavily modified news-agencies' pictures and propagandised items.* After the 1952 coup, the newsreel often contained extracts from speeches by the officers' leader, General Naguib, who became Egypt's first president in 1953 – then by Colonel Nasser the following year. It was shown at the start of a two-film programme and again before the main picture, usually an Egyptian movie with French and English subtitles. The first film would be a Hollywood musical, a British production or a European one with Egyptian and French (or English) subtitles. But American films were becoming more numerous and beginning, under the officers' regime, to take over from the European pictures that had shaped Alexandrian filmgoers' taste for 50 years. Comedy films were

---

* Newsreels were shown in Egyptian cinemas for decades and updated weekly before television was officially launched in 1958.

CHAPTER 36 Sleepy Streets

particularly popular with Egyptians. Cinéma Liberation screened Bob Hope films with Dorothy Lamour and Bing Crosby, Jerry Lewis and Dean Martin pictures, and Laurel and Hardy comedies – as well as (British) Norman Wisdom films and those of the French comedian Louis de Funès. Living up to their nickname, the con-twins charged entry fees at their basic, open-air -facilities although they received subsidies and free equipment from the regime's *Isti'lamat*.

A makeshift desk served as the box office next to a stand selling refreshments from two big iceboxes containing pop drinks, both sizes of Birra Stella and gelato. The two projectors were elevated on rostra behind a bare space with crooked rows of seats in three tiers. These comprised two rows of low wicker armchairs with cushions; then several rows of bamboo and wooden-framed chairs, caned with dried bulrushes; and rows of wooden benches at the front, up close to the screen, that would give their 1 *piastre*-paying occupants a pain in the neck. The sandy ground was sprinkled with water before sunset to settle the dust; creepy crawlies – insects, centipedes and the odd scorpion – would occasionally be found. My parents did not allow us to attend, but we managed to watch selected films whenever we liked from the elevated veranda of our friends Loulou and her brothers, Halim and Selim. They were a Jewish family whose two-storey villa was one of two houses backing onto the space that became Cinéma al-Tahrir. The other residence belonged to a Jewish-Ottoman family from the Great War migration. Although their children were our friends too, they were not too keen on teenagers invading their veranda – even though their mother, *Tante Lena*, visited my mother, albeit infrequently. Her husband, *Oncle* Asher, was the grumpiest resident on the street – in total contrast to the welcoming Luolou's parents, *Tante* Nismah and *Oncle* Ishak (Yitzhak). The latter always had refreshments ready for the youngsters coming to watch films from their veranda. But my mother made sure we took gifts of her homemade cakes, *petits fours*, biscuits and *Oncle* Ishak's favourite coconut-flavoured cupcakes.

I look back with a mixture of gratitude, sadness and guilt on how kind *Oncle* Ishak and *Tante* Nismah were to the entire neighbourhood's children. Night after night, the Jewish couple entertained selfish teenagers watching films from their veranda for the whole summer. It made me realise that it was the people and their social network of contacts, and the favours they carried for one another – not just the architecture, history and politics – that made *my* Alexandria.

Watching the con-twins loading their lorry that warm July morning, we guessed that it must have been a new film release to attract viewers to watch a special newsreel marking the day: the third annual rally commemorating 26 July, the date of King Farouk's forced abdication

297

in 1952, which was held at Menasciyah. Although the location was officially the almost half-kilometre-long Muhammad Ali Square, formerly *La Place des Consulats*, Alexandrians call the area Menasciyah after Francesco Mancini, the architect who created the square with splendid buildings in the early 1820s and designed the surrounding vicinity.[2] Mancini who arrived in Alexandria in 1820 from the Papal States in Italy, served from 1837 to 1847 as chief engineer of the city's *Commissione d'Ornato*, during which time he designed the town plan.[3]

The NF, and later SF, commissars and trade-union leaders would bus the faithful and workers, on overtime pay (after slicing their cut off each worker's allowance) to the square to cheer for Colonel Nasser. The workers applauded and chanted on cue as Nasser ranted from the balcony of al-Boursa about fighting European colonial powers, singling out *les Anglais*. After *les Anglais* he would attack Israel, then hurls insults at rival regional leaders – particularly King Hussein of Jordan, whom he characterised as a British puppet, and the Saudi royal family.

The Summer Capital

I slowed our steps by Villa Jessica, the summer residence of *Elseniouravocato* (Signore Avvocato). I pointed out two hooded birds (wheatear) dancing on a branch to my sister, but I also hoped the *avvocato's* daughters would be up. I had a crush on Sonia, the younger of the two, who was two years my senior. She was lascivious and forward in initiating sex-play and touches. Sonia and Seeka (Jessica) came out to their veranda; we chatted about the afternoon event, which the neighbourhood teenagers were looking forward to: the big seaside summer kite show at *Plage* al-Asafrah at the far, eastern end of Sidi-Bishr. I used my own code to signal to Sonia to meet at two o'clock, the quietest time when fewer people would pass by our secret hiding place in cave-passages at the Devil's Hole.

Signore Avvocato was an Italo-Cairean lawyer. The villa belonged to his late paternal uncle, an Alexandrian Jew who owned a bookshop by St Katherine's Cathedral in Menasciyah. Like thousands of Caireans, the lawyer would move his business to his Alexandria practice alongside the Egypt's 'establishment' during the summer months. This tradition went back to Muhammad Ali Pasha, who consolidated his power from 1811, the year he massacred the Mamluks who had controlled Egypt for over 500 years.[4] The pasha made Alexandria the de facto capital of Egypt from 1820 onwards, spending more time in Ras El-Tin Palace.[5] Cairo wasn't founded until 969 AD on the site of Fustat (marquees/tents in Arabic), the military camp set by General Ibn el-As in 640 that served as capital of the new Egypt ruled by the Muslim Arabs, who turned their backs on Alexandria – she seemed to them idolatrous – and a thousand years of silence succeeded them.[6]

CHAPTER 36   Sleepy Streets

The recognition of Alexandria as summer capital was strengthened in 1822, when the consul generals began moving their consulates from Cairo to Alexandria. The same year, Muhammad Ali signalled independence from the Ottomans by issuing the first postal stamps of Egypt instead of the Ottoman state.[7] Six years later, Ali launched the official gazette *Alwaqaeh al-Rasmaiyah* (Egyptian Chronicles) in Arabic as a supplement to *Vekayi-i Misriye* (Turkish-language) official chronicles. It was the first Arabic-language newspaper in the entire region, but the first-ever periodical had been the four-page French-language *Courrier de l'Egypte*,* launched in Cairo on 29 August 1798 after Bonaparte established the Bulak (Bulaq) Printworks.[8]

The *Alwaqaeh al-Rasmaiyah* (founded 1828) remains the state's official gazette to this day – sold at 50 piastres. Other newspapers flourished later in the 1880s, like the *Egyptian Gazette, le Progrès Egyptian*, the *Egyptian Mail* and *La Bourse Egyptienne*.

Muhammad Ali's commitment to building a strong navy to advance his foreign policy also accelerated Alexandria's growth. He established a school for 1,200 navy cadets in Ras el-Tin. It was headed by his son, Said Pasha, after whom Port Said was named. New shipyards and a navy arsenal (to replace ships destroyed at the Battle of Navarino) were built by the French in 1829, employing thousands of workers of multiple ethnicities and many women. Beside hiring Alexandrians, migrants from Upper Egypt were also employed along with Arabs from the Libyan Desert, Armenians, Turks, Maltese, Italians, and French and British skilled workers.[9] By the mid-nineteenth century, Alexandria was integrated into world trade systems with hundreds of ships sailing in and out of her harbour.

Under Said Pasha's descendants, it became a tradition for the state organs, all the embassies (after independence in 1922) and Cairo-based departments to move to Alexandria in May or early June to escape the Cairean heat. As expected, it became an extended summer holiday for the families of civil servants, diplomats and other professionals associated with the summer move to Alexandria. Hence, most of them had a second home there – either owned or rented on a long lease. The Egyptian cabinet had its building overlooking Buckley *arrêt*, renamed *wizarah* (cabinet) on Rue d'Aboukir. The move of the seat of government to Alexandria was formalised in modern times by Khedive

---

* The French-language Egyptian Post, also called La Poste de l'Egypte, was launched on 29 August by Bonaparte to promote his polices. It was edited by French mathematician and physicist Joseph Fourier (1768–1830), one of the savants (scientists, engineers, artists and botanists) who accompanied the expedition and established the Institut d'Égypte (Egyptian Scientific Institute).

299

Tawfik thanks to his son, Abbas Helmi II, who followed the tradition when he succeeded Tawfik in 1892 and even used to hold a military parade to mark the official move. But many wealthy Alexandrians were, at the same time, leaving the city for Europe for the summer months. There were so many Alexandrians in Europe that the city's wide-circulation newspapers were on sale in Athens, Carlsbad, Florence, Marienbad, Naples, Paris, Rome, Vichy and Vienna. Alexandrians of the late nineteenth century saw *their* Alexandria as part of Europe, which they knew far better than they did Internal Egypt.[10] After trips to Alexandria, some Cairo school children rumoured to have answered in response to a geography-test question that the city was in Europe instead of Africa.[11]

CHAPTER 37
The 1936 Treaty and Journals

The Press
We turned north on Rue Dix-Huit (Eighteen), which was known as Rue L'mua'ahdah, referring to the 1936 Anglo–Egyptian Treaty of Cooperation signed with the Wafd party government (1936–7) of Prime Minister Mustafa al-Nahas Pasha (1879–1965).*

The 1936 Anglo–Egyptian Cooperation Treaty† realigned the two nations' relationship, reassigning high commissioner (HC) status to ambassadors.‡ Farouk had just taken the throne, returning from his

---

* Nahas Pasha was first elected to parliament in the landslide Wafd victory in the 1924 elections. He had become popular five years earlier when he was dismissed from the bench upon joining Wafd during the 1919 revolt. He was a judge and, judges not being permitted to join political movements, was exiled along with Sa'd Zaghloul Pasha. After Sa'd's death, Nahas became the best-known name in the nationalist movement for over half a century. Attended by hundreds of thousands, his funeral in 1965 turned into a protest against the Nasser regime as people chanted, 'Liberty died after you, Nahas.' Nahas, who became Egypt's nineteenth prime minister in 1928 and served in the position on four other occasions, was a friend of Britain and a staunch adversary of King Farouk until his last ministry in 1950, when he joined forces with the late king against les Anglais.
† Registered at the League of Nations in January 1937: The Treaty of Alliance Between His Majesty, in respect of the United Kingdom, and His Majesty, the King of Egypt.
‡ The British representative had been consul general from 1786 – but when Britain declared her protection over Egypt in 1914 due to war with the Ottoman Empire, the head of the British diplomatic mission became HC. The position became ambassador under the 1936 Treaty and Sir Miles Lampson (Baron Killearn, 1880–1964), who had been HC since 1934, became the first HM ambassador and remained so for another ten years. The treaty also predetermined withdrawing British military personnel from all bases, except for 10,000 troops and 400 pilots. A limited number were to remain in Alexandria for eight years, while the rest of the 10,000 soldiers were to be confined

301

naval-college training at Woolwich in London following his father King Fuad I's death. The 16-year-old king feared the Italians might attack from the west or the southeast. The second Italo–Abyssinian War had started in 1935 and was still going on; the Italians had been in Libya since the Great War. The treaty obliged Britain to defend the Kingdom of Egypt and Sudan against any attacks.

The first person we encountered on sleepy Rue Eighteen was Hamada, the 11-year-old son of *A'am* Hamdy, the news-kiosk vendor on Rue el-Mehata (la Gare Sidi-Bishr), doing the morning newspaper round. (He did a second one, with evening papers, in the late afternoon.) His morning round was short and quick, delivering mainly to a handful of elderly permanent residents; the rest were summer-only visitors. The majority of the men preferred to pick up their newspapers on their way to the cafés, to escape their wives' questions and demands at the breakfast table – and most of the holidaymakers were more interested in *plage* activities, pastime games and flirting with the opposite sex than in reading broadsheets.

Like today, in 1956, publications in Egypt needed a licence to circulate; licensing became strict after the Great War and even more stringent during the Second World War. In 1946, there were 441 licensed newspapers and weekly magazines in the country, 326 of which were based in Cairo with most of the rest in Alexandria. These numbers didn't include official journals or academic, school, army or private-member-club periodicals as these were impossible to count. The licensed Arabic publications included 34 dailies, 201 weeklies, 15 fortnightly, and 67 monthly journals. Besides Arabic, the largest number were French, Greek or Italian newspapers and magazines. There were also publications in Hebrew, English, Armenian, Turkish and Persian – totalling 30 dailies, 35 weeklies, 5 fortnightlies, 31 monthlies and 33 periodicals.

A large number of multiple-language journals and weeklies were exempted from the licence system because they were not sold publicly but by post to subscribers or club members; these included German publications (within the wealthy Swiss community) and Russian, Hungarian, Spanish, Czech, Hindi and Bulgarian periodicals. Of the 326 Cairo-licenced newspapers, 67 were in European languages while the Cairo-Arabic ones comprised 15 dailies, 105 weeklies, a

---

to the base at the Suez Canal to protect the waterway. The British troops were to be evacuated within 20 years, before the end of the treaty period on 26 August 1956. But the thorny issue that raised opposition was the treaty's terms for the withdrawal of Egyptian troops from Sudan whilst letting British troops remain there indefinitely. Nationalists, including King Farouk, saw it as an attempt by les Anglais to grab Sudan, thus seizing two-thirds of the Nile kingdom's territory.

CHAPTER 37   The 1936 Treaty and Journals

dozen fortnightlies and 60 monthly publications. Several periodicals and magazines were published by, and for, Egyptian Jews in multiple languages, including *La Vara* (in Ladino), but the majority of them were in Arabic – like *al-Kawkab al-Masry* (the *Egyptian* Star), *al-Kaleem* (the *Articulate*) and *Israel*; the last-named also had Hebrew and French editions. The three-language printed *Israel* also illustrated no sensitivity within a cosmopolitan society in publication mastheads like *Israel* or *La Messager Sioniste* (the *Zionist Messenger*). Small circulation newspapers in other ethnic minority languages like Albanian or Portuguese were, in 1946, still having difficulties sticking to their scheduled runs due to printing-paper shortages from the war years.[1]

Hamada let us have the customary read through his bundle. All the English and French dailies were gone; only magazines and Arabic papers were left. My sister was looking at *Life*, *Paris Match* and *Al-Musawar*. I looked at broadsheets: the oldest daily, *Al-Ahram*; the newly launched *Al-Gomhouriah* (*The Republic*), edited by *Yuzbaci* (Captain) Anwar Sadat; and the largest circulation daily, *Al-Akhbar*.

'The World Anticipates the President's Speech Today', read the headline on *Al-Ahram*'s front-page lead, predicting President Nasser would announce immediate actions in foreign policy and to 'liberate' the country's economy.

'The president will reveal plans to finance the construction of Aswan Dam', said a report without a byline, claiming that Britain's prime minister, Anthony Eden (1897–1977), had delayed a statement to the Commons about the UK's policy on financing the hydraulic project until after President Nasser's speech.[2] This was inaccurate reporting, as the issue had indeed been debated in the Commons a day earlier. The foreign secretary, Selwyn Lloyd (1904–1978)*, was answering questions put by former Labour minister of defence, Manny (Emanuel) Shinwell (1884–1986). Shinwell suggested linking the proposed aid to support Egypt's building of the Aswan Dam with the prospect of free passage to all shipping through the Suez Canal. But Lloyd replied, 'Financial assistance is not being provided by Her Majesty's Government to Egypt for the development of projects in that country. The question, therefore, does not arise.'[3]

A week earlier, the Americans had withdrawn their offer to finance

---

*Liverpool-born John Selwyn Brooke Lloyd (John Selwyn Brooke Lloyd, Baron Selwyn-Lloyd of Wirral), Conservative politician (MP: 1945–76; House of Lords: 1976–8), served as foreign secretary (1955–60) and later chancellor of the exchequer (1960–2) under Prime Minister Harold Macmillan (1894–1986), and Lord Privy Seal in the cabinet of Sir Alec Douglas-Home (1903–1995). He became Speaker of the House in 1970 until he left for the lords in 1976. He authored Mr. Speaker, Sir, November 1976.

303

the project – with Britain following suit the next day. I often wonder what the outcome would have been had Eden's government granted the aid to the Egyptians in 1956.

Projects associated with the Nile had always been, and remain, deeply engraved on the Egyptian national consciousness – ever since Herodotus had called Egypt 'the gift of the Nile' – thus enabling leaders to whip up popular support around the issue. Bringing larger areas under cultivation to meet the demand to feed Egypt's growing population (from four million in 1805 to over five million in the 1840s), Muhammad Ali in 1843 started with building *al-qanater* (a regulation dam) 26 kilometres north of Cairo, digging large canals and adding three more branches to the two natural tributaries canals that created the Nile Delta. The policy was continued by his dynasty. When the population reached 9,669,000 in 1897, Khedive Abbas Helmi II, pasha of Egypt and Sudan, built the Aswan Reservoir Dam from granite;* completed in 1902, it was the largest of its kind at the time.[4] Between 1907 and 1912, Helmi II ordered its enlargement and installed a hydraulic power-generation station upon completion.[5] When the population reached 14 million in 1926, Sa'd Zaghloul's government added water-storage and further electricity-generation capacity to the dam.†

Exploiting the country's ancient, deep, emotional link with the Nile to gain popular legitimacy, Colonel Nasser's regime wanted to build the Aswan High Dam in 1955 as the population exceeded 20 million. By mid-1956, an initial agreement of $200 million was negotiated with the World Bank after Britain and the US indicated they would provide $70 million in aid.

However, US Secretary of State John Foster Dulles (1888–1959) failed to reach an agreement with the Egyptian leader. When Nasser went to the Brioni conference (Brijuni, Croatia in then-Yugoslavia), hosted by Yugoslav president, Jozef Tito (1892–1980) on 19 July 1956 to launch the Non-Aligned Movement (NAM), Secretary Dulles announced that the US had withdrawn the offer. Britain followed suit the next day. The Americans became suspicious of NAM's aims, which arose

---

*Opened on 10 December 1902, the dam was designed by the former head of the Ottoman Empire Irrigation Department, British civil Engineer Sir William Willcocks (1852 [India]–1932 [Cairo]), assisted by prominent British civil engineers like Sir Benjamin Baker (1840–1907) and Sir John Aird (1833–1911), whose construction firm, John Aird & Co., was the main contractors on the project. .
† The work began in 1929 and lasted four years, adding 9 metres to the height and making the crest level 36 metres above the original river bed with a length of 1,950 metres – all from granite – and supplementing generation capacity as well as creating the main road linking the two major routes to Cairo and Aswan airports.

CHAPTER 37   The 1936 Treaty and Journals

out of the 1955 Bandung Asian and African States conference hosted by Indonesian President Ahmad Sukarno (1901–1970) – a gathering hostile to Western democracies. It was attended by communist and socialist world figures like Vietnamese leader Ho Chi Minh (Nguyen Sinh Cung, 1890–1969), with memories of the French defeat at Dien Bien Phu (1954) still fresh in Western minds, and China's premier, Zhou Enlai (1898–1976). Colonel Nasser's recognition of communist China and abandonment of Taiwan was the last straw.

A month earlier, the Soviet Union had offered Nasser a $1.1 billion loan, and in 1955 he signed an arms deal with the eastern bloc. Finally, the World Bank also suspended funding for the project when Nasser would not agree to their conditions, providing him with a pretext to nationalise the Suez Canal – allegedly to use its revenue to fund the dam. The dispute showed Nasser's incoherent foreign policy and total lack of long-term strategy; I have often discussed the issue with fellow historians. Having alienated his American supporters and antagonised the European powers by moving closer to the communist bloc, why didn't Nasser ask Moscow to finance the dam? The project was, in fact, later funded by the USSR and was completed in 1970. The Egyptians paid dearly, losing traditional Western markets for their exports, mostly cotton, which now had to go to the Soviet Union according to the dam's finance terms. A Soviet loan in 1956 could have spared the chain reaction triggered by Naser's reckless seizure of the Suez Canal.

The Egyptian newspapers on 26 July 1956 were hostile to Britain, while Eden's Tory government was still sympathetic to Egypt – attracting criticism from Israel's friends in UK, including some Conservative backbenchers. Two days earlier, Lloyd had been defending HM Government's policy of banning arms sales to Israel. Sir Robert Boothby (1900–1986) cited Czechoslovakia's 1955 supply of arms to Colonel Nasser as a move that had tipped the balance of power in the region against Israel.[6]

Al-Ahram on that day claimed that the British establishment was 'nervously' awaiting Nasser's speech while explaining his recognition of the People's Republic of China as 'a reply to France's move to supply jet-fighters to Israel'. Most of the stories were flavoured with anti-British epithets, while the foreign-affairs pages focused on the troubles in Cyprus, relabelling the odd terror incident there as 'a wide resistance movement against the British occupation'. Cairo newspapers' reporting on France was similarly biased – especially on Algeria and French parliamentarians' questions about the cost of war there.[7]

Most newspapers downplayed two items, confining them to few inches on the Crime pages. One was about an American journalist duped by two local men and a woman who had offered him a

305

riverboat trip to have a 'good time with the shapely girl'. They took his wristwatch and his wallet, which contained 1 pound and 50 *piastres*, then threw him onto a deserted stretch of the Nile bank. The other item was more interesting: the adjournment of an appeal hearing of 17 activists arrested for belonging to a communist organisation. Although Marxist groups had supported and backed the military coup, Nasser was intolerant of any political movement not coming under his control. He turned against all left-wing organisations within two years – targeting their ethnically Italian, Greek and French adherents – especially groups with high-profile intellectual Jewish members. Although left-wing pro-Nasser commentators today wrongly claim that the late authoritarian leader blocked the Islamists' advance, reports in the 1956 papers give early indications of strong Islamist influence within the military regime. The majority of the Free Officers group who staged the 1952 coup were, or at one point have been, members of the Muslim Brotherhood.

The Finance pages of *Al-Ahram* on 26 July 1956 reported that the career economist, Finance Minister Abd-el-Menem al-Qaysouny (1916–1987), had asked Alexandria's Bourse committee to meet the following week to change the day of rest, when trading was suspended, from Sunday to Friday. It was the start of the imposition of an Islamic character on secular Alexandria. Within four years, all the sequestrated and nationalised businesses were forced to change their weekend break from Saturday/Sunday to Thursday/Friday. In the early 1980s, they changed it again, to Friday/Saturday, after realising that they were losing four days of trade with the world financial markets every week. Egypt's Ministry of Islamic Endowments – headed by Ahmad al-Baquori (1907–1986), a member of the Muslim Brotherhood – moved £€6 million ($25 million) – or $240 million in today's money – from the department's rich coffers to be invested in trade and industry, and in the construction of social housing.[8]

Hamada and my sister were giggling at some pictures in the tabloid-sized magazines of the period: the Italian *Moda* and *Tempo*, which also had French and Greek editions, and the American *Life* and its competitor, *Look*. The French magazine *Paris Match*, which was then only a few years old, became popular with Alexandrian female readers. Although printed in Arabic script, the Egyptian magazines were notably written in the modern Egyptian media language rather than the Arabic of newspapers in Syria or Iraq. *Akher Saa* (*News-Flash*) was Egypt's answer to *Life*, but it faced severe competition from *el-Kawakeb* (the Stars), *Al-Ethnine wa-el-Dunia* (the *World on Monday*) and *Al-Musawar* (the *Photographed*).

Al-Musawar in fact became Captain Anwar Sadat's gateway to journalism in 1948 before he re-joined the army in 1950. The weekly magazine had been launched in 1924 by Emile Zidan (1896–1982) from Dar-Al-Hilal Publishing House, founded in 1892 by his father, Beirut-born Georgie Zidan Bey (1861–1914), who migrated to Cairo to study medicine then became an interpreter with the British Army in the 1880s. Zidan was inspired by the launch in 1915 of *Al-Latif-Al-Musawarh* (*Events in Pictures*); the latter lasted until 1929, focusing on international events with light-hearted and satirical commentary accompanied by pictures and cartoons lifted from some European presses. *Al-Musawar* began as a pro-monarchy, nationalistic, current-affairs weekly – a serious, upmarket version of *Al-Latif-Al-Musawarh* with fewer images and a national rather than an international focus. As the name implied, the stories featured *wougha'a* (notables and socialites), royal-family members, politicians and celebrities. Its Current Affairs and Culture sections hosted prominent columnists appealing to middle-class *effendis*. Although it was more upmarket than the popular contemporary *Akher Saa*, competition from the latter pushed *Al-Musawar* to add lifestyle and light sections to attract female readers. *Al-Musawar*'s stable sister – *el-Kawakeb*, launched in 1932 – focused more heavily on movie stars and dancers, while the monthly *Al-Hilal* was the group's intellectual journal with essays, literary criticism and book reviews. Another of their publications, launched in 1941 – *Al-Ethnine-wa-el-Dunia* – was like the British *Hello!* Magazine in the 1990s.

To boost its circulation, in 1948 *Al-Musawar* featured several good-looking female royals in military uniform as cover girls in a series on 'The Egyptian Woman on the Frontline'. These had been volunteers in the Women's Corps during the country's first war with Israel, and included King Farouk's sisters and other high-profile ladies. The magazine doubled its print run when it put the popular Princess Fawzia (1921–2013) on the cover.[9] Although she sported a military cap, the picture also showed the king's sister's femininity, in modest pose but wearing attractive maquillage, with her piercing light-blue eyes – more our own 'good-looking girl' than in her serious cover shot as Princess of the State for *Al-Musawar* in March 1939, on the eve of her wedding. This union was an arranged political marriage to then Prince (later Shah) Mohammad Reza Pahlavi of Iran (1919–1980). Fawzia was unhappy in her marriage, complaining to her brother via confidants in the Egyptian diplomatic service about 'unsophisticated' Middle Eastern court ways and the Iranians' 'lack of the European etiquette' to which she was accustomed. The Iranians claimed she ridiculed the Shah, according to a CIA report.[10] In 1945, the princess left her daughter behind and headed to Egypt for medical treatment,[11] never to return. A Cairo court annulled her marriage in 1946 but she did not remarry until two years later, after the Shah finally accepted the Cairo court ruling and signed the decree absolute document. The Alexandria-born princess was one of the world's best-known beauties, often compared to actresses Hedy Lamarr and Vivien Leigh. *Life* magazine called her the 'Queen of Iran' on their cover on 21 September 1942. Her photograph on that occasion was taken by Cecil Beaton (1904–1980), who associated the Alexandria-born princess with the wrong continent, Asia, – 'If ever Botticelli were reincarnated and wished to paint an Asian Venus...here is his subject in the Queen's features contained in a perfect heart-shaped face and pale but piercing blue eyes; crimson coloured lips curling like wrought iron volutes; and the way the dark chestnut hair grows beautifully from the forehead'.[12]

Like most current-affairs magazines, *Al-Musawar* had to appeal to a broad readership, especially when Moustafa Amin left *Al-Ethnine-wa-el-Dunia* to relaunch *Akher Saa** with his twin brother, Ali, spelling serious competition for the rest of the country's weekly titles. The effect of the Amins' popular journalism in Egypt was like that of Rupert Murdoch on Britain's Fleet Street in the 1980s. Their style pushed most magazines into shifting focus to beauty contests and society events, and all publications added *moda*-camera and *salle de mode* sections. During the 1940s and all through the 1960s, Egyptian magazines, especially outside Alexandria, were obsessed with *modat-el-plage* (beach fashion). One of the annual events was Miss Maillot, and in 1948 all the magazines competed to cover the Cairo Miss *Maillot-qate'atine* (two-piece *maillot*) pageant. The bikini, introduced by French fashion designer Louis Réard (1897–1984), had been first paraded at the end of the War, in summer 1946, by French model and dancer Micheline Bernardini as a way of saving on scarce material. Since cities like Cairo and Port Said followed Alexandria's Europeanised French culture and etiquette, and Franco-Italian fashion, Egypt's fashion and beauty industries followed France's by default. The country's fashion industry added two-piece swimming suits (concealing more than the bikini did) to *moda* shows.

One such extravaganza was held at the swimming pool of the iconic 1869-built Swiss-run Mena House near the Pyramids – which had been Cairo's first hotel when it opened in 1890. The rest of the Egyptian press tried to catch up with *Al-Ethnine-wa-el-Dunia*'s and *Akher Saa*'s coverage of the tabloid-style investigation into the disqualification

---

* The lifestyle consumer magazine had been established in 1934 by pioneer journalist, editor, and publisher Mohammed el-Tabi'i (1896–1976), but ceased circulation in 1940 due to the War.

CHAPTER 37 The 1936 Treaty and Journals

of the media's favourite contestant, British-born Cairean Maureen Fleming. She had the best figure, the prettiest face and a unique smile – but she was 'caught out', in the words of Egyptian-media fashion guru Charlotte Wassef, herself Miss Alexandria and Miss Universe in 1935. The former athlete and swimmer Fleming's fashion blasphemy was to clad herself in a makeshift *maillot* cut into two pieces instead of a proper custom-designed bikini. A man in a three-piece suit who stole the show by accidentally falling into the pool at the moment Fleming 'exhibited her fine figure' to the judges and spectators was 'unmasked', claimed one magazine – without hard evidence, but quoting 'friends of Miss Fleming' – as her boyfriend, who was accused of deliberately stage-managing the incident. Several girls who came in full *maillots* were booed and jeered at by spectators during the initial parade, so they all left. But some girls improvised by cutting out the middle of the garment then re-entering. The first prize was moved down to the second-placed contestant, the Alexandrian fashion mannequin Gabby Hawarry, followed by another British Cairean, Betty Law. Fleming went on to win the 1950 contest at Piscine Auberge, also near the Pyramids, this time with a proper two-piece bathing suit. The 1950 pageant was co-sponsored by *Akher-Saa*. The Amin twins persuaded Hotel Auberge's management to set up a kiosk so that the audience could bet on the contestants after their first parade. Whether a deliberate publicity stunt or Miss Fleming's 'karma', another fully clothed man fell into the pool – but this time 'out of sheer excitement at the parading beauties', *Akher-Saa* reported.

Coverage of *modat-el-plage*, especially in the summer months, sold newspapers. When the weekly *El-Geel* (new generation) was relaunched after it was paused in 1959, the publishers thought of a *plage*-fashion idea to promote the magazine by utilising a row started by Islamists. The magazine sponsored a competition to design *al-maillot al-shar'ie* (the Islamic *maillot*), with judges including celebrities, women columnists and commentators, and two Muslim clergymen from al-Azhar. The winner was a reverse of the improvisation that had disqualified Miss Fleming in 1948. The designer bridged the flesh gap between the two pieces by covering the navel and widening the bottom part of the garment, concealing an extra centimetre of the wearer's crotch and inner thigh. The two clergymen were pictured applauding enthusiastically in approval.

CHAPTER 38
Evacuation Day

Les Anglais' final departure
The front pages on 26 July 1956 reflected Nasser's growing popularity. This had held since 18 June 1956 with what pro-regime newspapers branded *Eid al-Gala'a*, marking the evacuation of the last remaining British troops from the Suez Canal base – ending 73 years, 10 months and 26 days of unwelcome military presence in Egypt.

The media focus on 18 June 1956 was not on Alexandria – where the British occupation had started on 14 July 1882, three days after the bombardment of the city by Admiral Seymore of the Royal Navy's Mediterranean Squadron – but on the much younger town of Port Said at the northern end of the canal, where it meets the Mediterranean. Named after Khedive Said Pasha, who selected the site, *Poursaeed* (the French pronunciation) – with its outer harbour, inner harbour and several massive dry docks – was constructed in 1868 on land reclaimed from marshes, Lake Manzala and the sea. Within a few years, the city became the world's largest coal-bunkering station, catering for the Suez Canal and ships passing through.

Holding the official *Eid-al-Gala'a* big day in Alexandria had a lower propaganda value from Nasser's viewpoint. The British had left Alexandria 20 years earlier as a condition of the 1936 treaty. They returned temporarily to protect the city against Rommel's advance, but quickly vacated their camps at the end of the War. So Nasser chose not Alexandria but Port Said instead, to mark the historic day.

'The President Raises Egypt's Colours on the Naval Building in Port Said today', *Al-Ahram* splashed on 18 June 1956, with a cartoon illustration of Nasser – with the heads of past nationalist leaders behind

CHAPTER 38   Evacuation Day

him – raising the flag. The paper issued a 32-page supplement on 'Egypt's Struggle Against Occupation'.[1]

The official Alexandria preparations were ordered by Cairo, but there were also spontaneously organised festivities by nationalists, realising their dreams of *tard-les Anglais* (kicking out the British) – a national goal passed down the generations for 70 years. Even Alexandrians of European origin joined in the festivities despite their apprehension and suspicion of the military regime's hidden intentions. The fever of excitement spread through all of Alexandria's ethnic communities: Greek, Italian, Jewish, Levantine and Nilotic-Egyptian, all looking forward to a new dawn. Their elders had memories of Muhammad Ali and his dynasty's crusade for independence from the Ottoman Empire and European powers, including *les Anglais*. Nasser was the first Egyptian leader since Muhammad Ali to stand up to the European powers. Many Alexandrians of a European ethnic background backed the new regime – especially the Greeks and the Italians, who had always identified themselves as Egyptians. The communists among them saw the army coup as a nationalist move forward. Like all Marxists, they weren't bothered with details about democracy and elections. But commercial aspirations were also a factor after the coup leaders had given assurances to businesses and non-Nilotic communities four years earlier.

Most Alexandrians hoped that Nasser's stance would lead to more liberalisation and the opening up of trade with the New World's affluent markets by breaking away from British influence. Britain had been, for half a century, Egypt's largest trading partner. Almost 30% (£€10.9m-worth – $53m) of all the country's imports came from Britain while about 24% (£€8.4m) came from America and the remainder from the rest of the world. Meanwhile, 30.8% of Egyptian exports (£€11.4m – $55m) went to Britain, £€2.9m worth went to America and £€7.1m to France.* There was a military parade in Alexandria on Evacuation Day, and the air force dropped slow-descending balloons with President Nasser's portraits on them. There was a ceremonial unveiling of a memorial dedicated to the 1882 bombardment of Alexandria. The parade and a folkloric festival were held at King Fuad Stadium, renamed the Municipality Stadium when the republic was declared in 1953. None of my family went but we watched the fireworks in the evening, high up in the sky above the Eastern Harbour, from our first-floor balcony in Sidi-Bishr. There were no high-rise buildings on Rue Nineteen blocking the view then.

---

* The Egyptian pound (£🅔) was then worth £1.12. Total Egyptian imports were £🅔35m, total exports amounted to £🅔35.9m – 1947/9 figures, Egypt's Ministry of Trade and Industry.

311

Several receptions and parties were held by many clubs, ethnic-community schools, trade bodies and university colleges. There were public festivities in venues like Sporting's Club, the Greek Club and the Swiss Club. Most performers, dance troupes and music orchestras were European-Alexandrians who were, ironically, demonised in a theatre play called *Al-Watan* (Motherland) performed in Teatro Muhammad Ali (Muhammad Ali Theatre and Opera House, formerly Teatro Zizania). Overall, it was a festival reflecting the city's cosmopolitanism. The Alexandria Greek Dance company; *Les danseuses de Madame Nichol* (Madame Nichol's girls), an Anglo–French dance school; the predominantly Italian Alexandria Symphonic Orchestra; the British-trained Alexandria Police Brass Band; the Egyptian Roman Orthodox Youth; and the Levant Club Dancers, who presented the Lebanese *dabke* dance.[2] A sub-headline in *Al-Ahram* informed its readers, 'A homing pigeon flew carrying Alexandria's greetings to the president'. There was no news in the following days about the fate of the poor, nameless bird or whether it reached Port said,[3] but there was a report of a Port Said woman smashing an *ollah* (a fired-earth water-cooling pot) on the quayside as the last vacating British ship passed. Breaking a pot after shaking off the last drop of water was an Egyptian folk superstition to block guests who overstayed their welcome from ever showing up again on one's doorstep.

In an exclusive interview with the president, *Al-Ahram* introduced their readers to the 1935 Alexandria student activist Gamal Abdel Nasser. Evidently, the junta's PR machine was paving the way for a personality cult associating Nasser with nationalism and ridding Egypt of *les Anglais*. This would simultaneously demonise Britain and the European powers and inject the Ourabists' oriental-Islamic concepts into the Egyptian collective mind in an early move to reshape the citizens' identity.

The newspaper, which always backed the government in power, continued the message of moving the country away from European modernity. Below Nasser's interview, an opinion piece was headed, 'The [British] Occupation's War Against Egyptian Education'. This was what we now call 'fake news', falsifying history and claiming that 'the Dunlop reforms have been deliberately designed to undermine the Arabic language and Islam while weakening Egypt's Oriental character'. It was the first time that a daily Egyptian publication had used this mixture of identity adjectives – 'Oriental', 'Arabic' and 'Islamic' – in one sentence; this combination of characteristics had not hitherto been presented in the public discourse. The columnist referred to the modernisation of the state-funded education system introduced early in the century by Scottish teacher and missionary Douglas Dunlop (1888–1922), the chief inspector in the Egyptian Ministry of Education.

CHAPTER 38   Evacuation Day

The Dunlop Reforms

Dunlop's reforms had introduced English into schools' curricula when the official languages had been French and Turkish. He also introduced the teaching of Arabic and its grammar as an independent subject, separate from Islamic Quranic classes. The attack on *niztham Dunlop* (the Dunlop education reforms) in the 1920s came mostly from al-Azhar clergy, Islamists and old-school Ottomanists who objected to Egypt's independence and to Atatürk's secularisation of Turkey as 'un-Islamic'. The Dunlop reforms led to many schools' curricula moving away from the domain of the Islamic 'Church' (al-Azhar) into that of Wizarat al-Ma'arif Alo'momiyah (the Department of Universal Knowledge – the official name of the branch of government responsible for education, culture, arts and sports). Al-Maarif,* especially under the French-educated Ali Mubarak Pasha (1823–1893)[4] in the 1850s had been, for over 100 years, the leading force in introducing modernity to Egyptian schools that were had formerly been run by the Islamic al-Azhar foundation.[5] The department also oversaw and funded activities and organisations in the realm of culture and the arts – like theatres, museums, music groups, and the translation of books and subsidising of smaller publishers. Today, the pre-1953 education department's tasks are undertaken by four departments: Education, Culture and Arts, Sports and Youth, and Media and Information. The scope of activities and the mission of the old Wizarat al-Ma'arif were remarkably progressive by the standards of the time, refining children's tastes and emphasising separation between faith and thought – concepts that remained in place until Colonel Nasser's regime started pumping money into al-Azhar's budget, turning the Islamic institution, in 1961, into a multi-college academic university.†

Al-Ahram's piece about education angered my grandfather, who knew both the author and Dunlop and praised the latter as a moderniser and a fair-minded man of integrity and sound judgement. By an ironic twist

---

* The department was first established in 1837 as the 'Bureau scolaire' by French-educated students sent by Muhammad Ali, and headed by Ali Mubarak, who was known as the father of modern education in Egypt – especially when he criticised al-Azhar and reduced their interference in schooling. It became the Department of Knowledge and Education in 1850 under another reformist khedive, Abbas Helmi I, grandson of Muhammad Ali.

† This theological institution (established in 970 AD) remained exclusively a centre for theological studies, Arabic language and Quranic interpretation until Nasser weaponised it by expanding its role through offering scholarships to students from Muslim nations. Then, in 1961, the Azhar and Education Act 103/1961 granted al-Azhar finance and opened it for colleges and institutions offering Medicine, Pharmacology, Civil Engineering, etc. – and also obliged it to accept students of both sexes.

of fate, the author of the article, writer and publisher Mohammed Said al-Eryan (1905–1964), was rewarded for backing the military regime with the closure of his publication, *Sindbad* (1950–60).[6] This was, in fact, what my grandfather predicted during a heated argument he had with Monsieur Eryan in June 1956 about his unfair and misleading article while they were having their morning *café turc* and scanning the newspapers at the café overlooking *Plage* Sidi-Bishr.

CHAPTER 39
Fuul, Ration Books and Smugglers

The shady Rue Eighteen was pleasant: all the villas and enclosures leading to chalet plots had trees with blooming fences of Russian vine; jasmine; roses; camellia; flowering basil, rows of red, pink and white *Nerium oleander*; and grapevine. Behind them stood elm, fig, guava, mulberry, pear and pine trees – some blooming, with moths, butterflies and bees busy at work. The fragrance of the trees and hedges filled our nostrils. Dewdrops were still moistening the greenery and iron gates, mixed with the damp carried by the sea breeze. The *plage* was only 60 metres away, down the sloping Rue Eighteen towards the Mobile Oil *benzina* on the corniche past Rue *Princesse Fawzia*, but we didn't reach it. We turned eastwards on the shady elm- and willow-lined Rue Cinquante-Deux. Its villas were fronted by fragrant fences, their petals dropping to the pavement. It was a long road; the odd gentleman was on his way to down town while his holidaying family were still asleep.

Bells jingled, heralding A'am Ali's approach. He was the *fuul medames* vendor who also dispensed the popular *belilah (blé au lait)*, the indigenous Egyptian breakfast. The term *blé au lait* (wheat with milk) was coined by the French when they encountered it in 1798. The wheat grains are soaked overnight, mixed with baking soda and served hot with milk and added sugar or honey. Ali's box-cart was pulled by his donkey, Farid, named after the famous singer, composer and movie star Farid al-Atrash. Stroking the working donkey gave a rare opportunity for the poor children of domestic servants to reconnect with their stolen childhoods. Some as young as eight were serving children older than themselves. They did not sound as if they were from Alexandria but from Cairo or the countryside, and they worked for *effendis'* families who sent them with containers to buy *fuul medames* and *belilah*. The

Alexandria Adieu

working children were talking to a clearly unimpressed Farid, who was tied to *A'am* Ali's two-wheel-wagon. The cart had improvised insulation to keep its two large, bottle-shaped, copper containers warm – with a small, smoky oil stove underneath each one.

We hurried along the road towards the open sandy area where the only evidence left of *Camp les Anglais* were the fading white chalkstones once marking entrances and paths, and a chipped, bare flagpole. The asphalt had faded into a lighter-grey, cracked surface, sinking under the sand as the trees got smaller and shorter until the greenery gave way to bright, creamy, vast, open sand with the air getting warmer – reminding us why we had left without breakfast that morning before the sun rose high in the sky, lashing the dunes with blistering rays. We planned to have breakfast with our cousins at *Tante* Ralia's, leaving our two younger siblings behind. In summer 1956, *Tante* Ralia was living, for the second year running, in a rented flat in a post-war villa block owned by the Arab Sheikh Gadaider.

Like many Bedouin tribespeople from the Libyan Desert, the sheikh and his extended family roamed the massive sandy area from Alexandria to Benghazi, weaving in and out along the 1100-kilometre coastal road. Many of them had families in Misrata, a further five-hour drive. The town had been founded by their forefathers, Egypto-Libyan Bedouins known by Alexandrians and most urban Egyptians as *el-A'rab* ('the Arabs'), bringing goods from Misr – hence, *Misr-ata* (originated in Egypt). Unlike his father and grandfather, who travelled on animal backs crossing back and forth over borders they did not recognise, Sheikh Gadaider's generation travelled in jeeps left by retreating German and Italian armies or bought in post-war auctions, repaired and upgraded by Italian mechanics. Many such Arabs had made fortunes from smuggling – especially during the War, dealing with both sides. After the War, they added another lucrative business: ration books.

When ration books were introduced during the War, and were reintroduced by Nasser's regime in the 1950s, they became another investment for the Bedouins' centuries-old smuggling enterprise. The Libya Desert tribesmen were registered in Egypt's *tamween* (supplies) scheme but were also counted as Libyan subjects, having pledged allegiance to the late King Idris, who had been exiled in Egypt before returning to Libya after the War. The king was helped by the British and King Farouk to train his forces at the military camps of Imbaba, a suburb northwest of Cairo, to liberate his country and gain independence. The Arabs' ration books exaggerated the number of family members, buying sometimes more than double what they needed from Alexandrian shops at subsidised prices to sell in Libya and making handsome profits. This game continued after the War and

CHAPTER 39   Fuul, Ration Books and Smugglers

was still going on in the 1960s. Ironically, in the 1980s, when the late Colonel Gaddafi nationalised supermarkets and subsidised imports, the tribesmen in Libya extended their activities along their western border with Tunisia. Thus, 'nanny-state' policies often result in achieving what they were intended to avoid. Nobody ever got a grip on the correct figures, but the number of ration books was always at least one and half times that of the population. Books were issued per household, permitting middle-class *effendis'* and wealthier beys' families to include domestic staff like cooks, *sufragie* (footmen), gardeners and chauffeurs. A family of three or four would have a ration book with eight to ten names, all within the rules – and the domestic staff would also be registered in their own families' ration books in another administrative district. Books were seldom updated, while officials never bothered checking records. Family members who died or were working elsewhere remained on the book; the same went for children who had flown the nest and set up families with their own ration books.

On top of all this, the regime's 1950s and 60s economic vandalism became a smugglers' dream. Familiar consumer goods disappeared from the shops or were priced out of the reach of the Egyptian poor. Imported fruits that had been in abundance even when Europe faced shortages during the War tripled in price when the Egyptian currency was devalued after 1958.

The regime, adopting Soviet-style economics, listed many goods as luxuries, banning their import and marking 'luxury' local products as 'for export only'. The latter included avocados, some varieties of grapefruit, mangos, refined rice and refined sugar. The ban also increased the cost of medical equipment, pharmaceuticals and mechanical spare parts, as most were British- and French-made and could now only be imported via third-party countries – both adding to the burden on the Treasury and fuelling a boom in black-market activity, corruption and associated organised crime.

Some of the so-called luxury goods to which Alexandrians had grown accustomed traditionally featured in the food festivities of several faiths in the multi-ethnic, cosmopolitan city – especially Sham-Ennessim (Easter Monday), a festival that all Alexandrians – and urban Egyptians in general – regardless of ethnicity, race or religion celebrated, mostly with picnics. (Its origins in Egypt actually predated the Christian feast, reaching back perhaps 5,000 years into ancient times.) This economic chaos generated a black market on an unprecedented scale. For Alexandria's Muslims, breaking fast during Ramadan and celebrating *Eid-el-Sughaier* (the lesser eid festival) relied on imported food items: dried fruit from Turkey, the Levant and southern Europe; *ringa* (Nordic smoked herrings); *baccalà* (salted cod); and *saumon fumé*. The festivities

317

of Copts and various other communities – including Greeks, Italians and Spaniards – also needed their imports – and all required a mixture for the New Year, a big season for everyone in Alexandria. The ban on imports covered all British and French goods, while imports from other countries were severely affected by the sequestration of banks and Jewish businesses. It was a massive social shock, since modern Alexandria had been at the heart of Europe's consumer markets since the 1820s. Many restaurants went out of business, leading to mass unemployment, but the poorest were hit hardest.

Most *epiceries* in Alexandria and central Cairo were traditionally Armenian, Greek, Italian or French – and they could no longer obtain many of their regular supplies, having to adapt by registering as *tamween* dispensers.

One of Alexandria's largest *tamween* contractors was Épicerie al-Wardyan by the Western Harbour. The Wardyan district was mostly inhabited by migrants working as dockers or tram-workshop labourers, with a minority of indigenous Alexandrians who were shopkeepers or ran many of the bars and cafés near the harbour. The area's population increased fourfold due to two booms – first in the middle to late nineteenth century alongside a massive increase in cotton exports, and the second during the building of Allied forces' stores at the start of the Second World War. The Arab tribes from the Libyan Desert got their monthly *tamween* from Wardyan grocers; the largest of these belonged to Monsieur Aziz, father of my late friend, Alexandrian movie star Mahmoud Azziz (1946–2016).

Besides *tamween*, Épicerie Monsieur Aziz also supplied the very few *cazionhat* (cafés, and the odd service station) on Traiq Al-Sallum, the northern coast road. This made him known along the coast, and he had scores of Arab sheikhs' ration books on his register. Each sheikh would send a son or a nephew with a lorry, collecting a whole month's supply for the extended family of up to 200 names on each book. They left their books at Aziz's shop in a corner house he owned, living on the second floor with his family. Since most of those Arabs were illiterate, Aziz exerted great power over them; they also knew he knew of their smuggling game. He used to shout and order them around. He reportedly kicked some of them and, in one incident, threw a tin of tuna at an Arab *tamween* customer, leaving him with a scarred forehead.

The Arabs finally took their revenge on Monsieur Aziz in 1964. They gave him a small jar of their natural remedies, which successfully treated his chronically painful haemorrhoids. When the magic tub ran out, he asked the Arabs for more, so the story goes, and they said that their *hakeem* (tribal quack) was away, giving him the prescription ingredients instead and advising him that he would find most of them in his store and from *el-attar* (the herbalist) next door. Aziz followed the instructions, making the gel, and went into his bathroom to apply it. The immediate pain – like acid in a wound – was of epic proportions, so the story goes, caused by a chain reaction between some of the mysterious ingredients. Driven by the unimaginably sharp burning, Aziz smashed down the bathroom door and ran out naked – screaming at his wife to rub ice from the freezer compartment into his buttocks, which were convulsing violently. Only an injection from the local pharmacist, who was summoned by the family, temporarily calmed him down. Aziz had to eat his meals standing up for the next couple of days. The man who gave him the prescription never showed up again, and his relatives always maintained that Aziz either misapplied the remedy or that the herbalists gave him an incorrect ingredient or the wrong weight on the scale.

CHAPTER 40
Memories of the North Coast Road

Maroula
In the 1950s and 1960s, the area that was once a battleground during the War remained a vast stretch of unspoilt, open sand with blue skies and a golden sea coast mostly unknown to *masarwah* invading Alexandria in the summer months. Alexandrians of good taste and old families frequented the Western Desert's north-coast area for a day's break, or longer when they had the means to do so.

We went a few times to unspoilt spots for day trips, taking umbrellas, folding chairs and a picnic, having a whole natural *plage* for ourselves and not a soul in sight. But a change in our family fortunes and the sale of our large automobile made those beaches less accessible than before.

I went a few times with Papa and friends on visits to graves in Alamein War Cemetery and spent the day on a deserted beach. One discovery of a tiny café came during a trip with *Oncle* Constantine, who shared my father's passion for rare stamps, and his daughter, Maroula. He collected us from our Sidi-Bishr villa in his old Citroën – with its fading leather interior, beautiful chrome trimming and large lantern headlights – which often needed *a manilvento* (Alexandrian for *maniglia di avviamento* -the starting handle) to turn several times before the engine would begin to tick over.

It took forever to leave Alexandria after a detour near Muxx dockyards to avoid driving close to the abattoir and leather-treatment complex, and another hour on the western coast road until we reached the Alamein railway. Past the station on another road, Papa and *Oncle* Constantine walked into the war cemetery to visit some friends' tombs. They had the customary flowers with them and went around some tombstones and prayed. After another 20 minutes' drive, we reached

CHAPTER 40   Memories of the North Coast Road

a makeshift structure of wooden-beam and rush-mat shading over some chairs and tables made from bamboo, dried bulrush and rough wood. My father said it was a service station for drivers on the road to Libya but had expanded into a café after the War. Even though it was a Sunday, there were very few customers being served by a couple of Arab girls in colourful dresses. They fetched water from a well, drawn out by a wind-driven pump rigged on a steel tower. I spat out the salty, cloudy drink.

Maroula, who was approaching 18, laughed. *Oncle* Constantine said the water contained healthy minerals, and I could have Coca-Cola afterwards. The drinks were stored in a cooling box made of old railway sleepers over ice blocks. The Arab girls served freshly caught fish and giant *gamberi* (prawns) all grilled on an open fire – a hole in the sand with raised stones and a grille resting on them. The café overlooked a wide bay, and the water was so beautiful – turquoise-blue and hugged by golden sand. We took turns to change into our *maillohat* in the café's little toilet but the two grown-ups stayed under the shade of the rush mats, chatting, smoking and drinking Stella. Apart from the odd lorry driver stopping, the only other customers were two families with three teenagers between them. Maroula and I arranged to play some racketball games with them.

In 1968, we drove in Suad's Fiat car to Alamein, but either we went to the wrong café or it had changed beyond recognition. A knot of sadness locked my stomach when I remembered my racketball and water games with Maroula and the other boy and girls. I smiled when I recalled the time we were changing in the toilets, Maroula in her two-piece *maillot* pinching my cheek painfully when she turned and caught my eyes glued to her backside – before pulling my face very close to her lips and whispering *ya-abieh* (naughty).

'Let us cool you off in the water before you get noticed', she said, with a playful whack from the back of her hand on the front of my swimming trunks. I lost touch with Maroula and her family after they left Alexandria; some acquaintances said they headed to Cyprus, others to South Africa.

Forty years after swimming with Maroula, and amidst the ugly vulgarity of a holiday resort on the spot, nobody remembered that the small café had ever existed – except one old Bedouin in Al-Alamaine Station, who said, *'matrah Manoli?'* (Manoli's site). I could not remember whether the owner was Manoli or even if the café had a name. Arab Bedouins took over the property in Dekhila, A'gamie and Burg el-Arab that were vacated by fleeing or expelled Alexandrian Jews during the second exodus. My friend, Dino, who went to his family villa in A'gamie 20 years later, was heartbroken at what he witnessed.

In 1982, he saw his childhood swimming pool full of rubbish and children relieving themselves on the edge of the pit. Arabs were sitting around smoking; they had taken over the property in the area and the northern coast generally.

Dodgy dealings in the municipality led to large plots around camps vacated by the British Army under the 1936 treaty falling to Arab Bedouins like Sheikh Gadaider – sandy areas west of Alexandria and in Ramleh, east of Victoria's tramline. Some built huts for weekend breaks, but nobody bothered about buying land. There was no easy transport and no utilities provided, with windmill-powered pumps bringing saline water and noisy generators used for power. Like ours, before we got an electric one in 1956, *frigidaires* were powered by oil while gas cookers were fuelled by pressurised gas cylinders that needed replacing every few weeks. My grandfather bought the land in Sidi-Bishr and Villa Alexandrine for less than two-thirds of a teacher's salary in 1930. During the War, some people – mostly Arabs – laid claim to unregistered plots. Those who couldn't afford a windmill water pump erected makeshift huts with no facilities, using battered tin boxes, bulrushes and any materials left over from *Camp les Anglais*. They claimed it was their home within the common law of *wadih-el-yad* ('laying hands on'). On the rare occasions when an official bothered to visit the plot, he lazily reported that the claim was plausible based on 'evidence of occupation' like the Bedouins' goats roaming the sand and picking a few shoots, or the shed where their daughters who usually looked after the herd left some possessions.

Preparing for the Kite Battle
Sheikh Gadaider owned a two-storey villa block where *Tante* Ralia lived, consisting of four spacious flats. The sheikh's large family lived in the two apartments on the upper-ground floor – the basement was a garage. *Tante* Ralia and *Oncle* Niroop paid him a low rent because it was far away from the town centre and he wanted company for his wife and daughter when he left for Libya during the winter. *Oncle* Niroop had lost his business in autumn 1954 after Nasser placed president Naguib, under house arrest,[1] alarmed the markets and investors. General Naguib in March 1954 wanted to make good on his pledge on the day of the 1952 coup, instructing the officers to hand power to a constitutionally elected government, but Nasser objected and a six-month power struggle ended with the latter's removing the president and detaining him.

Oncle Niroop found employment with an oil company in summer 1956 – and was promoted within three months to deputy finance director. He replaced a deported Jewish Ottoman of Balkan ethnicity

CHAPTER 40 Memories of the North Coast Road

who was naturalised but had had the misfortune of volunteering with the British Army during the War, thus acquiring a second (British) nationality. In October that year, *Oncle* Niroop and *Tante* Ralia moved to Menasciyah to be closer to their boys' schools.

Sheikh Gadaider's large tent during the summer months stood alone as a landmark for years. The nearest building was way behind the eucalyptus, casuarina and pine trees that started some 300 metres back from the sand where the chalkstone road linking to Rue Cinquante-Deux (Fifty-Two) began. To the north, the sea view from *Tante* Ralia's roof was stunning. We used to go up there to fly kites with some of the sheikh's boys. I encountered the dumbest of them, who had been the butt of jokes and teasing in 1956, 30 years later as a high-ranking official in Colonel Gaddafi's Libyan Foreign Ministry.

It was still around half past eight when my sister and I walked across the sand carrying *fuul* and *belilah* gifts. We had borrowed two of *A'am* Ali's containers for a deposit of 1 *piastre*, half of my sister's pocket money. I said I'd buy the refreshments, since she will get her *piastre* back upon returning the containers the next day. Although our cousins were delighted with our gifts, *Tante* Ralia was furious as she was not sure of *A'am* Ali's hygiene standards. On top of preparing eggs and pastirma, she sterilised our offering in the pressure cooker after one of her usual verbal tirades – and all the teens sat to a hearty breakfast before a day of kite flying.

Once in a blue moon, the odd wealthy youth flying a model aircraft attracted the curiosity of envious children and even adults. Such luxury was way beyond the affordability of most Alexandrian children; hardly any of us had heard of motorised flying models. We only flew kites, which had their own technology. They were made from bamboo sticks and a frame of tight, waxed string covered with coloured translucent papers or newspaper.

My other two cousins, who lived in the Turkish quarter, had come the night before and they prepared their kites so that we had our 'air force' of four kites in addition to those of our allies. The two largest ones belonged to Aldhai, a Turkish diplomat's nephew from a mixed marriage, and Stephano, the Italian grocer's son who went to my cousin's school. Vicks brought a kite made of light aluminium frame. Victor was a Jewish boy in my class; we called him 'Vicks' and teased him by leaving Vicks' nasal-stick newspaper ads pinned to his classroom desk. Other mischief included someone distracting Vicks while another boy sneaked up from behind and shoved a chalk stick into his nostril. These three boys' kites completed our seven-strong squadron ready for the air battle, but we later realised that the opposition outnumbered our air force by five kites. However, we had some secret weapons that our cousins had prepared – like adding razor blades to the kites' tails and weighing them down with sharp broken crystal pieces fallen from old chandeliers'. The latter trick both helped to balance the kites with shorter tails and knock holes in our rivals'.

The competition was reputed to be one of the strongest kite shows in the whole of Ramleh – a tradition whose origin nobody knew, but which had been mastered by Greco-Alexandrians and launched, according to the city's folklore, by the Greek-orphanage boys. The orphanages were amongst many other institutions that the Greeks had established in Alexandria from the nineteenth century onwards. Most institutions – like hospitals, orphanages, schools and community centres – were founded by non-Nilotic migrant communities – and, in this respect, the Greeks outnumbered all others.

CHAPTER 41
The Kites Battle

26 July 1956 was the teenagers' kite-battle day; we wanted to impress the girls whom we were dating, or hoping to date. Our multi-ethnic team alliance of Italian, Jewish and Turkish and the cheering girls headed for *Plage* al-Asafrah, past Miami. I infuriated our teammates when I was late for the start of the air battle. I had been showing off by diving into the Devil's Hole to collect silver coins thrown by *masarwah* holidaymakers, combined with a 'quickie' session with Sonia under the rocks' caves. Sonia, Seeka and their cousin Gabriella were my human shield from my angry team. Seeka, who came to watch the kite show, had an eye for my cousin, the Don Bosco Institute student nicknamed Pisa; when chatting to a girl he fancied, my cousin would subconsciously tilt vertically to the left like the Leaning Tower of Pisa. We performed well against the Greek 'air force' of a dozen kites: we only lost two while destroying three of theirs and damaging two others by cutting the tail of one and piercing another.

That evening, we skipped tea at *Tante* Ralia's and opted for sandwiches from the café by the *plage* entrance when the sun started its evening departure, turning the sea's surface orange-gold and extending Miami Rock's shadow over the bay. The avvocato's daughters, their Italian cousin Gabriella, and Pisa returned with my sister and me. We took a shortcut along a small, narrow path between two plots full of chalets overlooking the Egyptian (formally Royal) Automobile Club and turned west by Cinema Florida. It was screening James Dean's *East of Eden*. Many Alexandrian boys started copying Dean's hairstyle and rebellious outfits. As was the custom, the programme comprised two films and a newsreel; the other movie was a comedy with Abbott and Costello. We turned south by the Benzina Shell towards the open-air el-Montazaha cinema and the Rue Kenisate-el-kedissien (the Two Saints Coptic church), which was dedicated to St Mark the evangelist and Pope Peter I (of the Last Martyrs).[1] The church was the target of a 2011 New Year terrorist bombing by the Gaza-based Islamic Group, an offshoot of the Muslim Brotherhood. The bombing was a contributing factor aggravating the public mood and leading to the three-week protest in which President Mubarak's regime (1981–2011) was terminated by the army, the body behind almost every historical event altering the course of history in modern Egypt.

Alexandria owes her rebirth, with industrial projects and modern education, partly to Muhammad Ali's military ambitions. Ali's and Ibrahim Pasha's technology and science ventures and institutions helped to build a modern army to advance their ambitious foreign policy. Following the army's substandard performance in the Abyssinian war (1874-1876) Ourabi-led an officers' revolt to block Khedive Tawfik's European modernisation. The mutiny started a chain of events that led to the British occupation of Egypt in 1882. Seventy years later, history repeated itself; following its abysmal performance in the 1948 war against Israel, the Egyptian Army staged the 1952 coup, while Sadat's presidency was ended by his assassination by an army unit infiltrated by Islamists. The military, controlling the electoral machinery, determined the 2012 election outcome and underpinned the first 'civilian' president's short-lived Islamist regime (2012–13). Then got the 'credit' for his removal by siding with the prevailing anti-Islamists majority during a broader uprising in 2013, which insured the popularity of their chief, General Abd-el-Fattah el-Sisi, allowing him to win the 2014 elections.

We didn't go as far south as the church but turned west along Rue Princesse Fawzia to pick up some crêpes from the area's best-known *boulangerie* – a favourite of my younger brother, who could live on nothing but those crêpes with crème fraiche and icing sugar or banana and honey. He was just over three years of age when he got lost with a cousin three months his junior. When he could not give an address, he asked the policeman to take him to *Dükkanı el-crêperie*. Although there were several crêperies in the district, the constable knew exactly which one the child meant. Once there, the boy remembered the route to our villa. The policeman accompanied the two children all the way home and got a handsome reward from my grandfather.

Approaching the Montazah piazza's lawn on the corniche side of Rue Princesse Fawzia, opposite Sidi-Bishr Mosque hill, we saw the con-twins with a megaphone standing on a makeshift platform by a large screen showing moving pictures of President Nasser. Nasser's voice, unrelated to the film, was bellowing from loudspeakers. A small crowd shouted

CHAPTER 41 The Kites Battle

anti-*les Anglais* slogans and condemned de Lesseps,* mispronouncing the name *dailissebs*, just as Nasser did. We didn't know it at the time, but in his speech, Nasser's third mention of de Lesseps was a coded message to his armed agents to swoop on the Suez Canal Company offices.

---

* Ferdinand Marie, Vicomte de Lesseps (1805–1894), who developed the concept of the Suez Canal and convinced Khedive Said and Ismail to start the project.

CHAPTER 42
Nasser Betrays Eden

We paused for a few minutes by the rally, but we did not fully understand what was going on until we reached our villa up the road. *Maman* had hot food ready and called the three girls in to eat with my sisters. We gave the crêpe-wrapped pack to Bellitta to prepare for my brother. Pisa and I went to join another, older cousin who had come with *Oncle* Niroop. The boys grouped at one end of the first-floor veranda with hot-chocolate drinks listing to *Oncle* Niroop, Papa, and grandfather discussing as they sipped their after-dinner cognacs. They feared the consequences of Nasser's 'foolish move'. My grandfather repeated his 'I told you so', recalling President Naguib's replacement of the tarboosh with the *casquette les Anglais* in 1953.[1]

'Grabbing the Canal was an irrational move', Papa said. He added that most of the shareholders, who were Egyptians with investment holdings and pensions, would bear the brunt. *Oncle* Niroop said the canal's 100-year concession only had a few years before it expired:

'Nasser should have waited and negotiated a better deal, the closer we got to the end of the concession in 1968, the more the balance of the bargain would go Egypt's way.' He added that the crisis could escalate into a global one. It would give *les Anglais* an excuse to back out of their commitment to pay Egypt's millions owed in war debts.

'It seems *l'bek-bashi* [the Colonel] hasn't thought this one through', Papa said. My grandfather thought it was unwise of Eden to trust *el bek-bashi* Nasser against Churchill's advice.

'I wish Eden had listened to Churchill', he said, adding that he would pay good money to know what Sir Winston thought.

Eden had become prime minister a year earlier when Churchill had been forced to retire due to ill health. Sir Winston, the war leader,

CHAPTER 42   Nasser Betrays Eden

remained, in the eyes of Papa's and my grandfather's generation, the free world's leader and the wisest man on Earth. Eden had visited Cairo with Lady Eden in February the previous year (1955) when he was foreign secretary. Nasser, president by then, had met him in full military uniform. It was not seen as a good signal by Churchill – the mark of a dictator, in fact. Sensing something Hitlerian about the Egyptian colonel, Sir Winston warned Eden not to trust Nasser. Although Eden later said he felt uncomfortable with Nasser holding his hand to guide him, the Foreign Office's Camel Corps played down his anxieties. Arabists in the Foreign Office said it was nothing sinister but merely a sign that Nasser trusted him; the fact that they had walked hand in hand was a friendly gesture based on trust, according to Sir Humphrey Trevelyan (1905–1985), Britain's ambassador to Egypt during the Suez Crisis.*

Like a man who had survived the Hiroshima bomb only to move the next day to Nagasaki, Trevelyan was posted to Baghdad after relations were severed with Egypt. He arrived in the Iraqi capital during its 1958 turmoil – with a military coup and the public murder of the Iraqi royal family, whose bodies were dragged in the streets by mobs. The same hordes also ransacked the British Embassy, then held the ambassador, Sir Michael Wright (1901–1976), and Lady Wright under siege[2]. In 1961, Trevelyan also warned London of Iraq's threat to invade Kuwait[3]. Unlike their disastrous handling of the Suez Crisis five years earlier, this time, London officialdom followed Trevelyan's recommendation – which was to protect Kuwait from an imminent invasion without provoking a military confrontation. The only casualties were two royal marines, who suffered sunstroke and heat exhaustion.[4]

In 1955, Foreign Office specialists told Eden that Nasser's hand-holding was like the handshake in Western cultures – an assurance of peace. Others warned that in Eastern cultures, keeping the guest's hand ensures he will not reach for a blade to use against the host. Eden

---

* I interviewed Sir Humphrey in 1977 when I was covering Britain's diplomatic role in peace moves. The UK was president of the European Economic Community (EEC) from January to June that year, when the Middle East declaration was made that went further than UN Security Council Resolution 242 by calling for 'a national homeland for the Palestinian refugees who suffered for too long'. I also asked Sir Humphrey about James Callaghan (1912–2005) who had become prime minister a year earlier, and his suspicion of both Henry Kissinger (b.1923) and of the UK Foreign Office, which was biased towards the Arabs as he claimed he had discovered when serving as foreign secretary (1974–6). As expected, Sir Humphrey defended the Foreign Office but agreed with Callaghan's distrust of Kissinger. Callaghan was the only twentieth-century British PM to have held all four great offices of state: chancellor of the Exchequer, home secretary, foreign secretary and prime minister.

unwisely opted for the earlier explanation, saying he could trust Nasser and do business with him.

Eden had underestimated the effect of the British Labour Government's ill-advised foreign policy in the region, 1945–51, under Ernest Bevin (1881–1951), which failed to dissuade (if not outright encouraged) King Farouk from taking up arms to destroy Israel when it declared independence. That conflict sowed the seeds for what Nasser was to later exploit to his advantage, undermining Anglo–Egyptian relations and turning Arab countries' masses against Britain for 'handing Palestine to the Jews', as his propaganda claim was later taught in schools in Egypt. Ironically, the League of Arab States had been a British plan, and its prime mover none other than Anthony Eden himself as foreign secretary (1935–8 and 1940-5 and again 1951–55). Although Eden in 1942 presented the grouping as gathering regional support against the Nazi–Fascist alliance, the real long-term aim since the 1930s had been to establish an Anglo–Egyptian–Saudi axis to contain American influence and guard against Washington's plans to control oil supplies in Arabia. Nasser, for his part, had other ambitions that went beyond the original British aims. He backed violent groups in Algeria and attacked France, Britain and her traditional friends, the Arab monarchs – especially King Hussein of Jordan – on *Radio Sout al-Arab*. He had already signed an arms deal with the eastern bloc in 1955.

In 1954, Eden indulged Nasser's fantasy: he didn't publicly contradict his claim that the 1952 coup had forced *les Anglais* to leave Egypt, although Britain's vacating the canal base actually proceeded according to the 1936 treaty schedule.* As foreign secretary, Eden persuaded a reluctant Churchill to agree to a new friendship accord in 1954 with Nasser, which was in substance a mere rewording of the 1936 treaty. The treaty had been unilaterally abrogated by Nahas Pasha, the Wafd prime minister, in October 1951, backed by King Farouk. Nahas won the 1950 election after five of his predecessors had failed to amend some of 1936 treaty articles to keep Sudan as part of Egypt and end the British military presence there. His revocation resulted in unrest, culminating in a clash between the British Army and the Ismailia police in January 1952. The Wafd minister of the interior, Fuad Serageddin Pasha (1911–2000), ordered the Ismailia police force to resist the British troops, which laid siege to their Ismailia central station

The Egyptian police had failed to control the riots that broke out in Ismailia following Nahas' speech in October 1951, and which continued

---

* Signed in 1936, the treaty stipulated that the remaining British troops based in the canal zone would depart within 20 years, meaning the end of 1956. The last soldier left in June 1956, six months before the deadline.

CHAPTER 42   Nasser Betrays Eden

throughout that autumn. Egyptian extremists, described as terrorists by Defence Minister Antony Head (1906–1983), continued to attack British troops. There was evidence of Egyptian police shielding the armed radicals and aiding the attacks, which by 23 January 1952 had killed 33 and wounded 69 British personnel. The British commander sent messages to the deputy governor of Ismailia asking him to disarm the 600-strong police force. The police refused, and for several days the British commanders made every effort to avoid civilian casualties. Finally, an attempt to enter the Police Bureau Sanitaire (HQ) on 25 January was met by gunfire; infantry and armoured personnel carriers (APCs) were used. By the time the police surrendered, 41 policemen had been killed and 73 wounded, while three British infantrymen were killed and 13 wounded.[5] It was another day to be woven into the anti-*les Anglais* folkloric tableau next to the 1882 Bombardment of Alexandria, the 1906 Dinshawai, and the 1942 Abdin Palace incident.*

Nasser began commemorating 25 January as Police Day, a sombre event with a wreath-laying ceremony but not a full national holiday; he did not want another, semi-armed institution taking the limelight from the army. In contrast, Ourabi's 1881 march with mutineering officers on Abdin on 9 September was turned by Naguib and Nasser in 1952 into the '*Fellah* Day'. The coup regime abolished the old national holidays, established new ones revolving around the military or violent incidents involving the army struggling against some foe, real or imagined. The twenty-third of July, the day of the unconstitutional coup against the legitimate government and the elected parliament, became the official National Day; 6 October, the start of the 1973 Yom Kippur War against Israel, became Army Day.

Egypt's foreign minister, Muhammad Salaheldine Bey, who was in Paris in January 1952, rejected Britain's offer to calm the situation in Ismailia, lift military rule and negotiate a new arrangement if the Egyptians would call a halt to violent attacks.

'We won't negotiate, but we stick to our position until les Anglais evacuate the canal', he told journalists, adding that he wouldn't call his Paris meeting with Foreign Secretary Eden 'negotiations'.[6] Salaheldine

---

* Dinshawai: In 1906, British officers who had lost their way while shooting pigeons ended up in an altercation with the villagers of Dinshawai in northern Egypt – resulting in deaths and injuries, and a trial presided over by Christian minister of justice Boutros Ghali Pasha (1846–1910) (later the ninth prime minister of Egypt, 1908–10). Boutros-Ghali, a mixed court judge (minister of justice then foreign minister) who presided over the trial, handed down death, whipping and prison sentences. He was later assassinated, in February 1910. For a good account of the effect of the trial on nationalist movement see Lewis, Bernard Islam in History, Open Court Publishing, Chicago 1993 PP 384

Bey was to be replaced two days later as the two-week-old Nahas Pasha government resigned, and the king summoned Ali Maher Pasha (1881–1960) to form a new cabinet.

Scanning the Egyptian newspapers of that momentous week in 1952 indicates extreme moves from the Egyptians. The Wafd government issued a call to arms in response to British troops' 'attack' on the police station. Egyptian students called a general meeting to enlist in groups fighting *les Anglais*, while white-collar unions donated between 1 and 3% of their monthly salaries to 'the popular armed resistance cause'. It wasn't clear against exactly whom those parties were conducting the armed resistance, how the money reached them or who was accountable for its spending.

Contrary to claims made by Colonel Nasser's regime when nationalising the International Suez Canal Company, the ISCC in 1952 showed independence from any British influence by opening its Ismailia hospital, with its advanced facilities, to treat injured Egyptian policemen and placing its medical staff – as well as drugs, equipment and a fleet of ambulances – at the disposal of the city's Egyptian health authority. The ISCC's move in January 1952 was reported in 57 words – a small item on page 16 of *Al-Ahram*. There were also several calls and editorials appealing to the United States to send 'symbolic military units' to the canal zone.

Historians will continue to debate the British miscalculation – after their falling-out with Egypt's Wafd nationalist government – in helping the army officers overthrow King Farouk, whom they thought was backing Nahas Pasha in abrogating the 1936 treaty. Aware of the officers' plotting, Eden and the Foreign Office put their bets on a more friendly, new officer-led regime willing to give up Sudan. Sudan, a part of Egypt for over 100 years, was, in 1952, an Anglo–Egyptian condominium. Shortly before reaching a deal with Eden, Nasser consolidated his grip on power by removing the half-Sudanese President Naguib and refusing to hand power back to an elected civilian government. Nasser gave up Sudan immediately after signing the agreement with Eden.

Having blundered letting the military take over Egypt, Eden could have offered a 'carrot' to Nasser – such as entry into Commonwealth and trade agreements on favourable terms in exchange for protecting human rights in Egypt and negotiating a special status for Alexandria as a semi-autonomous free-trade zone. This would have covered thousands of third- and fourth- generation Europeans and Jews, who had built modern Alexandria and kept her as an economic powerhouse for the whole of Egypt. Eden's mistake was to fail to exploit Nasser's desire to build a monument associated with the Nile by agreeing to help finance the Aswan Dam and provide further aid linked to

CHAPTER 42   Nasser Betrays Eden

Nasser's commitment to moderate his economic policy, protecting investments and commerce in Alexandria and human rights in Egypt. Unfortunately, not many in Alexandria expressed this idea forcefully or debated it publicly – though it was discussed privately among retired politicians and over dinner parties in households like ours. Nobody at the time thought that the officers, claiming to be nationalists, would inflict the kind of demographic, social, cultural and economic damage that they did on Alexandria and on Egypt as a whole.

Nasser Appropriates Churchill's Speech, and 'Nationalises' Islam
In 1954, only Churchill was sceptical of Colonel Nasser – citing the illegitimacy of the 1952 military coup; his stabbing in the back of his leader, Naguib; and his reneging on the promise to reinstate civilian rule. In an ironic twist, Churchill's most famous Commons statement, on 4 June 1940 during Britain's darkest hour, '…we shall fight on the beaches, we shall fight on the landing grounds…' was appropriated by Colonel Nasser in November 1956 in response to the Anglo–French ultimatum that started the Suez War. Addressing the congregation, after the Friday prayer at al-Azhar Central Mosque, which was broadcast live on Cairo Radio, Nasser pledged to 'fight from house to house and from village to village, we shall fight with the aid of Allah'.

It should be noted that during this famous speech, Nasser not once said, '*Tahia Masr*' (Viva Egypt), a cry which Egyptian nationalists had been vocalising for over 70 years in every significant national march or uprising. Nasser was supposed to be the president of all Egyptians, including the Coptic fifth of the country's population, hundreds of thousands of third- or fourth-generation migrants of European descent from different non-Muslim denominations and indigenous Egyptian Jews. Many rabbis in Alexandria had blasted Israel for joining the plot concocted by Britain and France, who were also condemned in ceremonies in synagogues. Egyptian Jews saw themselves as patriotic citizens defending their country against external aggression. Nasser, however, didn't address the nation as a whole with all of its demographic components. He didn't make a speech from his office, parliament or Abdin Palace, symbolising the state's independence, but he chose al-Azhar Mosque, speaking to Muslims only. Repeating the word 'Allah' 12 times, Nasser appealed to the masses to turn the call '*Allahu Akbar*' (God is the greatest) into the national slogan. The pro-regime Arabic newspapers *Al-Ahram* and *Akhbar-el-Youm* had one word – '*Sanuqatil*' (we shall fight) – splashed in red across their front pages, with photos of Nasser at the mosque surrounded by cheering worshippers. Thus, after nationalising the Suez Canal, Nasser nationalised religion. He raised the Islamic standard of the Orient to march against Christian Europe and Jewish Israel.

333

This single event was hugely symbolic in changing how nationalism was redefined by Nasser. It marked his nationalisation of Islam and a significant landmark on the road to building his authoritarian populism. Phrases from the speech that Nasser had appropriated from Churchill, such as 'we shall fight' and 'Egypt was the grave of invaders', became fighting songs on the radio (and the records still get dusted off whenever there is a crisis with a foe). Meanwhile, the '*Allahu Akbar*' chorus took precedence over the new, official republican anthem, *Nasheed el-Huryah* (songs of freedom). Nasser's speech set the mood for generations, growing up with anti-Western groupthink and national paranoia, that the outside world – especially European colonialists and, by association, world Jewry – were conspiring against Egypt. When I covered North Africa and the Middle East as a roving correspondent in the region 12 years later, there were student demonstrations in most Egyptian towns – but they weren't marching for peace. While students worldwide rallied in 1968 for nuclear disarmament and against wars, Egyptian students called for battle. They demanded to be armed, to 'fight Israel and those beyond Israel' – words taken from another fiery speech by Nasser.

'It was hypocritical of Churchill', said Papa that momentous evening in July 1956, 'It was on his watch when *les Anglais* secretly helped and encouraged the conspiring officers to topple the King'. My grandfather nodded approvingly. *Oncle* Niroop said nobody had expected the military regime to go that far.

'Ha,' exclaimed my grandfather, 'there is worse to come, *de plus en plus.*' This had become his typical response to the new regimes' surprises since his tarboosh outburst in 1953.[7] 'I told you they were *les Anglais* servants; now they turn against their masters; the idiotic adolescents will ruin Egypt…'.

In June 1956, Britain relinquished the canal base. In appeasing Nasser, Eden was counting on building a long-term strategic partnership with Egypt, an ally in two world wars and a pillar of the 1942 British-devised League of Arabic States, launched in 1945 by Farouk and King Abdel-Aziz ibn Saud (1880–1953).

Like my grandfather, Churchill was proven right; Eden was wrong. After consolidating his grip on Egypt, Nasser hijacked the league and turned it into an instrument for furthering his pan-Arab ambitions and a canvas for his relentless crusade to destroy the Jewish state. To explain the psychology behind Nasser's personal obsession with destroying Israel, which was shared by many of his fellow officers, most likely his deep desire to revenge their humiliating failure in the war Egypt launched against the Jewish state 1948. His battalion came under siege from the Israelis and had to rely on their enemy's good will to get basic

CHAPTER 42   Nasser Betrays Eden

supplies for most of the war duration. This unhealthy fixation with defeating Israel led to taking a disastrous course. Nasser dismantled Egypt's liberal multi-party parliamentary democracy designed the system that has continued to rig every election until the present day, and moved closer to the Soviet bloc. He received $83m-worth of Soviet military weapons through Czechoslovakia only seven months after Eden's 1955 visit. His propaganda machine also attacked the 'Baghdad Pact' (the Central Treaty Organisation), a military and economic cooperation alliance formed in 1955 by the UK, Iran, Iraq, Pakistan and Turkey. The CTO was initially designed to serve as the southeastern flank of NATO, but President Eisenhower stepped back at the last minute from joining another Cold War alliance.

Eden continued to make pro-Arab overtures despite six months of Nasser attacks on Baghdad Pact. In his November 1955 Lord mayor's speech at the Guild Hall when the Prime Minister sets out foreign policy aims, Eden said that any settlement to the Israeli–Palestinian dispute should be based on the 1947 UN partition resolution. The speech was received with great satisfaction by Arab leaders.[8] But Nasser did not share the Arabs' warmth towards American Secretary of State Dulles' August 1955 initiatives to resolve the conflict with Israel.[9] 'Nasser won't participate in the American plan', Foreign Secretary Selwyn Lloyd concluded after meeting him in Cairo in March 1956; he advised the British cabinet that foreign policy should be realigned accordingly.[10] Eden was blind to Lloyd's 'crystal ball' predicting the wider long-term consequences of Nasser's rejection of a settlement with Israel. For the following fifteen years, Nasser's pan-Arabism propaganda promoted hatred for the Jewish state. By keeping his country in a semi-permanent state of war with a neighbour, the Egyptian leader created a mood of dependency on the army in a society controlled by his police state of authoritarian populism. His two-pronged tactics of anti-(Judaeo-Christian) Western sentiment and a permanent anti-Israel public mood was copied by other military dictators and pan-Arab despots. And, like all totalitarian regimes, was inseparable from their domestic policies thus became a foundation of their regional strategies, and led to the failure of reaching a peaceful settlement with Israel.

CHAPTER 43
Eden's Miscalculation

The next morning, Friday 27 July 1956, I accompanied my grandfather for a walk to Mandarah for coffee with his friends. Some were politicians of the old parliamentarian system under the monarchy. With his decades of experience and his intricate love-hate attitude towards *les Anglais*, my grandfather was fair and objective when appraising statesmen, even those he opposed. His friends agreed with his statement that Eden was a great patriot who believed in peace and cementing lasting friendships with former colonies and protectorates to strengthen the Commonwealth as a future growing free-trade bloc – and that Nasser was ill-advised to betray him. Like Papa and *Oncle* Niroop, these Wafd politicians were of the 'old school' – believing that politics should be separated from ideology in order to serve national interests and seek mutual benefits, while Nasser was cut from a different material. This middle-ranking officer-cum-authoritarian-populist-autocrat was an example of an ambitious ideologue.

While Nasser was thundering his fiery speech on 26 July, Eden was hosting a Downing Street dinner for the 21-year-old King Faisal II (1935–1958) of Iraq with Prince Regent Abd-al-Ilah (1913–1958) and Prime Minister Nouri al-Said Pasha (1888–1958). The three were brutally murdered, and their bodies dragged through the streets by mobs, during a Nasser-inspired and backed military coup two years later.[1] Also attending the dinner were Lloyd; Chancellor of the exchequer (Viscount Kilmuir) Sir David Patrick Fyfe (1900-1967); the leader of the House of Lords, (Marquess of Salisbury) Robert Gascoyne-Cecil (1893-1972); Secretary of state for the commonwealth (Earl of Home) Alec Douglas-Home (1903-1995); the chief of the air staff Sir Dermot Boyle (1904-1993). The news of Nasser 'pinching the Suez Canal',

CHAPTER 43 Eden's Miscalculation

as Eden put it, came during the second course. The story circulated years later about Nasser's action interrupting the dinner was an urban myth created by Kilmuir, according to Lloyd whose account is backed by accessible documents[2]. The crisis meeting only took place after the Iraqis had left No 10, although in a few minutes brief discussion all agreed that that public opinion would support decisive action. The emergency discussion continued, in a different room, after dinner with Eden, Kilmuir, Lloyd, Home and Boyle. They were joined by the First Sea lord and chief of staff Lord Mountbatten (1900-1979) as well as allies who were sent a message to attend; the French ambassador Jean Michel Chauvel (1879-1979) and the American charge d' Affaires Andrew Foster (1903-1963)[3]. The US ambassador, Winthrop Aldrich (1885-1974), had left London earlier in the day.

Before leaving Downing Street, the Iraqi Prime Minister Nouri Pasha – a shrewd, seasoned politician and a cornerstone of the CTO strategy – had a separate discussion with Lloyd and agreed that a decisive military action should be taken against Nasser[4]; but warned against acting in collusion with Israel at any cost, as this would result in a backlash empowering unpredictable and undesirable forces. The wily statesman was proven right*.

Making no reference to the Iraqi delegation's visit to the UK, *Al-Ahram* the following day sported the headline 'Panic in London in response to nationalisation', stating that Eden had called an emergency cabinet meeting for later that day (27 July 1956). The paper printed Nasser's speech in full, alongside other reports and analyses attacking Britain and assuring readers that the canal revenue would be used to finance construction of the Aswan Dam.

Although the press, which hadn't been nationalised yet, were toeing the official line, they were still showing independence and catering for the interest of their readers as shown by *Al-Ahram* on the same pages covering Nasser's action and Britain's response. The paper covered 'Marilyn Monroe's husband', the American author Arthur Miller (1915-2005) 'run with the McCarthy commission' publishing the couple's pictures. *Al-Ahram* also gave a considerable space to speculation on whether the 29-year-old Italian movie star Gena Loulou Brigida was expecting a child.

Eden made an urgent ministerial statement to the House of Commons about the Egyptian Government's unilateral decision to 'expropriate' the canal company without notice and 'in breach of the concession

---

*Nouri Pasha's concerns that Nasser would endanger the while region unless he was stopped swiftly with decisively swift action (military if necessary as long as Israel wasn't involved), was also confirmed to me by Sir Humphrey Trevelyan in my interview with him.

337

agreements'.[5] The statement was measured; he did not attack Nasser or his government, adding that HM Government was in consultation with other nations affected by the action. The condemnation of the Labour leader, Gaitskell, was more robust as he deplored the 'highhanded and totally unjustifiable step' and supported the government. In fact, all speakers backed Eden and strongly denounced Nasser's move, which was in breach of the Convention of Constantinople 1888*[6] which defined the use of the canal as an international waterway, and of the articles of the 1954 cooperation agreement he had signed with Eden.[7] Although international law, public opinion and the Labour opposition were on his side, Eden made a grave error by not seeking a UN mandate, as the leader of the opposition Hugh Gaitskell (1906-1963) had advised in the Commons.[8] He instead, unwisely, chose a military course of action that ended his career and inflicted unprecedented damage on British interests and on Alexandria – especially given that her people were the very folk who needed help through a wiser, more measured action. A series of Nasser-inspired or -backed military coups or attempts by militaries followed – in Iraq, Lebanon, Sudan, Algeria, Yemen, Syria, Mali, Libya and Somalia. They often also involved Nasser's secret service, the *Mukhabarat*. These coups quashed nascent democracies in North Africa and the Levant and unleashed brutal forces that still rampage through the region today.

The Masr Fellaheen's Revenge on Alexandria

Eden felt betrayed by Nasser, who, before seizing the canal, had also been frustrating British interests in the region. Nasser attacked the Baghdad Pact in his 26 July speech, saying Egypt would only join agreements that were 'exclusively Arabic'. CTO included nations that weren't ethnically Arab nor used Arabic language, like Iran, Pakistan and Turkey. This part of the speech was baffling for most listeners, especially Alexandrians, including my grandfather, Papa, *Oncle* Niroop and friends. The term 'Arab' at the time was more associated with a fancy-dress code or referred to Bedouins or *Higazis* (people from the Arabian Peninsula), while Arabic, for Egyptians, mean the language used by *fua'aha* and *sheiukh* (Quran reciters and the Muslim clergy). 'Arab' was not an adjective with which they would associate Egypt or Egyp-

---

* European powers, led by France (which controlled a majority of the canal shares and wanted to weaken Britain's influence) were concerned at Britain's control of the Suez Canal following its occupation of Egypt in 1882. Thus, a treaty was signed in October 1888 by Britain, France, Austria-Hungary, Russia, Spain, the Netherlands, Italy and the Ottoman Empire (including Egypt) to regulate the use of the Suez Canal as an international waterway open to all in peace and war; it has been a matter of dispute, but it was not finally implemented in 1904 after signing the Entente Cordiale.

CHAPTER 43 Eden's Miscalculation

tians. None of the Egyptian nationalists of generations born before 1955 ever thought of their country as an Arab nation or of themselves as Arabs. Arab nationalism was never part of the public discourse since none of Egypt's political movements mentioned it. Arab unity was first cited in waging war against Israel, as the initial collective action of the Arab League, but Egyptian nationalists were suspicious of the league as '*mashrou'h les Anglais*' (a British project) of little benefit to Egypt.

The Arab League was a British trap set by *les Anglais*, said *Oncle* Wahba, owner of the café where my grandfather and friends discussed the issue. The pro-*les Anglais* politicians had duped Farouk into falling for 'a devious plan by perfidious Albion', added my grandfather. He explained that pro-British politicians like Nakrashi and Nahas[*] had gone along with the idea, 'letting Farouk bite a British bait', launching the Arab League and dragging Egypt into the unwanted and disastrous 1948 war.

'It was the inevitable outcome of planting the idea of leading a pro-*les Anglais* Arab pact', he said about the signing of the Alexandria Protocol in October 1944[†] and the League of Arab States Pact in March 1945.[‡] My grandfather expressed a valid view prevailing among Egyptian nationalists that having perceived an independent Egyptian state under Muhammad Ali and his dynasty as a threat to their dominance, Britain and other European powers did not wish to repeat the experience.

Twentieth-century Egyptian nationalists always maintained that Egypt would be weaker politically and economically in an oriental Islamic or Arab block that would dilute her culture and independence and restrict her cooperation and association with Europe and its modernising influence. The Arab League, as some loose grouping or bloc – from the British and European powers' viewpoint – was an ideal replacement for the Ottoman Empire that did not present a challenge to the West. The grouping's first military action and subsequent wars were not against *les Anglais* or other former European colonial powers but against 'the Jewish gangs' in Palestine, as Egyptian media used the term coined by the British to describe Israeli armed groups. Eden's 1954 attempts to woo Nasser lent credence to this view, and the prime

---

[*]There were four Egyptian prime ministers between 1944 and 1948. Three of them went along with the plan to launch the league; two were Saadists (a splinter group from Wafd), who thought that Nahas had moved the party too close to the British and formed their own party. ; Ahmed Mahir/Maher Pasha (1888–1945) and Mahmoud Fahmi el-Nakrashi Pasha (1888–1948) – both assassinated by Muslim Brotherhood terror squads – and the third the People's party's PM Ismail Sidqi Pasha (1875–1950).
[†]Signed by the prime inisters of Egypt, Iraq, Lebanon, Syria and Trans-Jordan.
[‡]Signed (two months later, on 5 May) by the heads of state of Egypt, Iraq, Lebanon, Saudi Arabia, Syria, Trans-Jordan and North Yemen.

minister was aware of Nasser's choice of a role model: Ourabi Pasha (1841–1911). Ourabi saw Egypt as affiliated to an oriental Islamic bloc under the Ottomans, while modern liberal nationalists wanted an independent Egyptian identity. Within four years of removing President Naguib, Nasser developed the Ourabist caliphate concept with a pan-Arab theory to create a united bloc (made of the former Ottoman governorates), erasing Egypt's ancient identity in favour of a pan- Arab one. The 1952 military overthrow of King Farouk was a revival of the anti-modernity Ourabi officers' rebellion against Tawfik – a manifestation of Cairo-led, oriental internal Egypt's revenge on Europeanised urban modern Egypt – and Alexandria in particular. Seventy years after Ourabi's defeat in 1882, the *fellaheen* avenged him by overthrowing Khedive Tawfik's nephew, Farouk.

26 July 1952 went beyond the declared aims of the coup three days earlier, with the inward-looking, Islamic-at-heart Cairo imposing its will on European Alexandria. The day marked the beginning of the end – Alexandria's slow death as the most advanced and Europeanised city in the entire region. The barbarians arrived, marching in their khaki uniforms into the birthplace of modernity in Egypt – driving from the south, along the desert road. The unrefined *fellaheen* entered the city through her dusty southern outskirts, marching across her clean, sleepy streets in the shadow of Italian architecture on roads that were an extension of Europe. Their final destination was the tip of Pharos Island, where divine revelations had instructed Alexander to build the great city over two millennia before. They hesitated to adjust their military *casquettes* at the gates of Ras el-Tin Palace, the pinnacle of European Alexandria, before taking the very first action that ended the chapter of her modern Hellenistic era.

The conspiring officers timed their action for the summer when the establishment moved to Alexandria and many ministers travelled to Europe. After taking over Cairo with ease, the conspirators issued orders to seize royal Alexandria and subjugate her to the force of Masr (Cairo), also the name of Egypt itself. Alexandria, whom Muhammad Ali, copying Ptolemy Soter, had made the de facto capital, was different in geography, demography and culture. Masr's ill-educated army officers were mentally captive to a twisted view of history with hearts full of hatred for outward-looking European Alexandria. Hatred burning in Internal Egypt like embers buried under a thin veneer of modernity since 1882. Hatred generated by a single event: the bombardment of Alexandria on 11 July 1882 and the subsequent occupation by *les Anglais*. It became part of the national folklore, with internal, oriental and Islamic Egypt holding Alexandria responsible. London (in the shape of William Gladstone's government, 1880–85) had given permission a

CHAPTER 43   Eden's Miscalculation

month earlier for the bombardment of Alexandria by the Royal Navy's powerful, modern guns against the advice of British diplomats in Alexandria.[9] The diplomats strongly warned against military action or landing any marines to avoid further inflaming a volatile situation[10] – but their cautions were rejected, just as Eden ignored Nouri al-Said's advice 74 years later.

PART X
COUNTDOWN TO CONFLICT

CHAPTER 44
A Country Divided

The 11 July 1882 bombardment, a landmark that changed Alexandria's history, came as a peak of political turmoil that divided Egypt, in socio-political choices and mindsets rather than ethnically or geographically, into two nations – one embracing modernity and another resisting progress. Alexandria, surrounded by water with only a narrow link to Egypt's land mass, geographically marked this conceptual division. The British presence reinforced her semi-independent status by empowering the rich, independent Alexandria Municipality,[1] representing a modern multi-racial cosmopolitan metropolis.

Divisions in Internal Egypt reflected different outlooks on life, culture and social etiquette, pitting open-minded middle-class and European-educated Egyptians against pro-Ottoman Islamic-caliphatist inward-looking Egyptians. Apart from Alexandria, the European-minded middle classes remained minorities in isolated urban centres like Port Said and the industrial towns. The majority in the remainder of the country, backed by the powerful Islamic 'Church' (al-Azhar) and many wealthy landowners, were pro-caliphate *fellaheen* with a rigid, backward outlook. The latter had resisted Muhammad Ali's modernisation from the start – and, more than a century later, most of Naguib's and Nasser's Free Officers Action (FOA) recruits were drawn from the anti-modernity strata regarding their social background and thinking.

Les Anglais' occupation, which followed the bombardment, strengthened this resolve and deepened this division. The Internal Egypt majority always recalled that date, 11 July 1882, and subsequent events such as Dinshawai, surrounding these incidents with a mythology in order to recharge the energy of their anti-modernity and anti-secularism crusade. They kept folkloric hatred alive in many ways – especially by

CHAPTER 44   A Country Divided

simplified, superficial lessons in the general-education system without enough details to unpack the historical context of events. The animosity added to Internal Egypt's envy of Alexandria thanks to inward-looking Egyptians' failure to understand the semi-independent trade city's spirit and mind.

The 1952 military coup represented a phase of cultural and socio-economic wars between cities generated by class or religious divisions. Masr (Cairo) – which, with its *fellaheen* attitude, became a citadel of Internal Egypt – always saw Alexandria as a bridgehead for European influence and culture, undermining the Islamic character to which Masr clung. The coup was a replay of Colonel Ourabi's conflict, when his exclusively military rebellion had failed to defeat Alexandria 70 years earlier. In 1882, the internal conflict was also linked with international geopolitics such as European-power rivalries and the Ottoman sultan's backing of army officers against Khedive Tawfik's modernisation, culminating in British intervention. There are also similarities with the Suez crisis seven decades later. Both sets of events played their role in altering the course of history.

William Ewart Gladstone (1809–1898), who took office for the second time in 1880, had his own motives to intervene in Egypt: 37% of his investments, worth £40,567 (near $100 million in today's money), was in Egyptian government-issued bonds. No fewer than 65 other Westminster MPs also had investments in Egypt.[2] The need to protect the Suez Canal, as part of safeguarding the trade route to India, became an obsession of British policymakers, who established posts along the way from Gibraltar to Malta and Cyprus to the Persian Gulf – with whose sheikhs they had signed the Trucial Treaty 60 years earlier in 1820. As a result, the issue was discussed openly in London. In Alexandria, the British (and other European powers') anticipated move 'to protect Europeans' was only a pretext.[3]

Historians will continue to argue over the real motives behind the Gladstone government's policy of occupying Egypt. Was it dictated by market forces? The personal interests of MPs and the prime minister? A long-term national-interest strategy? Electoral politics back home?

Alexandria's 1880s troubles, which Gladstone used as a pretext for intervention, were insignificant compared with riots and deaths in Europe during 1848 uprisings, or in Paris in 1871 when thousands were killed. There was sectarian strife between Alexandria's Greeks and Jews before Easter 1881. A Greek youth was found dead at the harbour. Although there were no signs of assault on his body, many Greeks believed in the anti-Semitic myths about Jews taking Christian children's blood for the baking of the Passover *matzah*. The Greeks started attacking the Jews.

Such conflicts, however, had been bloodier in the Alexandria of the fourth and fifth centuries – although communities had their own separate quarters then, according to the period's records used by historians like Ammianus Marcellinus (330–400) in his *Res Gestae*. He recorded the Arian bishop George of Cappadocia struggle against the rest of the Alexandrians (the Hellenes), ending with his death in 361[4] Most conflicts were between Christians and Hellenes, to whom many historians inaccurately referred as 'pagans'. *Paganos* usually referred to country peasants, inappropriate in this context and in that period of history as a descriptor for sophisticated urban populations – especially the Alexandrians who called themselves 'Hellenes'.[5] Alexandria's late fourth-century communal violence resulted in the destruction of the great temple of Serapis*, the Hellenistic-Egyptian god and the city's protector, known as the Serapeum in 391 by a mob of Roman soldiers.[6]

Worse was the triangular conflict involving the Nicene Bishop Cyril (376–444), who became patriarch (pope) of Alexandria in 412; Orestes, the *Praefectus Augustalis*† of the Diocese of Egypt; and Alexandrian Jews, many of whom were expelled by Cyril after they clashed with his clergymen. These troubles culminated in the violent murder of the brilliant Hellenic Neoplatonist, philosopher, astronomer and mathematician Hypatia (350/370–415), who combined free-thinking and the idea of pure living. Hypatia, history's first female mathematician, constructed improved models of astrolabes and hydrometers and left a body of work and essays that was built upon by René Descartes (1596–1650), Gottfried Wilhelm Leibniz (1646–1716) and Isaac Newton (1642–1727).[7] There is a widely held belief among historians that Cyril planned Hypatia's murder due to her influence on Orestes, who – like many aristocrats, Christians and Hellenes – considered her his 'divine guide' into the realm of philosophical and cosmic mysteries. Such knowledge at the time was condemned by Christians like Cyril as 'paganism'. His followers ambushed Hypatia in her chariot, stripped her naked, dragged her into the Caesareum and murdered her[8]. She became '*Philosophiae Martyris*'.[9] The fourth-and fifth-century conflict was also a power struggle between Cyril and Orestes, who kept himself close to both Hypatia and her Hellene followers, and the Jews of Alexandria.

---

* The Serapeum was built by Ptolemy III Euergetes (280–222 BC; reigned from 246 BC) for the god Serapis, protector of Alexandria. The god was an Egyptian–Hellenistic deity to continue Alexanderia's binary culture of combining existing Egyptian beliefs and gods with Greek ones.

† Augusta Perfect was a unique title; the highest rank within the empire of governor of a crown domain which had a more illustrious rank than previous *vicarius* as both crown and religious. The Diocese of Egypt encompassed what is now Libya and most of Palestine.

CHAPTER 44   A Country Divided

The 1880s tensions represented another chapter of community conflicts but were on nothing like the scale of the fifth century, when the Jews had often fought back, because the nineteenth-century Jews were pacifists. When the police arrested a Greek Alexandrian for stirring up attacks against Jews after Easter 1881 trouble, many Greek traders rushed out of the bourse into Place des Consuls to free him, attacking any Jews they encountered. Many of the latter ran for safety into British and French consulates on the square. The wealthy de Menasce family (themselves prominent Alexandrian Jews) actually paid the Greeks large sums of money to quieten them down.[10]

Egyptian Identity v. Ottoman Caliphatism
Within and outside of Alexandria, Egyptians were forging their 'nationalism'; it was characterised by a negative attitude to others. These 'others' were the Europeans or anyone perceived as non-*ibn-balad* (non-Nilotic). For many Nilotic Egyptians, especially outside European Alexandria, this category included fellow Nilotic-Egyptian Christians and Jews whose communities predated the arrival of Islam by centuries. But the picture was complicated with more than one nationalism. The secular nationalism of the independent Egyptian identity was influenced and inspired by nation-states that had emerged earlier in Europe. This trend was led by the middle classes and European-educated urban Egyptians seeking independence from the Ottomans. The seeds of this nationalism, more evident in Alexandria, were sown early in the nineteenth century by Muhammad Ali, and it was continued by his descendants – especially Ismail and Tawfik. This trend was noticeably more evident in Alexandria. The other nationalism, to which most of Internal Egypt subscribed, was a pan-Islamism affiliated with the Ottoman concept of the caliphate and characterised by hostility to Europeans and non-Muslims in general.

Robust enforcement of the rule of law under Muhammad Ali made Egypt safe for travellers, investors and merchants to go about their business – a very different picture to that painted two decades earlier, when travellers had been 'surrounded by hostilities'.[11] Muhammad Ali dealt harshly with Islamists troublemakers. When a Muslim sheikh claimed that non-Muslims' butchered meat did not meet the Islamic-dietary conditions, Muhammad Ali ordered his exile; he wasn't pardoned until he publicly disowned all his earlier sermons.[12] Mindful of the danger that Islamists posed to the project of building a modern Egypt, the administration of Muhammad Ali (1805–48) was particularly wary of any Islamist-inspired opposition. A protest led by an Islamic sheikh claiming to be a *Mahdi* (inspired by Allah), who denounced 'infidels' employed by Muhammad Ali, was swiftly crushed.[13] A French consul wrote in 1812 that Muhammad Ali had bought most of the al-Azhar *ulama*, and those resisting his modernisation were exiled.[14]

The main obstacle to modernisation was the al-Azhar Islamic institution. Its teaching, influence, and *ulama* were always there – resisting modernity, individual liberty and cosmopolitanism, and trying to preserve pan-Islamic caliphatism. This priestly class saw the modernity project and the establishment of an independent Egyptian identity as threats to their interests and prestige, which relied on invoking Islamic jurisprudence in every aspect of daily life and encouraging people to refer to them for guidance. The *ulama* have even continued their reactionary mission into the post-1953 Republic era, up until the time of writing. Al-Azhar scholars planted the seeds of hatred for non-Muslim migrants, whom they branded 'foreign infidels', even though they were fully aware of European and other non-Muslim investors providing jobs for Egyptians who were too lazy or too unwilling to invest and create jobs themselves and mostly wanted employment in the civil service.

The Azhar-educated Egyptian historian Abd-el-Rahman el-Gaberty (1753–1826) chronicled the French expedition in his massive multi-volume *Tarikh-el-Gaberty* (el-Gabertey's Chronicles); he was critical of Muhammad Ali's reforms. In 1813, he called Europeans 'the enemies of our faith' who had become 'the companions and intimate friends of His Highness'. In el-Gaberty's book, Christians were guilty of helping the pasha's commercial enterprises, obtaining the best jobs and houses, employing Muslims as servants and suggesting new taxes.[15] But he didn't object to the Ottomans, or the Arabs before them, forcefully collecting poll taxes from Non-Muslims. And these 'enemies of our faith' were the French experts who remained after Napoleon's defeat and were employed by Muhammad Ali to build a modern navy and army, many industries and educational institutions.

Alexandria was less influenced by al-Azhar's reactionary Islamism than Cairo, but the city could not remain immune to their poisonous ideas forever. Sheikh Abdallah el-Nedim (1843–1896), the son of *fellaheen* immigrants to Alexandria, founded the Al-game'iyah al-Khairiah al-Islamiah (IKA – the Islamic Charity Association), indoctrinating children under the guise of Islamic teachings. The IKA didn't last long, so in 1878 he founded Gamiat al-Shuban al-Mulsimeen al Wataniya (GSMA – the Muslim Young Men's Association), which folded after two years but nonetheless served as a precursor to the Islamo-fascist organisation Misr-al-Fatat (Young Egypt – YE) that was active in the 1930s and 1940s.[16] Nasser elevated el-Nedim's status to that of national hero, naming a school and a street after him, while a tram stop was

CHAPTER 44   A Country Divided

renamed al-Shuban al-Muslimeen. The sheikh's bust was placed in *Khaldin-Green*, a municipality park in central Alexandria.

Alexandrian society of the nineteenth century was tolerant and free, enabling el-Nedim to stage a satirical play at Teatro Zizinia, critical of 'tyranny' while the khedive attended the opening.[17] No such public criticism or satirising of the ruling regime was tolerated in post-1952 administrations. El-Nedim published pamphlets calling for the embracing of Islamic rules through Quranic teaching projects, claiming that Europe was exporting corruption, the chaos of socialism, and anarchy to Alexandria.

Sheikh Hamzah Fathallah (1846–1918) was also critical of European culture. Although moderate by comparison, his reference point remained Islamic teachings, which he saw as superior to secular laws and other cultures. Al-Azhar-educated Fathallah, a migrant from Tunisia, started working on the weekly *Al-Kawakab al-Sharqi* (Orient Star), founded in Alexandria in 1873 by Syrian printer, publisher and journalist Selim el-Hamawi. Fathallah consciously introduced Bedouin Arab desert and Islamic vocabulary and metaphors into Egyptian poetry and Arabic print-press copy.* A case in point was his own poem in praise of King Oscar II of Sweden (1829–1907) when the sheikh was invited to talk about 'women in Islam' in Stockholm in 1889. In the early 1870s, Fathallah's message was closer to el-Nedim's – until he left for Tunis in 1874 to edit its government's official paper.† Fathallah returned to Alexandria to edit the weekly *Al-Burhan* (Evidence), funded by Khedive Tawfik to counter the inimical output of pro-Ourabi journals like Sheikh el-Nedim's publications. *Al-Ahram* and no fewer than seven other papers founded by liberal and progressive Syrian journalists who migrated from Beirut supported Tawfik. Fathallah left *Al-Burhan* and briefly backed Ourabi Pasha when Tawfik appointed him a defence minister in February 1882 to placate the Egyptian Army officers. Fathallah later disagreed with Ourabi, objecting to the use of the army for political change – a stance that he expressed in editorials in his 1882-launched newspaper *Al-I'Etidal* (Moderation). Fathallah joined the Ministry of Education as chief inspector of the Arabic language, but opposed the modernisation of curricula and teaching methods.

Al-Azhar-educated activists like el-Nedim and their Islamic

---

*Egyptian newspapers' copy was written in mostly modern Egyptianised Arabic text adding demotic language, marrying multiple cultures' vocabularies unlike the inflexible classical Quranic script used in al-Azhar, the only higher-education teaching institution in Egypt until the Muhammed Ali-founded schools in the early nineteenth century.
†The Al-Raed al-Tunisi (The Tunisian Guide) launched in 1860. It was later renamed Al-Raed al-Rasmi (The Official Guide) by the French administration in 1881.

publications were components of the other non-nation-state nationalism of the Islamic caliphate, with its anti-European and anti-modernity attitude. This viewpoint had associated Tawfik with the British and French ever since he had come to power in 1879 following the deposition of his modernising father, Ismail Pasha. The latter had accepted Anglo–French dual control (financial supervision by decree in 1876) after his debts, in 1875, reached £68.5 m (£77 M with 11% and depreciation repayment) or $7.42 billion in today's money (it was consolidated into £98.3 m in 1880) due to spending on infrastructure, schools, arts and the extension of the railways throughout Egypt (which at that time encompassed Sudan and parts of Ethiopia).[18]

The Nasser regime's revised school-history texts only focused on Ismail's spending on arts and festivals while leaving out the infrastructure underpinning Egypt over the last 150 years; this infrastructure was paid for by Ismail's borrowing during that period. His development, modernisation and expansion of Egypt into Africa was a continuation of his grandfather's and father's quest for a nation independent of the Ottomans and the Europeans. But, in one of history's ironic twists, the borrowing made Egypt vulnerable to European intrusion. In 1875, Ismail sold his remaining investment – 176,602 shares (44% of the Suez Canal Company) – to British Prime Minister Benjamin Disraeli (1804–1881) who borrowed £4 million ($653 million in today's money)[19] on behalf of HM government from Lionel de Rothschild. Incoming non-Muslim migrants enjoyed many privileges during his reign, which helped to generate a xenophobic nationalism with an Islamic tone. Ismail tried to shift the blame for the national financial difficulties and debts onto Europeans in Egypt. At the same time, Otto von Bismarck (1815–1898), Chancellor of the newly founded German Reich, threatened an intervention. Disraeli was wary of Bismarck's influence, and of the expansion of a German Empire. Britain and France responded by persuading the Ottoman Porte (Sultan Abdul Hamid II – r.1876–1909) to depose Ismail in favour of his son Tawfik. However, unlike Islamists like el-Nedim and Fathallah or Ourabi officers, who wanted to cling to the Ottoman Islamic caliphate, Tawfik continued the work of Ibrahim and Muhammad Ali in establishing a distinctive Egyptian identity in an independent state.

Several aspects of the progressive nineteenth-century rise of Alexandria were foreshadowed millennia earlier by Ptolemy Soter (Ptolemy I – 367–283 BC), who kept Egypt and her capital Alexandria independent – refusing to integrate her into Alexander's broader empire. Ptolemy Soter, who once called on people to 'imagine a whole civilised world as one under one King', could only see one power that this king would possess in order to unite the new emerging world. He saw the empire

CHAPTER 44 A Country Divided

of Alexander, Aristotle's pupil, as an empire of the mind – of episteme and of a progressive, shared intelligence, not simply a geographical territory with Alexandria in its domain. Twenty-two centuries later, Muhammad Ali, Ismail and Tawfik wanted an independent Egypt to break away from the backward Ottomans and unite – in culture, mind and the episteme of modernity – with Europe.

CHAPTER 45
Tawfik–Ourabi: the Constitution

Khedive Tawfik was eager to draft a new constitution when he replaced his father in June 1879, but saw the draft by his first prime minister, Mohammed Cherif Pasha (1826–1887), as giving too much power to the assembly (Parliament).* Some historians blame Tawfik, who acted as prime minister following Cherif's resignation in August 1879, for not taking on board the idea of a parliament with more democratic reforms. Wilfred Blunt (whose wife Anne was a granddaughter of Lord Byron) thinks this act triggered a domino effect of subsequent troubles.[1] Tawfik was caught between competing powers with conflicting interests. How to deal with the rebelling mid-rank army officers, with the assembly, and implement modernising reforms while keeping the European consuls sweet?[†]

In September 1879, Tawfik appointed the patriot Riyad Pasha (1836–1911), of Jewish and Circassian ancestry and known for his honesty and commitment to Egyptian independence. Riyad's 1879–80 reforms would recognise national courts alongside the mixed courts, suppress odious taxes and end *el-Sukhra* (*corvée* – forced labour using *fellaheen* to dig canals)[‡], and ban flogging[2]. Sukhra resentment in the

---

*Created by Ismail, the assembly was a parliamentary council of the representatives of 120 constituencies in Egypt, Sudan and parts of Ethiopia and Eritrea, whose members were opposed to European intervention in Egyptian affairs.
† Egypt was a province of the Ottoman Empire; thus, other nations were diplomatically represented by consuls rather than ambassadors. The embassies were in Constantinople.
‡ Corvée was a source of national resentment that was exploited by various trends to block large projects like the Suez Canal. After a couple of years using forced labourers (and paying them very little in agricultural products like honey) Napoleon III (1808–1873) in April 1864 compelled the French company in charge to end the practice and pay decent wages. Despite objections from European (especially British) financiers, the company also brought modern digging equipment from Europe, which

CHAPTER 45 Tawfik–Ourabi: the Constitution

national collective consciousness was exploited by Colonel Nasser; he referred to it in nationalising Suez Canal and was used by his regime in their propaganda to justify grabbing private institutions owned by non-Nilotic investors. In 1879 the wealthy clergy and landowners rejected these measures; the *sukhra*, after all, provided them with unregulated cheap labour. The Riyad–Tawfik reforms had to wait until 1891, when Egypt showed a surplus in its national budget.

The other power working against Tawfik was the Ottoman sultan. The Porte was suspicious of the khedive's and Riyad's reforms, which would have taken Egypt on an independent path away from the Ottoman sphere. The Ourabist officers were aware of Sultan Abdul Hamid II's desire to undermine khedivial authority in Egypt by supporting military dissent in order to block the country's path to independence. Riyad also made enemies when he suspended critical newspapers like *Misr* and *Tigara* (Trading), founded in Alexandria in 1878 by Syrian-born Armenian journalist Adib Ishaq (1856–1885). Ishaq's 1879-founded *Al-Mahrousah* gave space to Islamist troublemakers like Sheikh el-Nedim.[3] The Cherifists financed Ishaq, who left for Paris, to publish an opposition newspaper, *Misr al-Qahira* (Egypt of Cairo). Its title reflected the conflict of identities between a society seen by Tawfik and Riyad as European, modern, open, cosmopolitan and multicultural – as embodied by Alexandria – and inward-looking, Islamic, closed-minded Oriental Internal Egypt, as expressed and represented by Cairo pan-Islamists, the al-Azhar *ulama*, and pro-Ottoman landowners and the Ourabists.

Tawfik–Riyad's July 1880 decree of limiting military service to four years was interpreted by Ourabi as curtailing the power of the military, removing his loyal 'Egyptian officers' from his side by promoting them. Ourabi's phrase, 'Egyptian officers', was disingenuous and divisive: the army itself was Egyptian, and it had been founded by Muhammad Ali with the help of French officers who came with Bonaparte. Yet, the Ourabists denied the same nationality to fellow Egyptians based on ethnic background or religion while, hypocritically, complaining about discrimination[*]. Ironically, it was the ethnically French Suleiman Pasha al-Faransawi (Gen Joseph Anthelme Sève)[4] who was the protector of the *fellaheen* officers. Ourabi, who joined the army at the age of 14, was promoted quickly – thanks to Suleiman Pasha, and to Khedive Said Pasha's closeness to the military when he headed the navy. During his rule (1854–63), Said allowed Egyptian *fellaheen* to pass on land that

---

accelerated the work and reduced injuries among the labourers.
[*] Nasser, 75 years later, showed similar racism backed by the Islamists and far-right nationalists, Nasser stripped thousands of fellow Egyptians of their nationality.

they cultivated, and which was taxed, to their male heirs. The latter could thus join the officers' class, which was exclusive to landowners, and be promoted to the upper ranks – a practice that had been banned by his father, Muhammad Ali. Ourabi became a major by the age of 19 and a lieutenant-colonel by 20.

Ourabi accompanying Said, in 1863, to Medina in *Higaz* (Arabia), which exposed him to Said's *idées égalitaires* and respect for the *fellaheen*. This fitted Ourabi's al-Azhar education – since Islam, in theory, makes all Muslims equal regardless of rank or nationality. Khedive Ismail put an end to Said's promotion of *fellaheen* officers to the upper ranks, however. With personal baggage and political ambitions, the 41-year-old Colonel Ourabi Bey, joined by armed units, marched to Abdin Palace on 9th September 1881 with a petition of demands for Tawfik, including Riyad's resignation. The day was marked 71 years later by General Naguib military coup regime as Eid el-Fellah (Fellaheen Day).

Riyad resigned on 10 September, and four days later, Cherif Pasha formed a government making Ourabi the Deputy Minister of War with another promotion. Cherif Pasha demanded a guarantee of non-interference from the military, which gained support from parliamentarians alienated by Ourabi's orders and threats.

More politicians started liaising with Ourabist military officers, while the Cairo press was agitating against European influence and appealing to Muslim sentiment. Cherif Pasha's 1881 government lasted less than five months.

Cherif resigned on 4 February 1882, and Sami el-Baroudi (1839–1904)* became prime minister. A draft bill launched on 7 February proposed a radical, progressive update of the 1879 constitution, marking the start of Egyptian independence from the Ottoman Empire, and reorganised the balance of power between the government and elected parliament in its binary role of legislator and holding the former to account.[5] But it was rejected by the Islamist-leaning Ourabists because it protected the rights of non-Muslims. Setting a precedent for the army intervening in politics, Ourabi forced Baroudi to dismiss many 'Europeans' from state institutions.[6] The army began to dominate Egypt in many respects.[7] Within a month, a 'plot' by Turco-Circassian officers against Ourabi was 'uncovered', and a tribunal found 50 of them guilty. Ourabi pressured Baroudi to reject Khedive Tawfik's demand for the cabinet to review the cases

---

*Mahmoud Sami el-Baroudi was a nationalist army officer and poet, born to an Ottoman Egyptian father and a Greek mother. His poetry was taught as part of Arabic literature in Egyptian schools, and he was known as the 'Lord of the Sword and the Quill'.

and evidence. The 'guilty' officers were dismissed and exiled. This set a precedent for the 1952 military regime 70 years later: 'uncovering a plot' became its preferred method of settling scores or eliminating opponents within the ruling military. The 1952 coup officers, relying on Muslim Brotherhood support, emulated Ourabi, who obtained backing from Sheikh el-Nedim and the al-Azhar *ulama*.[8]

The Islamic, pro-Ottoman (not quite yet Egyptian) military version of nationalism saw non-Muslims' presence as undermining the 'Islamic character' of the land and making Nilotic Egyptians unequal. Interestingly, the '*aganeb*' (aliens/foreigners), to whom Islamic-leaning Ourabists referred, included non-Muslim fellow Egyptians. There was no Egyptian nationality per se; all were subjects of the Ottoman Empire.

Ourabi's military, pan-Islamic-caliphate move was a precursor to Nasser's military pan-Arabism taking over public life 75 years later. Like Ourabi, who did not recognise a national independent Egyptian identity, Colonel Nasser abolished the name 'Egypt' in 1958, calling his federation with Syria the United Arab Republic. Syria became *Iklim Chamali* (the northern province) and Egypt came to be known as *Iklim Ganoubi* (the southern province). The word 'Egypt' would not appear in the state's official name for 13 years. When the republic was renamed in 1971 by Sadat, Egypt's independent identity was not restored: it became instead the 'Arab Republic of Egypt'. In the 1940s, Sadat was close to both Muslim Brotherhood and pro-Nazi groups; in the 1970s, he became involved with the US Near and Middle East strategy of creating a pro-Washington Arabo-Islamic bloc to include conservative Arab monarchs who opposed modern liberalism.[9]

Except for calls by small nationalist parties like Hezb Misr al-Om (Mother Egypt Party), which were never given permission to contest elections, there was no attempt to restore a name with an independent Egyptian identity after the two uprisings in 2011 and 2013 that ended the First Republic.

I consider the end of the First Republic to be the 2013 uprising, not the 2011 fall of Mubarak, since the Muslim Brotherhood regime of Mohamed Morsi (1951–2019) was an extension of the totalitarian republic declared in 1953. There has been a laughably disingenuous claim (by Western establishments who swallowed Islamist propaganda) that Morsi's election was 'fair, free and democratic'; it was nothing but. Wily statesmen like former UK prime minister Tony Blair (b.1953) and the older American statesman Henry Kissinger (b.1923)[*] were under no such illusion. What was good for the goose wasn't good for three previous ganders? The army, which ousted Mubarak in February 2011

---

[*] Heinz Alfred Kissinger fled Germany in 1938, served as National Security Adviser (1969-1975) and Secretary of State (1973-1977)

following mass protests, was in full charge – as it had been since the 1952 coup – and ensured the outcome of the vote in advance. The Supreme Council of Armed Forces (SCAF) had a veto on who could stand in both parliamentary and presidential elections. Both were held under the very election law and rules and the same electoral commission under which Mubarak, Sadat and Nasser had been elected in ten polls since Colonel Nasser was elected in 1956 by 99.9% of the votes- as the official count put it[10]. It is an insult to the intelligence to suggest that the Egyptians, in the middle of uprising and anarchy, managed to clean and reorganise their 60-year-old, profoundly corrupt electoral structure along democratic lines in a few weeks – let alone change their indifference to the customary fixing of elections. The late Mohamed Morsi, a leading member of the extremist Muslim Brotherhood (who were the officers partners in the 1952 coup), is presented as 'civilian'. Would a leading member of the IRA's Council be regarded as 'civilian' in the UK – or elsewhere? Not only were the 2011–12 elections controlled by the Egyptian military but they also underpinned Morsi's regime. It suited the administration of US President Barack Obama (b.1961) and SCAF to have an Islamist president backed by the army, preferring a Pakistan model as a safer option to an unpredictable civilian government: a post-millennial re-run of 1952 favouring a Muslim Brotherhood-backed military coup, as opposed to an elected civilian government that might not dance to post-colonial Anglo-American tunes.

In identical circumstances, the army removed Mubarak in 2011 and Morsi in 2013 (to avoid wider civil conflict) following a mass uprising against the president (several million more in 2013, with hundreds of Muslim Brotherhood members heavily armed). So why one is called a coup and the other not? Both revolts ended with the status quo that had existed since 1952, real power back in the hands of a military establishment still enthralled by Colonel Nasser's doctrine of Arabo-Islamism, modelled on Ourabi's pan-Islamism. The development, inevitably, led to al-Azhar (as the official Muslim Church*) playing a more significant role, opposed to the concept of an independent nation-state that had inspired the modernising leaders Muhammad Ali, Ibrahim, Ismail, Twafik, Helmi II and Fuad I.

The presence in Alexandria of Khedive Tawfik in summer 1882 helped the Ottoman-leaning Islamists' propaganda to portray him as a renegade, and his modernisation and reforms as treason to the Islamic caliphate. Today, the Arabic version of Wikipedia, Al-Maerifah, controlled by pan-Islamists, labels Tawfik Pasha – in every mention, regardless of the context – a 'traitor' and an 'agent of the non-believers

---

* See glossary and usage.

CHAPTER 45   Tawfik–Ourabi: the Constitution

and enemies of Islam'. Programmes undertaken in Tawfik's later years as khedive included a reorganisation of Egypt's legal system, the reform of parliament (general assembly and the legislative council), the abolition of slavery and corporal punishment, and many modern agricultural and irrigation projects.

Ourabi: a Blueprint for the 1952 Coup
Tawfik enjoyed little domestic support outside Alexandria and urban middle-class centres, and was thus forced to meet the demands of Ourabi while in (the more Islamic, pro-Ottoman) Cairo. Ourabi, who was al-Azhar-educated and from a rural background, demanded an end to privileges given to the higher-ranking officers of Turkish, Circassian and Albanian descent.[11] His officers' rebellion, which violated the 1879 constitution and had no popular base, was the blueprint of the 1952 coup by middle-ranking officers who, similarly lacked a popular base.[12]

There are also similarities between the two moves in dealing with European powers, culminating in British military intervention. The first case resulted in British occupation in 1882; the second, in 1956, came with French support. Both strengthened the hand of reactionary, inward-looking military forces that ended modernity and democracy. In both cases, 70 years apart, the Egyptian Army's dreadful showing in external wars triggered the move. Middle-ranking officers used their defeat in the 1948 war against Israel as a pretext to stage the coup after falsely accusing the ruling elite of conspiring and supplying the army with defective weapons. The 1880s revolts grew out of disaffection with the generals after a disastrous campaign in Abyssinia. Hence, their alleged discrimination based on race was a smokescreen: they blamed the 'top brass', who happened to be ethnically non-Nilotic. Ourabi enjoyed the support of hardline Islamists. Most of the FOA were members of violent or Islamo-fascist organisations like *el-yad el-Khafiyah* (the blackhand) and the Muslim Brotherhood[13].

After the abysmal performance in Abyssinia, Ourabi turned army officers' disaffection with the upper ranks into an Islamic crusade against the infidel Europeans. Sixty years later, Islamist-influenced FOA conspiring officers turned the 1948 defeat in Palestine into an Arabo-Islamic campaign against the infidel Jews and their allies, the Christian nations who had voted for the UN partition of Palestine.

A year after the failure to destroy the Jewish state, the General Arab-Islamic Congress, held at al-Azhar University in Cairo, was addressed by General Saleh Harb (1889–1968). General Harb, a former chief of staff, sat in Ali Maher Pasha's 1939 cabinet, which refused to declare war on Germany. Like Colonel Ourabi, General

Alexandria Adieu

Harb had attended a Quranic school believing in the Islamic caliphate.* Addressing the 1949 congress,† he held a pistol in one hand and a copy of the Quran in the other, stating that 'it is this that must speak now'. Taking an oath on pistol and Quran was pivotal to the ritual of Muslim Brotherhood members' admission into the secret assassination squad *al-Gihaz el-Khas* ; it was also taken by the conspiring FOA on the night of the 1952 coup.[14] The oath (taken in a dark room before a masked sheikh) meant death for any member who exposes the organisation as explained by the MB leader Al-Banna to army officers joining his group.

The ritualised oath was introduced by Major Mahmoud Labib (1882–1951), the Muslim Brotherhood's agent for military affairs.‡ Nasser praised Labib's essential role on the record, but only after his death. Muslim Brotherhood literature claims that Labib was a founding member of the conspiring officers' group, crediting him with coining the title 'the Free Officers'. This was confirmed by Major Hessein Al-Shafie (1918–2005) of the armoured corps, who was Nasser's and Sadat's vice president (1961–65 and 1968–75).[15] Brotherhood literature hailed Major Labib's activities when he was in Germany in the 1920s, organising anti-British marches claiming to have been joined by Hitler and his supporter[16].

---

*In 1915, Saleh Harb was in the Libyan Desert helping Arab tribes fight the Italians, but he then turned against the British with his tribesmen, who held the Outer Oasis until 1918, before escaping to Turkey and being sentenced to death in absentia. He lived in exile until he was pardoned by King Fuad on the request of Sa'd Zaghloul's government in 1924, returning home with many pardoned Egyptian political exiles.
† As chairman of the Young Men's Muslim Association (founded 1927).
‡ Major Labib had been a member of Hezb al-Watani (see Chapter 45 – 'The British Bombardment – and Occupation') since 1908, before joining the Muslim Brotherhood in 1938. He was close to General Harb as they worked together against the British Army in the Libyan Desert in 1915–18. He too was tried in absentia and sentenced to death for high treason, fleeing to Turkey and then to Germany. He remained in Munich and only returned to Egypt after King Fuad pardoned all Egyptian exiles.

CHAPTER 46
The Bombardment of Alexandria
– and Occupation

Although the Muslim Brotherhood's hatred for the Jews did not extend to the British, they exploited the mounting anti-*les Anglais* emotions inflamed by incidents like that at Ismailia police station or Abdin Palace. This sentiment, increasingly tinged with invocations of Islam, built on earlier mythologies surrounding events like the bombardment of Alexandria and the 1906 Dinshawai incident.[1] The trial of the Dinshawai *fellaheen* is a case in point. The judge was the Christian minister of justice, Boutros Ghali Pasha (1846–1910), who later became the first Egyptian-born Coptic Christian prime minister. He was murdered in 1910 by British-educated pharmacology student Ibrahim Nassif al-Wirdani (1886–1910), marking the first political assassination in Egypt's modern history. The assassin's motives were totally political (Wirdani cited as motives for the murder Ghali Pasha's backing for extending Suez Canal concessions to help ease Egypt's economic burdens and his taking Britain's side over Sudan).

The Muslim Brotherhood (and far-right nationalists) rewrote history, suggesting that assassinating Ghali Pasha* was payback for his presiding

---

* Ghali's assassination almost led to a Muslim–Coptic conflict as Islamists marched chanting 'Muslim Wirdani slew Ghali- el-Nusrani [Nazarite]'. Coptic associations and groups called for a conference in Alexandria in 1911 to deal with threats from Muslims. They were persuaded to drop the idea by Ghali Pasha's son, Wassif Boutros-Ghali (1878–1958). The French law graduate Wassif, who became Egypt's foreign minister five times in Wafd governments (1924, 1928, 1930, 1936 and 1937), was preoccupied with the project of national unity between Copts and Muslims, a cornerstone of the Wafd-led 1919 uprising. Egyptian political folklore still accuses les Anglaises of 'divide and rule' by driving a wedge between Christians and Muslims. Wassif Boutros-Ghali explained to the planning committee of the Coptic conference that not only was his assassinated father against the idea of the conference but also that Wirdani's motives and plans were political rather than

over the Dinshawai trial, which generated strong populist anti-British sentiment at the time.* Wirdani's underground group was a splinter group from Hezb al-Watany (the Nationalist Party), founded in 1907 by Moustafa Kamel Pasha (1874–1908), a staunchly anti-British, French-educated lawyer who promoted the idea of a pan-Islamic league. The pro-Ottoman, caliphate views held by al-Watany were a reactionary response to the launch of the progressive, Egyptian-identity, nationalist Umma (Nation) Party under the motto 'Egypt for the Egyptians'. Umma was founded by a European-educated moderniser elite led by philosopher Ahmed Lutfi el-Sayyed bey (1872–1963). El-Sayyed bey's campaign to raise funds by direct donations succeeded in establishing an independent university. He turned down the officers' request to become president in 1953, branding their coup unconstitutional.[2]

There were hardly any liberals or nationalists with modernising outlooks who believed in pluralist parliamentary democracy among the conspiring FOA leadership – itself, far from being democratic or liberal. The officers belonged, by membership or political belief, to various trends, none of which was democratic. Some followed far-left Marxist groups whose leaders, coming from privileged landowning families or being radical intellectuals, were dismissive of parliamentary democracy. The majority of Naguib led officers were right-wing authoritarians or fascists from Young Egypt or the Muslim Brotherhood, which backed Nazi Germany in the 1940s. Almost all were *fellaheen* admitted to the army for the first time in 75 years when King Farouk relaxed the rules in the late 1930s. The 1880s revolt by Ourabi's group (made up of the sons of *fellaheen* with Islamist and reactionary leanings) set the precedent of Egypt's army controlling the country's political agenda. It also became the blueprint for the 1952 coup; the conspiring officers had learned the lessons of Ourabi's revolt. General Naguib's officers did not move before securing assurances from the Western powers that had the means to influence them in Egypt – namely, America and Britain[3] – to let them overthrow the country's legitimate government.[4] The 1952 coup officers exceeded Ourabi's ambitions, however – they reversed the roles: instead of the government using the army as a tool of foreign policy advancing national interests, the military took over politics completely, using its vast assets to control the country and set the political agenda.

In the 1880s, the Islamic-caliphate concept was the 'glue' holding

---

religious.
*Ghali's presiding over the Dinshawai tribunal was only added as a motive for the assassination to strengthen the defence case by Wirdani's lawyer, Ibrahim el-Helbawi Bey (1858–1940), who was the prosecution barrister on behalf of the British officers in the Dinshawai trial in 1906.

CHAPTER 46   The Bombardment of Alexandria – and Occupation

the Ottoman Empire's peoples and provinces together, despite its being a backward ideology clashing with enlightened identity nationalism as represented by Tawfik and his supporters – mostly in modern Alexandria. But troubles in Alexandria escalated in June 1882, especially with clergy agitators such as Sheikh el-Nedim invoking Islam. Fearing for their safety, British residents approached Charles Cookson (1829–1906), the acting British consul general in Alexandria, for protection.[5] Cookson discussed plans to defend Place Muhammad Ali (where most of the city's consulates were located) with other European consuls and with Greek and British naval officers.

War Office minister Henry Campbell-Bannerman (1836–1908) confirmed to the House of Commons the Admiralty's approval for Sir Beauchamp Seymour, commander of the Royal Navy Mediterranean Squadron, to take over the consulate to protect Cookson and staff.[6] The war ships stationed off the coast of Alexandria was based on recommendation, in September 1881, by the British consul in Cairo, Edward Malet. He was sympathetic to the opposition's calls for constitutional reforms in Egypt. Ourabi's excessive demands and lust for power pushed Malet towards Tawfik Pasha and Gladstone's intervention plans. He sent a telegram to the Gladstone cabinet on 13 February 1882, casting doubt on 'exaggerated reports' that the khedive's position was unstable, and repeated his advice of a show of naval force off Alexandria's coast.[7]

More British and French gunboats[*] arrived at Alexandria Harbour at the beginning of June 1882[8] as part of the European powers initiatives to hold a conference by their ambassadors in Constantinople to respond to Ourabi's unconstitutional challenge to the khedive's authority[9]. Unlike Ourabi, Tawfik saw Europe as a friend of Egypt. The sultan naturally wanted to keep Egypt under Ottoman rule, but he was also aware of Britain's support for Tawfik. So he devised a two-faced policy, sending two diplomatic missions to investigate matters. One was Ali Fuad Bey's mission, with a brief to support the khedive; the other, led by Ali Nizami Pasha, backed Ourabi, who was decorated by the sultan in June and warned by aides to avoid Egypt falling into the hands of foreigners (meaning Europeans).[10] Ourabi and his supporters were not Egyptian nationalists, instead favouring the caliphate, so they regarded Khedive Tawfik as an apostate of Islam and expressed a desire for the Ottoman sultan to depose him.[†]

---

[*] British and French gunboats were already anchored off Alexandria throughout spring 1882 with orders to communicate with their consuls, to support the khedive, and to land a force if the safety of Europeans required.

[†] While playing both parties off against each other, the sultan waited for a couple of months and sided with winners; he denounced Ourabi as a rebel after his defeat by the

On 11 June 1882, a fare dispute between two Alexandrians, a Maltese and his Muslim donkey driver, escalated as each insulted the other's religion – an everyday occurrence in this cosmopolitan city. However, accounts of what happened next vary. The Calcutta-based *Friend of India* reported, 'Serious riots have taken place in Alexandria today. The disturbance originated out of a fight between the natives and Maltese, twenty of the latter being killed and wounded. The English and Italian Consuls were both badly wounded. Order has been restored by the aid of the military'.[11] In another account, 'the Maltese slew his Muslim rival with a knife'[12] – or shot him with a pistol in a third version, resulting in an explosion. Reports varied, but indicated that 'Egyptian natives' – including policemen, and even skilled artisans – began attacking anyone who looked European by dress, shouting pro-caliphate Islamic slogans and calling for the protection of the 'Sultan', and on 'Allah, to destroy the unbelievers'. London-based papers reported serious riots in Alexandria, in which 'natives' armed with *nebabit* (long, thick sticks) attacked Europeans. Several Europeans were killed and wounded, and many houses were destroyed by the rioters. Cookson was injured, and the Greek consul (mistaken for an Englishman) was beaten up, while a navy engineer of from HMS *Superb* was shot dead.

The Greek and British consulates handed out weapons to their nationals, who took refuge in the buildings. The British deputy consul telegraphed, reporting that the Egyptian police had not intervened to protect consulates or Europeans. In London, the government came under pressure. Newspaper headlines reported danger to British subjects, and questions were raised in the Commons as to why the Royal Navy had not intervened to protect lives.[13] The Islamist agitator, Sheikh el-Nedim, held a rally denouncing Khedive Tawfik as 'unfit to rule'. Simultaneously, the Greeks – funded by a wealthy banker, Ambroise Sinadino – started arming themselves for protection.[14] But the consuls asked Admiral Seymour not to land sailors in order to avoid inflaming the situation and provoking further violence. Hence, the European warships' presence was counterproductive to the protection of their nationals.

By nightfall on 12 June, 50 ethnic-European Alexandrians and perhaps as many as 250 Nilotic Egyptians had been killed. Nobody knows the correct figures as Muslims, like Jews, bury their dead before sunset – thus, no accurate counts were made. Two days later, Khedive Tawfik arrived as part of the usual summer move of the capital to Alexandria. Ourabi's troops began to patrol the streets in order to do what the police had failed to do. Ourabi himself arrived three days later

---

British in September 1882.

CHAPTER 46 The Bombardment of Alexandria – and Occupation

and drove through Alexandria to a hero's welcome in the same carriage used by the khedive and drove in the streets as Tawfik did; although he had denounced the khediviate dynasty in Cairo two days earlier[15]. Ourabi's troops were reported to have helped many Europeans to take refuge aboard ships in the harbour. Why Ourabi didn't encourage them to stay ashore in Alexandria, to act as a human shield against bombardment, remains a mystery. Correspondence between consuls indicates that by 17 June, no fewer than 20,000 European and Levantine Alexandrians had moved onto the European ships for safety.

Historians still disagree over who was responsible for the violence, which provided the British with a pretext for intervention. Was it Ourabi, for his failure (or reluctance) to maintain law and order when he had the means at his disposal to do so? Was it Alexandria's governor, Omar Lutfi Pasha, who Wilfred Blunt suggests[16] 'deliberately' failed to nip the troubles in the bud in order to portray Ourabi as unwilling to maintain law and order?

No conspiring had been needed for the explosion, however. Inflammatory rhetoric from Islamists like Sheikh el-Nedim had agitated (less-educated) Muslims against non-Muslims (mostly Europeans). Many of the latter ill-treated (mostly Muslim) Nilotic Egyptians, while the powerful consuls in the city did little to control their Europeans subjects (who were often armed by consulate staff). It was a tinderbox waiting for a spark.[17]

Ourabi, el-Nedim and the al-Azhar sheikhs accused Cookson (who gave arms to several Britons and Maltese on 11 June) of collusion with Tawfik and Alexandria governor, Omar Lutfi Pasha, in organising the riots as a pretext for intervention. But Islamic theologian-reformist Sheikh Mohammed Abdou (1849–1905), who was exiled by the British and Tawfik for six years, discounted any motive on the part of Cookson other than defending British subjects.[18] Admiral Seymour claimed he needed protection after a one of his crew* was killed in the riots in Alexandria. On 4 July, Seymour sent 'a menacing demand', in which he threatened to bombard Alexandria unless coastal forts were disarmed and handed over to British forces.[19]

As expected, the Egyptian cabinet – headed by Khedive Tawfik himself – rejected Seymour's demand and decided to resist after meeting in Ras el-Tin Palace with the sultan's representative, Dervish Pasha. Tawfik had no choice in reality, since Egypt's government could not have accepted an unlawful demand by a foreign naval admiral. On 10 July, all European ships left Alexandria's waters. The French

---

* Reports on his identity differ: some claimed he was an engineering assistant, others suggested he was a personal valet to Seymour.

decided not to join the British action and sailed, with French consulate staff on board, to Port Said. Although the French lost politically, they won, what is known in modern times as 'the hearts and minds' of the Egyptians; Egypt, collectively, kept thinking in French and remained culturally French in many aspects, until this day despite 70 years of British control.

At 07:00 on 11 July, the bombardment commenced and went on until 17:15, destroying most of central Alexandria – including the British and French consulates – and silencing Ourabi's artillery, which was no match for the modern British weaponry.[20] The following morning, the 98-gun HMS *Temeraire* reconnoitred, then was joined by the 64-gun HMS *Inflexible* when Hospital Fort battery reconstituted its defences. Although most of Alexandria's 11 forts were flying white flags, HMS *Britten* signalled that negotiations (for a ceasefire arranged for 14:50 on 12 July) had failed and that bombardment was to resume.[21] As a result, a fire erupted in the wealthy commercial centre of town and was fanned by the wind. Wealthy Egyptian merchants' houses and stores were not spared as they were looted alongside the Italian, Austrian and French consulates, post offices, hospitals and schools. This included the homes of Portuguese consul Comte Max de Zogheb and Nubar Pasha. Most of Alexandria's residents had left – Europeans by boat and Egyptians by train and road to Cairo, which was still ruled by its pro-Ottoman politicians. There were reports that some of Ourabi's soldiers had joined Muslim Alexandrians enraged by the bombardment in looting and killing.[22] Ourabi neither made a stand to stop the initial 400 British marines and sailors from landing nor tried to protect the city, unilaterally or in arrangement with Seymour as part of the ceasefire he requested. Instead, he withdrew most of his troops around 13:00 on 12 July, leaving Alexandria unprotected[23]. In addition to looting and burning buildings, mobs of Arab-Bedouins and people from out of town also threw fine artworks onto the streets or set them on fire. There was a three-day gap between Ourabi's withdrawal and the first British troops' landing on 14 July to restore order; they were joined a few days later by troops from the garrison in Cyprus, beefing up their numbers to 3,800 by 20 July.[24]

Tawfik had been at the Mustafa Pasha Palace and barracks in Ramleh.* He returned with the cabinet to central Alexandria on 13

---

* Nasser renamed it after Mustafa Kamel, the pro-Ottoman old National Party leader. The barracks were initially named after the palace of Tawfik's French-educated (at the Paris Egyptian Mission School) uncle, Mustafa Bahgat Fazil Pasha (1830–1875), who was named heir apparent in 1863 when Ismail Pasha was the khedive but deprived of the throne when the line of succession was changed by the Porte in Constantinople to run father-to-son (Tawfik). Mustafa Pasha protested by leaving Egypt for France, where

CHAPTER 46 The Bombardment of Alexandria – and Occupation

July, accompanied by his cavalry. Some British marines who landed the next day were dispatched to join Tawfik's cavalry in Ras el-Tin; among them was 32-year-old Lieutenant Horatio Herbert Kitchener. His knowledge of Turkish and Arabic proved valuable in communication for many years to come.

Alexandria entered a chapter of her history dominated by British influence, which lasted over half a century and peaked during the Second World War. In the 1880s, the British garrison troops were stationed in Mustafa Pasha Barracks, Moharrem-Bey and Sidi Bishr camps. The two harbours became an essential base for the Royal Navy; which proved to be strategically vital, during the Second World War. In 1901, a former Royal Navy officer, Sir George Morice Pasha, became the port-authority director.[25] By the start of the Great War, a quarter of Alexandria's police force was British; many others were Italians, having served since the 1850s.[26]

---

he became the patron for the radical Young Ottomans/Turks. (Yeni Osmanlilar) group in opposition to the Porte. He then returned to Egypt and became finance minister in 1869, then the minister of justice for one year in 1871.

CHAPTER 47
The Alexandria–Misr Rift

The Road to the 1952 Coup

There was little discussion in the Gladstone cabinet on the dispropor-tionate use of force, especially after Ourabi's guns were silenced on 12 July. The situation in 1882 was also different from that in 1802, when Britain had pulled out of Alexandria after defeating the French – even letting French scholars and scientist[1] keep their boxes full of artefacts, drawings and studies of Egyptian sites. The term 'international law' was not much in use in the 1880s; there was no United Nations, only the calculation that the threat of another superpower intervention would serve as a deterrent.

As Tawfik and the British were consolidating their positions in Alexandria, Cairo remained loyal to the Ourabists and their caliphate concept. Instead of using nationalist terms like *Moqawma* or *Defa'h* (resistance or defence), Cairo declared '*gihad*' (Arabic jihad, meaning an Islamic crusade) against Alexandria, denouncing Khedive Tawfik as a traitor. The official *Egyptian Gazette* led the call to arms – 'Make haste, O people of Islamic ardour' – and quoted Quranic war verses to fight 'the unbelievers'[2]. Cairo's notables – the al-Azhar *ulama* and the equally reactionary Coptic Church – declared a new government headed by Ourabi Pasha in the city, while Alexandria, assisted by the British, began preparations to confront the Ourabist forces surrounding her. Gladstone's cabinet in 1882 claimed that occupation would be temporary, to restore Khedive Tawfik's legitimate rule, and an expedition force led by General Sir Garnet Wolseley (1833–1913) was dispatched. The 'temporary occupation' lasted 73 years.

Alexandria's newspapers, loyal to Tawfik in the summer of 1882, reflected gratitude to the British as friends and protectors.

CHAPTER 47   The Alexandria–Misr Rift

'A spy carrying instructions from Ourabi was arrested in Gabbari, near the western harbour', reported *Phare d'Alexanadrie* on 11 September 1882. *Al-Ahram* ran the same report, but added, 'Les Anglais arrest agents and spies working for Ourabi on daily basis, this shows how alert they were in protecting the city'. Reflecting the official position, the *Egyptian Gazette* reported on 5 September 1882 that 11 Egyptian officers who fought against the British at Tel-El-Kebier had left Ourabi's side and sworn allegiance to the khedive. *Al-Ahram* reported that middle- and lower-ranking officers were growing increasingly unhappy about Ourabi's association with rebellious Arabs (Bedouin tribes), causing trouble on the southern edge of Lake Mareotis.[3] It praised *les Anglais* 'for lifting Egyptian corpses with respect and burying them with dignity', adding that these had been thrown into the Ismailia Canal 'by the rebels', whose act the paper invited its readers to compare with the 'humanity showed by les Anglais'.[4] This incident followed one of the battles at Tel el-Kebier between 'the Ourabi-led rebels', who numbered about 15,000, and *les Anglais*, who lost 2 dead and 54 injured against an estimated 35 rebels.

Alexandria's papers condemned Ourabi's action of hauling earth and debris to block part of the Ismailia Canal and reported the arrival of more British troops, saying that General Wolseley's troops had surrounded and stormed the rebels' fortifications and were chasing them. *Al-Ahram* published the details of the Porte's order to arrest Ourabi and exile him for treason, causing the British intervention and starting the land war. The papers reported British Consul General Malet warning European consuls in Alexandria to rein in their nationals and stop them attacking Egyptians.[5]

In addition to the Ismailia police-headquarters incident in 1952, which was small and confined when compared with the events of 1881 and 1882 in Alexandria, another major incident was the burning of Europeanised central Cairo on 25 January 1952 by the Muslim Brotherhood and other Islamic-leaning activists and some army officers from the FOA, according to Nasser's collaborators who later fell out with him.[6] These arson attacks, followed by ransacking and small-scale rioting, were later discovered to have covered for the looting of expensive stores. Alexandria, where Islamists had no base or support in 1952, did not witness any rioting and kept calm. The military coup was initially planned by the FOA for early 1955 because the officers could not dent the popularity of Nahas Pasha's Wafd government, but the burning of khediviate central Cairo led to the government's resignation.[7] The military brought their coup forward, and the fires were cited by Naguib and Nasser to justify it.[8] The incident also strengthened the Muslim Brotherhood's hand in the country.

Ourabi, who never called for Egypt's independence, nor made a stand in Alexandria when his army outnumbered the British marines twentyfold, was held by Nasser's military regime in more generous and higher esteem than true nationalist leaders like the Wafd leader Zaghloul Pasha, who led the 1919 revolution that secured Egypt's independence in 1922. The Zaghloul-Pasha-led Wafd party was elected in a landslide victory in 1924, winning 179 of the 211 parliamentary seats. Egyptian newspapers in 1924 called the event 'The Nation's Day'. *Al-Ahram's* headline flagged up the vote by stating that 'the day completes a chapter that started on 15th May 1808 when representatives of all trends and strata of Egypt endorsed Muhammad Ali to start the victorious journey of a triumphant struggle and progress raising the nation's flag everywhere'. Although the patriotic rhetoric was romantic, the paper was surprisingly impartial, advising the readers to vote for the candidate whose credentials they thought would best serve their constituents. This was in marked contrast to the same paper's reporting 42 years earlier, when it condemned Ourabi and the rebels. Representative democracy, which was celebrated in 1924, proved to be anathema to the military regime 30 years later.

On 22 July 1952, Hessein Serry Pasha (1894–1960) – who had, as Egypt's 25th prime minister, led the government (1940–2) during the Second World War until *les Anglais* forced King Farouk to replace him with their friend, Nahas Pasha – tendered the resignation of his three-week-old government. *Al-Ahram*, which went to print before the conspiring officers took over, reported on 23 July that the king had called the independent Naguib el-Hilaly Pasha (1891–1958) – who had been Egypt's 29th prime minister – from his Alexandria home (six bus stops along Route 25 from our villa) to form a government. El-Hilaly Pasha had resigned 20 days earlier.

Al-Ahram's 23 July 1952 edition reported Egypt and France voting against Britain in the Hague International Court of Justice (ICJ). Britain had sued Iran for nationalising its 51% share in the 1908-founded Anglo–Persian Oil Company (renamed the Anglo–Iranian Petroleum Company in 1935) but it was decided, by nine votes to five, that the case wasn't within the ICJ's jurisdiction. The newspaper also reported, with reference to Iran's democratically elected prime minister, 'Dr Mosaddeq's parliamentarian popular Victory in Iran', and the Shah asking him to form a government.

CHAPTER 48
The 'Voice' of the Coup

On 23 July 1952, Papa and my grandfather, contrary to their custom, weren't debating over the morning papers that they had discarded on the veranda coffee table but were in deep discussion about the army, the king and *Yuzbashi* (captain) Anwar Sadat. At 07:30, Radio Cairo had been interrupted by Captain Sadat pushing the newscaster aside and reading the first declaration of the military officers' 'action' to take over the government in the name of the chief of staff, Major-General Mohammed Naguib Bey. Army tanks had surrounded Broadcasting House on Rue Sherifien and the Marconi Electronics building housing the transmission equipment and placed armed guards in both.

'A Peaceful Military Action by the Army' said *Al-Ahram's* front-page splash the following day (24 July 1952), adding that Major-General Naguib Bey had replaced Hydar Pasha (1888–1957) as a chief of staff.

'The new military leadership contacted the American and British embassies,' the newspaper reported, quoting an unnamed Army HQ source, 'assuring the two embassies that the Army action was exclusively internal, to carry [out] radical reforms and not connected with, or affected by, any external factors. The two embassies were satisfied by the Army assurance.'[1]

My grandfather and father initially agreed that it was a palace coup by King Farouk to control the government after recognising the voice on the radio. The 33-year old Anwar Sadat had been promoted to captain by the king, who had reinstated him to the army 30 months earlier.* Besides the rebellious officers, Sadat joined other underground groups with conflicting ideologies and aims. He trained *Gama'at el-Ightialat*

---

* Sadat was promoted to major by Naguib Bey on the morning of the coup.

(the Assassinations Group – AG), which murdered the Wafd finance minister, Amin Osman Pasha (1898–1946), and attempted to assassinate his equally pro-British wartime prime minister, Nahas Pasha, on several occasions.[2] The group had been founded by the 20-year-old aristocrat Hessein Tawfik (1925–1983), son of Ahmed Tawfik Pasha, a minister in the Department of Transport. Among the AG was Mohammed Ibrahim Kamel (1927–2001), who later resigned as foreign minister of Egypt (1977–8), objecting to the signing of a peace treaty with Israel. Sadat was also close to the Muslim Brotherhood and the shady armed *Al-Haras Alhadidi* (the Iron Guard), who took orders directly from the palace, although most of their operations were unsuccessful due to internal squabbles and differing ideologies – ranging from far-right to extreme left.

The Guard had assassinated the Muslim Brotherhood leader Hassan al-Banna in February 1949 after the MB, on his orders, carried out a series of bombings and murders of judges and politicians including Egypt's 27th prime minister, Fahmy el-Nakrashi Pasha. But Al-Banna's followers were careful not to leave behind forensic evidence that would be admissible against their leader in a court of law. In addition to setting the area around Place de Opera alight in 1952, almost all of the Brotherhood's violent activities were terror attacks against fellow Egyptians – Jews and Christians – like the bombing of Cinema Metro, which killed several people in May 1947. The MB carried out attacks on Jewish-owned department stores with dynamite in summer 1948 – including Cicurel, (David) Dawoud Ads, Benzion and Gatteno, and Me'adi Land Company's head office. Besides bombing the Jewish quarter in Cairo, claiming many lives, the Brotherhood also destroyed the offices of the Société Orientale de Publicité and threw hand grenades at Cairo police chief Salim Zaki's automobile[3]. In March 1948, Sheikh Al-Banna ordered the murder of Judge al-Khazendar, head of the Alexandria appeal court. Al-Khazendar had, a year earlier, presided over a hearing that upheld the lower-court jailing of MB members on terror charges.[4] Al-Banna's men were so ruthless that they threw hand grenades at the judge's neighbours, who chased and cornered them.[5]

Nakrashi Pasha, during his second ministry in 1948, acted under martial law (imposed when war with Israel broke out) to dissolve the Muslim Brotherhood as a terrorist group; this followed a police raid on their premises that exposed the extent of their involvement in terrorism.[6]

The twice prime minister, Nakrashi split from the Wafd party in 1938 along with his predecessor, Ahmed Maher (Mahir) Pasha, and established the Saadist Institutional Party. Maher, Egypt's 26th prime minister, was assassinated by a Muslim Brother (a defector from

Wafd) for declaring war on Germany. Nakrashi, as prime minister (9 December 1946–28 December 1948) had objected to attacking Israel. There were calls in the media to block Israeli independence (generated mostly by the Brotherhood and pro-Nazi elements in the Egyptian establishment). King Farouk was coming under public pressure from Islamist-led demonstrations calling for war against the Jewish state. Besides breaching UN resolutions, Nakrashi Pasha argued, a war would harm the national interest by losing government friends at home and abroad.[7] Nakrashi feared that a state declaring war on 'the Jewish gangs'[8] would lend them legitimacy[9] and speed the free world's recognition of Israel.* The intelligence service had advised Prime Minister Nakrashi pasha against involving the army in a guerrilla war,[10] preferring clandestine support if he wanted to help the Palestinians. They suggested backing the Khartoum-born Brigadier Ahmed Abd-el-Azizi (1907–1948), who retired from commanding the Eighth Brigade in order to train (mostly Islamist of several nationalities) volunteers 'to fight the Jews in Palestine'. The operation was run on the Egyptian side by air force intelligence and army officers with Islamist leanings.†

The Iron Guard
The origins of the pro-Farouk Iron Guard can be traced back to the 1930s, when several Egyptian officers were recruited into the Iron Guard of Egypt (IGE) by Aribert Heim (1914–1992) when he had secret funds in Cairo.[11] When Heim was exposed, after the War, as 'Dr Death' for his experiments at Mauthausen Concentration Camp, the Austrian doctor escaped to Latin America and then to Egypt – converting to Islam and living in Cairo from 1956 onwards as Tarek Faried Hessein.[12]

The members of the revived Iron Guard that emerged in the 1940s were motivated by anti-British feelings, but most had sympathies with far-right tendencies corresponding to Islamism.[13] The outfit was the brainchild of Farouk's personal physician, navy doctor Youssef Rashad, and his manipulative, attractive wife, Nahid Rashad (b 1917).[14] Mrs Rashad was made lady-in-waiting for Farouk's sister, Princess Fawzia, after the latter escaped her unhappy marriage in Iran. The Rashads

---
*Egypt did not officially recognise Israel until 30 years later, in the peace treaty signed 26 March 1979 following de facto recognition with President Sadat's 20 November 1977 visit to Jerusalem.
† These included lft Abed-el-Menem el-Naggar a member of the FOA; pro-Islamist Captain Kemal el-Dine Hessein, a 2nd Artillery officer (and Nasser's education minister); Muslim Brotherhood military-liaison officer Abd-el-Hady Shaaban; and Captain Abed-el-Azizi Hammad, who became head of the presidential palace administration under Naguib.

recruited loyal army officers for the Iron Guard to gather military intelligence for the king, who did not trust *les Anglais* or their allies, Nahas Pasha and his Wafd ministers. The British were spreading anti-Farouk propaganda – mostly what we would now call 'fake news' – inventing stories about the King's corruption and immoral lifestyle.

Dr Rashad later became head of royal palace security, while his wife gained Farouk's confidence. In a report to the king, Mrs Rashad exaggerated Sadat's role as a 'patriot', helping the clandestine work of the Iron Guard against *les Anglais* and their collaborators. She was behind Sadat's reinstatement to the army, from which body he had been dismissed in 1946 whilst standing trial for Osman Pasha's assassination. Mrs Rashad subsequently turned double agent – working with her FOA-member lover, the extreme Marxist-internationalist-turned-anarchist Captain Moustafa Kemal Sidqi.[15] An undisciplined, violent, drunkard womaniser, Captain Sidqi was later sectioned by the officers' regime because he was against fighting Israel.

'Why should Egyptian workers fight their equally exploited Jewish workers for the benefit of the imperialists?' asked one of his 'incriminating' pamphlets, found in a home shared with his wife, the celebrity dancer Taheyyah Carioca (1915–1999), when she was arrested in 1953 by the military coup regime. Carioca was released four months later for lack of evidence.[16] Most pre-1952 groups regarded the captain as unstable and too unpredictable to be trusted. Another secret group was established by the palace within the ranks of the police, led by Brigadier Mohammed Wasfi, who planned to assassinate Captain Sidqi before the 1952 coup put an end to such internal fighting. Sadat's links in this web of spies and assassins led many, like Papa and my grandfather, to believe that the coup was Farouk's move against the opposition. But the third president of Egypt proved to be a Machiavellian 'chamaeleon', who, repeatedly, repositioned his sails to catch a favourable wind.

CHAPTER 49
The Spy, the Officer, his Dancer and her Lover

Sadat's 1946 arrest in connection with the assassination of Osman Pasha wasn't the first. He was jailed during the War for organising an attempt to fly General Aziz al-Misri Pasha (1879–1965), along with the Allies' war plans to General Rommel, who was advancing on Alexandria from the Libyan Desert in 1942. The plot failed when the aircraft developed a mechanical failure and crash-landed in the desert. The arrest of the pilot led to Sadat's arrest.

The conspirators on that occasion included Egyptian, British and European anarchists known at the time by the amusing label the rebellious left-wing imperialists. The best known among them was Count László Almásy (1895–1951), an Austro-Hungarian explorer and pilot who had mapped the Libyan–Egyptian Desert and was a socialite in the high societies of Cairo and Alexandria[1]. Knowingly or naively, the anarchists were used by German spies who met them at the *dahabiya* (houseboat) of Egypt's top star, Hikmet Fahmy (1907–1974), who spied for Rommel[2]. Fahmy was a top society celebrity, often travelling in a motorcade followed by media photographers. Sadat was a first lieutenant in the Signals Corps of the Egyptian military intelligence. His friends – the Irish-American Peter Muncaster (who was, in fact, the German spy Hans Gerd Sandstede) and Hassan Gaafer Bey (who was the German spy Hans Eppler, 1914–1999) – had asked Sadat to fix a broken radio-communication transmitter, which was vital to the operation, at Fahmy's houseboat.[3] Alexandria-born Eppler was the adopted son of a wealthy Egyptian father from an influential family and a German mother. Sadat later noted in his diaries[4] that the transmitter was hidden inside a gramophone and could still transmit upside down when the gramophone was playing.

The two disguised Germans and the officers frequently met at the Kit-Kat, a top Cairo nightclub by the Nile, where other Egyptian and British army officers watched Fahmy perform. The Kit-Kat was also frequented by wealthy Egyptians (sometimes escaping German air raids on Alexandria), spies, Jewish underground activists and smugglers from many different communities in central Cairo's cosmopolitan society. Fahmy was also reported to have performed in Vienna nightclubs in the 1938-39 attended by top German officers, including Heinrich Himmler (1900–1945)[5]. She was introduced to the Germans by a new lover she had met in Austria, the Alexandrian half-German Hassan Gaafer.[6]

Sadat and air force pilot Hassan Ezzat became close friends during their service in Sudan, then part of the Egyptian Kingdom. Flight Lieutenant Ezzat recruited Sadat and others to his underground group, the Patriotic Officers (PO), who assassinated *les Anglais* and their collaborators. The PO joined the FOA (Free Officers Action) after the War[7] Sharing Fahmy's and her friends' hatred of *les Anglais*, the two officers were instrumental in flying General al-Misri Pasha to meet Rommel. They recruited pilots angered by pressure to dismiss al-Misri as chief of staff. Al-Misri, of Circassian ethnic background, was fluent in Turkish, German and Arabic. He had worked with Thomas Edward Lawrence 'of Arabia' (1888–1935); together, they had taken British arms to Arab tribesmen led by Sherif Hussein of Mecca (1853–1931) to rebel against the Ottomans in he Great War.[8] Al-Misri helped the army officers plotting their coup, and was recognised by Nasser as their godfather. Nasser wanted al-Misri to replace Naguib as president, but he retired in 1954 after serving as an ambassador to Moscow in 1953.[9]

Al-Misri – and Egypt in the Second World War

Al-Misri had been a military guardian to Crown Prince Farouk when he attended the Royal Military Academy in Woolwich (1935-6) – and, ironically, in 1935 was commended by the then-British High commissioner, Sir Miles Lampson (1880–1964). King Fuad I wanted al-Misri to guide the 14-year-old prince to 'grow up like ordinary people' as he was concerned about the lavish lifestyles of Hassanein Bey and Madame Hassanein, who were keeping house with the prince. Al-Misri was 'known as a strict disciplinarian', wrote Lampson in June 1935 after his audience with King Fuad before sending Prince Farouk for military training in England.[10] Sending sons for military training in Europe was a tradition in the dynasty. The young Fuad, who was considered for Albania's throne, received his military training at the Italian Military Academy in Turin while living with Ismail Pasha in exile in Italy. Ironically, when Victor Immanuel III was removed, he chose

CHAPTER 49   The Spy, the Officer, his Dancer and her Lover

Alexandria. When Farouk abdicated six years later, he also sailed from Alexandria to exile in Italy. Lampson and Fuad wanted more English influence to balance the court's Italian and German effects on young Farouk.[11] But the relationship between Lampson – who became an ambassador after the 1936 treaty – and Farouk was to deteriorate badly during the War in a way that harmed Anglo–Egyptian joint interests.

In 1940, when Britain called on Egypt to join the Second World War Allies as stipulated by the 1936 treaty, Maher Pasha's government refused to join 'unless Italy attacked Egyptian territory'. Although it was officially neutral, Egypt was the main base for British military operations in North Africa and the Levant. Despite this neutrality, the Luftwaffe and Italian Air Force carried out deadly air raids on Alexandria in summer 1940, and the Egyptian press criticised the government's lack of transparency in concealing the number of casualties from these raids on Alexandria.[12] Ironically, the forces of Italian dictator Benito Mussolini (1883–1945) crossed the Libyan border into Egypt within a few weeks, and the Italians and Germans began subjecting Alexandria to relentless air attacks from nearby airfields in the Libyan Desert. The removal of General al-Misri was a wise move. Some officers in the Egyptian Armoured Corps near El-Alamein discussed whether or not to follow their orders to protect the southern flank of the British forces against Rommel's advancing Afrika Korps in May and June 1942 – according to Major Hessein Al-Shafie, who had been trained in England in 1938.[13] The British troops withdrew in disarray, leaving much gear and equipment behind, to make a stand at El-Alamein, the narrowest passage towards Alexandria. But the Egyptian Armoured Corps were disciplined and stood their ground, protecting the southern flank of the Allies south of El-Alamein. Meanwhile, the Egyptian Corps of Engineers were clearing mines dropped by the Germans in harbours and the Suez Canal.

Apart from ideological Islamo-Fascists and those attracted to Nazi ideas, many Egyptians sympathised with the Germans only to spite *les Anglais*. The young King Farouk was still very popular in 1940 with his social activities setting up charities, modernising projects, educational improvements and social services. He was putting his own money into charitable projects, and his sisters were founding hospitals, orphanages and schools. In November 1940, Egypt was officially neutral in the War despite the Luftwaffe attacks on Alexandria and the Suez Canal.

The 20-year-old Farouk was reluctant to join the conflict, so he called upon the independent Serry Pasha to invite other party leaders to head a coalition government, excluding the pro-British Wafd party. Lampson pressed King Farouk to replace Serry Pasha's government with a Wafd administration led by his friend,

Nahas Pasha.[14] Nahas-led Wafd was the most popular party in Egypt; Lampson thought it would be more effective in swinging public opinion behind the Allies and against the Axis powers, thus reducing the influence of pro-German elements among the King's circle.[15] When Farouk resisted the idea, Lampson obtained London's permission to have British Army tanks surround the palace on 4 February 1942, forcing the king to summon Nahas to form a government.[16] The incident backfired as it turned away a large section of public opinion, pushing more Egyptians into supporting pro-Axis groups at the expense of liberal political parties. Like the bombardment of Alexandria in 1882 and Dinshawai in 1906, with their mythical folkloric additions, the Abdin Palace incident left deep wounds in Egyptians' collective mind.[17] Indeed, during my interview with him, Major-General Naguib mentioned the episode as a turning point in the Egyptian Army's attitude towards Farouk.

When Tobruk fell to Rommel on 21 June 1942, four months after the Abdin Palace incident, Lieutenant Sadat, Flight Lieutenant Ezzat and other officers were drinking at the Kit-Kat Club's bar where Fahmy danced. The newspaper delivery boy announced, 'El-Alman [the Germans] took Tobruk in a single day as he handed the evening papers to the barman and customers. He reportedly approached a table where some British officers were sitting by the 'Egyptian playboy' Hassan Gaafer (the German spy Eppler), saying, 'El-Alman are on their way to Cairo, Sir. Maybe in a few days, Rommel Pasha will be drinking here with his officers.'[18] When the evening papers arrived at the Egyptian Army officers' table, one officer read out a headline loudly whilst the others ordered champagne. Sadat shouted, 'Perform the Tobruk waltz, Hikmet!'[19]

This was on the very day that Churchill was in the United States trying to get help from across the Atlantic. According to Eppler, top officers like General al-Misri, who had been introduced to him by Sadat, used to supply the Germans with useful information. The Kit-Kat was a valuable source to gather intelligence for the German spies; known by his Muslim name, Eppler made sure not to be seen mixing with Sadat and other Nazi-sympathising officers at the club but instead joined his 'friends', the British Army officers.

Flying al-Misri to meet Rommel was part of 'Salaam/Salam', a German military intelligence operation started (31 October 1941- Ended 30 June 1942) with finding a route by Von Almasy of getting two German agents from North Africa into Cairo to obtain information and to arrange for the sympathetic Egyptian general to meet the German field-marshal; its culmination became known as 'Operation Condor'[20]. Condor was - a hidden transmitter using the

CHAPTER 49 The Spy, the Officer, his Dancer and her Lover

novel *Rebecca* by Daphne du Maurier to reset the code daily[21, 22] The operation was run by Gaafer Bey (Eppler), who had joined the German *Abwehr* (military intelligence) as an operator in 1937[23] assistant, the second agent, was the radio operator Hans Gerd Sandstede, disguised as the Irish-American businessman Muncaster. Eppler had a budget of £€ 1 million (U$ 5 million at the time) to cover the operation's expenses and his lavish lifestyle in Cairo,[24] The role of his 1930s Vienna lover Fahmy was crucial.

'Part of her loyalty was our romance, not just her politics', he later boasted in interviews.[25] When the British arrested him after a stand-off at the Nile houseboat (on 24 July 1942), Fahmy spat in his face, pretending not to have any connection with 'this dirty Nazi'. He rewarded her later by buying her a nightclub in Cairo after his release in 1946.[26]

The English Patient
This extraordinary chapter of history, with its real characters and events, has generated television dramas, novels and films; some took poetic licence to extremes. The Egyptian movie *Al-Gassosuah's* (The Spy Dancer) opens with British tanks surrounding the Abdin Palace. Portrayed as a patriot, Fahmy hopes that the Germans will make a pact with the Egyptians to end 60 years of British occupation. But, still under the watchful eye of the Mubarak regime – part of the military coup First Republic – the 1994 film's false and vindictive portrayal of King Farouk as a cartoon pantomime villain bears no relation to reality.

The 1960 British war film *Foxhole in Cairo*, starring the Mexican dancer and actress Gloria Mestre (1928–2012) as Fahmy (renamed Amina), is much closer to actual events – apart from a fictional subplot about a British Army unit 'busting' the German relay transmission truck and intercepting transmission. In reality, the German spies called Sadat to repair the transmitter at Fahmy's home because it had not received the expected coded signal from Rommel's HQ. In fact, there was nothing wrong with the radio equipment;[27] the messages sent by Condor were received correctly, but the German officer in charge of the operation – known only as 'Angelo', and whose identity was never revealed – had ordered all radio stations in the Libyan Desert not to reply to messages.[28] The British, on the other hand, *did* intercept Condor's transmissions by a young intelligence analyst Jean Howard at Bletchley Park, but couldn't decode them in time before all German stations became silent on the orders of the agent Angelo[29]. Sadat thought that the two Germans most probably did not really want to send messages but were in Cairo simply to have a good time.[30]

Alexandria Adieu

The 1959 German film *Rommel ruft Kairo* (Rommel Calls Cairo) was more sympathetic to Colonel Nasser's revised version of history.

Using many Egyptian actors and actresses, *Rommel Calls Cairo* did away with historical accuracy and presented Fahmy and others in fictional oriental costumes closer to Islamic tastes, with no resemblance to the authenticity of Cairo's fashion and culture in 1942. Several Nazi officers had moved to Egypt after the War and, having been given new identities, were playing a significant role in Nasser's anti-Jewish and anti-British propaganda. After consulting the former Nazi advisers in Cairo, the Egyptians put their conditions to the filmmakers to permit filming in Egypt.[31] *Rommel Calls Cairo* presented a false picture of Egypt's socio-cultural life, showing 1940s Cairo as a purely Islamic city with little modern European influence. It was rewriting the past to fit Nasser's narrative, justifying pro-Nazi Islamists' actions and their violence against the forces of the free world armies, and the expressions in the movie were also altered to sound closer to the military regime's 'Newspeak'.

Yet another version was presented in the 1970 French movie *Le Mur de l'Atlantique* (The Atlantic Wall). But the most colourful adaptation of this episode – with a broader Hollywood licence – came in the 1996 film *The English Patient*, based on the novel by Michael Ondaatje (b.1943). It presented Count László Almásy, played by Ralph Fiennes, as a romantic hero; however, in the MI6 file on the group of plotters, he is referred to as 'a shabbily dressed homosexual bungling German intelligence officer with a fat and pendulous nose, drooping shoulders and a nervous tic'.[32] Ironically, it was the British intelligence who helped Almásy escape from Hungary when he was arrested after the War by getting Ala'eddin Moukhtar, a cousin of King Farouk to bribe Hungarian communist officials to release him[33]. Almásy's name was mentioned in a coded message deciphered at Bletchley Park, the UK's wartime code-breaking centre in Buckinghamshire, as a pilot making a dramatic flight to the Great Pyramid at Giza to extract two Hungarian agents.[34] Eppler was arrested with the others and was sentenced to death, but his influential family persuaded King Farouk to reduce the sentence to 10 years imprisonment. He was released in 1946 and immediately contacted by the KGB, but he declined the offer and moved to France[35]. When the 1942 al-Misri plot failed, Ezzat and Sadat were arrested alongside the German spies and Fahmy in July that year. The pair were imprisoned in *Sign el-Aganeb* (the 'aliens' jail'), where they recruited the jail officer, First Lieutenant Khalid Mohey el-Dine (1922–2018), who later joined the FOA.[36] Helped by Mohey el-Dine, the two escaped and changed their names and appearances Ezzat was

CHAPTER 49   The Spy, the Officer, his Dancer and her Lover

driving a lorry delivering supplies to British camps, while Sadat was his loading assistant. They were also gathering details and information about *les Anglais* to be given to anti-British underground groups.[37] The charges against the pair dropped in September 1945 when the state of emergency was lifted at the end of The Second World War; they resurfaced again a few months later[38].

CHAPTER 50
Plotters, Assassins and Fascists

Most Egyptian nationalist groups of the 1930s and 40s were more interested in fighting each other than fighting *les Anglais*. When the extreme right-wing Young Egypt founded the 'Green Shirts' as their para-military wing in 1935, the centrist Wafd party responded two years later by establishing he 'Blue Shirts' to defend itself against. Both groups went underground when all para-military groups were banned in 1938. The most violent extremist group was the Islamo-fascist *al-Gihaz al- serri* (Special Service – SS), the clandestine assassination squad of the Muslim Brotherhood. The Blues were, like Wafd during the War, pro-British. The Brotherhood never attacked British targets but targeted Egyptians instead – including Muslims. There were various loosely connected cells of zealous young Egyptians like the teenagers' AG (Assassinations Group), targeting British soldiers and British military vehicles with improvised firebombs in a disorganised, sporadic fashion.

Flight Lieutenant Ezzat, held in high esteem by the older Egyptian generation, used to drive with lieutenants Mohey el-Dine and Sadat at night near the army barracks 'and shoot, shoot, at *les Anglais* and their collaborators', Ezzat told me in 1983.[1] Their assassination campaign extended from the canal zone to Cairo, 'liquidating collaborators'. However, Mohey el-Dine edited out these assassinations from his 1982 memoir.[2]

Ezzat's book, which detailed several army officers' participation in terror attacks and plotting with the Nazis and the Muslim Brotherhood – and Nasser's role in arson attacks – was banned and had all copies confiscated by the FOA's 'Revolutionary Command Council' when Nasser appointed himself prime minister and minister of the interior

CHAPTER 50   Plotters, Assassins and Fascists

in April 1954. Ezzat and Mohey el-Dine were forced into exile and remained 'in the cold' for years. Ezzat, who settled in Italy running a marine-engineering consultancy, had fallen out with Sadat when the latter vetoed a proposal by the Revolutionary Command Council (RCC – the leadership of the FOA coup) to make him head of the Air Force. Sadat argued that the idealistic, romantic-nationalist Ezzat would prove inflexible in the post if political expediency called for pragmatism. Ezzat, and Mohey el-Dine, whose tanks had secured central Cairo on the night of the coup, in fact opposed the Arabisation of Egypt and were critical of Nasser's erasing the word 'Egypt' from the official name of the state,[3] his economic policy and his involvement in the North Yemen civil war. Following an army coup in 1962 in Yemen, the dethroned Imam Muhammad al-Badr (1926–1996) started resistance from neighbouring Saudi Arabi. Nasser sent over 70,000 troops in support of the coup during a war that lasted until 1970, with the loss of 10,000 Egyptian soldiers and many more civilian lives. The military and economic disaster was later dubbed 'Egypt's Vietnam'[4]

First Lieutenant Sadat was expelled from the army when he was arrested for the second time in 1946 for involvement in assassinating Wafd politician and anglophile Osman Pasha, whom he branded 'a British puppet'. Sadat made 'lists for liquidation', saying to AG assassins – who preferred killing Jews – that killing one collaborators was like killing a 1000 of *les Anglaise* and killing one of the latter equalled killing 1,000 *Yahudis*.[5] The accusation of collaboration with *les Anglais* was a powerful card to play against political opponents, so Sadat overlooked Osman's documented patriotic efforts. During the 1935 and 1936 talks with British High Commissioner Lampson, Osman repeated demands that Britain must agree to pardon students and troublemakers arrested during riots and attacks on British personnel. Over a lunch hosted by the Lampsons[6] for Osman and his British wife, Lady Catherine Gregory, they devised a formula – namely, setting up a commission to re-examine the evidence against the troublemakers for a retrial.[7] Osman also played a significant role in amending drafts of the 1936 treaty to advance Egyptian interests and end affiliation between the embassy and British personnel and officers employed in Egyptian institutions.[8]

Ezzat suggested disguising himself as a Nubian messenger delivering flowers from Lady Lampson and shooting Osman at home while Sadat drives the getaway automobile. The latter disagreed, insisting on a 'public execution' when Osman visited his friends at the British Embassy in order 'to make an example of him'. Fearing civilian casualties in the inevitable crossfire with the police, Ezzat objected. They split, and Sadat recruited zealous AG teenagers whom he was training in firearms use. The AG drafted a Sadat-approved liquidation list of Wafd

379

Alexandria Adieu

leaders who 'betrayed the 1919 revolution by collaborating with *les Anglais*'.⁹ Sadat was charged with conspiracy to murder and tried, in February 1947, along with 16 AG suspects. The 1947–8 trial attracted comprehensive press coverage, especially when AG collaborators tried to assassinate key eyewitnesses and staged a daring armed raid on the court house to snatch legal documents but extracted the wrong files. Tawfik was sentenced in absentia to 12 years. He managed to escape with Sadat, helped by a sympathetic police officer, Salah Zul-Faqqar (1926–1993), who was promoted by the coup regime in 1953; after leaving police service, he was rewarded with leading roles in films subsidised by Nasser.

The Romantic Hero

In the 1947–8 trial, the crown prosecution failed to prove Sadat's direct involvement beyond reasonable doubt, and he walked free. The only evidence was his admitting to training the students on the use of firearms, but he denied any knowledge of their aims. Sadat always arranged an escape hatch, according to Ezzat. On the night of the 1952 coup, Sadat took his wife to a cinema in central Cairo and accused a man of harassing her, staging a fight. He punched the innocent man and insisted on calling the police to make a record of the incident – handy alibi had the coup failed.

The 30-year-old Lieutenant Sadat's anti-British-occupation speech from the dock during the AG assassination trial made him a pin-up for schoolgirls like the 15-year-old Jihan Raouf (1933-2021), daughter of Egyptian surgeon Dr Safwat Raouf and Sheffield-born music teacher Gladys Cotterill. The teenager later became Sadat's second wife when she was still under the age of 16, after meeting him at a summer party. Jihan let her Egyptian half have the better of her English half, believing in the nationalists' slogan 'Egypt for the Egyptians'. It was becoming evident that *les Anglais*' presence was not just a military but a multifaceted dominance of the country's institutions and a set of alliances with the ruling elite. Ironically for the country's cosmopolitan ethnic communities such as Jews and European-educated Egyptians, *les Anglais* were also the protectors of their way of life. The nationalists' hatred for the British extended to middle-class Alexandrians, ethnically non-Nilotic migrants and non-Muslims – especially the Jews.

'The British had built roads from Cairo to canal zone towns and cities and airports and other infrastructure that all Egyptians used,' Jihan Sadat noted, 'but they did little for the majority of *fellaheen*. In rural areas, child mortality was almost 50%, while more than two-thirds of adults had parasites affecting their kidneys and livers from drinking untreated water.'¹⁰ *Les Anglais* have not trained native members of the Egyptian civil service or built the type of institutions that they had in British India. Their presence was one of 'protecting' rather than considering Egypt part of their empire or another 'jewel in the crown'. The bitter irony following the Abdin Palace incident was that anti-Farouk black propaganda (generated by both the British and the country's anti-modernity forces) associated the king with corruption and injustice, and portrayed him as a puppet in the hand of *les Anglais*. In reality, he was very much anti-British to his last day on the throne.

After Sadat's acquittal, his diaries detailing his imprisonment, trial and escape were serialised in *Al-Musawar*. Sadat was given a job by Emile Zidan – the publisher of the parent magazine *Migalat al-Hillal* (The Crescent), a monthly intellectual journal – which he quit when King Farouk reinstated him in the army. There were no intelligence or security checks on Sadat or his associates. This was another error by Farouk, to be added to his many miscalculations – like permitting *fellaheen's* sons into the military against traditional wisdom, thinking they would be his allies against *les Anglais*, dislike for whom had clouded his judgement and led to the growing influence of German sympathisers his court. Until his assassination three decades later, Sadat never really flew his true colours on a recognisable mast. He always proclaimed Egyptian nationalistic slogans – but so did many fascists and misguided, foolish extremists and lone violent activists. Perhaps his subconscious awareness of this matter was at work when choosing the title for his last book, *In Search of Identity*,[11] published shortly before the 'chamaeleon' officer's demise.

CHAPTER 51
The Officers' Conspiracy

Sadat's 23 July 1952 broadcast on behalf of Major-General Naguib Bey appealed for calm.

'The country has passed a most troubled period in history', he said, referring to the army's abysmal performance in the war that Egypt had launched against Israel in 1948. He blamed the defeat on 'agents of corruption'. There was no mention of overthrowing the king, a republic, or a revolution. The coup leaders didn't spin the label 'revolution' until several years later; it was instead 'The Blessed Action', a phrase coined by the Muslim Brotherhood. Farouk's popularity sank in 1949 after he divorced Queen Farida. The British generated rumours that Mrs Rashad[1] had been behind the divorce as part of a campaign to blacken his name following a disagreement on running Sudan while encouraging separatist movements.

Enter the CIA

The months leading up to the coup witnessed several ministerial changes in government. Farouk suspected that Britain and the USA were secretly undermining him[2]. He warned the US ambassador to Cairo, Jefferson Caffery (1886–1974), 'You will be sorry if I get turned out'. Farouk should have realised from the ambassador's cold response that the Americans were up to something. Their strategy was to take over the old European powers' spheres of influence by encouraging changes, mostly by undemocratic means[3][4]

Kermit Roosevelt (1916–2000), a Middle East operative with the CIA, had already reported to Caffery that he was in contact with officers opposed to Farouk, who were not communists and with whom he could do business.[5] Roosevelt had established the network

CHAPTER 51   The Officers' Conspiracy

of American Friends of the Middle East, and successfully plotted and executed operation Ajax, the overthrow of the Iranian nationalist prime minister, Mohammad Mosaddegh (1882–1967).[6] He had met with Colonel Nasser in 1950, and was liaising with him[7]

The CIA operative Miles Copeland repeated to me that Roosevelt tried to persuade King Farouk to stage a palace coup in order to undermine the opposing officers in the army and to regain his popularity by clearing the palace and the government of politicians and pashas whose reputations were tarnished by allegations of corruption[8]. But having failed to penetrate the ring surrounding Farouk, Roosevelt gave up; the CIA placed their bets on the officers, who showed encouraging signs and warmth towards The United States.[9] After reading the CIA brief, Ambassador Caffery decided not to take Farouk seriously as it was only a matter of time before a new regime sympathetic to the US would emerge.[10] Copeland lists many of Nasser's fiery speeches and attacks on regional leaders as predictable, and the way in which Nasser was manipulated into taking apparently radical, revolutionary decisions that actually served American interests.[11]

Copeland also confirmed that Naguib and Ali Sabri (1920–1991),* accompanied by Air Force Intelligence Captain Abd-el-Meneim El-Naggar, met and liaised with British diplomats at the Cairo embassy one week before the coup.[12]

Nasser insisted on changing the phrase 'Anglo–American imperialism' to 'British Imperialism' and on removing all negative references to America in pamphlets issued by the FOA before the 1952 coup.[13] The officers were betting on the United States' anti-colonial attitude, to assist them – it was seen as a 'code' for helping military coups by sympathetic officers to take over the British sphere of influence.[14]

The CIA's contact among the conspiring officers was Captain Abd-el-Mene'm Amin (1912–1996)[15] of the artillery corps; he conveyed the Egyptian officers' admiration of America's role in the world.[16] Amin, 12 days after the coup in 1952, presided over the military tribunal that ordered the summary execution of the Marxist leaders of the striking textile workers[17] and life sentences for the remaining participants.[18] Immediately after the trial, Amin hosted a meeting for Ambassador Caffery, accompanied by CIA officers, with General Naguib and Colonel Nasser to reassure the Americans of their anti-communism credentials.[19] Amin was later marginalised by the regime when he became Egypt's ambassador to the Netherlands, and then to Germany after Nasser overthrew Naguib. Amin resigned

---

* Sabri was a staunch Nasserite. He held several ministerial posts, including prime minister and vice president, and was a secretary-general of the Socialist Federation.

in 1956, accusing Egyptian intelligence of undermining his mission.[20]

Despite reports of suspected conspiracy in the army, the king decided to go ahead with the traditional move to Alexandria as summer life carried on there as usual. Lieutenant-General Hessien Sirry-Amr, the Frontiers Corps commander-general, reported the officers' plotting to defence minister Hydar Pasha. Prime Minister Serry Pasha, who had received a similar report, urged the king to arrest the conspiring officers but Farouk detested the idea. Egyptian royalists accused Hydar Pasha of betraying king and country. He was the maternal uncle of Nasser's closest friend, and later defence minister and vice president, Major Abed el-Hakim Amer (1919–1967).

Hydar played down the officers' reported mutiny as 'a storm in a teacup to do with various wings rivalry within the officers club committee'.[21] In a bid to control it, therefore, Farouk suspended the officers' club's executive committee. The king's miscalculation was based on Hydar Pasha's advice – and on his naive belief in his officers' patriotism, since it was he who had let them into the military ranks that had been previously closed to them. Colonel Nasser himself had had his application to the military academy rejected by the vetting committee, due to a criminal record after having twice been arrested among police troublemakers in Alexandria and Cairo in 1935. Nasser sent an appeal to the palace; he was later admitted to the academy in 1937 by the minister of defence, Ibrahim Kheiry Pasha, who overruled the institution's vetting committee.[22]

Hydar's 'a storm in a teacup' assessment was, however, not entirely irrelevant. In fact, the writing had been on the wall since the officers' club committee elections in January 1952. According to Naguib, his lead officers objected to the nomination of General Sirry-Amr Bey to chair the club committee because he was 'the king's man'.[23] But Sirry-Amr always maintained that Naguib, Nasser and their group fundamentally objected to the mostly Sudanese and Nubian Frontier Corps' representation in the predominantly northern Egyptian officers' club committee.[24] Colonel Nasser tried to assassinate General Sirry-Amr by firing on his car in Cairo on 8 January 1952.[25] The general's younger daughter, Souzy Sirry-Amr Hanem, accused the chief of staff, Hydar Pasha himself, of planning the attempt on her father's life by playing a trick over the phone to get him to where Nasser had set his ambush.

Although it was members of Nasser's cell that opened fire on Sirry-Amr's automobile, the would-be assassins accompanying the colonel were strange bedfellows: left-wing Captain Kemal Rifa'at (1921–1977), later Egypt's ambassador to the UN (1971–4), and Captain Hassan el-Tuhami (1924–2009), of Islamist leanings and later secretary-general of the Islamic Conference but who, following the Yom Kippur War, conducted secret peace talks with the Israelis. Nasser's assassins' cell also included the Alexandria-born Muslim Brotherhood member and pro-Nazi wing commander, Hassan Ibrahim (1917–1990), who had tried to reach Rommel with Gen al-Misri.[26] Nasser, who missed the general and hit a passing woman and her child,[27] fled the scene. He said later in his memoir that he stayed up all night praying for the injured woman not to die.[28] Her screams ringing in his head made him give up the idea of public assassination and focused his mind on arranging a coup instead.[29]

Both British Intelligence and the CIA started working with the conspiring officers in earnest immediately after the officers' club elections crisis.[30] The British were also keen on working with Naguib and Nasser and on getting rid of Farouk, and details have emerged over the last 30 years about British Intelligence aiding the officers to overthrow the king.[31] Eden, for instance, later confirmed that orders were given to British forces in Egypt not to help the country's legitimate head of state uphold the constitution – and his policy was promised to Major-General Naguib in person by British diplomat John Hamilton.[32] Later, in January 1952, according to Copeland, the officers assured the British that Egypt was ready to give up Sudan, then a part of the Nile Kingdom, which was, at the time, at the very heart of the Egyptian Government's dispute with London.[33]

Prime Minister Serry Pasha resigned on 22 July. Farouk called the reformist Naguib el-Hilali Pasha to form a government, which was sworn in at Ras el-Tin Palace at 16:00 the same day.

Time Runs Out
When new reports confirmed the conspiracy, Farouk issued the order to arrest the plotters at 21:00. But it was too late; they brought forward the coup date by a whole month after a warning from their agents.[34] The prime suspects were Mrs Rashad (by telling her lover Captain Sidqi)* and Hydar Pasha.

General Naguib, who replaced Hydar Pasha as chief of staff in the coup regime, spoke of his predecessor with fondness and respect when I interviewed him in 1983. Hydar was not arrested as other top brass were, nor did he have any of his wealth or land touched in the September 1952 land reforms. General Sirry-Amr was (falsely) implicated by the coup officers in an alleged defective-weapons deal. This was a myth concocted by the officers to justify their poor performance in the war with Israel. Sirry-Amr was later cleared by the court in a 1954 trial.[35]

---

*See Chapter 47 – 'The "Voice" of the Coup'.

Nasser was wary of Naguib's popularity in Egypt and with the European powers. Naguib's stand-off with Nasser in 1954 proved that he was genuine in his pledge to restore the country's parliamentary system, thus making him a better choice from the standpoint of the Western powers. This explains Nasser's action, immediately after the Anglo–French ultimatum in October 1956, of taking Naguib from his house arrest north of Cairo to a secret location deep in the desert. General Naguib himself didn't know where he was. Nasser was concerned that *les Anglais* might send their special forces to free Naguib and put him up to contest a swift election.[36]

The 1882 balance of power between the European powers and the Ottoman Empire had shifted by 1952. In the nineteenth century, the British (and other European nations) had been keen to block Ottoman governorates achieving independence as nation-states. By the 1950s, however, the former Ottoman provinces had already become internationally recognised, established states – and Egypt was the most advanced of them in the Levant region. During his 16 years on the throne, Farouk had proved to be more challenging to Britain than his cooperative uncle, Tawfik, back in 1882. The British assessment of Nasser – that he was not of the same mettle as Muhammad Ali – had led Eden and the Foreign Office to badly miscalculate. They believed that they could 'invest' in the officers' regime and guide it in order to retain Egypt's Westminster-style parliamentary system. The Americans saw a chance to speed up their seizure of the old European colonial powers' domain of influence – and indeed they helped Nasser even before Suez, with generous aid from President Harry Truman's (1884–1972) Point Four Program.* Finally, of course, Nasser was 'saved' by President Dwight Eisenhower in November 1956, after British and French troops had landed in the canal zone.

---

*The Point Four Program offered technical assistance for 'developing countries'. It took its name from the fact that it was the fourth foreign-policy objective mentioned in Truman's inaugural address in January 1949.

CHAPTER 52
The Move Against Alexandria

The Naguib-led officers did not drag out their conflict with the legitimate head of state for months, as Ourabi had done 70 years earlier. They moved swiftly against the institution of the monarchy and against Alexandria herself: by 07:00 on 25 July 1952, all the royal palaces were surrounded by tanks. The officers appointed Ali Maher Pasha to head a new government in the Wizarat building, the cabinet's Alexandrian summer home on Rue Abukeir.

Maher Pasha had refused to join the Allies' war against the Nazis in 1939.[*] Egypt's 23rd prime minister was a politician from the old liberal era, who debated bills in parliament and carefully considered economic repercussions. As my grandfather had predicted, he soon resigned – after 46 days in office, in fact, following two major stand-offs with the officers. The first was over their summary execution, in breach of existing laws, of workers who went on strike on 12 August at the Kafr-el-Dawar textile works. The second – and the last straw for Maher Pasha – were the economically disastrous land reforms announced on 9 September. He had resigned two days earlier in a stormy meeting with the officers, at which he tried to amend the draft land-reform act. General Naguib (in 1983) claimed that he agreed with Maher Pasha; breaking down large farms into smaller plots made them economically unsustainable and caused hardship to small farmers who accumulated massive debts.

After betraying their king in violation of the constitution, the officers demanded his abdication, accusing him of 'breaching the constitution'. Their false accusations that he had trafficked in defective arms and

---

[*] Maher Pasha had previously been in office three times: January–May 1936, 1939–40 and January–March 1952.

munitions proved to be a fabrication after lengthy legal cases in the Nasser regime's courts. Several of the junta's promises were disingenuous and were only made to placate Western ambassadors.

On the first day of the coup, the army officers had assured what they called 'our friends the foreign nationals in Egypt' that the army considered itself entirely responsible for protecting their persons and property. The junta didn't want to provide a pretext for British troops – still at the canal base – to intervene in order to safeguard lives, as had happened 70 years earlier.[1] The 'foreign nationals' in the military regime's 'Newspeak' meant Egyptians born to second- and third-generation migrants and those who held dual nationality or were long-term residents. They were expelled four years later, had their property confiscated and their businesses nationalised – especially the Jews – and many were stripped of their Egyptian nationality.

There was hardly enough support for the coup officers to create a significant mass momentum, but they exploited existing social factors to gain popularity. On the human level, there had been social injustice and a growing feeling that the upper classes trading and dealing with ethnically European Egyptians had been abusing privileges that came at the expense of the Nilotic-Egyptian poor. Such sentiment was exaggerated and exploited by socialists and Islamists to undermine the king and the status quo. On a larger scale was the rivalry between the two concepts and between Alexandria, the resurrected city-state, and Ottoman Egypt. *Masr* (Cairo) was leading *Masr* (Egypt), and Alexandria, a vital organ, was located outside of the nation's body – an illegitimate child who still had her umbilical cord connected to Europe and was, always, a 'foreign' cosmopolitan being that was growing out of control. Both contemporary and historical factors were entrenched in Internal Egypt's political and cultural trends – either by conviction, education, family affiliation, or faith (the last-named of which led people to staunchly take an anti-modernity stance, viewing secularism as anti-Islamic). Its inhabitants believed that Alexandria had provided both an excuse and a 'landing ground' for British intervention – just as she had been the entry point for the Napoleon-led French expedition in 1798, held responsible by al-Azhar's Islamists for introducing ungodly modernity to the Muslim caliphate. (Similar to the way communists in China viewed Hong Kong people's liberal culture as a Trojan horse for western imperialism, reactionary forces in Internal Egypt believed that Alexandria's Europeanism had acted as a Trojan Horse in their oriental Islamic country.)

The Revisionists of Alexandria's History

Many secular intellectuals – mostly left-wing, liberal public-opinion formers in the west, especially in influential media – aided the reaction-

CHAPTER 52   The Move Against Alexandria

aries' Orwellian reinvention of Alexandria – notably in associating cosmopolitanism (in a negative way) with imperialism. This was a message of the Marxist movement – whether Third International or Stalinist – later adopted by the left-liberal western mainstream media. In reality, the cosmopolitanism that started in Alexandria, and the presence in the city of hundreds of thousands of ethnic Europeans and non-Muslim former subjects of the Ottoman Empire, helped the Egyptians to formulate their own independent, modern national identity separate from that of the Islamic caliphate.

Zizinia, a 1997 Egyptian television series scripted by Osama Anwar O'kasha (1941–2010) and produced by Gamal abd-el-Hamid (b.1951), was a rare work touching on this reality. Set in Alexandria during the Second World War, the drama explored the origins of the Egyptian identity through Nilotic Egyptians' relations with migrant communities. Its primary weaknesses were inaccuracies as the producers couldn't resist the, often negative, stereotyping of non-Muslim Alexandrian-born residents as *khawagat* (aliens).

Another case in point is the mural *The School of Alexandria* in the main hall of the former Belediye of Alexandria (Governorate House in the coup regime's 'Newspeak') by French-trained artist Muhammad Nagi (1888–1956). He depicted Egyptian Alexandrians who happened to be ethnically non-Nilotic as distinctively alien, sometimes standing a step removed from the Nilotic crowd, as American academic Deborah Starr has observed. The painting is described underneath (by the republican regime) as 'a monumental celebration of the rich amalgam of religious and cultural traditions to which modern Egypt is heir', with an obvious subsuming of Alexandria into broader Egypt. Among the *alienate personis* was the legally Egyptian national Cavafy and another great Alexandria-born poet, writer, journalist, scholar, Giuseppe Ungaretti (1888–1970). Ungaretti was a significant contributor to twentieth-century Italian literature in the experimental Hermeticism movement (hermetic poetry). The two figures stand in the 'European' side of Nagi's frame, as noted by Starr in her subjective study of (selective) literary Alexandria in her 2009 *Remembering Cosmopolitan Egypt*.[2]

Starr, inaccurately, refers to the Alexandria-born – and thus legally Egyptian national – Ungaretti as 'Italian', not Alexandrian of Italian background, Italian-Alexandrian, or Italian-Egyptian. I wonder whether she would label current British politicians like London Mayor Sadiq Khan or British Home Secretary Priti Patel as (respectively) 'Pakistani' or 'Indian' or ' foreign' in a book or a newspaper column?

In her book, Starr uses terms that did not exist during the lifetimes of those mentioned or during the period her book covers – a period that I have personally witnessed. The jargon used in Starr's book was not in the public discourse until it was introduced by Colonel Nasser's military regime decades later as part of a process to change Egypt's identity and rewrite the history of Alexandria and Egypt. Starr repeatedly miswrites Nagi's name as 'Naji'. The artist himself wrote it and pronounced it 'Nagi'; the Egyptian State Information Department uses 'Nagi' (with 'g') since no Egyptian, past or present, pronounces (or writes) it with a 'j' – only Arabs do. Starr repeatedly and wrongly uses the label 'Arab' to refer to Alexandrian writers who predated Nasser's imposition of a pan-Arab concept in the 1960s. Works like Starr's, consciously or unconsciously or out of carelessness, perpetuate the nonsensical misconception that Alexandrians were 'Arab', which is also a concealed form of Western liberal-left racism that lumps together all peoples and nations south and east of the Mediterranean and in the Levant as being of one single race.

During a coffee break in a one-day seminar on media freedom in 2014, I mentioned to a co-panellist, who happened to be a North American born BBC high-profile journalist, that I had attended the annual Defence and Security International Conference in Bahrain as part of the British delegation a day earlier. I added that the DSIC organisers grouped delegates at country-designated tables during lunch.

'...so we sat around the Union Flag', I said, before adding as a light-hearted observation, 'but we were outnumbered by the Americans spilling over from the Stars and Stripes table into ours'. The supposedly informed BBC 'star' said, 'The Americans outnumbered the Arabs?' Puzzled by her question since I had already mentioned that there were scores of different nationalities delegations, I responded, 'Who mentioned Arabs? The Union Jack on the British delegation table?'

The BBC international journalist responded, 'Ah, multiple identities!' I shook my head in bemused astonishment: 'What identities? What are you talking about?' But, as is common at such gatherings, she was saved by someone butting in and diverting the conversation line. I thought in detail about this encounter and why this high calibre 'informed' BBC star's mind could only imagine two races, Americans and all other delegations (in the annually held international conference DSIC attended by several nationalities) grouped all as one race: 'Arabs'. And what was her 'multiple identities!' comment about? This fellow-journalist, who often joined me in covering events like the annual DSIC, isn't a run-of-the-mill, superficial young graduate new to the media, but an award-winning, respected, area-specialist foreign correspondent – so where had the confusion in her head come from? Do BBC senior international correspondents and their researchers check facts of ongoing current affairs like DSIC ?

CHAPTER 52 The Move Against Alexandria

It was evident that senior BBC staff, their researchers and producers don't bother to research the historical background of, and the basic facts about, places they cover, like Egypt, which explains their ignorance of its identity.

For a journalist, ignoring the historical background of a subject they cover is like driving a car through a crowded city without a rear-view mirror.

Besides representing a totalitarian ignorance prevailing within the Western left-liberal intelligentsia – perpetuated by the (far-from-enlightened) media comfortable with parroting the false new orthodoxy – there is a BBC groupthink, reflecting the way that the institution has been pushing millions to believe. Influential Western organisations – the BBC among them – misinform viewers by replacing Egypt's true identity with a false one. Using graphics as a visual symbol of a location is a case in point. There is a basic rule for using iconic pictures like a monument or a site, unique to a country or a city to make it recognisable without adding text or speech. A viewer would immediately think of *la Tour Eiffel* for France, Big Ben for London or the UK, the Statue of Liberty for the USA, The Acropolis for Greece and the Pyramids and Sphinx for Egypt.* However, the BBC television service, especially World TV and BBC Arabic in particular, has, over the past few years, started replacing the iconic Pyramids and Sphinx with graphics of mosque minarets for The Egyptian capital – a subliminal message reprogramming viewers' minds in order to redefine Egyptian identity as exclusively oriental Arabic-Islamic. Not only this projection dismisses the presence of over 12 million Christians and millions of secular, agnostic and other non-Muslim Egyptians, but, such misinformation slowly erases from viewers' memory the reality of 220 years of European modernity, 2,000 years of Christian culture, another 500 years of Hellenic-Ptolemaic history and 5,000 years of indigenous Egyptian civilisation associated with the world's oldest nation.

Such a view – an Orwellian rewriting of history – sits within a group of modern works underpinning the revisionist allegations that Alexandria as a cosmopolis only existed in Western literature and in Lawrence Durrell's novels. This view, paradoxically, comes from a left-wing liberal school that claims to be politically correct and anti-colonialist but is in fact deeply racist.

---

* When choosing graphics in a visual medium like TV or cinema, it is important to consider the uniqueness of the picture to the geographical location and how it makes the country, or city, recognisable to the viewers to bypass any language barrier. There are mosques everywhere (including Scandinavia), but the Sphinx next to the pyramids exist in one country only.

In Chapter 5 of her book, Starr explores the cycle of autobiographical works by three Alexandrians: Youssef Chahine in his films, and Edwar al-Kharrat and Ibrahim Abdel Meguid in their historical novels.

Starr stretches the imagination by claiming that their works 'assert that cosmopolitanism is inseparable from imperial pedigree'. The three belong to the left and communist trends.

In his novel *Clouds Over Alexandria,* Meguid's message refutes Starr's claim: '…They [the architects] *were* all Egyptians….' replies the historian Iesa Salmawi to the question 'Didn't the Egyptians build anything at all?' from the student Bashir noticing the predominance of Italian-sounding names among architects who constructed Alexandria's landmarks.[3] The Alexandrian Meguid owns and embraces what Starr labels 'Italians' as Egyptians rather than strangers who became a bridgehead for imperialism.

The other two figures cited by Starr, Chahine and al-Kharrat, were close personal friends of mine who saw themselves as Alexandrian first, Egyptian second and never as Arab. Al-Kharrat was arrested among Egyptian communists objecting to Nasser's Arabisation of Egypt after federation with Syria, while Chahine fled into self-exile for similar reasons. They would be turning in their graves at the thought of being labelled 'Arab' by Starr's interpretation – and in their works and discussions with me, neither associated cosmopolitanism with imperialism. On the contrary, they portrayed Alexandria's daily life as a manifestation of cosmopolitanism, advancing European modernity, that became inseparable from the Egyptian national independent identity and the struggle against Ottoman rule and, later, against British military presence and influence. The mosaic that Chahine presents in his Alexandria Trilogy shows cosmopolitanism as the foundation of the city's life and national (identity) independence. Al-Kharrat belonged to a Marxist movement that included Jews and was multi-ethnic in its membership, struggling for an independent Egyptian identity.[4]

By associating cosmopolitanism with imperialism and creating a false reality, the so-called progressives among revisionists and the liberal establishment in the West provided backward, undemocratic, extreme right-wing forces in Egypt with justifications for their ethnic-cleansing actions, finishing off the modernity and multi-ethnicity of Alexandria.

CHAPTER 53
Alexandria's Identity: Durrell

The other side of the coin was that the Alexandrians themselves did not fit within Ottoman Egypt. 'From Alexandria' will always be the answer when someone of my generation is asked where they came from, not 'from Egypt'.

Lawrence Durrell wrote, in his *Alexandria Quartet*,

The Alexandrians themselves were strangers and exiles to the Egypt which existed below the glittering surface of their dreams, ringed by the hot deserts and fanned by the bleakness of a faith which renounced worldly pleasure: the Egypt of rags and sores, of beauty and desperation. Alexandria was still Europe - the capital of Asiatic Europe if such a thing could exist. It ['she'] could never be like Cairo, where his whole life had an Egyptian cast, where he spoke ample Arabic; here [in Alexandria] French, Italian and Greek dominated the scene. The ambience, the social manner, everything was different - cast in a European mould where somehow the camels and palm-trees and cloaked natives existed only as a brilliantly coloured frieze; a backcloth to a life divided in its origins[1]

The only reminder of some Islamic tone in the quiescent rhythm of life in pre-1960 Alexandria would have been the occasional muezzin call from the odd minaret before the post-1980 loudspeaker outbreak. The seasonal oriental-Islamic colours added to the Euro-Mediterranean tableau, such as the Ramadan food ingredients in the Turkish quarter's markets or the non-Alexandrian expressions by *masarwah* on the Ramleh tram in the summer season – but everything else was incontrovertibly Alexandrian. For one group, Alexandria was the melting pot, the hybrid cosmopolitan entity; for others, the cosmopolis was made up of 'islands' of multiple ethnic communities who, to connect with other islands, needed to wade in fords made of the mongrel first group. Alexandria was both a reality and a myth, a dream and a once-in-a-lifetime experience that would never be repeated. Whether fantasy or real, Alexandria was a different story and a different vision for each individual Alexandrian. Even among my own relatives and post-War school friends, their settings and images differ – especially when you meet them in the diaspora. Each of them, whether scattered across the globe or still in the city, has their own image of *their* Alexandria – a vision different from all others. Some painted their pictures with ambiences from which they were snatched at the time of their departure; others coloured their picture of Alexandria with their happiest or saddest experiences. But it could be weirdly different for those who remained behind, depending on how they lived.

Some remained in an isolated bubble with a few like themselves; others cocooned themselves, holding on to the last view of Alexandria before closing their mental Sonnenberg Tunnel* hatch when the cultural holocaust thundered above. Worst were the ones who went with the flow, not noticing the regression and the decay around them.

'If there exists such a thing as the Alexandrian myth, it is because she stood, for the best part of a century, as the symbol of an open Mediterranean unlike the sea of today, sealed along all its coasts by petty nationalism', wrote the Greco-French historian Ilios Yannakakis (1931–2017), '...Alexandria was one of the last places where one could marry individual expansion to liberalism with traditional community ties'.[2]

Al-Mahrousah Sails Away

The hatred of inward-looking *fellaheen* in Internal Egypt for Alexandria, which they neither understood nor considered to be part of their post-Ottoman Muslim caliphate, finally reached boiling point on 26 July 1952. The *fellaheen* army officers forced the legitimate head of state, King Farouk, to abdicate to his son, the (constitutionally rightfully exiled King) Ahmed Fuad II. There had been no republican movement in Egypt in the years leading up to 1952. Still, the inward-looking anti-modernity forces associated the Muhammad Ali dynasty with modernity, cosmopolitanism and 'un-Islamic' Europeanisation. Like Alexander and the Ptolemies before them, Muhammad Ali's dynasty were Macedonians of Greek affiliation – not belonging to the southern shores of the Mediterranean. Like Cleopatra, the last Alexandrian Hel-

---

* The 1550m-long road tunnel was the world's largest mass-civilian nuclear fallout shelter; it could accommodate 20,000 civilians in the event of a nuclear war or some other massive disaster.

lenic queen of Egypt and the last of her dynasty, Farouk was the last of the reforming dynasty that revived Alexandria and introduced some modernity to what was otherwise an Ottoman backwater.

On his last day on the throne at Ras el-Tin Palace, Alexandria's closest point to Europe, Farouk turned down the offers made by the faithful sections of his armed forces – especially the Egyptian Navy and the Sudanese Palace Guard – to resist the officers' illegal act. They pleaded with Farouk, explaining that the coup leaders might control a section of the armed forces but were not recognised by the rest of the military units, which remained loyal to their constitutional chief: the king himself. In fact, the conspiring officers didn't manage to have all royal palaces surrounded until 30 hours after announcing the coup, and the Sudanese royal guards had no intention of surrendering. Farouk refused, saying that he would not go down in history as the king who started a civil war in his own country. He declared that no crown was worth Egyptians spilling the blood of fellow Egyptians, and abdicated in favour of his son.

'Egypt was not an easy country to rule' were King Farouk's last words to General Naguib on board the Royal Yacht *al-Mahrousah*, wishing him and the kingdom he was leaving behind luck and success in a new era. Naguib bade him farewell, and promised a return to civilian administration after holding an election.[3] Seventy years later, the Egyptians are still waiting for those first fair elections and a civilian government free from military control.[4]

The End of Modernity – Naguib's Revision

Farouk's words rang true in General Naguib's mind after he was ousted by Nasser in 1954 and watched the ideals of his Blessed Action (rebranded 'revolution' later) fade away. He would repeat 'revolution' with a sardonic irony, accompanied by a shake of the head and a short, embittered laugh mixed with the sigh of a disappointed, helpless man. Two years before he died, I went to see him with a local fixer. I was researching material for a film that I had been commissioned to script about the recently assassinated President Sadat, who a decade earlier had eased the harsh conditions of Naguib's house arrest laid down by Colonel Nasser. Naguib repeated King Farouk's words of a country that was not easy to rule. Nasser apologists and some revisionist historians claim that many Egyptians welcomed the 1952 coup. They point to the way in which the poor and impoverished saw the *khawagat* (meaning non-Nilotic Egyptians and non-Muslims) looking down on *fellaheen* and exploiting them. The revisionists interpret the much-delayed emotional reaction of 'the poor' as welcoming the 'Blessed Action', seeing

Alexandria Adieu

the republic's tough stand against the European powers (albeit three years later) as a new hope for long-awaited justice.

'Did the lot of the *fellaheen* and the Egyptian poor improve in the new republic under your "Blessed Action"?', I began.

'See for yourself...' was President Naguib's answer after a long pause – a reply mixed with a sardonic laugh as he pointed to the bare room where cockroaches ran on the cold, fading floor tiles. 'And I was a general in the army before the cou...[cut, short cough]...revolution!'

Farouk's departure in 1952 marked the beginning of the end of the royal Alexandria that had had a mind, heart and soul, drawing the curtain on a long chapter of modernity that started in the city and gave birth to an age of enlightenment not only in Egypt but throughout the region. This modernity – which had taken six generations* to establish since Napoleon landed in 1798, ushering in a new dawn – was overturned in 15 years because it had been built on a narrow base of semi-secularism (not quite the French *laïcité*) and mostly in Alexandria – while outside, in Internal Egypt, the modernity experiment had been limited to commercial urban centres and central Cairo. Internal Egypt's society had never been secular, nor had it embraced modernity except for several enlightened pools within strata of the middle classes: educated *effendis* in communities not connected geographically but, like small islands, linked by shared semi-progressive thought and liberal cultural attitudes.

I argue that modernity in Egypt was generated and sustained, for 180 years, by the dynamics of four main factors that revived Alexandria and tried to pull urban Egypt with her, but it could not draw in rural Egypt and its *fellaheen*. The rest of Egypt instead remained inward-looking, locked in the Ottoman-Islamic caliphate mentality. First were the dynamics created by the enlightened ruling establishment founded by Muhammad Ali Pasha and his dynasty, who were ethnically and culturally European and thus not intellectually bound by the oriental, Arabo-Islamic shackles that viewed European modernity as ungodly. Alexandrians saw their society as an extension of Europe – particularly France, Italy and the central European countries rich with arts, culture and social etiquette. The second dynamic was the work of European-educated Egyptians in Muhammad Ali's *be'tha*[5] since the 1820s. They set up Egyptian universities, providing secular and non-religious-based education for the first time since the Arab invasion in the seventh century.

The military-backed presence of a British administration[6] was a third factor. It checked the Egyptian Government under King Fuad and

---

* Modernity became the familiar way of urban life in the 1920s.

CHAPTER 53   Alexandria's Identity: Durrell

Prime Minister Zaghloul Pasha, setting a political structure emulating the liberal, multi-party Westminster parliamentary system alongside an independent judiciary and robust working tools imposing the rule of law. This helped unrestricted trade, the free market and a free press that spread to industrialised Egypt. Until the 1880s, the developing Egyptian press was crude, experimental and didactic towards its loyal readership. The British presence helped Egyptian media develop more professional standards and engage in public debate, giving writers and thinkers a platform from which to argue economic, political and social issues. These included women's rights and other early feminist topics. Although after the 1919 revolution, the press became partisan, it retained high professional standards. The positive impact of the British presence began to wear off after the signing of the 1936 treaty, which dramatically reduced British influence on Egyptian public life – including its positive aspects.

What contributed most to modernity, however, was Alexandria's cosmopolitanism – my fourth dynamic – which seeped into urban centres thanks to the multi-ethnic society that tended to opt for European customs and etiquette. The ethnic European migrants engaged in commerce, construction, manufacturing, education, medicine, the arts and culture. The Europeanised Syro-Lebanese Christians, Armenians and Jews played a significant role in that culture – especially in establishing its modern press. The 1850 massacre in Aleppo and the trouble in Mount Lebanon, culminating in the 1859–60 civil war between Christians and Druze that led to European intervention combined with repressive Ottoman rule, prompted many Syrian writers to flee to Egypt, establishing journals in their new home.

Beirut-born actress and journalist Roes el-Youssef (1898–1958), who was born Fatima Youssef but abandoned by her Muslim family after her mother's death and brought up by a Christian family, launched the liberal enlightened weekly *Rose El-Youssef* in 1925. The magazine still runs today, but was turned into a propaganda platform after its 1960 nationalisation by Colonel Nasser. In 1892, Syrian Christian migrant Hind Noufal (1860–1920) launched, in Alexandria, the first Arabic-language women's fortnightly journal – totally secular and liberal, enlightened and progressive-leaning – *Al-Fatat* (The Young Woman). It only lasted a few years but was a blueprint for progressive women's publications to follow, like the weekly *L'Egyptienne* (1925–40) published in French by feminist leaders, the half-Circassian Huda Shaarawi and her disciple Siza Nabarawy (1897–1985). Although it was elitist, it set the agenda for the feminist movement of the time, which was mostly egalitarian and progressive – unlike the ideologically female-supremacist feminism of the twenty-first century.

Alexandria Adieu

The non-Nilotics, whom Egyptian Muslims called *khawagat*, also invested heavily in Alexandria and Egypt to establish schools, hospitals, housing estates, sports and cultural clubs, community centres and newspapers. Nilotic Egyptians who benefitted from those institutions (and the many employed in them) copied them, establishing their own European-style organisations, clubs and associations. It was a chapter of the cosmopolis in which all races and cultures were accepted as equal citizens; Farouk's departure marked the end of this chapter.

'Did you know that I turned down the palace's offer to make me a field marshal on the morning of 26th July?' General Naguib shouted after me as I stood at the door waving back at the ageing, fragile first president of Egypt, who sat on his sickbed in his humble abode. By the time we went back for filming, Egypt's first president had become too ill to participate alongside other personalities who had made history during that period: former FOA members, diplomats, ministers and prime ministers under the monarchy and the republic, as well as Sadat's comrades-in-arms, his widow and his sister. The interviews told part of Egypt's story between the 1919 revolution and 1980, but from an angle different from the post-1952 revised version. Nasser's men, especially those ousted by Sadat, tried to blacken the latter's name. He was the devil in contrast to their saint, Nasser. Nobody denied Nasser's dictatorial ways; unnecessary, costly wars; or his calamitous economic policies – but all of them, who were financially and socially privileged as his regime's elite, justified these 'small sacrifices' for the greater good. None of them, however, was able to give a comprehensible or quantifiable definition of that 'that greater good.'

CHAPTER 54
Nasser's Defiance: The Suez War

Colonel Nasser was the first ruler of Egypt since Muhammad Ali Pasha to defy the Great Powers of the day and take an independent position. His stance was admired by many left-wing European commentators condemning the persistence of nineteenth-century-style 'gunboat diplomacy'; however, the reality was different on the ground. In the nineteenth century, the European powers preferred dealing with a single, weak, hegemonic entity – in this case, the fragile Ottoman Empire – to emerging independent states run by an educated elite with nationalistic ambitions that threatened their dominance. The nineteenth-century Great Powers even plotted with the Ottoman Porte in Constantinople to curtail leaders who might become an irritating power – like Muhammad Ali, who was pushed back inside Egypt.

Like Alexander and the Ptolemies, Muhammad Ali was an outward-looking moderniser who recognised the tremendous economic and cultural benefits that Europe could contribute to Egypt. He dealt with European powers in collaboration and sometimes rivalry – but also with challenges, and even confrontations. Nasser, by contrast, had a *fellaheen* Islamic mentality that was inward-looking. Once in power, he turned his back on Europe and saw the entire West as one hostile bloc; he focused on the Arab and Muslim countries, and dealt with the Soviet bloc while depriving the Egyptian people of the benefits they had enjoyed, since 1798, through contacts and involvement with Europe. By severing relations with Europe and expelling ethnic minorities, Nasser reversed 160 years of progress in Alexandria and Egypt.

As with the debate over Gladstone's true motives and the broader strategy that led to Britain's invasion of Egypt in 1882, the jury is still out on the real reasons behind Eden's blindness to the 1882 lesson of the hatred generated by the bombardment of Alexandria. The absurd 1956 ultimatum given to Egyptian and Israeli forces to disengage was similar to Admiral Seymour's demand to disarm Alexandria's forts: both were designed to be rejected as a pretext for military intervention. On 29 October 1956, ten Israeli armoured brigades invaded Sinai, routing Egyptian army units and advanced towards Suez Canal. An Anglo–French ultimatum was issued to Israel and Egypt on 31 October to withdraw their forces 10 miles (16 kilometres) west and east of the canal; it meant letting the Israelis advance (inside Egyptian sovereign territory) within 10 miles of the canal.

Britain and France had secretly signed the Protocol of Sèvres in Paris with Israel on 24 October. Like Ourabi, who tried to block the canal in order to stop General Wolseley's advance in 1882, Nasser sank 40 ships, blocking the waterway before issuing a 'complaint against France and the United Kingdom' to the UN Security Council (UNSC). The two countries launched air raids on Egyptian airfields and selected, strategic targets. My father's office in the magnificent nineteenth-century Italian-designed Poste Egyptienne building received a direct hit by a rocket that missed Marconi's communications centre a block away. On 31 October, the UNSC's Resolution 119 (dealing with Nasser's complaint) was vetoed by Britain and France. It was moved on 2 November 1956 to the UN General Assembly (UNGA), where the Great Powers could not use their veto on organising a peacekeeping force.

The Anglo–French invasion began on 5 November, provoking worldwide condemnation. The USSR threatened direct military intervention to end hostilities. Livid at Eden's (unwisely) keeping him in the dark, President Eisenhower refused to come to Britain's aid and forced the British prime minister to accept a UN ceasefire on 6 November 1956. Hostilities ended the next day – implementing UNGA Resolution 1001, which established the first UN Emergency Force, UNEF-I.* The British and French completed withdrawal of their troops by 22 December, enabling the militarily defeated Colonel Nasser to claim a (political) win. He declared 23 December 'Victory Day', giving him unstoppable momentum in spreading his radical influence throughout the region. Eden also failed to understand that in a post-Second World War world, a European power could not intervene with 1882-style impunity – especially not if it tried to hoodwink the United States in the process.

---

*In May 1967, Colonel Nasser ordered UNEF-I to leave; moved his army towards Israel's borders; and laid maritime siege to the Gulf of Akaba, which triggered the Six-Day War. UNEF-II was established after the Yom Kippur War of 1973 by UNSC Resolution 340.

CHAPTER 54   Nasser's Defiance: The Suez War

Although, in 1882, Internal Egypt was still influenced by Ourabi and his Ottoman affiliation, powerful, enlightened forces opposed him and were sympathetic to Britain and Europe. Strong and growing modernising trends and institutions were present from the 1860s onwards in Alexandria. This included Khedive Tawfik himself, who supported and welcomed Britain's routing of Ourabi's reactionary forces. Those enlightened forces were weakened in 1956, and Alexandria was fast losing her prestige and modernising influence after the 1952 coup – especially as international superpowers, including the USSR and USA, increasingly stood against Britain. Eden's unwise action generated support for Nasser even among the descendants of the European Alexandrians who had welcomed British intervention to protect them 70 years earlier. Unlike 1882, most – especially the ethnically Greek and Italian Alexandrians – saw themselves as Egyptians, and rushed to defend their country against Britain and France.[1]

With Nasser now riding a wave of popularity, the Egyptian middle classes, especially Alexandrians, paid a heavy price in losing their way of life; personal freedoms; civil liberties; and, above all, their livelihoods thanks to the imposition of a radicalised, state-run economy. Shortly after the Suez War ceasefire in November 1956, Colonel Nasser sequestered all British- and French-associated enterprises, including banks, investments, trade companies and property. Over 15,000 businesses, most of which were in Alexandria, were seized, causing widespread unemployment and ruin to the lives of hundreds of thousands of Alexandrians and Egyptians whose trade and purchasing ability had been trickling down to thousands of the poor who lost their jobs in the ruined businesses.

Most dangerous of all was Nasser's ability – with the help of a willing, often hysterical, media – to disseminate misinformation and mobilise public opinion against an imaginary conspiracy of world colonialism. This planted the seeds of hatred of 'others' in the normally peaceful hearts of many Egyptians. From late November 1956 and throughout the 1957 academic year, secondary schools and university students of both sexes were encouraged to volunteer in the 'Popular Resistance Students' Brigades'. These youths were given training on outdated Lee–Enfield 303 rifles, learning how to make Molotov cocktails, aim and shoot, reassemble and clean rifles that they could hardly lift – as my older lover, the Cairo University student, jokingly mused. The Anglo–French troops who landed in Port Said had not ventured into Egypt itself, and had left within days. So nobody among the volunteering students really knew who they were supposed to shoot at or who to resist. The Jews? *Al-khawagat*? *Al-aganeb*? But, farcically, there *were* scores of all three categories among the Students' Brigades – as witnessed by my elder relatives, like my cousin Pisa in the Italian Don Bosco School and another cousin reading Law at Alexandria University.

The majority of *khwagat* and *aganeb* knew no other homeland but Alexandria, where they had been born and raised. Of course they would defend their land and the country that they represented on the world stage, whether in cultural events like Miss World and film festivals or in sports like the Olympics. So the multi-ethnic Alexandrian students carried on marching with the 303 rifles, not really knowing at whom they should aim them. Nobody put this question to the sergeant barking orders at the trainees or the NF commissars lecturing them on how to hate Westerners. Although this zeal faded away a few months into the 1957 academic year, it left the aggressive hatred towards the 'other' in many hearts. But who was that adversary, the 'other', in the city of their own birth?

PART XI
THE FALL OF ALEXANDRIA

CHAPTER 55
The Ethnic Cleansing of Alexandria

Alexandria was founded in the fourth century BC by Macedonians, not by Egyptians or their Persian rulers (the Thirty-first Dynasty). She flourished into the capital of the Hellenic world and its seat of learning for 1,000 years until the Arab invasion. The seventh-century turmoil sent her into another millennium of decline and hibernation; the colonial Arab rulers neglected Alexandria, letting the Canopic branch of the Nile west of the city silt up and dry. In her 'second coming', in the nineteenth century, Alexandria's population grew from 13,000 in the early century to 527,000 in 1927. The figure during the Second World War was 800,000, of whom over 500,000 were non-Nilotic migrants.

The modern city-state of Alexandria was not built by the Arabs, the Mamluks, the Ottomans or Egypt's British 'protectors' (1914–22), but by the Alexandrians themselves in all their racial multiplicity and religious diversity – the Alexandrians whom the new military regime was now alienating by calling them *aganeb* and *khawagat*. The immigrants who built this city-state brought talent, expertise, economic opportunities and investment, besides stability and security. These 'foreigners' in fact had deeper roots and a more extended history in Alexandria than did most Nilotic-Egyptian families – like that of Nasser himself, whose parents didn't immigrate to Alexandria until after 1910.[*] The

---

[*] Nasser's parents were immigrants, who moved to Alexandria after World War I. His father, Abd el-Nasser Hessin el-merrie was born in 1888 in Asuit, south Egypt, and his mother, Fahima Hussein, was from Menia, also in the Upper Egyptian countryside. There is a large body of Arabic writing attesting that Nasser's great-grandfather was an immigrant from the Yemeni Qahtan tribe who settled in Asiut in the eighteenth century.

Nasser regime's propaganda used misleading, right-wing-nationalist expressions like *aganeb* to alienate fellow Egyptians from the country's ethnic minorities. Legal nationality, especially in Alexandria, did not correspond with ethnicity. For example, over a quarter of the 300,000 referred to as Greek did not have Greek citizenship. Most were legally Egyptian, and many belonged to diverse ethnic groups like Georgians, Armenians, Bulgarians and Jews from Asia Minor, to name but a few, because they had been born in Greek settlements on the Black Sea. In independent Egypt, after 1923, they were no longer Ottomans. The ones born to Egyptian fathers (not mothers) became Egyptian, but they were also categorised according to the regions their grandparents had inhabited and which became states after the Great War. Armenians, Siro-Lebanese, Albanians, Austrians, Persians, North Africans (many of whom were also counted as French), when asked, would say that they were 'Alexandrians'. The biggest shock for many was becoming legally stateless, as they discovered when they left on a temporary (exit-only) Egyptian travel document.

Unlike Muhammad Ali and his family, who dealt with European powers on different levels, Nasser became a menace for Britain; the European powers; the region; and, mostly, for Alexandria herself. He inspired and backed troublemakers. Military coup leaders copied his style in holding their former colonial powers to account, blaming them for the ills that their own economic policies inflicted on their countries, and in targeting Jews and ethnic migrants.

Although Nasser was directly responsible for Alexandria's ethnic cleansing, including the deportation and departure of most Egyptian Jews, the late Israeli leader David Ben Gurion (1886–1973) shares a great deal of the blame. Activating sleeper cells of Egyptian Jews to bomb Western and Egyptian institutions in Egypt causing incidents like firebombing key service centres, which generated internal reactions in order to make life uncomfortable for the country's Jews and encourage them to leave for Israel, had a devastating effect on Alexandrian Jewry.[1] However, hostility was also shown by Egyptian institutions towards their country's Jewry. Not only the Islamic *ulama* of al-Azhar but also the Coptic Church clergy were hostile to Israel. Pope Shenouda III (1923–2012), as the 117th patriarch of Alexandria (1971–2012), banned Egyptian Copts from the pilgrimage to a Holy Land under Israeli occupation. Also, the Egyptian establishment (which Britain did not attempt to dissuade, if not indirectly encouraged)[2] tried to block Israel's independence, and the biblically generated suspicion of Egypt ran deep in the new Jewish state.

Israeli Military Intelligence (in its Hebrew abbreviation, AMAN) launched Operation Susannah, activating a sleeper cell of Egyptian

CHAPTER 55   The Ethnic Cleansing of Alexandria

Jews to bomb Western and Egyptian institutions in Egypt. The aim was that these attacks could be blamed on Egyptian opponents of Nasser, hoping to show his regime as unstable and unworthy of support. It started with the bombing of the Alexandria Central Post Office, followed by six other buildings in Alexandria and Cairo.

The arrested Susannah activists were put on trial in Egypt. Eight Egyptian Jews were found guilty (two sentenced to death) of sabotage and arson. The scandal, known as the Lavon Affair, cost Pinhas Lavon (1904–1976) – Israel's defence minister from 1954 to 1955, who approved the operation – his job.[3] The operation triggered a chain of events – with retaliation attacks by each side on border posts, Israel growing closer to France in its aims for a nuclear programme and Nasser seeking Soviet-bloc arms and the escalation that culminated in the Suez War two years later.[4]

When the Egyptian security arrested Jewish sleeper cells, Israel retaliated by attacking Gaza, killing 39 Egyptians. Nasser responded with a Soviet arms deal that angered American and British leaders, who then withdrew previously pledged aid to build the Aswan Dam. The Israelis' ill-advised plan increased Nasser's popularity and harmed Egypt's Jews; it helped Islamist and Arab-nationalist propaganda in stirring anti-Jewish sentiment. This makes four men responsible for what befell Alexandria's Jewry: Colonel Nasser; Anthony Eden; Guy Mollet (the socialist prime minister of France from 1956 to 1957), instrumental in involving Israel in the Suez War; and David Ben Gurion (Israel prime minister 1948–54 and 1955–63). Whenever you encountered Alexandrian Jews in the diaspora world, they'd curse Nasser and Ben Gurion in the vulgar Alexandrian equivalent of 'a plague on both their houses': '*koss-om dool a'ala dool*' ('cursed be the c***s that spat out both').

This was history repeating itself, with a move spelling economic and cultural disaster for Egypt. Spain's expulsion of its Jews in 1492 was a disaster, depriving the country of their commercial and cultural contribution and thus throwing Spain into centuries of dark ignorance. But those Jews became a gift to many provinces and cities of the Ottoman Empire – especially in economy, education and the arts. The departure of a fifth of Alexandria's people was a gift to countless towns and provinces from the west coast of Canada to Europe, to Israel, and all the way to Australia with their contributions in arts, culture, economics, industries and cuisine – leaving Egypt to enter another long dark age. Alexandria University's female students in the 1950s were indistinguishable from their Sorbonne counterparts – and today, they look like something crawling out of Kandahar souks. If 26 July 1952 was the beginning of the end of modernity in Egypt, then 26

Alexandria Adieu

July 1956 saw a shifting of gear to speed up the sunset of modernity, entering a chapter similar to Alexandria's fall to the Arab army in 645 AD. The slow death of Alexandria began by depriving her of the oxygen generated by her children.

When 26 July came the following summer, our kite-battle allies, Vicks and his brother, were not there. Nor was Stephano; his family *épicerie* was closed. Two summers later, Gabriella and my older lover's naughty guest, as well as a quarter of my classmates, were not there – nor anywhere in Alexandria or Egypt. Summer seasons passed until we no longer watched Cinema Liberation films from our friends' veranda: Loulo, Halim and Selim, along with *Oncle* Ishak and *Tante* Nismah, had gone. The Cairo avvocato and his daughters weren't there; they too had been harassed, his licence revoked after he was accused of facilitating the transfer of property and business shares for some English and French businesses. They fled. And, eventually, when the con-twins set up their customary big screen and loudspeakers by the green near Sidi-Bishr Mosque to broadcast Colonel Nasser's 26 July speech, I too was not there.

CHAPTER 56
The Second Arab Conquest

During my last visit to Alexandria, Egypt was enduring its first-ever veiled first lady. Naglaa Mahmoud (Mrs Morsi) (b.1962) was wrapped in a dull grey Iranian-style *chador* covering her head, shoulders and upper body. The streets were subjected to volleys of incomprehensible Quranic verses and Islamic chants fired from cassette players in taxis and stores. The effect resembled a teen-fashion shop on London's Oxford Street – but instead of continuous, tasteless pop music it was the Quran blaring out.

Holding out to the last breath before falling into the hands of strangers who never understood her culture, the Hellenistic city had deluded me on my few and far-between visits into believing that it could, culturally, survive. Unlike the Islamisation that had followed her seventh-century Arab conquest by war and poll tax, Alexandria was finally conquered by the modern political forces of Colonel Nasser and his successors. As with almost all totalitarian regimes, the process of the Arabo-Islamisation of Alexandria came in stages. Nasser began by weakening Alexandria's economic and commercial independence with demographic upheavals that eroded her cosmopolitan identity. His union with Syria in 1958 was the first stage in forming a super-federation among half a dozen or so former Ottoman provinces. A nation becomes totally conquered not by losing wars but by losing its memory and, subsequently, its identity. Nasser's Arabisation was a deliberate and systematic, Orwellian process of erasing Egypt's memory of a national identity forged by Muhammad Ali's dynasty as separate from any external links, especially ideological ones. Nasser made Egypt a province of an ideological Arab caliphate made up of former Ottoman provinces.

Architecture and publicly displayed statues and monuments have been integrated components that formed Alexandrians' identity, ancient and modern; the direction in which they face are 'footnotes' to her identity, similar to the manner in which a pharaoh's face on an Egyptian temple would guide a reader deciphering its hieroglyphs to their starting point. The statues of modernisers like Ismail Pasha, Muhammad Ali Pasha, and the nationalist leader Sa'd Zaghloul Pasha (to name but a few) were, in Alexandria, placed facing northwest – towards Europe – turning their backs on the south and east. Noticeably, statues erected after the 1952 coup turned their back on Europe and faced south or east.

Nasser knew that there was more than one Egypt that he was plotting to lead. The coup led by General Naguib started with small units in Cairo and Alexandria, and initially found cautious, lukewarm backing from the country's lower-middle classes – including many ethnic Europeans. Nasser was fascinated by Latin American military coups that gained popularity among the downtrodden workers and peasants, and he sought similar recognition.[1]

The urban centres of economic and cultural activities, like Alexandria, were Europeanised and multiethnic. In Alexandria and the military academy, Nasser's own education and social life were mostly secular. His wife, the Alexandrian Tahiah Kazim (1920–1992), daughter of a wealthy merchant of Iranian background, dressed in her generation's French-styled Alexandrian fashion. She spoke European languages and socialised with Nasser in diplomatic receptions as Egypt's first visible first lady, since the actual 'first first lady', Aicha Labib-Naguib, was seldom seen in public; however, she too dressed in the contemporary prevailing European-styled fashion.

Aware of the different constituencies within Egypt, Nasser played to several galleries: the urban middle classes, rural *fellaheen* and Islamists. But what made it easier for the last-named to take over the country's urban areas was the regime's draining of the cultural 'wells' that fed the complex Egyptian identity. In the 1950s, Colonel Nasser began to acquire Islamic credentials under a revolutionary guise; his administration made tremendous efforts to project an Islamic profile.

Postal stamps designed before 1953 bore ancient Egyptian images like the Pyramids, Sphinx and temples, and cultural icons redolent of modernity like the royal opera house and royal Alexandria's various features. By contrast, stamps and banknotes issued under the republic bore Islamic and oriental symbols, and pictures of sites from the Islamic Fatimid (tenth–twelfth century) quarters of Cairo.

To attract the nation's rural population, and thus broaden the regime's relatively narrow urban base, Nasser needed these Islamist credentials.

CHAPTER 56   The Second Arab Conquest

At the same time, however, he wanted to maintain the secularist pretence to ensure his leadership's survival. The regime imposed a minimum 50% quota of seats in the rubber-stamp parliament for 'fellaheen and workers'. Simultaneously, Nasser massively funded al-Azhar[*] and founded *Izha't al-Quran kareem* an Islamic broadcasting service.[†]

Nasser's duplicitous strategy of appealing to both secularists and devout Muslims was emulated by the country's third president, Mubarak, and the fifth,[‡] Abd-el-Fatah el-Sisi (b.1954)[§]. The Mubarak regime fought Islamist terrorists with bullets but increased al-Azhar's funding, expanded its role and encouraged the spread of Islamic evangelist television channels. President el-Sisi, hailed by the masses as a saviour from the Muslim Brotherhood, sends double signals. While his regime is locked in a fight with Islamist terrorists, he flies the Muslim devotion flag. His daughter, Aya, dresses conservatively and wraps her head and neck in a large *écharpe*. The first lady, Entissar Amer-el-Sisi (b.1956) appears in less-conservative dresses, wearing subtle make-up, but tucks her hair, as Islamists demand, under bonnets and *écharpes* a bit smaller than her daughter's.

---

[*] Nasser allocated scholarships to students from Muslim countries in Africa and Asia to study at al-Azhar, and also expanded its educational role to include historically secular disciplines like the sciences, engineering and medicine.

[†] Nasser launched this, Egypt's first Quranic and Islamic broadcasting service, 1964 under the pretext of protecting Islam from falsified copies of the Quran circulating in bookshops.

[‡] Egypt's fourth president was the speaker of parliament, Sufi Abu Taleb (1925–2008), who served as an interim president for nine days until the MPs voted by majority to appoint Mubarak as president. Egypt's fourth president was the speaker of parliament, Sufi Abu Taleb (1925–2008), who served as an interim president for nine days until the MPs voted by majority to appoint Mubarak as president.

[§] Egypt's sixth president was an interim leader: the head of the constitutional court, Chief Justice Adli Mansour (b.1945). In constitutional terms, he was the president for one year – between the overthrow of Morsi in a popular uprising in June 2013 and the election of el-Sisi in 2014.

CHAPTER 57
Paving the Way for Sadat's Islamisation.

The Nasser regime's New Year's Eve 1958–9 rounding up of communists and secularists opposed, among other things, to erasing Egypt's name after the federation with Syria early in the year had far-reaching consequences. The January arrests[1] of communists and secular opponents became an annual pre-emptive tradition for years, and a setback for culture and the arts. The vast majority of contributors to Egypt's literary and creative industries were communists – most of them *Nahda*-educated – who, after being released following years of detention, were silenced, fled (mostly to France or the USSR), cowed or bought to promote the regime's Arabism.

Despite their misunderstanding of economics and hostility to parliamentarian democracy, the younger generation of communists at the 1970s universities continued their forebears' mission of advancing culture, literature and the creative arts. Displaying opinions, analysis, art and literary criticism besides current affairs, the communists' wall magazine (two A1 sheets joined together, displaying comment, analysis and cartoons) became like London's Speakers' Corner and a barometer for middle-class attitudes.

Seeing the phenomenon as a threat, Sadat's security organs financed and armed Islamic-group thugs to destroy the displays and disperse the debate gatherings by force, making these incidents appear like purely student disputes. The decisive 'battle' came in 1977. Mass protests in January of that year, sparked by the removal of subsidies on essential goods, turned into riots after the police and prisons released criminals who were awaiting trial to loot, burn and destroy; meanwhile, pro-Sadat Islamists firebombed nightclubs, cinemas, art galleries and cultural centres. Using the riots as a pretext, Sadat rounded up communists;

410

CHAPTER 57   Paving the Way for Sadat's Islamisation.

200 of their leaders were given long sentences, while not a single Islamist thug was arrested.

The communists made up the bulk of culture and arts bodies, theatre production, music bands and film societies. The heavy blows of 1977 led to the ending of most cultural activities in Egypt. The resultant vacuum on the campuses (and in society in general) was filled by Islamic groups spreading anti-Enlightenment culture and harassing female students to take up the veil. The classical, open-minded strong *filles d'Alexandrie*, whom I encountered in the 1960s – and who were celebrated by Durrell and al-Kharrat, disappeared behind a facial, as well as mental, *higab*, *niqab* or *burka*.

The Egyptian left (of all shades) made a fatal, historical error in joining moves by Nasserites and the far-right to reverse peace with Israel instead of campaigning to restore parliamentary democracy. Had they called for democracy, human rights and citizens' freedoms during Sadat's stand-off with Nasser's agencies in May 1971, they would have put he earlier, and his Western backers, on the spot and galvanised internal and international support. Instead of forging links with the Jewish and world peace movements, the Egyptian left went further than far-right groups in denying fellow-Egyptians their legitimate nationality. In the 1970s and 80s, the celebrated 'revolutionary' singing duo,[2] composer Sheikh Imam Eisa (1918–1995)[3] and his Egyptian-vernacular lyricist Ahmed Fuad Negm (1929–2013),[4] sang against such peace-taking measures with anti-Semitic, xenophobic and racist lyrics. The duo's 1984 rewording of the classic folk song '*Salma, ya, Salamah*',[5] objected to late Cairo-born singer Dalida (1933–1987)[6] returning to her Egyptian homeland. Their version also condemned her for 'appropriating' *Salma*, which, ironically, the two have themselves appropriated.

Sadat's Pact

Once installed as president, Sadat rekindled his 1940s association with the Muslim Brotherhood.[7] The Americans, unwisely, aided his Islamisation in order to erase the legacy of Nasser, which was seen as an extension of Soviet influence. One key figure in this project was the Egyptian–Saudi dual-national, Istanbul-born Kamal Adham (1929–1999), who reshaped the Saudi intelligence service in cooperation with the CIA. Sadat, claiming the title the *Mo'emen* (the believer in Allah) for himself, and Adham brought back into the country exiled Muslim Brotherhood leaders – like Sheikh Sha'rawi,[8] who had been in Saudi Arabia.

The battle for Egyptians' hearts and minds – which had raged for seven decades between two trends represented in the progressive, modernising Nation party and the pro-Islamic caliphate-reactionary Hezb al-Watany (Nationalist party)[9] – reached its climax in 1977. Sadat decided the outcome; he named as the victor his Watany party (founded in 1978), which became the ruling party until the overthrow of the Mubarak regime in 2011. The resultant regressive transformation in society was swift and almost effortless, to the surprise even of Adham himself.[10]

Beside Islamism, Sadat emphasised his 'fellaheen roots', using national television to give interviews from his childhood village in the Delta sporting designer *fellah* outfits. Once exclusive to cadets from the upper classes and more highly educated social strata, the police forces became open for *fellaheen* with their strong Islamic cultural background and anti-modernity attitude. They also ran state security in the 1970s, rounding up left-wing students, secular activists and intellectuals.

In the seventh century AD, Alexandria had been the last of Egypt's cities to fall to the Arab army after two years of siege, and the very last to convert en masse to Islam. After the 1977 defeat, she was also the last city to surrender to Islamist forces as she held out until the end of the twentieth century. The city's cosmopolitanism and strong economy guarded against the *fellaheen* migrants with their minds shaped by Quranic *kuttab* teaching and hostile calls from al-Azhar and its *ulama*.

The clergymen rejected modernity and carried a hatred for the head of *frengeh* (Napoleon) and his ungodly ending of their control of society. They handed their hatred for modernity down the generations. Al-Azhar's revenge on modernity was a dish waiting to be served cold, mostly by non-graduate Islamic teachers, *fe'ies*, who came low in the hierarchical professional and class order *fe'iat* (social classes).* *Fellaheen* boys who couldn't afford to complete al-Azhar's seminar but who managed to learn the Quran by heart became *fe'ies*, packing the entire Muslim 'gospel' into *kuttab* boys' heads without their understanding it. *Fe'ies* were the stuff of urban jokes and stand-up comedians, revolving around their greed, hypocrisy and homosexuality. Following the loss of her status after the 1952 military coup, it was only a matter of time before Alexandria gave in to the combined dark forces of Islamism and rural newcomers without culture or taste.

---

*The class explanation was a more plausible origin of the word fe'ie than the suggested corruption of faqih. Faqih meant a learned Islamic jurist, who would require a higher level of seminary study at al-Azhar (equivalent to a Master's in Islamic theology), but a fe'ie holds no school qualification. A fe'ie was never held in high esteem by the populace, and always referred to in a dismissive way.

CHAPTER 58
A Tale of Two Daughters

Tante Zouzo's tragic story was highly symbolic. Her mother's sudden death left her older teenage sister, Naomi, to play the maternal role for the ten-year-old Zouzo and her brothers, aged seven and five. After finishing French schooling in Alexandria, Zouzo and her friends wild behaviour raised eyebrows even by Alexandria's hedonistic standards. During her father's terminal illness, her guardianship was moved Naomi and her much older al-Azhar clergyman husband. This older widower, whom Naomi had married under pressure from her dying father, had two sons much older than his teenage wife. What mattered was the farmland, which the late father had inherited from Zouzo's mother, next to Naomi's husband's large plot. Naomi, in turn, wanted to secure finances and care for her younger siblings' education.

Naomi's husband, Sheikh Hassan, became Zouzo's de facto guardian. He forced Naomi to agree to Zouzo marrying his son, who was older than Naomi and 15 years Zouzo's senior. She kept rejecting the older *fellah*; her Alexandrian *chellah* also teased her about *le fiancé paysan*. Still under 21, Zouzo gave in to a combination of pressure by her older sister and a trick by the suitor. He turned up in a handsome suit and pretended to be a modern man, taking her to a seaside restaurant and promising her a honeymoon in Europe.

The next day, after the wedding in Cairo, they travelled to his village. Getting off the train, Zouzo stepped from the courteous Jekyll's company into *'un autre monde'*. Her remark was met by a smack from 'Sheikh Hyde's' slipper as she was dragged by the hair into a waiting horse-drawn carriage. He ordered her to be obedient and never to utter a word of French again. She was isolated in his father's country house, only allowed pocket money at his pleasure until he died in 1972. Her spirit was broken.

Alexandria Adieu

In 1950, *Tante* Zouzo didn't resemble the girl in the pictures with my mother, looking much older than the latter. She was a nervous wreck with a schizophrenic attitude to life – a frightened little mouse in the sheikh's presence, always covering her hair in a single-colour, dark *écharpe*. Away from the husband, mostly when she was with *Maman* and old friends, she enjoyed the old life: champagne and piano playing, but always with sad melodies. Only after an extended stay with my mother would the old Zouzo emerge, making a pun (in French) or commenting on fashion. She only drank and smoked when alone in Alexandria, not when she stayed with the sheikh and her children in a wooden chalet, part of her inheritance, half a mile from our villa.

She was the only one among her old, all-women circle of friends who would not change into a *maillot* or sunbathe on the *plage*. Zouzo would sit with an *écharpe* wrapped around her head or a wide-brim hat and large sunglasses concealing most of her face. She feared someone would tell her husband or, worse, that one of the mostly Italian photographers roaming the *plage* with a box camera and tripod would snap her. This would invite harsh punishment; she would receive a beating, with the slipper on her head, if the sheikh smelled cigarettes on her breath in the bedroom. Another time, after they had been married for many years, the sheikh discovered two Birra Stella bottles hidden by their 17-year old son in the fridge in their Cairo home. Although she had known nothing about them, she carried the scar from one of the bottles on her forehead for the rest of her life.

Zouzo's clergyman *fellah* husband entered into partnership with a businessman from a Gulf Arab country. They bought four villas in Alexandria and turned them into high-rises, with a mosque included in the development, that ruined a once-beautiful road with gardens and trees. The same era (the late 1970s to the end of the twentieth century) also witnessed good Muslim *fellaheen* from Egypt and businessmen from Arabia systematically dismantling other facets of Alexandria's cultural identity. Offering prices that freeholders or long-lease holders could never dream of paying, they started with nightclubs, then theatres and cinemas, followed by iconic art galleries and bars – turning them into wedding parlours, blocks of flats or commercial buildings.

The last time I saw *Tante* Zouzo was during my 1974 trip to Cairo covering the post-Yom Kippur War talks. She invited me for lunch and tried to match-make me with her recently graduated medical-doctor daughter. Like most Egyptian girls of her generation, she had good looks and a good sense of humour, but I didn't find her attractive; she wasn't Alexandrian, nor was any of her siblings. They took after their father in customs and outlook on life. Her older brother became influential in the central state-security agency, which was no longer

CHAPTER 58 A Tale of Two Daughters

run by the Western-educated upper middle classes. The agency became semi-militarised under Nasser. It was one of the regime's three tools for imposing Nasser's *diktat* along with the *Mukhabarat* and its secret arms, and the SF (Socialist Federation) and its sub-organisations. When Sadat took over, he used the same tools to broaden the country's Arabisation in order to encompass Islamisation. With this mindset, officers like Zouzo's son found a sense of superiority when he ruled parts of Alexandria. He didn't need to become an Alexandrian, like thousands of migrants who settled on her saffron soil had done for generations, but Alexandria had to conform to his view of the world. Instead of enforcing the law, the state-security apparatuses and police broke the law to advance an ideologically backward political agenda. The likes of the late sheikh's son went further, enforcing their own Islamic morality on the Maid of the Mediterranean.

In 2008, I was invited to a relative's daughter's wedding in Alexandria. The bride had stayed with us briefly during her studies in England, so naturally my daughter was invited too. We bought generous quantities of champagne and drinks, four times the allowance at Alexandria-Nuzha Airport's duty-free shop (owned by Egypt Air, the same airline that had stopped serving alcohol a couple of years earlier to conform to Islamic teaching). As the girls wanted to hold a hen party for the bride, the host sent one of her office *sa'ies* to buy more drinks for the many unexpected guests who all came to meet my daughter. After two hours of driving around, he couldn't find any available. The day coincided with some obscure date in the Muslim calendar, and the sale of alcohol had been 'voluntarily' banned on police 'advice' following a call by a radical imam.

No alcohol was served at the extravagant wedding party held at a top Alexandrian hotel, the city's best entertainers were noticeably self-censoring. This was a different world from the fun at the merrier (and financially more modest) weddings I had witnessed in the 1950s, with performers' bawdy jokes and sexy *balady* dancers when champagne (or a cheaper equivalent, depending on affordability) was served. It turned out that the groom's father had insisted on such boredom after recently landing a prestigious university post where the upper echelon, who were top-table guests at the wedding (none was a relative, but this was career diplomacy), had become staunch believers in the new-found Islamic morality. But Alexandria, already losing her mind, was still holding onto a few threads that Cleopatra had woven into her soul. In keeping with their old traditions, the bride's friends held a normal Alexandrian after-party at which champagne flowed, doubling the bill that the poor bride's father had to pay the delighted hotel manager – who must have been praying for more of such two-eras-in-one, schizophrenic weddings.

EPILOGUE:
The Gods Abandoned Alexandria*

Alexandria slipped through our fingers; Papa's prophecy came true. My last evening in Alexandria. How long had I walked since the taxi dropped me at the corner of Rue Sultan Hessein? I hadn't bothered to learn the new, alien name of the street. I must have been walking for 150 years since sunset, returning from a Sidi-Bishr that I no longer recognised.

I walked down the narrow back streets; on my left (eastwards) lay the start of el-Missallah neighbourhood, with its fancy leather shops where I once bought a handbag for the dancer Suad. I wanted to pass Rue de l'église Debbanè, the church erected by the Alexandrian Debbanès who had built a theatre and schools in the nineteenth century, and turned left along Rue Fuad. Here, the great Italian and French buildings still resisting the onslaught of ugliness, but for how long?

I reached the great arch on the left, leading to Teatro Zizinia, renamed Muhammad Ali Theatre, built by Bovio for Zizinia in the nineteenth century. This great neighbourhood still smells of Cavafy's Alexandria; he lived around the corner. Where is that big, dusty, bronze bell that had remained on the ground for as long as Alexandria could remember? Did it really belong to the Greek Orthodox cathedral, and nobody could lift it up there? Another few stitches embroidered in Alexandria's folkloric tapestry.

I walked among great Italian architecture, trying to remember what the facades used to look like. Unlike the human ear's ability to filter out

---

* In certain paragraphs here, I insert some of Cavafy's famous poem 'The God Abandons Antony' to reflect the mood of losing Alexandria when her gods abandoned her or, rather, were driven out of the city.

EPILOGUE: The Gods Abandoned Alexandria

noise when listening to a familiar piece of music, the eyes can't remove the hundreds of ugly signs that pockmarked Avoscani's, Bovio's and Loria's creations.

Alexandria *did* slip through our fingers.

Earlier in the afternoon, after having had a long lunch at Athinèos, gazing at a storm above the Eastern Harbour, I asked the first cabbie at the rear of the Italian consulate, '*share's kenisset Debbane*'. A stupid look on his face and a head shake. The second didn't know three equally famous roads. 'Take me to Rue Princesse Fawzia', and I opened the door and sat in the back of the third taxi. He didn't recognise the street either.

'*Game'h Sidi-Bisher, S'il vous plaît, ya usta*'; he sped eastward. Without the odd glimpse of the corniche, I wouldn't have recognised Alexandria as we drove through a continuous jungle of ugliness that was an affront to the eyes. Wait a minute; I know where we are! This is the Montazah Green by Sidi-Bishr Mosque; it looked smaller, squeezed by intimidating high-rise blocks.

'So we were going through rue Princesse Fawzia, *ya Usta*; don't you know the name of this famous road?' The driver looked at me.

'This is Khalid ibn-el-Walid road, *ya pasha*; how long have you been away? you forget?' *I* forgot? Who *has* forgotten Alexandria? *Me*?

Who the f*** is Ibn-el-Walid?

What had he given Alexandria, or done for the city, to merit replacing a more significant name – the princess who set up a charitable orphanage and a school in the area – with his name? The seventh-century Arab warrior who fought the Persians and the Iraqis had never set foot in Egypt, and I doubt if he could have pointed to Alexandria on the map!

I wanted to take a look at the rocks of the Devil's Hole, or Miami, but all seemed like a different cosmos…

I must have doubled back – memory-dreamwalking through boulevard Cherif, Rue Tawfik and St Katherine's Green – because I looked at the Bourse clock. It was suddenly midnight; I marched on the drumbeat, watching the invisible procession going by; I hear the exquisite music and voices mourning, and I listen, against the Alexandrian poet's advice. Goodbye to Alexandria, that is leaving. No, my ears aren't deceiving me, and I am not fooling myself; this was not a dream, this is not my final declaration as I listen with deep emotions to the voices, to the exquisite music of that strange long, long, long procession leaving Alexandria.

Alexandria, the capital of memories with history's paint strokes, adding more layers to the tableaux of time. I followed the long, invisible procession, passing through 2,300-year-long streets. The procession reached Fathy Mahmoud's bright white (Maid of the Mediterranean) *Europa and the Bull*, with its blinding white sails bringing the light

Alexandria Adieu

from Europe (or were they shining Alexandria's light to the whole world, as her lighthouse did for centuries?). The procession passed tombstones, with many names: Lucky my dog, Esther Cohen, *Oncle* Moheb, Shlomo Cohen, *Tante* fortune, *Tante* Carlota, *Usta* Franco... many more in the locked dusted, destroyed, cemetery; the unknown Greek soldiers and many others who defended Alexandria and fought during the War; and the names of those who built Alexandria. All fading on crumbling tombstones...

I wander in the old central streets laid down by Dinocrates like a lone survivor of a devastating earthquake, what was familiar in Alexandria for thousands of years crashing about my senses.*

The familiar names, faded on decaying signs, once marked the clinics of good doctors; Max Salama, *Docteur* Labib, *Docteur* Caracatsanis, *Docteur* Orvand.

Hotel Cecil's residents' privilege – Montgomery's Bar serves drinks all night; but I have already packed. In a couple of hours or so, I will say goodbye to her, to Alexandria that is leaving.

Our Alexandria was a unique culture and world on her own. Alexandria's mind was the love child of 4,000 years of the Egyptian civilisation's knowledge and wisdom and Greek philosophy, with all its understanding in many disciplines – infused by Alexander's spirit. Will his grave be found in our lifetimes?

Alexandria was a tableau painted by the quills of Durrell, Cavafy, and Forster. Alexandria was the energy sparked between the minds of intellectuals, between two lovers walking along the corniche as the Mediterranean waves massaged their aroused emotions, the spark in their shy kisses under giant trees hugging their moon-reflected shadows on the bank of al-Mahmoudiya Canal. Alexandria was music, concerts, drama, parties, poetry, paintings, opera, ballet, *balady* dance, and old china raining down from windows at midnight every New Year.

Say goodbye to her, to Alexandria leaving.

Alexandria was the minds, experiences, agonies and ecstasies of her children who walked, crawled, begged and danced on roads paved with the pages of history; her people, the finest stardust in the universe's centuries, whose bones, sorrows and dreams became her saffron soil. The Alexandrians, all of them intellectuals, street-sweepers, writers, artists, singers, vendors, waiters, soldiers, bakers, investors, merchants, dancers, doctors, actors, travellers, prostitutes, nuns, nurses, sailors, saints, sinners, dock-workers, teachers, tram-conductors and pickpockets preying on new immigrants searching for a better life. Have I missed anyone?

---

*Here, I use some phrases from Durrell's Quartet, when the character of Darley wanders the streets of Alexandria.

EPILOGUE: The Gods Abandoned Alexandria

Ah, yes, of course, barmen. I bought the barman another drink, downing my last Cecil cognac before turning away from the bar.

Shall I go firmly to the window and listen with deep emotions and try to see, to find out what happened to them? The heroes and heroines in the tapestry telling my story of Alexandria.

I once knew their addresses.

I consciously decided that I didn't want to see any of my Alexandria lovers. The youngest ones still alive among them would be septuagenarians by now. I want to remember them, as and where I left them: beautiful, young, sexy and alluring.

Farida the unique one; Suad the nightclub dancer; Nadiya the comedian; Nariman the rebel, the seductive Cairo university student and her girlfriend; *les filles* Haroun; Handy Huda; Mouna-Mouth; Maroula the mermaid; Naughty Neta; Faiza Fassad; Flirty Francesca; Shafikah Shafaief; Sexy Sonia; Shiny Shams, and the mysterious, nameless girl with whom I made love in the dark on a train in 1968 without our saying a word to one another. Love doesn't stop because of time–space–distance separation?

I still love them; we have bodily parted, but I, with each girl, consciously or subconsciously, have taken up emplacements in each other's mind forever. The girls were, individually or collectively, my sensual biological Alexandria; each one has hung her portrait in my gallery of prose.

It was still dark, before dawn, when I asked the taxi taking me to the airport to do a detour through the empty streets of Alexandria…I got out of the cab on the corner of what was once the mouth of the Ptolemaic canal, past the modern Bibliotheca Alexandrina at the foot of Cape Silsilah. I stood in the cold, wet breeze gazing with a crowded head at the Eastern Harbour.

The driver must have thought, 'this *khawaga magnoon*, who speaks like a true Alexandrian, but he was still a mad *khawaga* wasting his money going in the opposite direction'

But this *khawaga magnoon* wanted to stand looking at Fathy Mahmoud's *Europa and the Bull* sculpture: Zeus's voyage with Europa from Tyre, ending with his ravishing her in Crete, where the story of Alexandria began.

Crete? Will the plane fly over Crete?

I hadn't finished my Buck's Fizz when the hostess instructed me to buckle my seatbelt for take-off.

Was the flight route retreating Zeus's voyage carrying Europa, the reverse of the journey to founding Alexandria?

My Alexandria was not any city; she was a whole cosmos, a unique concept, a living being with mind, heart, spirit and memory.

Alexandria Adieu

My Alexandria of the mid-twentieth century, in the peak of her beauty, was a complex of ten centuries of the accumulated legacy.

Alexandria, a child of Cleopatra and a mother to Hypatia, had been poisoned in her prime, aged and decayed in a mere 30 years.

It took a thousand years from the Arab invasion until the rebirth of the city of Alexander at the hands of another Macedonian builder of nations, Muhammad Ali...how long would it take this time before a second rebirth?

But, before the chapters of her second-coming story could be completed, the gods abandoned Alexandria...

Listen...the final declaration – listen to the voices, to the exquisite music of that strange procession, and say goodbye to her, to the Alexandria you are losing.

The plane climbed, first southwest, then turning slowly over Lake Mareotis, making half a circle over Alexandria heading northeast. I looked out of the window; the great city getting smaller, swallowed by the mist of a widening gap between us...I waved, ...Alexandria...Adieu.

Notes

Prologue; : Alexandria…Where?
[1]From Cavafy's 1898 poem 'Waiting for the barbarians', *C.P. Cavafy: Collected Poems* (Translated by Keeley, Edmund and Sherrard, Philip), Princeton University Press, Princeton, NJ, 1975.

Chapter 1 – The Trianon – and a Trio of Writers
[1]One needle was still visibly standing in a photograph taken in 1860 during construction of the square on land reclaimed from the sea. See Haag, Michael, *Vintage Alexandria: Photographs of the City 1860-1960*, AUC Press, Cairo and New York, 2008, p. 27.
[2]See Chapter 7 – 'Tram Number 4, Old Alexandria'.
[3]Scores of books written about the Obelisk were published, but the easiest read and most comprehensive account is D'Alton, Martina, *The New York Obelisk, or How Cleopatra's Needle Came to New York and What Happened When It Got Here*, Metropolitan Museum of Art/Abrams, New York, 1993.
[4]Forster, E.M., *Alexandria: A History and a Guide*, Whitehead Morris Limited, Alexandria, 1922. Most recently, with an introduction by Lawrence Durrell, was the Tauris Parke paperback edition: New York, 1974.
[5]*New York Times*, 28 April 1930.
[6]Lagoudis Pinchin, Jane, *Alexandria Still: Forster, Durrell, and Cavafy*, Princeton University Press, Princeton, NJ, 1977 is one of the best books written about Alexandria and those three great writers.
[7]Haag, *Vintage Alexandria*.
[8]The title of the Alexandria Quartet's 1957 first volume: Durrell, Lawrence, *Justine- A Novel*, E.P. Dutton & Co. Inc., New York, 1957.
[9]Translated by Edmund Keely and Philip Sherrard in the book *C.P.Cavafy*, Princeton University Press, Princeton, NJ, 1992.

Chapter 2 – Gare-Ramleh: Alexandria's Heart and History
[1]See Chapter 15 – '*Plages* and Policemen'.
[2]Reid, Donald Malcolm, *Whose Pharaohs?: Archaeology, Museums, and Egyptian National Identity from Napoleon to World War I*, California University Press, reprint, Los Angeles, 2003, pp. 150–1.
[3]'The History and Heritage of Gianaclis Wines in Egypt', *Cairo 365*, 11 November 2010 edition.
[4]See Chapter 50 – 'Plotters, Assassins and Fascists' on Nasser sending troops to Yemen and the civil war there.
[5]Rifaat, Ibrahim, General, *Mira'at el-Haramine, Travels in Higaz* (Arabic), Amiri Publishing and Printing, Cairo, 1925.

Chapter 3 – The Hotel Cecil
[1]Homer (translated by Robert Fitzgerald), *The Odyssey, Book IV*, Vintage Classics, London, 2017, pp. 355–9.
[2]Meyers, O.H. and Mond, Robert, *Temples of Armant, a Preliminary Survey, The Text*, Egyptian Exploration Society, London, 1940.

Alexandria Adieu

[3]Diodorus Siculus, *The Library of History, Book XVIII*, The Loeb Classical Library, 1947.
[4]Roller, Duane W., A guide to The Geography of Strabo (Strabo: Geographica- XVII), Cambridge University Press, 2018, pp. 941–8

Chapter 4 – The Hyphenated Alexandrians
[1]Hirst, Anthony and Silk Michael, *Alexandria Real and Imagined*, Centre for Hellenic Studies, King's College London, 2004, Chapter 11, pp. 204–5.
[2]Navet-Grèmillet, Marie- Cècile, Penelope Delta et Alaxandrie: une femme grecque a la confluence des langues et des cultures, thesis, Montpellier University, 1998 , p. 337.
[3]Reimer, Michael, *'Colonial Bridgehead: Social and Spatial Change in Alexandria, 1850–1882'*, International Journal of Middle East Studies, 20 (4), November 1988, pp. 531–53.
[4]Kokkinidis, Tasos, 'The Greeks of Alexandria', *Greek World Reporter*, 12 October 2019.
[5]ibid.
[6]See Chapter 2 – 'Gare-Ramleh: Alexandria's Heart and History'.
[7]Heyworth-Dunne, James, 'An Introduction to the History of Education in Modern Egypt', Luzac and Co., London, 1939.
[8]Navet-Grèmillet, P 500; Wright, Arnold and Cartwright, Henry, Adolphus, *Twentieth Century Impressions of Egypt. Its history, people, commerce, industries and resources*, Lloyd's Greater Britain Publishing Company, London 1909 P 321; Benaki Museum Archives No 820, 'The Benakis Museum hosts exhibits related to founders'.
[9]See Chapter 2 – 'Gare-Ramleh: Alexandria's Heart and History'.
[10]See Chapter 43 – 'Eden's Miscalculation'.
[11]Archives, Alexandria Chamber of Commerce.
[12]Interview with Sinai Greeks, *Sada-el-balad News*, 18 January 2020.
[13]Mylona, E, *A presence without Narrative: The Greeks in Egypt 1961-1976*, Ethnikon Kentron Koinonikon Ereunon (the Greeks abroad) a 1972 special issue of the *Journal of the Hellenic Diaspora*, the Greek National Centre of Research, Pella Publishing, Athens, 1972, p. 70.

Chapter 5 – Doctors and Dayas
[1]Wills, Adrian, 'Herophilus, Erasistratus, and the Birth of Neuroscience', *Lancet* 354 (9191), 13 November 1999, pp. 1719–20; Vrettos, Theodore, *Alexandria: City of the Western Mind*, Free Press, New York, 2001, pp. 66–70; Grant, Mark, *Galen on Food and Diet*, Routledge, London, 2000; Nutton, Vivian, 'The Chronology of Galen's Early Career', *Classical Quarterly* 23 (1), 1973, pp. 158–71. See also Serageldin, Ismail, 'Ancient Alexandria and the dawn of medical science', *Global Cardiology Science & Practice* 4, December 2013.
[2]Burrow, Gerard N., *'Clot-Bey, Founder of Western Medical Practice in Egypt'*, Yale Journal of Biology and Medicine, July 1975, pp. 251–7; Clot, Antoine B., *'On the Medical Institutions of Cairo'*, British and Foreign Medical Review, Quarterly Journal, October 1838, pp. 592–3.
[3]*Azhar Journal*, #1202, section 709, 29 January 1980.

Chapter 6 - The Annual Flower Parade
[1]Mizrahi, Maurice, 'The contribution of Jews to Egypt's Economic Development', in *L'Egypte et ses Juifs, le Temps Révolu,: (19e et 20e siècle)*, Diffusion Payot, Lausanne, 1977, pp. 85–93.
[2]Vertos, Theodore, *Alexandria: City of the Western Mind*, the Free Press, New York, 2002, p. 1476 (Kindle edition); also: Brown, Chip, 'The Search for Cleopatra: Archaeologists search for the true face—and the burial place—of the "world's first celebrity"', *National Geographic*, July 2011.

Chapter 7 – Tram Number 4, Old Alexandria

Notes

[1] Agayev, Elnur, 'The Mediterranean Visit and the Book of the Travels of the Russian Monk-Traveller Vasily Grigorovich-Barsky in the First Half of 18th century', *CEDRUS: The Journal of MCRI*, European University of Lefke, Cyprus, 2016, pp. 675–88.
[2] Severus of Ashmumeen (ibn al-Muqaffa, d.987) wrote the history of the Coptic patriarchs of the ninth century. His best-known work (in Arabic) was *Lampe de l'intellect*. Young, M.J.L. and Ebied, R.Y., *The Lamp of the Intellect of Severus ibn al-Muqaffa, Bishop of Al-Ashmunain*, Peeters Publishers, Leuven, 1975.
[3] St Mark The Evangelist, Basilica di San Marco website, Venice: http://www.basilicasanmarco.it/storia-e-societa/san-marco-evangelista/?lang=en.
[4] ibid.
[5] See Chapter 1 – 'The Trianon – and a Trio of Writers'.
[6] *Jackson's Oxford Journal*, 9 December 1820.
[7] See Brier, Bob, Saga of *Cleopatra's Needle*, *Archaeology*, The Archaeological Institute of America, Boston Vol 55 No 6 Nov/Dec 2002
[8] Sarba, Mark *Ancient Egyptian Obelisks, a Tragic Incident at Sea, and Marine Art* Zip06-Shore Publishing • 05 April 2017
[9] The Graphic, London, 21 September 1878.
[10] Dannenfeldt, Karl H., 'Egypt and Egyptian Antiquities in the Renaissance', *Studies in the Renaissance*, January 1959, pp. 7–27.
[11] Pennington, Benjamin, T., 'Paleoenvironmental surveys at Naukratis and the Canopic branch of the Nile', *Journal of Archaeological Science*, 7, January 2016, pp. 180–8.
[12] Reimer Colonial *Bridgehead* P 93; Mabro, "*Alexandria 1860-1960*," PP 247-253

Chapter 8 – 'Rue France, Stamps and Homework'
[1] Masters, Bruce, 'The 1850 Events in Aleppo: An Aftershock of Syria's Incorporation into the Capitalist World System', *International Journal of Middle East Studies*, 22, 1990, pp. 4, 6, 7.

Chapter 9 – 1,000 Guinnieh, and a Home in Moharrem-Bey
[1] Woodhouse, C.M., *The Battle of Navarino*, Hodder and Stoughton, London, 1965, p. 191.
[2] Cowles, Loyal, 'The Failure to Restrain Russia: Canning, Nesselrode and the Greek Question, 1825-1827', *International History Review*, 12(4), 1990, pp. 688–720.
[3] Durrell, Lawrence, *Balthazar*, Faber and Faber, London, 1958, p. 234.
[4] Tzalas, Harry E., *Farewell to Alexandria*, American University in Cairo Press, New York, 2000, p. 166: translation of the Greek *Alexandria ad Aegypum* first published in 1997. Tzalas is the founder and president the Hellenic Institute for Ancient *and* Medieval Alexandrian Studies.
[5] Weinthal, Benjamin, 'Ex-Israeli envoy reveals large number of Ashkenazi Jews lived in Cairo', *Jerusalem Post*, 6 January 2021.
[6] *Cahiers d'Alexandrie*, 1965 and 1966 series, Archaeological Society of Alexandria.
[7] Haag, Michael, 'To Alexandria with Eve Durrell', MichaelHaagBlogspot, 22 November 2011: http://michaelhaag.blogspot.com/2011/11/to-alexandria-with-eve-durrell.html

Chapter 10 – A Tale of Two Cities
[1] Abdallah, Abdelfattah, Dr, *Alexandria Amidst Fragrant History and Saffron Soil*, Author House, Bloomington, IN, 2016, p. 47.
[2] Wahby Tapia, Ricardo, *Memories of Alexandria: From a Void to Nothingness*, Author House, Bloomington, in, 2013, p. 127 (Kindle edition).
[3] Abu-Lughod, Janet, 'Tale of Two Cities: The Origins of Modern Cairo', *Comparative Studies in Society and History*, 7 (4), July 1965, pp. 429–30.
[4] Philip, John, *Reminiscences of Gibraltar, Egypt and the Egyptian War 1882 - from the Ranks*, Antony Rowe Ltd, Eastbourne, 1893. Sergeant Philp was present at the two battles of Kassassin, and also fought at the Battle of Tel-el-Kebir. At Kassassin, his head was 'creased' by a bullet and he attributes his survival to his chinstrap chain, which

Alexandria Adieu

deflected the lead-shot. His memoirs are a fascinating insight into an NCO's life, and should appeal to anyone interested in the Victorian army and the British Empire at the height of its power.

[5]Baer, Gabriel, *Studies in the Social History of Modern Egypt*, University of Chicago Press, Chicago, 1969, pp. 192–99.

[6]Butler, Alfred Joshua, *Court Life in Egypt*, Chapman and Hall Limited, London, 1887, p. 121.

[7]Johnston, Shirley and Sonbol, Sherif, *Egyptian Palaces and Villas, Pashas, Khedives and Kings*, Abrams New York 2006 PP25-26; 'Ras el-Tin Palace: Description, facts and history', *Sharm Club*, December 2018.

[8]Pallini, Christina and Riccarda Scaccaborazzi, Annalisa, 'British Planning Scheme for Alexandria and its Region 1834-1958', in Carlos Nunes Silva (ed.), *Urban Planning in North Africa*, Ashgate, Abingdon, 2016, Chapter 15, pp. 188–96.

[9]Wilkinson, John Gardener, Sir (1797–1875, known as the father of British Egyptology), *Handbook for Travellers in Egypt*, Murray's Foreign Handbooks, John Murray, London, 1880, p. 101.

[10]Rochfort Scott, Charles, Major-General (1797–1872), *Rambles in Egypt and Candia*, Colburn, London, 1837, Vol. I, p. 43.

[11]Butler, *Court Life in Egypt*. It was translated by Egyptian scholars like the other works of this remarkable 1877 Oxford graduate and PhD: *Ancient Coptic Churches of Egypt* (1884) and *The Arab Conquest of Egypt* (1902).

[12]For a detailed and well-researched further read on this section, see: Mansel, Philip, *Levant: Splendour and Catastrophe on the Mediterranean*, Yale University Press, New Haven, CT, 2011.

[13]Baer, Gabriel, 'The Beginnings of Municipal Government in Egypt', *Middle Eastern Studies*, 4 (2), January 1968, PP. 118–39.

[14]'Notes on Portraits of Nubar Pasha' by Theodors Rallis, which was offered by the artist as a token to friendship to Chakour Pasha: Sotheby's catalogue for the Greek Collection, 15 November 2006.

[15]Reid, Donald Malcolm, *Whose Pharaohs?: Archaeology, Museums, and Egyptian National Identity from Napoleon to World War I*; University of California Press paperback, Berkeley and Los Angeles, CA, reprint Los Angeles, 2003, pp. 150–1.

Chapter 11 – Language

[1]Orwell, George, *Nineteen Eighty-Four*, Penguin, London, 2008.

[2]Abdallah, Abdelfattah, Dr, *Alexandria Amidst Fragrant History and Saffron Soil*, Author House, Bloomington, IN, 2016. PP 29-33 (ebook edition)

[3]The 2020 genetic analysis found that Egyptians have only 17% Arab genes, 4% Jewish, 3% southern European and 68% North African, while the Lebanese had 54% Arab genes: https://www.ncbi.nlm.nih.gov/pmc/articles/PMC5844529

[4]El-Behary, Hend, 'DNA proves that Egyptians are not Arabs', Egypt Independent, 17 January 2017.

[5]Greater Alexandria's population grew from 1,249,034 on the eve of the Suez Crisis to 5,807,051 in 2019 – *World Population Review*: https://worldpopulationreview.com/world-cities/alexandria-population

[6]See Meguid, Ibrahim Abdel, *No One Sleeps in Alexandria* (Translated by Wahab, Farouk Abdel), American University Press, New York, 2006 – a detailed account citing newspaper reports of the raids and the mass exodus by *fellaheen* migrants. Also: Borghas, Valerio, *Sea Devils, Italian navy Commandos in WWII*, Naval Institute Press, Annapolis, MD, 1995.

[7]This was a letter he sent to King Philip III about the ill-treatment of the native Inca and their aspirations; see Hamilton, Roland (ed./trans.), Felipe Guaman Poma de Ayala's *The First New Chronicle and Good Government: On the History of the World and the Incas up to 1615*, University of Texas Press, Austin, TX, 2009.

[8]Pratt, Mary Louise, 'Arts of the Contact Zone', *Profession, 1991, pp. 33–40:* https://www.

jstor.org/stable/25595469?seq=1
[9]ibid.

Chapter 12 – Invasions and New Expressions

[1]See Wissa, Mariam, *The Last Revolt of Bashmur (831 a.d.) in Coptic and Syriac Histography* (Chapter 9 – 'Migration Histories of the Medieval Afroeurasian Transition Zone'), *Studies in Global Social History*, 39 (13), 2020, pp. 247–60; Brooks, E.W., *'The Relations Between the Empire and Egypt from a New Arabic Source', Byzantinische Zeitschrift*, 22 (2), August 2009; Goddard, Hugh, *A History of Christian-Muslim Relations*, New Amsterdam Books, Chicago, 2000.
[2]Some of the books that survived the burning of the Bibliotheca Alexandrina and were kept in Constantinople were translated on commission by the Medici family to establish their Platonic Academy in Florence in 1445: see Osman, Ahmed, *Out of Egypt: the roots of Christianity revealed*, Century Random House, London, 1998; Field, Arthur, M., *The Origins of the Platonic Academy of Florence*, Princeton University Press, Princeton, NJ, 1990. The works of the Alexandria School of Medicine, mathematicians, and philosophers – especially the Neoplatonists, like Hierocles of Alexandria, Hypatia and Philo of Alexandria – were unearthed by Renaissance philosophers: Iversen, Erik, *The Myth of Egypt and Its Hieroglyphics in European Tradition*, Gec Gad Publishers, Copenhagen, 1961, pp. 88–9, 124–45, 150–3.
[3]'the people of Alexandria', from a letter by Hadrian, 134 AD, in Plutrach V quoted in Vertos, Theodore, *Alexandria: City of the Western Mind*, Free Press, New York, 2002, pp. 179–80.
[4]Vertos, *Alexandria: City of the Western Mind*, p. 122.

Chapter 13 – Alexander: the Democratisation of Knowledge

[1]Pollard, Justin and Reid, Howard, *The Rise and Fall of Alexandria: Birthplace of the Modern World*, Viking-Penguin, New York, 2006.
[2]Tierney, Michael, 'Aristotle and Alexander the Great', *Studies: An Irish Quarterly Review*, 31 (122), June 1942, pp. 221–8.
[3]Arrian, *Anabasis* (translated by Robson, E.I.), Harvard University Press, Cambridge, MA, 1929.
[4]Diodorus Siculus, *Bibliotheca Historica*, translated by Oldfather, C.H., Harvard University Press, Cambridge, MA, 1933.
[5]Rufus, Quintus Curtius, 'Book 10', *Historiae Alexandri Magni* (edited by Hett, W.S. and Bolchazy-Carducci), Wauconda, IL, 1987.
[6]For the definition, see Dakhila, Jocelyne, 'The Lingua Franca from the Sixteenth to the Eighteenth Century A Mediterranean "Outside the Walls"?' *New Horizons, Mediterranean Research in the 21st Century*, 10, January 2016, pp. 91–107.
[7]Pratt, Mary Louise, 'Arts of the Contact Zone', *Profession*, 1991: https://www.jstor.org/stable/25595469?seq=1
[8]El-Tahtawi, Rifa'ah, *Takhlis el-Ibrees Fi Talkhis Paris* (Arabic- e-book), Noor Books, Cairo, 2014.
[9]See Chapter 24 – 'Youssef Chahine: Alexandria's Struggle with Internal Egypt': philosopher Dr Taha (Hessein) Hussein's (1889–1973) trial for blasphemy. Professor of Theology, Nasr Hamid Abu Zeid (1943–2010), was, for his critical analysis of the scripture, taken to court by Muslim colleagues and had to flee Egypt permanently with his wife. The critical essays of Judge Sheikh Ali Abd-el-Raziq (1888–1966), known as the father of secular Islam, led to his expulsion from the judicial establishment.
[10]Abu Zaid, Nasr Hamid, 'Mmashruʻ al-nahda bayna talfiqiyyat al-tabaqa wal-turath al-talfiqi' (The renaissance project as a pragmatic accommodation and falsification of the past), *al-Muhit al- thaqafi*, 1 March 2002; Abu Zaid, Nasr, Hamid And Nelson, Esther R., *Voice of An Exile: Reflections on Islam*, Greenwood Publishing Group, Westport, CT, 2004.
[11]This event itself didn't take place in history but was rather a creation of Cavafy's

imagination – see: Dimaras, C. Th. and Hass, Diana, 'Cavafy's Technique of Inspiration', *Grand Street*, 2 (3), Spring 1983, pp. 143–56.

Chapter 14 – The 'Devil's Hole'
[1] Tzalas, Harry, E., 'Twenty years of underwater archaeological and geophysical surveys in Alexandria by Greek Mission (1998-2017)', paper presented to the Hellenistic Alexandria Conference, Athens, December 2017.

Chapter 15 – Plages and Policemen
[1] See Chapter 2 – 'Gare-Ramleh: Alexandria's Heart and History'.

Chapter 16 – My Love Tutor
[1] Forster, E.M., *Alexandria, A History and a Guide*, Whitehead Morris Limited, Alexandria, 1922, p. 16.
[2] See Chapter 23 – 'Film Houses: a Way of Life'.

Chapter 17 – A Mischievous Generation
[1] Meguid, Ibrahim Abdel, *No One Sleeps in Alexandria* (translated by Wahab, Farouk Abdel), American University in Cairo Press, New York 2006, location 1458 in Kindle edition.

Chapter 18 – Schoolchildren Grow Up Fast
[1] See Chapter 17 – 'A Mischievous Generation'.
[2] Al-Kharrat, Edwar, *Girls of Alexandria* (translated by Liarder, Frances), Quartet Books, London, 1993, p. viii.
[3] ibid., p. 56.
[4] See Chapter 1 – 'The Trianon – and a Trio of Writers'.

Chapter 19 – The War Generation
[1] See Chapter 10 – 'A Tale of Two Cities'.
[2] Lampson, Miles, Sir, *Politics and Diplomacy in Egypt: The Diaries of Sir Miles Lampson-1935-1937* (edited by Yapp, M.E.), Oxford University Press, Oxford, 1997, p. 535.
[3] ibid., p. 310.
[4] Copeland, Miles, '*The Real Spy World*, Weidenfeld & Nicolson, London, 1974. See also Chapter 45 – 'The British Bombardment – and Occupation'.

Chapter 20 – Hats, Hantours and Harlots
[1] Abdallah, Abdelfattah, Dr, *Alexandria Amidst Fragrant History and Saffron Soil*, Author House, Bloomington, IN, 2016. PP 77-82

Chapter 21 – The Railways: Politics and Play
[1] Bailey, Michael R. (ed.), *Robert Stephenson - The Eminent Engineer*, Ashgate, Farnham, 2003, p. 150.
[2] Misr railroad Station, Alexandria, Egypt, The Victorian Web, 31 July 2020: http://www.victorianweb.org/history/empire/egypt/alexandria/8.html.
[3] Helmi, M.A.M., Helmi, A. and Ibrahim, M., *Egyptian Railways in 125 Years, 1852-1977*, Egypt National Rail Publications, Cairo, 1977, p. 4.
[4] Ettouney, Osama M., 'Railways Along The Nile Valley: The Early Years 1851-1879', *Railroad History*, 20, Spring–Summer 2010, pp. 60 and 63.
[5] Wiener, Lionel, *Egypt and its Railways, Parts I & II* (in English; originally in French, Brussels, 1932), Egyptian National Railway Publications, Cairo, 1974, p. 76.
[6] Hughes, Hugh, *Middle East Railways*. Continental Railway Circle, Harrow, England 1981. PP 12
[7] Helmi et al., *Egyptian Railways in 125 Years*, p. 4.

[8]Ettouney, 'Railways Along The Nile Valley', p. 63.
[9]Strage, Mark, *Cape to Cairo: The Rape of a Continent*, Harcourt Brace Jovanovich, New York, 1973, p. 153; Hughes, Hugh *Middle East Railways*, p. 17.
[10]Bailey, *Robert Stephenson*, p. 293.

Chapter 22 – Cairo Interlude

[1]Like many demotic Egyptian words, this term for 'bridge' was derived from Ottoman Turkish – in this case, *köprü*; many Ottoman phrases for fashion, home furniture and architecture were, in turn, taken from French and Italian.
[2]Ramadan, Ahmed, 'The Bridges over Troubled Water', *Egypt Independent*, 11 December 2010.
[3]See Darwish, Adel, 'Cairo Clash over Eiffel's Bridge', *The Independent*, London 1 April 1995.
[4]Greene, David Mason, *Greene's Biographical Encyclopaedia of Composers*, Doubleday and Company, Garden City, NY, 1985; Predota, Georg, 'Verdi: Aida, Premiered Today in 1871', *Interlude.hk*, 24 December 2018; Grutz, Jane, 'An Opera for Egypt', *Aramco World*, 64 (5), October 2013, p. 10.
[5]Pallini, Cristina, 'Italian Architects and Modern Egypt', paper for the Aga Khan Program for Islamic Architecture at the Massachusetts Institute of Technology, 2004, pp. 39–50; Khalil, Mahmoud Ali, 'The Italian Architecture in Alexandria', Master's thesis, Kore University of Enna, Sicily, 2009, pp. 19–20.
[6]There is a detailed description of Ismail's visit to Paris with the Egyptian delegation, made up of various technocrats, and the Egyptian exhibition as well as the reception in the court, by Egyptian-born French writer Robert Solè from diaries and news reports of the 1860s: Solè, Robert, *Le Sèmaphore d'Alexandrie*, Seuil, Paris, 1997.
[7]Predota, 'Verdi: Aida, Premiered Today'.
[8]See footnote in Chapter 2 – 'Gare-Ramleh: Alexandria's Heart and History'.
[9]See Chapter 45 – 'Tawfik–Ourabi: the Constitution'.
[10]Police commander Salah Shadi (1921-1989) a member of the Muslim Brotherhood SS (Special assassination Squad), claimed Nasser and other FOA participated in the arsons that started at casinos near the opera house. *Ikhwan-on-Line,* 14 August 2008
[11]My interviews with Gen Naguib 1982–3. Also Naguib's memoirs: Naguib, Muhammed, *Kunt Ra'isa le-Misr* (I was President of Egypt, a memoir), Modern Egyptian Publications, Cairo, 1984, See also Chapter 46 – 'The Alexandria–Misr Rift'.
[12]Meguid, Ibrahim, Abdel, *Clouds Over Alexandria* (translated by Heikkinen, Kay), American University in Cairo Press, Cairo, 2019, p. 74.
[13]In 1999, archaeologists claimed it to be between 7,000 and 9,000 years old by studying 'precipitation-induced weathering': Williams, Paige, 'How Old is The Sphinx?', NBC News, 11 February 1999.

Chapter 23 – Film Houses: a Way of Life

[1]The Egyptian pound (£€) was worth £1.20 at the time of the Suez War; it fell to one-twenty-fourth of this value over the subsequent 60 years to £1= £€20.
[2]The French franc, accepted in Alexandria and equal to 4 Egyptian *piastres*.
[3]See Chapter 11 – 'Language'.
[4]El Hadari, Ahmed, *Tarikh el-Cinema fi Misr - 1896-1930* (History of Film in Egypt), Cairo Cinema Club Publications, Cairo, 1989.
[5]Abou-Chadi, Ali, *A Chronology of the Egyptian Cinema in One Hundred Years 1896-1994* (translated by Amin, Nora), Supreme Council for Culture, Cairo, 1998.
[6]El Bendari, Mona and El Ebiari, Mervat, *El Cinema el Tasgiliya fi Misr,* Supreme Council for Culture and National Centre for Cinema, Cairo, 1981.
[7]Shimi, Said, *Tarikh el Tasweer el Cinema'I fi Misr: 1897-1966*, National Council for Cinema, Cairo, 197; *The Birth of the Seventh Art in Alexandria*, The Bibliotheca Alexandrina Publications, Alexandria, 2007 PP 12,17, 49
[8]Ibid PP 49, 273, 181-4, 312-15, 373; Elhami, Hassan, *Tarikh el Cinema el Misreyah*

(History of Egyptian Cinema), Sondouk el Tanmeyah el Thaqafiyah, Cairo, 1995.
[9]Mahmoud, Ali, *Mozakirât Mohamed Karim fi Târîkh el Cinema el Misreyah*, Akâdimeyat el Founoun, Cairo, 2006.
[10]Darwish, Mustafa, *Dream Makers on the Nile - A Portrait of Egyptian Cinema*, American University in Cairo Press, Cairo, 1998.
[11]El Ghandour, Mona, *Sultanat el Shasha: Ra'idât el Cinema el Misreyah* (Pioneering Women in Egyptian Cinema), Riyad el Rayyes Books, Cairo, 2005.
[12]'Bahiga Hafez', feature in *El Helal*, 10, October 1965, pp. 27–31.
[13]Farid, Samir, *Safahat Maghoula min Tarikh el Cinema*, The Supreme Council for Culture, Cairo, 1994.
[14]Bibliotheca Alexandrina, Alexandrian Cinema archives.

Chapter 24 – Youssef Chahine: Alexandria's Struggle with Internal Egypt
[1]See Chapter 10 – 'A Tale of Two Cities' for Suleiman Pasha (General Sève).
[2]Forster's lover, Muhammed Al-Adl, was a tram conductor and the phrase Hermes psychopompós' also 'means conductor of the souls', Hagg also suggests that Al-Adl was Forster's muse for the book. Haag, Michael, *Alexandria: City of Memory*, American University in Cairo Press, Cairo, 2005, pp. 109 and 54.
[3]Prisse d'Avennes, (Achille Constant Thèodore Émile) ; Émile Bernard, *Petits mémoires secrets de la cour d'Egypte, 1826-1867 suivis d'une Étude sur les almées*, J. Bernard, Paris, 1930, pp. 29, 30.
[4]Abu Zaid, Nasr Hamid, 'Mashru' al-nahda bayna talfiqiyyat al-tabaqa wal-turath al-talfiqi', *al-Muhit al- thaqafi*, 1 March 2002.
[5]Darwish, Adel, 'Professor Nasr Hamed Abu Zaid: Modernist Islamic philosopher who was forced into exile by fundamentalists', *The Independent*, London 14 July 2010.
[6]See Chapter 56 – 'The Second Arab Conquest' and Chapter 57 – 'Paving the way for Sadat's Islamisation'.
[7]Raziq, Ali, Abd-el, *Islam and the Foundations of Political Power* (edited by Filali-Ansary, Abdou; translated by Loutfi, Maryam), Vol. 2, Edinburgh University Press, Edinburgh, 2013, p. 144.
[8]Ali, Souad T., *A religion, not a state: Ali' Abd al-Raziq's Islamic justification of political secularism*, University of Utah Press, Salt Lake City, UT, 2009.
[9]Emara, Muhammed, 'Egypt between the secular state and theocracy', *The Best Known Twentieth Century Debates – Volume I* (Arabic), Al-Manhal, Cairo, January 2011.
[10]Abu Zaid, Nasr Hamid and Nelson, Esther R., *Voice of An Exile: Reflections on Islam*, Greenwood Publishing Group, Westport, CT, 2004.

Chapter 25 – Naguib Mahfouz, Censorship and 'Alexandrian Man'
[1]See Chapter 50 – 'Plotters, Assassins and Fascists'.
[2]Sadat, Jihan, *Woman of Egypt*, Simon & Schuster, New York, 1987 and *My hope for peace*, Simon & Schuster, New York, 2009.
[3]Wilde, Oscar, *The Artist as Critic: Critical Writings of Oscar Wilde* (edited by Ellmann, Richard), W.H. Allen & Co., London, 1970. Part I: 'A Dialogue', pp. 948–56.
[4]Nietzsche, Friedrich, *The Birth of Tragedy from the Spirit of Music* (translated by Smith, Douglas), Oxford University Press, Oxford, 2008.

Chapter 26 – Change and 'Uglification'
[1]See Chapter 18 – 'Schoolchildren Grow Up Fast'.

Chapter 27 – Heikal's Paradox: a Schizophrenic Attitude to Culture
[1]Vatikiotis, P.J., *The Modern History of Egypt*, Weidenfeld & Nicolson, London, 1976, pp. 179–83, 203, 235–6.
[2]See Chapter 47 – 'The Alexandria–Misr Rift'.
[3]Darwish, A, 'Youssif Idris - Egyptian Novelist, playwright and writer', *The Independent*,

London 3 August 1991: https://www.academia.edu/38345792/Youssif_Idris_-_Egyptian_Novelist_playwright_and_writer

Chapter 28 – Alexandria and God
[1] See Chapter 1 – 'The Trianon – and a Trio of Writers'.
[2] Forster, E.M., *Alexandria: A History and a Guide*, Whitehead Morris Limited, Alexandria, 1922, p. 19.
[3] ibid., p. 45.
[4] ibid.
[5] There is a lengthy and excellent exploration and analysis of Forster's ideas in: Lagoudis Pinchin, Jane, *Alexandria Still: Forster, Durrell, and Cavafy*, Princeton University Press, Princeton, NJ, 1977, pp. 82, 86, 100–13, 115–18, 124–8, 130, 132–3 and 147–8.
[6] Al-Ghazali, Hamid Abu, *Al-Maqsad al-Asna fi Sahrh Asmaè Allah al-Husna* (translated by Burrell, David B. and Daher, Nazih), Islamic Texts Society, Cambridge, 1992. Also, see why the Quran is a better source since there is no single-authority official list: Morgan, Diane, *Essential Islam: A Comprehensive Guide to Belief and Practice*, ABC-Clio, Santa Barbara, CA, 2010, p. 10.
[7] Forster *Alexandria: A History and a Guide*, p. 34.
[8] Durrell, Lawrence, *Justine- A Novel*, E.P. Dutton & Co. Inc., New York, 1957, p. 193.
[9] ibid., p. 77.
[10] ibid.
[11] Lagoudis Pinchin, *Alexandria Still*, p. 135.
[12] Al-Kharrat, Edwar, *Filles d'Alexandrie* (Girls of Alexandria) (translated by Liardet, Frances), Quartet Books, London, 1993.

Chapter 29 – Miss World
[1] Durrell, Lawrence, *Justine- A Novel*, E.P. Dutton & Co. Inc., New York, 1957, p. 67.
[2] Personal chats with Eric Morley in the 1970s.
[3] Morley, Eric, *The Miss World Story*, Angley Books, Maidstone, 1967.

Chapter 31 – Songs Move Closer to Allah's Politics
[1] Darwish, Adel, 'Sheikh Sharawi - The Man who Perfected TV Evangelism and helped Islamise Egyptian Society', *Academia.edu* 1998: https://www.academia.edu/38336056/Sheikh_Sharawi-_The_Man_who_Perfected_TV_Evangelism_and_helped_Islamise_Egyptian_Society; Obituary: Sheikh Mohamed Mutwali Sharawi, The Independent, London 22 October 2011.
[2] See Chapter 37 – 'The Treaty and the Journals'.

Chapter 32 – Leila Murad: Alexandria's Songstress
[1] See Chapter 31 – 'Songs Move Closer to Allah's Politics'.
[2] Teveth, S., *Ben-Gurion's spy: the story of the political scandal that shaped modern Israel*, Columbia University Press, New York 1996, p. 81; Lutz, James and Lutz, Brends, *Global Terrorism*, Psychology Press, Hove, 2004, p. 46; for general comprehensive reading on the affair, see: Golan, Aviezer, *Operation Susannah, as told by Marcell Nino, Victor Levy, Robert Dassa and Philip Natanson* (Foreword by Golda Meir), Harper & Row, New York, 1978.
[3] Hussein, Taha, *Mustaqbal al-thaqafah fi Misr* (Arabic), dar el-Maarif, Cairo, 1938.
[4] See Chapter 33 – 'Cosmopolitan Festivities'.

Chapter 34 – Alexandria's Jews – a Second Exodus
[1] See details in Chapter 53 – 'Nasser's Defiance: the Suez War'.
[2] Roumani, Maurice, 'The Final Exodus of the Libyan Jews in 1967', *Jewish Political Studies Review* 19 (3–4), October 2007, pp. 78, 79, 80–8; De Felice, Renzo, *Jews in an Arab Land: Libya, 1835-1970*, University of Texas Press, Austin, TX, 1985, pp.

Alexandria Adieu

258–61.

[3]Basri, Carol, 'The Jewish Refugees from Arab Countries', *Fordham International Law Journal*, 26 (3), Article 6, 2002.

[4]For details of such measures, which forced many Jews to leave although they were not 'officially' deported, see André Aciman's account of the intimidating phone calls after his father's factory and firm were sequestrated – incidentally, putting Egyptian workers out of a job: Aciman, André, *Out of Egypt: A memoir*, Harvill Press, London, 1996. On the mounting pressure on Jews who 'chose' to leave, see Lagando, Lucette, *The Man in the White Sharkskin Suit: A Jewish Family's Exodus from Old Cairo to the New World*, HarperCollins, New York, 2007.

[5]Anderson, Sonia, *An English Consul in Turkey: Paul Rycaut at Smyrna, 1667-1678*, Oxford University Press, Oxford, 1989, pp. 30, 234, 244.

[6]There is a good study by Bernard Lewis (1916–2018), the first Western historian to be granted access to the Ottoman archives: Lewis, Bernard, *Ottoman Observers of Ottoman Decline, Islamic Studies*, Vol. 1, Islamic Research Institute, Islamabad, 1962, pp. 71–8. On printing and the Tulip Revolution, see: Sabev, Orlin, 'The First Ottoman Turkish Printing Enterprise: Success or Failure?', in Dana Sajed (ed.), *Ottoman Tulips, Ottoman Coffee: Leisure and Life style in the Eighteenth Century*, Tauris Academic Studies, 2007, pp. 63–89; Clogg, Richard, '*An Attempt to Revive Turkish Printing in Istanbul in 1779*', *International Journal of Middle East Studies* 10 (1), 1979, pp. 67–70; Erginbas, Vefa, *Forerunner Of The Ottoman Enlightenment: Ibrahim Muteferrika and His Intellectual Landscape*, Sabanci University Press, Istanbul, 2005, pp. 1, 46–47; Erginbas, Vefa, 'Enlightenment in the Ottoman Context: İbrahim Müteferrika and His Intellectual Landscape', in Geoffrey Roper (ed.), *Historical Aspects of Printing and publishing in Languages of the Middle East*, Brill Publishing, Leiden, 2014, pp. 53–89.

[7]Kramer, Gurdun, *The Jews in Modern Egypt, 1914-1952*, I.B.Tauris, London, 1989, pp. 31, 162–3, 233.

[8]Meguid, Ibrahim Abdel, *Touore el-A'anbar* (Birds of Amber) (translated by Wahab, Farouk Abdel), American University in Cairo Press, Cairo, 2005.

[9]Lagnado, *The Man in the White Sharkskin Suit*, p. 160.

[10]See Aciman, *Out of Egypt*.

[11]For more detailed accounts, see Carasso, Lucienne, *Growing Up Jewish in Alexandria: The Story of A Sephardic Family's Exodus from Egypt*, CreateSpace Independent Publishing Platform, North Charleston, SC, 2014.

[12]Montasar, Farah, 'Jews of the Nile' (extracts from older interviews with Egyptian-Jewish communist Youssef Darwish [1910–2006] on his memories with Alexandrian-French Jew Jacques Hasson [1936–1999] – part of the research on the film *The Jewish alley of Old Cairo*, released 2015), *Al-Ahram Weekly*, 21 June 2015.

[13]Pollard, Justin and Reid, Howard, *The Rise and Fall of Alexandria: Birthplace of the Modern World*, Viking-Penguin, New York, 2006, pp. 191–2.

[14]Josephus, Flavius, *Josephus: the Main Manuscripts of the Minor Works: The "Vita" and the "Contra Apion"* (introduction by Thackery, H. St., J.), the Loeb Classical Library, 1926. Part II *Contra Apion*, p. 40; also: Josephus, *The Antiquities of The Jews* (translated by Whiston, William), Project Gutenberg E books, Book XX, pp. 100–1: https://www.gutenberg.org/files/2848/2848-h/2848-h.htm

[15]Vrettos, Theodore, *Alexandria: City of the Western Mind*, Free Press, New York, 2001, pp. 25–7.

[16]See Wilensky, David A.M., 'A Karaite Prayer: Little-K known Jewish community builds center to tell its story', Jewish News of Northern California, 16 February 2017: https://www.jweekly.com/2017/02/16/a-karaite-prayer-little-known-jewish-community-builds-center-to-tell-its-story. See also: El-Kodsi, Mourad, (Arabic) 'Ash-Shubban Al-Qarra', in *The Karaite Jews of Egypt from 1882-1986*, Wilprint, Cairo, 1937, reprint in 2007.

[17]Hosni, Yousra Abdel-Aziz, *Alexandria: Historical and Archaeological Guide*, American University in Cairo, Cairo, 2010.

[18]Maged, Mira, 'Alexandria's Eliyahu Hanavi synagogue welcomes 180 Jews to celebrate

grand opening', *Egypt Independent*, 18 February 2020.
[19]Ragson, Adam, 'Historic synagogue in Alexandria set to be reopened following major renovation', *Times of Israel*, 23 December 2019.

Chapter 35 – The Rest of the 'Mosaic'
[1]*Al-Ahram*, 24 July 1952, quoting the coup leader General Naguib's assurances to citizens and to embassies.
[2]Boyd, Douglas A, 'Development of Egypt's radio, "Voice of The Arabs" under Nasser', *Journalism Quarterly* 52(4), 1975, pp. 643–53.
[3]Partner, Peter, *Arab Voices: BBC Arabic Service, 1938-1988*, BBC Publications, London, 1988, pp. 166–75.
[4]See Harvey, Ian, *Nazis in Cairo, Patterns of Prejudices*, Volume 1, Issue 3, Routledge, Oxford, 1967, pp. 6–8; Sharnoff, Michael, 'Defining the Enemy as Israel, Zionist, Neo-Nazi or Jewish: The Propaganda War In Nasser's Egypt, 1952–1967', Posen Paper in Contemporary Antisemitism, Vidal Sassoon International Centre for the Study of Antisemitism, Jerusalem 2012.
[5]See *Associated Press* Report on NBC News, 'Egypt Faces Questions on Nazi Fugitive's Past', 09:50 GMT, 6 February 2009; also see: Paul Rose (1935–2015) former Labour MP, Manchester Blackley, speech in the commons: *Hansard*, Commons Debates, 25 January 1968, Vol 757 col. 678.
[6]Dawisha, Adeed, *Arab nationalism in the Twentieth Century: From Triumph to Despair*, Princeton University Press, Princeton, NJ, 2003, pp. 147–59.

Chapter 36 – Sleepy Streets
[1]See Chapter 27 – 'Heikal's Paradox – a Schizophrenic Attitude to Culture'.
[2]Khalil, Mahmoud Ali, 'The Italian Architecture in Alexandria', Master's thesis, Kore University of Enna, Sicily, 2009, pp. 18–22 and 73.
[3]Pallini, Cristina, 'Italian Architects and Modern Egypt', paper for the Aga Khan Program for Islamic Architecture at the Massachusetts Institute of Technology, 2004, p. 3.
[4]Philipp, Thomas and Haarmann, Urlich, *The Mamluks in Egypt, Politics and Society*, Cambridge University Press, Cambridge, 1998, pp. 68, 118.
[5]Dodwell, Henry *Muhammad 'Ali*, Cambridge University Press, Cambridge, 1967 (originally published 1931), pp. 19–20, 73.
[6]Forster, E.M., *Alexandria: A History and a Guide*, Whitehead Morris Limited, Alexandria, 1922, p. 46.
[7]Philatelic society of Egypt, *L'Orient Philatelique*, 128, October 1974.
[8]*Verdery, Richard N., 'Brief Communications: The Publications of Bulaq Press', Journal of the American Oriental Society, 91 (1), 1971, pp. 129–32.* For more on the subject, see Section 2, 'Press, media and society', in Cameron Michael Amin, Benjamin C. Fortna and Elizabeth Frierson, *The Modern Middle East, a Sourcebook for History*, Oxford University Press, Oxford, 2006; for the history of the printworks see: *Bulaq: El-Amirya Press*, www.bibalex.org *(Rt 25-06-2020).*
[9]Overton, Derek James, 'Some Aspects of Induced Development in Egypt under Muhammad Ali Pasha and Khedive Ismail', MA thesis, Simon Fraser University, Burnaby, British Columbia, 1971, pp. 45, 58.
[10]*Phare d'Alexandrie*, 11 December 1898.
[11]For an amusing account of Caireans' 1920s attitude to the khedive's previous modernisations and to Alexandria, see: Solè, Robert, *Le Tarbouche (Birds of Passage)* (translated by Brown, John), Éditions du Seuil, Paris, 1992.

Chapter 37 – The Treaty and The Journals
[1]Tourist Department, Ministry of Commerce and Industry, *Egypt: a guide*, Al-Hilal Publishing House, Cairo, 1947, pp. 43 and 64.
[2]*Al-Ahram*, 26 July 1956.

Alexandria Adieu

[3] *Hansard*, 25 July 1956, vol. 557, cols 413–4.
[4] See Roberts, Chalmers, 'Subduing the Nile', in *The World Works: A History of Our Time*, V 2861-70, Doubleday, Page & Co., New York, 1916 print.
[5] There was a height limit to avoid damaging the Temple of Phiale on an island in the Nile. Its height was increased by 5 metres in 1907–12 – see 'Aswan Low Dam', Grace's Guide to British Industrial History: https://www.gracesguide.co.uk/Aswan_Low_Dam; Novokshechnov, V., 'Laboratory studies of the stone masonry in the old Aswan Dam', *Materials and Structures*, 26, 1993, pp. 103–10; Sir Murdoch MacDonald obituary 1957, Grace's Guide: https://www.gracesguide.co.uk/Murdoch_MacDonald
[6] *Hansard*, 24 July 1956, vol. 557, col. 275.
[7] *Al-Ahram*, 26 July 1956.
[8] Ibid.
[9] *Al-Musawar*, 12 November 1948.
[10] Anderson, Jack and Whitten, Les, 'CIA: Shah of Iran a dangerous ally', *St Petersburg Times*, 11 July 1975.
[11] Stadiem, William, *Too Rich: The High Life and Tragic Death of King Farouk*, Harper Collins, New York, 1991, p. 278.
[12] Shawcross, William, *The Shah's Last Ride: The Fate of an Ally*, Simon & Schuster, New York, 1988, p. 58.

Chapter 38 – Evacuation Day
[1] *Al-Ahram*, 18 June 1956.
[2] *Al-Ahram*, 18 June 1956.
[3] ibid, p. 4.
[4] Kenny, Lorne M., 'Ali Mubarak: Nineteenth Century Egyptian Educator and Administrator', Middle East Journal 21, 1967, pp. 35–51.
[5] Hunter, Robert, 'Egypt's High Official in Transition from a Turkish to a Modern Administrative Elite, 1849-1879', *Middle Eastern Studies*, 19 (3), 1983, pp. 277–300.
[6] See Chapter 7 – 'Tram Number 4, Old Alexandria'.

Chapter 40 – Memories of the North Coast Road
[1] For full details of the power struggle inside the officers' Revolutionary Council, see Chapter 53 – 'Alexandria's Identity: Durrell'.

Chapter 41 - The Kites Battle
[1] See Chapter 7 – 'Tram Number 4, Old Alexandria'.

Chapter 42 – Nasser Betrays Eden
[1] See Chapter 19 – 'The War Generation'.
[2] Trevelyan, Humphrey, Baron, *The Middle East in Revolution*, Macmillan & Co., London, 1970., PP 133-35
[3] Ibid, PP 180-81
[4] Darwish, A. and Alexander, G., *Unholy Babylon: The Secret History of Saddam's War*, Gollancz, London, 1991. PP 31-33
[5] *Hansard*, 31 January 1952, vol. 495, cols 362–5.
[6] *Al-Ahram*, 26 Januray 1952.
[7] See Chapter 18 – 'The War Generation the Traboosh row'.
[8] Trevelyan, Humphrey, Baron, *The Middle East in Revolution*, Macmillan & Co., London, 1970. PP 45
[9] Selwyn-Lloyd, Baron, *Suez 1956: A Personal Account*, Jonathan Cape, London, 1978. PP 59-60
[10] ibid. PP 61.

Chapter 43 – Eden's Miscalculation

Notes

[1] For details on 14 July 1958 in Iraq and the role of Colonel Nasser's intelligence, see: Darwish, A. and Alexander, G., *Unholy Babylon: The Secret History of Saddam's War*, Gollancz, London, 1991 pp.17-18; and Trevelyan, *The Middle East in Revolution*. PP133-135

[2] See Selwyn-Lloyd, Baron, *Suez 1956: A Personal Account*, Jonathan Cape, London, 1978 PP 74; Also minutes taken by cabinet secretary made no mention of the dinner being interrupted and that the meeting took place after the Iraqi guests left No 10, according to Downing Street Press Secretary William Clark (1916-1985), see William Clark Papers, *www.bodley.ox.ac.uk* file 7, Clark diary, 26-27 July 1956.

[3] Lloyd PP 74-5; Andrew B Foster telegram from London Embassy to The State Dept, 5 A M, 27 July 1956, historicaldocuments/frus1955-57v16/d2

[4] Lloyd, PP 74, 106; Eden, Anthony (The Earl of Avon) *The Memoirs of Sir Anthony Eden: Full Circle*, cassell, London 1960 PP 472-3

[5] Suez Canal Company (EXPROPRIATION), *Hansard*, 1956, vol. 557, cols 777–80, House of Commons Debate, 27 July 1957.

[6] European powers, led by France (which controlled majority of the canal shares and wanted to weaken Britain's influence) were concerned of Britain's control of the Suez canal following its occupation of Egypt in 1882, thus a treaty was signed in October 1888 by Britain, France, Austria-Hungary, Russia, Spain, The Netherland, Italy and the Ottoman Empire (including Egypt)to regulate the use of Suez canal as an international waterway open to all in peace and war; it has been a matter of dispute, but it was not finally implemented until in 1904 after signing the *Entente Cordiale*.

[7] *Hansard*, 1956, vol. 557, cols 777–80, House of Commons Debate, 27 July 1957.

[8] ibid.

[9] Most European consuls in meeting with British consul(Cookson) deputy Henry Calvert, advised Seymour not to land any sailors in Alexandria to avoid aggravating a volatile situation following tension between local Muslims and Europeans according to Calvert cable, see : Kusel Bey, C.F,Baron de *An Englishman's Reminiscences of Egypt*, John Lane Publishers, London 1915 PP72,74, 176; John Ninet: Ninet, John, *Lettres d'Egypte 1879-1882*, Éditions du CNRS, 1979 PP PP 187-8 12 June 1882; Malet, Edward, Sir, *Egypt 1879-1883 Vol 1* (edited by Sanderson, Basil, Lord), J. Murray, London, 1909 PP 402 (Sir Edward Baldwin Malet (1837–1908), - was a friend of Sultan Abdul Hamid II (1842–1918)- served as consul general in Egypt 1879–83. But Cookson also on 18 June 1882 discussed plans to defend the consulates and the square, see Malet PP 434,437

[10] For a good detailed account of the events and trouble in Alexandria, the bombardment and Gladstone's plans, see the Swiss journalist and traveller (also for a general flavour on the mood in Alexandria) Ninet, John, *Arabi Pacha*, Wentworth Press, Sydney, 2018,

Chapter 44 – A country Divided

[1] See Chapter 10 – 'A Tale of Two Cities'.

[2] Jenkins, Roy, *Gladstone: A Biography*. Macmillan, London-New York, 1995 PP 507; Shannon, Richard, Gladstone : Heroic Minister 1865-1898 PP 298, 303; Auchterlonie, Paul, 'A Turk of the West. Sir Edgar Vincent's career in Egypt and the Ottoman Empire', *British Journal of Middle Eastern Studies*, V 27,1 2000 PP 51; on correspondence, and the role of press reporting see: Blunt, W., *The Secret History of the English occupation of Egypt: A Personal Narrative of Events*, Alfred Knopf, New York, 1922.

[3] Shannon, Richard, Gladstone: Heroic Minister 1865-1898, Penguin Books, London, 2002 PP 302; See Chamberlain, M.E., 'The Alexandria Massacre of 11 June 1882 and the British Occupation of Egypt', *Middle Eastern Studies*, 13 (1), January 1977 PP 14-39; Blunt, *Secret History of the English occupation of Egypt*.

[4] For a good account of the conflict and Bishop George's Bishopry see: Kaplow, Lauren, *Religious and Intercommunal Violence in Alexandria in the 4th and 5th Centuries AD*, *The McGill Journal of Classical Studies* Vol IV, McGill University, Montreal 2005 PP 6-9

433

Alexandria Adieu

(whole essay PP2-26).
[5]Chauvin, Pierre, *A Chronicle of the Last Pagans* (translated by Archer, B.A.), Harvard Revealing Antiquity, Harvard University Press, Cambridge, MA, 1990.
[6]Watts, Edward, J., *City and School in Late Antique Athens and Alexandria*, University of California Press, Los Angeles, 2006 PP 117,119
[7]Watts, Edward, J., *City and School in Late Antique Athens and Alexandria*, University of California Press, Los Angeles, 2006 PP 114-5, 197-198, 200, 2008, ; Dzielska, Maria, *Hypatia of Alexandria* (translated by Lyra, F.), Harvard University Press, Boston, MA and London, 1996. PP 18, 26, 55, 67, 98,141
[8]On murder of Hypatia see: Watts, Edward, J., *City and School in Late Antique Athens and Alexandria*, University of California Press, Los Angeles, 2006 PP 114-5, some historians reported that Christian monks were involved in Hypatia's murder, Kaplow quoted several sources, Lauren, *Religious and Intercommunal Violence in Alexandria in the 4th and 5th Centuries AD, The McGill Journal of Classical Studies* Vol IV, McGill University, Montreal 2005 PP 15-18
[9]Whitfield, Bryan J., 'The Beauty of Reasoning: A Reexamination of Hypatia of Alexandria', *Mathematics Educator*, 6 (1), 2016 PP 14-20
[10]- Ninet, John, *Lettres d'Egypte 1879-1882*, Editions du CNRS, paris 1979 P 122; Hassoun, Jacques, *Alexandrie et autres récits*, L'Harmattan, Paris, 2001. PP 223-37
[11]As traveller Eliza Fay (1756–1816) wrote on 25 July 1779, passing through Egypt: Fay, Eliza, 'Original Letters from India', *New York Review of Books*, 2010. PP 72,73
[12]St. John, James Augustus (1795–1875), *Egypt and Mohammed Ali or, Travels in the Valley of the Nile- In two volumes* (Vol. I), Longman, Rees, Orme, Brown, Green & Longman, London, 1834 P 41-2.
[13]Fahmi, Khaled, *All the Pasha's Men: Mehmed Ali, His Army and the Making of Modern Egypt*, Cambridge University Press, Cambridge, 1997 P 95.
[14]Driault, Edouard, *Mohamed Aly et Napoleon*, Société Royale de Géographie d'Egypte, Cairo, 1925. PP 160
[15]Al-Gaberty, A.,R.,H., " A'gaeb al-Athar Fi al-taragem wa-al-Akhbar" (or Aja'b al-Athar fi at-Tarajim wa al-Akhbar.), The Egyptian Books House, Cairo, 1998 edition. Vol III P 316, IV P 229,
[16]On the likes of Nedim and his influence that led to failure of liberalism later see: Vatikiotis, P.J., *The History of Egypt From Muhammed Ali to Mubarak*, Weidenfeld and Nicolson, London, 1985. P104, 184, 294, 317-8,330
[17]Nadim, Abd al-Fattah, *Sulafat al-Nadim fi Muntakhabt Abd Allah a-Nadim*, Volume 2 (Arabic), ⊠Al matba'h al game'h, Dar el-Ketab publishing Cairo, 1914, reprint, Pranava Books, Delhi, 2020. PP 33
[18]Dawkins, Clinton, 'The Egyptian Public Debt', *North American Review*, 173 (539), October 1901. PP 487- 489, 104
[19]Buchanan, Donal Scott, 'The British Invasion of Egypt And The Political Press, 1882', MA thesis, Texas Tech University, Lubbock, TX, 1997, pp. 33, 29, 30.

Chapter 45 – Tawfik–Ourabi: the Constitution
[1]See: Vatikiotis, P.J., *The History of Egypt From Muhammed Ali to Mubarak*, Weidenfeld and Nicolson, London, 1985 PP 142,144, 146-9, 160; also see. Blunt, Wilfred S., *Secret History of the English Occupation of Egypt: A Personal Narrative of Events*', Alfred Knopf, New York, 1922.
[2]See : Brown, Nathan J., 'Who Abolished Corvee Labour in Egypt and Why?' *Past & Present*, 44, August 1994, pp. 116–37; Spillmann, Georges, THE DIGGING OF THE SEUZ ISTHMUS, History of the Two Empires, Foundation Napoléon - les archives: https://www.napoleon.org/en/history-of-the-two-empires/articles/the-digging-of-the-suez-isthmus
[3]See Chapter 43 – 'The Bombardment of Alexandria'.
[4]See Chapter 10 – 'A Tale of Two Cities'.
[5]Priewasser, Robert, 'Between Authoritarian Rule and Shura: Participatory Elements

and Traditions in the Egyptian State since the 19th Century', MA thesis, Universität Wien, Vienna, 2012. PP 17-23
[6]Katba, Kemal, *An Historical Accounts of Prime Ministers of Egypt 1878-1952*, The Egyptian Chronicles.com, Cairo, 2003, Chapter #4 The Third Cherif Pasha Cabinet
[7]Scholch, Alexander, *Egypt for the Egyptians!: The Socio-political Crisis in Egypt 1878-1882* Ithaca Press, Oxford 1981 P 193
[8]See: Mirza, Mansoor, Ahmed, 'Between Umma, Empire and Nation: The Role of the Ulama in the Urabi Revolt and the Emergence of Egyptian Nationalism', PhD thesis, London School of Economics, London, 2014. PP 180-83,205-10
[9]November 1988 interview with Sheikh Kamal Adham (1929–1999), founder of Saudi Arabia's *Mukhabart al- A'amah* (Intelligence Service).
[10]Caruthers, Osgood, *NASSER RECEIVES 99% OF THE VOTE; Acclaimed as First President of Egypt, The New York Times,* 25 June, 1956
[11]For a further account, see Abbas Helmi II papers, Durham University Library.
[12]Jordan, C.T., 'Urabi and Nasser, the Parallel Path', Arabic 311, Revolution in Egypt Blogs, College of William & Mary, Williamsburg, VA, 23 December 2014.
[13]See: abd al-Raouf, Abd, el Monem, *Arghamtu Faruq 'ala al-tanazul (I forced King Farouk to Abdicate)*- Azhr'a publications, Cairo, 1986 PP 9, 15, 21, 23, 25, 27, 41-61, 128; Ramadan, Abd, El-Azim, *Al-Ikhwan al-Muslimun wa al-Tanzim al-Sirri [The Muslim Brothers Secret Apparatus]* General Book Publishing Organisation, Cairo 1993 P158 ; (FOA member) Mohey el-Dine, Khalid, Maj *Al'an 'atakallam* [Arabic] (Now I speak), Al-Ahram Publications, Cairo, 1992 PP 43-47; Ahmad Mansour (presenter) *Al-Jazeera* interview with FOA member Gamal Hammad Part-II 20 November 2008; Podeh, Elie And Winckler, Onn, *Rethinking Nasserism : Revolution and Historical Memory in Modern Egypt* university Press of Florida, Gainesville, Florida 2004 PP 61, 183. On FOA connections with "Young Egypt", see : Podeh, Elie, *The Drift towards Neutrality: Egyptian Foreign Policy during the Early Nasserist Era, 1952-55 Middle East Studies*, Taylor & Francis Ltd, Abingdon, 1996, Vol 32 Jan 1996 PP 159-178; Rethinking Nasserism : PP124, 183
[14]My interviews with General Naguib, Cairo, 1983; with Khalid Mohey-el-Dine, London 1980; with Hassan Sabry el-Khouli, 1983 and with Ahmed Hamroosh, 1983 (all members of FOA); and with Hassan Ezzat, 1982.
[15]Al-Shafie's interview with Al Jazeera TV, 2 February 1999.
[16]*Assagh Mahmoud Labib mo'asses Tanzim al-ikhwan fi al gayish* (Major Labib the organiser of Muslim Brotherhood cells inside the Egyptian Army) *Bawbaet alharkat al-Islamiayh* (the gateway to Islamist movements), https://www.islamist-movements.com/38431, 18 December 2020

Chapter 46 – The Bomadrment of Alexandria- British Occupation
[1]See Chapter 42 –'Nasser Betrays Eden'.
[2]Confirmed by his nephew, Mohsen Lutfi, secretary general of the Egypt Mother Party, in an interview, 2005.
[3]Gordon, Joel, *Nasser's Blessed Movement: Egypt's Free Officers and the July Revolution*, Oxford University Press, New York 1992 PP 27, 35; Hamroosh, Ahmed, *The Story of 23 July Revolt*, Arabic Studies and Publishing Institute, Cairo, 1977; McLeave, Hugh, *The Last Pharaoh: Farouk Of Egypt 1920-1965*, McCall Publishing, New York 1970 PP 271-2(according to McLeave, from British embassy correspondence 'diplomat John Hamilton assured Naguib personally that on Eden's instructions the British wont intervene to uphold the constitution' ; Zalan, Kira, 'How the CIA Shaped the Middle East', US News and World Report, 16 January 2014: https://www.usnews.com/opinion/articles/2014/01/16/the-great-game-and-the-cia-shaped-the-modern-middle-east
[4]John Hamilton of the British embassy communication with Naguib and the officers mentioned by: Thornhill, Michael, Britain, *The United Sates and the Rise of an Egyptian Leader: The Politics and Diplomacy of Nasser's Consolidation of Power 1952-4*, *The English Historical Review*, Oxford University Press, Oxford 2004 Vol 119 No 483

Alexandria Adieu

PP 893-95; Ambassador Caffery (US in Cairo) report 8 May 1952, *Foreign Relations of the United States, 1952-1954, Volume IX The Near and Middle East*, US Govt Printing Office, Washington 1986 P1800 ; Copeland, Miles, *The Real Spy World*, Weidenfeld & Nicolson, London, 1974.
[5] Sir Charles Cookson didn't become consul general until ten years later (1891–7). In 1882, he was acting on behalf of the consul, Edward Baldwin Malet (CG 1879–83), who was reported to have been seriously ill – although Foreign Office minister Charles Dilke (1843–1911) told the Commons that he only had 'a mild attack of fever' (*Hansard*, Commons Debates, 19 June 1882, vol. 270, col. 1614).
[6] *Hansard*, Commons Debates, 26 June 1882, vol. 271, cols 382–3; Malet PP 434,437; Royle, Charles, *The Egyptian Campaigns 1882 to 1885*, Hurst & Blackett, 1900 PP 21,41,42, 46; more detailed account in Blunt, Wilfred S., *Secret History of the English Occupation of Egypt: A Personal Narrative of Events*', Alfred Knopf, New York, 1922. PP 254-261
[7] Galbraith, John S. and al-Sayyid-Marsot, Afaf Lutfi, 'The British Occupation of Egypt: Another View', *International Journal of Middle East Studies*, 9 (4), November 1978. PP 471-487
[8] See Royle Charles, The Egyptian Campaigns 1882-1885, Hurst and Black, London, 1900, pp. 36, 38.
[9] Deringil, Selim, *The Ottoman Response to the Egyptian Crisis of 1881-82, Middle East Studies*, Taylor & Francis Ltd, Abingdon,1988, Vol 24 1, PP 3-24.
[10] Deringil, Selim, 'The Ottoman Response to the Egyptian Crisis of 1881-82', *Middle Eastern Studies*, 24 (1), January 1988.
[11] *Friend Of India*, 17 June 1882.
[12] *Friend of India*, Cairo dispatch, 12 June 1882.
[13] *Hansard*, Commons Debate, 26 June 1882, vol. 271, cols 382–3.
[14] Blunt, *Secret History of the English Occupation of Egypt*. P236
[15] Scholch, Alexander, *Egypt for the Egyptians!: The Socio-political Crisis in Egypt 1878-1882* Oxford 1981 PP 254, 246
[16] Blunt P 314
[17] As a proof, several correspondence and reports that the consuls repeatedly asked their subjects remaining in the city after 12 June 1882 Not to carry firearms See : Scholch, Alexander, *Egypt for the Egyptians!: The Socio-political Crisis in Egypt 1878-1882* Oxford 1981 P 250; Royle, Charles, *The Egyptian Campaigns 1882-1885*, Hurst and Black, London 1900, P 56
[18] Blunt P 314; also see Chamberlain, M.E. *The Alexandria Massacre of 11 June 1882 and the British Occupation of Egypt, Middle East Studies* Vol13 No 1, Taylor & Frances Ltd, 977 PP 14-39;
[19] Dispatch by the correspondent of the *Brisbane Courier*, 6 July 1882.
[20] For details of the battles, Royal Navy ships, Ourabi's forts and their battery, see: Map XX 'Bombardment of Alexandria'; see also the *Liverpool Daily Post* special telegrams, afternoon 11 July to 8 PM 13 July 1882; also, *Daily Telegraph* dispatches from 6 July to 13 July 1882.
[21] Royle, Charles, *The Egyptian Campaigns 1882-1885*, Hurst and Blackett, London, 1900. PP 63, 85; Kusel Bey PP 199-201
[22] Royle, Charles, *The Egyptian Campaigns 1882-1885*, Hurst and Black, London, 1900 P 102; Ilbert, Robert, *Alexandrie, 1830-1930: Historie d'une communaute citadine*, Institute français d'archéologie orientale, Cairo, 1996 Vil I P228-9; For more details, see Swiss journalist John Ninet described the situation in his diaries and letters, as he observed it from his hotel nearby (next to the Scottish church in the French Gardens): Ninet, John, *Lettres d'Egypte 1879-1882*, Éditions du CNRS 1979.
[23] Royle, Charles, *The Egyptian Campaigns 1882-1885*, Hurst and Black, London, 1900 P 102; Ilbert, Robert, *Alexandrie, 1830-1930: Historie d'une communaute citadine*, Institute français d'archéologie orientale, Cairo, 1996 Vol I P 95.
[24] 'The Ruined Egyptian City; the Dreadful Scenes Enacted in Alexandria', *New York*

Times, 14 July 1882.
[25]*Edinburgh Gazette*, 11 June 1901.; Ilbert, Robert, Alexandrie 1830-1930 Cairo 1996.
[26]Ilbert, *Alexandrie 1830-1930* Vol I P 258 Fahmy, Khaled, '*The Police and the People in Nineteenth-Century Egypt*', *Law and Society in Nineteenth-Century Egypt*, *Die Welt des Islams (International Journal for the study of Modern Islam)* Brill publications, Leiden Vol 39(3), November 1999. PP 340—377.

Chapter 47 – The Alexandria–Misr Rift
[1]Napoleon brought with him 160 scientists, engineers and artists whose task it was to study everything there was to find out about Egypt. And they founded the institute of Egypt in 1798. There are 1000s of essays, a good summary is on LindaHall museum exhibition: https://napoleon.lindahall.org/napoleon_scientist.shtml.
[2]Quran 9:5
[3]*Al-Ahram*, 7 September 1882.
[4]*Al-Ahram*, 11 September 1882.
[5]*Al-Ahram*, 12 September 1882.
[6]Police commander Salah Shadi (1921–1989), a member of the Muslim Brotherhood SS (Special assassination Squad), claimed that Nasser and other FOA officers participated in the arson attacks that started at casinos near the opera house. Ikhwan Online, 14 August 2008.
[7]Testimony of FOA member Major Gamal Hammad (1921–2016), who, like Ourabi, was an al-Azhar-educated Islamist. He was loyal to Naguib and, after falling out with Nasser, he joined the diplomatic service (his interview with Al Jazeera TV, 17 November 2008).
[8]My interview with General Naguib, May 1983. Also Naguib, Muhammed, *Kunt Ra'isa le-Misr* (I was President of Egypt, a memoir), Modern Egyptian Publications, Cairo, 1984.

Chapter 48 – The Voice of the Coup
[1]The six-line item had no byline, *Al-Ahram*, 24 July 1952.
[2]My interviews with Sadat friend and wartime comrade Hassan Ezzat, London 1982, and his memoir of their underground struggle Ezzat September 1982; Ezzat, Hassan, *Asrar Ma'rakat al Huriyah* (The chronicles of the Freedom Battle), Cairo Publishing House, Cairo 1953 PP 18-19, 79-80, 87..
[3]Vatikiotis, P.J. *The History of Egypt from Muhammad Ali to Mubarak*, Weidenfeld and Nicolson, London, 1985 P 364
[4]Quoting Abd el-Aziz Kamel (former Egyptian minister of Islamic endowments and a former member of the Muslim Brotherhood SS special squad) *Islamist-movements.com*, 22 March 2021 gives details of the Assassination of justice al-Khazendar by the Muslim Brotherhood,,and the details of the trial of the assassins (Hassan abd-elHafez and Mahmoud Said Zienhum) and about his meeting with their leader Al-Banna in April 194; Askar,el- Fattah, Abd *How Did The Muslim Brotherhood Murder Justice al-Khazendar, Chabab Masr,* Cairo 9 May 2012; The Muslim Brotherhood Arabic site *Wikipedia al-Ihwan Al Muslimeen Ikhwaneiki.com* 7000 words article doesn't deny the assassination but try to justify it in contexts that it was "one off" seen by the assassins as " a nationalist act".; - El-Qaradawi, Youssef, Sheikh,*ibn alqariyah wal-kutab*)Personal memoir), Part I, Ashrooq Publishing, Cairo 2002, Chapter 17: (Kindle Edition 2020)
[5]'Political Crime Series – Assassination of Al-Banna', Al Jazeera TV, 27 January 2007.
[6]Interview with Fuad Serageddin Pasha, Garden City, Cairo, November 1983.
[7]Vatikiotis, P.J. *The History of Egypt from Muhammad Ali to Mubarak*, Weidenfeld and Nicolson, London, 1985. P364-366; Stadiem, William, *Too Rich: The High Life and Tragic Death of King Farouk,* Carroll & Graf New York, 1991 PP 276, 280 Jaber, Karam *Two Swords.. with the Qur'an in between, Rose al-Yusuf,* 25-31 December 1999, Cairo
[8]The British name for the underground Jewish groups like Haganah, Stern and Irgun

Alexandria Adieu

– copied by Egyptian media.
[9] Interview with Fuad Serageddin Pasha, Garden City, Cairo, November 1983.
[10] Interview with Amin Howaidy (1921–2009), FOA member, former head of Egyptian Intelligence and former defence minister, Cairo, November 1983; Stadiem P 280
[11] Conversations with Miles Copeland, CIA Cairo operative in the 1950s, Oxford October 1981.
[12] 'From The Briefcase of Dr. Aribert Heim', *New York Times*, 4 February 2009.
[13] See Reid, Donald, 'Political Assassinations in Egypt 1910-1954', *International Journal of African Historical Studies, 15 (4), 1982, pp. 625–51.*
[14] Nahed Rashad's passport record: DOB 1915, Married 1938, No specific DOD 1983 or 1998)unreliable Egyptian sources); see: interview with 1st lieutenant (retired) Ibtisamatl Abdallah (b 1928, joined the Women's Brigade with Nahed Rashad in 1948), *Adoustour Magazine* (doctor.org), 18 April 2015.
[15] My interviews with Hassan Ezzat, london Mayfair hotel, Sepetmber 1982 and Khalid Mohey el-Dine, London, June 1980.
[16] 'Carioca Tells Her Story after her Release', *El-Kawakeb*, Cairo, 16 February 1954.

Chapter 49 – The Spy, the Officer, his Dancer and her Lover

[1] Bierman, John, *The Secret Life of LASALO ALMAZY: The Real English Patient*, Viking, London, 2004, pp. 20–21.
[2] On the recruitment of Almásy and others to the Abwehr by its chief, Nikolaus Ritter, see: Kelly, Saul, *The Hunt for Zerzura*, John Murray, London, 2002; also Gross, Kuno, Rolke, Michael and Zboray, András, *Operation Salaam László Almásy's most daring mission in the Desert War*, Belleville, Munich, 2013.
[3] Carell, Paul, *Foxes of the Desert*, Macdonald & Co., London, 1960, p. 223; also confirmed by Hassan Ezzat.
[4] Sadat, Anwar, *Asrar -althawra-al-Masryiah* (A Diary of the Egyptian Revolution), National Publications House, Cairo, 1965.
[5] Salah, Mahmoud, *Sadat and the Spies*, Modern Arabic Publications, Cairo, 2005 PP 22-23,26
[6] Carell, Paul, *Foxes of the Desert*, Macdonald & Co., London, 1960.PP 201,203,213; also see *Operation Condor (i) Operations of Worl War II CODENAMES.infor*
[7] Interviews with Hassan Ezzat,, london September 1982 and Khalid Mohey el-Dine, London, Covent garden June 1980
[8] For more details about supporting Arab tribesmen see: Lawrence, T.E., *Seven Pillars Of Wisdom: a triumph*, The Reprint Society, London, 1935.
[9] Confirmed by Hassan Ezzat and Ahmed Hamroosh
[10] Miles, Lampson, Sir, *Politics and Diplomacy in Egypt: The Diaries of Sir Miles Lampson-1935-1937* (edited by Yapp, M.E.), Oxford University Press, Oxford, 1997. p 253
[11] ibid. PP 252,
[12] *Al-Ethnine-walel-Dunia* issue 318, June 1940.
[13] Al-Shafie's interview with Al Jazeera TV, 2 February 1999.
[14] Hosny, Hessein, Dr, *Years with King Farouk, a historic account by his private secretary*, Shrouk Publications, Cairo, 2001. PP 156-161
[15] Ibid. P156-162 on Abdin; on popularity of Nahas and Lampson analysis see : Lampson, *Politics and Diplomacy in Egypt*; also on the mood in the country: my chat with Lady Lampson, July 1991 Egyptian embassy reception, London.
[16] Hosny, *Years with King Farouk*. PP 158-160
[17] My interviews with members of the FOA and with Fuad Sirag el-Dine Pasha November 1983 Cairo; also Naguib, Muhammed, *Kunt Ra'isa le-Misr* (I was President of Egypt, a memoir), Modern Egyptian Publications, Cairo, 1984,.
[18] Carell, Paul, *Foxes of the Desert*, Macdonald & Co., London, 1960 P 201
[19] Ibid P 203
[20] ibid. PP 205-208, 213-4
[21] MI5 file KV-2/1467. UK National Archives

Notes

[22] For more details on Eppler, the role of Almasy and the of wealthy anarchists in Cairo in 1940s see: Mosley, L.O., *The Druid: The Nazi Spy who Double-Crossed the Double-Cross System*, Athenaeum, London, 1980.
[23] Mosley, Leonard Oswald, *The Cat and The Mice: The Story of John Eppler*, Harper, New York 1958,.
[24] Gross Kuno, Rolke, Michael and Zobary, Andras; *Operation Salam: László Almásy's most daring Mission in the Desert War* Belleville Publishing, München 2013.
[25] Andriotakis, Pamela, 'The Real Spy's Story Reads Like Fiction and 40 Years Later Inspires a Best-Seller', *People.Com Archive*, 1980: https://people.com/archive/the-real-spys-story-reads-like-fiction-and-40-years-later-inspires-a-best-seller-vol-14-no-24.
[26] Ibid. ; and for more colourful details see: Eppler, Johann, *Operation Condor: Rommel's Spy*, Futura, London 1978
[27] Sadat, *Asrar -althawra-al-Masryiah*.
[28] Verlag, Hannen, *Henri, Die Wustenfuchse*", Hannen Verlag GmBH, Hamburg 1958.
[29] A young intelligence analyst at Bletchley Park, Jean Alington (later Jean Howard) had followed the signal trail, but the warning sent to the British HQ in Cairo arrived late after much delay due to activities in the Libyan desert anticipating the imminent attack of Rommel; and by the time it was decoded there all the stations were silent on the orders of Angelo (see : Gross, Kuno, Michael Rolke and András Zboray *Operation Salaam László Almásy most daring mission in the Desert* War, Belleville, München 2013.)
[30] Bierman, John, *The Secret Life of LASALO ALMAZY: The Real English Patient*, Viking, London 2004 PP191-92; my chats with Hassan Ezzat, June 1982
[31] According to a film technician whose father worked in the Egyptian film industry at the time. Neither name could be revealed on their requests
[32] MI5 file KV-2/1467. UK National Archives; Bierman, John, *The Secret Life of Laszlo Almasy: The Real English Patient*, Viking, Penguin Books, London, 2004.
[33] Albo d'Oro delle Famiglie Nobili e Notabili Europee, vol XIV, Florence 2000, pp. 811-812
[34] Kelly, Saul, *The Lost Oasis: The True Story Behind 'The English Patient'*, John Murray, London, 2002.
[35] Follett, Ken, *The Key to Rebecca*, Hamish Hamilton, London, 1980.
[36] My Interview with Major Khalid Mohey el-Dine, 1980.
[37] My interviews with Ezzat, and: Ezzat, Hassan, *Asrar ma'arakat al-hurryah* (The chronicles of the battle for freedom), Tahrir Publications, Cairo, 1952.
[38] Fadhl, Bilal, *Asadat wa ma adrak*? -I (who was Sadat? part I), *Ala'rbi al-Gadid*, London, 25 December 2015

Chapter 50 – Plotters, Assassins and Fascists

[1] Ezzat, Hassan, *Asrar ma'arakat al-hurryah* (The chronicles of the battle for freedom), Tahrir Publications, Cairo, 1952.
[2] Mohey-el-Dine, Khalid, *Wa-alan-atakalam* (Only now I can testify), al-Ahram Publications, Cairo, 1992.
[3] See Chapter 44 – 'Tawfik–Ourabi: the Constitution'.
[4] Aboul-Enein, Youssef, Lt Commander. 'The Egyptian-Yemen War: Egyptian Perspective on Guerrilla Warfare', *Infantry Magazine*, 93 (1), Jan–Feb 2004, pp. 18–28.
[5] Wasim Khalid, the youngest member of the AG, took Sadat, who trained the group on the use firearms, as his role model. See Khalid, Wasim, *The Diaries of Wsim Khalid: al-Kifah al-Sirri dhid les anglais* (The Armed Struggle Against the British), General Egyptian Book Publishing Board, Cairo, 2014.
[6] Conversation with Lady Killearn in 1996.
[7] Miles, Lampson, Sir, *Politics and Diplomacy in Egypt: The Diaries of Sir Miles Lampson-1935-1937* (edited by Yapp, M.E.), Oxford University Press, Oxford, 1997, pp. 550, 645.
[8] ibid., p. 866.

[9] Khalid, *The Diaries of Wsim Khalid.*
[10] Interview with Mrs Sadat, Giza, Egypt, 1983. She also repeated it in her first book: Sadat, Jihan, *Woman of Egypt*, Simon & Schuster, New York, 1987.
[11] Sadat, Anwar, *In search of Identity: An Autobiography*, Harper Collins, New York, 1978.

Chapter 51 – The Officers' Conspiracy

[1] See Chapter 48 – 'The "Voice" of the Coup'.
[2] Conversations with King Farouk's second cousin, Adel Sabit, London 1988; also see his book: Sabit, Adel M., *A King Betrayed, The Ill-Fated Reign of Farouk of Egypt*, Quartet Books, London, 1989.
[3] Morsy, Laila, Amin, 'American Support for the 1952 Egyptian Coup: Why?', *Middle Eastern Studies*, 31 (2), April 1995, pp. 307–16; for more detailed reading on the wider CIA activities, see: Wilford, H., *America's Great Game: The CIA's Secret Arabists and the Shaping of the Modern Middle East*, Basic Books, New York, 2013, pp. 135–9.
[4] In fact, Farouk failed to understand that it was American contribution in aiding officers that was undermining his reign. The correspondence between American embassy in Cairo and State department indicate that Caffrey bargained with military coup officers to protect Farouk's life and persuade him to abdicate but also stopped the British intervening and thus letting America take over British influence in the new Egypt. See State Department archives NA RG 59, Box 415 774-00/7-2532, No 416, 23 July 1952 from London [US embassy] secretary of State (Top Secret); also: British Foreign Office archive: FO.371/9687- 1952, From Alexandria to Foreign, 26 July 1952 reported Caffery to his British counterpart: 'I have again contacted Naguib who has repeated his earlier assurance re. king's personal safety'.
[5] My 1983 chat with Miles Copeland, CIA Cairo operative in the 1950s, Oxford. See also: Copeland, *The Real Spy World*, Sphere Books, London, 1978, p. 62; also, Roosevelt confirmed this in 1984 in an interview in Washington with Mohamed Abd El-Wahab Sayed Ahmad for his PhD Thesis (No 10672698) to the School of Oriental and African Studies, 'Us-Egyptian Relations from the 152 Revolution to the Suez Crisis of 1952', London, April 1987. The American plans in pushing for a coup were reported to the Foreign Office by HM ambassador in Cairo Sir Ralph Stevenson (1895–1977) on 27 January 1952: FO.371/96879, 1952, from Cairo to Foreign Office, No. 195.
[6] Copeland, Miles, *The Game of Nations: The Amorality of Power Politics*, Simon & Schuster, New York, 1971, pp. 51–3.
[7] ibid., pp. 63–5; also see: War is Boring, 'How the CIA Set the Stage for Egyptian Strongmen to Last', Medium.Com, 25 November 2015: https://medium.com/war-is-boring/how-the-cia-set-the-stage-for-egyptian-strongmen-to-last-721362a1a4b5
[8] According to Copeland (in *The Game of Nations*) and Roosevelt (who admitted as much to Mustafa Amin), the CIA Project FF ('fat f***er') was to pressure Farouk to reform and move closer to America; also see: Holland, Matthew F., *America and Egypt: From Roosevelt to Eisenhower*, Praeger (Greenwood Group), Westport, CT, 1996, p. 27.
[9] My chat with Copeland, Oxford, 1983; Aronson, Geoffrey, *From Sideshow to Centre Stage: U.S.Policy Towards Egypt. 1946-1956*, Lynne Rienner Publishers, Boulder CO, 1986, p. 51; Naggar connecting CIA with Nasser: US National Security Archive (USNA), RG 59, CDF, 774.00/8-952, Cairo to State Department, Cable 315, 9 August 1952, and subsequent minutes; for more in-depth read on above, see: Copeland, Miles, *The Game Player: Confessions of the CIA's Original Political Operative*, Aurum Press, London, 1989.
[10] Copeland, Miles, *The Game Player*].
[11] Copeland, *The Real Spy World*, pp. 177, 179.
[12] Ibid. Also in my interview with him, Naguib did not contradict Copeland's claim – but he insisted that they had wanted to assure the Americans and the British of the peaceful intention of the movement. He added that all the betrayals

of the aims of their 'patriotic' movement happened after he had been ousted from power by Nasser.

[13]Hamroosh, Ahmed, *Qisat Thawrat 23 yulio* (The story of 23rd July), Arabic Research and Publication Institute, Cairo, 1977; and my interview with Hamroosh in 1983. Also Copeland, *The Game Player*.

[14]Morsy, *American Support for the 1952 Egyptian Coup*, pp. 307–16; my 1983 interview with Ahmed Hamroosh (1921–2011). Also, my interview with General Naguib in 1982.

[15]Ass'ad, Karim, 'All Nasser's Men', Ida'at, Ida2at.com/revolution-command-council-abdulnasser-men/, 31 January 2019; on the way the US Embassy in Cairo trusted Amin for years and his assuring them of then-officer's pro-American attitude and getting rid of anti-Western officers, there are various cables kept at the US National Security Registry – e.g. RG 59 774-00/112-2952, & RG 59 Box 9 Box 4075-774-00/9-5, & G 59 774-00/9-7, & Box 4015 774-00/9-18, & R6 4026 774-55/10-255 – all throughout 1952.

[16]My interview with Naguib, 1983. Also, interview with Miles Copeland, Oxford, 1983. Copeland confirmed that the CIA held four meetings with the coup officers between January and July 1952 to assure themselves that they could do business with them. Also, see: Copeland, *The Game of Nations*.

[17]See Chapter 18 – 'The War Generation'.

[18]'All the Revolution's Men', *Al-Ahram Weekly*, 595, 18 July 2002.

[19]Naguib, Muhammed, *Kunt Ra'isa le-Misr* (I was President of Egypt, a memoir), Modern Egyptian Publications, Cairo, 1984. Also my interview with Naguib, 1983.

[20]My interview with Khalid Mohey el-Dine, 1980.

[21]From General Sirry-Amr's papers as read to me by his daughter, Souzy Sirry-Amr, 2019.

[22]Abde-el-Nasser, Hoda, Dr, 'A historical sketch of President Gamal Abdel-Nasser', Nasser Foundation, Cairo. Also: Alexander, Anne, *Nasser (Life & Times)*, Haus Publishing, London, 2005.

[23]My Interviews with General Naguib, 1983, and with (member of FOA) Hassan el-Tuhami in 1983.

[24]My interview with General Sirry-Amr's daughter, Souzy Sirry-Amr, 2019.

[25]From General Sirry-Amr's papers as read to me by his daughter, Souzy Sirry-Amr, 2019. Also my interview with Khalid Mohey el-Dine, 1980.

[26]See Chapter 49 – 'The Spy, the Officer, his Dancer and her Lover'.

[27]My interview with Hassan el-Tuhami, 1983.

[28]See: Litvin, Margaret, *Hamlet's Arab Journey: Shakespeare's Prince and Nasser's Ghost*, Princeton University Press, Princeton, NJ, 2011.

[29]Nasser, Gamal Abdel, *The Philosophy of the Revolution* (introduction by Badeau, John S. and contribution by Gunther, John), l, Buffalo, NY, 1959. Also: Stephens, Robert, *Nasser: A Political Biography*, Pelican, London, 1971.

[30]My 1983 interview with Ahmed Hamroosh, although he insisted that they were not conspiring with a foreign power but wanted to secure America's help because they didn't trust the British.

[31]Wilford, *America's Great Game*, pp. 136–8.

[32]McLeave, Hugh, *The Last Pharaoh: Farouk Of Egypt 1920-1965*, McCall Publishing, New York, 1970, pp. 271–2 refers to British embassy correspondence reports from the archive. Also: Zalan, Kira, 'How the CIA Shaped the Middle East', US News and World Report, 16 January 2014: https://www.usnews.com/opinion/articles/2014/01/16/the-great-game-and-the-cia-shaped-the-modern-middle-east

[33]Copeland, *The Game Player*.

[34]My interview with General Naguib, 1983. Also: the first edition of Naguib, Mohammed, General, *Masir Misr* (Egypt's Destiny: A Personal Statement), Dar-Diwan, Cairo, 1955 was confiscated and banned by Nasser's regime.

[35]N Court case (520/1954) judgement of 17 Nov, 1954, Egyptian court circulars, 18

Alexandria Adieu

November 1954.
[36]My interview with General Naguib, 1983.

Chapter 52 – The Move Against Alexandria
[1]Naguib, Muhammed, *Kunt Ra'isa le-Misr* (I was President of Egypt, a memoir), Modern Egyptian Publications, Cairo, 1984; my interview with Naguib, 1983; also: reports in *Al-Ahram*, 24 July 1952.
[2]Starr, Deborah, *Remembering Cosmopolitan Egypt: Literature, Culture, and Empire*, Routledge, London, 2009.
[3]Meguid, Ibrahim Abdel, *Clouds Over Alexandria*, (translated by Kay Helkkinen) Hoopoe, branch of American University in Cairo Press, New York, 2019. P191
[4]Al-Kharrat, Edwar, *City of Saffron* (translated by Liardet, Frances), Quartet Books, London 1989; see chapter 53 Alexandria's identity.

Chapter 53 – Alexandria's Identity: Durrell
[1]Durrell, Lawrence, *The Alexandria Quartet Justine Baltzhar Mountolive Clea*, Faber and Faber, London, 2012, p. 509.
[2]Yannakakis, Ilios and Ilbert, Robert, *Alexandrie 1860-1960 Un modèle èphemere de convivialité: communautès et identitè cosmopolite*, Autrement, Paris, 1992.
[3]My interview with General Naguib, 1983. Also: Naguib, Muhammed, *Kunt Ra'isa le-Misr* (I was President of Egypt, a memoir), Modern Egyptian Publications, Cairo, 1984.
[4]Contrary to the false belief pushed by Islamists and the Western media, Egypt's 2011–13 elections were neither free nor fair. See Chapter 45 – 'Tawfik–Ourabi: the Constitution'.
[5]Egyptian students sent to be educated in Europe; see Chapter 12 – 'Invasions and New Expressions'.
[6]See Chapter 9 – 'A Tale of Two Cities', where 'The independent belediye' records Lord Cromer ending European consuls' resistance to an elected independent Alexandria Municipality collecting taxes.

Chapter 54 – Nasser's Defiance: the Suez War
[1]See Chapter 34 – 'Alexandria's Jews – a Second Exodus' and Chapter 35 – 'The Rest of the 'Mosaic' on Greek and Italian communists going to fight the British in Port Said, and Jewish rabbis condemning Israel in Alexandria's synagogues in 1956.

Chapter 55 – The Ethnic Cleansing of Alexandria
[1]For further details read Golan, Aviezer, " OERATION SUSANNAH, as told by Marcell Nino, Victor Levy,Robert Dassa and Philip Natanson,- Forwaed by Golda Meir", Harper & Row, New York 1978.
[2]See: Zamir, Meir, 'The Role of MI6 in Egypt's Decision to go to War Against Israel in May 1948', *Intelligence and National Security*, 34 (6), 2019, pp. 775–99.
[3]Golan, Aviezer, *Operation Susannah, as told by Marcell Nino, Victor Levy,Robert Dassa and Philip Natanson* (Foreword by Golda Meir), Harper & Row, New York, 1978.
[4]Weiss, Leonard, 'The Lavon Affair: How a false-flag operation led to war and the Israel Bomb', *Bulletin of the Atomic Scientists*, 69 (4), Chicago, 27 November 2013, pp. 58–68.

Chapter 56 – The Second Arab Conquest
[1]My interviews with General Naguib and Ahmed Hamroosh (both 1983), and several chats with Muhammed Hassanein Heikal.

Chapter 57 – Paving the Way for Sadat's Islamisation

Notes

[1] The January arrests were commemorated in folk songs among left-wing Egyptians who romanticised the phenomenon – like 'January Wind', penned by the late communist-movement Egyptian-vernacular lyricist Ahmed Negm while he was in jail in January 1977. See: 'For culture and Humanity', https://www.anfasse.org – Nigm-22-poems- 18 March 2007 (Arabic).
[2] Mustafa, Dalia, 'Negm and Sheikh Imam: The Rise and Fall of Political Song in Egypt' (Arabic), *Alif: Journal of Comparative Poetics*, 21, 2001, pp. 130–60.
[3] Darwish, Adel, 'Obituary: Sheikh Imam', *The Independent*, London, 9 June 1995.
[4] Abdul-Latif, Emad, 'Ahmed Fuad Negm', Oxford African American Studies Centre: https://oxfordaasc.com/view/10.1093/acref/9780195301731.001.0001/acref-9780195301731-e-50522.
[5] For the origin of this folkloric song, see Chapter 2 – 'Gare-Ramleh: Alexandria's Heart and History'.
[6] See Chapter 29 – 'Miss World'.
[7] For more details, see: Guirguis, Max, 'Islamic Resurgence and Its Consequences in the Egyptian Experience', *Mediterranean Studies*, 20 (2), 2012, pp. 187–226.
[8] See Chapter 31 – 'Songs Move Closer to Allah's Politics'.
[9] Both launched in 1907. See Chapter 46 – 'The British Bombardment – and Occupation'.
[10] Conversations with Kamal Adham between 1989 and 1991.

INDEX

A

Abazah, Wageih Captain 265
  Abazahs, the, 269,
Abd-al-Ilah, of Iraq Prince, 336
Abdellah, Abd el-Fattah Dr 109, 121
Abd-el-Raziq, Ali Sheikh,
  Al-Islam-wa-Osoul-Alhokm, 221
Abdel-Rahman, Omar Sheikh 258
Abd-el-Wahab, Muhammed, 263
Abdin Palace, 381
Abdou, Mohammed Sheikh, 361
Abu Taleb, Sufi Dr, , 409
Abu Zaid, Hamed Nasr, 220, 425, 428,
Abdul Hamid II, Sultan, 348, 351, 433
Abu el-Abbas, el-Morsi, 260
Abukeir , 149, 195
  Bay of, 27
  Rue Abukeir, 29, 54, 79, 115, 173, 210, 266, 387
Abwehr (German military Intelligence), 375
Abyssinia, 355
  Italo- Abyssinian War, 302
Abyssinian War 326
Achillas, 82
Acropolis, 391
Adham, Kamal, 411-2, 435, 443
Adib, Abd-el-Hay, 197
Adieu Bonaparte (1985), 216–217
Aflaq, Michel, 122
Ahmose I, 199
Al-Ahram, 234, 303, 305-6, 31013, 332-3, 337, 347, 365-7, 430, 435, 437, 4412
Aird, Sir John, 304
Akaba, Gulf of, 55, 400
Akhbar – el Youm, 303
Al-Akhbar, 303
Alamein, El, 37, 195, 215, 321, 373
  Battle of, 7
  Railway Station, 320
War Cemetery, 320
Albumasar, 77
Al-Burhan, Hamzah, Sheikh, 347
Aldrich, Winthrop, 337
Aleppo, 284
  Massacre, 87, 397, 432
Alexander the Great, 31, 126, 127, 130–135, 218, 287, 344, 348–349,
394, 399, 420
  Binary culture, 131, 344
  Building Alexandria, 20, 28, 36, 39, 76, 130-31, 249, 340
  Death, 132, 287
  Tomb, 19, 76, 77, 132, 242
  Vision of God Amon, 77, 130-31
Alexandria Belediye/ Municipality, 13, 26, 33, 45, 109, 111-3, 116, 118-9, 138-42,152,154, 166, 210, 228, 267, 311, 322, 342, 389
Alexandria Institute of Theology, 24
Alexandria, University of 244
Alexandria's tongue (Language), 122–125
  Demotic Alexandrian, 120, 122
Alexandrinologists, 19, 39, 29, 132
Alexandrinology, 11, 97, 224
Alexandros ho Megas, 126
Algazaeriayh, Ourada (Ouarda l'Algérienne), 253, 354,
Alitalia, 25
Al-Latif-Al-Musawarh (Events in Pictures), 307
Allen, Woody, 263
Allenby, Edmund Field Marshal Edmund, 103
Ali, Muhammad Pasha, 17, 52, 54, 191, 386, 399, 404, 420
  The Army, 28, 118, 93, 299, 326, 351, 352
  Dynasty, 21, 68, 130, 220, 394
  French connections & expertise, 24, 116, 127, 193, 313, 346, 348, 396
  Independent Egyptian Identity, 299, 311, 339, 345, 348, 354, 366, 407
  (dealing with) Islamism, 345-46,
  Place Muhammed Ali (M. Ali Square), 83, 85, 87, 112, 298, 359
  Projects and modernisation, 7, 23, 28, 33, 54, 65, 77, 82, 84, 93, 97,127, 190, 220, 342
  Palais Ras el-Tin & Alexandria Summer capital, 116-17, 132, 133, 134, 462, 298, 304, 340, 396
  Statue, 201-02, 408
  Teatro & opera House, 312, 406
Almásy, László Count, 371, 376, 438, 439
al-Nahda (the renaissance), 14, 219, 220,

444

EPILOGUE: INDEX

230, 235, 410, 425, 428
al-Qaeda, 48,
Ambron, Aldo, 95
Ambron, Gilda, 95
Ambron, Villa & Celebrities, 94–98
 and Durrell, 95, 97
Amer, Abed el-Hakim Major (later Gen), 254,384
Amer-el-Sisi, Entissar 409
Amin, Abde-el-Mene'm Captain, 383
Amin, Ali, 172,309
Amin, Mustafa, 172, 308, 309
Amir, Aziza, 213
Ammianus Marcellinus (Res Gestae), 344
Amun, 77, 132
Amunites, 28
Anderson, Ingrid, 245
Anfoushy, 249
Angel, Leon, 267
Anglo–Egyptian Treaty, 192, 301
Anglo–Iranian Petroleum Company, 366
Anglo–Persian Oil Company, 366
Antiquekhaneh, 198
Anti-Semitism, 265–266
Antoniadis, Sir Jon, 119
Antonius, George, The Arab Awakening, 32
Antony, Mark (83–30 BC), 17, 29, 143
al-Qaysouny, Abd-el-Menem, 306
Arabia, 33, 37, 43, 124, 257, 268, 330, 339, 352, 372, 411, 414, 435
Arabian Nights, 256
Arabian Peninsula, 207, 338
Arabs, 14, 21, 40, 122, 224, 238, 329, 335, 346, 390, 403, 424
 As seen by Egyptians, 9, 13, 339
 Bedouins, 9 , 299, 316, 318, 322, 362, 365,
 Invaders/Occupiers of Egypt, 81, 82, 126, 128, 133, 149, 287, 298
Arian of Nicomedia (Arrian), 132, 246
Anabasis, 132, 425
Aristotle , 131, 349
Ashkenazim, 97
Ashour, Sheikh, 258
Assassinations Group (AG), 368, 378
Assiyash-Aldawliah (International Politics), 231
The Association Internationale Nebi Daniel, 288
Assyrians, 126, 128
Asuit, 403
Attarin, 23, 53, 90, 275, 283
Attarin (Herablists), 65
Attarin Mosque, 46
Atatürk, Mustafa Kemal, 196

Athinèos, 18, 19, 25, 77, 89, 171, 242, 251, 417
Atiyah, Michael, 32
The Atlantic Wall, Le Mur de l'Atlantique, 376
Austro-Hungarian Empire, 49
Austro-Hungarian Society, 191
Avoscani, Pietro, 23, 31, 117, 202, 205, 417
Aybak, Izz al_dine,33
Ayyubid Dynasty, 33
Azab, Khalid Dr, 139
Azhar, Al, 13, 15, 66, 67, 133, 162, 218, 219, 220, 221, 224, 267, 268, 309, 313, 333, 342, 346, 347, 352, 354, 409, 412, 413, 437,
Azhar Journal, 422
 Clergy/ sheiks/Ulama, 14, 65, 67, 351, 353, 361, 364, 404
 Islamists, 388
 University 355
Aziz, Mahmoud abd-el, 318

B

Bab-el-Hadid, 197
Babylon, 131, 132, 432, 433
Bacos (Bachchus), 33
Badrkhan, Ahmed, 266
Bahary, 116
Baines, Edwin C., 190
Baker, Sir Benjamin, 304
Banco Italo Egiziano, 95
Al-Banna, Hassan, 215, 282, 356,368, 437,
Barakat, Daoud, 234
Baring, Evelyn – see Lord of Cromer
Barillet-Deschamps, Jean-Pierre Bey, 206
Bashmurite Revolution, 126
Bastet, 88
basturma,, 261
Baudrot, 78
Bayoumi, Mohamed,214
BBC, 66, 79, 391, 447
 Arabic Service, 391, 431
 External Service, 292,
 Journalists, 182, 390
 TV, 182, 391
 Woman's Hour, 180
 World Service, 79
Beaton, Cecil, 308
Beeley, Harold Sir, 78
Belon, Pierre, 82
Beltagi, Ibrahim Sheikh, 251
Benakis, Emmanuel, 53, 55, 422,
Ben Gurion, David, 404, 405
Benyamine, (fuul restaurant) 26

445

Alexandria Adieu

Benzion, 368
Bashmur, 126, 425
Beir Masoud, (also see Devil's Hole), 141, 143, 151
Binachi, Emmanuel 53
Bibliotheca Alexandrina, 9, 28, 79, 84, 128, 131, 139, 199, 236, 419, 425, 427
Big Ben, 391
Birra al-Ahram, 41–42, 233
Birra Masriyah, 233
Birra Stella, 17, 18, 25, 41, 42, 43, 45, 73, 146, 156, 241, 261, 276, 294, 297, 414
Bismarck, Otto von, 348
Black Sea, 53, 291, 404
Blair, Tony, 353, 447
Bletchley Park, 375-6, 439
Bombardment of Alexandria, 217, 356, 357, 361-62, 374, 400, 426, 433,
Bonaparte, Napoleon, 65, 82, 116, 118, 126-7, 183, 203, 216, 281, 287, 299, 345, 351, 388, 395, 411, 421
Booth, Captain 81
Boothby, Sir Robert, 305
Boumédiène, Houari, 254
Boutros-Ghali, 331, 358
  Boutros Dr, 231
  Boutros Pasha, 331, 357
  Wassif, 357,
Bovio, Enrico, 23
Boyle, Sir Dermot, 336, 337
Brazilian coffee production, 40
Brazilian coffee Stores, 39, 40
Breccia, Annibale Evaristo Bey, 19
British Airways, 25,
British Council, 20, 78
British European Airlines BEA, 25
British Institute, 28, 78
British East India Company, 117
British Overseas Airways Corporation BOAC, 25
Britten, HMS 362
Buckley, 33, 299
Budapest, 145
Burg el-Arab, 7, 321
  Airport, 37
Burgazzi, Giovanni, 94
Al-Burhan, 347
le Burn-Rushdy, Eugenie, 31
Bush, George W., 235
Butler, Dr Alfred Joshua, 117, 424

C

Caesareum, 344
Café le Bourse., 89
Café Petrou, 223, 227
Café Pullman, 39
Café Splendide, 90, 447
Café Vue-Splendide, 83
Caffery, Jefferson, 382-3, 436,440
Cairo,
  British embassy, 379, 383
  Fatimid quarter, 223, 379, 408, 435, 441
  Fire and Riots, 365
  Miss Maillot contest, 308-9
  Newspapers, 299, 302,305, 307
  Opera House, 202, 205
  Khediviate Cairo, 302, 203
  revenge on Alexandria, 340
Cairo Radio, 148, 253, 263, 333, 367
Cairo Road, 147
Cairo University, 221, 232, 268, 401
Callaghan, James, 329
Callimachus, 236
Campbell-Bannerman, Henry 359
Camel Corps, (Foreign Office's Arabists), 329
Camus, Albert
Caligula, 76
Canal la-Farkha, 85, 94
Canudo, Ricciotto, 263
Carioca, Taheyyah, 370, 438
Carlton, 33
Carter, Henry Captain, 81
Carter, Howard, 198
Cavafy, Constantine Peter, 7, 18, 24, 29, 43, 77-8, 219, 230, 239, 246, 389, 416, 418,
  Alexandrian Kings, 134-5
  The City, 22
  and Durrell (building on Cavafy's work), 236
  and Forester, 19, 43, 78, 216
  The God Abandons Antony, 416
  and (inspiration for) Liddell, 20
  Waiting for The Barbarians, 7, 295, 421
Cecil Hotel,35, 37-9, 418-9
Central Treaty Organisation (CTO), 335
Chakour, Joseph Pasha 26, 41
  Rue Cahkour, 26
Chahine, Youssef, 197, 211, 213
  Alexandria... Why?, 50, 215–218, 265
  Alexandrie encore et Toujours, 216
  An Egyptian Story (1982), 217
Chakour, Joseph Pasha, 26, 41, 118, 424
  Rue Chackour Pasha, 26
Champollion, Jean-François, 47
  Rue Champollion, 47, 78
Chatby, 28, 29, 53, 79, 210, 212, 250,

446

EPILOGUE: INDEX

260
Cherif, Mohammed Pasha, 350, 352, 435
　Boulevard Cherif Pasha, 87, 112, 417
　Rue Cherif Pasha, 40, 78
Chicorille, 40
Chevalier, Maurice (1888–1972), 28
China, 305, 388, 459
Chubra , 23
Churchill, Sir Winston, 37, 328–329
Cinéma Alhambra, 255
Cinéma al-Nile, 210
Cinéma Amir 49,
Cinéma Amir-Raghib Pasha, 210
Cinéma Anfoshi, 210
Cinéma Armenian Club, 210
Cinéma Bandarli and Dorès, 212
Cinéma Concordia, 83
Cinéma Couronnement, 84
Cinéma de Jésuites, 210
Cinéma el-Montazaha, 326
Cinéma Empire, 21
Cinéma Ferial, 209, 215
Cinema Florida, 325
Cinéma Fuad, 165
cinema institute, Alexandria, 214
Cinéma Hadra, 210
Cinéma Karmouz, 210
Cinéma la Concorde, 90
Cinéma La Guitèe, 210
Cinéma Libération, (Cinéma al-Tahrir) 296, 406
Cinéma Majestic, 26
Cinema Metro, 368
Cinéma Moharrem-Bey, 210
Cinéma Muxx, 210
Cinéma Odeon, 210
Cinéma Park, 26
Cinéma Pathé, 212
Cinéma Plaza, 165
Cinéma Radio, 215
Cinéma Rex, 83
Cinéma Rialto, 210
Cinéma Rio, 165
Cinéma Roi, 209
inéma Royale, 165,
Cinéma Ritz, 215
Cinéma Riviera, 210
Cinéma San-Stephano, 210
Cinéma Sporting, 210
Cinéma Star, 210
Cinéma Strand, 215'
Cinéma Widad, 210
Chauvel, Jean Michel, 337
Claridge's, 77, 78
Saint Claudia, 81

Cleopatra, (Egyptian film), 213
Cleopatra, (Queen VII) 28, 31, 35, 72, 134, 135, 143, 151, 236, 237, 246, 248, 394, 415, 420, 421, 422, 423,
　and Antony, 17, 72,
　Bain Cleopatre, and district, 28, 210, 275
　Books collection, 129
　Foreign policy & ambitions, 93, 132
　Needle (s), Alexandria, 17
　London, 17, 81,
　New York, 17, 421
　Pond, 247
Clot, Antoine Barthelemy Bey , 65, 67, 422,
Cohen (later Durrell), Eve, 49, 78, 97
Cohen, Nick, 182
Colosseum, The 205
Condor, 'Operation Condor', 374
Conservatoire d'Alexandrie, 94
Connolly, Cyril , 21
Constantine II, King 27
Constantinople, 116, 127, 132, 280, 281, 350, 359, 362, 363, 399, 425
　1888 Convention of, 338,
Cookson, Charles, 359, 360, 361, 433, 436
Copeland, Miles, 383, 385, 426, 436, 438, 440, 441,
Coptic (Orthodox)Church, 82, 99, 219, 266, 364, 404, 424
Coptic Church of Mar Gerges and school, 29, 108
　of Nairobi, 67
　of St Mark, 219
　of the Two Saints, 326
Coptic, Conference, The, 357
Coptic Dishes, 276
Coptic Eid, 260
Coptic Hospital, 67
Coptic Language, 124, 126, 127
Coptic Patriarchs, 423
Coptic saints, 238
Copts, Rue de l'eglise, 80
Côte d'Azur, 250, 251
Crete, 137, 419
Crowe, Colin, Sir, 78
Cromer, Earl of , 82, 118
Courrier de l'Egypte, 299
Cyril, Nicene Bishop, 344

D

Daniel, Naby, 79, 115
　Mosque of, 79
　Rue Naby Daniel, 52, 77, 82, 210, 288

447

Alexandria Adieu

Danseuses de Madame Nichol, Les 157
Dar-Al-Hilal Publishing House, 307
Dar-es-Salaam, 37
Darweesh, Sayyed, 24
Darwish, Youssef, 285
Dawoud Ads, 368
Debbanès, 416
de Lesseps, Ferdinand Marie, Vicomte 327
Dean, James, East of Eden, 325
de Botton, Gilbert, 32
Delta, (Nile Delta) 9, 54, 86, 98–99, 126, 164, 169, 191, 199, 200, 287, 304, 412
Descartes, René, 344
Devil's Hole, The 117, 139, 148, 151–3, 298, 359, 417
Dinocrates, 20, 25, 28–29, 36, 94, 136, 188, 205
Dinshawai, 331, 342, 357, 358, 374
Disraeli, Benjamin, 348
Diodorus Siculus, 36
Dixon Brothers, the 81
Doge Giustiniano Particìaco (Particìpazio), 81
Don Bosco Institute, 325
Doulas-Home, Alec, 303, 336
Drikos, Andrea, 18
du Locle, Camille, 203
Dulles, John Foster, 304, 335,
Dunlop, Douglas, 312
Durrell, Lawrence, 6, 18–22, 37, 238-9, 244, 411, 423, 429
   Alexandria Quartet, 19, 49, 95- 6, 236, 393
   Justine, 21-2, 95-6, 189, 238-9, 246, 421, 429
   Prospero's Cell, 96
   Quartet, 96, 189, 238, 418
   and Alexandria's identity, 393
   and Cavafy, 18, 236
   and Eve Cohen, 49, 78, 97
   and Forester, 18, 421
   and the left revisionists critics, 96, 236, 391

E

East India Docks, 82
Eastern Harbour, 35, 43, 68, 70, 72, 95
Écharpe, 40
École franciscaine, 94
Eczanet Joannides, 64
Eczanet Mizrahi, 64
Eden, Anthony, 303
l'eglise Copts, Rue de 80
l'église Debbanè, Rue de, 416
Egoth Hotel & Group, 38
Egyptian Air Force, 250, 265
Egyptian Broadcast and Television Service, 252
Egyptian Film Industry Chamber (EFIC), 264
Egyptian Gazette, 19, 43, 216, 299, 364, 365
Egyptian-Jewish Karaite, 262-3
Egyptian Mail, 19, 43, 216, 299
Egyptian Medical Syndicate (EMS), 66
Egyptian Roman Orthodox Youth, 312
Egyptian State Information Department, 390
Egypt's Ministry of Trade and Industry, 311
Eiffel, Alexandre Gustave, 200, 427
Eiffel, La Tour, 391
Eighteenth Dynasty, 36, 199, 450
Eppler, Hans (also see Hassan Gaafer), 371, 374, 375, 376, 439
Eisa, Imam Sheik, 411
Eisenhower, Dwight, 277, 386, 400
el- Baroudi, Mahmoud, Sami, 352,
Eid-el-Kebier, 260, 271
Eid-el-Sughaier, 260, 272, 274, 317, 450
El-Eid (Easter), 272, 275
Eliot, T.S. - The Criterion, 21
Eliyahu Hanvi Synagogue, 288
Etam, 40
English Boys School (EBS), 166
English Girls School (EGS), 147, 166
English Patient, The 376
Erasistratus, 62
al-Eryan, Mohammed Said, 314
Euclid, 79
Europa and the Bull, 117, 137, 417, 419
European Economic Community (EEC), 329
Evrópi, 137
Excavation and Antiquities Act, 198
Exton, Clive, 182
Ezzat, Hassan Flt lieutenant 215, 372, 374, 376, 378-80, 435, 437-9

F

Fahmy, Khaled, 437
Fahmy, Hikmet, 371-2, 374-6
Fahmy, safia – See Safia Zaghloul
El-Amirah Faiza, school, 167, 179
Faiza, Princess, 67, 240,
Princesse Faiza school, 11, 167
Faika, Princess, 67, 240
Faisal, of Saudi Arabia King, 33

EPILOGUE: INDEX

Faisal II, of Iraq King, 336
Farida, Queen, 67, 240,
Kahavat Farouk, Café Farouk, 84, 91
Farouk, King, 7, 89, 118, 148, 161, 180, 182-3, 209, 285 301, 369, 376
   Abdication, 95, 297, 340, 373, 394-5
   And Count Almasy, 376
   and Arab countries, Arab League, 33, 50, 334, 339
   and army, promoting fellaheen officers, 50, 358, 381
   and the British, 184, 302, 330, 332, 339, 366, 370, 372-4, 385-6
   and Charities, 67, 373
   CIA plotting against Farouk, 382-3
   coronation day, 72, 84
   and Farida, 89, 107, 240
   Foreign Policy, 301-2, 316, 373
   and Islam-Muslims-Muslim Brotherhood, 269, 382
   and Palestine, 307, 330, 369
   and 1952 Coup, 367, 370, 374-5, 384-5, 395-6
   and al-Wafd, 184, 330, 332, 366, 373
Farouk, Roi 240
Al-Faroukyiah School, 49
Al-Fatat, magazine 397
Fathallah, Hamza Sheikh, 347-8
Fathia, Princess, 67, 240,
Fathy, Hassan Dr, 56
Fattookie, Ourada (see lgazaeriayh, Ourada, Ouarda l'Algérienne),
Fawzia, Princess, 240, 307, 369,
Fawzia, Princesse Clinica, 67
Fawzia, Rue Princesse, 11, 145, 315, 326, 417,
al-Fayed, Dodi, 29
Felipe Guaman Poma de Ayala
First New Chronicle and Good Government, 125
Female genital mutilation (FGM), 66–67, 223
Feminism/feminist, 31, 66, 82, 114, 166, 177–178, 397
Ferial, Princess, 209, 240
Ferrol, 81
Fille du Nil (Daughter of the Nile), 213
Fiorello, Leopoldo, 211
First World War, 17
Fitzmaurice, steamer, 81
Fleming, district and tram Arret, 33, 191, 309
Forster, Edward Morgan, 18–22, 43, 78, 151, 216, 230, 236, 238–239, 246
   Alexandria: A History and Guide, 19, 219
   Howards End (1910), 19
   A Passage to India (1924), 19
Foster, Andrew, 337
Fourier, Joseph Dr, 299
France, 117, 133, 155, 212, 246, 284, 311, 362, 366, 376, 391, 410
   Influence on Egyptian education and culture, 226, 268, 288, 299, 308, 396
   Rue France, 87–92, 187
   Suez Canal, 338, 348
   Suez War, 55, 78, 266, 292, 333, 400-01, 405
   Tension with Nasser, 305, 330
Franco–Prussian War, 202
Freeman, Sir Ralph, 200
Free Officers Action (FOA), 342
French Gardens, the, 74, 83, 145, 436
Friend of India, 360
Fuad, Ali Bey, 359
Fuad I, Ahmed King, 68, 82, 82, 139, 141, 182, 195, 201, 233, 240, 269, 302, 354, 356
   and the Arabs/Muslims, 33, 269
   and the British, 372-3
   and charities, 68
   and democratic reforms, 396
King Fuad Stadium, 311
Rue Fuad, 25, 31, 49, 77-8, 209, 416
Fuad II, Ahmed King, 89
Prince Ahmad Fuad II, 89
Fyfe, David Patrick Sir (Viscount Kilmuir), 336-7

G

Gaafer, Hassn Bey, 371-2, 374-5, (also see Eppler)
Gabaliyat-al-o'llel, 188
el-Gaberty, Abd-el-Rahman, 346
Tarikh-el-Gaberty (el-Gabertey's Chronicles), 346, 434
Gable, Clark, 149
Gaddafi, Muammar, Colonel, 253, 323
Gaitskell, Hugh, 338
Galen, Claudius, 62
   On Anatomical Procedures, 62
   Antidotes, 63
   Hygiene, 63
Galloway, Thomas, 117
Gallipoli, 37, 189
al-Gma'a al-Islamia, 258
Gama'at el-Ightialat, 367 (see Assassinations Group)
Gamil-Aziz, Morsi, 251, 253-4, 356, 259
Gare de Ramleh, 25, 27

449

Alexandria Adieu

Garnier, Charles, 203
Al-Gassosuah's, 375
Gascoyne-Cecil, Robert (Marquess of Salisbury), 336
Gatteno, 368
General Bank of Alexandria, 55
Gezirah Gabr-el-Khour, 247 (see Île de Miami,)
Gheit-el-Enab, 103
Gianaclis, 73
Gigliotti, Pietro, 245
al-Gihaz el-Khas, 356
Giuseppina, Filomena, 245
Gizyah, 127, 218, 238, 282, 287
Gladstone, William Ewart, 12, 340, 343, 359, 364, 399, 433
Glymenopoulo, 33
Al-Gomhouriah (The Republic), 303
Gordon, Charles Pasha, 196
Gorst, Sir Eldon, 82
Greco-Roman museum, 236
The Great Pyramid, 207–208
Great War, the 14, 19, 24, 31, 37, 74, 76, 78, 103-4, 123, 133, 141, 155-6, 169, 180, 189-90, 295, 297, 302, 363, 372, 404
Greek Alexandrians, 18, 33, 54, 55, 88, 242, 283, 345, 401. See also Italian Alexandrians
Greek Club, 312
Greene, Rue, 47, 94
Grenfell, Francis Wallace, Field Marshal, 191
Grieve, Andrew, 182
The Guardian, 182

H

Haag, Michael, 20, 95, 97
and the Durrells (Lawrnce & Eve), 20, 97
Hadad, Ahmed, 267
Hadrian, Traianus , Emperor, 50, 425
Hafez, Abd-el-Halim, 252, 259,
Hafez, Bahiga, 94, 213
Hafez, Ismail Pasha, 94, 202
Saraya-el-hakanyiah el 87
el-Hamawi, Selim, 347
Hamdy, Baligh, 253–254, 256
Hamilton, John, 385, 435
Hammad, Abed-el-Azizi , 369
Hammam, Sayyed ,84
Hamroosh, Ahmed Major, 435, 438, 441, 442,
Hannux, 40
Al-Haras Alhadidi -See Iron Guard,
Harb, Saleh, General, 355-6

Hassanein, Ahmad Pasha 372, 442
Madam, Hassanein, 372
Hatata, Sherif Dr, 66
Hatem, Abdel Kader, Dr, 292-3
Hatshepsut (1507–1458 BC), 199
Head, Antony, 331
Hebrew, 129, 280, 302, 303
Heggy, Tarek Dr, 10
Heikal, Muhammed Hassanein, 222, 235
    Damaging Egypt's identity, 233
    Influence on culture and media, 230-31, 442
Influence on Nasser, 233
Propaganda Machine, 233-4
Heikal, Muhammed Hessein Dr, 214
Heim, Aribert, 369, 438
Abbas Helmi I, Pasha, Khedive , 23, 84, 191, 193, 288, 313
Abbas Helmi II, Pasha, Khedive, 82, 83, 145, 207, 212, 300, 304, 354, 435
Himmler, Heinrich, 372
Hind Noufal , 397
Hellenic Institute for Ancient & Mediaeval Alexandrian Studies, 242
Hello! Magazine, 307
Helmy, Sherif Dr, 10
King Herod of Jerusalem, 129
Herodotus, 52, 304
Herophilus (335–280 BC), 62
Hessein, Kamal el-Din Prince, 82
Hessein, Kemal el-Dine Captain, 369
Sultan Hessein Kamel - see Kamel, Hessein pasha
Higaz, 33
El-Hilaly, Ahmad Naguib Pasha, 366
Hippocrates , 62
Hitchcock, Alfred, 72
Hitler, Adolf, 233, 356
Horizon , 21
Horowitz, Anthony, 182
House of Lords, 336
Hulbert, Henry (1827–1895), 17
Hussein, Fahmia (col Nasser's mother), 403
King Hussein of Jordan, 32, 298, 330
Hussein, Saddam, 235
Hussein, Sherif of Mecca, 372
Hussein, Taha, 11, 268
    Clash with Islamic clergy and trial for blasphemy , 268, 425
    Modernise language and education, 80, 221, 268
    Mustaqbal al-thaqafah fi Misr, (The Future of Culture in Egypt), 268, 429
Hydar Pasha, 367, 384-85

EPILOGUE: INDEX

Hypatia, 79, 246, 344, 420, 425, 434

I

Ibn- Abd- al-Wahhab, Muhammed, 43
Ibn-al-As, Amr, General, 128, 238-9, 249, 287, 238
Ibn al-Hakam, Marwan, Caliph, 82
ibn-Marwan, Abd-al-Aziz, 82
ibn Saud, Abdel-Aziz King, 334
Ibrahim, Hassan wing commander, 358
Ibrahim Pasha, 31, 33, 43, 54, 84-5, 97, 134, 187, 326, 348, 354
Mosque, 25, 43-4
Ibrahim Pasha, Rue 233
Ice Cold in Alex, 43
Iconomopolous, Leonadis, 190
Ideal Film, 211
Ideal-Titra Film, 211
Idris of Libya King, 253, 278
Idris, Youssif, 231, 429
Al-I'Etidal, 347
Il-cinema egiziano, 211
Île de Miami, 142
Indian Ocean, 190
HMS Inflexible, 362
Inner Egypt, 44, 121, 133, 162, 167, 216, 284
'Inta Omry', 257
Institut d'Égypte, (Egyptian Scientific Institute), 299
l'Institut français, 79
International Court of Justice (ICJ), the Hague 366
'International Pageant of Pulchritude', 245
International Suez Canal Company (ISCC), 332
Irma la Douce, 189
The Iron Guard, 369–370
Iron Guard of Egypt (IGE), 369
Ishaq, Adib, 351
Iskandrani, Hassan Pasha Admiral, 93
Iskandrani, Rue 94, 101, 160
Islam, 24, 43, 61, 67, 96, 109, 118, 127, 133, 158, 161, 163, 164, 216, 221, 237, 238, 264, 267, 275, 282, 288, 312, 334, 345, 352, 355, 357, 359, 369, 409, 412
Islamic Charity Association, 346
Islamic Conference, 384
Israel, (newspaper) 303
Israel, 45, 195, 234, 259, 298, 303, 305, 331, 337, 411,
and Egyptian Jews, 264, 266-7, 277-8, 286-7, 404-5
and 1948 war of independence, 264, 269, 307, 326, 330, 334, 355, 339, 369-70, 382
and Peace with Egypt, 47, 368-9, 384
and Suez War, 55, 266, 277, 333-5, 400
and Yom Kippur War, 331, 385
Israeli Girls School- Alexandria, 26
Israeli Hospital - Alexandria, 48-50, 187, 266, 279,
Israeli Military Intelligence, 404
Italian Alexandrians, 53, 88, 291, 401
Italian Military Academy, 372
Italian School, 166
Al Ittihad, 260
Italo–Abyssinian War, 302

J

Jardins Francais, 74 – see French Gardens
The Jazz Singer, 211
Jedda, 33
Jerusalem, 129, 238, 257, 369, 423, 431, 453
Jews, 23, 26, 28–29, 52, 153, 368
Johnson, Boris, 148
Josephus, Flavius, 287
Le Journal Pathé, 212

K

Kafr-el-Dawar, 387
Kafr-el-Zayat, 99
al-Kaleem (the Articulate), 303
Kamel, Abd el-Aziz, 437
Kamel, Hessein Pasha, 82, 94
Rue Sultan Hessein Kamel, 25, 82, 416
Kamel, Mohammed Ibrahim, 368
Kamel, Moustafa Pasha, 358
Kamose, 199
Karaite Jews, 97, 262, 267, 286-7
Karim, Mohammed 155, 212, 214
al-Kawkab al-Masry (the Egyptian Star), 303
Al-Kawakab al-Sharqi (Orient Star), 347
Kelly, Grace, 71-2, 110
el-Khadim, Saad 97
Khan, Sadiq, 389
Khairy, Badi'e, 24
Khalafallah, Mohammed Ahmed, 221
al-Kharrat, Edwar, 103, 154, 167, 243, 392, 411
Banat iskandriah, 166-7, 426
City of Saffron, 103, 154, 442
Filles d'Alexandrie, 243, 429
Girls of Alexandria, 103
Rama and the Dragon, 103
Khartoum, 196, 369
Khashoggi, Adnan, 32

451

Alexandria Adieu

al-Khazendar, judge, 368, 437
Kheiry, Ibrahim Pasha, 384
El- Khouli, Hassan Sabry, 435,
El-Khouli, Lutfi , 231, 235,
Khomeini, Ruhollah, 47
Kishk, Abdel Hameed Sheikh, 258-9
Kissinger, Henry, 329, 353
Kitchener, Horatio Herbert Lieutenant (later Lord), 82, 191, 363
Hôpital Kitchener- Kitchener Memorial Hospital, 191
Kit-Kat, 372, 374
Kom-bakir, 188, 189
Kom-el-Dikka Hill, 76–77, 110, 162, 191-2
Kulthum, Umm, 251, 252, 259, 263, 280, 283
Kupiri Abbas, 207
Kupiri Abu el-Ella, 200
Kupiri al-Gezira, 201
Kupiri al-Giza, 207
Kupiri Imbaba, 200
Kupiri Ismailia, 200
Kupiri Qasr-el-Nile, 201-02

L

Labib, Mahmoud Major, 356-7, 435, 449
La Bourse Égyptienne, 299
Lagnado, Lucy, 284
The Man in The White Sharkskin Suit, 284, 430
Lagoudakis, Ioannis, 94
Lagoudis Pinchin, Jane, 19, 429
  Alexandria Still, 421, 429
Lamarr, Hedy, 71
Lamour, Dorothy, 297
Lampson, Jacqueline Lady, 438
Lampson, Miles Sir (Baron Killearn), 183, 372-4, 379, 426, 438, 439
L'ancienne Méditerranée, 117, 137
Lasciac, 190
Laurent, tram Arrêt and district, 31
Laurent, Edourad, 31
  Plage Laurent, 31
Laurent, Rue 31
Lavon Affair, the, 405
Lavon, Pinhas, 404
Lazarietta, 28
Lazhogly, Mohammed Bey, 83
League of Arab States, 330, 339,
  Alexandria Protocol, 339
  Arab League, 29, 50, 339
League of Nations, 301
Lee–Enfield 303 rifles, 142, 401
L'Egyptienne, 178, 397

Leibniz, Gottfried Wilhelm, 344
Leigh, Vivien, 308
Lemmon, Jack, 189
Levant Club Dancers, 312
Liberation Board, 232
Libya, 20, 122, 149, 234, 253, 278, 302, 316, 317, 321, 322, 338, 344, 430, 453
Libyan Desert, 316
Libyan–Egyptian Desert, 371
Liddell, John Robert, 20
  Unreal City, 20
The Life and Pains of Christ the Lord, 268
Life Magazine, 80, 177, 303, 306, 308
Lloyd, Selwyn, 303, 305, 335-7
Look, 306
Lord Cromer, 82, 118
Loria, Giacomo Alessandro, 37, 45-6, 417
Lorio Palace, 18
King Louis-Philippe I, 117
Lumière, Auguste Marie Loius Nicolas, 212
Lumière, brothers, 212
  Alexandria's Lumière Cinematographe, 212
Lumière, Louis Jean, 212
Lumière, La Ville, 177
Lutfi, Omar Pasha, 361
Luxor Massacre, 258
Lyceum Ballroom, 245

M

Ma'arif, al-(min of Education) 61, 90, 268, 313
Ma'arif, al- (publishers and bookshop), 39
Macmillan, Harold, 303
Madhi, Zozou 159
Maher, Ahmed Pasha, 368, 339
Maher, Ali, Pasha 33, 332, 355, 373, 387
Mahfouz, Naguib, 222, 223, 225, 226, 227, 230, 235, 428
The Thief and the Hound, 103
Miramar, 222, 223
Mahmal, 33
Mahmoud, Fathy , 137, 417, 419
Mahmoud, Mohammed Pasha, 211
Mahmoud, Naglaa (Mrs Morsi), 407
Mahmoudiyah Canal, 84–85, 104–106, 110–111, 115, 134, 188
La Maison Francaise, 40
da Malamocco, Buono, 81
Malet, Edward, 359, 365, 433, 436, 455
Mamluks, 21, 133, 298, 403

452

EPILOGUE: INDEX

Mancini, Francesco, 87, 298
Maniscalco, Alfonso, 77
Manolagas, Caliope 223
Mansour, Adli Chief Justice, 409
Manzala, lake 310
Mareotis, lake, 36, 85, 111, 365, 420
Marine (Greek) Club, 68
Mariette, Auguste Pasha, 198
Le masque rouge, 148
Matossian, 73
Mauthausen Concentration Camp, 369
Mazloum, Ahmed Pasha, 32
  Mazloum, Arret, 32
McCarthy commission, 337
Me'adi Land Company, 368
Mecca, 33, 101, 264, 271, 372
Mehatet-Masr, 190, 195, 197
Mehatet el-Ramleh, 25, 27, 209, 215
Medical and Public Health Act, 188
Meguid, Esmat Abd-el Dr, 29
Meguid, Ibrahim Abdel, 103, 283-4, 392, 424, 426, 427, 430, 442
  Birds of Amber, 283
  Clouds Over Alexandria, 206, 392
  No-One Sleeps in Alexandria, 103, 162
MENA (the Middle East and North Africa region), 44, 97, 292
Menasce, de, Baron, 94
Menasce, de, Bekhor, 48,49
Menasce, de (family), 345
Menasce, de, Baron Jacques 119
Menasce, Rue, de, 48, 49, 94,160
el-Merrie, Abd el-Nasser Hessin (Col Nasser's father), 403
La- Messager Sioniste (the Zionist Messenger), 303
Mestre, Gloria, 375
Hôtel Métropole, 18
Metzger, Albert, 37
Metzger, John, 38
Metzger, Patricia, 37
Mier du dieux, 94
Middle East News Agency, 292, 293
Migalat al-Hillal, 381
Miller, Arthur, 337
Misr-al-Fatat, (young Egypt) 346
Misr and Tigara, 351
al-Misri, Aziz Pasha General, 371-4, 376,
al- Missallah, Rue, 82
Mixed Provisional Municipal and Commercial Committee (MPMCC), 116
Mizrahi, Togo, 213, 266
Mohammed, Ahmed, fuul, 26
Moharrem, Bey Admiral, 93
Moharrem Bey, Rue, 45, 47, 84, 93-4, 98, 101-2, 162, 172, 191, 273,
Mohey el-Dine, Khalid, 1st lieutenant (Major later), 376, 378-79, 435, 438, 439, 441
Al-Mahrousah, Royal yacht 351, 394, 451
Moukhtar, Ala'eddin, 376
Monroe, Marliyn, 337
Montazo, Cinema, el, 326
Montazah Green (also Piazza Lawn), 260, 417, 326
Montazah Palace, 145,
Monte Carlo:
night Club, 28, 250
Radio, 79, 292
Montefiore, Moses Haim Sir, 288
Montgomery, Bernard Law Fld Marshal, 37
Montgomery's Bar, 37, 418
Mordechai, Lillian (see , Murad Leila)
Mordechai, Ibrahim Zaki Effendi, (See Murad, Zaki)
Morice, Goerge Sir Pasha, 363
Morley, Eric, 246
The Miss World Story, 246
Morsi, Mohamed, 353-4, 407, 409, 456
Mosaddegh, Mohammad, 382
Mosaddegh, Mohammad, 383 – also Mosaddeq, 366
Mother Egypt Party, 353
L'mua'ahdah, Rue, 301
Mountbatten, Lord, 337
Mousa, Nabowiya, 166
  Girls School, 166
Al-Musawar, 177, 303, 306–308, 381
Mubarak, Ali Pasha, 313, 432
Mubarak, Hosni, 38, 182, 234, 296, 326, 353-54, 375, 409, 412
Mukhabarat, al , 14, 66, 253, 254, 338, 415, 456
Muncaster, Peter, 371, 375
Murad, Leila, 213, 262-66, 269, 280
Murad, Maurice 265
Murad, Zaki, 262
Muslim Brotherhood, 38, 137, 215, 220, 242, 258, 269, 282, 288, 306, 326, 339, 353–358, 365, 368, 378, 382, 385, 409, 411
Muslim caliphate, 388, 394
Muslim Young Men's Association, 346
Mustafa Pasha, barracks, 30, 362, 363
Mustafa Bahgat Fazil Pasha, 30
Mutran, Khalil, 234

N
Nabarawy, Siza, 397

453

Nabil, Zouzo, 255
Nachmias, Victor, 45
El-Naggar, Abed-el-Menem, 145, 149, 173, 195, 210, 266,369, 383, 387
Nagi, Muhammad, 389-90
Nagui, Effat, 97
Naguib, Aisha Labib, 408
Naguib, Mohammed, (Gen, Lft Gen, Bey) 144, 161, 184, 201, 292, 296, 322, 328, 331-3, 340, 342, 352, 358, 365, 367, 369, 372, 374, 382, 383-85, 427,-28, 431, 435, 427, 436, 438, 440, 441, 442
Nahas, Mustafa Pasha, 301, 330, 332, 339, 365-66, 368, 370, 374, 438
Nahdat-Masr, 220
Nakrashi, Fahmy el Pasha, 207, 339, 368-69
Napoleon III, 203, 350
Nariman, Queen, 240
Nasser, Ellithy, 51
Nasser, Gamal Abdel Colonel, 78, 90, 138, 144, 184, 225, 232-34, 241 , 285, 296, 342, 354, 372, 398, 406, 411
Assassinating opponents, 384-85
Death, 298
Economic policies, 170, 229, 316, 331
Expelling Jews, Dual nationals and residents, 45, 48, 55, 105, 277-78, 286, 287, 292, 310-11, 401, 404-5
Propaganda Machine, 79, 122, 230-31, 282, 289, 312, 351, 376, 397
Sout al-Arab 'Voice of the Arabs', VoA, 292–293
and Arabisation of Egypt, 224, 233, 290, 353, 379, 392, 407
and Cairo arson attacks, 365, 378, 427
and the CIA operators, 382-83, 385
and communists, 79, 291, 306, 410
and disputes with regional leaders, 33
and eastern bloc, 305
and Islam, (with Muslim Brotherhood and empowering al-Azhar) 220, 258, 306, 313, 333–34, 354, 356, 369, 408-9
and nationalisation /sequestration of assets, 25, 30, 37, 266, 401
and Mohammed Naguib, 322, 332, 386, 395
and Pan Arabism, 199, 232, 234-5, 335, 379
and socialism, Socialist Federation, 222, 231-32, 244
and Suez Crisis , 55, 78, 303, 326-30, 336-39, 399-401

and USSR, 305, 335, 405
Orwellian Changes, 48, 112, 121, 201, 206, 207,346, 348, 362, 408, 415
Weaponising Arts and Culture, 215, 222-23, 252-54, 259, 380
National Bank of Egypt, 45
National Democratic Party (NDP), 296
National Geographic, 80
Nationalist Federation (NF), 232, 296
Navarino, Battle of, 93, 299, 423
Nazli, Queen, 118
el-Nedim, Abdallah Sheikh, 346-8, 351, 353, 359-61, 434
Negm, Ahmed Fuad, 411
Nelson, Horatio, Admiral, 164
Newton, Isaac, 344
New York's World Trade Center, 258
Nietzsche, Friedrich
Alexandria-Mann, 225
The Birth of Tragedy, 225
The Night of Counting the Years, 198
Nile Delta – see Delta
1919 revolution, 23, 82, 181, 235, 366, 380, 397, 398
Nineteenths Dynasty, 199
Nizami, Ali Pasha, 359
Non-Aligned Movement (NAM), 304
Nubar, Boghos Pasha, 83, 118, 326, 424
Nubar Pasha, Rue 148
The Rusted Nubar statue, 83
Nubians, 120, 126
Nuzha, 37, 111, 119, 185, 212,
Nuzha Airport, 7, 29, 415
Nuzha Bridge, 84
Nuzha Gardens
Nuzha Palace, 29
Nuzha Park, 75, 85, 272

O

Obama, Barack, 354
Olga, The (ship), 81
Omar Effendi,(stores) 39–41
Ondaatje, Michael, 376
Oreco, 40
Orestes, the Perfect of Egypt 344
Orfanelli, Alvise, 213
Orwell, George - Nineteen Eighty-Four, 121, 253, 292
Oscar II, of Sweden King, 347
Osman, Amin Pasha, 368, 370, 371, 379
Osman, Ahmed, 425
Ottoman Caliphate, 287
Ottomans/Ottoman Empire, 21, 53, 54, 82, 97, 116, 127, 133, 181, 190, 280, 299, 311, 340, 345, 346, 348–350, 372, 403–405

454

EPILOGUE: INDEX

Ottoman Sultan, 343
Ottoman Turkish, 281
Ourabi, Ahmed Lt Colonel Pasha, 6, 74, 350, 351, 387, 401, 427, 434, 439, 442
  anti-modernisation/anti-Egyptian identity, 326, 340, 348, 353, 359, 366
  and British occupation of Egypt, 55, 360-62, 364-5, 436
  influence on Nasser & 1952 military coup plotters, 331, 340, 347, 352-4, 358-9, 400
  his hatred of Alexandria, 343, 355, 360-62, 364
  his Islamism, 30, 352, 354-5, 437
  and military rebellion, 30, 231, 326, 352, 355

P

P. & C. Habig, 187
Pakistan, 335, 338, 354
Le Palais Regina. 37
Palestine, 20, 49, 50, 121, 234, 264, 265, 266, 281, 330, 339, 344, 355, 369
Panayiotis, Café, 84
  Maria, 84
Papaelia, Marina, 245-46
Paris, Egyptian Mission School in, 362
Paris Match, 80, 177, 306
Pastroudis, 49, 77
Patel, Priti MP, 389
Paul, of Greece King, 27
People of the Cave, 223
Pergolesi, Corrado, 18
Pericles of Athens, 130–131
Pericles, George, 18
Perrier, Denise, 246
Peter El-Gawly, 82
Peter I, Pope (of the last Martyrs), 80, 326
Peter VII, Bishop, 82
Petrou, Nikos, 223
Petrou, Panayoti, 223
Le Phare d'Alexandrie, 216, 365
Pharos Island, 36, 76, 126, 249, 260, 340
Place des Consuls, 54, 201, 212, 345
Place du Ismail, 74, 83
Plato, 131, 237
Pope John III of Samanoud, 82
Pope Shenouda III, 404
Le Progrès Egyptian, 299
Portman, Eric, 147
Port Said, 54, 55, 160, 291, 299, 308, 310, 312, 342, 361, 401, 442
La Poste de l'Egypte, 299
La Poste Egyptienne, 89

Poursaeed, 310
Praefectus Augustalis, 344
Proteus, 36, 137
Protocol of Sèvres, 400
Ptolemian Dynasty, 236
Ptolemies, 20, 27, 72, 95, 130, 132, 133, 137, 239, 394, 399
Ptolemy I. See Soter
Ptolemy III, Euergetes, 344
Puskás, Ferenc, 102

Q

Qadin, Ferial, 240
Qubla fi al-Sahra'a, 264
Quintus Curtius Rufus, 132

R

Raouf, abd el-abd elMoneim abd major, 435
Raouf, Jihan 380, 435 – see Jihan sadat
Raouf, Safwat Dr, 380,
Radio Cairo, 253
Radio Monte Carlo, 79
Al-Raed al-Rasmi, 347
Al-Raed al-Tunisi, 347
Rameses II, 199
Rainier of Monaco, prince, 71
Rameses II, Hotel 200
Ras el-Tin, Palace, 72, 84, 116-17, 298, 299, 340, 361, 363, 385, 395, 424
Rashad, Nahid (Nahed), 369-70, 382, 385, 438, 457
Rashad, Youssef, Dr, 369-70
Rassafah, Rue 84, 94
Reader's Digest, 80
Réard, Louis, 308
Regie Scuole Littorie, 29
Revolutionary Command Council (RCC), 378–379
Rhakotis, 36, 188
Rifaat, Ibrahim Pasha, 32–33
Mira'at el-Harmaine, 33, 421
Rifaat, Ahmed, Pasha, 191
Rifa'at, Kemal, 384
Ritsa (sea urchins), 42
Riyad, Mustafa Pasha,, 350-52
Roman Empire, 62
Rommel, Erwin, 37, 43, 46, 201, 281, 289, 310, 371-5, 385
Rommel ruft Kairo (Rommel Calls Cairo) 376
Roosevelt, Kermit, 382
Rose El-Youssef, 397
Rosetta, 50, 86, 128, 191, 195, 273
  Nile Branch, 86
  Rue Rosetta, 19

455

ABC# Alexandria Adieu

Stone, 47, 124
Rossi, Mario, 25, 260
de Rothschild, Lionel, 348
Royal Navy, 310, 341,
Royal Opera House (1869), 23
Royal Opera Orchestra, 245
Rushdy, Hessein Pasha (& Tram Arret), 30
Rustom, Hind, 255-6
Rustom, Leila, 262
Ruyssenaers, the Dutch Consul, 219

S

El-Saadawi, Nawal, Dr, 66
Saad-el-Dine, Mursi, Dr CBE, 78
Saadist Institutional Party, 368
Sabri, Ali, 383
Sadat, Anwar Captain, 6, 68, 78, 145, 222-3, 231, 254, 296, 326, 353, 354, 356, 368, 395, 437-9,
　Announcing 1952 military coup, 367
　Islamisation, 121-2, 221, 398, 410-12, 415, 428
　Journalism, 303, 306, 381
　King Farouk Court and Iron Guard connection, 370, 381
　Muslim Brotherhood connection, 215, 257, 367, 411
　Peace with Israel, 234, 369
　Nazi connection, 371, 374-6
　underground violent activities, 215, 367, 372, 377-80
Sadat, Jihan (jehan), 223, 380, 428, 440
Sah'ua (Islamic awakening), 267
al-Said, Nouri Pasha, 293, 336-7, 341
Said, Edward, 32
Said, Khedive Pasha, 54, 84, 190, 193, 219, 293, 299, 310, 336
Saint Mark the Evangelist, 80
Salama, Max Dr, 51-2, 64, 288, 411
Salem, Ahmed, 148
'Salaam/Salam' (operation), 374
Salone de Vere, 40
San Stephano, Arrêt and district, 32
San Stephano, Hotel 31
Sandstede, Hans Gerd, 371, 375
Santa Lucia, 242
Saudi Arabia, 33
Savants (scientists, engineers, artists and botanists with 1798 French expedition), 299
el-Sayyed, Ahmed Lutfi bey, 358
Shaaban, Abd-el-Hady 369
Al-Shafie, Hessein Major 356, 373, 435, 438
Shagart el-Dur, 33

al-Sha'rawi, Mohammed Metwalli Sheikh, 257-9, 385, 411
Schultz, 33
Second World War, 30, 46, 54, 363, 366, 372, 403
Sedaris, 39
Sednaoui, 40
Serageddin, Fuad Pasha, 330, 437-9
Serapeum, 344
Serapis, 239, 344
Seymour, Beauchamp Admiral, 359-61, 400
Shaarawi, Huda, 397
Shafik, Doria, 178
Shafiq-Kamel, Ahmed, 257, 259, 460
Shalom el-Riady (Shlomo the athlete), 266
Shalom-fi-al-police (Shlomo the policeman), 267
Shalom-wa-A'bdou, 267
Sham-Ennessim, 260, 272
Sheikh Sayyed, - see Darweesh
Shepheard's Hotel, Cairo 37
Serry, Hessein Pasha, 188, 366, 373, 384, 385
Sève, Joseph Anthelme, colonel 118, 182, 351, 428, 453
Sidi Bishr/Sidi-Bishr, 5, 27, 31, 65, 74, 98-9,107, 112-14, 136-40, 142, 145-6, 149-50, 154-5, 170, 173, 176, 183, 187, 210, 223, 227-8, 26-2, 269, 272-3, 298, 311, 314, 320, 322, 326, 363, 406, 41-7, 456
　Rue la Gare Sidi-Bishr, 302
Sidi-Gaber, 33, 173, 195, 260
Sidqi, Ismail Pasha, 339
Sidqi, Moustafa Kemal, Captain, 370
Silsilah, 72, 137, 419
Sinadino, Ambroise, 360
Sindbad, magazine, 80, 224, 314
el-Sisi, Abd-el-Fatah, 409
Sirry-Amr, Hessien Bey, lt General, 384-85, 441
Sirry-Amr, Souzi hanem, 384, 441
Siwa, 77, 131, 132, 185
Six-Day War, 51, 55, 143, 153, 224, 240, 250, 265, 278, 286, 400
Socialist Federation (SF), 222, 232, 296, 383, 415
Société Orientale de Publicité, 368
Socrates, 131
Sofia, Queen of Spain, 26
Soter, 39, 132, 236, 340, 348
　Rue Soter, 55
　Tram arrêt Soter, 28, 55
Souk el-Khiet, 88

EPILOGUE: INDEX

Soviet Union, 210, 305
Spectator, The 80
Sphinx, 198, 208, 391, 408, 427
Spinks, Sir Charlton, 192
The Spy Dancer, (Al-Gassosuah's)375
Starr, Deborah, 389–390
Remembering Cosmopolitan Egypt, 389
Staurazio, monk 81
Stella, see Birra Stella
Stephenson, Robert, 191
St Katherine's Cathedral, 83, 90, 298,
St Katherine's Green, 417
St Katherine, Place, 40
St Mark, 80
St Mark's Chapel, 80
St. Mark's Church, 82, 219, 326, 423,
St Mark's college, 184
Strabo, 39
Strada dell' amore, 94
Sudan, 197
Sudanese Palace Guard, 395
Suez Canal, 70, 201, 202, 343, 350, 351
   Suez Canal Company, 327, 332, 348, 453, 460
Suez War, 51, 57, 61, 79, 146, 170, 209, 229, 265–266, 292, 333, 401, 405
Sukarno, Ahmad, 305
Sukhra, 350
Suleiman Pasha (el-Faransawi) – see Sève, Joseph Anthelme Colonel
Suleiman Pasha, Rue 118
Sultan Hessein, Rue 25, 82
Superb, HMS 360
Supreme Council of Armed Forces (SCAF), 354
Susannah, Operation 404
Swiss Club, 312
Syria, 24, 53, 77, 199, 224, 233, 234, 254, 277, 278, 306, 338, 339, 353, 392, 407, 410

T

Tahtawi, Sheikh Rifa'ah el-, 133, 425
Takla, Bisharah (1852–1901), 231
Takla, Salim (1849–1892), 231
Tatwig, Rue 83, 84
Tawfik, Ahmed Pasha ,368
Tawfik, Hessein, 368, 380
Tawfik, Muhammad Pasha Khedive (viceroy), 17, 83, 118, 198, 207, 293, 300, 340, 362, 386
   Constitution and reforms, 350-52, 355, 359
   British occupation, 354-5, 360-61, 363-4, 401
   Modernisation and independent

Egyptian identity, 198, 293, 326, 345, 347-9, 359
Rue Tawfik, 40, 45, 183, 417
Tel-El-Kebier, 365
Temeraire, HMS 362
Thatmos III, 36
Theodore, Priest 81
Theon, 79
Thumosis III, 199
To Catch A Thief, 72
da Torcello, Rustico, 81
Tossizza, Michel, 54
Tossizza, Theodore, 54
Toson, (Muhammed Ali's son)
Toson, Omar Prince, 68
Trenet, Louis Charles Augustin, 28
Trevelyan, Sir Humphrey, 329, 337
Trianon, 17-19, 25, 43-5, 83, 89,
Truman, Harry (Point Four Program), 386
Tuhami, Hassan, Captain, 384
Tulip Era, 280
Turkish War Cemetery, 295
Tutankhamun , 199
TWA, 25
Twenty-Fifth Dynasty , 128
Tyre, 137, 419
Tzalas, Harry, 10, 96, 423, 426,

U

Umma Party (The Nation), 358, 435
UN Emergency Force UNEF-I, 400
UNEF-II, 400
UNESCO, 205
UNGA Resolution 1001, 400
UN General Assembly (UNGA), 400
Ungaretti, Giuseppe, 389
United Arab Republic (UAR), 233, 353
United States, 17, 332, 374, 383, 400
UN Security Council (UNSC), 400
UNSC Resolution 340, 400
UNSC's Resolution 119, 400
USSR, 305, 400, 401, 410
Uzbek Ibn Kathir, 77

V

Valencia, 81
La Vara, 303
Vekayi-i Misriye, 299
Venice, 81, 217
Venus, 247, 308
Verdi, Giuseppe, 202-3, 205
   Aida, 202, 427
Viceroy Abbas Helmi I Pasha (1812–1854), 191
Victoria, College, 32, 184, 211

457

Quarter and Terminus, 27, 32, 322
Queen, 29, 322
Victor Immanuel III, 372–373
Vieille Bourse, Rue 41,
Vienna, 83, 145, 217, 300, 372, 375

W

Wabour-el-Maiyah, 163
Wafd, 31, 301, 330, 332, 336, 339, 357, 365, 369, 370, 374, 379
   Party, 23, 154, 184, 193, 301, 366, 368, 373, 378
Wagdy, Anwar, 264
Wahby Tapia, Ricardo, 109
Alwaqaeh al-Rasmaiyah, 299
Wassef, Charlotte, 245, 309
al-Watany Party / Hezb al-Watani (national party), 356, 358, 412
Wells, H.G., 35
Western Harbour, 86, 88, 116
Whitehead Morris Limited, 236
Wilde, Oscar, 43, 219, 224, 428
Wilder, Billy, 189
Willcocks, Sir William, 304
Wingate, Sir Reginald, 191
Wirdani, Ibrahim Nassif al-, 357-58
Wissenschaft, 225
Wolseley, Grant General Sir, 364-5
World Monuments Fund, 288
Wren, Christopher, 205
Wright, Michael Sir, 329

Y

El-Yad el-Khafiyah (The Black hand), 355
Yahia el-hob (Vive l'Amour), 263
Yom Kippur War, 51, 68, 286, 331
Young Egypt (YE), 346
Young Men's Muslim Association, 356
Youssef, Fatima, 397
Youssef, Khalid, 213

Z

Zaghloul, Saad Pasha, 23-24, 31, 82, 166, 181, 301, 304, 356, 366, 397, 408
   Boulevard Saad Zaghloul, 18, 26, 39, 40
   Place Saad Zaghloul, 23, 27, 35-36
Zaghloul, Safiyah, 53, 82,
Zaki, Salim 368
Safiyah Zaghloul, Rue 25, 209, 210
Zananiri, George Pasha, 147
Zayed, Hala, 63
Zeinab, 213
Zidan, Emile, 307, 381

Zidan, Georgie, 307
Zizinia , Menandre de Comte, 31
Zizinia, Stephen Count, 31
Zizinia Senior, 31, 54, 416
Zizinia, Teatro, 23, 31, 83, 118, 347, 416
Zizinia, Television series, 389
Zogheb, Max de, 118, 362
Zeus, 132, 137, 419
Zeus-Amun, 132